Edited by:
Jonathan Crawshaw
Pawan Budhwar
Ann Davis

Human Resource
Management

(2nd Edition)

Strategic and International Perspectives

Los Angeles | London | New Delhi
Singapore | Washington DC | Melbourne

CONTENTS

PART ONE STRATEGIC ISSUES IN HRM

PART TWO HRM IN PRACTICE

PART THREE   HRM IN CONTEXT

DETAILED CONTENTS

PART ONE STRATEGIC ISSUES IN HRM

1

INTRODUCTION: CONTEXT AND CHALLENGES FOR HRM

Jonathan R. Crawshaw, Jude Preston and Alastair Hatch

2

HRM AND FIRM PERFORMANCE

Anastasia Katou and Pawan Budhwar

3

ORGANISATIONAL CHANGE AND HRM

Katty Marmenout and Achim Schmitt

4

HRM AND THE ETHICAL ORGANISATION

Carole Parkes, Helen Borland,
Thierry Nadisic and
Jonathan R. Crawshaw

5

GLOBALISM, MULTINATIONAL ENTERPRISES AND HRM

Charmi Patel and
Pawan Budhwar

PART TWO HRM IN PRACTICE

6

WORKFORCE INTELLIGENCE PLANNING

Judy Scully, Paul Turner,
Michael Gregson, Ben Clegg,
Joanna Parker and Paul Hunt

7

RECRUITMENT AND SELECTION

Stephen A. Woods, Lara D. Zibarras and
Daniel P. Hinton

8

DIVERSITY IN ORGANISATIONS: HRM AND INTERNATIONAL PRACTICES

Lilian Otaye-Ebede, Vincenza Priola
and Elaine Yerby

9

LEARNING AND DEVELOPMENT

Margarita Nyfoudi and Helen Shipton

10

REWARD STRATEGIES AND SYSTEMS

Ann Davis and Vidu Badigannavar

11

PERFORMANCE MANAGEMENT AND MOTIVATION

Arup Varma, Pawan Budhwar and
Peter Norlander

12

WORKPLACE RELATIONS AND REGULATIONS

Kathy Daniels

PART THREE HRM IN CONTEXT

13

HRM IN SMALL AND MEDIUM SIZED ENTERPRISES (SMES)

Nicholas Theodorakopoulos and Safa Arslan

14

HRM IN THE NOT-FOR-PROFIT SECTORS

Jennifer Surtees, Karin Sanders, Helen Shipton and Louise Knight

LIST OF FIGURES

LIST OF TABLES

GUIDED TOUR

R KNOWLEDGE OBJECTIV

ct on the changing nature and context of
in terms of the environment in which the
mporary organisation operates.
ribe the implications of these changes for
ging people at work.
e the nature of HRM and its evolution.
the range of roles, activities and pro-
cluded in HRM.
kills and knowledge areas requir
ts and others undertaking
organisation

KEY SKILLS OBJECTIVES

- Explore and describe what it is that y
  want from work.
- Recognise that different people hav
  different views on work and the emplo
  ment relationship.
- Take other people's views into acco
  when working in groups or teams
  Set out the key requirements
  HRM role within an organisa
  arguments from

Knowledge and Skills Objectives highlight everything students should achieve by the end of the chapter. The CIPD boxes indicate the modules relating most closely to the chapter content.

DEBATING HRM

The merit of decentralising the HR

Read the article 'HR business partne
tiveness' by Caldwell, R. (2008) at ww
docs/HRMJ.1748-8583.2008.00071.p
   TASK: *Split into two groups.*

1   One group should research the
    decentralising the HR function.

2   Groups should identify case
    decentralised or centralise

3   Groups should be prep

Debating HRM boxes present the key contemporary challenges and dilemmas faced by HR professionals.

ONLINE STUDY TOO

Thinking about joining the CIPD?
    Peter Cheese, CEO of the CIPD, s
companion website.

https://edge.sagepub.com/crawshaw2

Online Study Tools boxes direct you to handy resources on the website to help you study or read further at crucial points in the text.

INTRODUCTION

This introductory chapter has
evolution of human resource ma
professional discipline. Se
    required by HR

HRM IN PRACTICE

People management and the Ca

Cadbury Brothers, run by Joh
family of Quakers, started tradin
19th century they were so suc
and chocolate to the Queen. To
Cadbury, who were John's sor
George opened a new factor
The 'Bournville' factory, as
excellent access to trans
its workforce. At his

HRM in Practice boxes provide examples of unique or unusual real-world HRM examples.

Mid-chapter and end of chapter **Case Studies** offer a link between theory and practical challenges in the international HR environment. Each case study ends with questions for students to explore.

CASE STUDY

Reorganising the HR function at AE

AE Housing is an established charity
England and Wales. The organisatior

- London and the South East
- Wales and the West of England
- Midlands and the North

Due to a reduction across their fu
levels from 1800 to 1250 empl
the three geographical reg
    Prior to the re

GRADUATE INSIGHTS

First impressions of HR work

The following is taken from a conversati
of the MSc HRM and Business programm
of a large Multinational Enterprise (MNE)

Author: Can you briefly describe your jo
Rich: Yes, well obviously I am curre
responsibilities have varied a
abouts) each in different der
not just HR. This is impor
about all aspects of th

thor: In terms of HR th

pr

Graduate Insights present reflections from recent graduates and current students in worked-based training.

HR practitioner skills

The CIPD's HR 'Profession Map' (www.c
profession/hr-profession-map/) outlines a nu
tional HR skills and individual behaviours t
requirements for HR practitioners to be truly
include:

- Functional Skills – Organisation design, or
  opment, resourcing, learning and tale
  performance and reward, employee eng
  relations and service delivery.

- Behavioural Skills – Curious, decisiv
  encer, personally credible, collabo
  courage to challenge and role m

ASK: Reflect upon your deve
w you will b

Developing Key Skills sections contain a number of tasks/activities aimed at developing the core HR, management and leadership skills expected of university graduates.

CHAPTER SUMMARY

The key points that we have identifi

- Studying HR is about trying to un
  control, coordinate and motivate

- 'Exactly what is HRM?' is a hea

- Definitions of HRM tend to ma
  spective on people manager
  management; (3) that inv
  organisation's sustain
  mployme

End of **Chapter Summaries** list the key points indentified in the chapter.

e managers in the dev…
function is facing a number of imp…
ernal business environment. These includ…
2) the global economy, (3) changing demographi…
lation, (4) pressure to deliver more environment…
business performance and (5) how to effectively m…

REVIEW QUESTIONS AND EXERCISES

1. Evaluate the differences, if any, between personnel m…
2. Describe and evaluate Ulrich and Brockbank's (2005…
3. What, if any, contradictions may there be betwee…
   'business partner' and 'employee advocate' HR rol…
   Evaluate the advantages and disadvantages of o…
   lain how external environmental factors m…
   les.
   se organisation. Resear…

Review Questions and Exercises are provided at the end of each chapter for additional study.

…nce framew…
Why is it difficult to evalu…
organisational performance?

EXPLORE FURTHER

Muller-Camen, M., Croucher, R. and Leigh, S. (…
Study Approach. London: Chartered Institute of …
good book exploring HRM through the case study
contract, absence and turnover' in particular p…
issues linking HRM practices, the psychological…
towards and behaviours at work.

Schuler, R.S. (1989) Strategic human resou…
157–184. Although this article was now writt…
review of the key theoretical development…

The Chartered Institute of Personnel …
…bsite is worth exploring as it wil…
…rofession.

Explore Further sections list key articles highlighted in the chapter and identify key source material for students to follow up.

Glossary terms are highlighted in the text to help you spot key words and terms. A short explanation is provided in the **Glossary of Terms** section at the end of the book.

…s on
…ch views
…to achieve
…et al., 1997).
…related to the
…g, clear goal or
…asurement and
…e bureaucratic

…hose people
…ctive, or in
…its goals.
…n rela-
…ove

Hard HRM   Those HR policies and practices that enable the close control and coordination of employees – viewing employees as an organisational resource to be effectively utilised.

Soft HRM   Those HR policies and practices that aim to elicit the affective (emotional) commitment of employees to the organisation and its …

COMPANION WEBSITE ⑤SAGE edge™

Human Resource Management: Strategic and International Perspectives is supported by a companion website. Visit https://edge.sagepub.com/crawshaw2e to take advantage of the learning resources for students and lecturers.

FOR STUDENTS

- **Interactive multiple choice questions** allow you to test your knowledge of each chapter.
- **Free selected Sage journal articles** are available for each chapter to further develop your understanding.
- **Weblinks and video links** highlight real-world examples.
- **Podcasts** from the contributors of each chapter introduce key topics and provide useful tips and advice for when you are revising.

FOR LECTURERS

- **Instructor's manual** contains tutor's notes and answers to chapter questions and exercises to support your teaching.
- **PowerPoint slides** present key concepts from the chapters.

NOTES ON THE EDITORS AND CONTRIBUTORS

EDITORS

Jonathan R. Crawshaw is Senior Lecturer in Human Resource Management and Organisational Behaviour and Deputy Head (Research) of the Work and Organisational Psychology Group of Aston Business School, Aston University. Jonathan's research and teaching interests include organisational justice, behavioural ethics and careers, and he has published in leading academic journals on these interests. He is currently HRM Track Chair of the British Academy of Management, Associate Editor of *Social Justice Research* and Editorial Board Member of the *Journal of Management*. He has also guest edited special issues for the *Journal of Business Ethics, Human Relations* and the *Thunderbird International Business Review*.

Pawan Budhwar is Professor of International HRM and Joint Director of Aston India Foundation for Applied Research at Aston Business School, UK. He received his PhD from Manchester Business School. He is the co-founder and first President of the Indian Academy of Management, an affiliate of AOM. Pawan has published over 100 articles in leading journals on topics related to people management, with a specific focus on India. He has also written and/or co-edited 15 books on HRM-related topics for different national and regional contexts. He is the co-Editor-in-Chief of the *British Journal of Management* and an Associate Editor of *Human Resource Management*, a Fellow of the Academy of Social Sciences, the Higher Education Academy, the British Academy of Management and the Indian Academy of Management, and a chartered member of the Chartered Institute of Personnel and Development (CIPD).

Ann Davis is a Reader in the Work and Organisational Psychology Group at Aston Business School, UK. Her background is in both work psychology and HRM, and she is a chartered member of the CIPD and Associate Fellow of the British Psychological Society. She has taught introductory and advanced courses in the field of people and work for over 20 years. She has published in a variety of peer-reviewed journals in HRM and psychology, her work focusing on the construction and enactment of the employment relationship, primarily from the employee perspective.

CONTRIBUTORS

Safa Arslan is a PhD researcher at the Work and Organisational Psychology Group at Aston Business School, UK. Safa's interest areas of research are human resource management and firm performance, small and medium businesses, and entrepreneurship. His PhD study has been funded by the Ministry of National Education, Republic of Turkey.

Vidu Badigannavar is a Senior Lecturer in HRM at the Aston Business School. He holds an MSc and PhD from the London School of Economics. His research interests are in the areas of HR and performance outcomes of labour–management partnerships and employment relations in emerging economies. Vidu has published widely in leading journals such as the *British Journal of Industrial Relations, Advances in Industrial and Labor Relations* and the *Industrial Law Journal.* Prior to joining academia, Vidu spent over a decade working in the industry as an HR manager in the IT industry and later as a policy research officer with international trade union federations in South and South East Asia. Vidu's research has been funded by the Nuffield Foundation, the British Academy-Leverhulme Trust, DFID, the British Council and the Sir Ratan Tata Trust.

Helen Borland is Senior Lecturer in Business Sustainability at Aston Business School, Aston University. Helen's research and teaching interests are in the ecological sciences and philosophy of sustainability and how these may inform business. Helen has published in a variety of leading academic journals, as well as in the practitioner and popular press. She works on a number of consultancy and grant-awarded projects, including an EU Climate Change Leadership project.

Ben Clegg is a Professor of Operations Management at Aston Business School. He specialises in process and operations improvement using soft systems thinking and extended enterprise modelling. He teaches, trains and consults in this field.

Kathy Daniels is Senior Teaching Fellow at Aston Business School, teaching employment law and employee relations. Prior to this she was a senior HR manager in the manufacturing sector. Kathy writes extensively, primarily covering all topics relating to employment law. She carries out a range of roles for the CIPD, including contributing to HR Inform and the 'Law at Work' programme.

Mike Gregson, after a successful career in the banking sector, spent several years in the Workforce Intelligence and Planning Function of Birmingham City Council, as strategic lead for the design and deployment of strategic HRM including workforce planning, talent management and human capital intelligence metrics. In 2014 he moved to join the newly formed Acivico, where as Head of Commercial he leads on business development, communications and marketing, HR, legal and organisational effectiveness. Michael is currently studying for his PhD at Aston, and is in addition a lean six sigma black belt.

Alastair Hatch is an HR professional with over 15 years' experience within the public sector. After holding various HR roles in local government, the NHS and the Civil Service, Alastair has since 2014 worked for Highways England as Reward Manager, where a key role has been to advise and support the transition of employees from the Highways Agency to Highways England while at the same time delivering core reward strategy and activities.

Daniel P. Hinton is a Lecturer in Psychology at the University of Wolverhampton, where he teaches on the MSc in Occupational Psychology programme. His research is focused on selection and organisational assessment, particularly the application of ability tests for selection. Through his consultancy, he has worked with a diverse range of clients both within the UK and internationally, developing psychometric tools and delivering HRM solutions to clients in both the public and private sectors.

Paul Hunt is the Managing Partner of Higgs & Sons, a Top 200 law firm based in the West Midlands, England. Paul is a solicitor, having qualified in 1990. He specialises in complex commercial contracts in a wide range of manufacturing and service industries, his knowledge and experience from his management role allowing him to bring a grounded commercial perspective in his advice to clients. Paul is also passionate about the development of people and has worked with his management team to promote bespoke learning and other innovations within the firm.

Anastasia Katou is Assistant Professor of Organisational Strategy in the Department of Business Administration at the University of Macedonia, Greece. She received her MBA from the University of Sunderland, UK, and her PhD from Cardiff University, UK. Her research interests include human resource management, organisational behaviour and business strategy, with a focus on organisational performance. Her work has been published in leading academic journals, including the *Journal of World Business* and *Human Resource Management*.

Louise Knight is a Senior Lecturer in the Engineering Systems and Management Group at Aston University. She is co-Editor-in-Chief of the *Journal of Purchasing and Supply Management*, and has served as Convenor and Track Chair of the British Academy of Management SIG for Inter-organizational Relations: partnerships, alliances and networks. Her work on procurement strategy and capability, collaboration and network learning has been published in a wide variety of journals including *Human Relations*, *Public Money and Management*, *Health Policy* and *Management Learning*.

Katty Marmenout is a Visiting Professor of Organisational Behaviour at Ecole hôtelière de Lausanne, Switzerland, holding a PhD in Management from McGill University. Building on her practical experience in management consulting, her main research interests lie in the impact of mergers and acquisitions on employees, women leaders, and equality and diversity in the workplace. Her work has been published in leading academic journals, including the *Journal of Applied Behavioral Science* and *Human Resource Management*.

Thierry Nadisic is Associate Professor of Organisational Behaviour at EMLYON Business School, France. In 2009 he completed his PhD in Management at HEC Paris and won the HEC Foundation Prize for dissertation of the year. Thierry contributes to knowledge and practice on how to enrich and improve human relationships. His research, which has been published widely, addresses issues of fair management and well-being at work. His training and coaching activities emphasise leadership, change, team management and growth of teams and individual executives. He disseminates his work through conferences, articles in the media, and on his blog at www.thierry-nadisic.com, and through co-publication of the French magazine *Psychologie Positive*.

Peter Norlander received his Bachelor of Science degree from the Cornell School of Industrial and Labor Relations, and his doctorate of management from the UCLA

Anderson School of Management. He is an Assistant Professor at Loyola University, Chicago's Quinlan School of Business in the Institute of Human Resources and Employment Relations.

Margarita Nyfoudi is a Senior Lecturer in Human Resource Management and the Associate Director of the BA (Hons) in Human Resource Management at Birmingham City Business School. Her research interests include workplace learning, managerial development, employee communications and leadership with a particular focus on multi-level modelling. She received her MSc and PhD in HRM from Aston Business School, for which she was awarded a PwC scholarship and an Aston University graduate teaching assistantship respectively. She is a Fellow of the Higher Education Academy, an elected Council member of the British Academy of Management and an associate member of the CIPD.

Lilian Otaye-Ebede is a Senior Lecturer in HRM-Research with Liverpool Business School, UK, holding a PhD in Management from Aston University. Her research interests are in the areas of strategic HRM, employee relations, diversity management, international HRM and employee well-being. She has published academic papers in world leading journals and has extensively presented her research. She is currently an Editorial Board Member of the *Journal of Organizational Effectiveness: People and Performance*, an Associate Member of the Higher Education Academy (AHEA) and an Academic Member of the CIPD.

Joanna Parker is HR Director at Higgs & Sons. Her first HR Manager role was for a global law firm DLA Piper, after which she joined a national law firm with over 2000 partners and staff. Joanna was offered her first Director's appointment by Clarke Willmott where she was awarded HR Director of the Year by the profession's recognised journal *The Lawyer Magazine*.

Carole Parkes is Professor of Responsible Management and Global Issues, University of Winchester, UK, and previously Director of Social Responsibility and Sustainability at Aston University. Carole is Chair (UK & Ireland) of the UN Principles of Responsible Management Education (PRME) and International Advisory Committee member. Carole's research interests and publications are in CSR, ethics and HRM with a focus on the role of business in human rights and poverty and sustainability.

Charmi Patel is an Associate Professor in HRM within the Strategy and International Business Group at Henley Business School, University of Reading, UK. Her research interests include strategic and international human resource management, employee–organisation relationships, organisational justice, counterproductive workplace behaviours and occupational health within cross-cultural contexts (especially India). Findings from her research have been published in refereed international journals such as *Human Resource Management, Journal of World Business, Human Resource Management Review, International Journal of Human Resource Management* and *European Journal of International Management*.

Jude Preston has over 15 years' experience and knowledge of both strategic and operational levels of HRM and business management as well as leadership training, learning and development and change management. She has worked in various large blue chip organisations in a range of industries, from engineering and railways, to residential care and e-fulfilment, prior to transitioning to an academic career in 2011. She is a Teaching Fellow in the Work and Organisational Psychology Group at Aston Business School, where she teaches on several undergraduate and post-graduate courses within her academic group. Jude also runs her own consultancy company, which specialises in providing learning and development services to the rail engineering industry.

Vincenza (Cinzia) Priola is a Senior Lecturer in Organisation Studies at the Open University in the UK. Her interests focus mainly on how organisational practices affect the ways in which employees experience work. Her research concerns issues of employee and managerial identities, gender, sexuality and diversity in the workplace and how the concepts of brand and branding are experienced within organisations. Her book: *Branded Lives: The Production and Consumption of Meaning at Work* (co-edited with Matthew Brannan and Elisabeth Parsons) is published by Edward Elgar. Her latest work has been published in *Organization Studies*, *British Journal of Management* and *Gender, Work and Organization*. She is an Associate Editor of the journal *Gender, Work and Organization*.

Karin Sanders is Professor of HRM and Organizational Behaviour, co-Director of the Centre for Innovation and Entrepreneurship and Head of School, School of Management at the UNSW Australia Business School, Sydney, Australia. Karin has published in a range of peer-reviewed journals on various aspects of the HRM Process approach, informal learning, innovative behaviour and methodology. She sits on the editorial board for several international journals, like *Evidence-based HRM*, *Human Resource Management Review* and *Human Resource Management* and is Associate Editor of the *International Journal of Human Resource Management*. Karin is an elected member of the Executive Committee of the HR Division of the Academy of Management.

Achim Schmitt is Associate Professor of Strategic Management and Director of the EMBA and MSc in Global Hospitality Business programmes at Ecole hôtelière de Lausanne, HES-SO, University of Applied Sciences Western Switzerland. After more than 13 years in strategy consulting, he has worked at the University of Geneva (Switzerland), Columbia Business School (USA) and Audencia Business School (France). Achim holds a PhD from the University of Geneva and obtained his Habilitation at the University of Paris-Dauphine in France. His research focuses on organisational decline, corporate turnarounds and strategic management. He currently serves on the scientific board of the International Association of Strategic Management (France) and the Editorial Board at *Long Range Planning*.

Judy Scully is Senior Lecturer in Work and Organisational Psychology at Aston Business School. Her areas of research expertise include: emergency preparedness and evacuation, health service management and user engagement, SHRM and inno-vation in the public sector. She worked with the Workforce Intelligence Planning Team at Birmingham City Council for three years. As an investigator of a research bid team she has been awarded a number of large-scale research grants that have informed publications. These include: the NHS National Staff Survey, believed to be the third largest staff survey in the world: EREBUS (Engaging Research for Business Transformation) and INDEX (Innovation Delivers Expansion). She has recently been part of a team working with Network Rail. In 2005 Judy was awarded the Chancellors Medal and in 2014 she was given an Astonishing Academic Award.

Helen Shipton is Professor of Human Resource Management at the Nottingham Business School, Nottingham Trent University where she leads the Centre of People, Innovation and Performance. Helen is interested in HRM, creativity and innovation, and has published in leading peer-reviewed journals such as *Human Resource Management Journal*, *British Journal of Management* and *Journal of Organizational Behavior*. Helen is on the editorial board of *Human Resource Management Journal* and *Human Resource Management Review*.

Jennifer Surtees is a Solutions Consultant at Thomas International, a large global 'people assessment' organisation. Jennifer gained her PhD from Aston Business School, Aston University in 2016. Her research focused on inter-organisational innovation in the medical device sector, exploring the collaboration between SMEs and the NHS. During the course of her research degree Jenny has completed a secondment within the NHS Technology Adoption Centre. She achieved her MSc in Human Resource Management and Business in 2010 from the Aston Business School and is an Affiliate Member of the CIPD.

Nicholas Theodorakopoulos is Reader in Strategic Entrepreneurship Development and Head of the Work and Organisational Psychology Group at Aston Business School, UK. Nicholas's specialist areas of research, academic publications and teaching include strategic entrepreneurship, learning and innovation and diversity at work. His research has been funded by a host of organisations and has been published in a variety of internationally renowned peer-reviewed journals. He often acts as a coach and investor in early stage small businesses.

Paul Turner has held professorial positions at universities in Birmingham, Cambridge and Nottingham. He has held other senior management and non-executive roles in Europe and Asia. Paul has chaired European HR and Talent Conferences, and was a judge on European HR Excellence and CIPD People Management Awards. He is the author or co-author of *Workforce Planning* (2010) and *HR Forecasting and Planning* (2002), both published by the CIPD.

Arup Varma is Professor of Human Resources and Employment Relations at the Quinlan School of Business, Loyola University Chicago. His primary research interests lie in performance appraisals, expatriate issues and HRM in India. He has published over 75 book chapters and articles in leading journals, and has presented over 90 research papers at leading management and psychology conferences globally. Arup is also co-founder and past President of the Indian Academy of Management.

Stephen A. Woods is Professor of Work and Organizational Psychology at Surrey Business School and a Chartered Occupational Psychologist. He is known for his work on personality and psychometric assessment, recruitment and selection and vocational development, which he publishes in journals and scholarly books. As a practitioner, Steve has worked with a wide array of organisational clients, both in the UK and internationally.

Elaine Yerby is a Senior Lecturer in HRM at the University of East London and leads a variety of strategic HRM modules. She is a Chartered Member of the CIPD and is Vice Chair of the East London CIPD Branch. Her research interests focus on the role of gender in careers and managerial practice, diversity in the workplace and the relationship between HRM and organisational development.

Lara D. Zibarras is Senior Lecturer in Organisational Psychology at City University London and Associate Director for Research at the Work Psychology Group. As a Chartered Occupational Psychologist and Associate Fellow of the British Psychological Society, she has conducted extensive selection assessment research in high-stakes settings, focusing on the applicants' perspective, and use of innovative assessment methods such as situational judgement tests. She has published widely in academic journals and consulted for public and private sector organisations in the areas of selection, training, development and psychometric assessment.

PREFACE

It is two years since the first edition of this text was published. During this time, HRM has continued to experience considerable turbulence as the Global Financial Crisis recedes but new social and political challenges emerge. Human Resource Management as a profession needs to be aware of these challenges and respond to them in an ethical and sustainable manner, bridging difference between sectors, cultures and value systems and generating novel, evidence-based solutions to the problems with which it is presented. Students of HRM need to be able to demonstrate their awareness of these issues and integrate them into contemporary contexts both to ensure effective HR operation and to enhance their own employability.

In this new edition, we have further explored the international context for HRM, not just for multinational corporations (MNCs) but also for small businesses and not-for-profit organisations. Consideration of the international dimension in all its aspects, including cross-cultural working, MNCs, diversity and equality and international business, is simply a part of the organisational landscape. The diversity of students within the average university-level programme itself offers a degree of exposure to such issues uncommon even a decade ago. Therefore, this book seeks to provide a comprehensive introduction to HRM to students who are new to the field, but who will be seeking employment in a global market, working with diverse colleagues and across national borders.

The core theme of ethics within and sustainability of the work environment continues to play a significant role in the discussion and development of HRM. We believe that this agenda must be front and centre in our understanding of how organisations respond to new challenges. Our history as a profession has intermittently lost sight of the Human component of human resource management but our origins sit squarely within this discourse. We now are in a position to impact strategically on business operation while having a professional duty to safeguard ethical practice and demonstrating the courage to challenge inappropriate, unfair and unsustainable decisions, as both the Chartered Institute of Personnel and Development (CIPD) in the UK and the Society for Human Resource Management (SHRM) in the USA remind us. Focusing our attention on the triple bottom line of people, planet and profit provides a more broadly based set of performance outcomes than just financial viability and economic return. However, this requires that we are aware of the evidence and can create persuasive arguments in support of our values. We cannot, and indeed need not, rely on simple exhortation. Increasingly we see evidence of a positive link between good practice and good performance and we can effectively communicate this association through our thoughtful practice and responsible behaviour.

A criticism that is often made of those transitioning from education to work is that they are unprepared for the reality of the workplace. While graduates are well-informed and knowledgeable, their ability to apply that knowledge to their workplace experience is sometimes limited. This text seeks to address this shortcoming. Drawing on our excellent reputation for employability, and with the cooperation of our own students and graduates, we include real-world examples and current debates throughout the book. Recognising and analysing the challenges that arise where theory meets practice, generating creative, agile and applicable solutions, and communicating them effectively and with voice are key graduate skills. We have embedded through the text features designed to be both thought-provoking and developmental, encouraging you to explore linkages between theory and practice and develop your own vision of what reflexive HR practice looks like. While we cannot provide you with work experience, we hope you will identify a flavour of the reality of work, and for those of you already in work, that our interpretation and analysis offer alternative perspectives on the work experience.

This book therefore integrates a rigorous understanding of current HR theory and practice with real-world illustrations and examples of HR in practice, and highlights the challenges and controversies that arise when theory meets practice. It adopts a stance which recognises that effective functioning of an organisation is not simply measured by the financial bottom line, but by the outcomes for a wider range of stakeholders. This is located in the broader social, economic and political context.

The book is primarily designed as core reading for students who are having their first introduction to the field of HRM, either on a specialist HRM programme or as a part of a more generalist business or management programme. It serves as an introductory HRM text for both undergraduate- and postgraduate-level students, including those on general MBA programmes. The text provides a concise introduction to the field of HRM, balancing the needs of rigour in learning and teaching with relevance in the development of competence and thinking performers. It is suitable both for HR specialists and for non-specialist students who will, as future managers, be expected to implement HRM in the workplace, and indeed themselves be subject to HRM as employees. It seeks to encourage students to reflect on their own position in relation to key debates and to take a critical stance on the dominant managerial rhetoric surrounding HRM and how this would influence their own behaviour in the workplace.

The book has also been written to support students studying for level 5 (Intermediate) and level 7 (Advanced) qualifications from the CIPD. At the beginning of each chapter the units at each level that are addressed by the chapter content are identified.

STRUCTURE OF THE BOOK

The book is divided into three main sections. The key aims identified above are referenced throughout all three sections.

PART 1: STRATEGIC ISSUES IN HRM

The first part of the book (Chapters 1 to 5) lays out a range of overarching themes in contemporary HRM strategy. These reflect the aims identified earlier, and bring to the fore contextual features that shape the environment for HR practice. Chapter 1 discusses the nature, development and role of HRM, locating the field within the broader theoretical and practical landscapes. Chapter 2 moves on to explore HRM at a strategic level, focusing on recent debates around and evidence for the effect of HRM on firm performance. Chapter 3 raises the issue of organisational change, a constant in the business environment, and considers its implications for HRM. Chapter 4 focuses on issues of ethics and the role of HRM in promoting ethical, fair and sustainable organisations. Finally, in Chapter 5, the impact of the international context on HRM is explored. How do and how should organisations operating across borders and with diverse workforces adjust their approach to HRM to recognise and accommodate difference?

PART 2: HRM IN PRACTICE

Part 2 (Chapters 6–12) covers the core functional areas for HRM, taking a broadly 'employee lifecycle' approach. This begins with workforce intelligence planning (Chapter 6), which identifies the future demands for skills and behaviours across the workforce and their conversion into implementable actions in support of strategic objectives. Chapter 7 moves on to recruitment and selection, possibly the most recognisable of HR activities. Drawing on contemporary literature in both HRM and work psychology, the chapter reviews theory, practice and ethics in recruitment and selection. Diversity and HRM (Chapter 8) critically examines a range of perspectives on diversity management and their implications for HRM policy and practice. Chapter 9 turns to the place of learning and development in organisations. Focusing primarily on individual (rather than organisational) learning, it contrasts more traditional approaches to training in organisations with more individualised learning-based approaches to development. Chapters 10 and 11, 'Reward Strategies and Systems' and 'Performance Management and Motivation', could be viewed as a pair. A key theme in relation to reward is the establishment of fairness in the assessment and distribution of all forms of reward, both intrinsic and extrinsic. This is examined at some length, looking also at ways of establishing fair procedures and the meaning of fairness in this respect. Chapter 11 looks at how motivation can be managed in organisations, in part through the allocation of reward, but also through a broader set of performance management practices with their roots in work psychology and motivation theory. Finally in Part 2, workplace relations and regulation (Chapter 12) are explored. While different jurisdictions operate different workplace regulations, the chapter here will focus on the principles of workplace regulation and issues of power among different stakeholders in organisations.

PART 3: HRM IN CONTEXT

The final part of the book explores two sectors which are sometimes argued to be overlooked by much of the contemporary HR literature and yet place specific demands on HR operation and employ a significant number of people. Specifically, these are small firms (Chapter 13) and the not-for-profit sectors (Chapter 14). Both of these sectors can be difficult to define; however, they have increasing socio-economic significance both locally and globally. Chapter 13 explores the nature of people management in specifically entrepreneurial small firms and explores the usefulness of conventional and novel people management practices in such firms. In Chapter 14, the range of not-for-profit organisations is first outlined, along with the challenges they face. The influence of the political environment on not-for-profit strategy and orientation is explored.

PEDAGOGICAL FEATURES

In order to ensure that the three core aims identified earlier are achieved, the book contains a number of learning features in each chapter.

KNOWLEDGE AND SKILLS OBJECTIVES

Each chapter begins with a set of knowledge and skills objectives that students should achieve by the end of the chapter. It also indicates the CIPD modules which relate most closely to the chapter content, both for Intermediate (level 5) and Advanced (level 7) study. The skills objectives are also mapped against the Developing Key Skills features/boxes throughout the chapter.

DEBATING HRM

A key feature of the book is that it presents the challenges and dilemmas that are faced by HR professionals in the workplace. Each chapter highlights key contemporary debates and suggests questions and activities which students can consider to encourage more detailed and creative exploration of the issue.

HRM IN PRACTICE

In each chapter there are examples of excellent, unique or unusual HRM practice drawn from real-world examples. These are included to highlight the range of HR practice and to encourage students to think innovatively about HR issues.

CASE STUDIES

Each chapter contains two case studies, one short case mid-chapter and a longer end-of-chapter case. Each case has a set of accompanying questions which students can explore individually or in groups to broaden their learning. This serves to enhance the linkage between the theory presented in the chapter and the practical challenges faced by HR professionals in the international environment. Again reflecting the key aims within the book, the case studies and the HRM in Practice features have been selected specifically to address both international examples, particularly from emerging economies, and examples which illuminate issues of ethics and social responsibility. While not every chapter will include both BRICs and ethics examples, across the text the illustrative pieces are drawn from a wide range of national contexts.

GRADUATE INSIGHTS

In order to enhance and make real the lived experience of HRM, each chapter includes some insights obtained from recent graduates or current students undergoing work-based training. These again relate specifically to the subject matter of the chapter and may be observations, specific problems faced or difficulties encountered, or reflections on a role which the student/graduate has undertaken.

DEVELOPING KEY SKILLS

Each chapter contains a number of tasks/activities aimed at developing the core HR, management and leadership skills expected of university graduates. The skills identified within each chapter will be particularly pertinent (though not limited) to the topic and focus of the chapter and are outlined in the skills outcomes at the beginning of each chapter. While these activities may not be a replacement for real work experience, in some small way they provide an opportunity for students to start 'doing' HR, thus further enhancing their professional development and employability.

REVIEW QUESTIONS AND EXERCISES

At the end of each chapter, and following a bulleted chapter summary, a set of review questions is included. Of these, some are related to the curriculum content, either from the CIPD or that which is commonly covered in HRM modules, some are more reflective questions which students can follow up on as additional study, and at least one is an experiential exercise designed to broaden students' experience of HRM through either work-based or simulated activities.

EXPLORE FURTHER

Having purchased this book, you will have access to the full-text articles published by Sage which are referenced in the book. Key articles in this respect are highlighted in each chapter. An annotated further reading section is also included for each chapter, which identifies key source material on which students should follow up. Indications as to the significance of these sources and their specific contribution to knowledge are included for these sources.

ACKNOWLEDGEMENTS

First, we would like to thank all the authors who have contributed to this edited textbook. Without your expertise and commitment to the project this book would not exist, and for this we are truly grateful.

Second, we would like to thank all the team at Sage for their unerring support for and commitment to our book. We extend particular thanks to Commissioning Editor Kirsty Smy, who expertly supported and guided our original book proposals, and to Senior Development Editor Sarah Turpie, who has guided and supported us throughout the development and completion of this second edition. Without the support, patience and persistence of both of you this book would not have been written.

Third, we would like to thank all the reviewers who have been involved throughout the project and those academics who have provided invaluable guidance on their use of the first edition and how best to develop this second edition. Your commentaries have been insightful and informative and we hope you can recognise your influence in how the book has developed. We continue to attend to your input on tone, content and usefulness of our book.

Finally, we would like to thank all the authors and publishers who kindly agreed to grant us permission to reproduce the copyright materials in their various publications. These materials are an essential component of this book and without your kind permissions this would not have been possible.

PUBLISHER'S ACKNOWLEDGEMENTS

We would like to extend our warmest thanks to the following individuals for their invaluable feedback on the proposal and the draft material for this book:

Ziming Cai, University of Nottingham

Paul Hill, Northumbria University

Frances-Louise McGregor, University of Huddersfield

Steve McPeake, Ulster University

Daniela Rudloff, University of Leicester

Sally Sambrook, Bangor University

Martin Sposato, Middlesex University

Carola Weissmeyer, Keele University

PART ONE
STRATEGIC ISSUES IN HRM

CHAPTER 1

INTRODUCTION: CONTEXT AND CHALLENGES FOR HRM

Jonathan R. Crawshaw

Jude Preston

Alastair Hatch

CHAPTER KNOWLEDGE OBJECTIVES

- Reflect on the changing nature and context of work in terms of the environment in which the contemporary organisation operates.
- Describe the implications of these changes for managing people at work.
- Outline the nature of HRM and its evolution.
- Identify the range of roles, activities and processes included in HRM.
- Discuss the skills and knowledge areas required by HRM specialists and others undertaking HRM responsibilities within organisations.

KEY SKILLS OBJECTIVES

- Explore and describe what it is that you want from work.
- Recognise that different people have different views on work and the employment relationship.
- Take other people's views into account when working in groups or teams.
- Set out the key requirements for an HRM role within an organisation.
- Make arguments from different points of view.

This chapter also provides indicative content for the following CIPD Intermediate and Advanced level modules:

CIPD INTERMEDIATE LEVEL MODULES

5CHR Business issues and the context of human resources

5HRF Managing and coordinating the HR function

5DVP Developing professional practice

CIPD ADVANCED LEVEL MODULES

7HRC Human resource management in context

7SBL Developing skills for business leadership

GO ONLINE

This chapter comes with loads of online tools to help you to go that extra mile in your studies!

- **Multiple choice questions** to help you test your knowledge and revise for exams
- **Journal articles** so you can read further for assignments and essays
- **Videos** and **podcasts** to help you understand how complex concepts work in the real world

Visit **https://edge.sagepub.com/crawshaw2e** to access these resources for this topic.

INTRODUCTION

This introductory chapter has three main aims. First, it will explore the nature and evolution of human resource management (HRM) as both an academic field of study and a professional discipline. Second, it will outline the potential roles, skills and competencies required by HR professionals – themes that will be returned to throughout the remainder of this book. Finally, it will introduce a number of contemporary people management challenges which organisations face, and the HR implications of these challenges; again, these are issues that will be revisited throughout the remaining chapters of the book.

Human resource management (HRM) The organisational function that deals with issues related to its workforce. HRM may also be seen as a particular 'perspective' on people management – one that emphasises a strategic and integrated approach.

WHAT IS HRM?

We could answer this question by simply listing all the activities undertaken by an HR department or HR professional. A quick look at any number of HRM textbooks, HR-related websites or company profiles, and we could soon compile a fairly extensive list of these activities and responsibilities (see Figure 1.1). In this diagram, we have arranged the HR activities into four broad categories: operational, strategic, administrative and people-focused activities. However, it should be borne in mind that these categorisations are by no means definitive – many activities can reasonably be argued to fit into more than one of these category types. This can take us only so far, however, with organisations varying considerably in the activities undertaken by their HR functions. For example, despite the existence of a fairly complex and sophisticated HR function, an organisation may not have an HR presence at the senior management/executive board level. One would expect that within such an organisation, HR's role in strategic decision making might be fairly minimal. Some organisations don't have a distinct HR function at all – this is common in many SMEs. On a more practical level we know that working for one organisation is often very different from working for another despite the two perhaps employing similar HR policies and practices.

In other words, the way we are organised, directed and controlled, the employer's expectations of us and our contribution to the organisation, and our day-to-day experiences of work and treatment at the hands of our employer can vary greatly. Is this a function of whether one organisation has an HR department and another does not? Is this because one organisation employs certain HR activities that another does not? In short, the list of management activities presented in Figure 1.1, which is neither exhaustive nor definitive, tells us nothing about why these activities are undertaken

Operational HR Activities	Strategic HR Activities	Administrative HR Activities	People-focused HR Activities
• Business partnering • Advice to line managers • Recruitment • Selection • Learning and development • Training • Management development • Reward and benefits management • Performance management • Disciplinary & grievance proceedings • Dismissals • Redundancy • Employment law advice	• Executive Board membership • Strategic decision making • Workforce planning • Succession planning • Organisational (job) design • Talent management & development • Policy development	• HR-related administration • Upkeep of personnel records • Pay, and managing the payroll system • Pensions • Health & safety • Equal opportunities monitoring	• Employee engagement and motivation • Career management • Counselling • Occupational psychology • Occupational health • Change management

FIGURE 1.1 Common HR activities

by organisations, the methods used or how effectively they are implemented, their ultimate goals, or the relative role, power and influence of the HR function within the organisation.

Let's start instead, therefore, with a definition. Storey (2007: 7) defines HRM as 'a distinctive approach to employment management which seeks to achieve competitive advantage through the strategic deployment of a highly-committed and capable workforce using an array of cultural, structural and personnel techniques'. Storey's is a commonly cited definition and, although there are others, most are fairly consistent in their emphasis on similar assumptions and themes. So what are these assumptions?

1. That HRM is one particular, but not necessarily dominant, approach to the management of people in organisations. Thus HRM may be seen as the enactment or operationalisation of a particular 'perspective' or 'philosophy' on people management.

2. That HRM has a strategic role to play in helping an organisation achieve sustained competitive advantage. Many refer to this as HR 'adding value' to the organisation.

3. That an investment in a highly skilled and motivated workforce, through effective HRM policies and practices, is the 'one best way' to secure one's competitive advantage.

4. That HRM presents a unitaristic view of the employment relationship. In other words, the achievement of organisational goals and objectives is the sole purpose of employers and employees, and it is commitment to these goals that is sought from all stakeholders in the organisation. This is an alternative to a more pluralistic perspective on the employment relationship, which would recognise the importance of the different and often competing objectives or goals of different stakeholders – for example, employers, employees, trade unions, shareholders and governments. These perspectives are further discussed in Chapter 12.

Despite the definition and description presented above, let us not be under any illusion: HRM is still a heavily contested term. Indeed, for many, this is still the single most important, and yet unanswered, research question facing HRM scholars (e.g. Mayrhofer et al., 2000).

THE EVOLUTION OF HRM

We may get a better handle on exactly what HRM is if we attempt to understand its origins and evolution as an academic and practitioner field. After all, 50 or 60 years ago you may have been hard pressed to find mention of HRM in academic circles and few organisations that would have had a specifically-named 'HRM' function or department. While the exact nature of HRM and its evolution will vary from country to country (more of which later in Chapter 5), most seem to agree that the origins of 'modern HRM' are based in the workplaces and universities of the USA.

An excellent recent article by Bruce Kaufman exploring the historical development of American HRM (Kaufman, 2014) identifies a complex and multifaceted development of the field. Here we simplify this to what we believe are the three key stages of this evolution: (1) the social reform movements and emergence of industrial relations and personnel management; (2) the human relations movement and expansion of organisational behaviour as an academic discipline; and (3) the transition from personnel management to the more strategic HRM. For some, the recent focus placed on business ethics and social and environmental sustainability has led to a new, fourth stage in this evolution, with the emergence of sustainable HRM – one which focuses on delivering these competing economic, social and environmental goals (e.g. Freitas et al., 2011). We summarise below each of these four evolutionary stages of HRM.

The emergence of industrial relations and personnel management (circa 1890s–1930s)

Modern HRM is said to have its historical roots within the social reform movements of the late 19th and early 20th centuries. More enlightened employers, such as Robert Owen and George Cadbury in the UK, strove to improve the appalling working conditions that faced many men, women and children of this time. In the same period a growing number of labour movements across the newly industrialised world – the National Catholic Welfare Council in the United States and the Welfare Workers' Association in the UK – were also pushing for improved employment rights on a number of issues. For example, during this period great strides were made in regulating and legislating around long working hours, the use of child labour, and improved health and safety at work.

A growing 'labour problem' (e.g. Leiserson, 1929) associated with mass manufacturing and large-scale employment – manifested in greater conflict (and thus poorer relations) between employees and management – also saw a growing interest in the effective strategic management of the labour force at this time. In line with Classical Management Theory, in particular notions of bureaucracy (Weber, 1946) and the division of labour (Henri Fayol, 1841–1925), Frederick Taylor's *Principles of Scientific Management* (Taylor, 1911) is recognised as one of the most influential theoretical and, ultimately, practical people management developments of this period. Scientific management argues that greater workplace productivity is achieved through more rationalised and efficient modes of production. In short, Taylor and others placed their faith in a scientific, statistically-based analysis of the workplace to constantly strive for ever greater efficiencies in the production process. Efficiency, it was concluded, may be attained through:

1. The increasing mechanisation of the workplace

2. The simplification and routinisation of work

3. The extrinsic, output-related reward-based motivation of employees.

On the surface such principles do not appear to put people, and by this we mean employees, and their effective management at the forefront of managerial practice. In fact, however, a central concern of Taylor's studies was the motivation of workers (see Pryor et al., 2011). He simply concluded that motivation, and thus the efficient performance of employees, would be gained through the design of clear, simple and repetitive tasks, and the use of reward systems based on being paid for piecework. Indeed, these ideas are still very much in evidence today in many organisations and their departments, such as call centres, fast food outlets and contemporary car manufacturing plants.

Importantly, new workplaces driven by these principles of scientific management were required to engage more fundamentally than ever before, with issues of effective job design, workforce planning, training, reward and performance measurement – all core activities associated with the burgeoning field of 'personnel management', as it was known at this time. Indeed, it is reported that while in 1918 only a handful of firms in the USA had a personnel department, 10 years later one-third of companies with over 250 workers had one (Kaufman, 2014). Interestingly, it was also during this period that today's two largest bodies supporting the HR profession came into being – in the UK the Chartered Institute of Personnel and Development was formed in 1913 as the Institute of Industrial Welfare Workers, while a little later in the USA the Society for Human Resource Management was formed in 1948, as the American

Society for Personnel Administration – again perhaps reflecting the growing importance of personnel management, and HRM as a profession at this time.

HRM IN PRACTICE

People management and the Cadbury 'model village'

Cadbury Brothers, run by John and Benjamin Cadbury, two brothers from a family of Quakers, started trading in Birmingham around 1824. By the middle of the 19th century they were so successful that they were manufacturers of cocoa and chocolate to the Queen. Towards the end of that century George and Richard Cadbury, who were John's sons, had taken over the business from their father. George opened a new factory and site in the Bournbrook area of Birmingham. The 'Bournville' factory, as it became known, was unique not only because of its excellent access to transport links but also because of the facilities it provided to its workforce. At his own cost, George Cadbury built a 'Model Village' comprising hundreds of new homes and cottages for his workers. This 'factory in a garden' was designed around the new 'Garden City' movement that was emerging in the UK. All homes had gardens, with the site also containing sports fields, swimming pools, gardens, churches, schools – all designed to improve the standard of living for the Cadbury workforce. Workers were also provided with cheaper rail fares from the local station into Birmingham. This factory was built not only upon Quaker principles – there was no pub, and alcohol was not available to be bought within the village – but also on important business principles: that a happy, healthy and highly motivated workforce is good for business.

Source: the Cadbury website at www.cadbury.co.uk/the-story

Human relations and organisational behaviour (circa 1930s–1970s)

Towards the middle of the 20th century, although with its genesis in the Hawthorn Studies of the 1930s, there was an explosion of academic research in the overlapping fields of industrial and organisational psychology, industrial anthropology and sociology that began to heavily influence management theory and personnel management practice. A key strand of this research became known as the human relations movement and took a particularly 'behavioural', 'psychological' and 'emotional' perspective on the employment relationship, rejecting, at least on the surface, the 'rational economic (wo)man' assumptions of Taylorism and scientific management. This research was particularly interested in exploring the potential relationships between organisational efficiency, organisational performance and employees' positive emotions, attitudes and behaviours at, and towards, work.

Today such work is more commonly aligned with the academic discipline known as organisational behaviour. Although it is beyond the scope of this textbook to explore all of the individual avenues of enquiry that make up the field of organisational behaviour, research on topics such as leadership, organisational culture, team or group working effectiveness, interpersonal relations at work, organisational commitment, job satisfaction and engagement, organisational justice and individual personality differences, all have at their centre concerns regarding the improvement of working lives and the potential positive effects on individual, team and organisational effectiveness (e.g. Woods and West, 2010). It is within this period of academic endeavour that contemporary notions of HRM – and indeed the term HRM – began to emerge.

From personnel management to the more strategic HRM (circa 1970s – the present)

One of the most confusing aspects of studying, and even working within, HRM is the often interchangeable use of various phrases and terms for 'HRM'. Consider for a moment whether there are any real differences between departments labelled HRM, Human Resource Development (HRD), Personnel, People Management and Development, Human Capital Management, and Labour Concepts Management (yes, that is a real department!). These issues are further compounded by the ever-expanding range of job titles held by 'HR' professionals. We could, therefore, simply accept this situation and not place too much importance on a name or a job title, instead referring more generally to people management and investigating more closely what each organisational function or individual practitioner does.

However, within the academic literature at least, a dichotomy is often proposed between notions of personnel management and HRM, with the more strategic and business-focused HRM often presented as evolving from the more operational, administrative and employee-focused personnel management (Storey, 1989). Notions of strategic HRM, as opposed to a more operational and functional personnel management, gathered pace in the 1960s and 1970s, with the work of Michael Beer and colleagues at the Harvard Business School proving particularly influential. The 'Harvard Model' of HRM emphasises the importance of a close alignment between a firm's business and HR strategy and the development of a high-commitment workforce (for more, see Chapter 2). This is pitched as a contrast to 'personnel management practices' that are viewed as a rather ad hoc collection of more bureaucratic, controlling and reactive people management policies (Caldwell and Storey, 2007). Figure 1.2 summarises these main differences.

Career exploration

- Research global job sites (e.g. www.jobsite.co.uk/) for HR-related job titles.
- TASK: Compare and contrast the different job titles. Using the person specification/job description, compare the nature and scope of these jobs.

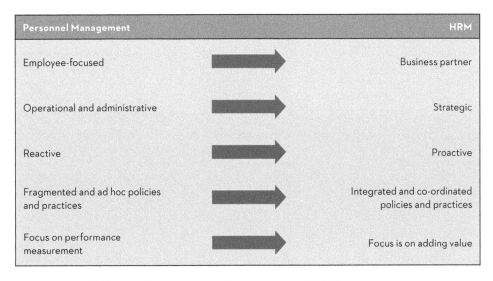

Personnel Management	HRM
Employee-focused	Business partner
Operational and administrative	Strategic
Reactive	Proactive
Fragmented and ad hoc policies and practices	Integrated and co-ordinated policies and practices
Focus on performance measurement	Focus is on adding value

FIGURE 1.2 Key differences between personnel management and HRM

At this same time, and closely paralleling debates around the transitions from personnel management to HRM, was the identification of 'hard' and 'soft' variants of HRM (for a review see Truss et al., 1997). Hard HRM is said to place an emphasis on the efficient utilisation of the workforce. In other words, hard HRM very much views employees as a 'resource' that needs to be effectively sourced and deployed to achieve organisational goals – like any other resource or raw material (Truss et al., 1997). As a result, hard HRM tends to focus on those HR activities and tools related to the close control and coordination of employees – for example, HR planning, clear goal or target setting and, most important of all, continuous performance measurement and assessment – and is therefore regarded as closely aligned to the more bureaucratic principles of personnel management.

Soft HRM, on the other hand, is said to place a greater emphasis on those people management practices and activities that are aimed at gaining the affective, or in other words, emotional, commitment of employees to the organisation and its goals. Employees are thus viewed in the more humanistic way extolled by the human relations, strategic HRM and high-commitment work practices (HCWP) work described above (e.g. Wood and De Menezes, 1998). Tight control of employees is thus potentially less important because highly committed employees are more self-regulating (Truss et al., 1997). Figure 1.3 summarises the main differences between hard and soft models of HRM.

Today the mainstream HRM literature suggests that effective HRM policies and practices are those that engage with both hard and soft notions of HRM – and thus the principles of personnel management and strategic HRM – and that these activities are not mutually exclusive. After all, hard HRM, which is associated with tighter control

Hard HRM Those HR policies and practices that enable the close control and coordination of employees - viewing employees as an organisational resource to be effectively utilised.

Soft HRM Those HR policies and practices that aim to elicit the affective (emotional) commitment of employees to the organisation and its goals.

High-commitment work practices Those policies and practices designed and implemented by organisations in order to elicit the affective commitment and engagement of some or all of their employees.

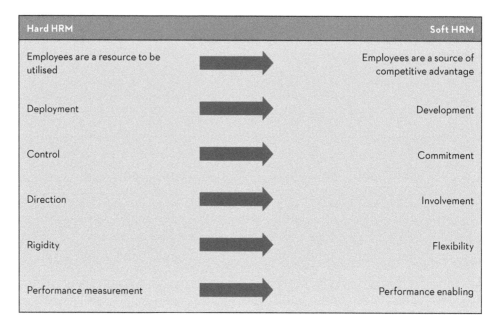

FIGURE 1.3 Hard and soft HRM

practices such as performance measurement and management, may provide greater work-related clarity and focus for both employers and employees. At the same time, a greater involvement in decision making and flexibility – soft HRM – may present more enriching and rewarding work for employees and the associated attitudinal and behavioural benefits for employers.

Sustainable HRM (2000s – the present)

The last 20 years or so have seen an increasing interest in business ethics, social responsibility and environmental sustainability. Ever more high-profile organisational ethical and environmental scandals have driven this interest, and many firms have reacted by focusing on their strategic approach to delivering their business in an ethical and both socially and environmentally responsible way.

Many see the HR function as best placed to help organisations deliver this sustainability agenda (e.g. Parkes and Davis, 2013). After all, delivering a more ethical and socially and/or environmentally responsible organisation can only be done through one's people. Thus, for authors such as Freitas et al. (2011), this period sees a new phase for HRM – one where effective HRM seeks a balance between 'economic prosperity, social equity and environmental integrity' (p. 232) – a theme we return to later in this chapter and book.

GRADUATE INSIGHTS

First impressions of HR work

The following is taken from a conversation held with Rich (real name withheld), a recent Aston University graduate of the MSc HRM and Business programme. Rich secured an HR position on the Graduate Development Programme of a large Multinational Enterprise (MNE).

Author: Can you briefly describe your job roles and responsibilities?

Rich: Yes, well obviously I am currently still part of the graduate scheme here which means that my roles and responsibilities have varied a lot over the past 12 months or so. I have spent around three months (or thereabouts) each in different departments and as such I have had experiences of different parts of the business, not just HR. This is important, however, because it is obviously really important for an HR person to know about all aspects of the business.

Author: In terms of HR then, what experiences have you had? What are your first impressions?

Rich: I am beginning to understand the structure of the department much more and the different roles that exist in it. Here, we have HR Advisors who are responsible for different parts of the business. Each Advisor has a team of people providing HR advice and support to managers and employees in their part of the business, with the Advisors reporting to the Head of HR. We also have a lot of HR advice and support via our online portal. In fact, part of what I have been doing to date has been helping to develop and upkeep our online HR site. I have also been introduced to some policy work and been allowed to sit in a number of meetings – mainly planning and advisory meetings, that sort of thing.

Author: And your first impressions of HR here?

Rich: Yes, good. There looks to be a lot of interesting work going on, you know. It's not just answering phone queries and stuff (although there is that of course). Like I said, there is policy writing and important planning meetings around recruitment and training and development. My feelings are that HR is taken quite seriously here and that the company recognises the importance of getting HR decisions right.

Author: And what skills do you think you will need to become an effective member of the HR team here?

Rich: Oh, I don't really know yet. I would say quite general skills really. Obviously, you would want a good understanding of HR stuff – particularly employment law – but I would say it is equally important to be able to work well with your colleagues, share information, be professional, keep to deadlines and be reliable, those sorts of things. Oh and definitely be able to work under pressure and to deal appropriately with some very sensitive situations.

CRITICAL PERSPECTIVES ON HRM

Before we go any further, it is important to recognise that there is a well-established 'critical' perspective on the HRM debate. Some scholars believe that the reality of 'HRM in practice' has been an all-too-dominant focus on those practices associated with hard HRM without the requisite engagement with soft HRM policies and practices (Caldwell, 2004; Legge, 2005). In other words, HR is principally about gaining the control and compliance of employees and not on facilitating their autonomy and affective commitment. Indeed, some authors present evidence that there has been very little engagement by many organisations in HRM in any form or at any level. Others criticise HRM for being 'old wine in a new bottle'. In other words, HRM is simply a 'faddish' collection of terms for many managerial practices that have existed within the workplace for many years. Indeed, this has been the response of many critical scholars to debates around the proposed transition from personnel management to strategic HRM; that HRM is nothing more than a repackaging of old ideas (for a review, see Legge, 2005).

Importantly, these perspectives and opinions often lead critical scholars to conclude that the principles of HRM perhaps hide a much darker, more sinister, managerial agenda. Drawing on Marxist critiques of the labour process, HRM is thus viewed, not as a path to greater employee enrichment and satisfaction at work, but instead as a managerialist agenda and rhetoric for the ongoing exploitation of people at work (e.g. Keenoy, 1990). Indeed, there is some fairly compelling evidence that such beliefs and conclusions may have some weight. For example, the continuing erosion of employees' job security; evidence of ever longer working hours (Gillan, 2005); growing numbers of reported cases of stress-related illnesses (CIPD, 2012a); and the ever-growing distance between the pay and rewards of those in the lowest and highest paid positions (Woods, 2010a). Fifty or so years of HRM appear to have not, one may argue, led to the utopian workplaces HRM scholars and practitioners perhaps promised.

HRM ROLES AND RESPONSIBILITIES IN ORGANISATIONS

While noting these important critical perspectives on HRM, our attention now turns to a number of competing models that have attempted to frame, summarise and explain the different roles, responsibilities and activities of HRM described in the previous sections. Here we present two (but there are more!) that are still heavily influencing both theory and practice – Storey's (1992) 'Strategic/Tactical' model and Ulrich and Brockbank's (2005) 'HR Leader' model, itself an update of an earlier model (see Ulrich, 1997a). We then explore recent cross-national research evidence for the enactment, and relative importance, of these roles.

STOREY'S (1992) STRATEGIC/TACTICAL MODEL

Storey noted that the role played by HR could be best described along two criteria: whether or not this role involved the direct intervention of the HR function in the employment relationship; and whether or not the function and its activities were principally strategic or tactical (operational) in nature. HR roles are thus defined along two dichotomous axes:

1. *Level of intervention*: where 'Interventionist' HR is directive and proactive and 'Non-interventionist' HR is reactive and non-directive.

2. *Strategic or tactical focus*: where 'Strategic' HR is focused on macro business-related concerns, and 'Tactical' HR is focused on more day-to-day operational (micro) people management issues.

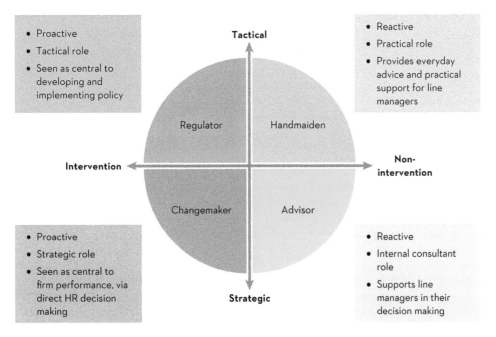

FIGURE 1.4 Storey's (1992) strategic/tactical HR roles

Within this two-by-two matrix, four potential roles for HR are thus observable: the Handmaiden, which sits in the tactical and non-interventionist quadrant; Advisor, which is strategic and non-interventionist; Regulator, which is tactical and interventionist; and Changemaker, which is strategic and interventionist. Storey (1992) argued that all may be present within an organisation, but that most likely one would be dominant. These four roles are summarised in Figure 1.4

ULRICH AND BROCKBANK'S (2005) HR LEADER MODEL

Ulrich and Brockbank proposed five potential HR roles within organisations – the Functional Expert, Employee Advocate, Human Capital Developer, Strategic Partner and HR Leader roles. Like Storey, they attempted to develop a model that recognised, and integrated, the complex (and often competing) strategic and operational functions and responsibilities of HR within organisations. Figure 1.5 illustrates and summarises these roles.

There are obvious similarities between Storey's (1992), and Ulrich and Brockbank's (2005) models. Both recognise a complex mix of operational and strategic roles for HR and also the potentially contradictory nature of these roles – for example, it may not be easy to rationalise and carry out both of Ulrich and Brockbank's 'employee advocate' and 'strategic business partner' roles. Indeed, many others have also commented on the potential 'role conflict' facing HR professionals trying to balance and enact an ever more complex range of duties and activities (e.g. Caldwell, 2003).

Functional Expert	Employee Advocate
An operational, tactical role;	An operational, tactical role;
Provides knowledge and expertise in all areas of HR policy development and implementation	Provides a communication bridge, to build trust between management and employees

HR Leader

A corporate governance role;

Overlays all the other four roles, providing essential HR leadership to integrate the other functions;

A 'player' within organisations, demonstrating contribution, the value added and leadership including in ethics and sustainability, as well as more direct HR-related issues

Human Capital Developer	Strategic Partner
A strategic role;	A strategic role;
Sources, develops, retains and deploys human capital to meet the strategic needs of the business, while balancing these with individual career needs	Partners management at all business levels, providing advice and leading change;
	Works with line management to improve team or business unit performance

FIGURE 1.5 Ulrich and Brockbank's (2005) HR leader model

Despite these concerns, as we have discussed previously, the pervading HRM rhetoric has proposed an increasingly strategic and less operational role for the HR function; but what does the research evidence tell us about the reality of these roles and this proposed transition in practice?

RESEARCH EVIDENCE: AN INTERNATIONAL PERSPECTIVE

The research evidence is, at best, mixed. In the US a number of studies into the changing roles of HR departments have presented a fairly negative picture. For example, in 2001 Lawler III and Mohrman (2003) surveyed 150 medium to large US companies; this was a follow-up to two earlier studies. They concluded that there had been very little change since their first survey in 1995, in the way that HR spends its time – that is, more time is spent on traditional operational HR activities and not as a strategic business partner.

The findings are similar in the UK. Caldwell (2003), in his 1999 survey of 98 UK companies, found that 82 per cent of them reported that Storey's 'HR advisor' was their most dominant role. In other words, strategic but non-interventionist, thus again falling short of the strategic business partner/change agent roles proposed in these models. A more recent 2007 survey of 787 small, medium and large UK organisations carried out by the CIPD supports these findings. While it reports that on average the HR function has doubled the proportion of time it spends on 'strategic inputs' at the expense of 'administrative activities', at the same time the amount of actual time the HR function spends on providing support to line managers and HR administrative tasks is still very dominant (CIPD, 2007).

We also see similar trends in the research carried out in other parts of the world. In China, Zhu et al. (2005), in a study of 328 managers from across state-, private- and foreign-owned enterprises, reported no significant differences between levels of strategic HR participation between their earlier survey in 1994/5 and the more recent survey in 2001/2. Indeed, in both state-owned and foreign-owned enterprises strategic-level participation of the HR function had seemingly dropped over this period. In India, Srimannarayana (2010), in a study of 293 managers, also concludes that HR is mainly engaged in Ulrich's (1997a) administrative expert and employee champion roles – that is, those non-strategic-focused roles. In their comparative study of 457 Brazilian and Peruvian managers, Coda et al. (2009) concluded that while HR departments in both countries were generally viewed positively in their delivery of operational HR activities, strategic roles and duties were not seen as effectively performed.

Interestingly, one country where there may be some firmer, more positive, evidence of this transition to a more strategic role for HR is Australia. In a comparative study of HRM roles across a number of countries, Bowen et al. (2002) reported that the status afforded the HR function in Australia was the highest of any country in their study, and significantly higher than in the USA. The importance and influence of HR in Australia seems to be confirmed by a later study by Sheehan et al. (2006) who, in a survey of 1372 members of the Australian Human Resources Institute (AHRI), reported that 20 per cent of respondents identified strategic development as their primary HR role. In response to a question regarding the level of importance of various HR activities over the past five years, they also rated strategic integration of HRM policies the highest, with 47 per cent of respondents rating this as very important.

HRM IN PRACTICE

Innovative HR from Asia

'Next Generation HR' is the CIPD's global research project into innovative HR practices. While the first stage focused on UK-based companies, the second focused on data drawn from HR leaders in 27 companies operating across the Asia–Pacific region (e.g. India, China, South Korea). Although findings from this phase are mixed, they are also particularly interesting. Perhaps challenging traditional notions of 'Eastern' countries seeking (and often struggling) to implement 'Western' HR thinking, the findings instead provide evidence that some of these HR leaders are coming up with new and highly innovative HR solutions to deal with many of the common challenges facing organisations across

(Continued)

(Continued)

the globe – for example, securing sustainable business growth, talent management and retention and employee engagement. Connor (2011) summarises these findings as follows, suggesting the best HR leaders often:

- Have a more fluid interpretation of HR structures, thus allowing faster implementation cycles for HR strategy.
- Effectively unlock new ideas by being business-, context- and organisationally savvy.
- Master the art of creating a sense of purpose through harnessing the press, the project and the organisation behind a big idea.
- Engender employee engagement by focusing on promoting a culture of accountability, authenticity and adaptability.

It is clear that notions of strategic HRM and HR best practices are being both adopted and adapted by the best HR leaders across the Asia–Pacific region. It is also clear that 'Western'-based HR leaders may learn a lot from these new perspectives on the profession.

Sources: CIPD (2010) *Next Generation HR Asia*. Research Report. Accessed online at: www.cipd.co.uk/binaries/hr-strategies-for-growth-in-asia_2012-overview.pdf (accessed 16 April 2016).

Connor, J. (2011) Eastern time. *People Management*, 27 January: 22–25.

DEBATING HRM

Convergence or divergence in HRM practices: implications for international HRM

Read the 'HRM in Practice' box above and access and read the article by McGaughey and De Cieri (1999); it can be found at www.tandfonline.com/doi/pdf/10.1080/095851999340530. You may need to use a Shibboleth login to access this article.
  TASK: *Split into two groups.*

1   One group should research evidence for global convergence in HRM policies and practices and one for continuing divergence in HRM practices.

2   Each group should then outline the opportunities and challenges that either convergence or divergence poses for HR departments and practitioners.

ORGANISING THE HR FUNCTION

How does one organise the HR function to best deliver the dual strategic and operational roles described above? The key dilemma is how one may unburden, or at least significantly reduce the burden on, one's HR professionals from their day-to-day operational and administrative duties so that they may have more time and space to engage more effectively with their strategic roles. As a solution, Ulrich (1997b) outlined a 'three-legged' organising model of the HR function, consisting of integrated HR business partners, HR centres of excellence and HR shared services. More radical solutions to this challenge have also included the outsourcing part of, if not all of the HR function and/or the introduction of new technologies supporting eHR and HR self-service models. These are all briefly described below.

HR BUSINESS PARTNERS

Notions of HR business partnering are heavily contested (Caldwell, 2008). However, the CIPD describes HR business partners as key, potentially senior HR professionals who are embedded within the various functions or departments within the organisation so that they may work closely with managers to influence, direct and implement business strategy (CIPD, 2012b). Business partnering is thus viewed as an alternative to the more traditional, centrally-located HR professional. It is argued that by decentralising this role, HR professionals are closer to core business functions and can thus better understand business needs and more effectively implement and influence business strategy. Despite these proposed advantages, they are not without their problems. Poor implementation and the problem of creating silos of knowledge – in terms of both the perceived problems and challenges facing the organisation and the solutions developed – have both been cited (CIPD, 2012b). Despite this, Caldwell (2008) estimates that in the UK around 400–600, mainly large, organisations have implemented some form of HR business partnering role.

HR CENTRES OF EXCELLENCE

HR centres of excellence are based around the core functional areas of HR practices, for example reward, learning and development, talent management and engagement (CIPD, 2012b). They are made up of highly skilled and knowledgeable HR professionals, and their aim is to add value to the business through innovative developments and solutions within these functional areas (CIPD, 2012b). HR centres of excellence are thus seen as a vital cog in HR's contribution to, and influence on, both the strategic direction of the business and the effective development and deployment of its human capital.

HR SHARED SERVICES

One of the most important trends in organising the HR function has been the introduction, by firms, of an HR shared service. HR service centres often take the form of a call centre that is commonly geographically separate from the main organisation and its subsidiaries. Their aim is to centralise and streamline the more administrative roles of the HR function, for example the upkeep of personnel records, although more recent work has suggested that such centres may also have an active role to play

HR business partners Key (potentially senior) HR professionals who are embedded within the various functions/ departments within the organisation so that they may work closely with managers to influence, direct and implement business strategy.

HR centres of excellence The core functional areas of HR practices and expertise, e.g. careers, reward, learning and development, talent management and engagement.

HR shared service HR shared service centres often take the form of a call centre that is commonly geographically separate from the main organisation and its subsidiaries. The services they provide often (but not solely) focus on administrative activities associated with payroll, recruitment, the upkeep of personnel records and training procurement.

in providing more transformational HRM (CIPD, 2012c; Maatman et al., 2010). The centralisation of these more transactional HR activities is said to present a number of benefits including improving the quality and consistency of service to employees and other potential customers; an ability to more easily share best practice across the HR function; reducing costs by avoiding a duplication of efforts; and freeing up time and space for other members of the HR function to focus on strategic-level concerns (CIPD, 2012c).

However, they are not without their critics (see Cooke, 2006). Some argue that such service centres require a completely new skill set – project management and service delivery, for example – that may not be held by HR professionals, and that investment in these skills may be patchy and costly. Others suggest that such restructuring may potentially create (albeit temporary) confusion regarding people's roles and responsibilities, thus leading to greater inefficiencies, poor customer service, increased costs and low morale in the HR team (e.g. Sparrow et al., 2004). Service centres may also be viewed – by both those working within them and those using their services – as being disconnected from the business and the employees that they support (Maatman et al., 2010). Despite these potential issues, however, a 2007 CIPD survey suggested that around one-quarter of UK organisations may have introduced some form of HR shared service provision (CIPD, 2007).

eHR AND HR SELF-SERVICE

eHR Any HR activities that are carried out via, or utilise, electronic systems, i.e. web-based systems.

The next logical step in this devolvement or decentralisation of the HR function is to empower or enable individual employees to access relevant HR services directly through sophisticated eHR technologies. The services provided by such systems have now gone way beyond the simple upkeep of personnel records, access to application forms or policy documents and on to online holiday requests, absence recording and more recently to online appraisals, CV checking and automated responses to a range of HR enquiries (Woods, 2010b). Again, the principal benefits here are the streamlining and cost savings associated with such systems, as well as the proposed freeing up of time for HR professionals to focus on more added value activities (*Personnel Today*, 2008).

HR self-service systems The devolvement or decentralisation of the HR function in order to empower or enable individual employees to access relevant HR services directly.

However, again, HR self-service systems are not without controversy or challenges. Uptake of such systems has been relatively poor and HR departments are failing to keep up to date with new technologies (Woods, 2010b). Moreover, despite having such

ONLINE STUDY TOOLS

Video case study: Pepco

Solidify your understanding with this example of how a large, complex organisation introduced, operationalised and evaluated a new shared services model of organising their HR.

https://edge.sagepub.com/crawshaw2e > Student Resources > Chapter 1 > Videos technologies employees may also be unwilling to utilise them effectively, preferring instead a more traditional interface with the HR function (Woods, 2010b). Such radical moves to streamline large areas of HR responsibility are also viewed as evidence of the further dismantling of the HR profession, with many departments undergoing significant downsizing and deskilling of HR jobs (Legge, 2005).

DEBATING HRM

The merit of decentralising the HR function

Read the article 'HR business partner competency models: Re-contextualising effectiveness' by Caldwell, R. (2008) at www.bbk.ac.uk/orgpsych/staff/academics/caldwell/docs/HRMJ.1748-8583.2008.00071.pdf
    TASK: *Split into two groups.*

1   One group should research the evidence FOR and the other evidence AGAINST decentralising the HR function.

2   Groups should identify case examples of organisations that have successfully decentralised or centralised their HR.

3   Groups should be prepared to feed back and defend their position in class.

OUTSOURCING THE HR FUNCTION

HR outsourcing simply refers to the use of another party to deliver all or part of this function and its services, with various reports suggesting that nearly all organisations have, at some point, outsourced parts of their HR function (e.g. Gurchiek, 2005). Many SMEs may outsource more strategic HR roles, buying in HR consultancy if and when it is needed, rather than burdening themselves with the high fixed cost of maintaining an HR function (CIPD, 2011) (see Chapter 13). Alternatively, and perhaps more commonly, it is the operational and transactional HR activities that are outsourced, by larger organisations, so that they may streamline and rationalise their service delivery while allowing the HR function to focus on more value-added activities (Belcourt, 2006).

HR outsourcing   The use of a third party (organisation) to deliver all or part of the HR function and its services.

Outsourcing presents organisations with certain challenges, including decisions regarding what to outsource, whom to outsource them to, for how long and how to manage this relationship (e.g. Sako and Tierney, 2007). As in many areas of HR, there are mixed messages regarding the potential gains of outsourcing the HR function. Although recent research has suggested that promised cost savings rarely materialise (e.g. Cooke et al., 2005) and that many organisations have scaled back their outsourcing activities, there is also evidence that decisions to outsource have again begun to pick up, albeit perhaps cautiously (CIPD, 2011). Table 1.1 lists a range of potential benefits and challenges to outsourcing the HR function.

TABLE 1.1 Potential benefits and challenges of outsourcing HR (CIPD, 2011)

Potential benefits	Potential challenges
Reduced costs	Decisions on what to outsource – as a rule, do not outsource what you don't understand
Increased efficiencies and speed of response	Loss of tacit knowledge
Access to the provider's sophisticated eHR systems	Loss of control over HR processes and decision making
Access to new HR expertise and knowledge	Disconnect between day-to-day operational decisions made by the outsourcing provider and the strategic HR decisions made by the central function
Reduced risk	
HR function freed to be more focused on strategy	

LINE MANAGERS AND HRM

To some extent the implementation of any one or more of these organising models assumes that line managers will take on a lot more responsibility for implementing and delivering HR activities, solutions and advice (e.g. Budhwar, 2000). As far back as 1999–2000, a survey of 4050 organisations from across 22 European countries showed a significant movement to greater line management responsibility for the HRM role, and significant convergence across countries in this trend (Larsen and Brewster, 2003). But what are the proposed benefits and challenges of this devolvement of responsibility for HRM to line managers?

On the one hand, the literature presents a strong case for the benefits of this move. Line managers are closer to their employees and, perhaps more importantly, to their customers or service users and are thus more aware of their needs. Skills shortages and training needs, for example, are thus more swiftly and efficiently identified and resolved or delivered. Performance issues, including sickness absence and poor-quality work, are also more readily identified, understood and dealt with. In short, line managers know their business and their team and are thus best placed to quickly and efficiently identify HR-related problems and to solve them (Whittaker and Marchington, 2003).

ONLINE STUDY TOOLS

Writing an essay? Expand your knowledge

Take a look at Gainey and Klaas (2004) on the outsourcing of training and development, which focuses on what impacts client satisfaction. Available via the companion website: https://edge.sagepub.com/crawshaw2e

Student Resources > Chapter 1 > Videos

MINI CASE STUDY

HR outsourcing by Indian SMEs

A recent 2012 article in *The Times of India* newspaper has highlighted a growing trend for Indian SMEs and family-run enterprises to outsource their HR functions to third-party providers. This, it reports, is a reaction to the increasing war for talent that all Indian firms are facing. Rituparna Chakraborty, the vice president of the Indian Staffing Federation, explains: 'With rising competition and the need for professionalism, many family-run businesses are understanding the significance of hiring the right people, managing them better, making them more productive and becoming compliant to their requirements. So they seek professional intervention from HR outsourcing organizations to bring in experience, systems, processes and technology.' It is these complex interrelated HR challenges of talent acquisition and engagement, performance management and compensation that are providing the real dilemma for today's Indian SMEs. As Makrand Appalwar, MD of Emmbi Polyarns (a rapidly growing woven sack manufacturer), says, 'The size of our organization does not financially justify employing a whole host of HR executives with individual specializations. So we outsourced our HR and that has enabled us to improve the efficiency of our in-house HR team. By outsourcing our HR, we could get immense help, support and hands-on experience from senior HR executives.'

CASE STUDY QUESTIONS

1 What are the key drivers for outsourcing HR outlined in this report?

2 What are the particular benefits and threats for SMEs and family-run businesses of outsourcing their HR? Explain your responses to this question.

3 What alternative HR organising models could SMEs and family-run businesses use? Outline the strengths and limitations of these alternatives.

Source: *The Times of India* website at http://articles.timesofindia.indiatimes.com/2012-10-16/india-business/ 34497470_1_hr-functions-performance-management-small-firms

On the other hand, there may be many practical challenges facing line managers in this role. They may not want it, nor have the necessary time or competence to deal with the day-to-day HRM functions (Larsen and Brewster, 2003). For example, how knowledgeable are line managers of recent employment law updates, and how much time do they have, and should be expected to spend, to stay updated with this essential, yet rather specialist, information? A lack of training or technical experience in HR may lead to poor decision making and avoidable, potentially very costly, employment tribunals. The benefits of devolving responsibility for HRM may therefore be lost as managers need constant hand-holding and guidance in order to avoid these costly errors and inefficiencies (Renwick, 2000).

More fundamental may be the unwillingness of HR professionals to share their knowledge and expertise with line managers, thus potentially precipitating their own redundancy from the organisation (Renwick, 2003). Indeed, such a shift raises the question of whether HRM can ever really gain prominence and influence in organisations if it gives up these core roles (see also Blyton and Turnbull, 1992). What is certain, however, is that line managers do now commonly share with HR the responsibilities for many HR roles and thus this relationship needs careful management. Based largely on Whittaker and Marchington (2003), the following guidelines are proposed:

1. Attempt to gain line manager 'buy-in' by clearly communicating not only the importance of this role but also exactly what is required.

2. Ensure the careful recruitment, appraisal and reward of these line managers, making sure this HR role is clearly reflected in these activities.

3. Give line managers the time and space to deal with HR issues.

4. Provide managers with the requisite knowledge, skills and competencies needed for the role (Renwick, 2003).

5. Make sure HR provides consistent and valuable support.

CONTEMPORARY HR CHALLENGES

PESTEL The common acronym used for the political, economic, social, technological, environmental and legal factors that may influence strategy and affect the performance of an organisation.

The wider political, economic, social, technological, environmental and legal (often presented as the acronym **PESTEL**) environment in which organisations find themselves presents ongoing challenges and opportunities regarding the most effective and efficient way to organise work in order to enable the continued success and survival of the firm. Importantly, these contextual factors are in constant flux, and the challenges posed 10, 20, 30 years ago are not the same as those posed today or those that will be posed 10, 20, 30 years from now. In your studies you will often read phrases such as, 'In the current changing environment …' or 'In today's dynamic and fast changing world …', but what exactly are the key macroeconomic issues facing organisations today and into the near future? Drawing on recent research (e.g. Burke and Ng, 2006; Gratton, 2011) we attempt to provide a useful summary – although we stress that this is not meant to be prescriptive and definitive.

HR practitioner skills

The CIPD's HR 'Profession Map' (www.cipd.co.uk/cipd-hr-profession/hr-profession-map/) outlines a number of core functional HR skills and individual behaviours that are essential requirements for HR practitioners to be truly effective. These include:

- Functional Skills – Organisation design, organisation development, resourcing, learning and talent development, performance and reward, employee engagement, employee relations and service delivery.

- Behavioural Skills – Curious, decisive thinker, skilled influencer, personally credible, collaborative, driven to deliver, courage to challenge and role model.

TASK: Reflect upon your development of these different skills. Plan how you will begin to fill identified gaps in (or further enhance) your HR skills profile.

THE INTERNATIONALISATION OF BUSINESS

Perhaps the most dominant force affecting work and organisations is the continuing globalisation and internationalisation of work. The growing power and influence of new economies such as Brazil, Russia, India and China, known collectively as the BRIC nations, but also other emerging economies, particularly in Eastern Europe, South East Asia and South America, present new opportunities and challenges for organisations operating both within and outside of these countries (e.g. Budhwar, 2012). They obviously provide new markets and customers as well as opportunities for cross-border alliances and foreign direct investment (FDI). As education and skills levels improve in these and other countries they may also provide organisations with new sources of knowledge and expertise to be employed and utilised (Gratton, 2011).

However, operating effectively with, and within, emerging economies raises a number of important HR challenges for multinational enterprises (MNEs). Specifically, international human resource management (IHRM) professionals are required to develop HR policies and practices that are responsive to local economic, institutional and cultural conditions while also integrating and supporting their global activities (Sparrow et al., 2009). The emergence of new economies is also likely to further diversify one's workforce as inward investment promotes a greater movement of people both into and out of their respective countries. Managing such diversity in organisations is thus another key HR challenge that will only accelerate in importance over the coming years (Gratton, 2011). The challenges of international HRM are explored further in Chapter 5.

THE GLOBAL ECONOMY

Lots has been written about the HR challenges posed by the recent (and past) global financial crisis (GFC) and emergence from these crises. It is widely accepted that during recessions it is common for employees to be laid off, hours to be reduced, recruitment frozen, training budgets scaled back and pay raises and bonuses to be limited or again frozen (for a review see Lai et al., 2016). In other words, HR budgets, and the employment relationship, are severely affected and the experience of many HR departments during the recent GFC was no different. A key challenge for HR, therefore, is how to maintain an adaptable, affectively committed, motivated and high-performing workforce during these uncertain times. Effective HR planning that reduces the need for short-term, and psychologically damaging, redundancies is seen as one important response to these challenges (Bramham, 1987). Another is to make sure that employers are not seen to be exploiting the recession, using it as an excuse to drive down wages while pushing ever more demanding performance management targets. Such opportunistic behaviours were reported, for example, by a recent study into the post-GFC HR challenges facing India's IT sector (Malik, 2013).

As an economy recovers, so the HR challenges change. Growth brings job creation and suddenly organisations may find retaining and attracting top talent become key challenges. Pay demands are likely to emerge and, as recruitment increases, training needs and budgets will also increase. The post-recession organisation may be very different (structurally and operationally), and again this may throw up specific HR challenges associated with, for example, recruitment, training, job design and reward. Of course, an organisation's treatment of its employees during the tough recession times may directly affect its ability to attract and retain employees when the economy starts to recover, and so a consistent and fair approach to people management during both periods is essential.

DEMOGRAPHIC TRENDS

We have already briefly described above how the increasing internalisation of business is likely to lead to organisations with ever more culturally diverse workforces. Importantly, migration, and the movement of labour, is no longer simply a concern regarding the migration of individuals from developing countries to developed countries but also of individuals of developed countries migrating to new emerging economies around the world. Within this context, managing and valuing diversity is an increasingly salient issue for HR professionals (Burke and Ng, 2006).

Demographic changes are not, however, limited to issues of cultural and national diversity. Lower birth rates and increasing longevity across many regions of the world, not just in developed or Western economies, is helping to create an ageing workforce (Gratton, 2011). This has a number of HR implications, be they pension provisions, retirement ages, the effective retention and utilisation of older workers, challenging stereotypes regarding older employees as well as managing attitudinal differences between the generations (e.g. Lawler III, 2011). In short, HR clearly faces a number of important challenges if it is going to respond effectively to these demographic trends and help organisations deal with these issues of diversity (Burke and Ng, 2006; Gratton, 2011).

TECHNOLOGICAL DEVELOPMENTS

A major factor in shaping the way people work is technology, and technological advances are only going to quicken (Sparrow, 2000). Perhaps one of the most established debates within this particular domain is around notions of virtual working. New forms of communication are allowing more and more people to work remotely and not only on relatively simple tasks. The information storing and sharing capabilities provided by new cloud technologies, for example, are said to be set to revolutionise the 'globalisation of research and development' (Gratton, 2011: 248) by significantly cheapening the costs of blanket connectivity, and thus communication and information sharing possibilities, across the world. As highlighted earlier in this chapter, advances in technology are also influencing the way HR itself is organised, with the emergence of ever more sophisticated HR information systems (HRIS). HR's ability not only to adapt to technological changes but also to adopt appropriate technologies to promote the effective and efficient delivery of its services is thus of paramount importance.

HR information systems The technologies used to design, deliver and support one's HR strategies, policies and practices.

DELIVERING SUSTAINABLE PERFORMANCE

Just a cursory glance at the popular press suggests a growing concern with the overlapping notions of corporate social responsibility (CSR), business ethics and environmental sustainability. In sum, many organisations are now being challenged not only to achieve economic success and competitive advantage – in increasingly competitive markets – but also to do so while meeting strict ethical principles. Protecting and respecting human rights, responding to wider societal needs by increasing community engagement, and leaving the smallest imprint on the Earth's reportedly diminishing and increasingly fragile natural resources by minimising carbon emissions all present their own challenges (e.g. Greenwood, 2002; Shen, 2011). Elkington (1999) referred to this as an organisation's 'triple bottom line' of economic, social and environmental performance. Ulrich and Brockbank (2005) made explicit HR's potential role in providing leadership on these issues, perhaps through leading culture change initiatives, influencing leadership training and development, promoting fair and just employment policies, and through the development of new competency frameworks that reflect the core values of ethics and sustainability. Chapter 4 provides a more thorough assessment of HR's role in promoting more just, ethical, socially responsible and sustainable organisations.

MANAGING CHANGE

To some extent, the importance of change, and effectively managing change, emerges as a direct consequence of all of the above. Thus, as the pace of technological, industrial and demographic change accelerates and markets become increasingly volatile, the ability to change swiftly and efficiently becomes a much-needed skill if one is to survive and prosper. In recent times we have seen, for example, how even iconic high street retail brands have floundered as they failed to keep up with technological advances and changing consumer attitudes and behaviour in their respective markets. Examples include HMV and BHS in the UK, and the global giant Sony.

While learning how to drive and manage change successfully is arguably a skill needed by all business units and managers, it is perhaps even more so for the HRM function (Gratton, 2011). As business strategies need to adapt to the changing environment, the people need to follow, with successful change requiring the sustained commitment of all employees in the organisation. As the HR function can be seen as the major caretaker of the human resources of the organisation, it is largely responsible for making sure that people are prepared to embrace change, and that they can understand why there is a need to reorganise, to acquire new skills and to attract new talent. Chapter 3 explores in more detail the key drivers of change and of HR's central role in both leading and implementing change.

Corporate social responsibility (CSR) Refers to the responsibility of organisations for their impact upon society – both locally and globally.

Business ethics The study of the moral challenges, dilemmas and responsibilities of business organisations, and their potential evaluation of, and responses to, these challenges.

Environmental sustainability Meeting the needs of the present without compromising the ability of future generations to meet their own needs.

CASE STUDY

Reorganising the HR function at AE Housing

AE Housing is an established charity promoting and offering sheltered housing across England and Wales. The organisation operates in three geographical areas:

- London and the South East
- Wales and the West of England
- Midlands and the North

Due to a reduction across their funding streams, the organisation reduced its staffing levels from 1800 to 1250 employees 12 months ago and, while it still operates across the three geographical regions, its work is now more focused on the key metropolitan areas. Prior to the restructure, AE Housing managed its operations as three distinct regions, each reporting to a Chief Executive's Office based in central London. Each region was led by a Regional Director with dedicated support from its own Finance and HR teams. Following the restructure, AE Housing is now nationally focused with a management team consisting of:

- 1 × Chief Executive Officer
- 3 × Directors of Housing
- 1 × Director of Finance and IT
- 1 × Director of HR

The HR Department maintains its regional support to the business but is now focused on a centralised model whereby HR business partners make use of experts who are operating nationally in fields such as recruitment, reward, case management and learning and development.

Control over HR decision making has been increased and the Chief Executive has had feedback from the recognised trade union that the application of policies is more consistent across the regions. Feedback from the Directors of Housing to the HR Director is less complimentary as their view is that the HR function does not always support the local needs of the business due to the 'one size fits all' application of policies.

Within the HR team, the three business partners each have a region to support and there are some differences in what they believe the level of HR service offering should be. Their colleagues working in the centralised areas of expertise have had limited formal training but have learned the requirements of their roles quickly.

As part of the restructure, the headcount of the HR team was reduced from 30 to 15 employees (reducing the HR-to-organisation ratio from 1 to 45 to approximately 1 to 60). The change in the ratio of employees to HR has meant that HR has necessarily changed its service offering and managers have had to take on more responsibility for the management of their staff.

The changed service offering has increased the negative feedback from the Directors of Housing to the HR Director as they believe their managers have less time to focus on 'the day job'. The Chief Executive has a different view in that she believes she pays her managers a salary to manage their staff and therefore it should not be seen as something outside the duties of the job.

CASE STUDY QUESTIONS

1. Describe the key challenges the HR Director faces in ensuring the consistency of decision making while addressing the local requirements of the rest of the business.

2. AE Housing has created experts in key HR disciplines. Highlight the risks and opportunities in switching to this model (both for HR and the rest of the business). What steps should the HR Director take to manage the risks and maximise the opportunities?

3. As a new HR business partner in AE Housing, examine the dilemma you face in ensuring managers are appropriately supported and empowered to make decisions. How would you address this?

4. The way in which the HR function is organised, and the service the function offers, has changed significantly. What are the unintended consequences of implementing such a change? What steps should the HR Director take to recognise and manage those unintended consequences?

CHAPTER SUMMARY

The key points that we have identified in this chapter are the following:

- Studying HR is about trying to understand how and why organisations source, organise, control, coordinate and motivate their employees.

- 'Exactly what is HRM?' is a heavily contested question.

- Definitions of HRM tend to make four key assumptions: (1) that HRM is just one perspective on people management; (2) that HRM is a strategic perspective on people management; (3) that investment in people (human capital) is the way to secure an organisation's sustained competitive advantage; and (4) that HRM is a unitaristic view of the employment relationship.

- HRM has evolved from earlier theoretical work, first in scientific management, then later in organisational behaviour.
- There may be important differences between personnel management and HRM.
- A number of theoretical models have been developed that have explored the roles and responsibilities of the HR function. These include, but are not limited to, Storey's (1992) strategic/tactical model and Ulrich and Brockbank's (2005) HR leader model.
- We are witnessing a number of emerging trends in models of how HR is organised, including HR business partnering, HR shared services, HR outsourcing and eHR technologies.
- The role of line managers in the delivery of HR is becoming increasingly important.
- The HR function is facing a number of important challenges posed by changes in the external business environment. These include (1) the internationalisation of business, (2) the global economy, (3) changing demographic trends, for example an ageing population, (4) pressure to deliver more environmentally or socially sustainable forms of business performance and (5) how to effectively manage change.

REVIEW QUESTIONS AND EXERCISES

1. Evaluate the differences, if any, between personnel management and HRM.
2. Describe and evaluate Ulrich and Brockbank's (2005) HR leader role.
3. What, if any, contradictions may there be between Ulrich and Brockbank's (2005) 'business partner' and 'employee advocate' HR roles?
4. Evaluate the advantages and disadvantages of outsourcing the HR function.
5. Explain how external environmental factors may affect HR policies and practices. Give examples.
6. Identify a case organisation. Research its strategic business objectives. What role do you think its HR function has in delivering these business objectives? Provide evidence for your answer.
7. Reflect upon your own work experience – this could be paid or unpaid, or an internship or placement experience. How was the HR function organised in this organisation? Was it largely centralised or decentralised? Was there an HR shared service or other technologies? Was it outsourced? However it was organised, do you think this HR function was effective in delivering its services to you?

EXPLORE FURTHER

Caldwell, R. and Storey, J. (2007) The HR function: Integration or fragmentation, in J. Storey (ed.) *Human Resource Management: A Critical Text*, 3rd edn. London: Thomson Learning, pp. 21–38. An excellent and critical review of recent research, exploring the nature, design and role of the HR function in contemporary organisations.

Gratton, L. (2011) Workplace 2025 – what will it look like? *Organizational Dynamics*, 40: 246–254. This is an excellent article proposing a number of important future challenges for the HR function. Other articles in this special issue may also be of interest.

The CIPD website at www.cipd.co.uk/. Although some areas of this site are only open to CIPD members, this is still worth exploring as it will provide you with lots of very useful information regarding the profession.

GO ONLINE

Visit the companion website for **interactive quizzes**, explanatory **videos** and **podcasts**, **journal articles** to use in your essays, and **weblinks** to useful resources.

https://edge.sagepub.com/crawshaw2e

CHAPTER 2

HRM AND FIRM PERFORMANCE

Anastasia Katou
Pawan Budhwar

CHAPTER KNOWLEDGE OBJECTIVES

- To explore and explain the contribution of SHRM to firm performance.
- To investigate the relationships between business strategy and HRM.
- To examine the different theoretical perspectives on SHRM.
- To examine competing conceptualisations of high-performance work systems.
- To examine issues in SHRM research.

KEY SKILLS OBJECTIVES

- To collect and analyse relevant data and information relating to HR strategy formulation.
- To be able to develop and implement an HR strategy and plan.
- To understand the nature and challenges of working in a strategic HR role.
- To be able to evaluate the contribution of HR policies and practices to organisational performance.

This chapter also provides indicative content for the following Intermediate and Advanced level CIPD modules:

CIPD INTERMEDIATE LEVEL MODULE

5CHR Business issues and the context of HR

CIPD ADVANCED LEVEL MODULE

7HRC Human resource management in context

GO ONLINE

This chapter comes with loads of online tools to help you to go that extra mile in your studies!

- **Multiple choice questions** to help you test your knowledge and revise for exams
- **Journal articles** so you can read further for assignments and essays
- **Videos** and **podcasts** to help you to understand how complex concepts work in the real world

Visit **https://edge.sagepub.com/crawshaw2e** to access these resources for this topic.

INTRODUCTION

Over the past two decades, research for the causal links between human resource management (HRM) and business performance has dominated both academic and practitioner debate (Purcell and Kinnie, 2007). Research on HRM was focused on the examination of the theoretical foundations of HRM, aiming to reveal its underlying assumptions, and on issues related to the validity of the techniques used in investigating the HRM–performance relationship. However, 'the nature of the interaction between HRM and performance, and particularly the search for conclusive evidence of the decisive positive impact of the former on the latter, is for many the whole subject area's "Holy Grail"' (Boselie et al., 2005: 67).

In this chapter we explore the dominant approaches on how HRM influences firm performance. The chapter has four aims. First, it examines the interaction between HRM and business strategies in determining the firm performance, by investigating the relationships between business strategy and HRM. Second, it will explore the theories on which the HRM–performance relationship is based, by examining the different theoretical perspectives in strategic human resource management (SHRM). Third, it will explain the causal link that takes place between the two end-points (i.e. HRM and performance) in this relationship, by examining competing conceptualisations of high-performance work systems. Fourth, it will summarise the problems encountered when investigating the HRM–performance relationship, by examining multi-level issues in SHRM research. In general, this chapter refers to the so-called modelling of HRM with firm performance, which examines the steps through which HRM influences firm performance. On the basis of these models, we explore the evidence relating HRM practice to firm performance.

In order to understand the HRM–performance relationship, we start by introducing two major concepts that underpin this relationship. The first concept is strategic management, which refers to the managerial decisions and actions that may improve performance in an organisation. The second concept is strategic HRM (SHRM), which refers to the processes that link HRM policies and practices with the strategic objectives of the organisation.

High-performance work systems (HPWS) An approach to organisational design and management which aligns the organisation with the environmental context as well as the systems, structures and processes. The approach seeks to achieve organisational effectiveness and high levels of performance.

STRATEGIC MANAGEMENT

In a management context, the term strategy is defined as 'the formulation of organizational missions, goals and objectives, as well as the action plans for achievement, that explicitly recognize the competition and the impact of outside environmental forces'

Strategic management Denotes a pattern of managerial decisions and actions undertaken by senior managers in order to improve performance in an organisation.

(Anthony et al., 1996: 8). The classical approach to strategy refers to the readiness and capacity of managers to take decisions and actions, through long-term planning, in order to accomplish performance goals. Accordingly, strategic management is defined as a field that deals with managerial decisions and actions in order to improve the long-run performance of organisations. Strategic management consists of several serially dependent components or steps, which determine the strategic management process in an organisation (also called the strategic management model). These include:

1. **Organisational identification** through the development and identification of one's current purpose and mission, goals and objectives and one's values and culture.

2. **Environmental analysis.** Dependent on how the organisation is identified in step 1, managers assess its internal environment and its external environment. The internal audit and the environmental scan may take the form of a SWOT analysis (Strengths, Weaknesses, Opportunities and Threats). The PESTEL framework, as discussed in Chapter 1, may be a better option for describing the external macro-environment.

3. **Strategy formulation** aims to identify the basis for the firm's competitive advantage. Strategy formulation is dynamic, in the sense that it is subject to change as environmental conditions change and must be kept flexible as it deals with the future, which is hard to predict with certainty.

4. **Strategy implementation** requires effective exploitation of resources, optimum utilisation of management systems and effective activation of HR practices. However, the intended strategy (i.e. the formulated strategy) may differ from the realised strategy (i.e. the actual strategy that the organisation is following), due to unforeseen forces affecting the process of strategy.

5. **Strategy evaluation** refers to the activities that determine how well the formulated and implemented strategy (either intended or realised) has achieved the goals designated by the organisation. In cases where the actual results fall short of the expected results, managers will have to take corrective actions. There is therefore a feedback loop from strategy evaluation to all other steps in the strategy management process.

Strategy formulation can take place at the corporate, business or functional level. The corporate-level strategy refers to the overall strategy of the organisation. The business-level strategy refers to the strategy of a business unit in the organisation that deals with managerial decisions and actions. The functional-level strategy formulation refers to the philosophies, policies and practices that support the operation of the major functions within the business unit. As HRM is a functional area within a business unit, then it may be assumed that it is at this level that the majority of HR strategy decisions will be made. Schuler (1989), for example, identifies three distinct HRM philosophies, that is, fundamental values and guiding principles adopted in managing people: accumulation, utilisation and facilitation. Additionally, Armstrong (2006) identified four areas of HRM policy, that is, how certain things will be done in specific areas of HRM. These policies will be dependent on the underlying HRM philosophy adopted and be consistent with the organisation's values:

1. Employee resourcing (e.g. planning, recruitment, selection, separation, talent management)

2. Employee development (e.g. training, development, careers, performance management)

3. Employee rewards (e.g. job evaluation, compensation, incentives, benefits)

4. Employee relations (e.g. participation, involvement, communication, health and safety).

STRATEGIC HUMAN RESOURCE MANAGEMENT

Having introduced in the previous section strategic management, we now turn our attention to **strategic human resource management**. Wright and Snell (1989) suggest that strategic HRM deals with those HRM activities used to support the firm's competitive strategy. Additionally, Armstrong and Long (1994) support the view that strategic HRM refers to the overall direction the organisation wishes to pursue in achieving its objective through people.

Strategic HRM The processes that link HRM policies and practices with the strategic objectives of the organisation in order to improve performance.

DEBATING HRM

HR on the board

Read the chapter by Brewster, C. (1994) Human resource management in Europe: Reflection of, or challenge to, the American concept?, in P. Kirkbride (ed.) *Human Resource Management in the New Europe: Perspectives on the 1990s*. London: Routledge, pp. 56–92.

For some time now, board membership of a senior personnel/HR person has been identified as one of the major influences on whether the HRM department is involved in various aspects of organisational strategy. Therefore, the board membership of an HR specialist has been taken as being a proxy for HRM strategic involvement, or integration. Authors (e.g. Brewster, 1994; Budhwar and Sparrow, 1997) found that representation of the personnel function at board level is, for some countries, in ascending order, as follows: Italy (18 per cent), India (29 per cent), Germany (30 per cent), Turkey (30 per cent), Ireland (44 per cent), Denmark (49 per cent), United Kingdom (49 per cent), Switzerland (58 per cent), Finland (61 per cent), France (84 per cent), Sweden (84 per cent).

TASK: *Divide into two groups.*

1 One group should gather recent research evidence with respect to the benefits of representation of HR at board level and the other group should argue in favour of no representation of HR at board level.

2 Each group should then outline the opportunities and challenges that either representation or no representation poses for HR departments and practitioners.

We have to bear in mind that although strategic HRM is sometimes used interchangeably with HRM strategy, they are not the same thing. HRM strategy involves a central philosophy of the way people are managed in an organisation, and the translation of this into HR policies and practices that are integrated with business strategy and within them. The next section will focus on strategic HRM as a theoretical framework rather than HRM strategy as the road map for achieving particular organisational outcomes.

THEORIES OF STRATEGIC HRM

In recent years two theoretical frameworks have dominated the field of strategic HRM: the resource-based view and the integration approach (Paauwe, 2009).

Resource-based view
A theoretical framework whereby HRM influences performance according to the human capital held by the organisation.

The resource-based view (RBV) argues that HRM influences performance according to the human capital held by the organisation (Barney, 1991). The human capital of an organisation consists of the people who work therein and on whom organisational success depends (Bontis et al., 1999). Where other organisational resources (technology, information, finance, etc.) are generally available, the only area where competitive advantage can be gained is through the unique contribution of the people within the organisation. Pfeffer (1994) argues that organisations wishing to succeed in today's global and dynamic environment must acquire and develop employees who possess better skills and capabilities than their competitors. For any resource to be a source of competitive advantage it must be rare, valuable, inimitable and non-substitutable; the HR practices of the organisation can lead to competitive advantage through developing a unique and valuable human capital pool. Within this theory we can distinguish three possible approaches:

1. **High-performance management**. This refers to the development of a number of interrelated HRM processes that together improve organisational performance (Stevens, 1998).

2. **High-commitment management**. This refers to the development of mutual commitment within the organisation, based on high levels of trust, that eventually influence performance (Wood, 1996).

3. **High-involvement management**. This refers to the treating of employees as partners in the organisation through communication and involvement, ensuring that high performance will ultimately be achieved (Pil and MacDuffie, 1996).

HRM IN PRACTICE

Managing human capital at a great place to work

Robert Levering and Milton Moskowitz, the authors of a best-seller book in 1981 called *The 100 Best Companies to Work for in America* and co-founders of the Great Place to Work® institute, argue that 'your company can be a great workplace, and you have the power to make it happen. It begins with an investment in building trust throughout your organization. The return will be a more vibrant enterprise, more innovative products and more satisfying relationships. Employees who trust their managers give their best work freely, and their extra effort goes right to the company's bottom line. Managers who trust their employees allow innovative ideas to bubble up from all levels of the company. Employees who trust each other report a sense of camaraderie and even the feeling of being part of a family. Together they deliver far more than the sum of their individual efforts.' Specifically, Robert Levering says that 'a great place to work is one in which you trust the people you work for, have pride in what you do, and enjoy the people you work with' (www. greatplacetowork.net).

Supporting the view that trust is the single most important ingredient in making a workplace great, Levering and Erb (2011) argue that in managing human capital companies should take steps to show an individual how his or her work directly ties in with the company's strategy and purpose, and leaders should share with employees their personal side of information, such as emotional reactions to news and personal takes on values. These steps will build a high-trust workplace culture that makes the company more effective and efficient. Specifically, '30 years of research, in over 40 countries around the world, has shown us time and again that investing in a high-trust workplace culture yields distinct, tangible business benefits. Our studies of the 100 Best Companies show that great workplaces enjoy significantly lower turnover and better financial performance than industry peers' (see Figure 2.1).

The integration approach to SHRM focuses more significantly on the link between HRM strategy formulation and performance. It emphasises the alignment of HR policies and practices within the HRM area and with other strategies across the organisation outside the area of HRM. Within this approach we distinguish three possible foci for integration: horizontal, vertical and combined integration.

Integration approach A theoretical framework whereby HRM strategy formulation focuses on the alignment of HR policies and practices with other business strategic objectives.

Horizontal integration

Here the focus is on the organisation developing a range of interconnected and mutually reinforcing HR practices, the argument being that such alignment will always produce superior results whatever the accompanying circumstances. Underlying this assertion is the premise that there exists a set of HR best practices that fit together and mutually reinforce each other. Synergy is a key emphasis of horizontal integration or, alternatively, of internal fit. Synergy will be achieved if the combined performance of a set of HR policies and practices is greater than the sum of their individual performances.

Synergy The concept explaining that the combined performance of a set of HR policies and practices is greater than the sum of their individual performances.

The assumption that best HR practices work in all contexts has been labelled as the universalistic model (Delery and Doty, 1996). According to Osterman (1994) and Huselid (1995), who are among the mainstream universalistic theorists, the underlying assumptions of this model are:

Universalistic or best practice model of HRM An approach arguing that the organisation is developing a range of interconnected and mutually reinforcing HR practices that will always produce superior results whatever the accompanying circumstances.

1. A linear relationship exists between HR practices and business performance;

2. Best HR practices are universally applicable; and

3. Internal fit is the key concept.

Although support for a universalistic approach to HRM exists, there are notable differences across studies as to what that approach should look like. Pfeffer (1994)

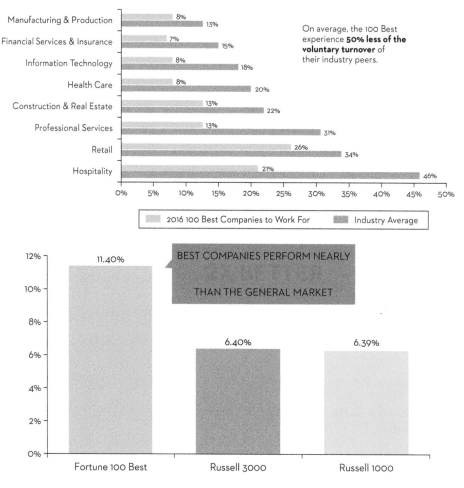

FIGURE 2.1 **Best companies to work for: statistics**

Source: '100 Best' data provided by Great Place to Work® Institute, Inc. (www.greatplacetowork.com/about-us)

Comparative data provided by BLS, '100 Best' data includes FT & PT turnover, BLS data include the same in addition to turnover for temp/contract workers. Copyright © 2016 Great Place to Work® Institute, Inc. All rights reserved.

Source: 'Stock Market Return', Russell Investment Group.

Equifinality The principle arguing that there may be many combinations of HR practices that result in identical organisational outcomes.

considers employment security, selective recruiting, high wages, incentive pay, employee ownership, information sharing, participation, empowerment, job redesign/teams, training and skill development, cross-training, symbolic egalitarianism, wage compensation and promotion from within to constitute significant best HR practices. There may be many combinations of practices that result in identical organisational outcomes (Doty et al., 1993), the so-called principle of equifinality. However, this challenges the concept of a universal 'best practice' model.

Vertical integration

Here, the organisation is seeking to develop a range of HR practices that fit the business's strategies outside the area of HRM. The logic here is that performance will be improved when the right fit, or match, between business strategy and HR practices is achieved. For example, generally, when pursuing an innovation strategy, organisations emphasise HR practices that encourage cooperative, interdependent behaviour and foster exchange of ideas and risk taking. For the quality strategy, the emphasis will be on seeking to enhance quality through ensuring highly reliable behaviour from individuals who identify with the goals of the organisation. For a cost leadership strategy, HR seeks to maximise efficiency through managerial monitoring and close control of employee activities (Schuler and Jackson, 1987). External fit, best fit and strategic fit are considered to be alternative expressions of vertical fit that determine the so-called contingency model (Delery and Doty, 1996).

According to Schuler and Jackson (1987), the underlying assumptions of this model are:

1. A non-linear relationship exists between HR practices and business performance;

2. The impact of the HR practices on business performance is different for the different levels of the critical contingency variable; and

3. External fit is the key concept.

Contingency model of HRM A view arguing that the organisation is developing a range of HR practices that fit the organisation's strategies outside the area of HRM in order to improve performance.

Combined integration

When an organisation formulates its strategy by combining internal and external fit it is called combined integration. This approach makes use of bundles of HR practices. The logic here is that different combinations of HR practices will lead to higher business performance, depending on the organisational context (MacDuffie, 1995). Richardson and Thompson (1999) argue that an organisation with bundles of interrelated HR practices that complement and reinforce each other (i.e. horizontal integration) should have a higher level of performance, provided it also achieves high levels of fit with its business strategy (i.e. vertical integration). Delery and Doty (1996) refer to this combined integration approach as the configurational model. According to MacDuffie (1995) and Delery and Doty (1996), who are among the mainstream configurational theorists, the underlying assumptions of this model are:

Configurational model of HRM An approach that suggests higher business performance is predicted by specific combinations or bundles of HR practices that best reflect the specific organisational context.

1. A non-linear relationship exists between configurations of HR practices and business performance;

2. Multiple unique configurations of HR practices result in maximal business performance, referring to the concept of equifinality;

3. The configurations are assumed to be ideal types that are theoretical constructs rather than empirically observable phenomena; and

4. Internal and external fit are both key concepts.

Developing an HR strategy

- On the basis of the three business strategies (cost, quality, innovation), explain the emphasis that managers should assign in adopting HR practices from the areas of resourcing (recruitment, selection), development (training, work design), rewards (compensation, incentives) and relations (involvement, communication).

- TASK: Read critically the study of Schuler, R.S. and Jackson, S.E. (1987) Organisational strategy and organisational level as determinants of human resource management practices. *Human Resource Planning*, 10(3): 125–141.

MODELLING HRM AND FIRM PERFORMANCE

We saw above three approaches to strategic HRM theory. These approaches suggest different routes through which HR practices contribute to business performance (Delery and Doty, 1996; Katou and Budhwar, 2010):

1. Universalistic or best practice models of HRM require that the key set of important strategic HR practices is identified, and that these practices influence business performance, maximising horizontal fit. The model suggests that business strategies and HR practices are mutually independent in determining business performance.

Horizontal fit The horizontal strategic alignment of the learning and development discipline with the other HR areas. Thus, an L&D manager needs to ensure that an employee is provided with training that corresponds to weaknesses traced in the performance appraisal.

Vertical fit Through a strategic needs assessment, the objectives of the L&D division are specified and linked with business strategy.

2. Contingency or strategic fit models of HRM require that a business strategy is identified, and then that we consider how individual HR practices interact with that strategy to result in business performance, thus maximising vertical fit. This is a sequential model, the choice of business strategy preceding the choice of HR practices.

3. Configurational or bundles models of HRM require that we first derive from theory internally consistent configurations of HR practices to maximise horizontal fit. Then we select a strategic configuration theory. Finally, we link the theoretically derived HRM systems to different strategic configurations to maximise vertical fit. This model advocates interrelation, suggesting that business strategies interact with HR practices in determining business performance.

Although there is no clear picture as to which of these models is strongest (Wood, 1999), there is at least some evidence that a contextual approach is preferable (Katou and Budhwar, 2010). Gerhart (2005: 178) writes that 'if studies of the HR–performance relationship continue to find no evidence that context matters, either the contingency theory central to strategic HR is flawed or the methodology'.

In practising HRM we have to distinguish between 'intended' HR policies, which are developed by the decision makers of the organisation, 'actual' HR practices that are implemented with respect to the intended HR policies, and 'perceived' HR practices which indicate how employees experience actual HR practices. Actual HR practices are those which are applied, usually through and by line managers, who undertake on a daily basis a whole series of actions that have an impact on how employees experience HR practices that are applied to them (Purcell and Kinnie, 2007). Although the process of successfully implementing HR practices depends on the skills of the line managers in communicating and dealing with problems, 'there is the risk that line managers simply fail to implement practices or may implement them badly' (Guest, 2011: 9), affecting in turn employees' responses.

HRM IN PRACTICE

HR best practice at Selfridges

Kinnie et al. (2005) conducted a two-year study into the implementation of HR best practices by line managers at Selfridges. In particular, the research focused on the changing attitudes (or satisfaction) of employees to a number of HR best practices including the performance appraisal, career opportunities, job influence, job challenge and respect shown by one's line manager. Results of the second year survey showed that employee satisfaction with this range of HR best practices had risen substantially across the board. As Purcell et al. (2003: 45) summarise, this case shows 'how organizations can focus developmental policies on the role of line managers and how these consequently have a beneficial effect on the staff that they manage. What happened in Selfridges was not simply luck in making good appointments but was the outcome of careful planning and forethought by the HR teams in the organization.'

THE GENERAL CAUSAL MODEL OF THE HRM–PERFORMANCE RELATIONSHIP

One drawback of the models presented above is that they focus on the two end-points of the HRM–performance relationship. At one end is HRM strategy and at the other end is business performance (operational or financial). But what happens between these two end-points? Exactly how do HR practices influence business performance? The mechanism, which remains unknown, is often referred to as the black box (Boselie et al., 2005).

Black box The unknown mechanism that is supposed to explain the influence of HR practices on business performance.

In trying to illuminate the black box, researchers initially concentrated on the skills, attitudes and behaviour of employees. This was based on the assumption that improved performance is achieved through people, in terms of better skills, attitudes and behaviour (Guest, 1997). This reflects a general consensus that HR practices do not lead directly to business performance. Rather, they influence human capital, in terms of employee skills, attitudes and behaviour, and it is these HRM outcomes that ultimately lead to performance (Katou and Budhwar, 2006; Wright et al., 1994). This process of A influencing B through C is known as mediation. Here, HRM outcomes (skills, attitudes and behaviours) positively mediate the relationship between HRM and performance. This is known as the mediating model (Paauwe and Richardson, 1997) or general causal model (see Figure 2.2).

General causal model The model that explains the HRM-performance relationship, whereby the precise mediating mechanisms through which HR practices influence business performance are indicated.

We can distinguish two types of linkages in this mode. There is a direct linkage from HR practices to business performance, which is also called the unmediated HRM effect. This suggests that HR practices have a direct influence on business performance.

The indirect linkage through HRM outcomes, which is also called the mediated HRM effect, indicates that HR practices influence HRM outcomes, which in turn influence business performance. It is not necessary for both direct and indirect linkages to be present at the same time. It is possible that a mediated effect may exist in the absence of an unmediated effect. In cases where both direct and indirect linkages are present, the intervening process is called partial mediation. In cases where only the indirect linkage is present, the intervening process is called full mediation. The final link in the diagram is labelled as reverse causality. The argument for this is that high-performing firms can afford HR practices (Huselid, 1995). Thus the performance outcome makes available to the organisation the ability to implement costly HR interventions. Few studies have investigated the strength of forward versus reverse causality. However, Katou (2012a) found that in small firms reverse causality from operational performance to HR practices is stronger than forward causality from HR practices to operational performance through employee attitudes and behaviour.

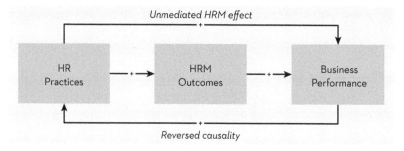

FIGURE 2.2 The general causal model of the HRM–performance relationship

While we have explored how the black box works, we have yet to decide on what it actually contains. All agree that HRM outcomes constitute the heart of the general linkage framework presented in Figure 2.2. Some researchers (e.g. Becker et al., 1997; Guest, 1997) add in further sub-boxes to such linkages. For example, attitudinal outcomes could be a sub-box consisting of employee motivation, commitment and satisfaction. Behavioural outcomes could make an additional sub-box containing employee presence (counterpart of absenteeism), employee retention (counterpart of turnover) and organisational citizenship behaviour (OCB), which refers to the work-related behaviour that goes above and beyond

Researching the relationship between HRM and performance

- Considering relevant data, explain the steps used in investigating the hypothesis that the relationship between HRM systems and organisational performance is mediated through the HRM outcomes of employee attitudes and behaviour.

- TASK: Go to the http://davidakenny.net/cm/mediate.htm website and 'learn how you can do a mediation analysis and output a text description of your results'.

that which is dictated by organisational policy and one's job description (Organ, 1988). However, this process produces two fundamental questions: How many sub-boxes explain the black box, and what is the content of each sub-box? Some authors demonstratively write that 'Until now there has been no consensus in the field of HRM with respect to this problem' (Paauwe, 2004: 58) and 'while we found plenty of acknowledgements of the existence of the "black-box", and some speculation as to its possible contents, few studies tried to look inside' (Boselie et al., 2005: 77).

DEBATING HRM

HR and economic crisis

Read the article by Katou, A.A. (2012a) Investigating reverse causality between human resource management policies and organizational performance in small firms. *Management Research Review*, 35(2): 134–156.

It is argued that an economic crisis hits small businesses more severely than large firms. As a result, small firms are trying to cut costs by reducing the budget of most HRM activities. It is further supported that because small firms cannot compete with large firms in reducing prices, they should concentrate more on the business strategies of innovation and quality enhancement of goods than on cutting costs.

TASK: In small groups of five students, discuss the case for and against cutting the budget of most HRM activities. You may also wish to discuss the view that although HRM policies lead to high organisational performance, it is high-performing firms that can directly afford HRM policies.

THE AMO MODEL OF THE HRM–PERFORMANCE RELATIONSHIP

In trying to unlock the black box a large number of models have been proposed, but one of the most influential is the AMO model from Appelbaum et al. (2000). They proposed an HRM–performance framework arguing that organisational performance is best served by employees who have the 'ability' to do the work, possessing the necessary skills and knowledge, who are 'motivated' to work and who have the 'opportunity' to arrange their skills in doing their work. Their model asserts that performance is a function of **A**bility + **M**otivation + **O**pportunity (i.e. AMO) (see also Boxall and Purcell, 2003; Purcell and Kinnie, 2007; Purcell et al., 2003).

AMO model This approach argues that organisational performance is best served by employees who have the ability to do the work, possessing the necessary skills and knowledge, who are motivated to work appropriately, and who have the opportunity to arrange their skills in doing their work.

The philosophy of the AMO model is that there is no specific list of HR practices that may influence performance. Instead, the whole process depends on HR architecture that covers policies designed to build and retain human capital and to influence employee behaviour. Thus, according to the HR architecture concept, there is a range of HRM policy domains (ability, motivation, opportunity) that are determined according to organisational context (e.g. industry, culture, country)

Performance outcomes The final and overall evaluation of the degree to which an employee has achieved specific targets set for him or her.

(Lepak et al., 2006). The basic HRM policies that are required in order to turn AMO into action are usually considered to be the following: recruitment and selection; training and development; career opportunities that are linked to ability and skill; rewards and benefits that are linked to motivation and incentive; and involvement, team working, work–life balance, job challenge and autonomy that are linked to the opportunity to participate.

The nature of front-line managers' strategic HR role

Four different aspects of management of people by front-line managers are usually identified, as follows (Purcell et al., 2003): implementing (i.e. putting HR policies into operation), enacting (making HR policies effective), leading (the small actions which front-line managers undertake on a daily basis) and controlling (i.e. controlling the behaviour of employees with respect to their job).

- TASK: Read critically the chapter by Marchington, M. and Cox, A. (2007) Employee involvement and participation: Structures, processes and outcomes, in J. Storey (ed.) *Human Resource Management: A Critical Text*, 3rd edn. London: Thomson, pp. 177–194.

- Reflect upon the critical role that front-line managers play in the development and continuation of employee involvement techniques.

In response to AMO policies, employees will develop organisational commitment, motivation and job satisfaction (attitudinal outcomes). These attitudes will lead to employees demonstrating a range of positive behavioural outcomes. Discretionary behaviour (i.e. making the right choices about how to do a job, such as speed, care, innovation and style) and organisational citizenship behaviour lie at the heart of the employment relationship and should be strongly connected to performance outcomes. Highly committed, motivated and satisfied employees are more likely to engage in discretionary behaviour and OCB to help the organisation to be successful. Therefore, it is argued that 'one of the prime functions of AMO policies is thus the way they help develop attitudes or feelings of satisfaction, commitment and motivation in most employees since these translate into discretionary behaviour, provided the job allows for it' (Purcell et al., 2003: 7).

However, the relationship between HRM policies and attitudinal outcomes is affected by the behaviours of front-line management. Nearly all policies are applied through and by line managers and therefore whether they implement those policies well or badly, consistently or inconsistently, will impact on the outcomes of the policies. This process of external influence is called moderation.

Performance outcomes constitute the ultimate impact of AMO policies, through the serial influence of employee attitudes and behaviour. These outcomes may be operational, such as effectiveness (i.e. if the organisation meets its objectives) and efficiency (i.e. if the organisation uses the fewest possible resources to meet its objectives), or financial, such as ROI (return on investment), ROE (return on equity) and ROCE (return on capital employed). Finally, reverse causality may be encountered from performance to employee attitudes, indicating that the success of the organisation brings positive attitudes to employees, because employees 'feel proud to tell people who they work for and want to stay working for the firm for the foreseeable future' (Purcell et al., 2003: 6).

MINI CASE STUDY

HR and ROI

Meta-analysis studies (i.e. methods focused on combining and contrasting findings from different studies) find that there is growing evidence that HRM positively affects organisational performance (Combs et al., 2006). It is supported that researchers find stronger relationships when examining high-performance work practices (HPWP) systems versus individual HR practices, operational versus financial performance measures and manufacturing versus service organisations (Combs et al., 2006).

Assume that you have recently been appointed as HR advisor for SingularLogic (http://portal.singularlogic.eu/english-home-page/1229/about-us), a leading software and integrated IT solutions group in Greece, which provides integrated solutions for the private and public sectors both in Greece and abroad. In addition, SingularLogic operates in various South East European countries through direct subsidiaries in Bulgaria, Romania and Cyprus, having set the foundations for substantial development in the region.

The Board of Directors of SingularLogic is sceptical because the consolidated turnover of the group reached €55.9 million for 2012, which was 5 per cent less than the consolidated turnover of the group in 2011. While you are based at the headquarters of SingularLogic in Athens, part of your role is to visit the group's subsidiaries and to audit their HR processes and practices. You are under pressure to demonstrate the business value of the HR function to the Board of Directors in terms of ROI (i.e. comparing the costs of HR programmes and activities to the benefits derived from them for assessing their worth to the organisation).

TASK: Go to www.competentiebeleid.be/assets/waarom/Measuring_ROI.pdf for information referring to the measurement of ROI in human resources by Phillips, J.J. (2007) *Measuring ROI in Human Resources*. Chelsea, AL: ROI Institute.

- Demonstrate the HR programme and activities value chain.
- Offer to the executives the types of ROI data.
- Indicate to the company how ROI for human resources will be implemented.

THE PSYCHOLOGICAL CONTRACT MODEL OF THE HRM–PERFORMANCE RELATIONSHIP

An alternative approach to illuminating the black box is to focus more directly on the relationship between employer and employee. While employees will typically have an employment contract, in recent years researchers have also begun to focus on the less codified elements of the relationship between employer and employee. This relationship is known as the psychological contract (see also Chapter 12). It is defined as 'an individual's system of belief, shaped by the organization, regarding terms of an exchange agreement between him/herself and the organization' (Rousseau and Greller, 1994: 385). Psychological contracts are informal and unwritten in nature, depending on the dynamic interaction between individuals and the organisation. They construct the expectation of both parties as to the nature of the exchange between the employer and the employee. There are two somewhat different types of psychological contract that can be considered (Rousseau, 1990). Transactional contracts tend to involve short-term, specific and monetary-related beliefs such as competitive wage rates and performance-based pay. Relational contracts are more concerned with a long-term relationship, characterised by both monetary and non-monetary reward including issues such as job security, loyalty, development opportunity, commitment and trust.

Given the turbulence in employment and employment types in recent years, a number of theorists and practitioners have argued that the traditional psychological contract is progressively replaced by the new psychological contract. The latter is described as an offer by the employer of fair pay and treatment in return for employee commitment to the work performed, considering that employees are responsible for their own career development as well as for their training and development (Robinson and Rousseau, 1994).

A major function of HRM is to cultivate a positive psychological contract that will lead to greater employee motivation, commitment and satisfaction, the attitudinal outcomes we earlier identified as a key stage in the AMO model of the HRM–performance relationship. In other words, psychological contracts can be treated as beliefs stemming from HRM policies and practices. Psychological contract fulfilment is focused on employers' promise fulfilment as perceived by employees; hence they are likely to reciprocate by fulfilling their own promises and perceived obligations (Conway and Briner, 2005). This is based on the notions of reciprocity and social exchange. If employers uphold their side of the bargain, employees will feel satisfied, committed and motivated, and so they will reciprocate by upholding their side of the bargain (Rousseau, 1995). Therefore, in this model, HR policies influence organisational performance as a result of psychological contract fulfilment.

The nature of the psychological contract itself, however, is shaped by the HR policies in operation. An initial interaction between the organisation and potential employees not only transmits the formal employment terms and conditions of the organisation to the potential job applicants but also communicates the organisation's beliefs about future employment. Thus an organisation that emphasises training and development

Psychological contract The unwritten expectations regarding terms and conditions of an exchange agreement between an employee and the employer.

may develop an expectation among prospective employees that they are part of its permanent employment (Gomez-Mejia et al., 2004). The components of employee reward may also serve to construct psychological contract terms by establishing the belief in the perceived value of employees; in other words, that they are worth their rewards in whatever form they are given (Gomez-Mejia et al., 2004).

GRADUATE INSIGHTS

Psychological contract during placement

A placement year in an organisation, or a year abroad, is integrated into many university degrees. Many students usually spend the third year of their course on work or study abroad or on placement, or a mixture of both. The placement year gives the student an opportunity to take on graduate-level responsibility and 'try out' a career path. The student will be able to put what he or she has learnt on their course into practice, while gaining valuable professional, and often paid, experience. A placement year enhances the student's graduate employment prospects and can help him or her make more informed career decisions. Over one-third of the placement students are offered graduate jobs by their placement employer (see e.g. www1.aston.ac.uk/study/undergraduate/placements/).

A placement programme usually involves a series of business and management training periods under the close guidance of a supervisor. At the beginning of the placement, a typical contract that constitutes the content of the placement experience, the intended learning outcomes and the structure of the relationship between the supervisor and the trainee is developed and signed between the organisation and the trainee. The typical contract helps to prevent later difficulties in cases where the supervisor or the trainee feels that obligations are not being met. In addition to the typical contract that sets out obligations about work and everyday practicalities of the supervision, supervisors and trainees draw up a psychological contract. This contract involves expectations of both parties and helps to develop a trusting and positive supervisor–trainee relationship. The usual insights of the graduate placement psychological contract refer to the hopes about the roles the two parties value most and to the expectations each of the two parties has of the other. Hawkins and Shohet (2004) propose that in cases where the expectations of the psychological contract can be made explicit and agreed upon, the process of learning will be improved.

Discussing with students about their psychological contract during their placement experience, Tom Brothwell (spending one year on placement at the University Laval, Quebec, Canada) said that 'The whole experience was second to none; not only academically but culturally as well as being great fun! It has certainly reinforced the international element of my degree and has set me apart from other graduates in the global job market.' Chris Rothwell (on placement at Microsoft) said that 'My year's experience here means that I'm able to take on responsibility much faster, allowing me to gain more experience and get a really fantastic start to my career.' Mark Boosey (on placement at Reuters) believes that 'I've learnt and experienced loads of important things that just aren't possible in university', while Chloe Piper (on placement at CSV [Community Service Volunteers]) said that 'I have learnt how to manage my time, work effectively within a team of volunteers, and how to manage responsibility, especially with cash. My communication skills have been immensely improved because I talk to a range of clients – some speak very little English and others have mental health issues and drug and alcohol problems. I have learnt secretarial and admin skills, as well as passing a food hygiene course.'

The appropriate use of HR policies can therefore create a positive organisational environment that will influence the degree of fulfilment of employer and employee promises (Purcell et al., 2003). Thus, HR policies determine the status of psychological contracts by shaping the day-to-day behaviours of the members in an organisation (Rousseau, 1995). Consequently, a major function of HR policies is to cultivate a positive psychological contract that will lead to improved organisational performance. Effective HR policies produce positive psychological contracts, generating positive attitudinal reactions, which consequently will improve organisational performance.

METHOD PROBLEMS IN INVESTIGATING THE HRM AND FIRM PERFORMANCE RELATIONSHIP

We have presented in the previous section three general models that describe the relationship between HRM and business performance. These models have dominated both theoretical and empirical research and academic and practitioner debate over the last 20 years or so (Gerhart, 2007). However, core questions about the relationship between HRM and performance are still unanswered (Camps and Luna-Arocas, 2012). This is because various problems have bedevilled research in this area, making our knowledge still unsure (Guest, 2011). These fall into five broad areas (Purcell and Kinnie, 2007):

1. The methodology framework followed

2. The performance measures used

3. The configuration of the HRM system

4. The theory that explains the causal link between HR practices and performance produced

5. The level of analysis used.

METHODOLOGY PROBLEMS

Common method bias The methodological problem arising from the fact that in surveys exploring the HR-performance relationship single respondents provide the measures of both HR practices and performance.

There are three main methodological problems within this kind of research. First, most studies exploring the HR–performance link used surveys addressed to single responders, such as a senior HR manager. This single individual is asked to describe both HR practices and organisational performance. The problem here is one of bias, specifically what is termed as **common method bias**. To overcome this problem, multiple respondents are used, or different sources are employed for collecting (dependent) performance measures and explanatory HR practices measures.

The second methodological problem is that survey studies tend to collect cross-sectional data, that is, all the data are collected at the same point in time. This does not allow us to make any inference about whether HR practice causes performance outcomes, whether performance outcomes cause HR practices or whether something entirely separately causes both. Cross-sectional research can only reveal associations and not the direction of causality in the relationship between HR practices and performance.

Third, most studies do not consider the lag effect, which refers to the time it takes an HR practice to impact on performance. The most logical design to address the time taken for HR practice to influence performance would seem to be measuring HR practice at one time and then, at a later time, measuring organisational performance.

PERFORMANCE MEASURE PROBLEMS

Our second research problem in relation to the HR–performance debate is to decide what measures of performance to take. With respect to performance, the most important problem refers to the use of objective (explicitly measured) or subjective (based on perception) performance measures. Referring to the objective data, although profitability is assumed to be a profound end goal of HRM, the problem is that there is no convincing methodology for measuring the influence of HR practices on profitability (Purcell and Kinnie, 2007). There are so many other factors which will intervene to influence profitability; consider, for example, the PESTEL framework discussed in Chapter 1. This has led many researchers to explore measures that are closer to the HR practices, for example employee turnover or absence (Harter et al., 2002). While both profitability and absence are objective measures, however, both objective and subjective measures are highly variable between sectors, economic philosophies and geographic areas. This brings the necessity of controlling for context (Gerhart, 2005). The controls used in the analysis are frequently categorised into organisational-level control variables (such as age and size of organisation) and individual-level control variables (Budhwar and Sparrow, 2002).

HR CONFIGURATION PROBLEMS

Another potential problem that makes drawing unequivocal conclusions difficult is the choice and definition of the HR practices used in the analysis. There are countless combinations of HR practices that result in identical organisational outcomes. Marchington and Grugulis (2000: 1114) stress that 'lists of HR practices are developed on the basis of looking at what other researchers have used or by constructing groupings of practices on the basis of factor analysis, and then attempting to impose some theoretical justification for this ex post facto'.

THEORY PROBLEMS

With respect to the theory problems, Boselie et al. (2005) report large disparities in the treatment of the components, emphasising the precise mechanisms that outline what is taking place between HRM and performance. As we discussed above, this is known as the black box problem. However, most theories assume that employee attitudes and behaviour constitute the heart of the HRM–performance relationship, which in fact reflect the mediating mechanism that links HRM with performance. Meta-analytical studies (e.g. Combs et al., 2006; Jiang et al., 2012; Subramony, 2009) describe the extent to which HRM policies and practices matter in determining performance. However, in addition to the causal links potential moderators may exist in the relationships between HRM and performance. There are usually three general approaches considering the moderation effects on the HRM–performance relationship. First, it is assumed that HRM features such as distinctiveness, consistency and consensus may moderate the HRM–performance link (e.g. Katou et al., 2014; Sanders et al., 2008). Second, organisational features such as climate, support and strategic activities may have a potential influence on the HRM–performance relationship (e.g. Chowhan, 2016; Neal et al., 2005). Third, context-related features such as industry or country type may moderate the relationship between HRM and organizational outcomes (e.g. Combs et al., 2006; Jiang et al., 2012; Subramony, 2009).

HRM content The individual HR policies and practices that make up an HRM system.

HRM process The method by which HR policies and practices are communicated to employees.

Furthermore, various models discussed above treat the HRM system as being composed of three parts: content, process and strength (Bowen and Ostroff, 2004; Katou, 2012b). HRM content refers to the individual HR policies and practices that make up an HRM system. HRM process refers to the method by which HR policies and practices are communicated to employees. **HRM strength** refers to how HR policies and practices are experienced by employees (Kinnie et al., 2005). HRM strength, which reflects organisational HRM climate in terms of a collective understanding of expected behaviours and incentives to adhere to them, is influenced by both HRM content and process. Since the introduction of the concept of HRM strength in 2004, it has been operationalised in a variety of personal ways by researchers (e.g. Bednall et al., 2014; Delmotte et al., 2012; Frenkel and Yu, 2011; Frenkel et al., 2012; Ribeiro et al., 2011), and in general it has been widely accepted in the HRM field (Ostroff and Bowen, 2016). However, it is argued that HRM process mediates the relationship between HRM content and HRM strength (Bowen and Ostroff, 2004).

LEVEL OF ANALYSIS PROBLEMS

One difficult challenge in HRM research refers to the level of analysis (i.e. plant, business unit, corporation): 'Plant-level studies provide the advantage of measuring HR practices quite specifically and probably most accurately'; 'Business level studies are the optimal setting for assessing the links between HR practices and business strategy'; and 'Studying these phenomena at the corporate level provides a tremendous advantage in the assessment of financial performance' (Wright and Gardner, 2003: 315). HRM can be related to outcomes in different ways at different levels of analysis (individual level of analysis with HRM outcomes at higher levels of analysis). However, this 'multi-level' approach to studying perceptions of and reactions to HRM systems will inevitably need to deal with the concept of variance at different levels of analysis.

Conceptualising and operationalising HRM system strength

- Considering that a number of researchers have focused on individuals' own perceptions of HRM system strength, conceptualise and operationalise HRM system strength in your own personal way.

- TASK: Read critically the study of Ostroff, C. and Bowen, D.E. (2016) Reflections on the 2014 decade award: Is there strength in the construct of HR system strength? *Academy of Management Review*, 41(2): 196–214.

CASE STUDY

AmBev Brazil

AmBev (America's Beverage Company; www.ambev.com.br) is a brewing company headquartered in Sao Paulo, Brazil. AmBev was established in 1999 with the merger of two breweries, Brahma and Antarctica. It is the biggest brewery company in Latin America and the fifth in the world. AmBev took a major step towards globalisation in 2004 when it merged with Interbrew, a leading brewery company based in Belgium, creating InBev. Starting an expansion plan, InBev acquired beverage companies throughout many countries, and finally bought Anheuser-Busch, which is America's leading brewer, creating the largest brewery in the world in terms of volumes produced, named AB-InBev.

AmBev produces and/or bottles beers (such as Antarctica, Brahma, Skol and Stella Artois) and soft drinks (such as Pepsi, Lipton Ice Tea and Gatorade). It employs 46,500 people, its revenue is US$15.7 billion, and its net income is US$5.1 billion (2012 figures). Based on the fact that AmBev was the dominant producer in Brazil, with a market share of 60 per cent, its internationalisation process was guided by the necessity to expand to countries with higher growth potential. However, AmBev firmly believes that the success of its internationalisation depends on the quality of its human resources; and it further believes that when a company has good quality human resources, when there is internal harmony and common vision, then the company is sure to succeed in implementing its goals.

To satisfy the need for quality of its human resources, AmBev helps its employees to discover and to develop their talents and skills, to face professional challenges, to manage their careers and to enhance their personal development. It tries to inspire them, to encourage them, to reward them and to take care of them. Emphasis is put on the health, education, experience and skills of employees. Specifically, AmBev has established 12 agricultural production centres where the company is delivering teaching programmes for young farmers on how to use efficient techniques for growing the ingredients necessary for the popular soft drinks that AmBev is producing. The shareholders of AmBev believe that its success depends on the following 10 dimensions (see www.ab-inbev.com/pdf/AB-InBev_Ten_principles.pdf):

1 Our shared dream energises everyone to work in the same direction: to be the best beer company in a better world.

2 Great people, allowed to grow at the pace of their talent and compensated accordingly, are the most valuable assets of our company.

3 We must select people who, with the right development, challenges and encouragement, can be better than ourselves. We will be judged by the quality of our teams.

(Continued)

(Continued)

4 We are never completely satisfied with our results, which are the fuel of our company. Focus and zero-complacency guarantee lasting competitive advantage.

5 The consumer is the Boss. We connect with our consumers through meaningful brand experiences, balancing heritage and innovation and always in a responsible way.

6 We are a company of owners. Owners take results personally.

7 We believe common sense and simplicity are usually better guidelines than unnecessary sophistication and complexity.

8 We manage our costs tightly, to free up resources that will support top-line growth.

9 Leadership by personal example is the best guide to our culture. We do what we say.

10 We don't take shortcuts. Integrity, hard work, quality and consistency are keys to building our company.

CASE STUDY TASKS

Assume that you are the newly appointed head of the HR Department of AmBev. You have the following tasks:

1 To present to the Board specific programmes that must be initiated in order to successfully deliver the 10 dimensions.

2 To explain to the Board how you would measure the value added of these programmes.

Source: AB InBev (2010) *Dream, People, Culture: 10 Principles*. www.ab-inbev.com/pdf/AB-InBev_Ten_principles. pdf. (accessed 8 July 2013).

CHAPTER SUMMARY

The key points that we have identified in this chapter are the following:

- This chapter has explained the potential contribution of HRM to sustainable firm performance. In doing so, the various theoretical perspectives that have been put forward to explain this relationship were evaluated.

- Concepts such as strategic management and strategic HRM that are related to the HRM–performance relationship are introduced. Strategic management refers to the managerial decisions and actions that may improve performance in organisations, and strategic HRM refers to the processes that link HRM policies and practices with the strategic objectives of the organisation.

- The theoretical frameworks of the resource-based view, whereby HRM influences performance according to the human capital held by the organisation, and the integration approach, whereby HRM strategy formulation focuses on the alignment of HR policies and practices within the HRM area and with other strategies outside the area of HRM, have dominated the field of strategic HRM.

- Three major models that explain the relationship between HRM and organisational performance have been critically presented. These are the universalistic or best practice models of HRM, arguing that the organisation is developing a range of interconnected and mutually reinforcing HR practices that will always produce superior results whatever the accompanying circumstances; the contingency or strategic fit models of HRM, arguing that the organisation is developing a range of HR practices that fit the business's strategies outside the area of HRM; and the configurational or bundles models of HRM, implying that the existence of specific combinations of HR practices that depend on organisational context lead to higher business performance.

- The general causal model of the HRM–performance relationship is presented whereby the precise mediating mechanisms through which HR practices influence business performance are explored. These mediating mechanisms, which are popularly referred to as the black box, assume that HRM outcomes such as employee skills, attitudes and behaviour positively mediate the relationship between HRM and performance.

- In trying to illuminate the black box, the AMO HRM–performance framework is explored, arguing that organisational performance is best served by employees who have the ability to do the work, possessing the necessary skills and knowledge, who are motivated to work appropriately and who have the opportunity to arrange their skills in doing their work. Additionally, the psychological contract HRM–performance framework is presented, whereby the state of the psychological contract, based on the notions of reciprocity and social exchange, mediates the relationship between HR policies and organisational performance.

- Important problems in empirical research demonstrating the causal links between human resource management and business performance, such as the methodology framework followed, the performance measures used, the configuration of the HRM system, the theory that explains the causal link between HR practices and performance produced and the level of analysis used, are presented. Although there is growing evidence that high-performance work practices affect organisational performance, these problems make the size of the overall effect difficult to estimate and produce mixed results.

REVIEW QUESTIONS AND EXERCISES

1. What is meant by strategic management? Explain the steps of the strategic management process.

2. What are the levels of strategy formulation? Discuss what is the focus of each strategy.

3. What is meant by strategic human resource management? Present the theoretical frameworks that have dominated the field of strategic HRM.

4. What is meant by black box? Explain the linkages between HRM and firm performance.

5. What are the basic properties of the universalistic, contingency and configurational models?

6. What are the core concepts in the AMO and the psychological contract HRM–performance frameworks?

7. Why is it difficult to evaluate the contribution of HR policies and practices to organisational performance?

EXPLORE FURTHER

Muller-Camen, M., Croucher, R. and Leigh, S. (2008) *Human Resource Management: A Case Study Approach*. London: Chartered Institute of Personnel and Development. This is a very good book exploring HRM through the case study approach. The chapter 'The psychological contract, absence and turnover' in particular provides a very useful summary of the key issues linking HRM practices, the psychological contract and important employee attitudes towards and behaviours at work.

Schuler, R.S. (1989) Strategic human resource management. *Human Relations*, 42(2): 157–184. Although this article was now written some time ago, it still provides an excellent review of the key theoretical developments in strategic HRM.

The Chartered Institute of Personnel and Development website at www.cipd.co.uk/. This website is worth exploring as it will provide you with lots of very useful information regarding the profession.

GO ONLINE

Visit the companion website for **interactive quizzes**, explanatory **videos** and **podcasts**, **journal articles** to use in your essays, and **weblinks** to useful resources.

https://edge.sagepub.com/crawshaw2e

CHAPTER 3

ORGANISATIONAL CHANGE AND HRM

Katty Marmenout
Achim Schmitt

CHAPTER KNOWLEDGE OBJECTIVES

- Identify the main internal and external forces that act on an organisation to trigger change.
- Discuss the different approaches to change, and the strengths and weaknesses of each.
- Acquire a solid understanding of the key steps in a successful change process.
- Understand the role of leadership and its implication for driving culture change.
- Appreciate the nature of human and organisational resistance to change.

KEY SKILLS OBJECTIVES

- To be able to perform force field analysis using Lewin's framework.
- To be able to distinguish between different approaches to change.
- To be able to plan a sustainable change effort according to Kotter's eight steps.
- To be able to identify the appropriate approach for cultural change.
- To understand behavioural change and how to manage resistance to change.

This chapter also provides indicative content for the following CIPD Intermediate and Advanced level modules:

CIPD INTERMEDIATE LEVEL MODULES

5CHR Business issues and the context of HR

5ODT Organisational development

CIPD ADVANCED LEVEL MODULES

7HRC Human resource management in context

7ODD Organisation design and organisation development

GO ONLINE

This chapter comes with loads of online tools to help you to go that extra mile in your studies!

- **Multiple choice questions** to help you test your knowledge and revise for exams
- **Journal articles** so you can read further for assignments and essays
- **Videos** and **podcasts** to help you to understand how complex concepts work in the real world

Visit **https://edge.sagepub.com/crawshaw2e** to access these resources for this topic.

ONLINE STUDY TOOLS

Video Case study: What is Urgency?

Solidify your understanding by watching an excellent explanation by John Kotter himself on the first step of his model: creating a sense of urgency.

https://edge.sagepub.com/crawshaw2e > **Student Resources** > **Chapter 3** > **Videos**

INTRODUCTION

> If you want to truly understand something, try to change it. (Kurt Lewin)

Heraclitus argued that there is nothing permanent except change. Indeed, all of life is change. At the micro or individual level, from birth to maturity, both our physical growth and mental development involve tremendous amounts of change. At the macro or societal level, as centuries and decades pass we witness huge developmental leaps and bounds. Thus it is not surprising that, at the organisational level, we similarly encounter changes throughout the lifecycle of a corporation. However hard to believe, all major corporations eventually started as an entrepreneurial venture launched by a visionary change agent, be it Walt Disney, Henry Ford or W.H. Smith. We can hardly imagine the amount of change these organisations have endured over the decades or even centuries of their existence.

Still, while change is part and parcel of life in general and of organisational life in particular, many people are reluctant to embrace change. Change implies leaving behind the familiar, the certain; it implies taking risks and looking for different solutions to new problems. These solutions may be superior but may require a great deal of learning and investment before they pay off and prove to be right. Change is filled with doubt. Changing may also result in less optimal situations, due to miscalculations, misfortunes or unexpected changes in the market. Overall, changing implies leaving our comfort zone and this alone may be sufficient to make individuals reluctant to change, as humans are programmed to avoid uncertainty.

While changing may be hard for individuals and organisations, the consequences of failing to do so may loom large. As such, change may be a bitter pill to swallow, but a much needed medicine. Failing to change course in line with environmental requirements may result in disappearance or organisational death. Who recalls a pioneering computer company named Digital Equipment Corporation (DEC)? DEC, founded in 1957, was a leading vendor of computer systems until it died in 1998 – acquired by Compaq, which itself disappeared as at it was acquired by HP in 2002.

As the pace of technological change accelerates and markets become increasingly volatile, the ability to change swiftly and efficiently becomes a much-needed skill. While learning about how to drive and manage change successfully is arguably a skill needed for all business managers and functional experts, it is even more so for the HRM function. Indeed, as business strategies need to adapt to the changing environment, the people need to follow. More so: in order to be successful, change efforts require the passion and commitment of all people in the organisation. As the HR function can be seen as the major caretaker of the organisation's human resources, it is largely responsible for making sure that people are prepared to embrace change, that they can understand why there is a need to reorganise, to acquire new skills and to attract new talent. In sum, changing requires doing things differently and the HR function's role is to enable individuals to do so in the best possible way.

In this chapter we first discuss the process and content of change, as well as different types of organisational change and how to implement them. Finally, we focus on the individual level and examine behavioural change and how we can effectively inspire and lead change.

CONTENT VERSUS PROCESS OF CHANGE

This chapter intends to provide students of HRM (and business management in general) with tools and skills that will enable them to initiate and lead change initiatives in organisations. While many of these tools appear simple to use, we cannot highlight enough the complexity of change. Executives enrolled in leading change programmes greatly appreciate the toolkit presented in this chapter, which they receive over the course of their training. Still, they often feel frustrated. From our experience, we can describe this problem as stemming from the difference between the **process** and **content** of change. As HR practitioners will often act as change agents in their organisations, it is crucial for them to understand this distinction, as they will need to alert and guide line managers to the implications of this distinction between process and content.

Change agent A person who indirectly or directly initiates change and assists others in understanding and implementing changes. Change agents are often referred to as catalysts for change.

While tools and models are essential elements to make change efforts successful, they relate to what we call the process of change. We can apply those models and implement change accordingly. If we follow the process and do it right, it should work, and accumulated evidence shows the usefulness of the tools described in this chapter.

However, in order to successfully implement change we also need a deep understanding of the change context. Unfortunately, none of the existing books on change management can provide an answer to your particular change issue. Each person or organisation, and particularly HR representatives, needs to examine the content and **context of change**, for example: What do we need to change? Where do we want to go and why? What is our vision? Finding the right answers to these questions is key and a prerequisite for successful change. Once appealing answers have been found to these questions, then the tools come in handy and following the process will lead to successful change. HR executives should appreciate, however, that without the foundation of an enticing vision for the future and a solid understanding of the specific context, the best-managed change process would only lead to disappointment and frustration.

GRADUATE INSIGHTS

Conducting a challenging change project at Renault

The following is taken from a conversation held with Julie, a recent EMLYON graduate of the General Management programme. The discussion highlights the difference between the process and content of change. Julie was entrusted with a challenging change project at her firm Renault. After completing the course in change management and applying the tools presented in this chapter, Julie was proud to be able to declare her first major change project a great success. We asked Julie what was the most challenging part of the change: the vision. She spent days and days thinking about the vision and designing the project: how to present and communicate it. She checked informally with her peers, superiors and subordinates to get input and ideas and to get a proper understanding of the context and the expectations of the different stakeholders. Once she had the vision, the process followed seamlessly: 'Once I had nailed down the right vision, following Kotter's steps (See Pages 68–70, this volume) was as easy as a piece of cake', recalled Julie.

ORGANISATIONAL CONTEXT AND CHANGE

Why does change occur in organisations? It occurs because organisations develop throughout time. Similarly to individuals, organisations experience change throughout their organisational life. A newly created entrepreneurial business, for instance, inevitably changes as its business succeeds and grows. Mature organisations change and adapt because globalisation, technological innovations and the development of our society do not allow them to stand still. Consequently, organisational change is important for every organisation because without change they risk losing their competitive edge or justification for existence. In this context, organisational change can be defined as a process by which organisations transform their present state to some desired future state. Organisational change does not take place spontaneously. It is the outcome of several forces that encourage change.

Organisational change The process by which organisations transform their present state to some desired future state.

Organisations are part of a complex, dynamic environment from which they require resources to produce a certain material or immaterial output (Beer, 1980). Given today's current dynamic nature of most markets, it is nearly impossible to find an industry or a firm that is not engaged in continuous or periodic innovation and reorientation. As an organisation constantly interacts with its environment in order to maintain critical resources, changes within the external (outside the organisation) and internal (within the organisation) environment may trigger organisational change. Correctly identifying the organisational context and reasons for change represents therefore a critical component of successful change management processes.

EXTERNAL REASONS FOR CHANGE

External reasons for change lie outside the organisation's boundaries and are situated within the macro environment. These external forces for change have been found to emerge from political, economic, social, technological, environmental and legal factors that can be analysed by using the PESTEL model (Aguilar, 1967) first introduced in Chapter 1:

External reasons for change Reasons for change that can be found outside of the organisation's boundaries and are usually situated within the macro-environment.

- **Political drivers for change:** Changes in government policy, ideologies, practices and systems (i.e. infrastructure, education, health system).
- **Economic drivers for change:** Changes in the economic climate, including economic growth, inflation, interest rates, taxation and exchange rates.

- **Social drivers for change:** Changes in socio-cultural values of the society that reflect people's behaviour, values, attitudes and expectations.
- **Technological drivers for change:** Changes in technological conditions leading to new technological developments for products and processes.
- **Environmental drivers for change:** Changes in environmental conditions (i.e. climate, weather) that alter conditions of the ecosystem.
- **Legal drivers for change:** Changes in regulatory systems that set legal boundaries in which firms operate (i.e. labour law, trade regulations).

INTERNAL REASONS FOR CHANGE

Internal reasons for change Organisational alterations in technology, primary task, people and administrative structures.

Conversely, internal reasons for change generally stem from organisational alterations in technology, primary task, people and administrative structures (Leavitt, 1964). Internal technological triggers for change refer to adaptations within the production of goods and services and include installation or replacement of plant, machinery, tools or the redesign of production processes. Modifications of an organisation's core business, for instance through changes of current services or products with which to serve current markets, summarise internal stimuli from primary tasks. The development of individual members and groups of people that constitute an organisation relates to internal people changes. Finally, changes within the formalised organisational structures, such as hierarchies, reward systems, control systems and working procedures, comprise change triggers based on administrative structures. As we can see, many of these reasons for change lie indeed within the realm of HR and are therefore relevant for appreciation by students of HR and HR practitioners.

Force field analysis Provides an environmental scanning tool that answers the question whether or not organisational change is necessary by comparing driving and hindering forces for change.

In general, external and internal reasons for change are often difficult to distinguish as they tend to overlap and are mutually reinforcing. In summarising the external and internal reasons for change, Kurt Lewin (1951) developed the 'force field analysis' model. Essentially, this model argues that each organisation is in a state of equilibrium between forces for change (driving forces) and forces against change (hindering forces).

Resistance to change The refusal to accept or comply with organisational change.

Driving forces characterise all external and internal aspects that tend to motivate change. Hindering forces restrain and decrease the driving forces and try to maintain the status quo. These hindering forces are often called resistance to change because they block change. Given that both forces exist in every change situation, they create a sort of equilibrium.

But what is the use of the force field analysis? The force field analysis provides a tool that answers the question whether or not organisational change is necessary. Organisations are in need of change when the total strength of all driving

Perform a force field analysis using Lewin's framework

Driving Forces	Hindering Forces

TASK: Pick an industry or organisation you are familiar with. Analyse the environment using Lewin's force field analysis. Can you foresee any changes?

forces outperforms the total strength of all hindering forces. This technique assumes that organisations are in a state of equilibrium or organisational balance. Change takes place when there is an imbalance between both types of forces and ends when the opposing forces are brought back into equilibrium.

MINI CASE STUDY

Change in the airline industry

Traditionally, travelling in Europe was characterised by either expensive air flights offered by established airlines (e.g. British Airways, Lufthansa, Air France) or by slow and expensive state-owned rail companies (e.g. British Railways, Deutsche Bahn, Société Nationale des Chemins de Fer Français). When the European Union deregulated air travel in the mid-1990s, low-cost airline companies (e.g. easyJet, Ryanair, Flybe) decided to enter the European air travel market and established business models that allow the companies to offer flights at low cost. Through a focus on the cheapest passenger transportation from one point to another, these companies aim to avoid all additional costs. Significant cost savings are achieved, for instance, by only selling tickets on the internet, hence bypassing traditional, margin-demanding travel agencies. In providing a real alternative that met the prevailing travel needs, low-cost companies steadily increased passenger numbers and could sustainably position themselves in the market. As a consequence, the traditional established airline companies witnessed a constant revenue decline. Today, all national carriers also set up low-cost subsidiaries and changed their business models as a reaction to the new market entrants and to defend their position within the air travel market. In this example, the deregulation of the European air travel market, the entrance of low-cost airline companies, declining sales and increasing cost sensitivity represent driving forces for national carriers to change. Conversely, the investments related to setting up a low-cost business model and partly abandoning their current market positioning represent forces against the change. By shifting and embracing a low-cost model in their organisations, national airline companies managed to reach a new organisational equilibrium.

CASE STUDY QUESTIONS

1 Identify the driving and hindering forces that changed the European airline industry in the mid-1990s.

2 Compare the European airline industry at the beginning and at the end of the 1990s. What changed? How did airline companies react to these changes?

Sources: Regani, S. and Dutta, S. (2003) *EasyJet – The 'Easy' Way to Succeed*. European Case Clearing House. Case reference #303-193-1. Accessed online at: www.thecasecentre.org/educators/products/view?id=20946

McCosker, P. (2003) *EasyJet – The Largest Low Cost Airline in Europe*. European Case Clearing House. Case reference #303-067-1. Accessed online at: www.thecasecentre.org/educators/products/view?id=20848

In this respect, a force field analysis provides an environmental scanning tool that helps to identify and evaluate all external and internal driving and hindering forces when dealing with change. The better the analysis of driving and hindering forces, the better the strategies to implement the desired change.

TYPES OF CHANGE AND CHANGE PATHS

First-order change
Organisational adaptations or variations made within an existing system without changing the system itself (incremental change).

Second-order change
A change which breaks with the past basic assumptions and transforms fundamental characteristics and attributes of the organisation (discontinuous change).

Organisational change can be classified into two fundamental different modes: first-order and second-order change (Watzlawick et al., 1974). First-order or continuous change refers to organisational adaptations or variations within an existing system without the system itself changing. As such, first-order changes are often considered incremental adjustments and result in variations of products, structures and processes (Quinn, 1978). In contrast, second-order changes are changes which break with the past basic assumptions and transform fundamental characteristics and attributes of the organisation. These changes are defined as discontinuous or second-order change. While the first is mostly referred to as incremental change, the latter is also characterised as deep change (Quinn, 1996).

Distinguishing between deep and incremental

TASK: Identify 10 changes you have read about or experienced first-hand and classify them into deep and incremental change.

In light of these general types of change, organisational evolution is based on both incremental first-order changes that improve the existing status quo and discontinuous second-order changes that fundamentally adapt to a new environment. In this regard, theorists argue that organisations evolve through periods of incremental changes disrupted by discontinuous periods of reorientation (Romanelli and Tushman, 1994). However, although the types of change differ, both distinct concepts of change have a common underlying logic: organisations do change throughout time and adapt themselves to external and internal changes in order to survive and remain successful in their respective markets. The question thus arises: how to adapt to these changes?

Paul Strebel (1994) has answered this question and proposes a set of eight generic change paths based on a diagnosis of the forces of change and resistance. The choice of any of these paths depends on the answers to a series of questions aimed at identifying the strength of the forces of change and resistance, and whether these forces can be avoided or contained (see Figure 3.1).

Reactive change
Organisations are faced with driving forces that exert so much pressure that change becomes obligatory.

The first question tries to identify the strength of a change force as determined by its current or future impact on the company's performance. Therefore, it is useful to perform Lewin's force field analysis first, as driving and hindering forces for change, when identified, will provide the answer to Strebel's first question. For instance, strong change forces and resistance cause performance to decline and require immediate organisational adaptation, also called reactive change. In these situations, organisations

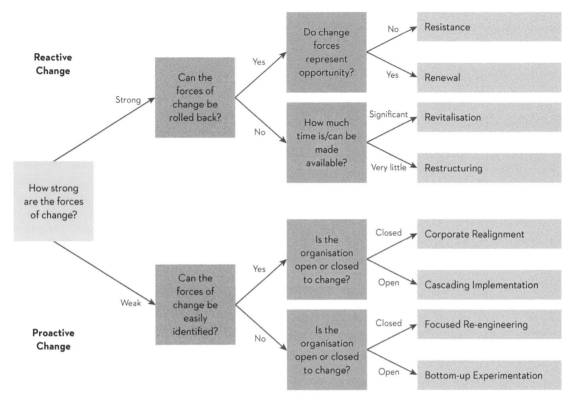

FIGURE 3.1 Strebel's change paths (Strebel, 1994).

Reproduced with permission of the Regents of the University of California.

are faced with driving forces that put on so much pressure that change becomes obligatory and requires a reactive change path. Conversely, weak change forces and low resistance characterise situations in which organisations are still doing well and the forces of change have yet to affect performance (proactive change path). Compared to reactive change, such **proactive change** situations are often more orderly and more efficient as changes can be analysed, planned and implemented under a sufficient amount of time and organisational resources.

Proactive change
Organisations are faced with driving forces that are foreseen in the future and thus haven't yet impacted organisational performance.

A reactive change path characterises situations under which organisations have to respond to strong forces of change and resistance. Under these conditions, Strebel argues for identifying the nature of the forces for change and the resources and time available by asking whether or not an organisation can resolve and neutralise the need for change:

- **Change forces can be neutralised:** If the forces for change are strong but can be resolved by organisational activity, then a less radical change associated with renewal or resistance will be appropriate. The organisation should follow a renewal path in which the change represents a business opportunity that can be exploited through stepwise change and adaptation. Conversely, if change forces represent a threat for the current business, then the change should follow a resistance path and instigate small internal adaptations that reduce the pressure exerted by the change force.

- **Change forces cannot be neutralised:** If the forces for change are strong and cannot be neutralised by organisational activity, then the organisation needs to implement a more radical change associated with restructuring and revitalisation. If sufficient time is available for implementing the necessary changes, the organisation should follow a revitalisation path based on slow, continuous, strategic, operational and/or cultural changes. When the time available is limited, the organisation has to apply a restructuring path in which changes are implemented with a high intensity and speed. These changes often entail a sharp shock to existing structures and systems, forcing immediate employee adaptation.

A proactive change path describes a situation in which the change forces have so far not affected the organisation. Such change situations usually leave more time available to implement potential changes. However, as the forces for change are weak, the organisation has more difficulties in specifying the change requirements and mobilising internal commitment for change. For instance, while senior management or HR may be mandated with an important change initiative, some stakeholders may fail to see the necessity for change as organisational performance is so far not affected. Hence, the initial question to ask in the case of proactive change situations is whether the forces for change can be easily identified:

- **Change forces are easy to identify:** When the forces for change are easy to identify, the organisation needs to transform the change forces into internal change drivers in order to mobilise commitment for change. In a situation in which the organisation is closed to change and does not realise the necessity for adaptation, then the company has to create awareness via the corporate realignment path. Organisations have to overcome inertia and create the organisational energy to support fundamental change. In contrast, when an organisation is open to change, required changes can be immediately addressed by a top-down cascading implementation.

- **Change forces are difficult to identify:** Creating support and commitment for change is difficult when change forces cannot be easily identified. In such a situation, the organisation needs to find a way to create a mobilising discomfort with the current situation while simultaneously communicating how things should be done in the future. If the organisation is closed to change, a focused re-engineering path aims at creating a changing mindset among employees that stimulates efficiency and effectiveness search processes in order to improve the organisation's current level of performance. Under circumstances in which the organisation is open to change, such search processes can be encouraged by experimentation through a bottom-up approach.

In concluding Strebel's model, a fundamental element when selecting an appropriate organisational change path is to assess the strength of the forces of change. Except for the resistance path (in which organisational change does not appear), all change paths actively deal with creating commitment for change inside the organisation. This allows an organisation to reactively or proactively address drivers for change and reach a new organisational equilibrium.

DEBATING HRM

Which change is easier - proactive or reactive?

Well, it depends. Both proactive and reactive change efforts have their particular sets of challenges. When initiating a proactive change project, we may have more time to reflect, involve people, be innovative and spend some available budget on the initiative, which may increase its chances for success. However, proactive change efforts often lack urgency as one does not feel the heat yet. Therefore, it may be more challenging to mobilise people.

Conversely, reactive change occurs mostly when there is a clear need to change, so people can be mobilised through a sense of urgency. However, reactive change often happens in times when less slack is available to reflect, be creative and take the time to involve everyone. Thus, reactive change may need to happen more in a rush and with smaller budgets, which may generate its own set of frustrations for employees who would like to have more time to contemplate the change.

TASK: *Split into two groups.*

1   One group should identify three cases of *proactive* change and perform background research to understand the approach and challenges associated with this type of change. The other group will do the same for cases of *reactive* change.

2   Both groups should identify key success factors and challenges for successfully managing their selected examples of proactive or reactive change initiatives.

3   Groups should be prepared to answer questions about their cases and defend their position in class.

THE CHANGE PROCESS: MODELS AND TOOLS

Models of organisational change represent an important source to gain a comprehensive picture when assessing change. These models help HR practitioners to provide answers to why change needs to happen, how change should happen and what should happen. One of the first change models was Kurt Lewin's three-phase model of planned organisational change: unfreeze, move and refreeze. The initial 'unfreezing' stage of Lewin's change model destabilises the current organisational equilibrium and creates a motivation and readiness to change. This stage challenges

Lewin's change model
A change model that describes a three-stage process of 'unfreezing', 'changing' and 'refreezing'.

current values, attitudes and behaviours. Throughout the subsequent 'moving' stage, the change situation is diagnosed, change activities selected and implemented. The final 'refreezing' stage aims at sustainably integrating the conducted changes and creating stability by reaching a new organisational equilibrium. While this change model has often been criticised for its simplicity, the underlying logic of initialising, managing and stabilising change processes has found its way into the majority of most existing change models.

Building on the Lewinian idea of a multi-stage change process, John Kotter (1995, 1996) developed his **eight-step model** for planning, implementing and sustaining change. According to Kotter, the organisational change process consists of the following eight steps:

Step 1: Establish a sense of urgency. The first step in changing an organisation is to create a sense of urgency in order to generate awareness of the need for change among organisational members. This stage aims at dislodging people from their comfort zone and counteracting complacency. It is important that stakeholders not only hear about the reasons for change but consciously understand them through compelling arguments or valid and dramatic evidence from inside or outside the organisation.

Step 2: Form a powerful guiding coalition. The second step is to carefully assemble a group of individuals who can actively guide the change and function as a team. The change team members (or guiding coalition) should be committed to the change project and possess the necessary knowledge, skills and capabilities to constantly drive the change throughout the organisation. They have to provide encouragement for the upcoming changes and immediately confront rumours among organisational members.

Guiding coalition A group of individuals who can actively guide the change and function as a team (also referred to as change team).

Change vision Describes the desired future state after the changes have been implemented and thus provides direction throughout the change process.

Step 3: Create a change vision. The third step is to formulate a change vision that focuses the change efforts and inspires organisational members to participate in the change. Such a change vision is developed and shared by all members of the change team and provides direction throughout the change process. It therefore needs to be imaginable, desirable, feasible, focused, flexible and communicable. Good change visions are communicated in less than five minutes and stimulate a reaction that signifies both understanding and interest.

Step 4: Communicate the change vision. The fourth step is to clearly communicate the change vision and the need for change. Communicating the change vision needs to address all organisational stakeholders and should be constantly repeated so that organisational members easily recall the desired changes. A good communication strategy is therefore based on simplicity, metaphors, multiple information channels, repetition, leadership-by-example and explanations of seeming inconsistencies.

Step 5: Empower others to act on the vision. The fifth step is to empower individuals to change their behaviour. This step entails removing obstacles that block the change, changing systems or structures that undermine the change vision and encouraging risk taking and non-traditional ideas, activities and actions. Failure to do so risks creating frustrated organisational members who refuse to participate further in the desired change process.

Step 6: Plan for and create short-term wins. The sixth step is to ensure that organisational members realise the progress of the implemented changes. Positive, visible short-term results will stimulate enthusiasm and motivation to further support the ongoing change process. Consequently, change processes need to plan for visible performance improvements as well as to recognise and reward employees involved in the improvements.

Step 7: Consolidate improvements and produce more change. The seventh step is to foster determination and persistence in encouraging ongoing commitment to the change progress – in other words, to **consolidate change**. Organisational change takes time as organisational members need to be trained and to adapt. Thus, the change process needs to continuously reinforce the desired changes and provide a supportive organisational context.

Step 8: Institutionalise new approaches. The final, eighth, step involves articulating the connections between the new behaviour and overall corporate success – in other words, **institutionalising change**. Furthermore, leadership development and succession ensure that the organisation institutionalises the new approaches. In this way, the implemented changes become visible and get anchored in the organisational culture, which then avoids falling back on old routines and habits.

Lewin's three-stage model and Kotter's eight steps both show that each change process consists of several stages, each lasting a considerable amount of time. Mistakes or failure in one stage can have significant negative impacts, jeopardising the success of the overall change process. Consequently, for HR practitioners to successfully implement a change process they need to engage in comprehensive planning, dedicated execution and constant monitoring.

Kotter's main intention behind his change model was to highlight critical elements within a change process. In this sense, Kotter's eight steps to transform an organisation should be understood as an iterative approach rather than a linear progression through a change process. Given the distinct complexity and dynamics of each change situation, there will always be some overlap between distinct stages. Of particular importance are the change vision and its communication throughout the entire change process. This comes with words and acts: nothing is more harmful to change than inconsistencies between what important individuals communicate and what they do. Failing to anchor the vision into the organisation risks turning change efforts into confusing and incompatible activities that can lead to wrong directions and outcomes.

DEBATING HRM

The merit of decentralising the HR function

Kotter's change management process is a useful tool to apply to a variety of change projects in the organisation. Provided a well thought-out vision is present, following Kotter's steps thoughtfully can produce valuable and sustainable change. Using Kotter's steps, debate with your group the merit of decentralising the HR function.

TASK: *Split into two groups.*

1   Discuss within each group whether each step in Kotter's model is of equal importance. Should leaders spend equal amounts of time, effort and resources on each?

2   One group should prepare a vision and develop each step to argue FOR decentralising the HR function. The other group should prepare to resist and provide arguments AGAINST decentralising the HR function.

3   Organise a debate between the two groups. Can following Kotter's steps help in resolving the resistance?

Using Kotter's eight steps

To prevent failure of a change initiative, Kotter created the following model consisting of eight steps:

1   Establish a sense of urgency

2   Create a coalition

3   Develop a clear vision

4   Share the vision

5   Empower people to clear obstacles

6   Secure short-term wins

7   Consolidate and keep moving

8   Anchor the change.

While this sequence is important, one may have to go back and forth to ensure maximum success.

TASK: Identify a change you have experienced. Using Kotter's steps, evaluate step by step how this change was managed. What could be done differently next time?

BEHAVIOURAL CHANGE

Organisational-level change inevitably depends on some degree of individual-level change, as members of the organisation need to change their habits and ways of working in order to realise the projected change in the organisation. Change is fundamentally about doing things differently. In general, habitual patterns of action serve us well; they allow us to respond quickly to an environment that we know well. In stable environments, our routine behaviours could survive over our lifetime. However, when circumstances change, our routines may no longer function well.

Famous management guru Peter Drucker used to say to his executive clients: 'Don't tell me you had a wonderful meeting with me. Tell me what you're going to do on Monday that's different.' As those who have tried to change their behaviour can acknowledge, behavioural change is not easy and old habits die hard. But why is it so hard to change? In order to understand why change is hard for most of us, we need to go to the biological roots of the problem.

As we learn behaviours, neurons form connections we refer to as neural pathways. As we perform behaviour patterns over and over, the neural pathways are reinforced until they become so engrained that they become habitual. Habitual behaviour is triggered by a certain stimulus in the environment. Presented with the same stimulus, we perform the same behaviour. While we have known for centuries that changing habitual behaviour is hard, advances in neuroscience provide a more optimistic outlook. Recently the static view of the brain has made way for the notion of neuroplasticity. This refers to the fact that our adult brain is constantly changing: new pathways and even new neurons are generated (Davidson et al., 2000). Thus, the ability of the brain to adapt and change is far greater than we previously thought. This is good news for anyone interested in change, as our brains appear to have a great capacity for it.

In order to change habitual behaviour, we need to replace the undesirable behaviour with a more functional alternative behaviour and thus create new neural pathways and reinforce them. This change in behaviour requires conscious effort and reflection on our part. This is why, under stress, we often revert to our old habits, or what is referred to in psychology as our dominant response (Forsyth, 2009). While initially it may require a great deal of effort and time to reinforce new pathways and inhibit old ones, eventually the new pathway should become solid enough to rely on. However, this happens only through recurrently performing the behaviour. In other words, a new behaviour is established through action, not merely by reflecting upon it or having good intentions.

Therefore, a bias for action contributes to effecting change (Bruch and Ghoshal, 2004). Self-perception theory can explain why taking action has a powerful effect on an individual (Bem, 1967). Because individuals infer their own attitudes from observations of their behaviour, engaging in new and functional behaviours in line with the desired change will alter the person's beliefs with respect to possible success. Thus, action results in a 'can do' attitude. Moreover, engaging in positively valued behaviours will increase our self-esteem (Branden, 1995) because everything we value in life requires action to be achieved, sustained or enjoyed. Action also allows for learning as initial trials provide feedback as to how one can improve during the next iteration. The reason some people have a hard time changing their behaviour is that they really value it under another name. Something in us does not want to give up the habit because it also stands for something we value. Therefore, to solve this intrapersonal ambiguity about the behaviour we want to change, we need to unbundle negative from positive elements (Ben-Shahar, 2009; Nir, 2008), or realise that striving for one does not need to mean giving up the other.

While tedious and hard, there is one very potent way to speed up the behavioural change process described above. We can do this by involving emotion or values. When change relates to something we find important or we have strong feelings about, we learn better and faster. We are more motivated and thus will exert more

Behavioural change
Transformation and/or modification of an individual's routine, habits and ways of working.

Neuroplasticity
Refers to the fact that our adult brain is constantly changing and generates new pathways and new neurons.

effort in order to accomplish and succeed in the change. John Kotter argues that in order to achieve a change in behaviour (Kotter and Cohen, 2002) the core method should proceed according to the steps see-feel-change. First, we need to help people see and visualise the issue at stake – in other words, create awareness in others. As a result, seeing something they had not seen before touches people at a deep level, evoking a visceral response and liberating emotions, such that emotionally charged ideas change behaviour.

See-feel-change
Individual change only appears if individuals first see and visualise the need for change (see), then understand and care about the change (feel), which finally leads to a change in behaviour.

HRM IN PRACTICE

DP World: see-feel-change

DP World was founded in 2005 through a merger of Dubai Ports Authority and Dubai Ports International. In 2006 DP World acquired UK-based P&O and became the third largest port operator globally. DP World operates more than 60 terminals across six continents and employs 30,000 people, mostly unskilled labourers. DP World's number one priority is stated as the safety of its people and the environment. One of the major concerns of its Global Safety and Environment Department is to reduce fatalities and the lost time injury frequency rate (LTIFR). In order to do so they devised a highly successful campaign, closely in line with Kotter's 'see–feel–change' sequence. The 'Come home safely' campaign was based on the concept of 'father and child' to make port operations employees appreciate the significance of their lives. Pictures of employees' children were gathered and used to create billboards to remind their fathers that they were waiting for them at home. Thus, safety meant more than not getting hurt, but being able to go home to their families. According to Ian Baking, Assistant Vice President for Domestic Operations, 'The campaign touches the emotions because it focuses on the values of each person and goes beyond mandating safety practices to workers. The campaign gives our occupational health and safety initiatives character and a human face. It is warm and personal and people respond because it touches their hearts.'

CULTURE CHANGE

HR executives are considered the guardians of an organisation's culture. Change efforts often involve a need to adapt priorities or values that are engrained in the company culture. When Intel was being challenged by new processor makers, Intel engineers, driven by speed and performance, had to adopt a new value: 'cost'. At first, they were totally uninspired by working on reducing cost. Only when they realised that they would not be able to continue working on speed if they continued to lose market share did they acknowledge that integrating the value of cost was important. As values drive behaviour, it is particularly important to have the culture aligned with current business needs. Culture is broadly understood as a system of shared values, symbols and meanings. In his ground-laying model of organisational culture, Edgar Schein conceptualises organisational culture as composed of three levels (visible artefacts, values and underlying assumptions).

Schein (1984: 3) defines organisational culture as 'the pattern of basic assumptions that a given group has invented, discovered or developed in learning to cope with its problems of external adaptation and internal integration, and have worked well enough to be considered valid, and therefore, to be taught to new members as the correct way to perceive, think, and feel in relation to those problems'. In simpler terms, an organisation's culture is a set of shared beliefs and values, indicating what is important on the one hand, and practices and norms, expressing how one is supposed to react or behave, on the other hand. While Schein's work predominantly focused on organisations, his model can be usefully applied to larger collectives such as societies and nations. Society moreover provides the macro context for organisations and individuals and it is not surprising, therefore, that the same values and norms are present across the different levels (individual, organisation and society).

Schein's definition also sheds light on how a culture emerges and evolves. First, we should note that organisational culture essentially results from learning to cope with one's environment, either internal or external. As members of a group face new situations, they try to understand their environment and develop rules of thumb or theories about how to deal with and behave in certain situations. Thus, individual and organisational learning will result. Internally, learning will take place about how to function as a group and how to best deal with getting organised in the workplace. The culture is perpetually being shaped and reshaped, as there is constant learning going on about how to deal with the environment and how to manage internal affairs. Finally, Schein stresses 'passing on' in his definition, because a decision to pass on a belief or a practice is an important indicator of the validity of a solution and of the agreement between members. This passing on often occurs by means of stories or myths of important events and heroes.

Relying on Schein's definition, we can also acknowledge that a culture will most develop or evolve in periods when a great deal of learning is taking place. This is, for example, the case at the inception of the firm or in phases of technological revolutions, market shifts or rapid economic growth. In those instances, old rules and ways of working may no longer fit the changed context and need to be adapted. A number of these adaptations may take place naturally, whereas others will be more stable and will require purposeful intervention by leaders. Naturally occurring adaptations to a culture (be it national or organisational) may be functional and self-sufficient; however, management may often feel the need to intervene in the process of cultural adaptation, either to speed it up or to make sure it goes in the desired direction.

There are two routes into changing a culture. Schein's model is helpful to understand the difference between the two. The bottom-up route, or the manifestation route, from assumption to artefact, is the one operating when the organisation is founded. The basic assumptions and unconscious beliefs, about human nature and the purpose of the organisation, held by the founders, become the basis of the organisation. This

Organisational culture A set of shared organisational beliefs and values, indicating what is important on the one hand, and practices and norms that express how one is supposed to react or behave on the other hand.

Applying Schein's model to culture change

Schein's definition and model of culture allows us to distinguish two routes to change a culture: the bottom-up route, or manifestation route, and the top-down route, or symbolic route. Both routes complement each other to effect change in the workplace.

TASK: On the basis of Schein's model and definition of culture, analyse and describe the culture of your school. Which assumptions, values and artefacts can you find? How could you change a particular element of the culture? Propose ideas following both routes.

route will also operate when new leadership with different assumptions takes over. A new leader may convey his or her beliefs to his direct reports, leading to a series of measures and changes in policy based on these beliefs. Indeed, what members assume is manifested in and shapes what they value and what they will create. However, this change route is very slow as it may take time for the basic assumptions to trickle down to other members in the organisation and until appropriate manifestations follow.

Therefore, the top-down or symbolic route, from artefacts to assumptions, may appear more appropriate as it assists the bottom-up desired change. A straightforward example would be the move from closed offices to an open-plan arrangement in order to create more collaborative working patterns and foster the value of teamwork. This route is similar to the natural way of learning to deal with new things in the environment. Whether the new office space is purposefully selected by management or accidentally imposed, individuals will have to go through similar learning and adaptations resulting in changes to deeper cultural elements.

THE ROLES OF HR IN MANAGING AND DELIVERING CHANGE

Chapter 1 introduced Storey's and Ulrich's models, which both emphasised the role of HR in relation to change and organisational performance. Both the roles of 'change-maker' (Storey, 1992) and 'strategic partner' (Ulrich and Brockbank, 2005) include change leadership as a key component of HR. Below we briefly review the different roles of HR in managing and delivering change.

INSPIRING AND LEADING CHANGE

As change involves leaving one's comfort zone and putting extra energy into trying to do something different, leaders need to inspire people, provide them with an enticing vision for the future and reassure them that they can achieve the change required. A prerequisite is then that they themselves are excited and convinced about the value of the proposed change. They need to lead by example and walk the talk, or else followers will easily perceive they are hypocritical and become disenchanted (Cha and Edmondson, 2006), refusing to adhere to the vision for change. Here the role of the HR professional is crucial. As a strategic partner to the business, he or she will often be informed and engaged in the change effort before others and as such will be expected to model enthusiasm for the change in question.

While fear (as a sense of urgency) can often cause people to jump start on trying to change their course of action, it is hard to sustain motivation based on fear as individuals become habituated or become helpless (Seligman, 1991). However, positive emotions have a more lasting and powerful effect on attempts to change behaviour. Recent advances in positive psychology in general and particularly the broaden-and-build theory (Fredrickson, 2009) offer promising tools for change agents. When we feel positive, our awareness expands and we can see more possibilities; moreover, positivity builds our capacity to endure hardship and allows us to continue in the face of resistance. Both broaden (as changing contexts are complex) and build (as change requires effort and persistence) aspects of positive emotions and are therefore highly relevant to change. A whole new field of study in Positive Organisational Scholarship is currently under development, looking into how principles of positivity can be applied in the workplace, and has found that inspiring and leading change from a positive angle has more chance to succeed.

Broaden-and-build theory Suggests that positive emotions broaden an individual's awareness and encourage novel, varied and exploratory thoughts and actions.

ONLINE STUDY TOOLS

Writing an essay? Expand your knowledge.

Rafferty, Jimmieson and Armenakis (2013) provide a multilevel review on change readiness in this highly relevant article.

https://edge.sagepub.com/crawshaw2e > **Student Resources** > **Chapter 3** > **Videos**

HRM IN PRACTICE

A culture of positivity at Prudential

One of Prudential's major challenges was to retain employees, and clients were worried about consistency of service. When senior leader John Kim was first introduced to Positive Organisational Scholarship (POS) during a visit to the University of Michigan, he immediately felt its importance for his business. Together with two senior HR executives he initiated a POS culture change. The purpose was to create the right environment for the people while increasing shareholder value. The guiding coalition was convinced that POS could do this, so they had a vision. Next, they gathered the top 100 executives and John Kim shared the vision, concluding with: 'you need to think deeply about whether you believe in this vision. If you do, then "get on the bus". If you don't, then this may not be the place for you.' Following this off-site meeting, each and every executive started to include POS ideas and practices in their daily business and in their interactions with their staff. Soon the culture became infused with POS language and principles. One year into the change effort, it was found that business units with higher scores on positive practices experienced a better work environment, more effective relationships with management and greater numbers of employees intending to stay with the firm. Financial performance also improved in relation to the extent to which positive practices were implemented. Positivity was paying off.

Based on: Vanette et al. (2006).

OVERCOMING RESISTANCE TO CHANGE

Overcoming resistance to change is a major issue for change leaders. But why do people resist change? Commonly, resistance to change is attributed to a low level of tolerance for change, an innate dislike of change or risk aversion. However, when Kotter and Schlesinger (2008) actually enquired why people resist change they found that the major reason was the desire not to lose something valuable; second came misunderstanding the change; and third, people had a different assessment of the change. When we examine these reasons we can see that most of them

Understanding why people resist change

Kotter and Schlesinger (2008) identified the major reasons for resisting change in the following order:

1   Desire not to lose something valuable

2   Misunderstanding the change

3   Different assessment

4   Low tolerance for change.

TASK: Recall seven instances in which people resisted a change effort (in your family, in an organisation or in society at large). Identify the real reason why they resisted the change.

can be resolved through Kotter's recommended process and particularly by increasing the clarity of the vision (step 3) and by communicating it in a way that people understand the rationale behind what is to be done and what they can gain from it (step 4). Next, empowering people and involving them in developing strategies and tactics to enable the change (step 5) can also lower their resistance while creating buy-in. Indeed, by inspiring and empowering employees at all levels, each and every one can become a change agent for the benefit of the organisation's success.

COMMUNICATING CHANGE

While in all change efforts the role of communication is crucial, frequent generic communication often represents a burden to already overloaded managers. Therefore, specifically targeted communication to affected workgroups is more effective: What do they need to know? What do they need to understand? HR practitioners who have previously been involved in change efforts are all too aware of the predominantly negative discourse and the high level of anxiety present in such situations. In the absence of timely communication by HR and top management, employees will rely on rumours which can rapidly spread through the organisation through contagion. In order to counter contagion of negative attitudes, HR practitioners can rely on transparent communication, which has particularly been applied in merger cases, as adopting realistic merger previews can reduce uncertainty experienced by employees. Providing realistic information allows employees to have a basis for action other than uncertainty and offers a validated alternative to rumours. By installing a programme of realistic communications about the change, HR remains in control of what is being said about the change and limits contagion of negative attitudes. Realistic previews focus on (1) providing frequent, honest and relevant information; (2) making sure employees are treated fairly; and (3) attempting to answer all questions employees may have.

MANAGING REDUNDANCIES

In some cases of change there are clear losers, and we cannot prevent those employees who have their job to lose from resisting a change effort. When layoffs are bound to happen, even if we explain it is better to cut some branches today than wait for the whole tree to go bad, we cannot expect those concerned to cheer. In those cases, we can only act ethically and fair, using principles of justice (see Chapter 4).

CASE STUDY

Change management at Pringle

The British cashmere knitwear manufacturer Pringle has a long tradition as one of the leading fashion producers. The company has been known for quality and enjoys a faithful group of customers. However, the company suffered substantial losses during the 1990s and needed to substantially downsize its employees from over 2000 to 180. These layoffs were necessary due to adverse exchange rates, stronger competition within the European market, an unsuccessful diversification into mass market sportswear and a decline in manufacturing quality. In fact, Pringle was on the brink of bankruptcy. In 2000, the Fang Brothers – a Hong-Kong-based investment company – decided to acquire Pringle for just €9 million in an approach to diversify their investment portfolio. One of the first activities of the new owners was to recruit Kim Winser. Kim had been working for over 10 years as senior executive for Marks & Spencer and was considered an expert in the British and European fashion market.

As soon as Kim took office, she quickly realised that Pringle's product portfolio was too big, did not yield any synergies and was poorly designed. Given that the brand had suffered substantially during the past years, the CEO decided to reposition Pringle in the market: away from a rather staid, middle-aged image towards a designer fashion brand. This was a major challenge, but as the company had lost its traditional customers Kim thought that she had nothing to lose. Kim considered the rejuvenation of the brand not as a risk but rather as an opportunity. Her confidence increased even more after she managed to convince her former Chief of Marketing at Marks & Spencer, Greg McAllister, to join Pringle. The arrival of the new CEO as well as the replacement of the Chief of Marketing ensured that employees at Pringle knew that changes were about to take place.

After having met with Pringle's senior managers, Kim decided on a relaunch of the fashion range of knitwear in just 12 weeks. While the production department had been very sceptical about such a short production cycle, Kim promised the employees an additional bonus if they reached this target. In a general assembly with the staff, she publicly announced that 'products have to change and this change has to be done fast'. This, she argued, was essential in order to present a new range at the forthcoming Italian trade fair.

(Continued)

(Continued)

However, some senior executives remained very critical of this approach and defended the company's prior strategy. According to this group, 'quality takes time'. Consequently, Kim only worked with senior executives who supported her change plan.

A couple of weeks into her new position, she realised that most of the workforce expected the factory to close, perhaps with manufacturing moving to the Far East. In a written email to her employees, Kim confirmed that manufacturing would remain in Hawick in Scotland. She further reinforced the Scottish link by branding the fashion merchandise 'Pringle Scotland' and explained: 'I have added a Scotland to the name because in a lot of countries worldwide, it is definitely a bonus. Pringle will be known for high quality Scottish cashmere!'

While Kim was trying to restructure the operations and keep the employees motivated, McAllister recruited new young designers. He also decided to move the design department from Scotland to London. After a long discussion with McAllister, Kim also moved the company headquarters from the prestigious Savile Row in London to a new, more modern building, which reduced office expenditure significantly.

However, some of the senior executives continued to resist these changes. In a meeting with her executives, Kim decided to terminate the contract with the existing Manufacturing Director after he repeatedly criticised her decision making. McAllister supported this strategy and decided to cancel the contract of Nick Faldo, a golfer, who had been Pringle's celebrity face for almost 20 years. For McAllister, Pringle needed something new and thus Pringle would merchandise its products on young and trendy models.

The relaunch of the marketing strategy was supported by a visit of the Princess Royal to the Hawick factory at around the same time as the redesigned sweaters were seen worn publicly by David Beckham, the internationally famous football star.

The target of the Italian trade fair was met, 20 per cent of the existing retail outlets were dropped and new retailers recruited, including Harvey Nichols and Selfridges. By the end of 2000 sales were increasing. Pringle decided to expand its production and hired an additional 80 employees, combined with investment in new machinery at Hawick. In 2001, sales increased about 30 per cent up on the previous year. By 2003, the business press was reporting the new found success of Pringle. Having consolidated its position in the UK, Pringle had plans underway for retail expansion in the USA and Hong Kong. Sophie Dahl (English author, cookbook writer and former model) became the 'new face' in Pringle's advertising.

CASE STUDY QUESTIONS

1   Explain and apply to the case John Kotter's eight steps for managing change effectively.

2   According to you, what could have been done better and how would you evaluate the overall change process?

3   What are Kim Winser's future challenges in managing change at Pringle?

Source: Adapted from Johnson, G., Scholes, K. and Whittington, R. (2008) *Exploring Corporate Strategy*, 8th edn. Harlow: Prentice-Hall, p. 538.

CHAPTER SUMMARY

The key points that we have identified in this chapter are the following:

- As environments change, organisations are prompted to follow and adapt. Performing Lewin's force field analysis allows one to generate a deeper understanding of the external and internal change context.

- Different contexts may require different approaches to change. Answering Strebel's questions and following his suggested change paths can shed light on how to proceed according to the context.

- Change is hard to achieve, but following a step-by-step approach as proposed by Kotter allows one to plan for successful change. Moving back and forth between steps may be required to ensure long-term success.

- Changing one's habits is difficult but not impossible. Behavioural change can be facilitated by involving emotions and values. Leading by example is the key to ensuring behavioural change throughout an organisation.

- To overcome resistance to change it is important to understand the actual reasons behind resistance. Most resistance can be undone by improved communication.

REVIEW QUESTIONS AND EXERCISES

1. Discuss the external and internal forces that create the need for organisational change.

2. Describe Kurt Lewin's force field analysis. According to Lewin, why is organisational change required?

3. According to Paul Strebel, how can an organisation select an appropriate change path? Describe the distinct change paths.

4. What are the fundamental elements of each change process based on Kurt Lewin?

5. Discuss Kotter's eight steps for leading organisational change.

6. Identify a process, policy or habit you would like to change in your organisation or school. Using Kotter's steps, design a detailed plan to accomplish this change. What appears to be the most challenging step?

EXPLORE FURTHER

Kotter, J.P. and Rathgeber, H. (2006) *Our Iceberg is Melting: Changing and Succeeding Under Any Conditions*. New York: St. Martin's Press. This book provides an easy-to-read and memorable fable describing a penguin colony needing to change. Kotter highlights each of the steps for successful change.

Bruch, H. and Ghoshal, S. (2003) Unleashing organizational energy. *MIT Sloan Management Review*, Fall: 45–51. Despite being written 10 years ago, still an important paper.

Find updated stories and insights from John Kotter at Kotter International: www.kotter international. com/news-and-insights. An excellent resource to find out more about Kotter's research, including important case examples.

GO ONLINE

Visit the companion website for **interactive quizzes**, explanatory **videos** and **podcasts**, **journal articles** to use in your essays, and **weblinks** to useful resources.

https://edge.sagepub.com/crawshaw2e

CHAPTER 4

Carole Parkes
Helen Borland
Thierry Nadisic
Jonathan R. Crawshaw

HRM AND THE ETHICAL ORGANISATION

CHAPTER KNOWLEDGE OBJECTIVES

- To explore, and explain, the growing debate on issues of ethics, justice, social responsibility, sustainability and human rights in organisations.
- To define notions of ethics, justice, social responsibility and sustainability.
- To explore relevant theory-informing issues of ethics and justice at work.
- To understand why managers/leaders behave (un)fairly and (un)ethically.
- To understand the role of ethical codes, policies and practices and the importance of HRM to the integration of social responsibility and sustainability.
- To discuss the role of HRM, and the HR profession, in delivering fair, ethical, responsible and sustainable organisations.

KEY SKILLS OBJECTIVES

- To critically reflect upon ethical dilemmas at work.
- To develop an awareness of the ethical, social responsibility and sustainability dimensions to strategic decision making and problem solving.
- To demonstrate ethical problem-solving and decision-making skills.
- To be able to advise others on issues of ethics, social responsibility, sustainability and human rights at work.
- To improve one's ability to make fair decisions and behave justly.

This chapter also provides indicative content for the following Intermediate and Advanced level CIPD modules:

CIPD INTERMEDIATE LEVEL MODULE

5CHR Business issues and the context of human resources

CIPD ADVANCED LEVEL MODULES

7HRC Human resource management in context

7SBL Developing skills for business leadership

GO ONLINE

This chapter comes with loads of online tools to help you to go that extra mile in your studies!

- **Multiple choice questions** to help you test your knowledge and revise for exams
- **Journal articles** so you can read further for assignments and essays
- **Videos** and **podcasts** to help you to understand how complex concepts work in the real world

Visit **https://edge.sagepub.com/crawshaw2e** to access these resources for this topic.

ONLINE STUDY TOOLS

Video case study: William McDonough Ted Talk

Go further in your studies by watching this very engaging Ted Talk on how green design can prevent environmental disaster and drive economic growth.

https://edge.sagepub.com/crawshaw2e > **Student Resources** > **Chapter 4** > **Videos**

INTRODUCTION

The globalisation of business and the complexities this creates present challenges that are unprecedented in human existence. Perhaps the greatest of these challenges is best summed up in the following question: How can the lives of all people around the world be improved in the context of a resource-constrained planet? While the issues this question raises are not new, the banking crisis and collapse of economic markets have refocused attention on the ethics and responsibilities of business. The interconnectedness between these events and the impact they have on people's lives have thus generated an impetus to call for a re-examination of the role of business in society. This is in line with the growing interest in the ethics of business and what is generally referred to as corporate social responsibility (CSR) and sustainability. In September 2015, the United Nations came together to agree the 17 Sustainable Development Goals (SDGs) that set out the agenda on key global challenges that include poverty, food, health, education, women, water, energy, economy, infrastructure, inequality, habitation, consumption, climate, marine, ecosystems, institutions for peace and sustainable development. The business community, represented by the UN Global Compact, pledged to work together with governments and civil society organisations and communities to achieve these goals by 2030 (see UNDP, 2015).

Corporate social responsibility (CSR) Refers to the responsibility of organisations for their impact upon society - both locally and globally.

As HR is the key function with responsibility for people in the organisation, what are the roles and responsibilities that these challenges present for HRM practitioners in organisations today?

This chapter will define the different terms and concepts used in this area of study, explore the issues related to these challenges, and provide a much-needed investigation of the potential roles and responsibilities of the HR function for promoting more ethical, fair, responsible and sustainable organisations. The chapter introduces and discusses a wide range of conceptual and empirical research in the areas of workplace ethics, justice, social responsibility, human rights and sustainability. A particular focus is also placed on providing students interested in both HR and non-specialist management roles with a range of tools and practical recommendations for promoting more fair, ethical, responsible and sustainable organisations.

This chapter is organised as follows. At the outset, we provide some definitions of the various terms used in relation to this area. We then explore the nature of the issues in more detail and examine the case for ethics, justice, social responsibility, human rights and sustainability as part of HRM strategy. We then set out the policies and processes for integrating these issues into the organisation.

THE ROLE OF HRM: A PRIMER

In order to examine the issues, we need to look at the relationship in theory and practice between the growing interest in the range of concerns relating to workplace ethics, justice, social responsibility, human rights and sustainability on the one hand and the role of HRM on the other.

The history of HRM is intertwined with the development of 'responsible business'. In Chapter 1 you saw that the evolution of HRM started with the social reformers, who were primarily concerned with the welfare of workers. The case study in that chapter refers to Cadburys and Edward Cadbury (son of a pioneer of corporate social responsibility, George Cadbury) who observed the link between the welfare of employees and 'good business': 'The supreme principle has been the belief that business efficiency and the welfare of the employee are but different sides of the same problem. Character is an economic asset; and business efficiency depends not merely on the physical condition of employees, but on their general attitude and feeling towards the employer' (Cadbury, 1912: xvii).

The role that HRM has played in promoting and maintaining ethical and responsible business practice has varied over the decades (and this will be discussed later in the chapter), but there are essentially two key aspects of the HRM role that should be highlighted at this point. The first is ensuring that the organisation's strategies, policies and practices (including those relating to HRM) are ethical and that the culture of the organisation is consistent with this approach. Critical to the operation of the organisation is the behaviour of those individuals that comprise it, and HRM has responsibility for the key policies and processes (such as recruitment and selection, training and development, performance review and organisational development) that can influence the culture and therefore behaviour within the organisation. Therefore, HRM professionals can play a key role in relation to embedding ethics, justice, social responsibility, human rights and sustainability.

The second is that the HRM profession itself models ethical behaviour through the individual professionals' conduct within the organisation. Professional HRM bodies around the world, including the US-based Society for Human Resource Management (SHRM) and the UK-based Chartered Institute of Personnel and Development (CIPD), have professional codes of conduct that place expectations of ethical behaviour on their members (Parkes and Davis, 2013). SHRM refers to 'serving all stakeholders in the most morally responsible manner and leading individual organisations to conduct business in a responsible manner as well as exhibiting individual leadership as a role model for maintaining the highest standards of ethical conduct' (www.shrm.org). The CIPD also sets out two particular standards for its members that relate to these roles. The first is described as the 'courage to challenge', defined as when individuals 'show courage and confidence to speak up, challenge others even when confronted with resistance or unfamiliar circumstances'. The second is the requirement to be a 'role model', defined as a person who 'consistently leads by example; acts with integrity, impartiality and independence; applies sound personal judgement in all interactions' (CIPD, 2009: 1).

WHAT'S IN A NAME?

One of the confusing issues in relation to this area of the business is that a number of terms are used to describe what is broadly referred to as the 'responsibilities of business'. Some of these terms have already been referred to, and so it is appropriate at this point to provide some definitions of the different concepts and the related areas of research and activity.

ETHICS

The American Heritage Dictionary (2007) defines ethics as 'the study of the general nature of morals and of the specific moral choices to be made by an individual in his or her relationship with others, and the rules or standards governing the conduct of the members of a profession', but explains that ethics also 'indicates an obligation to consider not only our own personal well-being, but also that of others and of human society as a whole'.

JUSTICE

In the context of the workplace, we focus on organisational justice. This is the psychological concept of fairness as perceived by the employee in relation to its three dimensions consisting of: (1) the distributions or outcomes (distributive justice); (2) the procedures by which those distributions are determined (procedural justice); and (3) the communication of the distributions (interactional justice) (Cropanzano and Greenberg, 1997).

Organisational justice The psychological concept of fairness as perceived by the employee.

HUMAN RIGHTS

Human rights are rights inherent to all human beings, whatever our nationality, place of residence, gender, national or ethnic origin, colour, religion, language, or any other status. We are all equally entitled to our human rights without discrimination. These rights are all interrelated, interdependent and indivisible (United Nations Office of the High Commissioner for Human Rights, n.d.).

Human rights Many ethical issues in HRM relate to issues of human rights. These include: freedom from discrimination, privacy, due process, participation and association, healthy and safe working conditions, fair wages, freedom of conscience and speech, work and dignity at work.

CORPORATE SOCIAL RESPONSIBILITY (CSR)

The European Commission (2013) defines corporate social responsibility as 'the responsibility of enterprises for their impacts on society'. To fully meet their social responsibility, enterprises 'should have in place a process to integrate social, environmental, ethical, human rights and consumer concerns into their business operations and core strategy in close collaboration with their stakeholders'. (See also the case study at the end of this chapter.)

SUSTAINABILITY

Sustainability is most often associated with the environmental domain and implies continuity and more long-term perspectives. This is encapsulated by the Brundtland Commission Report that describes sustainable development as 'development that meets the needs of the present without compromising the ability of future generations to meet their own needs' (United Nations Commission on Environment and Development, 1987).

ETHICS IN BUSINESS

ethics in business
Ethics in business
comprises principles and
standards that guide
behaviour in the world
of business (Ferrell et al.,
2008).

One common approach to ethics in all fields, including ethics in business, is the notion of 'doing good' or, to use the opposite and most frequently used phrase, of 'doing no harm' (Baron, 1996). This is never more relevant than in the business context of today. It is difficult to escape the catalogue of ethical scandals that have beset organisations in the public and private sectors over recent decades. Examples include (but are not limited to) the failure of our major banks, the explosion and oil spill in the Gulf of Mexico, and the collapse of a factory building in Bangladesh and the consequent loss of life of clothing workers producing garments for Western high street stores. The behaviour of business (locally and globally) is subject to constant scrutiny, and the 24/7 societies in which we live provide instant access to information (and misinformation). There are myriad media communication channels that place expectations on business organisations not just to behave ethically but also to provide visible evidence that they are acting responsibly.

The consequences of these expectations and public scrutiny have highlighted real concerns for the conduct of organisations and their leaders, with the resulting problems of reputational risk and a reduction in trust. The 2016 Edelman Trust Barometer reveals the largest ever trust gap (12 points) between the informed public and mass population, driven by income inequality and divergent expectations of the future (Edelman, 2016).

This lack of trust goes to the heart of the problem of 'business ethics' and the potential mismatch between an individual's ethics and those exercised in business. For some the notion of business ethics is an oxymoron, and they question whether ethics can be practised in business. If this reasoning is followed, then business may be seen as outside the realm of ethical enquiry or as morally neutral or amoral. Others may argue that ethics in business do exist but differ from ethics in other spheres and therefore may appear amoral in other spheres. However, it is our contention that business, politics and personal life should all share the same ethics as part of a moral community.

Critical thinking

Ethical theories enable situations to be viewed from different perspectives. Table 4.1 provides a pragmatic guide to assist with decision making.

TASK: Use the questions to explore ethical dilemmas that arise in personal and professional life. For example: in the workplace, the use of outsourcing or acceptance of gifts from suppliers; and in personal life, decisions about whether to buy ethical or sustainably sourced goods.

APPLYING ETHICAL THEORY

Ethical theory can appear to be remote from the practicalities of everyday decisions in the workplace, but from the earliest times, decisions taken in business are often justified theoretically and practically using arguments that stem from ethical theory. Indeed, Aristotle is recorded as stating that there is nothing as practical as an ethical theory. To make sense of the term 'ethics' it may be worth thinking of ethics as 'values in action' and to remember, when developing HRM strategies and policies, to consider whose values or ethics are being used in a business or where they come from.

Ethical theories provide rules that can be applied to any given situation, and most fall into two broad groups. First, there are those that base the judgement of the decision on the outcome of the actions, and second, those that do not look at whether the outcomes are desirable but at the underlying principles of the motivation to act (Parkes and Harris, 2008) (see Table 4.1).

TABLE 4.1 Ethical theory: a practical approach

Theory	Explanation	Questions
• Egoism	• Self-interest	• Is this in my own (or the organisation's) interest?
• Justice	• Fairness	• Am I treating everyone fairly? How fair are the systems, processes and outcomes?
• Utilitarianism	• Belief that value is determined by its utility; the 'greatest happiness principle'	• If I consider all consequences, who will be better off, who will be worse off?
• Virtue ethics	• Moral character	• Am I acting with integrity? What would a person of good moral character do in this situation?
• Feminist ethics /Ethic of care	• Care for others and relationships	• How would the affected parties feel? Which solution allows good relationships to be maintained?
• Discourse ethics	• Communication to resolve conflict	• What norms can be established? How can the situation be resolved and mutual respect be maintained?
• Ethic of rights	• Entitlement of others	• Whose rights need to be considered? Am I respecting fundamental human rights and dignity?
• Ethic of duty	• Duties to others	• Whom do I have obligations to in this situation? How should everyone act in this situation?

Adapted from Crane and Matten (2010). Reproduced with permission of Oxford University Press.

VALUES

In the previous section we suggested thinking of ethics as 'values in action'. This is because values (both individual and organisational) are important to consider in the context of ethics in organisations. Values have been defined as ideas or cognitions present in every group or society about desirable end states (Rokeach, 1973) and play an

Values (individual and organisational) Ideas or cognitions present in every group or society about desirable end states (Rokeach, 1973) and play an important role in driving individual behaviour within and outside the workplace (Schwartz, 1999).

important role in driving individual behaviour within and outside the workplace (Schwartz, 1999). They are a fundamental characteristic that both employees and organisations share, they operate at multiple levels (societal, organisational and personal) and play an important role in shaping the organisation's culture with regard to ethics. They are also important to consider because value statements have become a popular means of communicating what an organisation believes it stands for and how it wishes to be seen by its stakeholders.

HRM's role in the processes used to identify an organisation's values is vital because encouraging engagement in relation to the range of stakeholders (including employees) requires open discussion and critical awareness. Research by the Work Foundation (Wong et al., 2009) explores the link between individual and organisational beliefs and values and emphasises the impact of values on employee commitment and engagement. Similarly, a mismatch between individual and organisational values has the potential to have a negative impact on an employee's psychological contract. Martin and Hetrick (2006) highlight how 'values-based psychological contracts' can improve employee commitment where employees identify with an organisation as a form of cause or mission.

Reflecting on personal values

- List 10 key words that define the values that are important to you. Think about where the values come from (e.g. family, faith, education, experience, peer groups).

- Next, reduce the values list to five, focusing on those values that are most important to you.

- Finally, consider, of the five values remaining, which are the one(s) that you could never give up.

ORGANISATIONAL JUSTICE

Scholars of organisational justice have tended to seek answers to a number of important, and interrelated, questions regarding justice in the workplace: (1) What is justice at work? (2) Why does justice matter to employees? (3) How do employees make justice judgements regarding their work? And (4) What are the potential consequences of these justice judgements? (see Crawshaw et al., 2013).

WHAT IS JUSTICE AT WORK?

As introduced earlier, past research has identified up to four different 'types' or 'sources' of justice at work – termed distributive justice, procedural justice, interpersonal justice and informational justice. Often scholars have combined interpersonal and informational justice into one concept – interactional justice – and for parsimony we will also do so for the remainder of this chapter.

- **Distributive justice** refers to the fairness of outcomes one receives from one's employer. In other words, are the resources or rewards offered by an organisation distributed or allocated in a fair manner? In examining these questions, most research (at least Western research) has tended to assume that distributive justice is best understood in terms of equity. In other words, distributive justice is upheld when employees feel that they get (e.g. bonuses, promotion, access to training and development) what their performance or contribution to the organisation deserves or merits.

- **Procedural justice** refers to the organisational procedures and processes followed to make these reward or resource allocation decisions. Leventhal (1980) identified six procedural justice 'rules' which, when enforced, are said to promote greater employee perceptions of fairness regarding organisational procedures. These rules are:

  1. Voice/decision control: procedures that allow employees to influence the final decision.
  2. Accuracy: decisions that are based on the collection of accurate information.
  3. Representativeness: procedures that seek input from all stakeholders affected by the final decision.
  4. Bias suppression: procedures that promote objective decision making and suppress opportunities for personal bias (see Chapter 9).
  5. Correctability: procedures that allow employees to challenge decisions that have been made.
  6. Ethicality: ensuring that procedures uphold the pervading moral and ethical values of society.

- **Interactional justice** refers to the fairness of one's interactions with the decision maker – often one's direct line manager. Specifically, interactions that provide timely and detailed information or explanations of decisions and are carried out in ways that show respect for the individual are viewed as interactionally fair.

WHY DOES INJUSTICE MATTER AT WORK?

In their review, Cropanzano et al. (2001) propose a multiple-needs model of justice, suggesting that individuals may view justice as important for instrumental, relational and/or deontic reasons.

- **Instrumental perspectives on organisational justice.** These suggest that justice matters to individuals because a fair system is more likely (in the long term at least) to provide one with the best outcomes. Justice matters, therefore, because a just system will more likely help one achieve one's personal work-related goals (e.g. Cropanzano et al., 2005).

- **Relational perspectives on organisational justice.** Alternatively, others suggest that justice matters to individuals because being treated fairly by your manager(s) (and peers) suggests one is a highly valued member of the team and organisation. Thus justice matters because it helps to meet one's self-esteem and identity needs (see Tajfel and Turner, 1986).

- **Deontic perspectives on organisational justice.** Finally, others suggest that justice matters 'for its own sake'. In other words, justice matters because it is the basic human right of all employees to be treated fairly. In support of such perspectives, there has been some really interesting recent research that shows employees care about, and react negatively to, injustices even when they themselves are not the recipient of this mistreatment (e.g. Greenbaum et al., 2013).

HOW DO EMPLOYEES MAKE JUSTICE JUDGEMENTS AT WORK?

When it comes to answering questions on how employees make justice judgements, the literature has been dominated by three models – equity theory, fairness theory and uncertainty management theory:

- **Equity theory:** Adams's (1965) equity theory proposes that employees make justice judgements by calculating their own inputs (e.g. effort, skills, performance) into, and outcomes (e.g. pay, bonuses, promotions) from, the organisation and comparing this ratio with a significant other – commonly a peer carrying out a similar role either in their team or in another equivalent team within the organisation. Only when these ratios are in balance is one said to perceive a fair system (for a more detailed review see Cropanzano and Greenberg, 1997).

- **Fairness theory** suggests that individuals evaluate the (un)fairness of a decision by making three separate judgements – namely 'would', 'could' and 'should' judgements – regarding the decision (Folger and Cropanzano, 2001). First, for justice to be a concern at all, individuals must have a negative experience of some kind – for example, being passed over for promotion. This forces one to reflect upon this scenario and to evaluate how another, alternative scenario (i.e. getting the promotion) 'would' have felt. Second, individuals evaluate whether anyone can be blamed for this negative experience – in other words, 'could' the decision maker have acted differently? Finally, and only when these two previous conditions have been met, will one judge whether the decision maker 'should' have acted differently – for example, followed procedures more closely.

- **Uncertainty management theory (UMT)** is a reaction to these rather deliberate process models above, suggesting that individuals tend to use cognitive shortcuts or schemata when assessing the fairness of their experiences (Van den Bos and Lind, 2002). Emerging from earlier research on fairness heuristics theory (Lind, 2001), UMT argues that the sheer complexity and uncertainty that most of us face in our daily working lives lead us to rely on limited information or cognitive schema when judging the trustworthiness of our employer and our colleagues. This information therefore may be about the allocation of rewards (distributive justice), procedures followed (procedural justice) or our interactions with line management (interactional justice) – it just depends on what information is available at the time.

WHAT ARE THE OUTCOMES OF (IN)JUSTICE?

A vast amount of research has identified a whole range of emotional (e.g. anger), attitudinal (e.g. job satisfaction) and behavioural (e.g. organisational citizenship behaviour) outcomes of employees' injustice judgements (for a meta-analysis see Colquitt et al., 2001). However, research suggests that employees' behavioural reactions to (in)justice may come in three forms. Individuals may decrease their 'good' behaviours, increase their 'bad' reactions and may even start to behave in an 'ugly' way (Conlon et al., 2005). 'Good' outcomes refer to positive behaviours such as organisational citizenship behaviours towards the organisation (OCBOs) or the individual supervisors (OCBIs); 'bad' outcomes equate with withdrawal reactions (absenteeism, turnover, neglect and employee silence); and lastly there are 'ugly' or antagonistic reactions such as sabotage, theft and other retaliatory behaviours. While all three types of (in)justice have been shown to have a significant impact on these three types of behaviours, meta-analysis research suggests that procedural justice appears to be the strongest antecedent of 'good' behaviours, withdrawal reactions are best explained by distributive (in)justice, and interactional (in)justice has the strongest unique effect on more antagonistic reactions (Colquitt et al., 2001).

(IN)JUSTICE AND HRM

Experts and managers who incorporate fairness into the design and implementation of the HR policies of their firm can thus benefit from the numerous positive consequences identified above. Thus, when designing HR practices, HR professionals would do well to explicitly consider justice issues. Let us look at one specific case in point – personnel selection.

Personnel selection, whether relating to internal promotional decisions, decisions relating to the recruitment of new members of staff or redundancy decisions, is perhaps the most widely researched justice/fairness issue in HRM (e.g. Gilliland, 1993). As we will return to in subsequent chapters, there is a vast amount of research regarding the potential discrimination faced by various minority groups in the selection process and thus fairness/justice is one of the most important criteria for assessing the validity and reliability of assessment methods (see Chapter 7). Importantly, such unfair practices do not benefit any party (in the long term) – employees or candidates are more likely to react negatively (reduce performance or even sue the organisation) and employers are unlikely to benefit from selecting the best qualified and able candidates or staff available (e.g. Bertolino and Steiner, 2007).

Thus, whatever the exact nature of the assessment method (e.g. assessment centre or job interview), a focus on organisational justice theory can provide important insights into the design and delivery of effective assessment and selection. Let's look at some specific examples:

1. Panel interviews, rather than one-to-one interviews, are more likely to suppress bias (procedural justice) as multiple perspectives are taken on the suitability of candidates.

2. The development of explicit competency frameworks and the use of scoring mechanisms and templates against these frameworks in selection are more likely to promote the accuracy of decision making (procedural justice).

3. Sophisticated (and well-kept) personnel records are again more likely to promote accurate decision making, suppress bias and also promote greater transparency in the process.

4. Well-trained interviewers who actively listen, and treat candidates with the respect and dignity they deserve, are more likely to promote important interactional justice perceptions.

5. Organisations that communicate selection decisions in a timely and sensitive manner are again more likely to promote important interactional justice perceptions (e.g. Gilliland, 1993).

While this is clearly not meant to be an exhaustive list of all the potential justice-related considerations in well-designed selection processes, hopefully it provides a pointer to these important issues. Of course, these same issues arise when one is considering the design and delivery of other HR policies and practices including (but not limited to) issues around conflict management, redundancy, pay and reward, career management and learning and development; we will therefore return to these issues when discussing these practices in later chapters of this book.

CORPORATE SOCIAL RESPONSIBILITY (CSR)

There is a range of terms that come under the heading of 'social responsibility' that have gained popularity among business managers and the general public in recent years. The terms all refer to the general idea that businesses should take account of all the groups affected by what they do; not only shareholders and investors but also suppliers, customers, governmental and non-governmental organisations (NGOs), communities affected by their activities (locally and globally) and – central to our discussion in this book – employees. Some prefer to use the term social responsibility because 'corporate' may be inappropriate to organisations in the public sector or small and medium sized enterprises (SMEs). Similarly, others emphasise 'corporate responsibility' in relation to governance and responsibility. Another approach to implementing CSR is reflected in the term 'corporate citizenship'. As with the concept of citizenship generally, 'corporate citizenship' reminds us that organisations are embedded in wider systems and environments and in the idea that organisations are themselves actors within local, national and international settings. This underlines the political role that organisations may play (especially MNCs) in the societies in which they operate (positively or negatively). In effect, the idea of responsibility demands that we look beyond simplistic ideas that business is solely about making profit; that we look beyond the 'bottom line' to take account of a range of stakeholders and to respond to the economic, political, social and environmental context within which organisations have to work.

A more traditional view of corporate responsibility has revolved around three key responsibilities. These involve:

1. Producing goods or services that people want and that are safe and ethically provided.

2. Providing employment and treating those employed well.

3. Paying taxes to contribute to the society in which the organisation operates.

Some of what may appear to be fairly basic responsibilities may have been forgotten in recent times, particularly with regard to the payment of taxes. In the UK, three huge corporations (Google, Amazon and Starbucks) were brought before Parliament and questioned about their tax avoidance. The arguments made by companies that they can use the money saved to support good causes is an interesting one because this suggests that the companies should take the place of governments in allocating resources for society's needs. Starbucks found itself at the centre of a media and customer storm that led the company to change its approach to taxation and agree to pay tax in the UK. While what the companies were doing was not illegal, the public scrutiny that organisations are now subject to is, according to Janice Turner (2015) in *The Times*, 'throwing up a new set of ethics that are nothing to do with cool causes, biodegradable packaging or empathy for indigenous tribes. It is a dull, quotidian, almost timeless mark of good citizenship: do you pay your taxes?'

Carroll's (1999) model of corporate social responsibility sets out four aspects of responsibility – economic, legal, ethical and philanthropic obligations, with economic obligations forming the base of a pyramid on which the other layers rest. The economic drivers are important for organisations, but the danger of relying only on the 'business case' is that ethics and CSR become 'optional' (any ethical or moral case then being disposable). Similarly, while adhering to the law is not optional, it cannot deliver ethical and responsible behaviour on its own. An example of this involves the laws surrounding discrimination in employment, which provide a regulatory framework but do not replace effective policies and practices that aim to influence behaviour. Philanthropic activity has been the main way in which many organisations have seen their 'social responsibilities'. This is predominantly through charitable giving or related activities, and while this is laudable, it can still position ethics and CSR in economic terms as an 'externality'. The consequence of this is that organisations may have a disconnect between promoting a CSR policy in the community and behaving responsibly as an employer. In short, ethics and CSR should be much more about how a business makes its money and runs the organisation, rather than just about what it does with any excess profits. An authentic approach to CSR requires real engagement with all its stakeholders. If ethics and CSR are to be successful, the strategies and policies must be internally driven – which contrasts greatly with the popular use of ethics and CSR as a public relations or marketing gimmick.

Visser (2008) extended Carroll's work and adapted his pyramid model to be more appropriate for developing countries (Ragodoo, 2009). In this model, economic responsibilities are at the base of the pyramid and are deemed to be: providing investment, creating jobs and paying taxes. This is followed by philanthropic responsibilities that require setting aside funds for CSR community projects. The legal responsibilities are defined as ensuring good relations with government officials, and finally the ethical responsibilities call for the adaptation of voluntary codes of governance and ethics.

Garriga and Mele (2004) provide a useful overview of CSR theories. Their paper discusses four different types of CSR theory:

1. Instrumental theories, which outline the business case and set out social activities as a means to achieve economic results.

2. Political theories, which outline the power of organisations in society and the responsible use of this power.

3. Integrative theories, in which the organisation is focused on the satisfaction of obligations to stakeholders.

4. Ethical theories, based on ethical responsibilities of organisations to society.

In essence, the paper considers each CSR theory in relation to the four dimensions of profits, political performance, social demands and ethical values, and calls for an approach to CSR that integrates the four perspectives.

CSR AND HRM

At the start of this chapter, the importance of the role of HRM in relation to CSR was highlighted. In particular, this meant the role of HRM in ensuring that the organisation's strategies, policies and practices (including those relating to HRM, such as recruitment and selection, training and development, performance review and organisational development) are ethical and that the culture of the organisation is consistent with this approach. Thus HRM professionals can play a key role in relation to embedding ethics, justice, social responsibility, human rights and sustainability by integrating these issues into the value system of the organisation. In adopting a triple bottom line perspective (that embraces multiple stakeholders), there is an opportunity to widen the rather narrow economic interpretation of what 'effectiveness' in terms of strategic HRM means. Rather than assuming that 'strategic' relates mainly to the financial consequences of HRM policies and practices, the legitimate concerns of constituents (other than investors) can be recognised (McWilliams et al., 2006).

The raised public expectations, competitor pressures and increased levels of media scrutiny (with the associated reputational risk) also suggest that ignoring these issues is no longer possible.

This reorientation of strategy and policies has other, more positive benefits. There is growing evidence that the career choices of graduates, and thus recruitment for employers, are influenced by the sustainable development and CSR agenda of employers (HEA, 2007). Therefore, recruitment and, importantly, the retention of talented employees can be affected by the extent to which organisations are able to demonstrate their commitment in this important area (Turban and Greening, 1997). Many organisations now actively involve employees in CSR and sustainability initiatives as part of development initiatives including induction and management development programmes (see below).

SUSTAINABILITY

Sustainability is a widely used term, yet there seems to be a limited understanding of what we actually mean by the word. In business, sustainability is often used to refer to two related ideas. One is about the need to think about the longer-term survival of the business and not just about making 'quick profits'. The other is to think about the link between the survival of the business and the survival of the physical environment. However, from the literature we see that sustainability is, in fact, a very precise term that has its roots in the ecological sciences (Borland and Lindgreen, 2013), and as such is regarded as a scientific term.

HRM IN PRACTICE

Engaging employees in CSR and sustainability: PricewaterhouseCoopers (PwC) community engagement

'We create socio-economic value by using our skills and experience to engage with and help local communities, measuring our impact and encouraging a network-wide focus on capacity-building and education ... All PwC firms are involved in their local communities through a vast range of projects, from supporting youth education and leadership programmes to helping social entrepreneurs and local charities. This is a core part of our PwC culture, and we regularly contribute our time, skills and resources. While our goal is to make a difference in the communities where we work by sharing our time and knowledge, PwC people also benefit from new skills, enhanced personal fulfilment and deeper local relationships. The key areas for PwC commitments in 2014–2016 are as follows: 1. Harness the power of our network to scale responsible business behaviours, 2. Increase the positive social impact of our community activities, 3. Manage our impact on the environment, 4. Enhance the transparency and relevance of our CR reporting' (www.pwc.co.za/en/about-us/corporate-responsibility/community-engagement.html).

Further information on these activities and reports on progress are available at: www.pwc.co.uk/who-we-are/corporate-sustainability/community-involvement.html

For other examples, including those of SMEs, see the Business in the Community website: www.bitc.org.uk

HRM IN PRACTICE

Corporate responsibility competency map

One of the key challenges for HRM specialists in developing strategies, polices and practices in this area is the availability of sufficient people with the appropriate expertise.

Business in the Community provides an interactive online 'Corporate Responsibility Competency Map' that sets out key activities for both CSR specialists and HR managers. The competency map is a useful tool that can be adapted for application in recruitment and selection, training and development and performance management processes.

The map provides a range of activities including: Communications (external and internal), Community, Environment, Governance and Risk Management, Influencing Leadership, Marketplace, Measuring and Reporting, Policy, Programme Development

(Continued)

(Continued)

and Implementation, Supply Chain and Workplace. For each activity there are also: (1) Desired Business Outcomes, (2) Challenges, (3) Behaviours and (4) Resources.

The behaviours include: Achievement, Builds Relationships, Change Driver, Collaboration, Communication, Data Gathering and Analysis, Engages Others, Influence, Innovation, Integrity, Operational, Organisational Awareness, Organisational Commitment, Self-Confident, Strategic, Technical Expertise.

The competency map is available at: www.bitc.org.uk/services/training-bitc/cr-practitioners-key-skills

Porritt (2007: 33) defines ecological sustainability as 'the capacity for continuance into the long-term future, living within the constraints and limits of the biophysical world'. He further suggests that ecological sustainability is viewed as the goal, end-point or desired destination for the human species as much as for any other species, and can be explained, defined and measured scientifically. Finally, he asserts that the pursuit of ecological sustainability is both non-negotiable and pre-conditional, meaning that if humans want to have a long-term future on Earth they need to start behaving, and living, sustainably, which currently we are not doing. Judge (2002) summed up sustainability when he said: 'We can't make the Earth sustainable; it is sustainable – but whether with us, or without us, is our choice.'

This sobering statement implies that ecological sustainability is, in fact, a scientific imperative rather than a social nicety and this changes the orientation and, indeed, the priority in terms of the things we need to address urgently if we want to survive in the long term. This inevitably creates a hierarchy of priorities for the sustainability challenge, with ecological as the first priority. The social and economic elements thus become secondary as each is founded on and dependent on ecological sustainability (Porritt, 2007).

It is therefore important to distinguish between 'sustainability', which is ecocentric, and 'sustainable development' that is human-centric. The term sustainable development embraces the traditional three pillars of the triple bottom line – economic, social and environmental (Elkington, 1999). Porritt (2007: 33) defines sustainable development as: 'the process by which we move towards sustainability'. Sustainable development emphasises the importance of providing a sustainable human future. This distinction is crystallised by the report of the UN Commission on Environment and Development (the Brundtland Report) (1987), which recommends that sustainable development should be viewed as 'development that meets the needs of the present without compromising the ability of future generations to meet their own needs' (p. 383). However, the phrase was originally written in the context of the title of the report, *Our Common Future*, which referred to 'meeting the needs of all species' and not just the human species. Therefore, the original Brundtland Report phrase was written in the spirit of sustainability. Unfortunately, it is often used, today, in a limited context because it tends to be associated with exclusively human development and progress and not the development and progress of all species.

Debates about climate change polarise opinion around sustainability, but climate change is not the core issue; it is seen as one of the symptoms of our global lack of sustainability as human beings (Borland, 2009). The Earth (as a planet) changes and will continue to do so in order to adapt to different conditions and survive. The question is whether this is with us or without us and the most at risk from these changes are the most vulnerable communities and peoples in the world. Thus our lack of sustainability can be seen to be contradicting the ethical principle of 'do no harm' because it is driving society and organisations in a direction that is destructive to the environment, to other species and ultimately destructive to future human society (Porritt, 2007; Purser et al., 1995). This leads us to question whether our current lifestyles and business models are sustainable.

While there has been an increasing recognition of the need for sustainability strategies and policies in organisations, there can be confusion about what it really means in practice. For example, sustainable for what and for how long? Does this mean all existing species or just humans or both, and is it all humans? What role does business take in this and how do we measure success? In HRM research and practice, the concept of sustainability has been predominantly used to refer to organisation performance, and more specifically to how high-performing individuals and high-performance working translate into performance that is sustainable over the long term (CIPD, 2010). However, the wider debate about sustainability centres on one of the most challenging issues facing all human beings, and that is our lack of ecological sustainability: 'Human development has become almost inseparable from the, now, almost global conception of economic growth that is in many respects the antithesis of [societal] and ecological ends' (Blowfield and Murray, 2008: 323).

If we are to move to a more sustainable world, all actors, including governments, businesses, communities and individuals, need to play their part in committing to a shift in the way we live our lives. Although political leaders need to act with courage and commitment to reach global agreements, the real success will be the extent to which all organisations (and the general public) engage with the issues and commit to changing the way they conduct their business activities and live their lives. In short, what makes it possible for individuals to make the connection between the information they have, what they need to do in practice, and their behaviour?

The role of strategic HRM (in research and practice) is concerned with leadership, vision, organisational values, employee engagement, culture and changing attitudes and behaviour. It is also responsible for the processes, policies and practices; including requirements in recruitment and talent management, the training it gives employees, the expectations placed upon them through performance management and reward systems, as well as establishing codes of practice for what is considered appropriate behaviour. There are examples of companies using monetary and non-monetary rewards to support sustainability activities (e.g. rewards for 'green' behaviours or for working with others to promote sustainable products and services).

Borland et al. (2016) have developed a useful typology that categorises business strategies on the basis of the product, firm or industry approach towards ecological sustainability. They draw a distinction between 'traditional', 'transitional' and 'transformational' strategies.

TRADITIONAL STRATEGIES

Traditional business strategies (Porter, 1980, 1985) assume a limitless supply of physical resources, customers and new markets and a relentless development of products and services. Businesses are separate from society and the natural world and have no interaction with, or responsibility towards, either.

TRANSITIONAL STRATEGIES

Transitional business strategies are concerned with 'ecological efficiency' and are based on the five Rs: *reduce, reuse, repair, recycle* and *regulate* (Borland et al., 2016). The transitional approach incorporates familiar concepts such as CSR, environmental management, such as adoption of the International Organisation for Standardisation's (ISO) 14001 Environmental Management standard, and environmental regulation, such as the Environmental Protection Act of 1990.

Such a transitional approach has a positive effect in reducing usage, waste and damage to the environment from non-renewable resources and in the recycling of waste materials, and it can therefore be seen as 'less bad' than traditional strategies. However, a transitional strategy can also be seen as a 'bolt-on' to a traditional strategy, dealing with ecological concerns after products and services have been created, sold and consumed.

TRANSFORMATIONAL STRATEGIES

By contrast, transformational strategies offer a marked difference from traditional and transitional strategies in that concern for ecological sustainability provides the starting point, and also a sustainability vision that strongly influences strategic thinking within a company or an industry, leading to innovative business strategies. Transformational strategies adopt an 'ecocentric' perspective, whereby the future generations mentioned in the Brundtland definition of sustainable development (1987) refer to whole ecosystems and all species. Ecosystems may be defined as complex sets of relationships and interdependencies among the living resources, habitats and residents of an area, including plants, trees, animals, fish, birds, micro-organisms, water and soil (Stead and Stead, 2010). Healthy ecosystems are able to self-renew, self-manage and self-regulate, and do not require environmental management, doctoring and engineering by humans (Rolston, 1994).

Transformational strategies are also based on five Rs – *rethink, reinvent, redesign, redirect* and *recover* – and on 'eco-effectiveness', through harnessing the inherent effectiveness of ecosystems to self-perpetuate (Borland et al., 2016). In order to be eco-effective, industrial systems should be designed to be 'cradle to cradle' and closed loop, whereby energy and resources are transformed into products whose wastes are absorbed and reused, thus eliminating waste, rather than 'cradle to grave' and open loop where wastes are left as wastes (as is the case in traditional and transitional strategies).

SUSTAINABILITY AND HRM

HRM can play a key role in the shift towards developing transformational strategies for sustainability. Providing appropriate training, communication systems and reinforcement mechanisms is often seen as a starting point. However, to achieve fundamental change, the sophisticated interaction between many different organisational and contextual factors needs to be considered, including the challenge of engaging individuals and groups with a transformational business strategy (previously discussed) that embraces the needs of others and broader ethical and ecological principles. This includes making connections between behaviours at home and in the workplace. Who else, other than HR within an organisation, has a remit for strategic change and employee engagement and thus has the potential to make a difference? Critical to any change is the commitment of senior management, and HRM has a role in gaining buy-in from key stakeholders. Identifying 'sustainability champions' in different areas of the organisation can help to integrate and embed sustainability practices, but recruiting employees with ecological and scientific expertise (who understand the technicalities of the change required) may be the only way to make substantive progress.

MINI CASE STUDY

Ricoh UK

Ricoh UK has recently experienced a major reorganisation of staff and products. Previously, it was responsible for the manufacture of photocopiers to be sold across Europe. Since the reorganisation the UK site now has the responsibility for manufacturing and selling ink cartridges, with the photocopier business going to the French Ricoh site. The head office in Japan recognised that the UK site was more proactive than other European Ricoh sites at designing, implementing and manufacturing recycled or reconditioned products and creating a zero waste work environment. UK staff were seen as being more innovative with new ideas for products, processes, policies and practices. The senior managers in Japan were committed to diffusing this 'environmental ethos' throughout the company, with the UK site acting as a 'best practice' site. The senior managers, therefore, set them the challenge of converting not only the photocopier business but now the cartridges business too into a more sustainable business. The UK site has a 'products, processes and practices

(Continued)

(Continued)

champion' in their Environmental Officer, who has been proactive in converting not only the products, processes and practices, but also the staff, the physical buildings and the real estate on which the factory site stands. This 'holistic' approach is still novel but is now regarded as an exemplar for the industry, winning the company many awards and accolades. The Environmental Officer has instilled the virtues of 'personal responsibility' and 'individual leadership' in the staff in the UK and a group of staff are now active both at work and in their own time in promoting not only the environmental work of the company but also the importance of sustainability and the environment more widely among the general public and other companies. This work is supported by the senior management and is written into each individual staff member's personal development plan with identifiable goals and targets.

TASK: Using the concepts of transitional and transformational strategies described above, select either a product, a process, a policy or a practice in an organisation you are familiar with and examine what it would look like in a transitional (*reduce, reuse, recycle, repair, regulate*) or transformational (*rethink, reinvent, redesign, redirect, recover*) format using the 5Rs in each case. Assume you have senior management support for this activity.

GRADUATE INSIGHTS

Connecting HRM and sustainability

Yasmin Surran (not her real name) graduated with a BSc in Business and Management (with an HRM specialism) and was appointed to a graduate role with a large car manufacturer. The company has a proud history of pioneering low (and zero) carbon emission cars and was clearly committed to integrating sustainability principles into its product design and manufacturing.

Yasmin had observed that although employees were aware of the company products and the environmental awards gained by the company, there was limited awareness of why it was important to protect the environment. Many saw the zero emission cars as just another product line and an opportunity to sell more cars.

During her studies Yasmin had attended lectures on sustainability and the responsibilities of business and, as part of her role in HRM, was involved in organising employee training and communication events. Yasmin proposed including sustainability in these events and helped set up 'employee roadshows' on sustainability. Her actions were important because:

- Yasmin saw an opportunity to include sustainability (and the role the company plays in helping to protect the environment) and, importantly, why this is important to all our futures.

- The planned sessions aimed to enable individuals to make the critical connection between their own behaviours and the environment.

- They would also encourage sustainability to be part of their own decision-making processes and actions at home and in the workplace.

Many organisations have made inroads with recycling and carbon reduction schemes, but these are often easy targets. To make a real difference and embrace the challenges of the future, strategic HRM needs to be at the forefront of rethinking organisational strategies that really do change the way we use the Earth's valuable resources (Parkes and Borland, 2012).

CSR AND SUSTAINABILITY REPORTING

Many organisations now engage in CSR and/or sustainability reporting, with public limited companies required to publish these reports about their activities. While these are in the public domain, they are by nature 'self-reports'. Since 2000, a growing number of MNCs have adopted the Global Reporting Initiative (GRI) guidelines (www.globalreporting.org/) – a framework of internationally accepted guidelines and principles for companies and organisations to report on corporate responsibility and sustainability performance. It is based on 10 universal principles in the areas of human rights, labour, the environment and anti-corruption.

Corporate social responsibility (CSR) Refers to the responsibility of organisations for their impact upon society - both locally and globally.

Sustainability The capacity for continuance into the long-term future, living within the constraints and limits of the biophysical world. Sustainable development is the process by which we move towards sustainability (Porritt, 2007).

STRATEGIES FOR DEVELOPING AN ETHICAL ORGANISATION

The role of HRM in taking responsibility for influencing change towards more ethical, responsible and sustainable organisations has been discussed, but it is important to state that it is not simply a case of using mechanistic instruments such as changing structures or issuing edicts. Standards can be provided in policies and codes, but norms are established through factors that influence the broader organisational culture and subcultures, including managerial language and behaviours. Just publishing a 'code of ethics' or producing CSR and sustainability statements is therefore not sufficient – the principles must be interwoven into everything a business does. In the case of codes of ethics, Ferrell et al. (2008) argue that they need to be part of an effective ethics programme which is a process of continuous activities that are designed, implemented and enforced to prevent and detect misconduct. However, this requires the recognition that its code of ethics – just like CSR and sustainability – is part of the value system of the organisation and embedded into its core systems, including those for which HR is responsible.

In developing strategies for workplace ethics, justice, social responsibility, human rights and sustainability, it is important to pay as much attention to how such strategies will be implemented as to the strategies themselves. The key principles for implementation include (see also Webley, 2006):

- Establishing and clarifying the organisation's core values and principles. These are the threads that bind all the policies and principles together; ensuring that there is clear leadership throughout the organisation in establishing the core values and principles; and developing an understanding of the organisation's stakeholders, the nature of the relationships with and responsibilities towards them.

- Ensuring that the business strategy, ethical principles, CSR and HR practices are aligned; communicating consistently and effectively with all stakeholders; providing timely and appropriate training to reinforce values and principles; and reviewing strategy, policy, procedures and practices to ensure consistency and compliance.

HRM'S ROLE: A SUMMARY AND CRITIQUE

The responsibilities that HRM has for the key processes and practices in an organisation are brought together in a model by Verbos et al. (2007). The authors draw on literature from business ethics, positive organisational scholarship and management publications to outline the elements of positive ethical organisations, defined as 'those exemplary organisations consistently practicing the highest levels of organisational ethics. In a positive ethical organisation, the right thing to do is the only thing to do' (Verbos et al., 2007: 17).

Verbos and colleagues propose a living code that sets out the importance of organisational identity and brings together five key organisational processes (attraction–selection–attrition, socialisation, reward systems, decision making and organisational learning). This is supported by the interaction of ethical leadership and an ethical organisational culture – in other words, one that is characterised by heightened levels of ethical awareness and a positive climate regarding ethics.

However, there has been some criticism of HRM for not taking up the challenge to champion ethical and responsible behaviour or leadership in organisations. It can be argued that this may be due to the profession's drive to prove its business credentials by attempting to justify its role primarily in financial terms. Fisher (2000) provides three key reasons for this possible reluctance by HRM professionals. The first is what Fisher (2000: 68) calls 'quietism', where HR professionals are 'coerced' into siding with the organisation, whatever the cost. The second is 'neutrality', which could be a byproduct of a lack of opportunities to 'blow the whistle' because of the perceived power of organisational politics. The third reason is the acceptance of the business case justifying compromising personal ethical viewpoints (and where any resistance tends to be in the form of sarcasm).

This said, it would be wrong to label all HR professionals as ethically 'mute' and there are many encouraging examples of what Lowry (2006) describes as 'ethical reactivity', where HR managers choose to intervene in specific situations, and 'ethical assertiveness', where HR professionals have managed to reconcile the internal and external pressures to influence an ethical pathway (see also Parkes and Davis, 2013).

DEBATING HRM

Taking up the challenge

The history of HRM has strong connections with movements for more ethical and socially responsible business. In the UK, the CIPD now translates this into two behavioural requirements for HR professionals: having the 'courage to challenge' and being a 'role model' (CIPD, 2009).

TASK: In small groups, discuss the role of HR professionals in 'taking the lead' in promoting a more ethical organisation. How successful do you think they have been? Do you think this should be a leading role of HR professionals and departments? Why? Or why not?

CASE STUDY

CSR and sustainability reporting

In October 2011, the European Commission adopted a new strategy on CSR. The strategy places a strong emphasis on a core set of internationally recognised CSR guidelines and principles.

Five instruments together make up an evolving and increasingly coherent global framework for CSR: It highlights in particular the 10 principles of the UN Global Compact, the OECD Guidelines for Multinational Enterprises, the ISO 26000 guidance standard on social responsibility, the ILO Tripartite Declaration of Principles Concerning Multinational Enterprises and Social Policy, and the UN Guiding Principles on Business and Human Rights. The European Commission refers to these instruments as 'an evolving and recently strengthened global framework for CSR'.

The 10 principles of the United Nations Global Compact

The Global Compact (www.unglobalcompact.org) asks companies to embrace, support and enact, within their sphere of influence, a set of core values in the areas of human rights, labour standards, the environment and anti-corruption. Companies can sign up to the UN Global Compact, which subsequently commits them to submit a yearly communication on their progress.

The OECD Guidelines for Multinational Enterprises

These guidelines (www.oecd.org/daf/inv/mne/) are far-reaching recommendations for responsible business conduct that 44 adhering governments – representing all regions of the world and accounting for 85 per cent of foreign direct investment – encourage their enterprises to observe wherever they operate.

The ISO 26000 guidance standard on social responsibility

This is a voluntary international standard (www.iso.org/iso/home/standards/iso26000.htm) that provides guidance rather than requirements, so it cannot be certified, unlike some other well-known ISO standards. It is aimed at all types of organisations, not just enterprises.

(Continued)

(Continued)

The ILO Tripartite Declaration of Principles Concerning Multinational Enterprises on Social Policy

This declaration (www.ilo.org/empent/Publications/WCMS_094386/lang—en/index.htm) offers guidelines to multinational enterprises, governments and employers' and workers' organisations in such areas as employment, training, conditions of work and life and industrial relations. This declaration is the only ILO text that is also addressed to enterprises. The ILO provides a help-desk for enterprises on international labour standards.

The UN Guiding Principles on Business and Human Rights

The UN Guiding Principles (www.ohchr.org/EN/Issues/Business/Pages/BusinessIndex.aspx) define what governments and enterprises should do to avoid and address possible negative impacts on human rights by enterprises. On the basis of these principles, the European Commission has been developing an introductory guide to human rights for small businesses and guidance for three business sectors (SRSG, 2011).

In addition, for questions related to reporting and transparency, enterprises frequently refer to the Global Reporting Initiative and to the International Integrated Reporting Council (www.theiirc.org).

TASK:

1 Select three multinational companies (preferably from different sectors).

2 Go to the company websites to access their CSR/sustainability reports.

3 Consider the similarities and differences between the reports. You may find the guidelines and principles above useful in reviewing the reports.

CHAPTER SUMMARY

The key points that we have identified in this chapter are the following:

- Ethics, justice, CSR, sustainability and human rights are all issues that have been of increasing interest to organisations in recent years.

- The importance of these issues to the success of an organisation has gained momentum due to (inter alia) greater societal awareness and concern, media interest, the associated reputational risks, competitor drivers, ethical and moral arguments as well as an increasing recognition of the positive benefits for individual organisations.

- Each of these areas is distinct yet has important connections, and it is important to recognise the particular nature of the issues in an organisational context. For example, sustainability can be overlooked in HRM but for all individuals and society as a whole it is the key to the future for all of us and for all species. Similarly, human rights and the responsibilities of business are of growing importance and are likely to be a key concern for all organisations in an increasingly global economy.

- The role of HRM is critical to embedding all of these issues into the organisation because of the responsibility that HRM has for key processes and practices within the organisation. These include recruitment and selection, training and development, codes of conduct, organisational development, culture and values.

- Although the links between the historical development of ethical and responsible organisations and the HRM profession are interconnected, individual professionals can be conflicted because of the drive to constantly justify their existence through financial targets and the 'business case'.

- The growing recognition of the importance of these areas to organisations provides the opportunity for HRM professionals to validate the critical role of HRM as an essential part of organisational life rather than an 'add-on extra'.

REVIEW QUESTIONS AND EXERCISES

1. Ethics, justice, CSR, human rights and sustainability are issues and areas of activity that have moved further up the agenda for most organisations in recent years. Discuss three key reasons for this shift.

2. Think about two organisations that you believe have a positive image with regard to ethics, CSR or sustainability, and two organisations that have a more negative image. Explain the reasons for your choices.

3. Using the examples chosen for question 2, discuss the potential HRM implications of the different images for the organisations concerned.

4. How would you design an HRM strategy that enables connections to be made between the physical environment and home or work behaviours, and that is in line with a transformational strategy as described above?

5. Which HRM processes do you think would be the key to achieving this strategy?

6. What do you consider to be the role of HRM in relation to ethics, justice, CSR, human rights and sustainability?

7. Discuss the benefits and challenges for HRM professionals (and their organisations) in taking on such a role.

EXPLORE FURTHER

Parkes, C. (2012) The OD role of HRM in ethics, corporate social responsibility (CSR) and sustainability, in H. Francis, L. Holbeche and M. Reddington (eds) *People and Organisational Development: A New Agenda for Organisational Effectiveness*. London: CIPD Publishing, pp. 286–311. This chapter discusses ethics, corporate social responsibility (CSR) and sustainability in the context of business organisation, and their links with emergent theories and practices in organisational development (OD) and human resource management (HRM). It draws upon case study examples to illustrate how change towards 'responsible management' may be facilitated, exploring the contribution of emerging (Organisational Effectiveness) strategies in achieving this.

Parkes, C. and Borland, H. (2012) Strategic HRM: Transforming its responsibilities towards ecological sustainability – the greatest global challenge facing organizations. *Thunderbird International Business Review*, 54(6): 811–824. This article offers new insights into developing business strategies for ecological sustainability, highlighting the implications for strategic HRM activity through organisational effectiveness, leadership, values and, ultimately, HRM processes and systems.

Business in the Community at www.bitc.org.uk. This is a UK umbrella organisation that supports businesses with CSR and sustainability strategies and initiatives. The website has many examples eof different organisations' approaches to integrating CSR and sustainability, including those related to HRM strategies and practices.

GO ONLINE

Visit the companion website for **interactive quizzes**, explanatory **videos** and **podcasts**, **journal articles** to use in your essays, and **weblinks** to useful resources.

https://edge.sagepub.com/crawshaw2e

CHAPTER 5

GLOBALISM, MULTINATIONAL ENTERPRISES AND HRM

Charmi Patel

Pawan Budhwar

CHAPTER KNOWLEDGE OBJECTIVES

- Develop an understanding about the MNE (multi-national enterprise) perspective of international HRM.
- Critically evaluate the key approaches to HRM in a multinational context.
- Understand how MNEs develop HRM systems for their global operations.
- Critically analyse the global standardisation versus localisation debate.
- Highlight the key HR challenges faced by MNEs in the global context (especially in emerging markets).

KEY SKILLS OBJECTIVES

- Conceptualise a model of the working of MNEs.
- Develop HR-related skills and an understanding about the demands of working in a global context.
- Critically analyse and evaluate the working of key HR approaches in different settings.
- Develop research skills to analyse the what and why of HR challenges for an MNE.

This chapter also provides indicative content for the following Intermediate and Advanced level CIPD modules:

CIPD INTERMEDIATE LEVEL MODULES

5HRF Managing and coordinating human resources function

5CHR Business issues and the contexts of human resources

CIPD ADVANCED LEVEL MODULES

7HRC Human resource management in context

7RTM Resourcing and talent management

GO ONLINE

This chapter comes with loads of online tools to help you to go that extra mile in your studies!

- **Multiple choice questions** to help you test your knowledge and revise for exams
- **Journal articles** so you can read further for assignments and essays
- **Videos** and **podcasts** to help you to understand how complex concepts work in the real world

Visit **https://edge.sagepub.com/crawshaw2e** to access these resources for this topic.

INTRODUCTION

Recent advances in information technology, together with deregulation of labour movement in areas such as the European Community and liberalisation of the world markets, coupled with the phenomenon of globalisation, have fuelled an unparalleled surge in the growth of multinational corporations (MNCs). MNCs (or, as some would call them, transnational corporations, TNCs, or multinational enterprises, MNEs) have to make key decisions on how to manage across borders. In particular, there is a balance to be achieved between the drive for global coherence as an enterprise and being adaptive to the local environments in which they operate. These competing pressures for integration and differentiation represent a core challenge for the international human resource manager. Effective HRM is the key to success with respect to performance of MNEs globally (Budhwar et al., 2009) as it is the primary function through which these pressures are realised and reconciled. For the vast majority of organisations, the cost of the human resources who do the work is the single largest operating cost that can be controlled and adapted to the external MNE environment (see Chapter 10). HRM is crucial to the survival, performance and success of the enterprise with regard to both the cost and benefit sides of managing people internationally. This further becomes critical, given that international organisations need to deal carefully with a multicultural and diverse workforce in order to flourish in their overseas operations (see Chapter 8). Managers who work in a global environment are generally subjected to the impact of multiculturalism, regional and global change and dynamism to a much greater extent than managers operating in single-country organisations (Brewster et al., 2011; Evans et al., 2011).

Transnational corporation (TNC) An organisational form that is characterised by an interdependence of resources and responsibilities across all business units regardless of the organisation's national boundaries.

Multinational enterprise (MNE) MNEs or multinational corporations (MNCs) are those companies that are registered in more than one country and are involved in trade of products or services in various countries.

It is not surprising, then, that an MNE's choices in this context become complex and ambiguous as, from an HR perspective, the organisation grapples with the important questions of how much it should localise and how much it should standardise its HR systems across its international operations. What approach should an HR department take with respect to staffing and recruitment practices? How can an MNE develop its HR systems to fit its global portfolio? This chapter aims to provide students with a comprehensive introduction to the people management

Exploring HR challenges for MNEs

TASK: Imagine that you are an HR manager in a local company that has decided to go international. You have been charged with sorting out the HR function and key decisions for your international operations. What questions should you be asking, and why?

challenges facing MNEs and the management of human resources in an international context. In particular, it will cover: (1) what is meant by the term MNE, (2) the key approaches to HRM in a multinational context, (3) the debate about global standardisation versus localisation, (4) how MNEs develop their HRM systems for their global operations and (5) it will highlight the key HR and people management issues faced by MNEs in the global context. Overall, the chapter will help towards the development and review of management policy, practices and systems in the field of international human resource management (IHRM). It will enable the student to develop research skills to critically analyse the 'what' and 'why' of HR challenges faced by MNEs.

GLOBALISATION AND MNES

In simple terms, MNEs are those companies which are registered in more than one country and are involved in the trade of products or services in various countries. Similarly, the term TNC has been coined to describe an organisational form that is characterised by an interdependence of resources and responsibilities across all business units regardless of the organisation's national boundaries (Dowling et al., 2013). The term TNC has also been used to describe a particular type of MNE that tries to cope with large flows of mechanisms, products, resources, people and information among its subsidiaries, while simultaneously identifying their distributed resources and capabilities. However, not only does the international context affect MNE operation, but MNEs themselves also impact upon the international business context. As Dicken (2007: 107) states, 'the global economy is shaped by TNC through its decisions to invest, or not invest, in particular geographical locations. It is shaped, too by the resulting flows of materials, components, and finished products, technological and organisational expertise, finance, between its geographically dispersed operations.' There is no doubt that the scale of economic activity controlled by MNEs/TNCs today has grown sharply in the last 20 years and will continue to grow in the future despite the economic slowdown caused by Western recession. For example, world exports as a share of gross domestic product (GDP) have increased from under 20 per cent in 1994 to over 32 per cent in 2008. While global trade fell back in 2009 as a result of the global slowdown, it has been bouncing back in recent years. These statistics are a testament to the interconnected nature of the world economy today, that a crisis emanating in Western financial markets led to a worldwide recession, with world GDP falling by over 1 per cent in 2009 (Goldstein and Pusterla, 2010).

There has been more to globalisation than just a rise in world trade. There has also been a significant increase in foreign direct investment (FDI) by MNEs over the last 15 years. This increase has been especially strong in emerging economies such as the BRIC nations (Brazil, Russia, India and China). The advancement of globalisation has also been reflected in the number of companies establishing a presence in other nations, directly competing in overseas markets. Some evidence suggests that common factors such as the easing of trade barriers and tariffs and the ICT revolution have made these aspects of globalisation easier than before. For example, the Fortune Global 500, an annual ranking of the world's largest corporations by revenue, has seen the representation of companies based in BRIC nations more than double from 27 to 58 in 2005–2010 (PricewaterhouseCoopers, 2010). This growth, according to the 2010 PwC report, is expected only to rise in the near future, with some estimates suggesting that the number of new multinationals from emerging markets may rise as high as 40 per cent by 2024 compared to 2008. For example, on the basis of PwC growth analyses, India and China together are projected to account for 42 per cent of the total number of MNEs arising over the next 15 years. In 2009, China was the largest source of new MNEs, but by 2018 the report expects India to overtake China, with its projection to see 20 per cent more new MNEs than China by 2024. Similarly, countries such as Korea, Malaysia, Russia and Singapore together represent 36 per cent of all new MNEs in the projection period. The rest of the nations, such as Brazil and other major Latin American emerging economies (Mexico, Argentina, Chile, etc.), have relatively low numbers of new MNEs in both the base and projection periods (PricewaterhouseCoopers, 2010).

These new MNEs therefore are likely to operate in higher value-added business services or manufacturing sectors by locating different elements of their value-adding activities in different parts of the world. For example, a European pharmaceutical company may well have international R&D partnerships with competitors in the USA, and manufacturing joint ventures with local partners in India or China, where there are also many outsourced local sales of generic products to a local distribution firm (Evans et al., 2011). Thus for these transnational, boundary-less organisations or MNEs one of the significant challenges, among others, is to effectively manage sources of competitive advantage such as their human resources while maintaining a clear and consistent global business strategy in order to continuously improve organisational performance (Budhwar, 2012). HR professionals who anticipate internationalisation typically need to address the following issues (Brewster et al., 2011):

- Do we have a strategy for going international?
- To be successful, what types of managers will we need and how do we find or develop them?
- How can I find out about the way HRM is conducted in other countries: their laws, trade unions, labour market, expectations, etc.?
- What will be the impact of local cultural norms on our current ways of working? Can we adopt all or any of them in other countries?
- How will we choose whether to send expatriates or use local employees?
- How do we manage international moves if we choose to send some people out from home?
- How do we manage knowledge across geographical and cultural distance?

Exploring answers to these multifaceted questions, such as adapting people management practices to foreign subsidiaries and coordinating and controlling distant operations and challenges to foreign assignments facing today's MNEs, requires an understanding of HRM issues at three levels of analysis, namely: (1) cross-cultural management; (2) comparative HRM; and (3) international HRM (Brewster et al., 2011; Budhwar et al., 2009).

Budhwar and Sparrow (2002) and Edwards and Rees (2011) describe cross-cultural tradition being rooted in the ideology that every nation has its unique sets of deep-lying values and beliefs, and that these are reflected in the ways societies operate and in the ways that the economy operates and people work and are managed at work. Thus it is rooted in the

Cross-cultural management Is rooted in the ideology that every nation has its unique sets of deep-lying values and beliefs, and that these are reflected in the ways societies operate and in the ways that the economy operates and people work and are managed at work.

Comparative HRM Focuses specifically on the way that people work and explores the differences between nations in the way organisations manage their human resource processes.

International HRM Focuses on the way in which organisations manage their people resources across different dimensions of national contexts, but typically within the same firm.

culture and values of different regions and how they affect employees' perceptions and interpretations of work. The comparative HRM tradition focuses specifically on the way that people work, and explores the differences between nations in the way organisations manage their human resource processes. Such studies would, for example, explore the differences between HR practices in a firm based in Germany and a firm based in Japan.

International HRM and its more recent 'strategic' IHRM school of thought focuses on the way in which organisations manage their people resources across these different dimensions of national contexts, but typically within the same firm (see Chapter 1). For example, a US-based company might operate a performance appraisal system which depends on openness between managers and subordinates, each explaining plainly how they feel about the job being done. That firm operating in an Eastern context may face difficulties with such an approach, as such openness might prompt fears of 'loss of face'. Thus, replicating practices that have been successfully practised in home countries might prove to be more hazardous when it comes to adopting them to improve productivity and effectiveness in the overseas operations of MNEs. Thus IHRM investigates how MNEs manage the demands of ensuring that the organisation has an international coherence in a cost-effective way and yet is able to be locally responsive in terms of people management issues. IHRM therefore deals with both practices and a range of policy issues as well as strategy-related issues in terms of managing its human resources (Briscoe et al., 2011; Dowling et al., 2013). Here we will focus primarily on IHRM rather than cross-cultural or comparative HRM.

Analysing demands of working in a global context

TASK: As an International HR manager of an MNE, out of the three levels of analysis mentioned above, which level would be the most important one in terms of helping you to formulate cost-effective management practices?

MINI CASE STUDY

Barclaycard internationalisation strategy

Barclaycard was one of the UK's first credit cards and as one of the largest global credit card businesses has a rapid growth strategy. Apart from the UK, it operates in the United States, Germany, Spain, Greece, Italy, Portugal, Ireland, Sweden, Norway, France, Asia–Pacific and across Africa. In 2006, it employed 3000 staff, with 15 per cent based in the UK. To enable expansion during this time, Barclaycard International built a platform of people management processes (processes, structures and frameworks) to bring stability, governance and control. Primary agenda items for the HR team in 2006 with respect to the growing international strategy were international resourcing, international mobility, talent acquisition and the development of global policies and frameworks. Resourcing, then transferring, capability globally, either within an existing business or during the start-up and building of a local business, necessitated a range of preferred recruitment suppliers and the building of networks across them to transfer learning about: the management of different types of supplier and agency; assessment of their true global capability; and the availability of skills in each labour market. A new International Resourcing Business Partner role acted as a further support mechanism for HR business partners and business leaders to facilitate the acquisition of top talent through the negotiation of global preferred supplier arrangements for head-hunters and research institutions; the development of an employee value proposition and employment brand across countries; advising on global versus local process; sources of best practice; and appropriate geographical diversity in the use of international talent. Barclaycard's call centre in Dublin acted as a central platform and nursery for future international expansion. It moved from 10 employees in 1997 to 360 in 2006. Initially intended to support non-UK operations, the centre grew to serve eight countries including Ireland, Italy, Spain, France, Germany, Portugal, Greece and Botswana. Dublin was chosen because of the nature of the role, the employee base and the city's labour market. The recruitment population was well qualified, with intentions to stay in the country for around 12–18 months. Employees spoke (and were hired for) their mother tongue in the markets they served, requiring principles of cross-cultural management to be applied to a single internal labour market. Moreover, the acquisition of Banco Zaragozano enabled a new contact centre in Spain. Thirty-five employees moved from Dublin to Spain to help transfer practices. HR business partners dealt with: setting up legal entities to transfer employees; deciding the best mix of local recruitment; use of local job centres; assessing funding support; and understanding the implications and ramifications of local employment law and sector agreements. Rapid global expansion required the deployment of skills and experience in a multitude of countries at short notice, not always achievable at pace through local recruitment. A new international mobility framework reduced the cost and complexity of expatriating individuals by securing talented employees on global contracts with a premium for global mobility but only 'light' expatriate assignments. Rather than wait until Barclaycard International was in or near its markets, people were recruited ahead of the curve for target markets with investments made in forward market mapping. For example, research agencies and head-hunters were used to map a wider range of geographical labour markets, and researching people working in target roles. Global policies and frameworks operated on an exception basis (even if culturally uncomfortable, explicit guidance and global protocols governed activity unless it was illegal to do so) to ensure consistency, rigour, global governance and risk management. Finally, control monitoring processes were aligned with institutional requirements such as Sarbanes Oxley in areas like pre-employment screening policy. The case revealed a clear sequence of HR issues regarding choice of HR processes to be managed globally or in country and the role of local HR business partners developed in relation to recruitment and selection activity, and the emerging sophistication of insights into the behavioural implications of central HR policies within local cultures.

Adapted from Sparrow (2007).

CASE STUDY QUESTION

1   What does the case of Barclaycard International tell us about the ease with which MNEs can manage collaborative networking between various geographical locations?

MNES AND HRM

Bartlett and Ghoshal's (1998, 2004) basic premise is that MNEs are represented by units that need to be coordinated or integrated in some form and to some degree, spread throughout the world. In essence, MNEs are firms that need to be global and local (multi-domestic) at the same time. Because HRM activities and processes often facilitate issues of differentiation and integration, they represent a critical component in IHRM (Schuler et al., 2002). IHRM in that sense is about understanding, researching, applying and reviving all human resource activities in their internal and external contexts as they impact the process of managing HR in enterprises throughout the global environment to enhance the experience of multiple stakeholders (Briscoe et al., 2011). Therefore, and developing from Chapter 2, the key question here is: how does HRM contribute to the performance of multinational firms? Given the vast differences in HR practices and processes from one firm and culture to another, it is not surprising there is a great deal of controversy about this issue. To illustrate this further, Evans et al. (2011) highlight three different faces or roles of HRM.

The first face is that of a builder, that is, building HRM, which is getting the basic HRM functions, activities and processes in place while ensuring internal consistency. According to Evans et al. (2011), over time the builder becomes the custodian but often the responsibility lies with a specialised personnel or HR department. The second stage or face is that of realigning HRM so as to meet the changes in the external business environment. Advancement of new technologies, marketplaces and structure of competition calls for realigning the HRM function in order to implement new strategies effectively. Therefore, often this face of HRM is also referred to as the change partner, since it involves a partnership between line management and HR professionals. Both the above stages of HRM lead to a much broader and more complex concept of fit. Evans et al. (2011) argue that HRM needs to strive for internal fit and more externally oriented coherence while keeping five different factors in mind:

1. **The organisation's strategy** – its objectives such as financial returns; strategic growth such as market share, etc.; the balance between short-term and long-term objectives; its basis for achieving competitive advantage (superior quality, customer service, low-cost production).

2. **The external institutional environment** – the external social, political, legal norms and constraints.

3. **The workforce** – the implications of demographics such as age, gender, ethnic profiles and diversity.

4. **The organisation's culture** – whether work is viewed as egalitarian or hierarchic; whether collaboration or competition is valued in peer relationships.

5. **The technology and work organisation** – the skills required by technology; the degree of interdependence imposed by the work system; the degree to which technology and work design require judgement and creativity on the part of employees and related factors.

Therefore, at the builder stage for example, these various elements are often taken for granted. For example, the founding team might have a particular strategy; the institutional environment is that of the home country or region; the technology and work organisation factors are set. But all these factors will change over time with expansion or internationalisation, thus compelling organisations to realign or reconfigure their HR practices. Evans et al. (2011) explain that such realignment often takes quite some time to achieve. For example, it took Glaxo-Welcome 10 years to meet its goal of rapid product development by creating cross-functional team working to ensure changes in performance management, selection and development, technology, workforce, careers and deeper cultural norms and values. Similarly, it took Motorola a decade to build a premier local management cadre for its operations in China.

Nonetheless, an organisation cannot always go through constant realignment, especially in new high-tech software, professional service and e-based sectors where the process of change is quickening. Here the final face of HRM is that of a navigator steering through the dualities and paradoxes faced by these transnational organisations. It is described as steering via HRM as it is characterised by interlinks between strategy and HRM. The focus is on developing the capabilities of the organisation and its people to thrive in an environment of continuous change. It involves constructively managing the opposing forces such as short operating results and long-term growth, global integration and local responsiveness, and the need for change and continuity required by execution. These incongruities are at the heart of an MNE, hence the third face of HRM is referred to as navigator, that is, one who steers between such opposing forces (Evans et al., 2011).

LOCALISATION VERSUS STANDARDISATION

A key debate within the IHRM literature is the issue we have already noted of differentiation and integration, also referred to as the local versus global debate, as a defining feature of MNEs' operation. To further illustrate this tension as a critical component of duality theory, Evans et al. (2011: 55) write:

> All firms maintain corporate integration through rules, central procedures and planning and hierarchy. But as the needs for integration grow, more rules, more control and more bosses at the centre simply will not work, but instead [they] will only kill local entrepreneurship and drive away good people. So these classic tools need to be complemented with more informal mechanisms for coordination: lateral relationships, best practice transfer, project management, leadership development, shared frameworks, and the socialization of recruits into shared values. These tools of 'glue technology', as we call them, are to a large degree the application of human resource management.

Thus the proponents of duality theory argue that opposites and contradictions are not 'either/or' choices but 'both/and' dualities that must be reconciled. The nature of the international business strategic approach is therefore a key determinant of an organisation's eventual positioning on the integration–differentiation continuum. Harris et al. (2003) mention that the recurrent themes in the literature are the link between the strategy–structure configuration in MNEs and the competing demands for global integration and coordination versus local responsiveness. They further investigate that where global integration and coordination are important, subsidiaries must be globally integrated with other parts of the MNE and/or strategically coordinated by the parent company (Budhwar et al., 2009). In contrast, where local responsiveness is important, subsidiaries should have far greater autonomy and there is less need for integration. Factors that influence the need for integration in global business strategy include the following:

- Operational integration takes place in technology-driven businesses such as chemicals or pharmaceuticals where a small number of manufacturing sites can serve wide geographical markets, or in the case of consumer electronics firms where the company is unified according to products or markets that demand a high level of integration.

- Strategic coordination takes place when, in line with the firm's overall strategy, the MNE can select specific areas where there is a need for centralised management of resources. For example, significant resources such as research and development must be coordinated in terms of strategic direction, pricing and technology transfer, whereas most other functions are not.

- The influence of multinational customers exerts great demands on the coordination of resources, equipment, finance and people through global competition. For instance, a multinational customer can compare the prices in different regions; hence it is imperative for MNEs to coordinate pricing, service and product support worldwide.

HRM IN PRACTICE

MNEs in Spain

A recent survey study by Belizon et al. (2013) on HR practices and policies in 242 foreign MNEs operating in Spain identified a multiplicity of factors influencing subsidiary autonomy with respect to HRM. Results revealed that the highest levels of subsidiary autonomy existed in the policy areas dealing with employee involvement, the provision of information to employees, training and development and organisational learning. However, the level of subsidiary autonomy seemed to be slightly more limited in policy domains relating pay levels to market comparators, attitude surveys and suggestion schemes and succession planning for senior managers. Moreover, lower levels of HR subsidiary autonomy were found in MNEs coming from countries with a more flexible labour market, that is from countries very different from Spain where there is, comparatively, a highly regulated labour market. Conversely, higher levels of HR subsidiary autonomy were found in the MNEs originating in countries more similar to Spain regulation-wise, suggesting that MNEs coming from flexible labour market traditions are more used to 'strategic freedom' in deploying their preferred HR approaches, and are therefore likely to strive to do the same across borders.

On the other hand, factors that push the need for differentiation in global business strategy can include:

- Market demands, especially when local competitors define the market competition; local responsiveness is a common approach. This is equally true where products have to be customised to local taste or regulations, such as in the case of processed foods or fashion.
- Legislative demands locally, which may prevent full standardisation of services across the globe, leading to a requirement for more tailored approaches.
- Political demands, which can act as potential barriers to entry in some markets as they may require MNEs to set up a more autonomous subsidiary primarily staffed by host country nationals (HCNs).

MNES' DEVELOPMENT OF HRM SYSTEMS

De Cieri and Dowling (1999, 2006) identify six theoretical and empirical developments in the study of IHRM, which can be usefully applied with respect to the global versus local debate.

INSTITUTIONALIST THEORY

Rosenzweig and Nohria (1994) apply institutionalist theory by arguing that, of all functions, HRM tends to most closely adhere to local practices, in that they are often mandated by local regulation and shaped by local conventions. Within HRM, they see the order in which six key practices most closely resemble local practices as:

- Time off
- Benefits
- Gender composition
- Training
- Executive bonus
- Participation.

Many other HR issues could be added to this list. The underlying assumption for these rankings is that where there are well-defined norms for the HRM practice and they affect the employees of the affiliate organisation, they are likely to conform to the practices of local competitors (Harris et al., 2003; Morgan, 1986). Thus, from this perspective, factors such as the degree to which an affiliate is embedded in the local environment, that is, the subsidiary's dependence on local input and the degree of influence exerted on it from the local institutions; and the strength of flow of resources available at the MNE's disposal as well as the characteristics of the parent, that is, how far the MNE is willing to take risks in terms of employing HCNs, are some of the important determinants of an MNE to adapt to local conditions or standardise globally (De Cieri and Dowling, 2006).

RESOURCE DEPENDENCY THEORY

This theory views the exchanges of resources between an organisation and its constituencies as the main feature of the relationship. On the basis of such an understanding, the local environment in which the MNE is operating is valued in terms of it being the source of scarce resources, which are essential for organisational survival. The main idea is that of identifying the ability of external groups who have some command/power over the vital operations of an organisation. For example, there may be a scarcity of suitably qualified people in a certain country of operation, thus necessitating an MNE to transfer or send expatriates there. Or, for instance, legal issues such as work permits might restrict the general labour mobility. This theory thus highlights the importance of general external environmental conditions and the ability of an MNE to maximise the effectiveness of its human resources within the same environment (Harris et al., 2003).

RESOURCE-BASED PERSPECTIVE

This perspective views human resources as resources that are capable of providing sustainable competitive advantage. It therefore considers human resources as strategic assets that contribute to competitive advantage regardless of the power and politics within organisations. This perspective also ignores the impact of national culture on the ability to transfer knowledge and learning. Its key features are knowledge creation and learning, for example knowledge acquired by expatriates on assignment and diffused across the organisation (Evans et al., 2011).

TRANSACTION COST THEORY

Reed (1996: 39) defines this as 'adaptive adjustments which organisations need to make in the face of pressures for maximising efficiency in their internal and external transactions'. To minimise the costs associated with such transactions/exchanges, this perspective identifies environmental and human factors that are key features of organisational efforts. Environmental factors are asset specificity and uncertainty, whereas the human factors are bounded rationality and opportunism. Harris et al. (2003) argue that this perspective has direct consequences for HRM and the manner in which HRM practices are organised by an MNE to achieve a governance structure, which enables the management of multiple implicit and explicit contracts between employers and employees. However, this theory is limited in scope because it does not take into account social power and human agency.

STRATEGIC CHOICE PERSPECTIVE

The interaction between people and their environment is the key focus of the strategic choice perspective. Schuler et al. (1993: 420) define it as 'the process whereby power holders within organisations decide upon courses of strategic action'. This perspective takes into account social power and human agency by acknowledging the decision-making power of managers and the impact their values have on strategies and practices. Nonetheless, a key limitation is that it does not account for external pressures and the power of control systems within the MNEs (Schuler et al., 2002).

BEHAVIOURAL PERSPECTIVE

This perspective focuses on employees' behaviours within an MNE that mediate the relationship between strategy and firm performance. A core assumption of this is that HR practices aim to elicit and reinforce employee attitudes and behaviours. For example, Schuler and Jackson (2005) link HR practices to the types of behaviour required for different competitive strategies, for example equality, cost reduction or innovation. A drawback of such a perspective is that today's MNEs tend to adopt all three competitive strategies at the same time (Schuler and Jackson, 2005; Schuler and Tarique, 2005).

APPROACHES TO HRM IN MNES

Among the many people management issues facing an MNE is that of staffing and recruitment of its human resources. The staffing issues that MNEs confront are either not present in a domestic environment or are complicated by the international context in which these activities take place. For example, a UK-based MNE wishes to appoint a new finance director for its Russian subsidiary. It has to decide whether to fill the position by selecting from finance staff available in the company's parent country, the UK (a parent country national - PCN), or to recruit locally (i.e. look for a Russian finance director, a host country national - HCN). Alternatively it could choose to seek a suitable candidate from one of its other foreign subsidiaries (i.e. a third country national - TCN). The IHRM literature describes four primary approaches to dealing with the staffing issues of MNEs. Perlmutter (1969) claimed that the approach taken will depend on the decisions and assumptions made about key product, functional and geographical considerations. The four approaches are described below (Dowling et al., 2013).

Parent country nationals (PCNs) Employees whose nationality is the same as that of the headquarters of the multinational firm.

Host country nationals (HCNs) Employees whose nationality is the same as that of the local subsidiary.

Third country nationals (TCNs) Employees whose nationality is neither that of the headquarters nor of the local subsidiary – that is, a third separate country.

Conceptualising a model for MNEs

TASK: Each of these above theoretical perspectives has a value. If you were asked to make a choice between them, in what order would you put them, based on their value in explaining local versus global debate for an MNE?

GRADUATE INSIGHTS

HR work within an MNE

The following is a brief interview transcript of a recent MBA student outlining the challenges of HR processes in an MNE. Chris (name changed) works as an HR assistant in a large MNE with over 23 offices worldwide.

Author: Can you briefly describe your role or position within your company?

(Continued)

[Continued]

Chris: I work as an HR assistant here, in the head office in [the] UK. In that respect, my job is like any other kind, working in conjunction with the senior HR director/managers in managing our HR function in over 23 offices worldwide. I joined this company over two years ago. Earlier I was working for a company based in the UK.

Author: What are some of the typical HR management issues faced by your MNE? Are they different from, say, challenges you faced in your previous work, i.e. the domestic company?

Chris: Yes of course, in my previous work all we had to do was take care of day-to-day HR activities that is, payroll, selection, recruitment, training, etc. In my current company it's all this and much more. The complexities in managing 23 worldwide offices ranging from the Middle East, South East Asia, Europe and Africa, its employees, as well as employees being sent there from [the] UK ... I would say it's a different game. Our single most [difficult] challenge is sending an expatriate to these destinations, making sure they deliver what they were supposed to. Expatriate assignments are the only way we can ensure coordination of work and consistency in meeting our client's requirement. Then of course, there is the challenge of handling the local workforce, its laws, and regulations. ... Also expatriates come with their own problems especially if it's an employee who has a family, is married with children and all. Managing that entire process can be at times quite exhausting.

Author: What has the company/HR department done to ensure adequate resolution of these HR issues?

Chris: Our company has very cleverly singled out processes which are quite standard across our offices in different countries. Of course there are things that are done differently, for example in our Shanghai office, than here but overall the gist of it remains the same. For example, we incorporate 360 degree feedback in our performance appraisal process; this remains [the] same whether here or in China but the way it is carried out will differ significantly due to culture ...

ETHNOCENTRIC APPROACH

Ethnocentric approach An approach taken when strategic decisions are made at headquarters and key positions in both the domestic and foreign operations of an MNE are mainly filled by personnel from the parent country (i.e. by PCNs), with zero or very limited autonomy delegated to the foreign subsidiaries; an MNE is said to be following an ethnocentric approach.

When strategic decisions are made at headquarters and key positions in both the domestic and foreign operations of an MNE are filled by personnel from the parent country (i.e. by PCNs), with zero or very limited autonomy delegated to the foreign subsidiaries, an MNE is said to be following an ethnocentric approach. There are often sound business reasons for pursuing such an approach. It enables better organisational control and coordination of activities; it allows PCNs to develop international experience; and headquarters' (HQ) people are already well versed in company practices and therefore seen as the best people to do the job. MNEs may also adopt an ethnocentric approach in order to reduce risks. It might be difficult for established MNEs to find experienced personnel in a host country to carry out functions as expected at the headquarters.

An ethnocentric approach also has some limitations. These include:

- Fewer opportunities of growth development and progression for HCN staff, which may lead to reduced productivity and increased turnover.
- PCNs may have difficulty adapting to the host country, during which time they might make mistakes and poor decisions. This may include language difficulties, lack of awareness of local custom and practice, or ignorance of cultural mores.

- The style of operation from HQ may not fit well with local culture and practice, leading to cross-cultural issues.

- It is usually expensive to employ PCNs in such expatriate positions; they are costly to relocate and often demand high compensation packages. Not only is this an expense for the company, but it can lead to resentment among the HCNs with whom they are working.

POLYCENTRIC APPROACH

When an MNE treats each subsidiary as a distinct national entity it is said to be adopting a polycentric approach. Here, typically, the host country operation will be allowed more decision-making autonomy, and will be staffed primarily by HCNs. This approach overcomes some of the shortcomings of the ethnocentric approach. By employing HCNs the MNE eliminates language barriers, avoids the adjustment problems of expatriate managers and their families and removes the need for expensive cultural awareness training programmes. Employment of HCNs is usually less expensive and allows the MNE to keep a lower profile in sensitive political situations. It also leads to better continuous improvement and to maintaining a high morale of employees, which leads to low turnover as HCNs can see a career path within the organisation. A polycentric approach, however, has its own disadvantages. These include:

Polycentric approach
An approach adopted when an MNE treats each subsidiary as a distinct national entity. Typically, the host country operation will be allowed more decision-making autonomy, and will be staffed primarily by host country nationals (HCNs).

- Control and coordination can be problematic: an MNE could become a federation of independent national units with nominal links to each other and to corporate headquarters.

- Limited opportunities for PCNs as they will have limited exposure to international operations. Over time this will constrain strategic decision making and resource allocation.

- It prevents a global approach.

GEOCENTRIC APPROACH

The third approach Perlmutter identified is known as the geocentric approach. Here the MNE thinks more globally in terms of its operations, recognising that each part (subsidiaries and headquarters) makes a unique contribution with its unique competence. Nationality is ignored in favour of ability, and all the aspects of business are integrated into one. The main advantages of such an approach are that it enables an MNE to develop an international executive team, drawing talent from wherever it is found. This assists in developing a global portfolio and an internal pool of labour for deployment throughout the global organisation. It overcomes the limitations of both ethnocentric and polycentric approaches by providing pragmatism between the approaches. It supports cooperation and resource sharing across different units. Nonetheless, there are disadvantages associated with the geocentric approach as well. These include:

Geocentric approach
Within this approach the MNE thinks more globally in terms of its operations, recognising that each part (subsidiaries and headquarters) makes a unique contribution with its unique competence. Nationality is ignored in favour of ability and all the aspects of business are integrated into one.

- A geocentric policy can be expensive to implement because of increased costs associated with relocation, such as sending an expatriate or maintaining a standardised compensation pay policy.

- To successfully implement a geocentric policy requires a more centralised control of the staffing process, which has a longer lead time than a short-term solution. The subsidiary autonomy is lost, which may be resisted by the subsidiary.

- Moreover, if the host country wants an MNE to employ a high number of its citizens, it may use immigration controls in order to force the MNE to employ more HCNs, whereas the company may have been thinking of recruiting TCNs or PCNs. This is equally challenging for an ethnocentric approach.

REGIOCENTRIC APPROACH

Regiocentric approach
Refers to a geographical strategy and structure that are based within a particular geographical region of the world.

Geographical strategy and structure of the MNE are the main elements of the **regiocentric approach**. Staff may move outside their countries, but only within the particular geographical region. Regional managers may not be promoted to head-quarters positions but may enjoy a degree of regional autonomy in decision mak-ing. For example, a UK-based firm could create three regions within which their respective subsidiaries might be functioning: Europe, America and Asia–Pacific. European staff could be transferred throughout the European region (say a British manager going to Germany, a French manager to Belgium and a German to Spain). In the Asia–Pacific region European nationals would be rare, as would transfers from the regions to headquarters in the UK. There are several advantages of such an approach. First, it allows interaction between executives who are transferred to regional headquarters from sub-units in the region and PCNs posted to the regional headquarters. This enables better integration at regional level. Second, the MNE would reflect sensitivity to local conditions, since local sub-units are staffed almost totally by HCNs, thus recognising the need for differentiation globally. And lastly, it can be a way for the MNE to gradually move towards a purely ethnocentric or geocentric approach, depending on its experiences.

There are also some disadvantages of a regiocentric approach. These include:

- It can constrain the MNE from taking a global stance by creating a sort of federalism at the regional rather than the country level.

- This approach moves career prospects from national to regional level; however, it still limits movement to the parent headquarters.

Dowling et al. (2013) categorise managerial attitudes that reflect the socio-cultural environment in which the internationalising is embedded within three staffing categories. However, the nature of international business often forces MNEs to implement these options upon host adaptation with respect to staffing of its employees. For example, a firm might want to adopt an ethnocentric approach to all its foreign operations, but a particular host country might force the MNE to appoint its own citizens in key subsidiary positions. So, for that market, a polycentric approach might be mandatory. In such instances, a uniform approach is not achievable. The advantages and disadvantages of PCNs, TCNs and HCNs are as shown in Table 5.1.

DEBATING HRM

Staffing for MNEs

Robinson (1978: 297) states that 'The firm will opt for an approach of using parent-country nationals in foreign management positions by default, i.e., simply as an automatic extension of domestic policy, rather than deliberately seeking optimum utilisation of management skills.'

TASK: Discuss in small groups whether you agree with this statement. If so, what are its implications for MNEs?

Apart from these approaches, Dowling et al. (2013) recognise that external and internal contingencies facing the internationalising firm will also exert an influence on its staffing choices. These include context-specific, company-specific and local unit variables and their effects on IHRM practices.

The local context of the headquarters as well as of the subsidiary can be described in terms of both cultural and institutional variables. Cultural values may differ between those at the headquarters and the host country context. For example, Tarique et al. (2006) mention that cultural similarity acts as a moderator between MNE strategy and subsidiary staffing. Where parent and host country cultures are more similar, then parent country practices are more likely to be adopted successfully. The authors also found that MNEs tend to staff culturally distant subsidiaries with PCNs, which had a positive effect on labour productivity. Institutional variables such as the legal environment and the education system may directly affect staffing options and opportunities. Requirements to employ HCNs or the development of relevant skills and knowledge may limit, or indeed enhance, the range of staffing options available.

The structure, strategy, international experience, corporate governance and organisational culture of the MNE will also influence the strategy behind staffing and the approach an MNE takes. Equally, the nature of the establishment of the international operation can also vary quite considerably; that is, whether it is a joint venture, acquisition, merger or an investment project might also affect the staffing approach, which may be further dependent on the cultural and institutional environment. The strategic role that the subsidiary has to play for the MNE as a whole may be related to questions such as need for control, the locus of decision making, which might further impact the staffing choices. Selection, training, compensation, career

Evaluating HRM approaches in MNEs

- Read and reflect upon the above section.
- TASK: What freedom do you think an MNE has with respect to imposing its own approaches to HRM in its operations throughout the world? Do you think the given approaches help or further complicate matters for an MNE?

development (discussed in greater detail in Part 2 of this book) and use of expatriates, as well as repatriation in a broader firm context, also play an important role in the development of effective policies required to sustain a preferred staffing choice.

TABLE 5.1 Advantages and disadvantages of employing PCNs, TCNs and HCNs

Staffing choices	Advantages	Disadvantages
Parent country nationals (Nationality of employee is the same as that of the headquarters of the multinational firm; PCNs)	• Organisational control and coordination are maintained and facilitated. • Managers with potential are provided with international experience. • PCNs may be the best people to do a job, given their special skills and expertise. • There is assurance that the subsidiary will comply with company objectives, policies, etc.	• Adaptation to host country may take a long time (including family, etc.). • An inappropriate HQ style may be implemented by PCNs. • There might be big differences in compensation packages between PCNs and HCNs.
Third country nationals (Nationality of employee is neither that of the headquarters nor the local subsidiary; TCNs)	• A compromise between expertise and adaptation. • In comparison to PCNs, the salary and pay benefits of TCNs may be lower; hence they are less costly. • With respect to the host country environment, TCNs may be better informed than PCNs.	• The host country may resist hiring of TCNs. • TCNs may not want to return to their own countries after assignment and can create a challenge for the MNE. • TCNs can be costly and might struggle to adjust to their overseas assignment.
Host country nationals (Nationality of employee is the same as that of the local subsidiary; HCNs)	• Barriers such as language and culture are eliminated. • No extra costs with respect to hiring and immigration, e.g. visa costs. • Since HCNs stay longer in their positions there is continuity of management practices. • Government policies may dictate hiring of HCNs.	• They might be an impediment to control and coordination by HQ. • HCNs have limited career opportunity outside the subsidiary. • Hiring HCNs limits the opportunities for PCNs to gain foreign experience. • Hiring of HCNs alone could encourage federation of national rather than global units.

HRM IN PRACTICE

Coca-Cola's African story

Nothing symbolises globalisation and MNE quite as powerfully as Coca-Cola. The planet's favourite soft drink brand is pervasive, even in its poorest continent. Establishing its presence in Africa as early as 1928, when it opened its first production plant, Coca-Cola as of 2006 has operations in all 56 African countries, with 40 bottling firms operating 170 plants under licence as part of its 'franchise' system. The company has become Africa's largest private sector employer, with over 60,000 employees in the Coca-Cola system, which consists of the parent company, franchised bottling operations and distribution and a further 40,000 casual staff. Explaining its people management strategy in Africa, Githuku, head of the current corporate citizenship strategy, initiated by Alex Cummings, Africa Group President and Chief Operating Officer, explains: 'The idea behind our strategy is that it is not top down but bottom up.' On heading Coca-Cola's HR centre of excellence for Africa in 2004, Githuku transformed the existing HR department from a team of generalists into four specialist support functions: a transactional arm; a business partner arm; a specialist team including heads of talent development, HR information systems, total reward and organisational effectiveness; and a talent acquisition arm.

The new structure, which Githuku drew up with the help of consulting firm Mercer, reflected the results of research into how the HR function was spending its time and where it was adding most value to the business. The new model was also being adopted in the company's Atlanta headquarters in 2006. Githuku's ambitions are for Coca-Cola to move forward from its current 10–14 per cent expatriate leadership population and grow 'long-term players on the continent' from local talent. The next step would then be to export some of those players developed in Africa to other global divisions of the Coca-Cola Company. In Africa this commitment has translated into stringent targets for HR in human rights, workplace practices and health and safety terms. 'Our second challenge in HR is to adhere to the labour regulations with our bottling partners', says Githuku. 'Some have the ability to invest in HR and some don't.' She is concerned, given the difficult business environment in which Coca-Cola operates in some African countries, to prevent Colombia-style issues from emerging: 'We are not sitting back on our laurels.' In fact, since 2006 Coca-Cola has been working on labour relations issues across the entire system with the aim of developing a 'cross-functional, aligned approach' including skills development.

Adapted from Johnson (2006). Reproduced by permission of Rebecca Johnson.

KEY HR CHALLENGES IN GLOBAL AND EMERGING MARKETS

A critical component for MNEs, after staffing and local versus global approaches, is to manage an internationally mobile and diverse workforce. Traditionally, MNEs have deployed groups of managers/experts to disseminate corporate strategy and culture to local units and transfer competence across borders; such staffs have been labelled expatriates. Expatriates are those high-profile managers who are sent from headquarters to the host country to manage the control and coordination of activities and to establish the MNE culture within the host country. According to Harris et al. (2003)

Expatriates Groups of managers/experts who are sent to local units to disseminate corporate strategy and culture and to transfer competence across borders.

and Brewster et al. (2011), strategic targets addressed by an international assignment could be as follows:

- To improve business performance
- To foster the parent corporate culture in the subsidiary, or share cultural views
- To break down barriers between the parent company and subsidiaries
- To solve technical problems
- To develop top talent and future leaders of the company
- To open new international markets
- To handle politically sensitive business
- To control business improvement initiatives
- To improve trust and commitment of the subsidiary
- To reduce risks
- To train HCN employees in order to improve individual skills
- To improve team skills
- To implement knowledge practices, for example development, sharing, codification, combination, transfer and mapping of the organisation's knowledge
- To develop, share and transfer best practices
- To improve business relationships
- To develop networking processes at intra- or inter-organisational level
- To develop an international leadership
- To control financial results.

However, such ambitions also mean that there are significant challenges with respect to managing such an internationally mobile staff. The complexities of managing an expatriate have been the focus of much sustained academic research on IHRM over many years (see Dowling et al., 2013). Despite this focus, there are several key challenges that an MNE needs to face with respect to people management issues.

One of the first major challenges is to establish selection criteria for the international assignee. Companies' perception that international selection is a high-risk operation leads to a tendency to place over-emphasis on technical and managerial qualifications, to ensure that the job can be done competently. Sparrow et al. (2004) called the selection practice a 'coffee-machine system', which leads to selection of an expatriate from a small pool of known senior managers, then on to potentially discriminatory outcomes and to some serious failures. In fact, to avoid such high rates of expatriate failure many organisations have now adopted more sophisticated procedures such as psychometric assessments (see Chapter 7) of competencies and other approaches to suitability assessments (Harris et al., 2003).

The next challenge, after the appropriate selection of expatriates, is to manage the assignment cycle, including the high failure rate of expatriates. An expatriate failure in this context is defined as the premature return home of an expatriate manager (Tung, 1998). Though there is no real consensus in terms of statistics of such expatriate failure, experts argue that in some cases, such as within the US literature, the failure rates are extremely high (Evans et al., 2011). Therefore, preventing or minimising these will involve the HRM specialist to work on the following areas:

- **Preparation** – in terms of organisational training like cross-cultural workshops, pre-paid visits to the host country, factual briefing, assessment centres and field experiences, informal networking with other expatriates – these are some of the common approaches that an MNE takes in terms of preparing the expatriate for the foreign assignment.

- **Adjustment** – adjustment of an expatriate is, according to Black et al. (1991), based on four factors. Individual factors include self-efficacy, relational and perceptional skills, emotional stability, interpersonal and self-confidence skills. Non-work-related factors are particularly those that deal with the family situation. An inability of the spouse and children to readjust to a new cultural environment is a common source of difficulty. Therefore, if an expatriate is on a high culture novelty job then the social support they need from the MNE is a deciding factor in their adjustment at work. And lastly, there are job factors such as role clarity (lack of clarity on what is expected), role discussion, role conflict, role overload, which make it difficult for the expatriate to adjust in the host country.

- **Rewards** – the high costs of international assignments mean that much attention is focused on developing more cost-effective systems which will still provide an incentive for the expatriate to move. The key determinants of the system are cost efficiency, that is, making sure that the plan delivers the intended benefits in the most effective manner (including tax consequences); equity issues, that is, making sure that the plan is equitable irrespective of the assignment location or nationality of the expatriate; and system maintenance, that is, making sure the plan is relatively transparent and easy to administer. A balance-sheet approach is most popular among MNEs. This is designed to maintain standards of living for expatriates, irrespective of their assignment location.

- **Performance management** – the assessment of an expatriate's performance involves a complex range of issues, and research to date suggests a rigorous performance appraisal system for expatriates is far from universal (Dowling et al., 2013). A thorough, objective appraisal of an expatriate is likely to be highly complex. This is because the general difficulties of performance measurement are compounded in the case of expatriates by headquarters' lack of knowledge of the local situation (Schuler et al., 1991).

- **Repatriation** – a key issue after the international assignment is completed is that of repatriating the expatriate, that is, his or her homecoming. A critical issue in repatriation is the management of expectations (Harris et al., 2003). Work-related expectations of repatriates can include job position after repatriation, standard of living, improved longer-term career prospects, opportunities to utilise skills acquired while abroad and support and interest from supervisors and colleagues in the home country. Together, these concerns suggest that organisations need to devote more attention to their handling of the repatriation process. Examples of some of the best practice in this regard include:

- ○ Pre-departure career discussions
- ○ A named contact person at the home country organisation
- ○ A mentor at the host location
- ○ Re-entry counselling
- ○ Family repatriation programmes
- ○ Employee debriefings
- ○ Succession planning.

Moreover, the issue related to pursuing diversity management is critical. For example, to what extent should MNEs try to standardise their diversity programmes across their subsidiaries? In principle, the organisational structure of MNEs' diversity management activities should adopt the one that the firm has overall supported. This would then assume that an organisation adopting an ethnocentric or geocentric approach would have more or less standardised programmes across the world.

The challenge of recruiting female expatriates as part of MNEs' inclusive approach to HRM is an important one. Caligiuri and Cascio's (1998) model for predicting the success of female global assignees is based on four antecedents: personality traits, organisational support, family support and the attitudes of host country nationals towards working women or female expatriates. Dual-career couples and the implications of international working for work–life balance pose further important challenges for MNEs in terms of internationalising its workforce.

DEBATING HRM

The role of expatriates

The literature suggests that expatriate assignments do offer a number of benefits as well as challenges to MNEs in staffing their foreign operations.

TASK: *Keeping these in mind, in small groups discuss the following*:

1　Are MNEs justified in using expatriates?

2　Could MNEs' objectives be achieved through alternative means? If so, what are some of the other forms of international assignments?

CASE STUDY

AstraZeneca expatriate management

AstraZeneca is the one of the world's largest pharmaceutical companies, headquartered in London, UK and Södertälje, Sweden. In 2008, the revenues at AstraZeneca approximated US$31.6 billion, with a workforce of 66,000 employees. In 2009,

AstraZeneca had around 350 employees working on international assignments in 140 countries worldwide. These employees were on short-term, long-term or commuter assignment contracts. According to Ashley Daly, Senior Manager of International Assignments for AstraZeneca in the USA, the company's employees were mainly concentrated in Belgium, the USA and the UK, but they 'also have a significant presence in the Asia–Pacific and Latin America regions'. The company's policy states that for any international assignment, there has to be a strong business rationale. The company made sure that the career management of its employees during the assignment was consistent with personal development goals as well as the company's needs while ensuring the costs of international assignments were fair. The contractual arrangements for the assignment were also centrally managed; 'from the outset, if there is not a clear sense of how the international assignment experience can be applied at the end of the assignment term – at least in broad terms –the business should strongly consider whether an international assignment should even move forward', said Daly.

Once an assignment offer was made to a potential expat, AstraZeneca paired them up with an international assignment manager (IA manager), who briefed them on company policy and the opportunities for cultural and language training. Prior to the departure for their international assignment, employees were provided with adequate training on several issues such as leaving for the destination country, returning back to their home country, cultural differences, social do's and don'ts and, if necessary, training their spouse in the local language. Tessi Romell, Research and Development Projects and HR Effectiveness Leader at AstraZeneca, said that the company also helped connect new expats with those who had already served in that location.

At times, they also hosted follow-up workshops in the host county. Expats were in constant touch with their IA manager in addition to reporting to a line manager in their home country. Moreover, AstraZeneca saw to it that expats were given the necessary flexibility for them to achieve a work–life balance. 'AstraZeneca is really good at allowing people to manage their own time and being aware that we are working across different time zones. It's always something that we try to take into consideration so we don't have people [taking care of work matters] in the middle of the night', said Romell.

Furthermore, there were few complaints with respect to work–life balance from the company's expat employees. Romell explained, 'It's a combination of things that the company is doing and having a culture that is supportive of work–life balance, as well as encouraging individuals themselves to think about their own work–life balance.' Industry experts too felt that the practices followed by AstraZeneca, such as preparing the employees for international assignments, providing them with support and assigning an IA manager, were effective. They lauded AstraZeneca's practices, which were in contrast to those of many companies that rushed employees to foreign assignments without adequate support. With economic recession around the world continuing, some experts felt that organisations would be forced to reconsider the costs associated with international assignments. Some felt that global companies such as AstraZeneca would send fewer people on international assignments, or allot them to

(Continued)

(Continued)

shorter terms abroad. They even predicted that the high compensation and benefits generally associated with foreign assignments could also see cuts. Daly noted that although measures were taken to cut the costs around taxes, by sending expats on short-term assignments, completely cutting the costs was not always possible. When an expat has family, Daly pointed out, some aspects of expat packages such as host country support, educational counselling for expat children and spousal support played a critical role in ensuring expat success. These supports ensured that the expatriate family was able to settle down in the host country. Not providing them could result in employees not being able to focus on their new job, putting the company's investment at risk. According to Daly, 'Our recent focus has been less on reducing numbers of international assignees and more on making the right decisions about who goes on assignment; why they go; and perhaps most important, how the skills and experience gained abroad will be leveraged in their next role, post assignment.'

Adapted from Purkayastha (2010) IBS Center for Management Research, Casecentre.org

CASE STUDY QUESTIONS

1   What approach did AstraZeneca take with respect to internationalisation?

2   What should AstraZeneca do differently with respect to managing its expatriates? And why?

3   What decisions related to expatriates can organisations take to maximise the benefits to the company despite the ongoing economic recession?

CHAPTER SUMMARY

The key points we have identified in this chapter are:

- The meaning of the term MNEs and their rise due to globalisation.
- Cross-cultural HRM, comparative HRM and IHRM as the three levels of analysis in understanding the MNEs' functioning and management of their human resources.
- Approaches to staffing tend to be based on four key classifications, that is, ethnocentric, geocentric, regiocentric and polycentric. Based on any or a combination of these approaches, PCNs, TCNs or HCNs may be recruited by the MNEs.
- There are both internal and external contingencies involved while deciding on the local versus global debate of MNEs' operations.
- In order to transfer best practices and maintain control, among other things, MNEs often make use of expatriates.

- To minimise expatriate failure, the HRM specialist needs to work on preparation for the assignment cycle, adjustment, performance management and reward of the expatriate while on the assignment, as well as the issue of repatriation of an expatriate once the assignment/project cycle is completed.

REVIEW QUESTIONS AND EXERCISES

1. Highlight the key challenges faced by MNEs when internationalising.
2. Describe and evaluate the three levels of analysis that form the subject matter of IHRM.
3. Discuss Perlmutter's (1969) approaches to staffing and recruitment. What are their advantages and disadvantages?
4. Explain how external and internal factors may affect the staffing choices of MNEs.
5. What are the factors that influence the need for localisation versus standardisation in global business strategy?
6. Discuss the stages involved in managing the assignment cycle of an expatriate.

EXPLORE FURTHER

Dowling, P., Festing, M. and Engle, A. (2013) *International Human Resource Management*. London: Thomson. To look into the topics addressed in this chapter in greater depth, this book provides an excellent mix of conceptual models, empirical research and application of IHRM literature. The book also includes a wealth of case study materials and class discussion activities.

Budhwar, P. and Debrah, Y. (2001) Rethinking comparative and cross national human resource management research. *The International Journal of Human Resource Management*, 12(3): 497–515. This is an excellent journal review article that highlights the rapid development of the HRM discipline and the need for more cross-national and international HRM studies. The authors critically analyse five main HRM models on the basis of which a framework for HRM evaluations in different contexts is proposed. It is a good read to get a thorough background into international HRM theories/models and frameworks.

The Society for Human Resource Management website at www.shrm.org. This is the website of the main HR professional body in the USA and contains lots of useful information on IHRM and other related HR topics.

GO ONLINE

Visit the companion website for **interactive quizzes**, explanatory **videos** and **podcasts**, **journal articles** to use in your essays, and **weblinks** to useful resources.

https://edge.sagepub.com/crawshaw2e

PART TWO

HRM IN PRACTICE

CHAPTER 6

WORKFORCE INTELLIGENCE PLANNING

Judy Scully

Paul Turner

Michael Gregson

Ben Clegg

Joanna Parker

Paul Hunt

CHAPTER KNOWLEDGE OBJECTIVES

- To understand the difference between workforce planning, workforce intelligence planning and strategic workforce planning.
- To understand why and how national and international organisations need to plan their future workforce, and the role of HR in workforce intelligence planning.
- To understand the academic theories that inform the behavioural aspects of workforce intelligence planning, including those associated with skills, motivation, engagement and leadership.
- To understand the critique of workforce intelligence planning, and the need for robust evaluation studies.

KEY SKILLS OBJECTIVES

- To work as a team to design a workforce intelligence plan.
- To debate an HR strategy to implement a workforce plan.
- To use the research resources available for horizon planning.
- To agree a research evaluation design for workforce intelligence planning.

This chapter provides indicative content for the following Intermediate and Advanced level CIPD modules:

CIPD INTERMEDIATE LEVEL MODULE

5RST Resourcing and talent planning

CIPD ADVANCED LEVEL MODULE

7RTM Resourcing and talent management

GO ONLINE

This chapter comes with loads of online tools to help you to go that extra mile in your studies!

- **Multiple choice questions** to help you test your knowledge and revise for exams
- **Journal articles** so you can read further for assignments and essays
- **Videos** and **podcasts** to help you to understand how complex concepts work in the real world

Visit **https://edge.sagepub.com/crawshaw2e** to access these resources for this topic.

INTRODUCTION

> The workforce and workplace of tomorrow will be very different from those of today. Organisations need specific skills and attributes from their leaders. Employees will have markedly different needs and preferences, and workers will have different views based on their experiences, culture, ethnicity and education. (McKinsey, 2012)

Workforce planning (WP) has become an integral part of business planning in organisations. It is regarded as a core process of HRM that ensures organisations have the right number of people at the right time, in the right place with the right skills, which are aligned with the organisational strategy (Baron et al., 2010; CIPD, 2012). The addition of behavioural considerations to the workforce plan, the creation of measures of effectiveness and finally the conversion of these into implementable actions throughout the organisation is known as workforce intelligence planning (WIP). Both will support the organisation's efforts to achieve its strategic objectives and will be among the critical sources of intelligence for achieving competitive advantage (Nutt, 2010). Strategic workforce planning (SWP) complements WIP by including behavioural considerations, as well as highlighting the importance of planning for a 'right cost' workforce in a context of downsizing (Melchor, 2013). The role of HR in WP/WIP/SWP is integral to the design and implementation of the plan.

This chapter will explore WP, WIP and SWP in the context of both strategic human resource management (SHRM) and HR practitioner experience in the UK, the USA and Europe. It shows the HR tools that inform the implementation of WP/WIP/SWP and how theory and practice contribute towards the development of an evidence base for systematising and evaluating WP/WIP/ SWP. The chapter has four key areas of focus:

1. To define what we mean by WP, WIP and SWP and explain why these concepts are so important to the modern national and international organisation.

2. To understand why and how national and international organisations need to plan their future workforce and the role of HR in planning.

3. To understand how key behavioural aspects of SHRM, particularly skills, motivation, leadership and employee engagement, are integral to WIP and SWP.

4. To understand the critique of WIP and the need to develop robust and rigorous evaluation models.

In the first part we define what we mean by WP, WIP and SWP, and explain that including 'intelligence' in the concept means that in practice organisations also link skills

Workforce planning
'A core process of human resource management that is shaped by the organisational strategy and ensures the right number of people with the right skills in the right place at the right time to deliver short and long term organisation objectives' (Baron et al., 2010: 4). It can be described as 'an organisational attempt to estimate the demand for labour and evaluate the size, nature and sources of supply which will be required to meet that demand'.

Workforce intelligence planning 'Workforce intelligence planning is all about matching need with the right number of employees with the right knowledge, skills and behaviours in the right place at the right time' (Department of Health, 2012).

Strategic workforce planning The term is used in conjunction with workforce planning and workforce intelligence planning, and more commonly used in the USA and Europe. It signifies an HR system designed to have the right people in the right place at the right time, with the right behaviours (and at the right cost).

to behaviours. We outline the processes involved in developing a plan and explain why organisations need to undertake such HR activity. We then demonstrate how SHRM theory informs the core behavioural concepts of WP/WIP/SWP. These include workforce skills, talent management motivation, leadership styles and employee engagement models. The next section explains the use value of horizon and scenario planning. It will focus on the tools needed for these approaches, drawing on examples used for both the development and implementation of the workforce plan. We then address a critique of WP/WIP/SWP that suggests it requires an evidence base of evaluation studies. In consideration of this critique we explore a range of evaluation studies that could be operationalised to show WIP impact. Throughout the chapter we highlight national and international examples. Our main case study is Birmingham City Council (BCC), a UK public sector organisation where WIP evolved between 2007 and 2012. The BCC practitioner experience exemplifies good practice through the HR role and explains how the WIP plan was implemented.

Higgs & Sons, a professional firm of solicitors in the UK, provides a second case study. The work in progress on the WIP design at Higgs & Sons shows the importance of senior leadership and employee engagement, and explains how WIP will be implemented through a WIP model that will include evaluation.

WORKFORCE PLANNING, WORKFORCE INTELLIGENCE PLANNING AND STRATEGIC WORKFORCE PLANNING

WHAT IS WORKFORCE PLANNING?

Workforce planning has been around since the 1960s, but recent decades have seen a resurgence in interest from organisations in both private and public sectors. In the past it has been referred to as manpower planning (Bramham, 1975, 1989). Manpower planning is associated with a more centralised, number-crunching type of process, whereas workforce planning attempts to move away from this by allowing for a greater recognition of human resource management issues, especially those concerning skills, and is appropriate in a variety of organisational settings (Sinclair, 2004). WP also has roots in established HR concepts such as 'human resource planning' and 'succession planning' (Turner, 2002). Modern WP centres on the notion that an organisation's business strategy should shape its human resources strategy. However, despite recent attention, the implementation of WP is often problematic for HR practitioners and represents a significant business challenge (Laabs, 1996).

Manpower planning
A centralised, number-crunching type of process that predicts the number and types of staff skills required for current and future organisational needs. The process was discredited in the 1980s for not predicting the economic downturn.

The concept of WP can be difficult to describe, with many opting for the basic interpretation of 'getting the right staff with the right skills in the right place at the right time' (see e.g. Bradford Teaching Hospitals NHS Foundation Trust, 2008; CIPD, 2012; Department of Health, 2004; US Department of the Interior, 2001). However, such a definition can be criticised for lacking clarity. For example, how is 'right' defined – and by whom? Reilly (1996) provides more clarity in defining WP as 'a process in which an organisation attempts to estimate the demand for labour and evaluate the size, nature and sources of supply which will be required to meet that demand'. Regardless of how it is defined, WP aims to help organisations meet the challenges associated with operating in an environment which is subject to dramatic changes. In order to adapt and face the uncertainty it is vital to have a workforce that is appropriately skilled and completely engaged. WP provides organisations with detailed intelligence about the current deployment of its workforce and a strategy to make sure that it remains effective in the future. Considering the importance of such knowledge, WP can be an integral part of business planning in organisations. To add complexity to this area, scholars have highlighted key differences between WP and workforce intelligence planning. The addition of behavioural considerations to the quantitative analysis of the workforce plan, particularly leadership, staff engagement and the creation of measures of effectiveness and evaluation, and finally the conversion of these plans into implementable actions throughout the organisation, is known as workforce intelligence planning (WIP). Strategic workforce planning (SWP) originated in the USA in the 1960s, and is similar to WIP, particularly because it advocates the need for the 'right behaviours'. For example, Ulrich (2013) discusses the importance of senior leadership behaviour and points out that talent is not enough if employees cannot work together in a team. Following the 2008 economic crash, OECD (2011) research recommended that OECD countries improve the link between workforce planning and strategic planning. The study also muted the need for SWP evaluation. Focusing on the 'right cost' of the public sector workforce, Huerta-Melchor (2013) argued that SWP was essential for organisations in times of fiscal constraint as well as identifying the essential talent that is required to meet the current and future work plans. The study exemplifies Austria, Italy, Sweden, and acknowledges Australia, Canada and the UK as leading the way forward. Ward (2013) also draws on global examples, including the USA and China, to identify SWP best practice. In sum, there is a symbiotic global relationship between WP/WIP and SWP, which has developed over 50 years.

> **Workforce plan** In general, workforce plans are designed to be short term (one year), medium term (three years) or long term (five years plus). However, the more uncertain the situation, the more likely is the time plan to be shorter. It is also worthwhile being cautious about optimising such plans in organisations where planning can be regarded as continuously changing due to contextually specific external factors.

THE RELATIONSHIP TO HRM

It is the essence of modern WP that the organisation's business strategy should shape the human resources strategy (see Chapter 2). As part of its strategic planning, therefore, the organisation will need to forecast how many people will be in the workforce in future years, where the workforce will be based, and what skills and behaviours it should have. The relationship between human resource management and WP is defined by the CIPD as 'a core process of human resource management that is shaped by the organisational strategy and ensures the right number of people with the right skills in the right place at the right time to deliver short and long term organisation objectives' (Baron et al., 2010: 4). The CIPD argues that WP can be either 'hard' – which is about numbers of employees or potential employees – or 'soft' – which is more concerned with developing a strategic framework (CIPD, 2012).

The UK Department of Health National Centre for Workforce Intelligence (www.cfwi. org.uk) expanded the conventional definition of WP to include the link between skills and organisational behaviours in the process:

> Workforce intelligence planning is all about matching need with the right number of employees with the right knowledge, skills and behaviours in the right place at the right time. (CFWI Annual Conference, 2012)

The shift from WP to WIP and inclusion of 'intelligence' refers to the study of management and staff behaviour in relation to skill acquisition. In this context 'intelligence' refers to leadership behaviours and staff behaviour plus insight into the culture and change management of the organisation. By combining the quantitative analysis (number crunching) of WP together with an understanding of management and staff behaviour, culture and change management implications, WIP provides a holistic view of how an organisation should craft its people strategy to deliver strategic objectives in a rapidly changing environment.

WHAT HR AIMS AND ACTIVITIES ARE INCLUDED IN WP, WIP AND SWP?

The HR aims are to ensure that the organisation:

- Obtains and retains the quantity and quality of people it needs to achieve strategic objectives;
- Makes the best use of its human resources;
- Is able to anticipate the problems of potential surpluses or deficits of people through gap and demand analysis;
- Develops a well-trained, flexible and agile workforce that can adapt to an uncertain and changing environment; and
- Reduces its dependence on external recruitment when key skills are in short supply.

There are several HR activities that might be included in the process of WP and WIP. Among these are HR being actively involved in developing:

- Business plans
- Labour demand and supply forecasting
- Organisational design
- Succession management for all key positions
- Talent management and career planning
- Recruitment and retention planning to meet organisational objectives
- The creation of a flexible and agile workforce through multi-skilling and the right levels of learning, training and development
- Skill acquisition
- Senior leadership and line manager development
- Employee engagement techniques
- Horizon planning and scenario planning
- Developing a strategic plan over a one-, three- or five-year period and an operational plan over one year that informs the budget.

Whichever of these HR activities are included, it is important to note that WP, WIP and SWP are seen as dynamic HR tools. A precursor to WP, WIP and SWP is the agreement of the organisation's senior management team, engagement and buy-in from managers and HR responses that are both 'joined up' and integrated. Once the plan has been prepared, then communications with and engagement of the organisation's leaders and line managers will be critical success factors.

From the above discussion you can see that WP/WIP/SWP provides a huge challenge for HR, and implementation is not without difficulty. These difficulties include:

- HR planners not having access to business planning.
- WP/WIP/SWP given low priority by senior management.
- The HR function is not skilled to execute WP/WIP (Khatri, 2000).

HRM IN PRACTICE

Examples of WP and WIP in practice

WP, and more lately WIP/ SWP, is utilised in a wide variety of private and public sector organisations across the world. Examples below highlight some of the organisations where the HR function has engaged with WP.

- **Hewlett Packard** claims that the planning and staffing of projects will greatly influence the effectiveness of the organisation, customer satisfaction and staff morale (Firth, 2012). It therefore uses WP to match skills against projects worldwide. In addition, the company looks to the long term by a process referred to as 'Labour Strategy Optimization'. In both cases, WP is important to the company, delivering its objectives through the effective deployment of its people.

- **Starbucks** uses WP in both a strategic and operational sense as the organisation 'leverages quantitative and qualitative measures of the workforce current state and future state perspectives'. WP allows the company to identify and focus on the most critical aspects of the workforce, and the analysis is then used to inform a wide range of HR activity from talent management to the development of an employee value proposition (Kelly and All, 2013).

- **Tesco**, with some 500,000 employees worldwide, uses WP to establish the likely demand for new managerial and non-managerial staff. Regular reviews of workforce information and forecasts allow the company to anticipate and plan for the required staffing levels and achieve both flexibility in the workforce and the attainment of the company's strategic objectives (*The Times*, 2013).

- **Capital One** applies WP as part of the management of its global workforce by modelling 'outcomes like attrition rates, employee morale, and rates of promotion. Among the factors they consider in their models are aspects of the organizational chart – span of control, levels of hierarchy, which affects promotion rates, and positions that are reserved for developmental assignments' (Cappelli, 2009). The HR planning team works with the business unit leaders to develop models around their particular business plans to align the talent management practices with those business goals. The company approach helps the leadership of the business to look ahead at talent requirements and HR/labour costs.

- **Both the UK and USA Navies** apply WP tools as an integral part of their human resources activity. In the USA, workforce planning is used to 'link workforce requirements directly to the agency's mission and strategic and annual business plans; develop a comprehensive picture of where gaps exist between competencies the workforce currently possesses and future competency requirements; and identify and implement gap

(Continued)

(Continued)

reduction strategies' (Department of the Navy, 2013). In the UK, the Royal Navy has one of the 'most complex HR tasks in the UK when it comes to WP ... satisfying the level of demand for personnel, but avoiding an over-supply of staff'. In order to achieve these objectives there is a fine balance between 'focusing on recruitment and retention strategies'. WP provides the information on which such decisions can be made (Stevens, 2010).

- **The Australian public sector** uses WP in order to meet organisational objectives. The Australian National Audit Office (ANAO) describes WP as a key strategic activity of the organisation's corporate planning process, enabling it to best use its human capital to achieve its outputs and outcomes. Freyens (2010) cites a range of organisations applying these principles.

- **Boeing (US)** promotes an approach to SWP that incorporates having the right conversation with its business leaders, including questions designed to help leaders think critically about their workforce: 'Which skills make or break your business strategy? What is the culture of your workforce? Where does your skill pipeline reside?' (Peterson and Krieger, 2013: 43).

- **Texaco (US)** developed the Texaco Guide to Strategic Workforce Planning in 1994, the shared view being that, 'individuals exist within a larger talent context, and a plan is no stronger than its weakest component' (Ward, 2013: 15). The evolution has seen changes that reflect the criticisms of traditional manpower planning, and as part of the scenario planning now consider what are the pros and cons of virtual organisations.

- **The Raytheon Company (Homeland Security, USA)** views talent management as central to SWP. Its aim is to attract and retain high flyers in line with the business strategy (Motion, 2013). This work starts with understanding the current workforce and asks questions around what is driving the gap, for example replacement or growth. Canada and the USA have a successful track record of implementing talent management strategies designed around filling competency gaps (Huerta-Melchor, 2013). Talent management is complemented by new types of metrics for talent development principles (Shapiro and Davenport, 2013).

ONLINE STUDY TOOLS

Writing an essay? Expand your knowledge

Anderson (2004) discusses the metric of workforce planning in this classic article.

https://edge.sagepub.com/crawshaw2e > **Student Resources** > **Chapter 5** > **Journal Articles**

Whatever term (WP/WIP/WSP) is adopted, workforce planning has evolved to become an integral part of business strategy. The recognition of behavioural and cultural considerations in delivering strategy, and the essential role of HR in that process, marks the progress. A key objective will be to ensure alignment of the make-up of the workforce to the longer-term, sustainable aims of the organisation, including a built-in flexibility to allow for change (Turner, 2010).

GRADUATE INSIGHTS

Business transformation at Birmingham City Council (UK)

The case study below shows how Birmingham City Council (BCC) developed a WIP plan as part of its strategic activity, incorporating WIP into its Business Transformation Programme. To support this work the Council part-funded an ESRC PhD Case Award and a student (Ann) joined them for three years. Ann worked with the WIP team and focused on the line manager experience of the transformation process, noting particularly how they adapted to taking on more HR tasks as a part of their role. This included conducting focus groups with line managers to understand their perspective of being given more HR responsibility, and how that had changed their role. As Ann identified, the WIP team, who are part of the HR function, designed a five-step model (see Figure 6.1) that enables managers to examine drivers for change, assess the needs of the service user, and consider implications for job roles, ways of working and skills requirements.

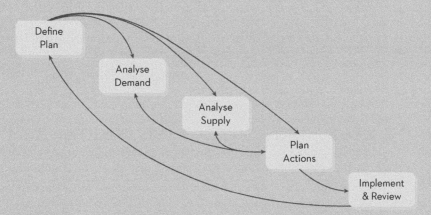

FIGURE 6.1 Birmingham City Council's five-step change model

Thus BCC:

- Conceptualised a WIP model;
- Adapted the plan to the new IT system that had been introduced;
- Integrated WIP with Business Planning; used Horizon Planning to identify, attract and build future skill needs; introduced a Talent Management Programme to identify leaders and retain people with the right skills and behaviours; identified and minimised barriers;
- Engaged the workforce with a new performance development review (PDR) system that is conducted by line managers; and
- Developed an intelligence hub with external organisations.

Ann also noted the importance of 'HR devolvement to line managers' at BCC and how this 'contributes towards staff engagement and innovative behaviour', themes that became central to her PhD research.

Understanding the Process of workforce planning, workforce intelligence planning and strategic workforce planning

Using the following texts as a support: Baron, A., Clarke, R., Pass, S. and Turner, P. (2010) *Workforce Planning: Right People, Right Time, Right Skills*. London: CIPD; Ward, D. and Tripp, R., with Maki, B. (eds) (2013) *Positioned: Strategic Workforce Planning that Gets the Right Person in the Right Job*. New York: AMACOM/American Management Association.

1   Identify the workforce planning definition and the key stages for its preparation.

2   Identify the additional behavioural, cultural and organisational factors included in WIP/SWP.

TASK: Working in teams, design a workforce intelligence plan for a case organisation of your choice.

WHY ARE WP, WIP AND SWP IMPORTANT?

THE HR FUNCTION IN RELATION TO WIP AND THE ORGANISATION

The HR role has a vital role to play in the development of WIP, for three reasons. First, HR will be critical to the development of competitive advantage and responsive to the dynamic nature of the global economy by having sufficient numbers of skilled people in place. Second, HR professionals will work on the development of the organisation strategy to implement WIP. Ulrich et al. (2012) have highlighted two competencies that will be important to HR professionals in implementing WIP: *strategic positioner* and *capability builder*.

- **Strategic positioner** – HR professionals can apply knowledge such as information about labour market dynamics, social forces and demographic trends as well as customer requirements, and place this in the context of developing their own workforces. Combining this information with knowledge of workforce behaviours will be the 'workforce intelligence' that will help to secure competitive advantage.

- **Capability builder** – HR professionals can transform individual abilities into an effective and strong organisation.

Third, the workforce plan will ensure the reduction of risk (Klosk, 2013). WP will equip HR with insights into the shape and structure of the organisation over time and minimise risk by helping the organisation to understand the nature of its current and future workforce and achieve its objectives even in difficult economic circumstances. This understanding enables HR to work with employees and provide skills that will make them more agile. The outcomes of these areas of focus are outlined in more detail as follows.

HR'S ROLE IN PLANNING THE CURRENT AND FUTURE WORKFORCE

Ulrich et al. (2012) suggest that HR professionals can provide insightful interventions about the current and future workforce. Based on this important HR role, a question facing all organisations is, how can we envisage the workforce in five, 10 and 15 years? The answer to this, which is sometimes referred to as 'workforce visibility', will determine almost every aspect of HR policy. Future workforce numbers, types of employees and location of employees are three areas of visibility that will come out of the WP and WIP. In turn this will determine recruitment and retention, training and development and reward and recognition. But, to be successful, the workforce plan will also provide insights into aspects of succession planning to senior teams, organisation design and the desired culture. The WP and the WIP/SWP are sources of intelligence across the spectrum of people's activity in the organisation.

- At a strategic level the WP/WIP/SWP will show what an organisation needs to do in respect of its human assets to achieve competitive advantage. It will show which aspects of talent management require most attention, whether there are sufficient skills in key areas and where there is a need for HR interventions.

- At an operational level, WP/WIP/SWP will provide intelligence on recruitment over the period of the plan or changes in business. It will provide visibility on redeployment or redundancy as the business strategy evolves and emphasis is placed on different areas (such as closing down older locations and replacing existing products or services with newer ones). It will provide insights on training needs in both the short and long term.

- To achieve this task, the organisation needs to understand demographic characteristics (Buahenee, 2009), such as an ageing workforce, and build these differences into any future plans. If the WP, WIP and SWP lead to actions that can build on the demographic differences, then this has the potential to add to organisational success:

  > Changing demographic realities, rapid technological advances, and ever-evolving globalization dictate that it's time to get focused and serious about creating diverse and inclusive workplaces that drive performance and spark innovation. (Deloitte, 2011)

HR'S ROLE IN PLANNING WORKFORCE AGILITY

Workforce agility is the organisation's human resource responsiveness that would allow it to deal with organisational change. Ulrich (1992) suggested that one of the key aims of planning is to develop flexibility, which means the adaptability and mobility of employees to undertake a range of tasks and/or employ a variety of skills. This is now often referred to as workforce agility. The CIPD (2011: 6) identified the characteristics of workforce agility as 'the ability to stay open to new directions and be continually proactive, helping to assess the limits or risks of existing approaches and ensuring that leaders and followers have an agile and change-ready mind-set to enable them, and ultimately the organisation, to keep moving, changing, adapting'.

Workforce agility The organisation's human resource responsiveness that would allow it to deal with organisational change and adapt quickly to internal and external opportunities and challenges.

Through workforce planning, an organisation can anticipate changes in both the marketplace and the workforce, and mobilise appropriate resources. A systematised approach to this process gives an organisation the ability to change more quickly than its competitors and effectively maximise its return on investments in talent. For private and public organisations, workforce planning can be the difference between a successful business offering and a missed opportunity.

In summary, the HR function has a role in collecting robust information and evidence-based intelligence on which it can act to build agility and responsiveness through its human resources that will allow it to be successful in an unpredictable economic environment.

MINI CASE STUDY

WIP in progress: Higgs & Sons (2015 – ongoing)

Higgs & Sons is a successful legal firm that employs in excess of 200 people. The HR Department has engaged the workforce in a 'My Future' HR initiative, and to maintain a cutting edge in HR in support of the firm's business strategy the firm's Managing Partner and HR Director agreed to introduce WIP into Higgs & Sons. The first phase of WIP has been designed to:

- Establish WIP in the HR Department and align it to the firm's business plan.
- Engage senior leadership in the design.
- Engage all employees, both legal and support staff, in the design.
- Include a focus on the wider enterprise – to ascertain how changes in wider stakeholders' needs (e.g. courts, insurance companies, Ministry of Justice) were changing and could affect WIP in Higgs & Sons.
- Understand the future client context by engaging with the wider enterprise.
- Conduct a formative and subsequent evaluation to ensure the sustainability of WIP.
- Design a WIP model which included internal and external factors.
- Design a 'One Team' survey.
- Pilot WIP in three areas.

Higgs & Sons gained funding from Innovate UK for a Knowledge Transfer Partnership (KTP), to which they also contribute. A KTP associate was appointed and joined the HR team under the supervision of the HR Director, as well as an academic supervisor from Aston University. Progress was monitored by Innovate UK.

In order to engage the workforce and partners in the WIP design and implementation, interviews and focus groups were initially undertaken with business owners and staff members, to identify their needs and glean innovative approaches from their experience. The findings highlighted a raft of employee and senior management ideas, as well as the IT package requirements for successful WIP implementation. The findings have informed a 'One Team' WIP plan that has been developed and will be put into practice at the next stage. The WIP planning design includes a systematised HR approach to WIP, a HR modelling tool and a 'One Team' annual survey to measure the impact of WIP as part of the evaluation. For example, the evaluation survey will identify the success of 'boundary spanners', who work across different departments, and understand how this improves the client base. Higgs & Sons will be able to measure the success of WIP as it progresses.

The intention of this project was to extend WIP to include the behaviours of external stakeholders and clients who are not part of Higgs & Sons but whose changing requirements may affect the overall number, type of skills and behaviours of Higgs & Sons' workforce. Understanding these exogenous forces should help strategic WIP implementation. For instance, the pace of change towards a requirement for fixed-priced legal work, unbundling and online delivery of services may influence and inform behavioural change in Higgs & Sons' culture towards a 'Managed Professional Business' (MPB) type operation in some disciplines rather than a more traditional 'Professional Partnership' (P2) type operation (Pinnington and Morris, 2003). Inevitably this will have a dramatic impact upon WP, WIP and SWP.

TASKS: *Discuss in a group:*

1   The practical implications of HR owning the planning process.

2   The types of behavioural tools that HR could introduce.

3   How HR will ensure that WIP is sustainable.

4   How to effectively include exogenous factors from key stakeholders in the planning process.

UNPACKING THE WP, WIP AND SWP DEFINITION THROUGH SHRM

The following three sections show how the behavioural concepts in the definitions of WP/WIP/SWP are evidenced in SHRM theoretical models. You will have seen that a lot of the discussion about WP/WIP/SWP has been from practitioners and consultants. Our next task is to consider what academic evidence can support WIP. Chapters 1 and 2 inform this part of the discussion.

Establishing a theoretical base is important, given that both WP and WIP have been critiqued for being practitioner-based and not having an evidence base to show that they work (Sinclair, 2004). In general, the 1960s are cited as the rise of workforce planning and the 1980s as the fall (Sullivan, 2002, cited in Sinclair, 2004). It is suggested that the fall coincides with the failure of workforce planning to identify the economic downturn despite the focus on head counting and the corresponding statistical quantitative analysis. While the 1990s witnessed a resurgence of WP, it has subsequently been viewed as an area of study that has not engaged the academic community. However, the introduction of behavioural issues has brought WIP/SWP closer to mainstream SHRM. The sections below show how management and SHRM theory can inform the behavioural 'intelligence' aspect of WIP.

SCIENTIFIC MANAGEMENT, SKILLS AND MOTIVATION

Early Management studies (Taylor, 1911; Trist and Bamford, 1951) and SHRM studies (Delery and Doty, 1996; Guest, 1997; Huselid and Becker, 1996; Katou and

Budhwar, 2006; Purcell et al., 2003) show us that we cannot separate the right skills from the right behaviours.

Contemporary organisations, such as the motor organisation Ford (Beynon, 1973) and outsourced call centres (Clegg et al., 2005), draw on management theory from the early 20th century to ensure that they have the right skills, abilities and behaviours required to execute workforce intelligence planning. 'Taylorism' workforce planning focused on skills and motivation and is based on Taylor's (1911) observations of the process by which a US steelworks recruited and organised its workforce, which he deemed as inefficient. As previously discussed in Chapter 1, Taylor redesigned the job role and skills required through a scientific method whereby skills were broken down into routine tasks to improve efficiency. By introducing a highly routinised design of skills, Taylor is criticised for likening humans to machines (Hackman and Oldham, 1980). Taylor also believed that the main motivational aspect to work is pay, an idea that has been greatly contested (Purcell et al., 2003). For WP the practice of breaking down skills into small tasks is still common to both production and knowledge areas. The latter area has become known as 'digital Taylorism' (Aston et al., 2009). There is some evidence to show that the routinisation of skills is dominant in the production and knowledge areas that are outsourced to other countries. For some transnational corporations, for example in Germany, this can amount to up to 80 per cent of the workforce (Aston et al., 2009). There is also a geographical shift of skill design in supply chains, such as clothing sectors, where management skills are also outsourced as well as routinised production skills (Sparrow and Brewster, 2006).

THE HUMAN RELATIONS MOVEMENT, SKILLS AND MOTIVATION

In contrast to the scientific management approach which advocates routine skill acquisition, multinational organisations, such as Google and Microsoft, have adapted a different behavioural model that was developed by the human relations movement at the Tavistock Institute, London. This theory stems from a study of British coal mining (Trist and Bamford, 1951). The research suggested that leadership had failed to understand or plan for the inevitable interdependent relationship between social and technical systems that was necessary for high productivity within the organisation; these weaknesses require increased consideration of exogenous forces which act upon the workforce. The study illustrates a different approach and links skills to behavioural issues, including leadership behaviours and staff motivation. The authors' findings highlighted the behavioural aspect of human relations, a model that is widely adapted today and informed the development of HR.

Theoretically, the two early management models discussed above are at different ends of a continuum. The important learning point is that different types of skill design can influence different behaviours. Currently, most international organisations use a combination of skills and consider behavioural issues when they plan their workforce.

SHRM MODELS AND THE HR FUNCTION

The human resource management debates from the 1980s onwards deliberated on how to ensure that workforce planning was completely integrated with the strategic needs of the business and operationalised through the organisation's business plans. Following Schuler and Jackson's (1987) argument for aligning workforce plans strategically, Schuler (1992) developed a five-stage planning model; while Budhwar and Sparrow (2002) proposed four generic strategies:

- Talent acquisition, that is, attracting the best human resource talent from external sources.

- Effective resource allocation, that is, maximising the use of existing human resources by always having the right person in the right place at the right time.

- Talent improvement, that is, maximising talents of existing employees by training and guidance.

- Cost reduction, designed to reduce the costs of personnel.

These four generic strategies are core to current workforce intelligence planning strategy. However, debate suggests that the HR function internationally is not generally skilled to execute WIP, particularly because HR is not aligned to the design and formulation of strategic planning (Purcell and Ahlstrand, 1994). A study in Singapore confirmed the difficulties for HR managers, who were conducting WP without being given the appropriate skills or being privy to a working knowledge of organisational strategies (Khatri, 2000). This raises the question of the competencies of the HR function in relation to the design, implementation and sustainability of WIP/SWP.

EMPLOYEE ENGAGEMENT AND WP/WIP

NHS Health Education England (2013) and the Department of Health National Centre for Workforce Intelligence (2012) emphasise employee engagement as a behavioural issue that is integral to the success of WIP. Both draw on the UK National Health Service (NHS) constitution to justify the 'need to engage staff in decisions that affect them and the services they provide' (NHS Health Education England, 2013: 10). As such, workforce engagement is important to WP/WIP/SWP because it is viewed as a means by which organisations can keep their workforce positively related to organisational commitment (Demerouti et al., 2001).

HR skills for WP/WIP

The HR function at Birmingham City Council used the Ulrich model (Ulrich, 1997) to develop six HR centres of expertise, each headed by an HR business partner. HR centres of expertise were established at the local level and focused on the development of a flexible workforce, agile working and the increased capability of manager–employee intranet use to implement performance development reviews.

TASK: Thinking about the key points in the Ulrich (1997) model and/or the Budhwar and Sparrow (2002) model, reflect upon the skills and competencies needed by the HR function to effectively implement WP/WIP.

DEBATING HRM

How SHRM models inform WP/WIP success

Engaging staff is a key theme of the SHRM models. For example, the universalistic model proposes that the involvement of staff in job design, staff engagement and empowerment strategies will improve commitment, motivation and job satisfaction (Boxall and Purcell, 2003; Huselid, 1995; Pfeffer, 1994). Similarly, contingency models take into account the engagement and behaviour of employees. Guest (2002) suggests two approaches. The first involves staff in decision-making processes such as effective team working (West, 1994).

The second approach suggests the use of HR tools to measure whether there is improved organisational performance (Guest, 1997; Huselid and Becker, 1996). For example, these can include staff engagement mechanisms such as staff surveys, staff involvement groups and quality circles to measure engagement. There is also broad agreement in configurational models that devolvement of HR practices to line managers contributes towards effective employee engagement which then leads to better organisational performance (Delery and Doty, 1996; Katou and Budhwar, 2006). Collectively, SHRM models evidence as to why key concepts of strategic human resource management debates relating to skills, motivation and engagement are essential for understanding the behavioural aspects of WIP/SWP.

TASKS: Working in groups and with reference to Chapter 2 and the overview above, debate the following issues:

1   Why do SHRM models encourage organisations to engage their workforce?

2   What types of staff engagement activities would support the HR function to measure workforce engagement?

3   How can the HR function encourage staff engagement through line managers?

There are a number of different definitions in the concept of employee engagement. For example, the behaviours identified in the Schaufeli et al. (2008) definition of work engagement are vigour, dedication and absorption. These engagement behaviours are seen to promote motivation and commitment and to drive innovation in the organisation. The HR activity to assess the extent of employee engagement has been a key theme in the SHRM literature. A comprehensive account of the SHRM models can be found in Chapter 2. The discussion below shows the types of HR activities that have been identified in SHRM studies as useful for measuring the extent of employee engagement in an organisation, and the rationale for implementing them.

LEADERSHIP SKILLS, MOTIVATION AND WP/WIP/SWP IMPLEMENTATION

In relation to the leadership involvement in SWP, Ulrich (2013: 277) raises the important question, 'What do our leaders need to be good at to make this strategy happen?'

He then suggests that the role of leaders includes being meaning makers, who enable their workforce to achieve positive meaning through their work contribution. Also, HR professionals contribute to this meaningful organisation by providing the appropriate architecture. Ulrich (2013: 282) suggests five ways by which HR can support leadership: build the business case for leadership; define leadership effectiveness from the outside/in (involving external and internal stakeholders); assess leaders; invest in leadership; and measure leadership (Kirkpatrick's scale, attitude, knowledge, behaviour and results are cited as an example).

With regard to the implementation of WP/WIP/SWP, research evidence tells us that while top team management needs to take ownership of the plan (Bass et al., 2003), implementation will generally be delivered by line managers (Purcell et al., 2003). A key behavioural aspect of workforce planning is the effect of different leadership skills on employee behaviour and engagement. These are important to workforce planning since the delivery of the plan will depend on both employee and leadership performance. These aspects of leadership are discussed below. First, the skills and behaviours of transformational leadership are shown to inspire and motivate. Second, the skills and behaviours necessary for line managers to deliver the organisation's plan are shown in transactional leadership. Both styles are necessary for implementing WP/WIP/SWP.

TRANSFORMATIONAL LEADERSHIP

The role of senior leadership is important for WIP because it can inspire employees to trust their leader through organisational change and perform at a higher level. However, there are different types of leadership, and the behaviours in some types of leadership are more inspirational than others. Two key studies (Bass, 1985; Kotter, 1995) argue for the importance of transformational or visionary leadership in organisational change. Both provide behavioural models that show the behaviours and skills to promote that vision through senior management. There are four components in the Bass (1985) model that show the leadership behaviours and skills necessary for organisational change:

- **Inspirational motivation:** leaders articulate a vision which is appealing and inspiring to followers (articulate an inspiring vision, set the task and promote optimism regarding the achievability of the vision).

- **Idealised influence:** display conviction, develop role-modelling behaviours consistent with a vision, appeal and influence staff at an emotional level.

- **Intellectual stimulation:** leaders stimulate and encourage creativity, gather evidence and ideas and put them into practice.

- **Individualised consideration**: mentor or coach and listen to staff concerns and needs.

Similarly, Kotter (1995) focuses on the role of senior management leadership and conceptualises an eight-stage process that is driven by the behaviours and skills of the leader who, in the face of organisational change, creates a sense of urgency and involves the workforce, builds a stakeholder coalition of leaders that produces intelligence, creates a vision, communicates change, empowers employees, provides short-term wins, consolidates gains and embeds change in the organisational culture (see Chapter 3).

TRANSACTIONAL LEADERSHIP AT THE LINE MANAGER LEVEL

In contrast, Mintzberg (2004) believes that the role of leadership should be focused at the line manager level. Mintzberg is somewhat sceptical of the success of WP, given that all planning is subject to change. Using IBM as the example, he argues that it is not enough to cite individual senior leaders as the only drivers of organisational change. He suggests that leaders should also be selected further down the organisation. Line managers are cited for this leadership role because they have their roots in the organisation and are closer to the workforce. (See Chapter 1, where Crawshaw and Hatch explain the case for and against line managers having HR responsibility.) The evidence-based model (Purcell et al., 2003) outlined below (discussed in Chapter 2 by Katou and Budhwar) also stresses the importance of line manager transactional style leadership. The model below shows how line managers can contribute towards leading WP/WIP/SWP.

DEBATING HRM

Leadership and WIP

Purcell et al. (2003) found that when employees are dissatisfied with their line manager this has a greater impact in terms of the lowering of commitment and productivity than does any other factor. In contrast, employees are more likely to go above and beyond their contract if front-line managers behave in a way that encourages positive attitudes and discretionary behaviours. Purcell et al. (2003) used the term 'black box' to signify how line manager leadership behaviours, together with recruiting people with the right skills, abilities and motivation, can potentially improve performance. Their study depicts a framework that specifies three minimal requirements for employee performance: ability, motivation and opportunity (the AMO model is presented in Chapter 2 by Katou and Budhwar). In essence, the model suggests that people perform better when:

- They have the Ability to do so, in terms of skills and knowledge.
- They are Motivated to do well.
- They are given the Opportunity to learn skills and contribute towards work success.

TASKS: *Working in groups:*

1   Discuss what evidence Purcell et al. (2003) have given us for understanding the importance of line managers' transactional leadership for WIP.

2   Discuss the strengths and difficulties of giving line managers HR responsibility.

3   Debate why senior leadership support from HR is viewed as important to implement WIP/SWP.

EXTERNAL INTELLIGENCE AND EVALUATION MODELS

The previous section showed how skills cannot be separated from behaviours, and how motivation, employee engagement techniques and leadership models are evidenced in management and SHRM models. All of these issues need to be considered in the design, implementation and sustainability of WIP/SWP. This section looks at some of the external intelligence that is available. The focus is on horizon planning and how organisations can use scenario planning to think outside the box to develop WP/WIP/SWP.

HORIZON PLANNING

Horizon planning is not just about looking within the organisation to understand the workforce skills and abilities, it is also about looking externally at the situational context to understand what trends are on the horizon. In general, workforce plans are designed for the short term (one year), medium term (three years) and long term (five years plus). However, the more uncertain the situation, the more likely is the time plan to be shorter. It is also worthwhile being cautious when optimising such plans in organisations where planning can be regarded as continuously changing due to contextually specific external factors. Consequently, most organisations turn to external government organisations to identify the external trends and statistics necessary for horizon planning and gaining intelligence. UK governmental and associated organisations most used for horizon planning include:

- Foresight website: www.foresight.gov.uk/horizonscanning/
- Social trend data: www.statistics.gov.uk/socialtrends37/
- Performance survey trend data: www.statistics.gov.uk
- OECD website: www.oecd.org
- Office for National Statistics website: www.statistics.gov.uk
- Institute for Public Policy Research (IPPR) website: www.ippr.org.uk/publicationsandreports/publication.asp? id=544

When we consider population trends, such as those raised by the census, these highlight policy issues that have a direct impact on the workforce **supply and demand**. Horizon planners (www.statistics.gov.uk/socialtrends37/) provide the data to justify the need to upskill the workforce in line with the global economy. Demographic characteristics are particularly important for WP/WIP. For example, in the UK the postwar double spike in birth rate and the year-on-year reduction of premature deaths have resulted in a growing number of people living beyond the age of 80. This means that we are entering a period of change where there will be a significant shift in balance of the population towards the older. By 2030 the population of England will have grown by 5 million and nearly 90 per cent of this rise will be of people aged 60 and over (www.foresight.gov.uk/horizonscanning/).

The finer detail informs us that generations X (born 1965–1977) and Y (1980–1990s) work better together than baby boomers (born 1950–1965) and that X and Y are more

Horizon planning   Horizon planning is not just about looking within the organisation to understand the workforce skills and abilities, it is also about looking externally at the situational context to understand what trends are on the horizon. These can be a range of trends such as demographic, economic and political trends. Most government organisations provide information on workforce trends on websites that are used by horizon planners.

inclined towards entrepreneurship and more likely to migrate to other countries in pursuit of business opportunities (Henwood and Pidgeon, 2013). X and Y are seen as responsible for the current economic growth in India and China. What does this mean for workforce skills in the UK and globally? Does this mean that the UK will experience a migration outflow of its skilled workforce to the more technically advanced economies, as predicted by international HRM? HR functions frequently approach these problems through an activity termed scenario planning, which is discussed below.

SCENARIO PLANNING – WHAT IF?

Scenario planning is 'a way of building a mind-set aimed at anticipation' (Turner, 2002) and is used by some organisations to analyse future situations. It can be a valuable and complementary process to workforce planning. Some scenarios that might be considered are:

- Serious shortfalls in a skill area that is critical to the achievement of the business objectives and on which delivery of the workforce plan is dependent. How would the organisation deal with such a problem? What would be the HR response?

- Serious behavioural failures in a sector where there has been a lack of leadership and staff motivation, and organisational efficiency has deteriorated to the point of serious neglect of the organisation's client base. How would the organisation approach this problem? How would the WIP plan incorporate the behavioural changes required?

- Market or economic conditions that were not anticipated in the strategic or workforce plan. How would the organisation deal with these? What would be the effect on the workforce? Is the organisation agile enough to deliver its objectives in the face of such changes?

- Changing requirements of key external stakeholders which include clients and customers, regulatory bodies, partners and suppliers and which may have social, economic and technical implications for any given organisation, causing them to have to rethink their workforce profile.

Frequently organisations will use horizon and scenario planning to recruit (internal and external) stakeholders with the appropriate expertise to attempt to think the unthinkable, and use this type of intelligence to decide how to plan their workforce. In the next section we address a valid critique of WP/WIP, namely that there is a lack of evaluation and performance measurement models that can validate the efficiency of WIP. Hence a range of models is considered for WIP evaluation.

THE CRITIQUE OF WP/WIP: EVALUATION

Although numerous organisations use WP/WIP, Sinclair (2004) suggests that it needs robust evidence to show that it works. SHRM theorists persistently strive to measure and evaluate performance and we consider how some of these models can be applied to evaluating WP/WIP. Traditionally, performance has been interpreted as measurable outputs, and is dependent on the skill that the individual brings to the job.

Scenario planning
Encourages staff to think outside the box and conceptualise a 'what if' situation. It is used by some organisations to analyse future situations. It can be a valuable and complementary process to workforce planning. For example, staff might be considered to think about how an organisation might survive if there were serious behavioural problems in the workforce that impacted on their core service or product delivery. Scenario planning also enables the managers to visualise the impact of an ageing workforce, consider succession planning and balance skill levels to address potential skills gaps.

However, effective performance relies at least as much on the staff behaviours as on how that skill is carried out (Davis and Scully, 2008). The models below incorporate the behavioural aspects of skills.

Evaluation of business plans and employee performance

A model that combines qualitative and quantitative methodology in a mixed method evaluation (Bryman, 2001) is Pritchard's (1990) model, where business plans and employee performance are integrated with productivity. Pritchard (1990) defines productivity as how well a system uses its resources to achieve its goals and objectives. This amounts to measuring organisational inputs such as WIP, and processes such as skill acquisition and behaviours, as well as performance outputs and achieving goals. Pritchard (1990) advises organisations to be aware that the goals they strive for are realistically challenging. In this model the evaluation of WIP starts at the developmental stage and continues through the evolution, to provide evidence of how it can better equip organisations with the capacity to survive in an unknowable future.

Competency evaluation

Competence has been cited as an integral feature of WIP/SWP because competence involves having the right skills, right place, right time (Ulrich, 2013). Sparrow and Hiltrop (1994) discuss employee performance in terms of competencies with respect to seven elements. These include:

1. Knowledge, to carry out the position and achieve the expected goals.

2. Skills, to carry out the job in an effective manner.

3. Positive attitude and values, to connect with the task.

> **Evaluating WP/WIP**
>
> The Department of Health National Centre for Workforce Intelligence (www.cfwi.org.uk) has developed a set of metrics that enables organisations to select and evaluate workforce planning models. This entails a mathematical representation based on workforce supply and demand. The models are designed for different types of organisation and different departments within organisations. They support organisations in assessing horizon trends in relation to their organisation, analyse workforce supply and demand, assess skill needs and assist talent management for their future workforce.
>
> TASK: Drawing on one or more of the models from the website above, outline your key criteria when designing a model to evaluate WP/WIP.

4. Traits, person-specific qualities and characteristics, whereby the individual responds to the role in an effective way.

5. Motivation, the drive to carry out one's job.

6. Self-image, through self-awareness.

7. Social role, an understanding of how to behave in a particular context, based upon social norms and expectations.

Competencies are recognised as a behavioural approach to evaluating performance because they focus on the behavioural approach to the task, as well as the skills, knowledge and abilities needed for the job. Boyatzis (1982) recognised this distinction in his work competencies, viewing the behavioural aspects of an individual as mediators that enhance or hinder work performance.

The evaluation models have identified the importance of including the behavioural aspects in WP/WIP/SWP. They have started to address two critiques of WP/WIP/SWP: first, that the area of study lacks evidence-based research and academic rigour; the second critique is that there is a lack of evaluation studies. A third critique of WP/WIP/SWP concerns the skills of HR implementation of WP/WIP/SWP. The case study below gives a practical example of HR skills.

CASE STUDY

WP modelling in Birmingham City Council (2007 – ongoing)

The WIP team within the HR Directorate at BCC helped with the strategic planning to support the organisation to introduce WIP. The maturity of the IT system enabled the WIP team to model scenarios regarding the workforce, budgets related to the employees, demographics, job families, ratio planning, voluntary redundancy costs and agency, management and leadership ratios. In addition, WIP was able to model relevant staff reductions in line with government austerity measures, to help BCC understand the challenges that it faced and how these would feed through to the relevant services and individual directorates of the Council. The complex modelling helped senior managers and strategic leaders to consider internal and external changes to their staffing needs:

- Managers could link the number of births to the number of school places required in the next three to four years, in order to estimate the number of head teachers required.
- Scenario planning enables the managers to visualise the impact of an ageing workforce, consider succession planning and balance skill levels to address potential skills gaps.

The capability of scenario planning has enabled BCC to test policies and financial plans against these scenarios and make more informed strategic decisions than it has been able to do before. Both micro and macro aspects have been built into the scenario planning, linking the WIP team with external agencies to obtain various data sets including employment data, demographic trends, industry trends and technology trends.

Challenges facing the BCC WIP team

The key challenges faced by the WIP team ranged from establishing data modelling techniques and influencing behavioural change to contributing towards developing a different culture within an organisation with a wide range of stakeholders. Increasing HR's capability was also fundamental to the success of workforce intelligence planning within the organisation. To achieve this objective, the WIP team ran a number of knowledge transfer sessions with HR business partners, HR leaders and the operations team to ensure understanding and use of the workforce planning techniques.

Another challenge for the WIP team included changing the behaviours of some of the key stakeholders, an example being the Human Resource Business Partners (HRBP) and the financial planners within the directorates. The key aspect of the behavioural change was the encouragement and coaching from the WIP team to facilitate HRBP and financial planners to work together and ensure the sharing of data and information, including planning ahead and exploring new service designs.

Talent management framework

Alongside the development of workforce planning modelling tools, the WIP team introduced a talent management and succession-planning programme. The programme works on a six-month cycle, in line with the Council's performance development review (PDR) for employees. Line managers lead the PDRs and follow a five-step process through the cycle, which involves: identifying critical roles; identifying talented individuals; agreeing succession and development plans with peers; putting in place plans with individuals; and reviewing progress.

CASE STUDY QUESTIONS

1 What are the workforce planning challenges at BCC?

2 How can senior leaders ensure that employees have the appropriate skills and behaviours?

3 As a senior manager, how would you use horizon-planning information to develop workforce intelligence planning?

4 How could HR managers most effectively balance workforce supply and development to changing stakeholder requirements?

5 How do line managers contribute towards WP/WIP?

CHAPTER SUMMARY

Conceptually and practically, workforce intelligence planning has evolved over the last four decades. The concept of workforce planning replaced the concept of manpower planning in the 1970s and by the early 21st century the thinking behind workforce planning changed. In addition to organisations having the right skills at the right time in the right place, there was a recognition of the importance of having the 'right behaviours' as well as intelligence into the organisational culture and change management. This point is important because the chapter has explained the difference between workforce planning, workforce intelligence planning and strategic workforce planning. A practical task is to provide the tools for the HR function to implement WIP. The chapter has outlined the tools required in the design of WIP. Strategically, this also means that the HR function will need to be involved in the design of the strategic business plan. Thus the HR function will transform as it designs and implements WIP, and this will include tapping into external intelligence resources such as SHRM evidence-based theory and practice as well as internal perspectives. The key points that we have identified in this chapter are that:

- Organisations need to engage in WIP/SWP so that they remain productive and competitive through periods of change and stability in the wider environment.
- Gathering intelligence from different sources is essential to WIP/SWP. Engaging the workforce is a prerequisite for WIP.
- Horizon planning, scenario planning and talent management are aspects of the toolkit for WIP.
- SHRM provides the evidence base for the core behavioural concepts in WIP/SWP.
- Senior leaders need to be visionary to influence the workforce.
- Line managers at all levels of the organisation are the key conduits for the implementation of WP/WIP/SWP.
- The critique of WIP stems from a weak evidence base, lack of evaluation, lack of external stakeholder input and HR not being involved in the strategic plan.
- Birmingham City Council has developed and implemented an innovative model for WIP.
- Higgs & Sons is pioneering the long awaited evaluation of WIP.

REVIEW QUESTIONS AND EXERCISES

1. Why has WP/WIP/SWP become such an important part of HR activity?
2. Why is it important to consider the behaviours of the workforce as well as their skills, knowledge and abilities?
3. What are the key stages of WP/WIP/SWP?
4. What skills and support does the HR function need to be able to execute WP/WIP/ SWP?
5. How can WIP/SWP be evaluated?
6. How can the HR function overcome the critique of WIP/SWP?

EXPLORE FURTHER

Francis, H., Holbech, L. and Reddington, M. (2012) *People and Organisational Development: A New Agenda for Organisational Effectiveness*. London: CIPD. An excellent practical text exploring different elements of people management and organisational effectiveness.

Lavelle, J. (2007) On workforce architecture, employment relationships and lifecycles: Expanding the purview of workforce planning and management. *Public Personnel Management*, 36(4): 374–385. An excellent article on contemporary issues of workforce planning and management.

Department of Health (DoH) National Centre for Workforce Intelligence publications; www.cfwi.org.uk. These are excellent sources for up-to-date statistics and information regarding the UK.

OECD Working Papers on Public Governance, No. 21, OECD Publishing; http://dx.doi.org/10.1787/5k487727gwvb-en These papers provide up-to-date information on SWP in OECD countries.

Pinnington, A. and Morris, T. (2003) Archetype change in professional organizations: Survey evidence from large law firms. *British Journal of Management*, 14(1): 85–99. Insight into the changing HR function of law firms.

GO ONLINE

Visit the companion website for **interactive quizzes**, explanatory **videos** and **podcasts, journal articles** to use in your essays, and **weblinks** to useful resources.

https://edge.sagepub.com/crawshaw2e

CHAPTER 7

RECRUITMENT AND SELECTION

Stephen A. Woods

Lara D. Zibarras

Daniel P. Hinton

CHAPTER KNOWLEDGE OBJECTIVES

- Understand the importance of recruitment and selection for organisational effectiveness and individual satisfaction, in the context of strategic human resource management.
- Understand the process of recruitment and selection, and methods used to attract and assess applicants and candidates.
- Appreciate the importance of fairness and ethics in the recruitment and selection processes.
- Understand the importance of reliability and validity in selection.
- Understand strategic and applicant-oriented perspectives on recruitment and selection.
- Understand the importance of fit in selection decision making and steps that can be taken in socialisation and integration of new recruits.

KEY SKILLS OBJECTIVES

- Develop a job or competency analysis framework for a specific organisation.
- Make informed choices about the appropriateness of different selection tools and methods.
- Evaluate the effectiveness of a selection process. Support and mentor new employees effectively through the organisational transition process.

This chapter provides indicative content for the following Intermediate and Advanced level CIPD modules:

CIPD INTERMEDIATE LEVEL MODULE

5RST Resourcing and talent planning

CIPD ADVANCED LEVEL MODULE

7RTM Resourcing and talent management

GO ONLINE

This chapter comes with loads of online tools to help you to go that extra mile in your studies!

- **Multiple choice questions** to help you test your knowledge and revise for exams
- **Journal articles** so you can read further for assignments and essays
- **Videos** and **podcasts** to help you to understand how complex concepts work in the real world

Visit **https://edge.sagepub.com/crawshaw2e** to access these resources for this topic.

INTRODUCTION

The importance of recruitment and selection in business and organisations is arguably the easiest concept to grasp in the practice of HRM. Consider for a moment the people you work with, either formally in employment, or informally in your studies or elsewhere. We can all relate to observations that people differ in their effectiveness at work and fundamentally in their strengths, skills and competencies. It is likewise easy to appreciate that jobs make different demands on people: simply consider the range of jobs in an organisation with which you are familiar.

Nevertheless, while it is very easy to understand the *need* for systematic and strategic recruitment and selection, developing an understanding of *how* to implement it at an organisational level is more difficult. This is particularly true in the context of strategic HRM because the vast majority of the recruitment and selection literature adopts a micro-HRM perspective, focusing on narrow issues and specific techniques. This leads to poor practice and a failure in too many (although certainly not all) organisations to apply an evidence-based approach to attracting and selecting effective and competent people.

In this chapter we will review some of the core issues and latest thinking in the recruitment and selection literature. Our chapter begins by contextualising and reviewing the foundations of effective recruitment and selection processes from a strategic HRM perspective. We draw heavily on the literature on selection that has accumulated in the field of work and organisational psychology, and consider specific assessment methodologies and their relative merits in different HRM contexts. We finally consider some of the wider ethical and social psychological issues associated with recruitment and selection.

EFFECTIVE RECRUITMENT AND SELECTION: A PRIMER

In this chapter, we define an effective approach to recruitment and selection as one that is:

- **Evidence-based**: this means that research and empirical evidence are used to inform the processes and procedures of recruitment and selection.

- **Systematic**: this means that processes follow a logical pathway whereby decisions are made sequentially and on the basis of sound analyses.

- **Strategic**: this means that recruitment and selection are performed with due attention to the strategic context of the HR function and the strategic needs of the organisation.

Recruitment The process of attracting people to join an organisation.

Selection The process of assessing people to determine their suitability to join an organisation.

The work and organisational psychology literature is rich in evidence about the validity of selection assessment methodologies and techniques (Woods and West, 2014). In this sense, the evidence base for effective recruitment and selection is wide ranging and high volume. The emphasis in most of this literature is on the effectiveness of systematic or structured techniques of selection (Zibarras and Woods, 2010). These might be defined as techniques that have a high degree of procedural methodology and clear processes of measurement and evaluation. The research literature, virtually without exception, points to the merits of such techniques (e.g. Schmidt and Hunter, 1998).

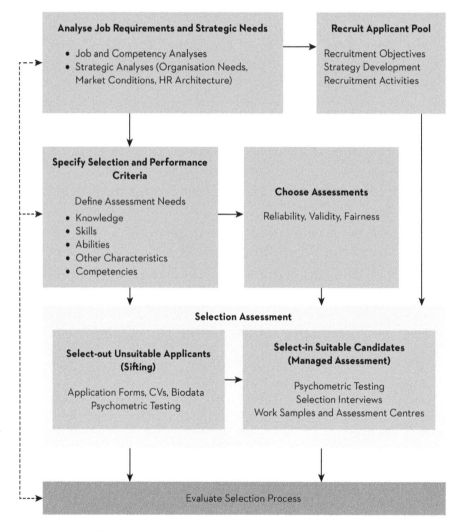

FIGURE 7.1 A model of the recruitment and selection process

Adapted from Woods and West (2014).

In systematic approaches to selection, a sequential process is followed that applies research or problem-solving logic to the recruitment and selection problem (e.g. Woods and West, 2014; see Figure 7.1). The process begins with job analysis, in which various techniques of research are applied to determine the work to be done and the various knowledge, skills, abilities and other characteristics/competencies that are required to deliver the work.

Based on the job analysis, recruitment activities are carried out to advertise and communicate job vacancies and attract job applicants by describing the tasks and person requirements alongside benefits and other information. Job analyses also guide decisions about selection criteria (i.e. upon what information will a selection decision be made?), and ultimately the choice of selection assessment techniques. Information about the reliability and validity of selection assessments also guides choices about which techniques to use.

Once selection assessments are chosen, and applicants attracted, the process of selection proceeds with the objective of narrowing down the applicant pool. Sifting techniques help selectors to make select-out decisions, rejecting those who are unsuitable because, for example, they do not meet the minimum mandatory requirements. Potentially suitable candidates are then assessed more carefully to determine who should be selected-in.

Once selected, recruits are managed into the organisation through induction and socialisation procedures, which we do not cover in this chapter. In reflective learning organisations, selection processes are evaluated to determine their effectiveness.

Many practitioners and academics present this kind of systematic process as robust and contemporary. While it is certainly robust, it is now more reasonable perhaps to see this methodology as quite traditional (Cascio and Aguinis, 2008). Developing a contemporary perspective on resourcing, recruitment and selection requires a better integration of the evidence base for structured and systematic recruitment and selection into a strategic HRM framework.

One key theme in the strategic HRM literature is the role of contingencies in the effectiveness of HR practices (e.g. Lengnick-Hall et al., 2009). Contingency theories emphasise that in certain scenarios specific practices are likely to be more or less effective than in others. This point is less frequently acknowledged in the traditional selection literature. Systematic selection as described above is typically grouped with other so-called high-performance work systems, and treated as universally effective (thereby constituting a potential practice for inclusion in the universal perspective, which identifies HR practices that always have a positive effect on performance; Lengnick-Hall et al., 2009).

It is possible to identify evidence for both positions, depending upon one's perspective. For example, the evidence from meta-analyses is consistently that structured selection is more effective than unstructured, informal techniques. Nevertheless, the utility of such techniques is predicated on being able to be very selective in decision making. The fact is that in some economies there is a dramatic under-supply of people with key skills and knowledge, meaning that selectors often do not have the luxury of selecting one person from a candidate pool of 20. Rather, they may be required to select one from three, one from two, or even two from every three candidates. So a selection ratio based on economic context is a key contingency that influences the effectiveness of structured selection practice.

Contingencies such as these and other strategic demands and objectives of organisations are central to the issue of effective strategic recruitment and selection, and we will return to these points later in the chapter, considering the application of selection in different contexts.

It is also worthwhile to consider the position of recruitment and selection alongside other core aspects of HRM. In particular, there is a clear interface of recruitment and selection with training and learning (Chapter 9), and with performance management (Chapter 11). While recruitment and selection help to ensure that people are recruited with as well developed competencies as can be reasonably expected, the processes of performance management and training and learning help people to integrate into the organisation and to ultimately be effective.

RECRUITMENT: ATTRACTING PEOPLE TO THE JOB

Given the importance of this stage of the recruitment and selection process, it is surprising that the findings of research are not more directive or insightful. Indeed, some critics point out that many findings from recruitment research are somewhat obvious (e.g. see critical evaluation by Ployhart, 2006). However, there is sufficient evidence to help practitioners in applying systematic approaches. Breaugh (2008) identifies the following key steps in recruitment activities:

- **Recruitment objectives**: identifying the specific recruitment need, the kinds of individuals to be recruited, the time frame for processes, and the required levels of performance and retention needed from the process.

- **Strategy development**: working out a strategy for the recruitment activity, in which key questions about who and where to recruit, how to reach targeted people and what to communicate during the recruitment are all considered.

- **Recruitment activities**: application of specific methods of recruitment to attract the applicant pool, typically involving decisions about who will do the recruitment, whether it will be outsourced, the nature of the information to be conveyed, and the use of various media.

Schneider's **Attraction–Selection–Attrition model (ASA**; Schneider, 1987) describes how people are attracted to organisations principally on the basis of their judgement about whether they fit with the job and organisation. Initial decisions may be based on perceptions of job fit, but during the recruitment and selection phase, according to the ASA model, applicants and organisations both enter into a kind of fact-finding exercise, designed to determine the degree of fit between them. When the person-to-organisation fit is high, the applicant is more likely to be selected. Within the organisation, employees who are a poorer fit are more likely to leave (attrition). The result of this is that, over time, an organisation will gradually become filled with people who fit well with the organisation. There are many benefits to this, such as employees tending to show high levels of job satisfaction and organisational commitment (Andrews et al., 2011). This

Fit   The extent to which a person perceives that they fit with their job, work environment, career or organisation.

model highlights the importance of subjective fit perceptions in decision making, with implications for how jobs are marketed during recruitment.

Other research has examined specific practices, which may need to be employed by the recruiter, dependent on the nature of the job and the job market as a whole. One example of this is in circumstances under which there is likely to be a large applicant pool for a particular job. This is a situation which is frequently faced by recruiters the world over, as the global economic recession has led to raised unemployment and fewer job positions in most countries. In these situations, recruiters often use realistic job previews to ensure a good fit between person and job characteristics. Such previews might highlight any negative aspects of the job in order to ensure the seriousness of the job application. For example, when recruiting for a recruitment consultant role, the recruiter might emphasise the heavy workload associated with the role and the high-pressure environment in which the successful applicant would be working, as well as highlighting the potential for commission and bonuses. Doing so would dissuade casual applicants from applying for the role. The administration of this and other practices is equally important. Chapman et al. (2005) found that receiving timely responses to enquiries and applications led to higher perceptions of the attractiveness of the recruiting company.

SELECTION: ASSESSMENT AND SELECTING PEOPLE FOR THE ORGANISATION

Much research in the area of selection might be considered micro-HRM. This should not necessarily be negative in its connotation, but is rather to say that the most impactful research is usually concerned with process and method. There are important insights for all HR practitioners. We will consider the strategic context of this evidence base after reviewing the key findings of the field.

JOB ANALYSIS

Before we can assess whether or not a candidate is suitable for the job we are recruiting for, we first need to establish what to measure. You probably have a fairly clear idea of the kind of things that make a salesperson effective in their job (for instance, they need to be confident, be outgoing, have good product knowledge, be friendly and so on). But what if you were recruiting for a very specialist role that you knew little about? How could you decide how to assess whether a candidate would make an effective food science technician, a nuclear physicist or even a Special Forces officer?

The answer is that we do this through a process called job analysis. Job analysis is the foundation of all selection processes. It is the systematic process by which HR professionals seek to better understand what a job role involves and what makes for an effective worker in that role.

Though the methods used to collect job analysis data are many and varied (for an overview see Woods and Hinton, 2016), there are two broad approaches to conducting job analysis. These approaches differ in their focus, the methods you might use to conduct them and their resultant outputs. Work-oriented job analysis seeks to break the job

Job analysis A systematic process designed to determine what a job role involves and what makes for an effective worker in that role. It produces either a job description (work-oriented job analysis) or a person specification (worker-oriented analysis).

down into its elements, the smallest units of work that it consists of, such as pressing a button, opening an application on a computer, or selecting an appropriate tool. These elements are grouped into job tasks, all of which may be grouped together to produce a job description, which is the eventual output of work-oriented job analysis.

KSAOs The knowledge, skills, abilities and other attributes/characteristics that make a worker effective in a particular role.

By contrast, worker-oriented job analysis focuses on defining the knowledge, skills, abilities and other attributes/characteristics (KSAOs) that make a worker effective in a particular role. KSAOs cover a very diverse range of characteristics of the job holder, such as their job knowledge, skills learnt for a particular job task, more generalised innate cognitive and physical abilities, motivation, attitudes, values and personality traits. Once defined, these attributes are drawn together to form a detailed 'person specification'.

Researching job analysis data

O*Net is a huge database of job analysis data, collected over a number of years by the US government. It is the first port of call for anyone conducting job analysis for a role.

TASK: Go to the O*Net online website (www.onetonline.org). Use the Occupation Quick Search function to find job analysis data within the O*Net database for a role that interests you. Read the profile for that role and find out the key job tasks that make it up and the key KSAOs that an effective worker needs to perform in this role.

In contemporary HRM practice, a very widely used approach to job analysis is competency modelling or profiling. Competencies can be defined as 'observable workplace behaviours [that can] form the basis of a differentiated measurement [of performance]' (Bartram, 2005: 1185–1186). Advances in competency modelling have aimed to standardise and understand the main classifications of job competencies (e.g. planning and organising, communicating and presenting), most recently by relating them to core aspects of individual differences in personality, motivation and ability (Bartram, 2005). The job analyst, either using their own expertise or through consultation with subject matter experts, identifies the competencies that best reflect the required behaviour in a particular job role. The identified behaviours then inform the behaviours that will need to be demonstrated in selection by the successful applicant for the role. For example, for a secretarial role, the job analyst would reason that the competency of planning and organising would be central to the role, due to the importance of the job holder being able to organise their own diary and those of others effectively. A competency framework would inform the job analyst of the level of this competency that would likely be required, and would detail the kinds of behaviour that would be demonstrated by someone performing at this level in a similar role. The successful applicant for the role would then be required to demonstrate behaviour at this level at selection, perhaps assessed through their performance on a diary-based work sample test (see below).

From a practical point of view, standardised competency models help practitioners to understand the broad competency domain, but specific companies typically have their own emphasis and contextual information to add, making competency models organisation- and job-specific. By their nature, competencies are flexible, allowing them to be applied across jobs at different levels of seniority, and to remain relevant as job requirements change over time. For these reasons, the recent trend is for senior managers to favour the competency approach over other forms of job analysis (Campion et al., 2011). The task of the HRM practitioner is usually to help devise competency models, develop descriptions of relevant behavioural content, and then identify specific competencies required for specific jobs and positions in the organisation.

MEASUREMENT ISSUES

Once a job description and person specification for the job have been generated, specific assessment methods can be chosen to best assess candidates for the role. However, it can be challenging to decide whether or not an assessment method is fit for the purpose of predicting the future job performance of a candidate.

Contemporary approaches to selection aim to increase the objectivity of a selection process, reducing the impact of a number of biases associated with the subjective assessment of candidates. According to Galin and Benoliel (1990), the most important of these are the halo effect, the similarity effect and the beautyism effect:

- **The halo effect**: the tendency for an assessor to generalise a good or poor rating of one of a candidate's attributes to all other attributes of that candidate. For example, an assessor may judge a candidate who is dressed smartly for interview as being competent in other, unrelated aspects of the job.

- **The similarity effect:** the tendency for assessors to rate candidates whom they perceive to be similar to them more highly than those they do not. This similarity can be something that is based on overt characteristics such as gender, ethnicity or age, or can be based on perceived similarity in more abstract terms, such as similarity in interests or personality traits.

- **The beautyism effect:** the tendency for assessors to rate candidates they perceive to be attractive more highly than those they do not.

These combined effects – termed idiosyncratic rating tendencies – are biases in perception that all of us are subject to as human beings. Together, these effects can account for around 62 per cent of the variation in assessors' subjective ratings of candidates (Scullen et al., 2000).

A key issue in employment selection is that, since human beings are immensely complex organisms, we can never predict how someone will behave with 100 per cent accuracy. When making the decision about whether or not to use a particular assessment method, assessment professionals base their judgements on a number of aspects of the method. The first of these are the method's reliability and its validity, often referred to collectively as its psychometric properties.

Reliability

The reliability of an assessment method, broadly speaking, is best defined as how accurate it is. If a method is reliable, we can be much more confident in its assessment of a candidate than if it were unreliable, as these assessments are less likely to be influenced by outside factors such as measurement error or assessor bias.

Idiosyncratic rating tendencies Biases in perception that give rise to variation in assessors' subjective ratings of candidates. Examples of idiosyncratic rating tendencies are the halo effect, the similarity effect and the beautyism effect.

Reliability A measure of how accurate an assessment method is.

Validity A measure of the degree to which an assessment method measures what it is supposed to measure.

Coefficient A number between 0 and 1 used as a measure of the reliability or validity of a selection method. The closer to 1 a coefficient is, the higher the reliability or validity.

Reliability is represented by a coefficient, a number between 0 and 1 that represents the degree to which measurements of the same thing using the same assessment method will agree with one another (a value of 1 representing perfect agreement between measurements and 0 representing no agreement).

Reliability is assessed in different ways for different assessment methods. Inter-rater reliability, for example, is a measure of the extent to which interviewers on a panel might agree with each other's ratings of some aspect of a particular candidate, giving him or her similar ratings. Low inter-rater reliability may indicate that assessors' ratings of a candidate are based more on idiosyncratic rating tendencies than on objective assessment of the candidate's attributes. By contrast, internal consistency is a measure of the degree to which questions within a test designed to measure a specific ability or personality trait might 'agree' with one another, a candidate scoring similarly across the different questions. Finally, test–retest reliability measures the extent to which scores on an assessment method at one time agree with scores at a later date, reflecting accuracy of measurement over time.

Validity

Validity, on the other hand, refers to the extent to which a method is measuring what it is supposed to measure. There are many kinds of validity, but the kind that is of most interest to HR professionals is criterion-related validity. This refers to the extent to which scores on a selection method reflect some kind of outcome. In the case of selection assessment, this outcome is most frequently the future job performance of a candidate. Criterion-related validity is represented by correlational data, taking coefficients between 0 and 1 (1 representing perfect prediction and 0 representing no predictive power whatsoever). In practice, methods with criterion-related validity values of 0.50 and above are considered strong predictors of job performance, although validities as low as 0.20 can represent meaningful predictive effects with impact for performance. Table 7.1 summarises the results of meta-analytic research on the criterion-related validity of several selection methods, which are described in the following subsections.

ASSESSMENT TECHNIQUES: EARLY-STAGE

Early on in the selection process – assuming recruitment has been effective – there will be many candidates, all of whom will be interested to some degree in the job on offer. The objective is to reduce the number of applicants in this pool to a more manageable size. This approach to selection is called selecting-out or sifting.

CVs

A curriculum vitae (CV; referred to in some countries as a résumé) is often the first contact that an applicant and an organisation will have with one another (Thoms et al., 1999). CVs typically include data such as an applicant's employment history,

TABLE 7.1 Summary of meta-analytic research on the criterion-related validity of selection methods

Method	Criterion-related validity
Ability tests	0.51 (Schmidt and Hunter, 1998)
	0.50–0.60 (Bertua et al., 2005)
Structured interviews	0.60–0.63 (Wiesner and Cronshaw, 1988)
	0.51 (Schmidt and Hunter, 1998)
	0.44 (McDaniel et al., 1994)
Situational judgement tests	0.19–0.50 (Christian et al., 2010)
	0.34 (McDaniel et al., 2001)
Work sample tests	0.54 (Schmidt and Hunter, 1998)
	0.33 (Roth et al., 2005)
Assessment centres	0.76 (Gaugler et al., 1987)
	0.39 (Arthur et al., 2006)
	0.28 (Hermelin et al., 2007)
Biodata	0.35 (Schmidt and Hunter, 1998)
Personality questionnaires	0.40 (Schmidt and Hunter, 1998)
	0.04 (Openness) – 0.22 (Conscientiousness) (Barrick and Mount, 1991)
Unstructured interviews	0.20–0.37 (Wiesner and Cronshaw, 1988)
	0.33 (McDaniel et al., 1994)
Résumé/Application form data	0.18 (Schmidt and Hunter, 1998)
Years of experience	0.10 (Schmidt and Hunter, 1998)
Years of education	0.10 (Schmidt and Hunter, 1998)
Interests	0.02 (Schmidt and Hunter, 1998)
Graphology	0 (approx.) (Neter and Ben-Shakhar, 1989)

qualifications and contact details; but beyond this, there is little standardisation of their content, different CVs varying widely in their layout and the information they provide. This lack of standardisation is problematic as inclusion of details such as a personal statement or academic grade point averages can influence whether an applicant is selected or rejected at this stage (Thoms et al., 1999). The other downside to using CVs for sifting is that it is relatively resource-intensive to sort through them in high volume, even when using some form of CV management system (Maheshwari et al., 2010).

Application forms

A more manageable way of handling the data collected by a CV is to force applicants to present in a structured way. By using an application form in place of a CV in a selection process, an organisation can control the information that candidates submit, rather than leaving the choice of whether to include or omit a piece of information in the candidate's hands.

In spite of the popularity of both CVs and application forms, the evidence for their predictive validity is poor. As they collect a diverse range of data about a candidate, the psychometric properties of individual data types within them tend to be examined rather than the candidate's suitability as a whole. Years of job experience, years of education and candidate interests have all been demonstrated to be poor predictors of future job performance, showing predictive validity coefficients of 0.18, 0.10 and 0.10 respectively (Robertson and Smith, 2001).

Within application forms, a growing practice is the inclusion of biodata items. These are questions that allow candidates' responses to be scored more objectively, theoretically allowing for better comparison between candidates. Biodata items can take many forms. For example, a biodata item designed to assess a candidate's experience of leading a team could either take the form of a scale on which a candidate was asked to rate the frequency with which they had led a team in the past two years, or could assess their experiences of leadership in a more open-ended, short answer-type way, the latter being scored against a set of pre-determined criteria.

The advantage of adopting a more structured biodata approach to collecting early-stage information about a candidate is clear: meta-analytic evidence suggests that biodata items are much better predictors of future job performance than the more conventional methods that typically make up CVs and application forms, showing validity coefficients of around 0.35 (Schmidt and Hunter, 1998). The inclusion of biodata items can, therefore, allow HR professionals potentially to raise the predictive validity of their early-stage assessment methods to acceptable levels.

ASSESSMENT TECHNIQUES: MID-STAGE

Psychometrics

Psychometrics are tools designed to assess hidden constructs, aspects of a person such as intelligence and personality traits that often cannot be measured or observed directly. We include them here as 'mid-stage' techniques. They are commonly used during late-stage assessment, though technological changes, coupled with their relatively inexpensive costs to administer to large groups, have meant that psychometrics are increasingly being used as part of the sifting stage (often as a second-sift) in many selection processes.

Predictive validity A form of criterion-related validity that measures the extent to which a selection method can accurately predict some important criterion in the future (most commonly future job performance) based on assessment scores in the present.

Psychometrics Standardised tests used in selection to measure hidden attributes of a candidate. Subdivided into ability tests and personality questionnaires.

Trait An individual's distinguishing characteristic, such as sensitivity or conscientiousness.

Ability tests

Ability tests are designed to measure some facet of cognitive ability (e.g. verbal reasoning, numerical reasoning, abstract reason, spatial rotation) or general mental ability as a whole (often referred to as GMA or '*g*'). In selection, HR professionals map key job tasks to the kinds of cognitive ability that they are likely to tap in to. For example, if a role required the job holder to run complex financial statistics, it is likely that a candidate with high numerical reasoning would be able to perform this task effectively (once given the necessary training). The HR professional would, therefore, test all candidates for the job on their numerical reasoning ability.

Meta-analytic research has consistently found ability tests to be the single best predictor of future job performance available (e.g. Schmidt and Hunter, 1998). Furthermore, they have been shown to predict success in a wide range of occupations (Robertson and Smith, 2001). The reason for these findings is still somewhat unclear, but the most frequently cited explanations are that high cognitive ability increases the likelihood of training success (e.g. Ackerman et al., 1995) and/or helps in the effective acquisition of job knowledge (e.g. Kuncel et al., 2010).

The major limitation of using ability tests for selection is that certain social groups appear to perform better on them than others. A vast amount of research has shown mean group differences between men and women (e.g. Jackson and Rushton, 2006), older and younger people (e.g. Hough et al., 2001), people from differing socio-economic status groups (e.g. Eckland, 1979) and – most markedly – people from different ethnic backgrounds (e.g. Berry et al., 2011; Cooper and Robertson, 1995). The implication of these group differences is that, when used for selection, ability tests may present the problem of adverse impact (see below). Furthermore, new meta-analytic evidence suggests that the predictive validity of ability tests is lower for some ethnic subgroups than it is for the White majority (Berry et al., 2014).

Adverse impact A potential outcome of a selection process in which a minority social group is disadvantaged compared to the majority group. Most commonly assessed through the comparison of selection ratios between social groups.

Personality questionnaires

In selection, HR professionals often use personality questionnaires to measure aspects of a candidate's personality that may be desirable for some tasks within a job role. Since personality reflects broad preferences for behaviour, these questionnaires can – at least in theory – be used to predict a wide range of on-the-job behaviours that a candidate is likely to display. All personality questionnaires fall into one of two broad categories: type-based measures, such as the ubiquitous Myers–Briggs Type Indicator (MBTI), seek to classify people's personality as belonging to one of a number of discrete types (for example, either 'introvert' or 'extravert'); by contrast, trait-based measures, such as the NEOPI-R, classify candidates as belonging somewhere on a scale (using the same example as before, the same candidate could lie anywhere on the scale between 'highly introverted' and 'highly extraverted'). Conceptually, only trait-based measures should be used for selection since, unlike trait-based measures, type-based measures do not allow for quantitative comparison between candidates, and are plagued with other scientific and theoretical limitations (see Woods and West, 2014; see also Chapter 2).

The use of personality testing for selection requires the HR professional first to develop an ideal personality profile. The ideal profile is a summary of the pattern of personality traits that would be best suited to the tasks of the target job, and is developed using job analysis data. Once this ideal profile has been created, the personality profiles of applicants for the role can be judged against this ideal profile, highlighting areas of consistency (indicating that a candidate would be well suited to aspects of the job that require personality traits of this kind) and areas of inconsistency (indicating that a candidate might potentially struggle with job tasks related to this aspect of their personality).

Personality questionnaires demonstrate predictive validity of around 0.30 (Schmidt and Hunter, 1998), although this increases substantially when good job analysis is used (Hogan and Holland, 2003). Similarly, the predictive validity of all personality traits is higher for jobs in which employees have a degree of autonomy and in which work is less structured than for those that are very structured and in which employees have less control over decision making (Judge and Zapata, 2015). Advances in understanding of the structure of personality are continuously clarifying the nature of relations between criteria and traits (see Woods and Anderson, 2016).

Moreover, recent research has highlighted the potential long-term benefits of assessing personality at selection. This research reflects new perspectives in performance at work that more clearly acknowledge the dynamic nature of performance in an organisation. When people start a new job, they typically experience a learning curve, during which they accumulate new knowledge about a job. Ability makes a difference to this acquisition of knowledge; however, once a person has acquired relevant job knowledge, performance motivation and, in many jobs, interpersonal competencies and personality traits make a difference for long-term effectiveness. In particular, high Big Five Openness has been demonstrated to predict the maintenance of performance over time (Minbashian et al., 2013). Research now indicates the long-term validity of personality traits for sustained performance (Lievens et al., 2009; Thoresen et al., 2004).

An often-cited limitation of using personality questionnaires for selection is that responses to them can be faked. In high-stakes selection situations, it is not unreasonable to expect some candidates to be tempted to deliberately create a more favourable impression of themselves than might be the truth. This practice is known as socially desirable responding behaviour (SDR) or impression management (IM). Despite concerns of practitioners, there is no academic consensus about the actual importance of faking in selection. More practically, there are a number of options available to address and mitigate potential SDR.

Instructions should be designed in such a way as to promote an honesty contract between candidate and assessor, as is becoming accepted practice in modern psychometric testing (e.g. Lievens and Burke, 2011). Psychometric test designers could also consider the possibility of including some form of social desirability scale in their questionnaires. These scales are made up of items (i.e. questions) that no one would realistically agree with unless they were trying to create a more favourable impression (for example, 'I have never told a lie'). With the advent of remotely administered online testing, concerns have been raised that SDR behaviour in personality assessment is likely to become more prevalent. However, recent encouraging research suggests that SDR behaviour may, in actual fact, be no more prevalent in remotely administered selection situations than it is under supervised conditions (Arthur et al., 2010).

ASSESSMENT TECHNIQUES: LATE-STAGE

Once the applicant pool has been reduced to a more manageable size through the sifting process, the task of selection becomes to identify the most suitable candidates. This process is often referred to as selecting-in.

Interviews

The most common form of late-stage assessment is the interview. Interviews may take the form of being unstructured, in which the interviewer(s) invite the candidate for a free-form 'informal chat', or structured, in which candidates are asked a pre-determined set of questions and there is only very limited scope for elaboration of answers or follow-up questions. Despite unstructured interviews being far more common in selection than structured interviews (Van der Zee et al., 2002), evidence for both their reliability (Campion et al., 1997) and predictive validity (Schmidt and Hunter, 1998) is poor. Conversely, a structured approach to interviewing seems to eliminate these problems, structured interviews consistently showing excellent inter-rater reliability (Huffcutt et al., 2013) and predictive validity coefficients of up to 0.56 (e.g. Schmidt and Hunter, 1998).

With the overwhelming evidence for the importance of structured interviews, a key question is exactly how one goes about designing them. There are well-established guidelines in the literature (e.g. Campion et al., 1988), but, broadly speaking, the key features of a structured process are:

1. Questions defined on the basis of job analysis to ensure job relevance.

2. Use of standardised procedures, including asking all candidates the same questions.

3. Use of rating scales to evaluate answers, with examples used to anchor the rating scales.

4. Use of interview panels to evaluate the answers given.

5. Active attention to fairness, ethics and discrimination, to be mindful of potential bias and to challenge it.

An extension of the structured approach is the competency-based interview, which specifically asks questions around key job competencies and requires answers to report past behavioural examples. The behavioural content of answers is evaluated in order to assess the competency evidence.

MINI CASE STUDY

Developing competency-based interviews for a small UK-based market research company

The managing director of a small market research company (25 employees) wanted to have competency-based interviews developed to use during interviews. Following initial meetings it transpired that the key problem with selection lay in the fact that there was no standardised interview or scoring format to use to select the market researchers.

The first step of this project was to conduct a job analysis which involved interviewing the current research executives. We aimed to gain input from a variety of sources (including managers, direct reports and clients) to get a holistic view of the two levels of job role – Research Executive (RE) and Senior Research Executive (SRE).

The output of the job analysis led to the development of a competency framework for both RE and SRE. Unsurprisingly, there were some competencies that were relevant for both, but other competencies were different and relevant to only one of the two levels. Based on the framework, competency-based interview questions were developed, along with marking criteria to assess the answers to each of the interview questions.

Before implementing the interview in a live selection process, the interviews were piloted on a group of current employees – this was to check whether the interview questions were suitable and also whether the marking criteria were appropriate.

Since the organisation was small and only recruited a couple of people each year, it was not possible to do a formal or large-scale validation process. However, candidates' interview ratings during selection were checked against later performance ratings. Two years later organisational turnover has reduced when compared to previous levels, which may indicate that the selection process is having a positive influence on candidates.

CASE STUDY QUESTIONS

1   Why do you think interviews were used as a job analysis technique in this case study?

2   What other methods of job analysis might have been useful?

3   In what other ways do you think the interviews could have been evaluated or validated in this small organisation setting?

Situational judgement tests (SJTs) Standardised tests used to assess a candidate's judgement in workplace situations based on hypothetical scenarios. Used to predict future behaviour or assess job knowledge.

Situational judgement tests

Situational judgement tests (SJTs) are designed to assess a candidate's judgement about a situation encountered in the workplace. Applicants are presented with hypothetical work-based scenarios describing a problem or dilemma, and they are asked to choose a response from a list of alternatives (Lievens et al., 2008). SJTs can take two forms, being either behaviour-based – in which a candidate responds to a situation in the way that he or she would be most likely to – or knowledge-based – in which candidates respond in the way that they judge would be most appropriate (McDaniel et al., 2007). This distinction can have a huge impact on the SJT in terms of its criterion-related validity (McDaniel and Nguyen, 2003) and how resistant it is to faking (Nguyen et al., 2005).

SJTs are developed on the basis of a thorough job analysis, to ensure that the content reflects situations that the employees may face in the working environment (Christian et al., 2010). SJTs tend to focus on testing attitudes and ethical values (such as integrity or empathy) that are not generally tapped into by other measures, rather than knowledge per se (Patterson et al., 2012b). The content and format of the SJT can be altered to fit the specific job role (Lievens et al., 2008). As such, they are increasing in popularity and are a flexible method for organisations to use during selection.

Using SJTs in selection can have a wide range of benefits. Evidence suggests that SJTs are reliable (McDaniel et al., 2007) and have good criterion-related validity (i.e. they predict subsequent performance) across a range of occupations (Patterson et al., 2009b), even up to nine years into the future (Lievens and Sackett, 2012). Additionally, SJTs have been demonstrated to predict other important behaviours such as organisational citizenship behaviours (OCB; Rockstuhl et al., 2015).

Work sample tests

In contrast to SJTs, work sample tests can be thought of as high-fidelity simulations of work. They are designed to assess – as the name suggests – candidates on a sample of the kind of work that they could typically expect in the job if they were successful at the selection stage. Probably the best-known example of the work sample test is the in-tray exercise, in which candidates must sort through and prioritise a number of competing work demands within a simulated in-tray or email inbox.

Empirical support for the use of work sample tests in selection is generally good. They typically display high levels of predictive validity (Schmidt and Hunter, 1998). Additionally, there is evidence to suggest that certain kinds of work sample tests – specifically psychomotor tests and group discussion tests – can be better predictors of performance even than ability tests, making them a viable alternative to ability testing, given their low adverse impact and generally favourable applicant reactions (Robertson and Kandola, 2011). There is, however, some evidence to suggest that the specific nature of the work sample used can influence how different groups perform on it: Harari and Viswesvaran (2014) found that females outperformed males on clerical work sample tests that involved typing and verbal comprehension, whereas males performed better if the work sample required spatial abilities.

Assessment centres

The use of assessment centres is considered here as a type of selection method, though it is perhaps better thought of as an approach to selection. Rather than being a physical building, as the name might suggest, an assessment centre is a series of assessment

Assessment centres
A series of assessment methods spread over one or a number of days, designed to assess candidates many times on many traits at once.

methods spread over one or a number of days, designed to assess candidates many times on many traits at once.

Competency A class of behaviour that is specific, measureable, observable and related to performance in a job.

The assessment centre approach revolves around the assessment of competencies. Once the relevant competencies for a role are identified, assessment methods are selected to enable assessment of those competencies in multiple exercises. A typical assessment method might require candidates to attend a structured interview, followed by participating in a group task, and finally to complete a work sample test and a measure of personality.

This multi-trait, multi-method approach has a number of advantages over individual selection methods. There are advantages of observing performance in different contexts, and there is evidence that assessment centres provide assessors with greater prediction of subsequent training success than ability tests do alone (Krause et al., 2006). Moreover, in a study comparing the incidence of legal proceedings based on nine types of selection method, Terpstra et al. (2002) found that assessment centres were only very rarely challenged by candidates and that, in cases where they were challenged, the cases were all dismissed.

Despite the clear advantages that the assessment centre approach promises, evidence for its predictive validity is somewhat disappointing. Validity coefficients of 0.28 (Hermelin et al., 2007) to around 0.39 (Arthur et al., 2006) are most commonly reported. Assessment centres are very resource-intensive to run, leading professionals to draw unfavourable comparisons between them and other, cheaper methods when making decisions on how to assess candidates (Hough and Oswald, 2000).

STRATEGIC APPROACHES TO ASSESSMENT

Our review of selection assessment methodology has highlighted a number of key findings about the choice and deployment of selection assessment techniques. How do these findings fit with a strategic approach to HRM?

One way to think about this question is to consider HR architecture (Lengnick-Hall et al., 2009). Tsui et al. (1997) identify how organisations typically have many HR systems that are deployed differentially for specific positions. Adaptation of approach while maintaining best practice is of key importance.

Choosing selection methods

Learn how to make informed choices about the appropriateness of different selection tools and methods by designing an assessment centre.

TASK: Use the job analysis data you identified using O*Net earlier on in the chapter to design an assessment centre matrix:

1   Choose six performance-related attributes (e.g. from under the 'Work Styles' heading in the O*Net page you accessed) that you want to assess.

2   Choose a maximum of five assessment methods from those described in this chapter that you could use to assess these attributes.

3   Mark on your matrix which attributes are going to be assessed by which selection methods, ensuring that each attribute is assessed at least twice and that no method assesses more than five or six attributes.

Here we review some specific case examples to illustrate applications of how contingencies can be incorporated into recruitment and selection methodology.

TALENT AND HIGH POTENTIAL SELECTION

Talent management is an often-quoted activity in HRM that might range in meaning from managing people generally through to managing top-level managers and directors. The most acceptable meaning is converging on the following (e.g. Collings and Mellahi, 2009):

1. Identification of key positions in a business that contribute to the achievement of strategic business objectives.

2. Identification of high-potential individuals, either external or internal to the business, that can be developed and managed in those positions.

When defined in this way, the strategic impact of talent management is obvious. Also clear is the role of sound and robust assessment and selection. Identifying high potential, selecting such individuals and keeping them is a critical HRM task.

The challenge for assessment and selection is first to understand the nature of high potential and precisely what high potential people are being selected for. Typically, when an employee or recruit is added to a high-potential pool of people, that person is put on a steep career trajectory that will involve experiencing multiple areas of a business and progressing quickly to a leadership role. The person is not so much selected for a job, rather for a career.

Silzer and Church (2009) review the literature on high potential and formulate a model capturing three key elements that define high potential individuals:

- **Foundation aspects**: high cognitive ability to facilitate learning, and key personality traits such as achievement orientation.
- **Growth aspects**: motivation to learn, and resilience to grow and develop.
- **Career aspects**: typically leadership, but also career-specific speciality or competence that might include technical excellence in a field.

One implication for assessment and selection is that a combination of assessment perspectives is needed. For foundation aspects, prospective assessment is needed to inform decisions, looking forwards at predictors of learning and performance maintenance. For career aspects, retrospective assessment is needed to examine capability and competencies developed through the career to date. For growth aspects, a combination of techniques may be needed to look at prospective and actual past learning and adaptation.

SELECTION OF DOCTORS

There are many examples of very specialist careers in which systematic and structured selection is all the more challenging. One such example is the selection of medical practitioners. In the last 10 years the UK National Health Service (NHS) has focused specifically on how doctors should be selected throughout their medical careers. Selecting the wrong person for the job can have serious negative consequences both for the NHS and, perhaps more importantly, patients (Patterson and Ferguson, 2007). The selection of doctors can be considered 'high-stakes' since candidates have trained for many years and personally invested time and money to become doctors. Furthermore, selecting doctors within the NHS is high profile, attracting both public and media interest with stringent levels of scrutiny and public accountability. Thus the NHS has to provide a robust selection process to ensure it is able to defend its decisions in the light of potential appeals (Patterson and Zibarras, 2011; Patterson et al., 2011). Research in this specialist area has focused on two main areas:

- Identifying selection criteria for success in the role of a doctor (via job analysis).
- Designing and validating selection methods and processes.

As discussed earlier in this chapter, the first stage of an effective selection system is to thoroughly analyse the relevant KSAOs associated with successful performance in a given job role, as this ensures that the correct competencies can be assessed during selection. In research conducted by Patterson et al. (2000), three methods of job analysis were conducted to analyse the role of a general practitioner (GP). Findings showed that personal and non-cognitive attributes such as empathy, sensitivity and communication skills were essential requirements for a doctor.

Situational judgement tests have been a valuable addition to the selection processes for doctors since SJTs can target professional attributes that are difficult to assess otherwise. SJTs have been specifically designed for speciality medical selection (relating to when doctors specialise in the specific field where they want to work, such as becoming a GP or a surgeon). Research evidence has shown SJTs to be excellent predictors of future work performance for GPs and in clinical medicine (Patterson et al., 2009a, 2009b). SJTs have also been used for selecting future surgeons, anaesthetists and dentists (e.g. Patterson et al., 2012a).

In addition, the assessment centre method has been used extensively in medical speciality selection. Since assessment centres (ACs) involve a number of selection methods and candidates are assessed by multiple assessors, they allow a wide-ranging assessment of an individual's effectiveness in a given job. The exercises used within ACs are generally high-fidelity, in that they closely resemble the job role. For example, in the GP assessment centre, the exercises

Evaluating a selection process

- Think back to a selection process that you either organised/delivered or participated in (i.e. that you attended as a candidate).
- TASK: Knowing what you know now from this chapter, evaluate its effectiveness:

1 Consider the recruitment stage – what was your experience like and how effective were the process, administration and communication? What could have been done differently?

2 Consider the selection and assessment stage – what techniques were used, and to what extent were they defensible and effective? How could they have been improved?

include a simulated patient consultation, which is exactly what a GP does on a daily basis. ACs have shown excellent predictive validity for GPs (e.g. Patterson et al., 2005), and among other specialties such as obstetrics, gynaecology and anaesthesiology (e.g. Gale et al., 2010; Randall et al., 2006). In the case of medical specialty, the differences in the various specialist pathways mean that there is likely to be utility in using assessment flexibly so that it is customised for each (see e.g. Woods et al., 2016).

APPLICANT PERCEPTIONS OF DIFFERENT SELECTION METHODS

Research has shown that applicants perceive selection methods differently in terms of 'fairness', with several studies conducted to compare cross-national perceptions of common selection methods (interviews, CVs, work samples, biodata, ability tests, references, personality questionnaires, honesty tests, personal contacts and graphology; e.g. Anderson and Witvliet, 2008). Findings indicate a relatively stable pattern of results with few cross-national differences in ratings of process fairness on these selection methods. Generally, interviews, CVs and work samples are rated most favourably, while personal contacts, graphology and honesty tests are rated least favourably, with very few significant differences found between countries. Similarities in applicant perceptions are more prevalent than are differences (e.g. Hulsheger and Anderson, 2009), suggesting that it may be possible to generalise findings internationally. Nevertheless, individual differences such as differences in personality traits and – in particular – core self-evaluations have been demonstrated to affect how different applicants react to assessment centres, even when controlling for differences in performance at selection (Merkulova et al., 2014).

OUTCOMES OF APPLICANT PERCEPTIONS

Research suggests that there are three types of outcomes typically resulting from applicants' perceptions of recruitment/selection processes. They can relate to:

1. **Attitudes** – where applicants' experiences during selection can influence their attitude (positively or negatively) towards the selection process, job or organisation (e.g. Van Vianen et al., 2004). For organisations this may have a significant impact on public relations because an applicant's attitude towards the organisation can influence how positively they discuss it.

2. **Intentions** – where applicants' perceptions relate to various intentions, such as job acceptance intentions (Truxillo et al., 2002), recommendation intentions (Anseel and Lievens, 2009) and litigation intentions (Bauer et al., 2001).

3. **Behaviours** – where applicants' experiences have been linked to some behaviours such as work performance (Gilliland, 1994) and subsequent reapplication among rejected candidates (Gilliland et al., 2001).

It is important for organisations to consider the applicants' perspective because negative experiences can result in the loss of good applicants from selection (Hulsheger and Anderson, 2009), having a detrimental effect on the utility of the process (Murphy, 1986).

Successful selection processes therefore require ongoing evaluation and monitoring of their quality from both the applicants' and the organisation's perspectives (Cascio and Aguinis, 2008). Positive candidate experiences may also be important for continued attraction since applicants are more attracted to organisations with better reputations (Turban and Cable, 2003), and fair selection processes may positively influence an organisation's continued ability to attract the best applicants and recruit effectively within a given job market (Schmitt and Chan, 1999).

More broadly, of course, there are benefits of good selection for employees as well as businesses. People tend to be more satisfied with work if they perceive a good fit between them and their job (Lauver and Kristof-Brown, 2001).

HRM IN PRACTICE

Assessing candidate reactions to selection methods in postgraduate selection for doctors (GPs)

As outlined earlier in this chapter, selecting doctors is a 'high-stakes' process since candidates have trained for many years and personally invested time and money to become doctors. Since this selection process attracts public and media interest, the recruiters within the NHS were eager to ensure that candidates perceived the selection methods to be fair. This is particularly important because the NHS is a monopoly employer, so if candidates do not get a position their career choices are limited. By ensuring that candidates feel the process is fair, this will reduce the likelihood that candidates may appeal against selection decisions (Patterson and Zibarras, 2011).

Using organisational justice theory as a model to explore candidate reactions, we explored perceptions of the GP selection process, focusing on the selection methods themselves, and perceptions of interpersonal treatment (whether candidates feel that they were treated appropriately). Data were collected over three consecutive annual recruitment rounds. Overall, findings suggested that the GP selection process was positively received, as indicated by the fact that all selection methods were judged to be job related and considered fair both in relation to characteristics of the methods themselves and to interpersonal treatment.

One interesting finding was that in the first recruitment round, initial reactions to the SJT were less positive than a clinical problem-solving test (which focused on clinical job knowledge). Since the SJT had been recently introduced, communication interventions were used to explain to candidates why SJTs were used in this setting and their relevance to the job role. Over the course of this study, there were significant improvements in the perceptions of the SJT. This highlights the importance of monitoring candidate perceptions in any organisation's recruitment and selection process, so that recruiters can be alerted to potential shifts in perceptions.

A full description of this research can be found in: Patterson, F., Zibarras, L., Carr, V., Irish, B. and Gregory, S. (2011) Evaluating candidate reactions to selection practices using organisational justice theory. *Medical Education*, 45(3): 289–297.

GRADUATE INSIGHTS

Annie's placement experiences

The following is taken from the reflections of a returning Aston University placement student (Annie). They are interesting because they highlight the importance of developing positive, supportive relations between the applicant and assessors, both in terms of applicant performance on the day of assessment and also when they start the job.

Annie: I competed for and was awarded the position of HR support officer with ABC. The application process was very competitive and consisted of two stages – a face-to-face interview and an assessment centre. As I had previously attended many interviews and assessment centres I felt more than prepared, however. This said, the pressure to secure a placement position was growing and as I entered the second stage of the selection process I was very anxious to succeed. The assessment centre consisted of the usual range of activities, psychometric testing, group exercises, interviews and also a presentation in front of my future manager and the director. We knew this in advance and so I researched and prepared extensively for this presentation as I felt this may be the key part of the day. Throughout the day I felt I made a good impression on the assessors and felt my confidence build. A supportive relationship had been established with the assessors which improved my performance and also helped me once I started my job some weeks later.

ETHICAL AND LEGAL ISSUES IN RECRUITMENT AND SELECTION

Recruitment and selection, like any human resources process, is governed by legislation. The exact nature of the legal framework that governs it varies between countries. In the UK, recruitment and selection processes must adhere to the terms of the Equality Act 2010, which seeks to protect candidates from both direct and indirect discrimination based on a number of protected characteristics (such as age, gender, ethnicity and so on; see Chapters 8 and 12 for further discussion). Similarly, equality in recruitment and selection in the European Union is governed by Directive 2006/54/EC and the Charter of Fundamental Rights of the European Union. The legal context is of obvious importance in selection, given the increased risk of litigation by applicants towards organisations that they believe have discriminated against them at the selection stage (Terpstra et al., 2002), and the positive push for responsible management.

Related to – yet distinct from – the legal context of recruitment and selection are the ethical issues surrounding it. From a legal perspective, there might not be specific legislation preventing the use of a particular selection method. Moreover, globalised business also adds the complexity of HR managers being responsible for the personnel of organisations operating in different legal contexts; the legal position in one location may be different from another, such as the inconsistencies between gender equality legislation in Western countries when compared to some Middle Eastern ones. Responsible and ethical practice, however, would still dictate that HR professionals take steps to ensure that the selection methods they use treat all candidates fairly, adopting ethical rather than legal viewpoints. See Chapter 4 for further discussion of these issues.

ENSURING FAIRNESS AND BEST PRACTICE IN SELECTION PROCESSES

Despite the differences in legislation between countries, there are a number of best practice steps that all HR professionals can take to ensure that their recruitment and selection processes are fair and legally defensible:

- **Combining methods:** As previously discussed, no assessment method can predict future performance with perfect accuracy. For this reason, high-stakes selection decisions should never be made on the basis of a single assessment score. This is particularly relevant when using psychometrics for sifting as candidates often do not get the opportunity to put their results in context.

- **Avoiding positive discrimination: Positive discrimination** is the intentional treatment of a disadvantaged group in a more favourable way than other social groups. It is most often seen in quota systems, whereby an organisation decides to, for example, specifically hire more women so that women are better represented in its staff. While this may seem fair and justified, in many countries it is illegal. Instead, organisations in this situation should use positive action, a legal approach to increasing the representation of a particular group that includes encouraging applications from members of this group and advertising in places that target this group (websites, publications, etc.).

Positive action An approach to increasing the representation of a particular group in an organisation that includes encouraging applications from members of this group and advertising in places that target this group. Distinct from positive discrimination.

- **Providing training for assessors:** In the case of the assessor biases highlighted by Galin and Benoliel (1990), there are a number of approaches that can be taken to reduce these subjective biases, thereby making assessment in interviews and assessment centres fairer and more reliable. Assessors can be trained to address their own biases in assessment in a number of ways, in much the same ways as they would be for the elimination of bias in performance appraisal processes. Rater error training is focused upon making assessors aware of their own tendencies to be influenced by sources of subjective bias. Frame-of-reference training is designed to make the meanings of terms in assessment (such as 'satisfactory', 'poor', 'outstanding') consistent across assessors, allowing assessors to classify interviewee responses more objectively. Methods such as these have been demonstrated to effectively reduce bias in assessment from sources such as the halo effect and rater leniency (e.g. Hedge and Kavanagh, 1988; Woehr, 1994).

- **Linking assessment methods to key KSAOs and competencies:** As a general rule, the more job-relevant an assessment method appears to applicants, the less likely they are to object to its being used for selection (Anderson et al., 2010). One way of ensuring job relevance is to choose assessment methods that are directly related to job analysis data for the role.

- **Monitoring the outcomes of selection processes:** Finally, fairness can only be ensured if the outcomes of selection are monitored in terms of how it has treated applicants from different groups. If proportionally many fewer people from a disadvantaged group are being hired as a result of your selection process than the proportion of those applicants from the majority group, it may be an indication that your selection process is showing signs of adverse impact (Bobko and Roth, 2010). If this is the case, you should immediately review your selection processes to see if any specific method may be unfairly disadvantaging members of a particular social group.

DEBATING HRM

Using recruitment and selection to encourage environmental sustainability in the workplace

Recently, organisations have been coming under increasing pressure to address environmental issues and to improve their environmental performance. In many industrialised nations, the government has set legally binding targets for reducing greenhouse gas emissions over both the short and long terms, informed by the Paris Agreement.

Some authors (e.g. Rimanoczy and Pearson, 2010) have suggested that HRM practices can support organisations in reaching sustainability goals and, as such, HRM practitioners have a key role to play in developing strategies for this purpose. One area where HRM strategies could be important in delivering organisational improvements is to use interventions throughout an employee's lifecycle in an organisation – for example by selecting individuals who are committed to the environment, or using induction programmes that focus on pro-environmental behaviour.

In a recent survey by Zibarras and Ballinger (2011), 21.6 per cent of the 147 organisations surveyed used 'recruitment and selection criteria that recognise environmental behaviour/commitment' at least sometimes as a method of encouraging employees to be pro-environmental in the workplace. However, this was ranked 14th out of 17 different HRM practices used in the organisations surveyed.

TASK: Working in groups, outline a case for and against using recruitment and selection criteria to select (or reject) candidates who show an aptitude for pro-environmental behaviour in the workplace.

(You can download details of the survey from: www.cubeproject.org.uk/wp-content/uploads/2011/05/BPS_DOP_GoingGreenAtWorkBook.pdf)

THE EMERGING USE OF SOCIAL NETWORKING IN SELECTION

One emergent trend in selection in HRM is the use of social networking by organisations in recruitment and selection. Although there are potentially many positives to be taken from the use of social networking for recruitment (e.g. Doherty, 2010), we include the issue in this section specifically because of the risks of social networking in selection.

There are very few data on the prevalence of the use of social networking for gathering data on job applicants, although Brown and Vaughn (2011) cite figures of 45 per cent of recruiting managers in 2009, rising from 22 per cent in 2008. One may assume further increases since then. There are important risks from the practice, which can be summarised by considering our criteria for effective selection, specifically that it should be evidence-based and systematic.

There is certainly no evidence of any validity of the use of social networking information for making selection decisions and, in terms of the systematic aspect of selection, Brown and Vaughn (2011) highlight the following issues:

- **Lack of job relevance:** organisations could place themselves at risk by potentially incorporating irrelevant information into their decision making. Selecting on the basis of data that is not job-relevant is a fundamental failing in selection that could be challenged.

- **Invasion of privacy:** there is an important ethical and social responsibility issue to be considered, particularly when the use of social networking extends to personal non-work sites such as Facebook.

- **Misunderstanding or assumption:** it is easy for managers to mistakenly make attributions about the nature of personal information such as photos, which are often viewed out of context. Biases can be introduced here.

- **Discrimination:** while organisations take steps to avoid discrimination in the evaluation of candidates from protected groups, it is often easy to ascertain membership of those groups through social networking sites, which may lead to the introduction of bias and discrimination.

- **Variability of information:** there is obviously no structure to the way that information on social networking sites is entered or reviewed, and this means that potential candidates or applicants are treated differently in terms of the information used to assess them.

Early research on applicant reactions to the use of social networking for recruitment and selection suggests that organisations should be cautious in using them, because applicants do feel that their privacy has been invaded, leading to perceptions of the organisation being less attractive as a potential employer (Stoughton et al., 2015).

One thing is certain, which is that social networking will remain a feature of people's lives, so there is a big responsibility for HR practitioners to get to grips with this issue in the coming years, and to inform policy and best practice in how and when social networking might be used in recruitment and selection efforts.

THE SELECTION DECISION: ISSUES OF FIT AND TRANSITION

Throughout this chapter, we have highlighted several areas of recruitment and selection practice that have received surprisingly little research attention. One such area is the selection decision, empirical examination of which is woefully light.

If one were to consider all of the evidence we have reviewed on selection assessment, it would seem that selection decisions should be a simple case of actuarial reasoning: add up any relevant selection scores and select the person scoring most highly. Managers typically see this as an inappropriate approach to take for one simple reason: it may not reflect fit between the recruit and their team.

One research study of note in the area of selection decision making is informative in this respect. Kristof-Brown (2000) reported that in an examination of selection decision making and the reasons behind the decisions, it is possible to differentiate the aspects of person–job and person–organisation fit. That is to say that most of the assessment of KSAOs and competencies feeds into perceptions of person–job fit (that a person is competent), whereas judgements of person–organisation fit are more subjective.

On the basis of these findings, one must probably conclude that selection decisions are rational – a weighing up of all relevant information – and that the challenge of HRM is to ensure that fair and ethical decisions are made that weight heavily the robust assessments used for selection, while simultaneously ensuring that inadvertent intra-group conflict due to poor team fit is avoided.

In this regard, there are steps that HR practitioners can take to facilitate transition, socialisation and fit. For example, the 'transition cycle' (Nicholson and West, 1989) highlights steps in transition to new jobs that recruits may need to navigate (preparation, encounter and adjustment). Support can be given to recruits at these different stages:

1. **Preparation**. This stage refers to the period prior to entering a new job role. It involves the formation of perceptions by the individual about what the new role will be like.

2. **Encounter**. The second stage in the cycle refers to the first days and weeks in the new role, involving a sort of reality check, by which the individual quickly learns about the basic characteristics of the job and the group of others that he or she will work with.

3. **Adjustment**. At this stage, the individual draws on the knowledge of the work and social environment that he or she has accumulated and develops his or her own style of fulfilling the work role.

Mentor and help facilitate transition for a colleague

One of the key challenges for any new recruit is to make the transition and adjust to a new work environment and organisation.

- TASK: Identify a new colleague in your team at work, or in your workgroup at university or college, and help them through the preparation and transition stages of the transition cycle.

- First ask if they have any questions for you about the team and the way people work – this helps with preparation. Second, help to facilitate informal encounter by introducing them to your other colleagues and team members, and explaining the roles that each person has. Try to facilitate networking by giving email addresses for the various people in the team. Your efforts should help to complement the formal induction offered by your organisation or institution. Reflect on the impact that this activity had for your colleague, and for you.

4. **Stabilisation**. In this fourth stage, the work associated with the job role becomes routine, with the person becoming more established in the role.

Moreover, in a development of the ASA model (the ASTMA model, incorporating Transformation and Manipulation), Roberts (2006) considers how, if managed properly, new recruits may grow to fit, or even effect change on, work environments and teams for positive benefit. Emergent thinking is also moving towards an acknowledgement of the effects of work on people, such that their attitudes, values and even personality traits may develop, deepen or change in response to integration in work environments (Woods et al., 2013).

CASE STUDY

Restructuring management and leadership in the international oil and gas industry

In this case study, we elaborate and focus on a specific issue – the challenges of recruitment and selection in a multinational oil and gas context. This scenario draws on the real-life experience of one of the authors.

The driver for change in this organisation was the need to develop as a world-class oil and gas business. Leadership and management were identified as the necessary catalyst. Presenting problems in these grades were:

- A lack of market competitiveness for excellent leadership and management – competitors had better developed leadership development and selection programmes.
- The attrition of talented leaders and managers who were leaving to join competitors that offered better salaries and benefits.
- A lack of skills in junior to middle management grades – managers and leaders at lower grades often lacked the competencies and skills to deliver strategy.

In response, corporate HR introduced a new, simpler executive hierarchy in order to standardise leadership and management grades across the whole business. There were to be only eight levels of management and leadership covering supervisors to chief executive. HR knew that to populate these new structures, it would need to blend an approach to:

- Identify and fast-track internal talent and high potential.
- Assimilate those competent at their current level.
- Recruit externally to key leadership positions (below chief officer and board).

A further complexity of the challenge was the international context of operations. In order to be world class, the organisation's strategy was to enhance international operations, particularly through development into new countries in Africa and through collaborative joint ventures with other operators. Leaders of the future may be called upon to work internationally, and would at the very least need a global mindset.

TASK: In this activity, you should discuss the scenario above. It is OK to make assumptions about the company but, in your discussion and in answering the questions below, you should state and be clear about these assumptions. Discuss in a group the challenges faced by this business and then answer the following questions with reference to material covered in this chapter:

1 What are the key steps that should be taken in approaching the challenges of recruiting and selecting people into these management grades?

2 How could HRM practitioners simultaneously ensure that recruitment and selection activities were fair and ethical, and adapted appropriately to meet the strategic needs of the organisation?

3 What are the other HRM processes and functions that are likely to influence the effectiveness of any solutions in this scenario?

CHAPTER SUMMARY

In this chapter, we have reviewed some of the key aspects of effective recruitment and selection in organisations, and considered these in the wider context of strategic HRM, together with practical applications in different kinds of business and situation. Key learning points from this chapter are:

- Effective recruitment and selection should be evidence-based, systematic and strategic. When recruitment and selection processes are conducted effectively, there are benefits for performance, for company image and perceptions of the organisation, and for people's well-being.

- Recruitment activity is under-researched, but there are some clear steps that help to make recruitment more effective and coherent. Social psychological theory tells us much about why people make decisions to apply to and join companies.

- There are well-evidenced structured techniques for assessing people for selection. However, a challenge for HR practitioners is to deploy these appropriately and adaptively in different contexts.

- In making selection decisions, practitioners need to carefully manage the impact of perceptions of person–team and person–organisation fit. Post-selection, there are steps to be taken to help recruits make the transition to the new company, socialise and integrate.

- Effective recruitment and selection must pay attention to fairness and ethical issues. These apply at recruitment, selection and policy levels.

REVIEW QUESTIONS AND EXERCISES

1. What are the potential outcomes for both individuals and organisations of poor recruitment and selection processes?

2. How has the role of the candidate changed in recent years in the process of recruitment and selection?

3. 'Managers aren't concerned with academic concepts like reliability and validity'. Discuss this assertion with reference to what you have learnt in this chapter.

4. As an HR manager of a large organisation, you are concerned that women are under-represented in your organisation. Outline how you would go about finding out if your recruitment and/or selection processes were to blame for this, and the steps you might take to resolve it.

5. Think of an organisation in which you have worked or of which you have some direct experience. On the basis of what you have learnt in this chapter, how could the organisation improve its recruitment and selection processes?

6. 'Due to the inherent problem of adverse impact, ability tests have shown themselves to be too risky to use for selection in organisations'. Do some further reading to come up with a reasoned argument for, or against, this statement.

7. Think back to a time when you had an interview for a job or for something at university. It was probably a stressful time for you. Spend some time reflecting on how it felt to be a candidate for that selection process. Note down some ideas about your experiences of the interview, what you thought of the interviewer, how they treated you, your perception of the organisation after the interview and any other relevant details. Perhaps your experiences of this interview even had some kind of lasting effect on you and your perception of the organisation or recruitment and selection in general. Once you have reflected deeply on your experiences, take those reflections and think how you could use this knowledge of what it's like to be a candidate and what you've learnt in this chapter to improve this selection process. Focus on how the experience could be improved for future candidates and think about the possible effects that improved applicant experience might have on the organisation.

EXPLORE FURTHER

Taylor, S. (2008) *People Resourcing*, 4th edn. London: CIPD. An excellent and practical text-book that guides you through all the stages of the people-resourcing process.

Brown, V.R. and Vaughn, E.D. (2011) The writing on the (Facebook) wall: The use of social networking sites in hiring decisions. *Journal of Business and Psychology*, 26(2): 219–225. An interesting paper that explores the emerging trend of employers using social networking information in the recruitment and selection process.

The O*Net online website at www.onetonline.org. This is a huge database of job analysis data, collected over a number of years by the US government, and is the first port of call for anyone conducting job analysis for a role.

GO ONLINE

Visit the companion website for **interactive quizzes**, explanatory **videos** and **podcasts**, **journal articles** to use in your essays, and **weblinks** to useful resources.

https://edge.sagepub.com/crawshaw2e

CHAPTER 8

DIVERSITY IN ORGANISATIONS: HRM AND INTERNATIONAL PRACTICES

Lilian Otaye-Ebede

Vincenza Priola

Elaine Yerby

CHAPTER KNOWLEDGE OBJECTIVES

- To understand how the concept of diversity has developed from an earlier focus on equal opportunities.
- To explore different perspectives on diversity management (DM), including mainstream and critical perspectives.
- To assess how different diversity perspectives have implications for the development and implementation of HRM policies and practices.
- To critically evaluate the links between HR diversity policies and diversity practices in organisations.
- To explore approaches to diversity across the globe.

KEY SKILLS OBJECTIVES

- To be able to link social, political and cultural contexts to ideas of diversity management.
- To be able to diversify diversity management interventions to fit in with the organisation's needs.
- To be able to develop HRM policies which are embedded in the organisation's cultural contexts.
- To be able to evaluate formal and informal diversity practices in organisations.

This chapter also provides indicative content for the following Intermediate and Advanced level CIPD modules:

CIPD INTERMEDIATE LEVEL MODULES

5CHR Business issues and the context of human resources

5HRF Managing and coordinating the human resources function

CIPD ADVANCED LEVEL MODULES

7HRC HRM in context

7LMP Leading, managing and developing people

GO ONLINE

This chapter comes with loads of online tools to help you to go that extra mile in your studies!

- **Multiple choice questions** to help you test your knowledge and revise for exams
- **Journal articles** so you can read further for assignments and essays
- **Videos** and **podcasts** help you to understand how complex concepts work in the real world

Visit **https://edge.sagepub.com/crawshaw2e** to access these resources for this topic.

INTRODUCTION

The concept of diversity is used to refer to social categories, such as gender, ethnicity, age, disability, religion and sexual orientation, which indicate groups who have been historically subjected to discrimination in society and work. In addition to these main categories, other dimensions such as social class and work or management status are often included when referring to diversity. Scholars distinguish these categories in several ways, but one of the most common is the distinction between visible (e.g. gender, race or ethnicity, age) and invisible (e.g. sexual orientation, religion) dimensions (Priola et al., 2014). Generally, discrimination on the basis of invisible dimensions is more difficult to detect and to expose and can cause stress in employees relating to their decision to disclose (or not) invisible categorisations (Claire et al., 2005; Ragins et al., 2007).

While categorisation may ease understanding of a specific social group, we need to be aware of the problems that such distinctions create. Social categories are often viewed as mutually exclusive groups in that one individual can only belong to one category – for example, either male or female, black or white, heterosexual or homosexual. In reality life is not so simple and we can all think of individuals whose identity is neither black nor white, or individuals who are neither homosexual nor heterosexual and so on. Social categorisation also has the potential to negate the concept of 'intersectionality'. Initial definitions of intersectionality focused on 'the ways in which race and gender interact to shape the multiple dimensions of black women's employment experiences' (Crenshaw, 1991: 1244). Although rooted in feminism, the concept of intersectionality in diversity can be attributed to any form of difference and several scholars (e.g. Kang and Bodenhausen, 2015; Nash, 2008; Wright and Priola, 2016) argue that intersectional research should, in fact, go beyond the categories of gender and race and should consider the impact of many other identities such as class, sexuality, disability and social status among others. Thus an individual can be discriminated against as a result of multiple dimensions of difference – for example, a working-class, black woman with a disability.

In addition to the essentialist view that social categorisation can create, we also need to be aware of the perils of stereotyping. Categorising implies a process of generalisation about members of a social group often based on clearly visible differences between the groups. Such process leads to the creation of stereotypes, which characterise vast human groups in terms of a few fairly crude common attributes (e.g. southern Europeans are loud), while neglecting the complexity and variety within groups. Internal homogeneity within groups does not exist (e.g. not all women are

Diversity Refers to social categories such as gender, ethnicity, age, disability, religion and sexual orientation, which indicate groups who have been historically subjected to discrimination in society and work. Other dimensions such as social class and work or management status are often included when referring to diversity within organisational life. Diversity is, thus, generally applied to recognising group differences and seeks to move beyond traditional characterisations of difference.

Social categories Generally refer to gender, race or ethnicity, age, sexual orientation, religion, physical and mental ability. Categorisation, while it can be useful in understanding the specific needs of social groups, can also lead to the formation of stereotypes, as individuals are often perceived to belong to only one category rather than allowing for category fluidity, and to possess all the characteristics of that category.

Discrimination Workplace discrimination can be overt or hidden and subtle but manifests itself when one social category is given preferable treatment, and/or another is disadvantaged, in relation to access to jobs, promotion, training or better terms and conditions in employment (formal) or is subjected to verbal and non-verbal behaviours limiting the respect, credibility and psychological well-being of individuals (informal discrimination).

feminine in their manners), therefore when referring to a social group it is important to be cautious in making generalisations.

The implications of social categories are important for both social and work lives, and, with reference to the workplace, it is necessary that workers develop awareness of diversity concepts and practices to facilitate inclusivity and participation of all workers in organisations. Organisations are not neutral in relation to social categories; however, they are often blind in neglecting the relevance of socio-demographic aspects to their functioning. Individuals come to work with their gender, sexual, racial or ethnic identities and these affect how they do their work, how they interact with others and how others interact with them. Organisational processes and practices, on the other hand, can systematically reproduce the dominant view, and in doing so exclude minority groups while promoting others (the dominant groups; see also Chapter 7 in relation to bias in selection). For example, when organisations arrange training courses during the evening or at weekends, they are excluding all employees with caring duties (more often women) from the opportunity to receive further training and potentially the opportunity to be promoted and progress further in their career (Danowitz et al., 2012). It is also argued that employers have overtly accommodated certain social categories more comfortably into organisational life compared to others and greater efforts have been focused on gender and disability issues when compared, for example, to sexuality issues with transgender employees still experiencing high levels of discrimination and violence. Organisational research on LGBTQ (lesbian, gay, bisexual, transgender and queer) employees reveals that sexual minorities and people transitioning or who have transitioned face considerable discrimination and disadvantage in the workplace. This highlights how perceived advances in organisational diversity management thinking and practice do not benefit all groups and ultimately individuals equally and that a focus on organisational practice providing a fair and safe place of work for minorities should be a priority on equality agendas.

Further caution is required when considering diversity issues around the world, given that social categories are not recognised in the same way or at the same level in different societies. Diversity literature has developed based on Western ideals and principles that underpin much of the current thinking on 'diversity management'; an important question thus concerns the extent to which diversity theories and practices become irrelevant in the context of societies and groups that have been shaped by specific historical, social, political, religious and cultural factors. This has led some authors to claim that diversity management is a mere rhetoric (Jamali et al., 2010) and that it assumes some meaning only when considered in the light of social, political and cultural factors.

Diversity management (DM) Generally refers to the business need for more diverse workforces to compete in new global labour and consumer markets. Inherently linked to the business case and liberal approach to equality, most DM approaches are grounded in the economic imperative to increase the diversity of employees within organisations.

The overarching aim of this chapter is to explore diversity within the context of HRM in a global perspective. The chapter begins with a discussion on the evolution of diversity and its legislative underpinning. We go on to discuss the business case argument for diversity management (a discourse that connects workforce diversity and enhanced organisational outcomes) and how it relates to HRM. Additionally, we discuss the relationship between diversity management and strategic HRM, culminating with a discussion on the future of international diversity management. Within the chapter there are a number of organisational examples and case studies which students can use to apply their learning. At the end of the chapter students will be able to critically evaluate the different diversity perspectives and the impact they have on organisational approaches to diversity management. In addition, students will have the opportunity to reflect on the relationship between strategic HRM and diversity management and the challenges and barriers associated with embedding effective diversity policies and practices in organisations. With a focus on different international and cultural contexts, the chapter aims to move beyond taken-for-granted assumptions and rhetoric about diversity management and expose students to the realities of embedding diversity initiatives within organisations. As students explore diversity issues in a range of organisational and international settings, as discussed in this chapter, they will have the opportunity to develop a critical understanding of contemporary diversity management approaches and practices.

LEGISLATIVE UNDERPINNING

The recognition of the need to pay attention to diversity in organisations began in the United States and has evolved over the years in terms of both conceptualisation and geographical extension, moving to Europe and, more recently, generating debates and interventions in newly industrialised countries. Social movements, followed by legislation, have influenced organisational practices and the development of diversity management policies and programmes across both public and private organisations.

Equal rights/opportunity legislation aims to achieve equality of opportunity for all by focusing on specific groups which have been discriminated against and ostracised in the past. The legislation on equal rights and opportunities also specifies equal employment opportunity (EEO), making it illegal to discriminate in the workplace against specific groups. In different countries equality legislation may or may not support affirmative action (also referred to as positive discrimination in the UK or employment equity in Canada), which represents a more proactive approach in defining measures that are designed to offset the effects of past discrimination and ensure the equal employment opportunities of disadvantaged groups. Affirmative action, for example, would include specific measures that encourage people from specific groups to apply for work (see Chapter 7) or training (Chapter 9). In the USA, laws were promulgated at the height of the civil rights movement in the 1960s and 1970s and have been amended regularly by the different administrations until recently. Initially, affirmative action was stipulated within the law (although in some cases enforcement has been patchy); however, since the Reagan presidency in the 1980s, legislative changes to curtail the administrative enforcement of affirmative action (AA) appeared to threaten the EEO/AA system (Burstein and Monaghan, 1986; Gutnam, 1993). More recently, and following a court ruling (in favour of Adarand in the 1995 *Adarand* v. *Pena* case), the Clinton administration concluded that affirmative action had not outlived its usefulness, but ordered agencies to eliminate or reform any practice that created employment quotas (used to increase the representation of minorities along the lines of their representation within the general population), led to the placement of unqualified individuals, discriminated against majority group members or continued after its goals had been met (Bureau of National Affairs, 1995; Yakura, 1995). Affirmative action as a practice was lately upheld by the Supreme Court's decision in relation to a specific case of university admission when the judge ruled that universities had a compelling interest in promoting class diversity (*Grutter* v. *Bollinger* 2003).

Human resource managers and EEO/AA specialists responded by developing efficiency arguments for their programmes (Kelly and Dobbin, 1998), initially by promoting EEO/AA practices as ways to formalise and rationalise personnel decisions, and eventually by developing business arguments for attracting a diverse workforce. While in the US affirmative action has been viewed as a 'business policy which has allowed industry to benefit from new ideas, opinions and perspectives generated by greater workforce diversity' (*Harvard Law Review*, 1989: 669) from an HRM perspective, EEO/AA specialists in the last two decades have recast equality measures as part of diversity management, touting the competitive and strategic advantages offered by practices such as anti-dsicrimination policies, training programmes and recruitment practices (Kelly and Dobbin, 1998). The emphasis on the strategic and competitive advantage buttressed the 'business case' for diversity (see later in chapter), which continues to dominate the contemporary mainstream literature (Kossek and Lobel, 1996; Özbilgin and Tatli, 2011; Subeliani and Tsogas, 2005).

Within the UK, legal compliance has been a major driver for employers to adopt diversity management policies. While significant demographic changes in British society and work environments in the last few decades have created the need to consider diversity issues in the workplace, approaches to equality within the UK have been highly influenced by European Union legislation. Despite the fact that the interpretation and implementation of EU legislation vary across member states in line with their gendered socio-economic contexts (Hoskyns, 1996; Ostner and Lewis, 1995), the EU framework has been an important influence on the national equality legislations of the EU members. For instance, the Amsterdam Treaty of 1997 introduced measures to reduce discrimination on the grounds of ethnicity, race, gender, age, religion or sexual orientation. In the UK, the Equality Act 2010 replaced and consolidated all previous equality legislation, including the Disability Discrimination Act 2005, the Equal Pay Act 1970 and the Race Relations (Amendment) Act 2000 (see also Chapter 12). The Act reforms, streamlines and harmonises the previous anti-discrimination legislation and covers nine protected characteristics, making it unlawful to discriminate on the grounds of age, disability (those who have, or have had, a disability), gender reassignment (no longer required to be under medical supervision), marriage and civil partnership, pregnancy and maternity, race, religion or belief (including lack of belief), gender and sexual orientation.

Equal opportunity (EO)
The term predates diversity management and is based on the principle of treating all people the same and not discriminating against people on the basis of particular characteristics, such as gender, race, ethnicity, sexual orientation, disability and age. In Western society EO approaches have become enshrined in employment law and reflected in policies of employment to prevent discrimination within the workforce.

In Asia, among the countries that have equality laws (in some cases these cover only specific groups which may not include all the above) there are examples of affirmative action in relation to specific groups. To illustrate, the Indian government classifies castes which are socially and educationally disadvantaged as Other Backward Classes. 'Reservation' is applied to improve their social and educational development. This allows a certain percentage of the total available vacancies in educational institutes and government jobs to be set aside for people from backward classes. Similarly, in China 'preferential policies' require that some of the top positions in government be distributed to ethnic minorities and women; also they require most universities to give preferred admission to ethnic minorities. Pakistan has also introduced quotas for the employment of women in the public sector and civil services (10 per cent), in national and provincial assemblies (20 per cent) and in local governing bodies (33 per cent) (Chaudhry and Priola, in press). The Japanese Equal Employment Law of 1985 (which came into force in April 1986) prohibits gender discrimination in relation to recruitment, hiring, promotion, training and job assignment.

In Canada, similar to the US context, the Employment Equity Act (EEA) requires firms to establish working conditions that are free of barriers to career advancement for four designated groups, specifically women, aboriginal peoples, persons with disabilities and 'visible' (racio-ethnic) minorities (Labour Program, 2013). The Equity Act also requires firms to report their employment statistics annually to the Canadian government, which acts as a driver for equality and diversity within organisations.

In Africa, the Black Economic Empowerment (BEE) programme was launched by the South African government in 2001 to deal with the inequalities of apartheid. The programme attempts to give previously disadvantaged groups (Black Africans, Coloureds, Indians and Chinese) of South African citizens some economic privileges which were previously not available to them. The measures include employment preference, skills development, ownership, management, socio-economic development and preferential procurement. Several other initiatives are present in other countries across the world; these above represent only a few examples.

As this chapter will go on to explore, the existence of equal opportunity legislation around the world has not automatically resulted in improved experiences within the workforce for diverse groups. Even within a supportive legislative environment, the historical, cultural, social and economic conditions of a country have a significant impact on the possibilities of creating fair and equal organisations and work opportunities.

FROM EQUAL OPPORTUNITIES TO MANAGING DIVERSITY

According to Goss (1994), there are two ways in which equal opportunities (EO) issues are located within HRM. The first approach is concerned with issues related to human capital and advocates the view that when opportunities to develop and progress for any particular group are obstructed, the result will be the sub-optimal use of human resources: 'Equal opportunities is a purely practical matter of outcomes that need not be concerned with the nature or origins of inequalities; what is important is the resource value of the employee, not their social status' (Goss, 1994: 156). Such a

---

Linking social, political and cultural contexts to diversity management approaches

Organisational approaches to diversity management are influenced by a range of macro-national forces external to the workplace, such as anti-discrimination and human rights laws. However, experiences of diversity management within the workplace are shaped by more than just organisational and legal contexts. Environmental scanning skills that take into account the full range of social, cultural, ethnic and religious factors that interplay with the legal framework are essential for HR and diversity specialists.

TASK: Consider factors beyond legal compliance with the law that could shape and influence the diversity management strategy for the faculty of a university business school. Taking these issues into account, draft a diversity management strategy document that could be presented to senior managers.

Human capital This approach advocates that when opportunities for any particular group to develop and progress are obstructed, the result will be the sub-optimal use of human resources. Adopting a resource-based view of the firm, the management of diversity is not concerned with inequality but with optimising the resource value of each employee.

Social justice Located within the humanistic view of HRM, the social justice approach views diversity management from a moral and ethical perspective and focuses on the processes that determine injustice. A social justice approach seeks to address inequalities by promoting the understanding and integration of social differences. The emphasis is therefore on the promotion of equality as a social duty for the employer rather than as an economic imperative.

Liberal approach to equal opportunity This approach suggests that equality of opportunity exists when individuals are enabled to freely compete for social rewards. Therefore the role of the policy maker is merely that of the referee, required to ensure that the rules of competition are not discriminatory and are fairly applied for all. The function of EO/DM policies is to devise fair procedures, avoiding direct and indirect discrimination.

Radical approach to equal opportunity This approach significantly differs from the liberal view in that it is more proactive in seeking intervention on workplace practices on the basis of moral value and social worthiness. The radical approach is concerned with the outcome of the contest and the distribution of rewards.

functionalist approach is in contrast with the humanistic view of HRM within which the social justice approach can be located. This views equal opportunities as a moral and ethical project that focuses on the processes that determine injustice and seeks to address inequalities by promoting the understanding and integration of social differences (see also Chapter 4 for further discussion of ethics and social justice in HRM). The emphasis is therefore first and foremost on the promotion of equality as a social duty for the employer; economic benefits may derive from this, but should not be the main concern.

Similarly, Jewson and Mason (1986) explore the differences between the liberal and the radical approaches to equal opportunities and discuss the conceptual and practical applications of both approaches in the workplace. They suggest that the liberal conception argues that equality of opportunity exists when individuals are enabled to freely compete for social rewards. Therefore, the role of the policy maker is merely that of the referee, required to ensure that the rules of competition are not discriminatory and are fairly applied for all. The function of EO policies is to devise fair procedures, avoiding direct and indirect discrimination; therefore, in terms of principles embodied in the policy, these are merely procedural ones. While acknowledging that talent and ability are individual attributes, liberalism ignores the social and structural causes of inequalities and what determined the abilities, or the lack of them, in the first place.

The radical approach significantly differs from the liberal view in that it is more proactive in seeking intervention on workplace practices on the basis of moral value and social worthiness. If the liberal approach is concerned with the rules and fairness of the procedures, the radical approach is concerned with the outcome of the contest and the distribution of rewards. Discrimination goes beyond the individual affected and needs to focus at the group level (e.g. black people, women, disabled people). Furthermore, concepts such as ability and talent are considered as the result of social traditions and artefacts, which have been developed by the ruling elite and therefore are embedded in relationships of power.

In terms of the implementation of EO activities, the liberal view requires the bureaucratisation of procedures (devising fair procedures), while the radical view requires the politicisation of decision making. Decision, for radical supporters, is interpreted as an opportunity to advance the interests of disadvantaged groups. Organisational officers are recommended to support, advance or favour members of disadvantaged groups whenever possible. In addition, supporters of the radical approach urge organisational decision makers to consider the implications for the various minority groups of all decisions as well as rules, regulations and organisational practices in general. To achieve the implementation of equal opportunities within a radical conception, the promotion of ideological consciousness of justice and fairness is advocated at all organisational levels: 'The raising of collective consciousness is conceived as an integral part of a long and enduring struggle. Indeed radicals may regard this as the most fruitful contribution that policy can make to the attainment of equal opportunities' (Jewson and Mason, 1986: 326).

With the change of political and social landscapes in the last 50 years in both the USA and Europe, the emphasis on equal opportunities as equal redistribution (and some argue equal recognition as well – see Fraser, 1997) of education, training, employment and career development opportunities has shifted to a less politicised emphasis on diversity. The terminology of equal opportunities is seen as associated with the politics of the 1960s and 1970s and a socialist approach to redistribution (of opportunities as well as resources), including affirmative action. As legislation in the USA moved away from affirmative action, and as more private sector organisations have introduced equality policies and programmes within their HR function, the emphasis on 'sameness' has shifted towards an emphasis on valuing 'difference', leaving space for what is referred to as diversity management (Cassell, 2001; Greene and Kirton, 2010; Thomas and Ely, 1996).

The term 'managing diversity' was first coined by R. Roosevelt Thomas, who was an early diversity consultant to Fortune 500 companies and in 1983 founded the American Institute for Managing Diversity. He later emphasised the business case for managing diversity in his 1990 *Harvard Business Review* article, arguing the link between diversity management and firms' competitive advantage, and acknowledged the connections with earlier EEO/AA efforts (cf. Kelly and Dobbin, 1998).

> A lot of executives are not sure why they should want to learn to manage diversity. Legal compliance seems like a good reason. So does community relations. Many executives believe they have a social and moral responsibility to employ minorities and women. Others want to placate an internal group or pacify an outside organisation. None of these are bad reasons, but none of them are business reasons, and given the nature and scope of today's competitive challenges, I believe only business reasons will supply the necessary long-term motivation. ... Learning to manage diversity will make you more competitive. (Thomas, 1990: 112–117)

Since then various arguments have arisen which have contributed to accentuating the business case for diversity in organisations, confining the moral case for social justice to more theoretical and policy-oriented debates. While the moral case for social justice suggests that, as a result of past discrimination against people of certain social groups, organisations as well as society are morally obligated to promote social justice and compensate those who have been intentionally and unjustly wronged (Kellough, 2006), the business case for diversity management in organisations refers to the demographic changes altering labour markets as well as consumer markets, which have created the need for organisations to attract different groups of workers. The argument here is that, when employees from diverse backgrounds feel appreciated and comfortable, they will contribute more to the organisation, increase their productivity, as well as lending cultural expertise. On the other hand, with changes in consumer markets and the need for organisations to reach new markets and newly wealthy minority groups, they will have to develop new products and marketing approaches. Attracting employees from these groups would allow the organisation to have access to customers' needs and tastes which would inform the development of products and services (Kelly and Dobbin, 1998). The focus, though, is on organisational business interest, rather than on moral interest.

As discussed above, the concept of managing diversity emerged initially in the USA, to move to Europe and Australia. However, as more non-Western corporations are operating in international markets, current attention is now being paid to how translatable and relevant the concept is for non-Western countries, particularly countries such as Brazil, Russia, India and China (the BRIC countries) where organisations and their economies are experiencing rapid growth. Cooke and Saini's (2012) qualitative study of managing diversity strategies and practices in Chinese and Indian organisations shows the different significance attributed to diversity management by Chinese and Indian managers. Their study revealed that Chinese managers interviewed did not see diversity management as an issue, while Indian managers attributed greater significance to diversity from both legal and financial added-value perspectives. The study also reported that it was rare to find a formal written policy on diversity management in Chinese and Indian organisations. Where it did exist, its focus was on avoiding conflict rather than adding value to the business or addressing social injustice. In acknowledging the small sample size of the study, the authors highlight the importance of the political, social and economic differences between China and India and the Western context from where the concept of managing diversity has originated.

EVALUATING THE BUSINESS CASE FOR DIVERSITY MANAGEMENT

According to the business case perspective, there is much scholarly interest in how to effectively manage a diverse workforce as a source of competitive advantage. However, research on the performance implications of diversity management has often produced contradictory findings (see reviews by Guillaume et al., 2013, 2015; Joshi and Roh, 2009; Shore et al., 2009; Van Knippenberg and Schippers, 2007). On one hand, researchers have reported beneficial outcomes for those organisations which proactively manage diversity; these include: greater innovation and competitive advantage (Bassett-Jones, 2005; Richard et al., 2004); the ability to attract and retain the best talent available; reduced costs, due to lower turnover and fewer lawsuits (Carlozzi, 1999; Cox, 1991; Cox and Blake, 1991; Cox, T.H., 1993; Robinson and Dechant, 1997). Other scholars have reported contradictory results in relation to retention and organisational performance (Sacco and Schmitt, 2005) and lower employee satisfaction and higher turnover (O'Reilly et al., 1989) among those organisations with an active diversity management policy.

An example of an organisation that implemented a diversity management programme, declaring the business case for its introduction, is Aeon, a major Japanese retailer, which employs more than 58,000 workers over 300 stores throughout the country. In an attempt to enhance the organisation's competitiveness, the executive team decided to further develop female employees' managerial skills in order to compete with foreign-owned retailers that have entered the Japanese retail market since 2003. The new business strategy was based on increasing the number of female merchandisers and targeting more female customers; the company also implemented a new promotion programme that would increase the number of female store managers (Taniguchi, 2006). The senior team was motivated by what is referred to as the 'information and decision-making' justification (Williams and O'Reilly, 1998) for having a more diverse workforce, whereby an increase in female managers would be justified by the need to achieve a greater understanding of the primary (female) customer needs.

The proportion of female managers in Japan is much lower than in other developed countries. At the time of this study in 2005, only 5.1 per cent of managerial positions were held by women and only 2.8 per cent were directors. Due to the cultural significance of longevity of service and the importance placed on long working hours in gaining access to senior positions, Japanese women have been penalised in relation to promotion opportunities and career development due to the prolonged periods of leave that most of them experience in order to fulfil caring responsibilities. The significant shortfall in the number of women in managerial roles was recognised as a serious social and economic issue by the Japanese government, which set a target to increase the percentage of female managers to 30 per cent by 2020. The low participation rate of female managers was evident at Aeon, which at the start of their own female positive action programme had only one female store manager. Following the implementation of the programme, the company experienced a 12 per cent increase in the number of female store managers, alongside stronger sales and profit growth (Taniguchi, 2006).

The authors of the study suggest that the success of the programme went beyond an 'information and decision-making perspective' and increased performance resulted from applying a 'competitive advantage justification' for the diversity initiative. As identified by Kidder et al. (2004), justifying diversity programmes based on needing to change due to competitive threats to the company is more acceptable to employees than change based on legislative requirements or social arguments. The entry of Western companies, such as WalMart, into the Japanese retail market was perceived as a significant threat and employees were willing to support the cultural changes needed to increase the number of women in management positions, as this was crucial to the survival of the company. The way in which the right contextual environment favours the successful implementation of diversity programmes highlights the complex and controversial relationship between diversity and organisational performance. Taniguchi's (2006) case study at Aeon stresses the need for alignment between the external context of the firm and changes to the internal organisational features, such as organisational culture and promotion processes and practices.

Such results highlight the complexity of diversity management in relation to the context within which policies and programmes are implemented, but also in relation to the various perspectives and ways with which policies and actions are implemented in practice in the workplace. As highlighted by Jewson and Mason (1986), the development of equal opportunity policies in the workplace often reflects a confused and contradictory deployment of different conceptions of equal opportunities (e.g. critical or mainstream) and this is reflected in the use of terms and concepts in an arbitrary and confused manner. Theoretical and conceptual distinctions, which are routinely applied in scholarly analysis, in practice are often confused, and antithetical philosophical positions (e.g. liberal and radical) are paradoxically amalgamated.

The conceptual difficulties in defining and 'managing' diversity also apply to the relationship between a successful equality and diversity programme and organisational performance. Organisational performance is generally measured via financial measures, such as profits and sales, but also by a range of variables such as employee turnover or employee engagement. The 'business case' for diversity management, which advocates a relationship between diversity and organisational performance, is problematic due to: (a) the confusions in translating diversity management perspectives into practical actions; (b) the power struggles that exist among the different factions in organisations; and (c) the numerous factors that influence performance as well as the lack of a consistent measure of performance itself. Furthermore, in light of the contradictory findings in relation to the relationship between diversity management policies and performance, it would be dangerous to support DM on the exclusive basis of the business case, particularly when an active organisational engagement with diversity does *not* correspond to increased performance. What should an organisation do when it emerges that supporting minority groups does not result in greater productivity? Should it just abandon DM practices? Should inclusion and equality values be embedded in organisational practices even when these do not produce financial gains? Should an organisation have a moral obligation to groups that have been historically ostracised? Reflecting on these issues will help students and practitioners to achieve their own assessment of the business case for DM.

ONLINE STUDY TOOLS

Video Case Study: Diversity and Inclusion at a Culture Organisation

Watch this informative account of diversity and inclusion at the British Council where a representative of the Diversity and Inclusion in India Forum interviews Rekha Verma, the head of staff planning and strategic initiatives.

https://edge.sagepub.com/crawshaw2e > Student Resources > Chapter 8 > Videos

DIVERSITY PERSPECTIVES AND HRM PRACTICES

As mentioned earlier, there is a divide between radical/critical diversity studies, which explore discrimination in employment around group-based disadvantages (e.g. Nkomo, 1992; Ogbonna and Harris, 2006; Parsons and Priola, 2013), and liberal/mainstream studies, which focus on equality procedures and investigate performance-related outcomes of diversity (e.g. Joshi et al., 2006; Nishii and Mayer, 2009). More specifically, the shift from equality based on legislation to diversity management has resulted in diverging views from HR scholars. On the one hand, mainstream scholars conceptualise the shift as a positive development, while on the other, critical scholars are alarmed by its potentially regressive implications for fairness at work (Dick and Cassell, 2002). The critique of diversity and the concerns over a shift from equal opportunities to diversity management have now become commonplace in critical diversity research circles (Tatli, 2011). The main concern of the critics is that the managerial and utilitarian conception of difference sidelines social justice arguments and obscures structural inequalities (Janssens and Zanoni, 2005; Linnehan and Konrad, 1999; Sinclair, 2006; Tatli, 2011). Given this divide, HR managers tend to develop HR diversity policies and practices based on the underlying organisational cultural perspective. For example, an organisation emphasising equality principles in its culture and practices is more likely to have HR policies and practices that are geared towards equality and fairness; while organisations that are more focused on human capital (see above) will tend to develop diversity policies oriented to the improvement of the organisational performance.

DEBATING HRM

From diversity to inclusion

The HRM perspective on diversity management has been criticised by scholars (e.g. Benschop, 2001; Benschop and Dooreward, 1998; Dickens, 1998; Truss, 2001) for representing 'employees' as a generic category and for avoiding engaging with the very different effects that HRM activities may have on different categories of personnel (Benschop, 2001). Furthermore, it has been argued that HRM needs to reflect the growing interest in the concept of '**inclusion**' (Kumra and Manfredi, 2012), rather than just focusing on diversity statistics. The assumption underpinning much of the HRM diversity management literature and practice advocates the business case, suggesting that organisational performance will be increased via broadening the range of groups within the workforce; however, critics challenge this position, arguing that performance gains will only be achieved once diverse groups feel 'included', not just represented. Inclusion is defined as 'the removal of obstacles to the full participation and contribution of employees in organisation' (Roberson, 2006: 217). Shore et al. (2010) noted that two key elements of inclusive practice are to encourage a sense of 'belongingness' and 'uniqueness' among all employees, who have to feel valued as unique individuals, not just as members or representatives of diverse groups. Inclusion theorists argue that the diversity management agenda has failed to move beyond the business case model and has ignored the unique talents and needs of individuals. It is argued that there is the need to rethink HRM approaches to diversity management from the perspective of inclusion, examining the implications of organisational practices for individual employees and thus the implications of such heterogeneity for organisational practices and how this heterogeneity influences the organisation's performance. How this is done poses another challenge for HR managers (Kumra and Manfredi, 2012).

TASK: *In small groups, discuss the following:*

1   What key issues need to be taken into consideration when designing HR practices to promote inclusion in the workplace?

2   Can the social justice perspective be reconciled with the business case in the implementation of inclusion policies and practices? If so, how?

Having said this, it is rare for contemporary organisations to be focused solely on either justice or the business case. Most tend to comply with equality laws as well as developing and implementing policies and practices that have the potential to improve the functioning of their organisations. A recent longitudinal study (Otaye-Ebede and Tatli, 2013) examined the changing discourse of HR policies and practices before and after the economic recession, describing ways in which HR/diversity and equality officers pitched workforce diversity policies and programmes internally in their organisations during the pre-recession and post-recession periods in the UK. The findings suggest that in times of economic crisis the business case for diversity was less emphasised, whereas the legal and moral discourses were more emphasised. This signals that building the legitimacy of diversity management solely on the business case is a dangerous move as it engenders the possibility of abandonment of equality, inclusion and diversity initiatives if they are not seen as profitable. As DM has arguably been built on the legacy of the equal opportunity legislation (Liff and Wajcman, 1996) and social justice arguments, social responsibility in addition to legal compliance should form the major driver for employers to adopt diversity management policies and implement diversity management programmes (Tatli, 2008).

It is obvious that the adoption of diversity policy does not necessarily result in workplace equality and inclusion; in fact, after more than 40 years of gender equality legislation, women are still a minority in senior roles in workplaces across the world. Among the sectors with the widest gender gap is the financial sector, still dominated by white, middle-class men in senior positions (see also Chapter 10). A new review commissioned by the UK Treasury and the Bank of England (HM Treasury and Virgin Money, 2016) has recently called for banks to set targets for gender diversity, suggesting that failing to meet this objective should result in cuts to top executives' bonuses. The successful example of the target of 25 per cent of female membership in non-executive roles in FTSE 100 company boards set in the UK in 2012, which has now, after four years, been met, has been highlighted as a powerful scheme to be emulated. The new scheme for gender equality in banking will not be enforceable by law but large institutions will tend to comply in order to avoid being named and shamed. There are other examples of gender targets set by banks but such interventions have often been limited in scope. For example HSBC, which employs less than a third of women in senior roles, has set the target of half the senior manager posts at the new Birmingham headquarters retail bank

---

Evaluating formal and informal diversity practices in organisations

Developing and implementing effective diversity strategies and practices is not straightforward; in fact, diversity management approaches have been criticised for not adequately addressing unequal outcomes and discrimination in organisations. Therefore, it is essential for HR and diversity specialists to continually review and critically reflect on all practices (formal and informal) of inclusion/exclusion within their organisations, and strategically develop organisation-wide plans for action as a means to remove barriers for disadvantaged groups.

TASK: Access, via their websites, the diversity strategies or approaches of three organisations of your choice. Taking into account issues explored in this chapter:

1   Evaluate the strategies in relation to the key barriers or challenges that the organisations could face in implementing these strategies effectively in practice.

2   Consider five ways in which the strategies or policies could be improved.

3   Which other strategies, that have not been considered by the three organisations you searched, do you think could enhance inclusion in practice?

Examples of companies to explore are:

Tesco: www.ourtesco.com/working-at-tesco/everyone-is-welcome/everyone-is-welcome-at-tesco/

McDonald's: www.aboutmcdonalds.com/content/mcd/corporate_careers/inclusion_and_diversity.html

Google: www.google.co.uk/diversity/

Civil Service: www.gov.uk/government/organisations/civil-service/about/equality-and-diversity

to be filled by women (to be opened in 2019). While positive, such a decision is limited to the UK headquarters and the retail branch only. As revealed by the Equality and Human Rights Commission (2016), recruitment to the boards of FTSE 350 companies (of which 90 per cent have no female executive director) remains 'shadowy and opaque' and still relies on the 'old boys network', which makes it difficult for women, but also for racial minorities and disabled people to get access to senior roles.

DEBATING HRM

The link between diversity management and corporate social responsibility (CSR)

An emerging area of academic and practitioner interest is to link diversity management to the wider CSR agenda and strategy of the organisation. CSR issues have recently risen up the strategic agenda as a consequence of unethical and illegal business practices in the finance sector that have been argued to have contributed to the 2008 economic crash and several high-profile corporate scandals, such as Enron and Arthur Andersen. While the concept of CSR was initially confined to how organisations can and should minimise the negative impact of their operating practices on the physical and social environment, increasingly CSR is analysed through a multiple stakeholder perspective, which considers the ways in which organisations can affect the lives of their employees, their local community and the wider society. It is argued that a broader interpretation of CSR could encourage organisations to implement social justice approaches to diversity management, as part of their internal management practices (Kumra and Manfredi, 2012):

1   How does linking diversity management within the wider CSR agenda and strategy of the organisation afford the opportunity for the greater promotion of social justice approaches to diversity management?

2   What are the potential organisational and structural constraints that may derive from such an agenda?

3   Would the integration of DM and CSR dilute the political importance of equality and diversity?

STRATEGIC HRM AND DIVERSITY MANAGEMENT

Diversity management has been defined as 'a process intended to create and maintain a positive work environment where the similarities and differences of individuals are valued, so that all can reach their potential and maximize their contributions to an organization's strategic goals and objectives' (US Government Accountability Office [GAO], 2005: 1). This definition clearly identifies the effective management of diversity as an important strategic goal for organisations. As noted in Chapter 2, strategic HRM encompasses those managerial decisions and actions which concern the management of employees at all levels and which are directed towards creating and sustaining competitive advantage (Miller, 1994: 114). Strategic HRM requires HR policies and practices to be linked with the strategic objectives of the organisation. However, the alignment of the HR strategy to the overall business strategy is not necessarily uncomplicated; rather, it is a complex and iterative process (Monks and McMackin, 2001) which is often contested for emphasising the business goal and mainly focusing on organisational performance rather than focusing on the employees' perspective. The link between SHRM and diversity management is further complicated by the emphasis of SHRM on organisational performance, which is seen as limiting diversity management to a business case perspective. In fact, many equality and diversity scholars and professionals contest the link with SHRM for its reluctance to move beyond the business case argument, largely ignoring arguments of social justice and fairness. While research has shown that often organisations justify their diversity management strategy in business terms, it can be argued that the role of an HR strategy should be to influence the strategic goals of the organisation with an emphasis on creating an inclusive work culture which, first and foremost, nurtures individual talent and diversity.

This latter issue has started to penetrate organisational thinking and practice. As the research findings began to mount that having written diversity policies and strategies based on a business case philosophy was insufficient in realising the full potential of a diverse workplace (Carlsson and Rooth, 2007; Ziegert and Hanges, 2005), strategic HRM practitioners started to promote diversity *and* inclusion. As the 'Debating HRM' feature 'From diversity to inclusion' in this chapter highlights, it is argued that organisations should seek to create a culture of inclusiveness focused on engaging and valuing the input of all employees. Inclusion puts diversity into action by creating an organisational culture of involvement, respect and connections, where the richness of diverse ideas, backgrounds and perspectives is harnessed to promote organisational performance and employee well-being (Kumra and Manfredi, 2012). The UK Civil Service, NHS, Google and other leading organisations now define their approach to diversity in these terms.

Unconscious bias
Refers to the associations we hold about people from different social categories, which exist outside our conscious awareness and have a significant influence on our attitudes and behaviour. In organisational diversity terms it is considered of particular relevance in recruitment and selection and performance appraisal, as unconscious bias means assessors can automatically respond positively or negatively to people irrespective of merit.

Related to the move towards 'inclusiveness' is the growth in practitioner and academic interest in unconscious bias. With its origins in psychology, organisational interest in unconscious bias has increased over the past few years supported by a body of evidence that has allowed the concept to become attributed as one of the reasons organisations have failed to fully utilise diverse talent and break down organisational inequality. Unconscious bias refers to the associations we hold about people from different social categories, which exist outside our conscious awareness and have a significant influence on our attitudes and behaviour. In HRM it is considered of particular relevance in recruitment, selection and performance appraisal, as unconscious bias means assessors can automatically respond positively or negatively to people irrespective of merit. Therefore the role of unconscious bias training is to understand the biases we hold and explore how to reduce their impact on organisational decision making with the objective of achieving fairer and more inclusive organisations (Equality Challenge Unit, 2013).

Several organisations have embraced the focus on unconscious bias. For example, PwC provides 'Open Mind' mandatory training biennially for all partners and interviewers and assessors. The training is designed to make employees think about the impact of unconscious bias on their working relationships, and consider situations where they can take action to be more open-minded to difference. The emphasis is on individual responsibility to challenge biased assumptions in themselves and others. (For more details see www.pwc.co.uk/careers/student/aboutpwc/diversity.html.) Similarly, Google is undertaking a multi-year project to understand how inclusive organisational cultures are built and sustained and how their employees can take conscious control of their actions, behaviours and cultural contributions. Beyond just training initiatives they are examining the verbal and physical cues that can influence employees' feeling of inclusion and their likelihood to engage in a particular activity (see https://rework. withgoogle.com/subjects/unbiasing/). For example, Google has sought to remove unconsciously biased cues from their workspaces such as the naming of rooms after famous male scientists (Cheryan et al., 2009).

While the organisational currency for inclusive cultures remains buoyant, our empirical understanding of the impact of these initiatives on effective equality and inclusion is still relatively weak. The emphasis on unconscious bias has been criticised for underestimating and masking the continued existence of explicit bias and discrimination in organisations. Inclusion strategies are accused of relaxing the motivations to achieve genuine equality behind a mask of harmony and reflective practice (Dovidio, 2013). Addressing calls for more empirical research to explore the links between inclusion and performance, Sabharwal (2014) identified the importance of supportive leadership and empowering employees with more information and resources as being essential for a genuine inclusive culture to emerge. Further sector- and industry-specific research which explores a full range of outcomes is required in order to build a more complete evidence base before inclusion and unconscious bias can be offered as a significant step forward in embedding workplace equality.

MINI CASE STUDY

'Unbiasing' at Google

Google openly states that it is not where it wants to be in terms of the diversity of its workforce. In the USA 70 per cent of employees are male and 60 per cent are white. Seeking to make sure that Google is an inclusive and fair place to work for everyone it has adopted a range of activities to improve the equality of their current workforce and future employees. Key activities include transparency in diversity profiling, a diverse range of benefits, infusing diversity into all people management practices and supporting initiatives to address gender imbalances in the participation in science and technology subjects in schools and higher education.

Underpinning its approach to diversity is unbiasing education. Unbiasing is the term Google uses to mitigate unconscious bias and to 'give your first thought a second look'.

(Continued)

(Continued)

Based on academic research that reveals that awareness of unconscious bias can lead to a reversal in biased outcomes (Lebrecht et al., 2009; Legault et al., 2011; Mendoza et al., 2010), Google argues that exposing our unconscious biases that underlie our beliefs is necessary for changing attitudes and behaviour.

Since 2013 Google has been educating employees and leaders (known as Googlers) in exploring their unconscious bias at work to start a conversation about 'unbiasing'. The aim was to provide a common awareness, understanding and platform to talk about unconscious bias. A key aim was to contextualise the debates within the language of technology and the computer science industry that employees could relate to. To illustrate, Google describes unconscious bias almost as a computer programme:

> Unconscious biases are the automatic, mental shortcuts used to process information and make decisions quickly. At any given moment individuals are flooded with millions of bits of information, but can only consciously process 40. Cognitive filters and heuristics allows [*sic*] the mind to consciously prioritise, generalise, and dismiss large volumes of input. These shortcuts can be useful when making decisions with limited information, focus or time but can sometimes lead individuals astray and have unintended consequences in the workplace.

Googlers attend unconscious bias workshops where they explore how to mitigate bias and build 'bias-busting actions into Google's people processes to ensure they yield fair outcome'.

Google acknowledges that there are still significant gaps in its empirical and practical knowledge on how to mitigate unconscious bias. But it believes that in order to create a workplace that supports and encourages diverse talents, ideas and perspectives, a platform and tools to begin 'unbiasing' are needed. Google believes the unconscious conscious is critical to creating a welcoming and inclusive workplace.

Sources: https://rework.withgoogle.com/subjects/unbiasing/ and www.google.co.uk/diversity/at-google.html

CASE STUDY QUESTIONS

1. Critically consider the strengths and weaknesses of Google's approach to unbiasing education.
2. What barriers do you think Google could experience in embedding unbiasing education?
3. Do you think this approach to addressing inequality can be effective? Why? Why not?
4. What do you think are the dangers in focusing on unconscious bias as opposed to both conscious and unconscious bias?

An example of an organisation that has integrated diversity management into its strategy is LANXESS. LANXESS is a multinational company whose business is the development, manufacturing and marketing of plastics, rubber, intermediates and speciality chemicals. It started in Germany but currently employs people from 31 different countries and has a strategic growth focus on the emerging economies of countries such as Brazil, Russia, India and China. In 2011, LANXESS established its Diversity and Inclusion initiative with the aim to achieve structured development of diversity by promoting equal opportunity and work–life balance in the traditionally male-dominated chemical industry. As part of this initiative, LANXESS reviewed and extended several human resource processes. One such diversity management measure, which LANXESS integrated into the organisational strategy, is the Senior Trainee Programme, which currently involves 13 highly qualified women and one man who, with the support of LANXESS, are returning to employment after a long period spent raising a family. The pro-gramme lasts 18 months and includes tasks and personal development training through mentoring and individual coaching. As stated in the company annual report: 'This initiative reflects the great importance of a diverse work-force for our competitiveness on global markets, for increasing our innovative strength and performance capabilities and for attracting and retaining promis-ing talents.' Another project introduced by LANXESS is the establishment of a corporate target to increase the propor-tion of women in mid-level and upper management by around 20 per cent by 2020. (Sources: http://lanxess.com/en/corporate/about-lanxess/diversity-inclusion/ and www.annualreport2012.lanxess.com/the-group/corporate-responsibility/employees/development-opportunities-and-diversity-for- international-markets.html.)

Strategic fit and diversity management

This chapter has explored the importance of HR and diversity management specialists adopting context-specific interventions to DM, including linking activities to the strategic goals and needs of the organisation.

TASK: Access the strategic plan of an organisation you are familiar with. Identify four key diversity management interventions that could support the achievement of the organisation's key objectives.

GLOBAL VERSUS MULTINATIONAL DIVERSITY MANAGEMENT

As this chapter has already explored, defining diversity and diversity management is not straightforward due to the different perspectives and approaches within the field. When considering international or global applications of diversity management from the perspective of an MNC, it becomes even more important to consider contextual factors that shape different societies' understanding and acceptance of issues relating to inequality, discrimination and diversity and how they can and should be managed by organisations that operate in international settings. In recent years we have witnessed the emergence of dissonant views from Africa, Asia and South America concerning the over-dominance of Western academic and practitioner diversity literature, which cannot fully address the different roles that race and religion have played in shaping diversity and equality experiences around the globe (Syed and Özbilgin, 2009). It is thus important for HR practitioners to understand the principles and debates in contemporary global diversity management.

Global diversity management strategy
A global diversity strategy in MNCs is centrally controlled by the head office and can be equally adopted across all subsidiaries; alternatively, the policies and practices are adapted to different national contexts within which the organisation operates.

HRM IN PRACTICE

The influence of the context

The environment within which organisations and their departments operate significantly influences their processes, operations and daily work activities. Research has shown that the external environment has far-reaching effects on the HR department's practices and policies. The enactment of workplace legislation affects nearly all HRM practices; for example, anti-discrimination legislation has influenced firms' selection processes and practices. In fact, with the enforcement of anti-discrimination legislation, unfair recruitment practices could potentially result in legal charges of discrimination and have repercussions on the company's reputation as well as having significant cost implications, in both settlement and legal costs. In order to protect themselves from these charges, organisations are obliged to conduct their hiring process in a rigorous and fair manner, whereby job qualifications and skills are mainly used as the selection criteria. Following the same arguments, HRM practices are also strongly influenced in various ways by the expanding cultural diversity of the workplace. In order to address the demographic changes in the workforce, organisations are introducing different measures to meet the different needs of employees. For example:

- Some firms are attempting to accommodate the needs of families by offering benefit options like extended maternity leave, on-site child care provision, flexible time and job sharing.
- Some organisations are attempting to accommodate the needs of older workers through skill upgrading and training designed to facilitate the acceptance and learning of new techniques.
- Some organisations provide a multi-faith prayer room for their religiously diverse workforce.
- Some companies are educating their low-skilled workforce in basic reading, writing and mathematical skills so that they can keep up with rapidly advancing technologies.

It is argued that due to the impact of globalisation and the internationalisation of organisations, labour markets and customer bases, multinational organisations have increasingly experienced the need to address issues concerned with diversity in different countries and thus to develop global diversity strategies (Kumra and Manfredi, 2012). Despite this, global diversity management as a field of study is still in its infancy

(Kumra and Manfredi, 2012; Özbilgin and Tatli, 2008). Evidence suggests that many multinational organisations simply rely on Western-centric ideals and approaches to diversity management and assume that these can easily be transported into their international subsidiaries and operations (Nishii and Özbilgin, 2007). However, such an approach has demonstrated many flaws and highlighted the need for global diversity management to consider the socially constructed nature of social categories. MNCs can choose to develop a global diversity strategy which, while remaining centrally controlled, is adapted to the different national contexts within which the organisation operates. Alternatively, organisations can opt to adopt a multinational diversity strategy. In this case organisational diversity policies are developed for each national context (e.g. in each subsidiary) by local professionals with consideration for the national culture(s) and how these are shaped by political, social, historical, legal and religious norms.

Nishii and Özbilgin (2007) highlight that when MNCs adopt a global strategy it is important to consider specific national contexts and understand how each country might differentially define and conceptualise diversity from a social, legal and political perspective (see also Chapter 5). In addition, they suggest that an organisational global diversity management approach should support and develop multicultural teams and develop cultural and global competences, in order to build effective relations between employees around the globe. While MNCs can operate within an overarching global diversity strategy, they need to build flexibility into organisational definitions of global diversity to allow for local variations that can take into account the specific social-historical context of a region. Multinational organisations implementing global diversity management practices should not rely on a one-size-fits-all approach and assume that practices that are effective in the home operating country can be replicated elsewhere.

For example HSBC, while having a workforce originating from over 150 countries, has recently been under pressure for the homogeneity of its senior managers, who do not demographically represent the wider workforce employed. Its diversity strategy reflects the human capital approach explored at the beginning of the chapter, and allows for diversity to be managed differently in each of its global operating regions. To illustrate, in the UK there is a focus on enhancing and supporting the contribution of women by encouraging more applications via the graduate recruitment scheme. On the other hand, in subsidiaries in Latin America wider social inclusion initiatives are the main focus as integrating different social groups within the workplace is a priority. The regions are encouraged to embed the value of inclusion within all

Developing HRM policies that are embedded in the national cultural context

Since global forces shape the diverse nature of organisations and workforces and the localities in which organisations are based, it is increasingly important for HR specialists to have a strong understanding of the cultural context(s) in which their organisations operate.

TASK: Research and design an expatriate HR strategy for an Australian company that has established a new operating base in China. The strategy should take into account the cultural context of the new operating country.

management practices, and this 'inclusiveness' approach is underpinned by a range of global management practices. HSBC has diversity committees or fora in all its business units across the globe. These committees include representatives from human resources and senior management from the different regions and coordinate and monitor the global diversity strategy. In addition, HSBC has a global diversity training programme for all management levels as well as region-specific training. The global training is focused on values and behaviours and openness to new ideas and different ways of working. (Source: Cresser, 13 July 2011, FT.com: www.ft.com/cms/s/0/b486efb6-ad34-11e0-a24e-00144feabdc0.html#axzz2HtAvhiuG.)

PRACTISING EQUALITY IN AN INTERNATIONAL CONTEXT

In addition to the development of a diversity strategy, whether global or multinational, senior-level buy-in and ownership of the diversity agenda are essential if diversity initiatives are to be successful. The HR function plays a significant role in the coordination and promotion of equality, diversity and inclusion activities in MNCs. Common activities and practices include:

- **Global diversity forum.** The main roles of such a forum are to coordinate the global diversity strategy and disseminate key diversity messages to all employees. It is considered important that the forum includes senior executives from all the global operations. To be effective it needs to have a decision- and policy-making function and to analyse diversity activities and statistics in all the regions where the multinational organisation operates. Global diversity fora are now commonplace in Fortune Global 1000, FTSE 100 and generally multinational organisations from a variety of industries, including energy, financial services, hospitality, manufacturing and pharmaceuticals.

- **Global employee networks.** These are employee-led networks for different groups within organisations. The groups are encouraged to self-form and self-organise but are usually supported and facilitated by the HR department. The networks are made up of employees who belong to a specific social category or have common interests, backgrounds or experiences. Examples of employee networking groups include women's leadership networks, global disabilities groups and LGBT (lesbian, gay, bisexual and transgender) groups. All employees are offered the opportunity to participate and join relevant groups. Networks are often set up in local regions and global opportunities to discuss and share experiences are then facilitated by the company.

- **Global diversity training.** Diversity awareness training has been a common feature of diversity management best practice for a number of years. Approaches to diversity training differ between: (a) activities focused on specific groups (e.g. middle managers or women) and (b) a holistic approach whereby all members of the organisation are exposed to the training. Many multinational organisations often seek to provide the training on a global basis using webcast formats and electronic training tools to access employees across the globe (Kumra and Manfredi, 2012). However, diversity training specially developed for the different national contexts is also desirable.

While MNCs are encouraged to have global diversity management practices, it is problematic to automatically assume that the above activities will work on a global scale, as their effectiveness has also been challenged in a domestic setting. To illustrate, diversity training has been criticised in Western contexts for failing to improve the position of women and ethnic minorities despite having been the most common form of diversity initiative in Western organisations for over 20 years. Research has shown how men and women value and respond to diversity training activities differently (Holladay and Quiñones, 2003), therefore generic programmes that are not tailored to a particular group do little to address cultural and behavioural attitudes towards diversity. Worse still, there is evidence to suggest that the training can actually increase incidents of discrimination and bias, when employees attempt to act upon their new learning without having the contextual awareness and sensitivity needed (Kumra and Manfredi, 2012), a point to consider when reading Chapter 9.

DEBATING HRM

Critical reflection on diversity management practices

As highlighted in the above discussion of commonly applied global DM practices and approaches, it is important to cast a critical lens on these activities to ensure that they are appropriate for global and international organisations and operations.

TASK: *Working in small groups,*

1   Use academic and professional literature to build an ethical case for and against the implementation of a global diversity management strategy (one global strategy to be applied across all the organisation's sites – with appropriate local variations you feel important).

2   Do the same exercise for and against the implementation of a multinational diversity management strategy (a different strategy for each regional/national context).

THE FUTURE OF INTERNATIONAL DIVERSITY MANAGEMENT

In order to support the development of international diversity management and move away from the current over-reliance on Western approaches to diversity management, an enhanced empirical research base that offers new insights and situated know-ledge of international approaches to diversity management is required (Özbilgin and Tatli, 2008). Building a greater understanding of national specific experiences and approaches to diversity management will support the design and implementation of more effective diversity management strategies. It also affords the opportunity to look beyond the dominance of the business case approach, which characterises much of the Western thinking on and motivations for diversity management practices. It can be argued that the limitations of current thinking and practices in global and international approaches to DM are evidenced by the continued inequalities and disadvantages that minority groups such as women, ethnic minorities, disabled or LGBT employees still experience in contemporary organisations.

GRADUATE INSIGHTS

Mandeep's experiences

The following is taken from a conversation held with Mandeep (pseudonym), a part- time MSc HRM student, who, towards the end of her studies, has commenced work as an HR assistant at a subsidiary of a large manufacturing company.

Q: What is your current role and what are your responsibilities?

Mandeep: I have been in this post for three months and I am currently working as an HR assistant. The HR office at the site where I work includes two other people and one is the HR manager, so my role is to support her, mainly with responsibility concerned with training and development.

Q: Does the job correspond to what you thought when you applied to the position?

Mandeep: Yes to be honest with you I feel that I have more responsibilities than expected. As it's only three of us there is a lot to do so I am empowered to take decisions as well as compiling forms, booking people into courses and so on. I am actually encouraged to provide suggestions and to take decisions, obviously as I have not been here long, I still check with the manager.

Q: Why did you want to work in HR?

Mandeep: I've always been interested in the human side of management and work so it felt natural to know more about HR and that's why I did my Master's and then sought work in this area.

Q: From your specific experience, what are the main differences between 'learning about HRM' and 'practising HRM'?

Mandeep: If I have to be honest we often learn on a bigger scale than what one often ends up doing. For example now I focus on T&D mainly of shop-floor workers. Very rarely we develop the courses ourselves as some are bought in and are delivered by consultants and others are delivered by supervisors and managers so as HR specialist we actually don't do the development or the delivery. From what I can see even my manager mainly focuses on administration rather than more strategic work.

HRM IN PRACTICE

Global diversity management at PwC

As the previous discussions have highlighted, diversity management in international contexts cannot be a one-size-fits-all proposition. PwC recognised that in order to implement a successful global diversity strategy it needed to empower local regions and take account of the cultural differences between headquarters and global offices.

As this 'HRM in Practice' example highlights, best practice needs to be adopted and adapted to meet regional differences and interests.

PwC has a Global Diversity and Inclusion Council, which is made up of members from all the global offices. This central council coordinates and promotes diversity management activities that take place around the globe. While the council advises and leads on global DM strategy, the organisation also recognises the importance of having diversity management leaders in regional offices who consult with employees on their needs in relation to diversity management. Therefore, in addition to having global role models (e.g. inspirational female leaders) the regions also develop diversity management initiatives that reflect the needs of the specific groups of employees in these areas. For example, in order to improve the position of women in the organisation, PwC invests in female talent around the globe and has developed a number of schemes such as bias awareness training, coaching schemes and reverse mentoring to support and improve the retention of female talent across the organisation. In addition to global activities, the regions implement initiatives that are tailored to the needs of their employees. PwC South Africa launched the AWARE programme in May 2007, which stands for Attract – Women – Advance – Retain – Empower and is tailored to the issues facing female professionals in South Africa. The programme seeks to retain female talent at all levels and support them in breaking the glass ceiling by strengthening the pathway to leadership positions.

This 'HRM in Practice' example highlights how multinational organisations can combine a 'global' approach with a 'multinational' approach (see 'Global versus Multinational Diversity Management' section above) to diversity. While maintaining a global strategy, the combination of the two approaches allows local regions to lead on and develop specific national diversity management initiatives which fit with the diversity issues of that context.

Source: www.pwc.com/gx/en/women-at-pwc/index.jhtml

International diversity management will only be effective in addressing inequalities in the workplace when it is targeted to and relates to the specific socio-economic, cultural, religious, political and historical national context of countries, and when there is an in-depth understanding of how power and dominance are framed in different contexts around the world (Bell, 2012). Even when it appears that issues relating to inequality and diversity are similar (e.g. in Southern Europe), it is important not to apply concepts and practices from one geographical context to other nations without examining specific national differences (Syed and Özbilgin, 2009). Global diversity management initiatives that ignore the situated nature of diversity and inequality are mere 'window dressing' for organisations that purport the need to address discrimination and disadvantage without changing the status quo (Jamali et al., 2010). This has led to calls for new approaches to global DM to be explored and for a greater emphasis on and promotion of nationally specific programmes of diversity management.

CASE STUDY

DM in Brazilian organisations

Few studies have examined equality issues in Brazilian organisations, and even fewer have focused on the role of HRM in the management of diversity in Brazilian companies. Brazil is currently the sixth largest economy in the world and home to leading companies and multinational operations. Its population is characterised by a rich mixture of several ethnic groups, particularly descendants of native Indians, Portuguese, African slaves and other immigrant groups, mainly from Europe and Asia. Following pressure from minorities and trade union groups, the Brazilian Federal Constitution promulgated in 1988 that employment is a fundamental right and that any type of discrimination is prohibited.

In the 1990s only a few subsidiaries of MNCs operating in Brazil had formal HRM equality and diversity practices and most local organisations did not have equal opportunity policies. In order to investigate (a) how Brazilian companies are currently incorporating diversity into their management practices and (b) what is the role of human resources in this context, Jabbour et al. (2011) conducted a study in 15 of the largest Brazilian organisations that had commenced a process of developing diversity management programmes. Their study, involving company observations and interviews with the CEOs and the HR directors at all organisations, revealed that Brazilian organisations are only now beginning to consider DM programmes.

The CEOs interviewed suggested that diversity management programmes were relatively new to Brazilian corporate life and that processes to actively address inequalities in the workplace were rarely formalised into policies, albeit the government was exercising pressure on large companies to establish quotas. Only four of the 15 participant organisations had diversity policies and the general consensus was that in Brazil the main driver for inclusion of minority groups in the workplace was the legal requirement to fulfil government quotas. Furthermore, most companies focused on one or a few specific groups (e.g. women or ethnic minorities) rather than having a general approach to inclusion. In spite of the lack of a mature system of equality practices, there was clear evidence from the interviews with HR managers that there was growing awareness and, in many cases, growing efforts to include DM in their people management practices that went beyond fulfilling the requirements of the law. Despite an overall positive view of the quota system established by the Brazilian government, there was also evidence from the CEOs and HR professionals that diversity management initiatives were likely to be more effective when managers and employees believed in the social and organisational benefits of inclusion and therefore went beyond compliance with the law and attempted to create inclusive workplaces. Only a small proportion of these large organisations (less than one-third), though, appeared to have an organisational culture with incentives for diversity and where top management actively supported the inclusion of all workers.

This study highlights key issues in equality and diversity practices. Equality should represent an organisational value emphasised within an organisational culture that encourages an inclusive work environment. Senior management should demonstrate a clear direction in showing the relevance of inclusion in everyday working life. The study also highlighted the importance of Brazilian law and its constitution in shaping future attitudes and behaviours towards diversity management in Brazilian organisations. Understanding the historical and social context of the country that leads to divisions and tensions between different ethnic and social groups in society is essential if diversity management strategies are going to be developed and implemented effectively.

CASE STUDY QUESTIONS

1   What are the important factors to take into consideration when trying to enhance the value of equality within an organisation?

2   Discuss whether and why the HR function is best placed to develop and implement equality and diversity measures across the organisation. What are the specific challenges to Brazilian organisations in their implementation of equality values and initiatives?

3   What are the likely practical challenges for an HR team responsible for implementing and coordinating an equality and diversity programme?

4   What methods could be used to improve awareness of diversity and equality issues within organisations in Brazil? Would these methods vary in your own country? If so, how?

CHAPTER SUMMARY

This chapter provided an overview of the main aspects of diversity study and practice in organisations. The key points discussed are:

- The concept of diversity is contested in its meaning as well as its different applications in both society and work. The reasons for its contested nature lie within the socially constructed nature of social categories, which have different connotations in different historic periods as well as in different cultures.

- In discussing the evolution of the concept of diversity as embedded in social and political processes, the chapter discussed the different theoretical (e.g. radical versus liberal) and practical perspectives (social model versus business case model) of equal opportunities and diversity and problematised the translation of diversity concepts into diversity practices.

- When considering diversity management in multinational organisations, an important aspect to acknowledge is the perspective taken by the parent company (e.g. global versus multinational).

- The application and implementation of diversity management policies and practices that have been developed in the country of origin across the different international sites have been widely criticised by scholars as well as practitioners; organisations are now aware of the need to develop culture-specific programmes. Global approaches that do not account for the different national socio-political experiences associated with social categories, and therefore are not sensitive to the different social customs and cultures, are bound to fail.

- In more recent years organisations have been urged to develop different diversity policies in different countries and therefore take a more 'multinational' approach to diversity management rather than a 'global' one-size-fits-all approach.

REVIEW QUESTIONS AND EXERCISES

1. What are the significant political and social changes that have influenced the development of EO/DM?
2. What are the challenges that organisations face when they have to develop DM policies?
3. What does the approach of DM as practice focus on?
4. Why is it important to focus on equality and diversity practices in organisations rather than focusing on the policy only?

EXPLORE FURTHER

Kirton, G. and Greene, A.M. (2015) *The Dynamics of Managing Diversity: A Critical Approach*, 4th edn. Oxford: Butterworth-Heinemann. The authors attempt to problematise the concept and practice of DM and argue that the study of equality needs to consider not only issues of discrimination, but also the needs of people in relation to their diverse cultures and identities. The text critically explores diversity as recognition of the differences and similarities between and among social groups, and how policies must reflect these.

Syed, J. and Özbilgin, M. (2009) A relational framework for international transfer of diversity management practices. *International Journal of Human Resource Management*, 20(12): 2435–2453. This article considers the implementation of DM across multinational organisations.

Guillaume, Y.R.F., Dawson, J.F., Otaye-Ebede, L., Woods, S.A. and West, M.A. (2015) Harnessing demographic differences in organizations: What moderates the effects of workplace diversity? *Journal of Organizational Behavior*. doi: 10.1002/job.2040

www.equalityhumanrights.com/ and www.edf.org.uk/blog/. Both sites are excellent sources of important up-to-date information on legislation and statistics regarding equal opportunities.

GO ONLINE

Visit the companion website for **interactive quizzes**, explanatory **videos** and **podcasts**, **journal articles** to use in your essays, and **weblinks** to useful resources.

https://edge.sagepub.com/crawshaw2e

CHAPTER 9

LEARNING AND DEVELOPMENT

Margarita Nyfoudi
Helen Shipton

CHAPTER KNOWLEDGE OBJECTIVES

- Explain what learning and development is and why it is important.
- Critically assess what self-directed learning, reflection, double-loop learning and social and intellectual capital mean for our understanding of learning and development.
- Outline and justify why an understanding of learning theory is necessary in order to promote effective, business-focused learning in the workplace.
- Appreciate the intellectual and practical value of the training cycle for managing formal learning events.
- Understand and assess the relative merits of informal versus formal learning.

KEY SKILLS OBJECTIVES

- Select a training intervention after having given due attention to the underlying theory.
- Design learning interventions with reference to the training cycle.
- Make appropriate plans to facilitate learning interventions by eliminating any hindering factors.
- Make appropriate links between learning and development (both formal and informal) and business strategy.

This chapter also provides indicative content for the following Intermediate and Advanced level CIPD modules:

CIPD INTERMEDIATE LEVEL MODULES

5LMS Developing leadership and management skills

5ICM Implementing coaching and mentoring

5CLD Understanding the context of learning and development

CIPD ADVANCED LEVEL MODULES

7LTD Learning and talent development

7DDE Designing, delivering and evaluating learning and development provision

GO ONLINE

This chapter comes with loads of online tools to help you to go that extra mile in your studies!

- **Multiple choice questions** to help you test your knowledge and revise for exams
- **Journal articles** so you can read further for assignments and essays
- **Videos** and **podcasts** to help you to understand how complex concepts work in the real world

Visit **https://edge.sagepub.com/crawshaw2e** to access these resources for this topic.

INTRODUCTION

Learning and development (L&D) is increasingly recognised as a function that contributes to the attainment of strategic organisational objectives. Indeed, L&D provides the mechanisms for knowledge creation and exchange, thereby driving organisational change (see Chapter 3) and renewal. L&D has been recognised as one of the core human resources functions (see Chapter 1). Both the promotion and retention of talent through rigorous developmental interventions lie at the heart of effective L&D. Bringing together this duality of function and purpose, we suggest that one of the L&D practitioner's main roles is to link individual needs with interventions that support the achievement of organisational objectives. It is therefore essential to shed light on the nature of learning and how learning might be enabled.

> Learning and development (L&D) A function that contributes to the attainment of strategic organisational objectives, providing the mechanisms for knowledge creation and exchange. L&D has been recognised as one of the core HR functions.

This chapter focuses mainly on individual learning and practices. Employees are those who primarily create, transfer and use knowledge. Without individual learning, higher levels of learning may not be achieved (for the team or the organisation). The first part of the chapter analyses the nature of L&D. Attention is drawn to contemporary issues, such as lifelong learning and self-directed learning, while clarification is provided regarding terms such as learning, training and development. Further, the theoretical perspectives that underpin adult learning are discussed. The intention is not to present an extensive review of existing learning theory (see Blanchard and Thacker, 2013; Conole et al., 2004) but to offer a practical guide to help the reader appreciate the value of each learning method in diverse organisational settings.

The second part of the chapter is concerned with analysis of the systematic training cycle, which provides a framework for the design and implementation of formal interventions. Although there is a shift towards informal learning, planned interventions play an important role in the alignment of L&D needs with business objectives (Harrison, 2009). It is essential to discuss the process for organising and implementing learning interventions by means of a comprehensive systematic training model.

After an initial consideration of the basic L&D issues, the third and final part of the chapter focuses on the issue of strategic contribution. In tackling this, reference is made to the importance of both the vertical and horizontal integration of L&D with organisational objectives and HRM practices respectively.

THE NATURE OF LEARNING
DEFINING LEARNING, TRAINING AND DEVELOPMENT

Over the past decade, learning rather than training has emerged as a priority for L&D departments in organisations. Yet, what is learning and what is training? In this section, we clarify key terms.

Learning Is a 'self-initiated, personal and intentional' process (Roberson, 2005: 29) that involves a change in cognition, action or interaction with others. This change may concern an individual's acquisition of a specific type of knowledge, skill or attitude.

Learning may be defined as a change in cognition, action or interaction with others. This change may concern an individual's development or improvement regarding a specific type of knowledge, skill, attitude or other attribute (KSAO). The word development refers to the acquisition of a new KSAO, while improvement indicates enhancement of already existing KSAOs. According to Matthews et al. (2004: 93), 'learning is the intended outcome of training'.

Training May be defined as 'planned instruction' (Armstrong, 2014: 308) with the purpose of achieving learning in order to improve performance (see Chapter 2) or satisfy development needs.

Thus, training may be defined as 'planned instruction' (Armstrong, 2014: 308) with the purpose to achieve learning in order to improve performance (see Chapter 2) or satisfy development needs. In other words, employees may participate in a training intervention either to improve a particular competence that will help them perform better at their current position or to develop competence that will enable them to perform well at a future position. It is important to note that although training is planned, learning cannot be planned and may or may not be achieved.

Education A formal procedure, led by one or more instructors with the purpose to achieve learning in one or more areas of interest.

Education stands close to the concept of training, due to the fact that the instructor plays a major role in both activities. Child education or pedagogy differs from adult education or andragogy (Knowles et al., 2015). While the former calls for students to adapt to the conventional curriculum, the latter is developed around the per se needs of adult learners (Lindeman, 1926). Education refers to 'an activity undertaken or initiated by one or more agents that is designed to effect changes in the knowledge, skills, and attitudes of individuals, groups, or communities' (Knowles et al., 2015: 11). In other words, education is a formal procedure, led by one or more instructors with the purpose to achieve learning in one or more areas of interest.

Development Refers to the acquisition or improvement of a portfolio of knowledge, skills or attitudes in a specific area of interest. It 'involves preparing someone to be something' (Matthews et al., 2004: 93).

Finally, development refers to the acquisition or improvement of a portfolio of knowledge, skills or attitudes on a specific area of interest. It 'involves preparing someone to be something' (Matthews et al., 2004: 93). Development is achieved through the accomplishment of many different types of learning, and thus it is a long-term process (Mankin, 2009).

CURRENT THEMES IN L&D

Current thinking focuses on learning rather than on training since the former represents the epicentre of training and development processes (Armstrong, 2014). This shift in focus has been accompanied by certain themes, such as self-directed learning, lifelong learning and continuous personal development. A holistic consideration of the nature of learning necessitates the exploration of these themes prior to the analysis of different theoretical perspectives.

Self-directed learning (SDL) Highlights individuals' responsibility for their own learning and promotes the transfer of learning.

The concept of self-directed learning (SDL) highlights individuals' responsibility for their own learning and promotes the transfer of learning. Learning is a 'self-initiated, personal and intentional' process (Roberson, 2005: 29). Thus, SDL is a type of learning that allows the individual to make informed decisions about the content, the process and the learning method with the intention to achieve customisable and thus more effective learning outcomes. SDL shifts control from trainers to learners.

SDL is linked with lifelong learning (LLL), since learning and development, as a life process, promotes change not only 'within the individual' but also 'for the individual's career choices' (Matthews et al., 2004: 113). In other words, L&D does not only arm the learner with skills, knowledge and abilities necessary for his or her current work position, but for his or her chosen career path as well. LLL may be defined as 'the on-going acquisition of knowledge and skills by study and experience throughout the duration of an individual's career' (Mankin, 2009: 37). According to Tuschling and Engemann (2006), the origins of LLL can be found in debates about alternative educational processes that took place in the 1960s and 1970s. At present, in a knowledge-based economy, it has become a major EU strategy (European Commission, 2006), and each member state needs to implement initiatives to promote LLL for its citizens.

DEBATING HRM

Personal learning

Imagine that you are an L&D practitioner in an organisation where the senior management supports self-directed learning, yet the employees are not inclined to engage in such activity.

TASK: What would you do? Could you find a solution that would benefit both the organisation and the employees?

In a YouTube video Professor Bill George from Harvard Business Executive Education shares his thoughts on the subject of lifelong learning (HBSExecEd, 2010). You may access the video through the link: https://youtu.be/VjlPOafjLJs

Jarvis (2006) indicates that reflection is necessary in order to implement learning interventions with impact. Reflective learning corresponds to Argyris's (1999) double-loop learning, according to which employees are encouraged not only to question existing practices (single-loop learning) but also to challenge the existing 'norms, values, policies and operating procedures' (Burnes, 2009: 149) that precede and orchestrate these practices and alter them if they are not appropriate. As will be explained later in the chapter, this alteration (change) constitutes the outcome of learning.

In the new era of lifelong and self-directed learning, the most appropriate method of learning appears to be workplace, on-the-job learning (Hager, 2004). Muller-Camen et al. (2009: 272) argue that when workplace learning is linked with 'a robust and well-operating appraisal or performance management scheme', it could 'enable each development activity to be planned and monitored as a natural part of everyday performance'. However, it is important to highlight that the employees need to get involved in the decision making in terms of their workplace development and also to be given a certain amount of autonomy. Otherwise, any planned development that has not been agreed with the individual employees may intensify their workload and increase their levels of fatigue and stress (Boxall and Macky, 2014).

Workplace learning serves as a platform for the development of intellectual capital, which is a source of competitive advantage (Nahapiet and Ghoshal, 1998; Noe and Tews, 2009). Intellectual capital constitutes both human and social capital. The former refers to the knowledge, skills, health and values that cannot be separated from the individual and are brought into the workplace (Becker, 1964). For Becker, education and training play a vital role in the development of human capital. Further, social capital could be described as 'the sum of the actual and potential resources embedded within, available through, and derived from the network of relationships possessed by an individual or social unit' (Nahapiet and Ghoshal, 1998: 243). While the concept of human capital existed in the past (Becker, 1964; Schultz, 1961), that of intellectual capital is relatively new (Edvinsson and Malone, 1997) and it highlights the importance of social interactions in the creation and sharing of knowledge.

HRM IN PRACTICE

Continuous professional development in the UK

The Chartered Institute of Personnel and Development (CIPD) in the UK has embraced the notion of reflective learning, as this way of learning enables the individuals to clearly link their 'professional development to practical outcomes', assume responsibility for their learning and thus appreciate the value of each intervention (CIPD, 2009). Moreover, CIPD members are recommended to transform this process into an instinctive activity, part of their everyday working life, in order to be able to intuitively trace new challenges and developmental opportunities. According to the CIPD, reflection constitutes the basis for its Continuing Professional Development (CPD) scheme, given that it enables the individuals not only to learn how to learn, but also to realise how they learn best and which skills are necessary for their future career progression.

THEORETICAL PERSPECTIVES ON LEARNING

Learning theories constitute the basis upon which the L&D interventions are designed and implemented. One of the biggest challenges for the L&D practitioner is 'to focus on those learning theories that are most relevant to a particular type of intervention and to build this into the design process' (Mankin, 2009: 111). In addition, given that learning constitutes 'the strategic competence for an entity experiencing change' (Brown and Gray, 2008: 21), an understanding of these perspectives enables the reader to get to grips with the way an organisation can implement change effectively (change which may concern the acquisition of certain skills or abilities by the employees; the improvement of a process; or the alteration of a procedure). This part is concerned with the main learning theories that are used to describe andragogy, that is, the way adults learn. Reference is made to behaviourism, cognitive learning, experiential learning and social learning theory.

BEHAVIOURIST THEORY

'Learning is a relatively permanent change in behaviour that occurs as a result of practice or experience' (Bass and Vaughan, 1967: 8). Regarding the behaviouristic perspective, the prominent theory is the operant conditioning and reinforcement theory (Skinner, 1953), according to which certain outcomes of past behaviour influence future activity. For example, when the trainer praises the learner for performing well, the learner will continue to study in order to keep receiving positive reinforcement and thus this individual will *learn to study* thoroughly. The drawback of this theory is that unless there is continuous reinforcement, the behaviour will not change into the desired outcomes. Behaviourism could be classified as an explanatory learning theory (Shipton, 2006), in which diverse rules, processes and routines guide the individual towards the desirable behaviour in terms of organisational procedures. Thus, for example, practitioners could adopt this perspective to design interventions on health and safety regulations.

COGNITIVE THEORY

Learning is 'a qualitative change in a person's way of seeing, experiencing, understanding, conceptualising something in the real world' (Marton and Ramsden, 1988: 271). For cognitive theorists, learning is not a mere change in behaviour, but rather a change in the way information is processed and the individual's mental schemata built or reorganised (Blanchard and Thacker, 2013). According to Piaget (1954), the two most crucial processes for learning are accommodation and assimilation. The former term refers to the creation of new categories or schemata, while the latter is used to describe the procedure when already existing schemata are enhanced with further information. For example, if an employee does not know what a spreadsheet is, he or she needs to attend training in order to create in their cognition a new category regarding spreadsheets. In later and more advanced training, this category will be enriched with further information regarding spreadsheets.

Cognitive theory could be regarded either from a normative or an explanatory perspective (Shipton, 2006). Specifically, from a normative perspective, the individual's mental schemata are enhanced with organisational knowledge; a case in point is a new employee who is learning about the history and the values of the organisation. On the other hand, from an explanatory perspective, focus is placed on situations where tacit knowledge is deemed of high importance and thus the organisation and individuals interchange knowledge and adjust accordingly. For instance, an employee has found a new, more effective way of executing a job task and he or she informs the supervisor, who in turn transfers the new knowledge to the other employees.

EXPERIENTIAL THEORY

Learning is 'the process whereby knowledge is created through the transformation of experience. Knowledge results from the combination of grasping and transforming experience' (Kolb, 1984: 41). This learning theory has been influenced by the experiential work of Dewey (1916), Lewin (1951) and Piaget (1970). The theory highlights the importance of experience in the learning process; while it attempts to provide an integrated model regarding adult development, in which the dimensions of experience, perception, cognition and behaviour are combined in order to create knowledge (Kolb et al., 2001). Kolb's (1984) learning style inventory constitutes a well-known model of the experiential paradigm, according to which learning takes place in four stages: (1) having a concrete experience; (2) reflecting on it upon observation; (3) drawing conclusions or realising that the learning has occurred; and (4) actively experimenting on what has been learnt. It is recognised that one learner may be more inclined to use different dimensions than another learner and thus two individuals may acquire different knowledge from a single experience. For instance, learning how to use factory machinery could necessitate practising with each piece of equipment per se for some employees, while other employees could find it more useful to understand the mechanical laws upon which the machinery functions.

SOCIAL LEARNING THEORY

'Learning is a remarkably social process. Social groups provide the resources for their members to learn' (Brown and Duguid, 2000: 137). Social learning theory constitutes another holistic theory, according to which the process of learning can be explained by the reciprocal interaction of behavioural, cognitive and environmental influences (Bandura, 1977). Bandura argues that human beings learn primarily through observation by modelling the behaviour of others; nevertheless, although learning may have taken place, it is not certain that there will be a change in behaviour such as performance improvement. According to the theorist, role modelling encompasses both learning acquisition and performance improvement; its effective implementation is subject to four critical conditions: attention, retention, reproduction and motivation. Specifically, attention is concerned with all the factors that affect a learner's focus; thus, for instance, an employee needs to be concentrating in the learning intervention he or she attends and not be distracted by factors such as limited time, noise, or even hunger. Retention represents the ability of the learner to categorise the information in such ways that he or she can easily recall; this could be done with the use of verbal or visual codes. A case in point is an employee who learns the importance of the company's suppliers by using symbols in front of their names. Further, reproduction is concerned with the ability of the learner to reproduce what he or she has learned and, in addition, to assess and evaluate their performance; the self-assessment questions at the end of a learning intervention could contribute towards this direction. Regarding motivation, Bandura argues that the learner needs to be interested in what he or she is being taught. Thus, for example, a sales assistant may be more motivated and interested in negotiation skills than in accountancy rules.

Social learning praises tacit knowledge which is transferred informally throughout an organisation; this informal type of learning is created either by passively observing (Bandura, 1977) or by

Social learning

- Think of an activity through which you have learnt something in the past by observing another person performing a specific task.
- TASK: Reflect on this experience. Was it an effective learning experience? Why?/Why not? How could you improve the effectiveness of such learning techniques?

interacting with colleagues (Dewey, 1916). As stated by Brown and Gray (2008: 19), since learning 'is fundamentally social' it should occur in the context within which individuals interact and interchange ideas. The so-called situated learning constitutes a variant form of social learning theory (Mankin, 2009), according to which learning is transmitted from and received in the place where it is created, as, for example, in the case of apprentices, who are guided by a community of expert practitioners who constitute their social network. Nahapiet and Ghoshal (1998) indicate that social networks are the key to the creation, transmission and retention of intellectual capital, which comprises human and social capital and ultimately offers competitive advantage. Finally, Jarvis (2006: 13), in an attempt to offer a holistic definition encompassing all the above theoretical perspectives, defines learning as:

> the combination of processes whereby the whole person – body (genetic, physical and biological) and mind (knowledge, skills, attitudes, values, emotions, beliefs and senses) – experiences a social situation, the perceived content of which is then transformed cognitively, emotively or practically (or through any combination) and integrated into the person's individual biography resulting in a changed (or more experienced) person. (Jarvis, 2006: 13)

In this regard, the theoretical perspectives of behaviourism, cognitivism, experiential learning and social learning are not exclusive and may be merged into an integrated whole. Thus, it could be argued that individual learning is the process of creating, through various combinations, a change in one's behaviour, mind or level of experience within the social context. This change constitutes the outcome of an effective learning intervention.

FORMAL AND INFORMAL WORKPLACE LEARNING

It is important to relate the above theoretical perspectives to workplace learning methods, which are not country-specific, but are practised in organisations in diverse parts of the world and in different types of organisations. In this way, the reader will be able to directly associate theory with practice and acquire a better understanding of the L&D contribution to the HR department and to the whole organisation. Workplace learning comprises formal and informal interventions. Formal may be described as any planned learning which is initiated by management; while informal is any naturally occurring learning which emerges without management's intervention (Shipton, 2006). Shipton and Zhou (2008) argue that both perspectives should be considered in the learning and development strategy of an organisation in order to satisfy both the strategic objectives of the firm and the individual learning needs.

FORMAL LEARNING

Although the most popular intervention continues to be classroom-based training, the use of coaching, mentoring and e-learning is growing (CIPD, 2015). Coaching is usually a one-on-one intervention between the employee (coachee) and the coach (peer, manager or external practitioner) that involves a set of techniques (questioning, active listening, reflection, goal setting and feedback) with the intention to help the

Coaching   Is usually a one-on-one intervention between the employee (coachee) and the coach (peer, manager or external practitioner) that involves a set of techniques (questioning, active listening, reflection, goal setting and feedback) with the intention to help the former achieve a personal, professional or performance-related goal that is specific and time-bound (Nyfoudi, 2016a).

Mentoring Involves a
one-to-one relationship;
yet it focuses more on
the individual and on
issues wider than those
concerning the job role,
such as the employee's
personal development and
career aspirations.

former achieve a personal, professional or performance-related goal that is specific and time-bound (Nyfoudi, 2016a). Mentoring also involves a one-on-one relationship, but it focuses more on long-term issues wider than those concerning the job role, such as the employee's career aspirations. Both interventions are based on behaviourism and cognitivism; for example, the coach or mentor offers immediate feedback to the learner in order to reinforce the desirable behaviour (behaviourism); or the employee is introduced to a new process for which there is a need to create new mental schemata (cognitivism). Social learning may also take place, for instance when the individual learns by interacting with the coach/mentor, who acts as a role model.

Another developmental activity used by the L&D function is e-learning. E-learning interventions use information and communications technology in order to deliver a customisable learning experience to the learner. One of the advantages of e-learning is that it may provide immediate feedback for the learner, and thus the correct behaviour is reinforced (behaviourism) instantly. In addition, e-learning is based on cognitivism, since it provides the learner with either new information (accommodation) or enhances his or her knowledge regarding an issue (assimilation). Further, e-learning is related to the experiential theory, given that the learner reflects on the degree of the acquired learning and is able to decide whether to continue into, for example, a more demanding module or repeat the latter one.

The shift towards a more self-initiated learning process encourages the use of e-learning. Still, it seems that HR managers are not fully convinced of its effectiveness. According to CIPD's Learning and Development Annual Survey (CIPD, 2015), only 12 per cent of the respondents include it among the most effective L&D practices. Thus, blended learning, a combination of delivery methods and learning methodologies, has surfaced as an alternative method (Sloman, 2007), which appears to be both effective and efficient for the current socio-economic climate.

Other methods of planned learning are job shadowing and job rotation; the former refers to the learning an employee acquires by observing what another individual does, in which way and at what time (Mumford, 1996). The latter involves the transfer of the employee to different work roles in order to expose the learner to new perspectives or practices. Both of these methods enable the further development of an employee's intellectual capital as the learner interacts with a wider social network.

INFORMAL LEARNING

Even though planned learning is necessary and its merits are widely recognised, research shows that most learning in organisations occurs informally (Shackleton-Jones, 2008). Informal learning activities might entail reflection on daily activities, keeping up to date by reading professional journals or books, asking for feedback from and knowledge sharing with colleagues, supervisors and customers (Sanders et al., in press). Research shows that these informal learning activities are related to organisational outcomes. For example, empirical research within six vocational educational training (VET) schools has shown that teachers' participation in informal workplace learning activities is positively related to the number of students that successfully graduate (Bednall et al., 2014). Informal learning takes place within communities of practice (CoPs), which have attracted the interest of both the academic and business communities (Mankin, 2009) as potential sources of competitive advantage. CoPs could be described as groups 'of employees who work together, learn from each other and develop a common understanding of how to get work accomplished' (Noe and Tews, 2009: 270). The learning occurring in CoPs and social networks is based on social learning theory. Individuals who share a common purpose or goal interchange ideas in a virtual or actual place and thus co-create or transfer tacit knowledge. This type of knowledge produced is very difficult to imitate and transfer outside the organisation and, ultimately, leads to competitive advantage for the organisation.

DEBATING HRM

E-social networks

Back in 2009, the head of BBC Academy, Nick Shackleton-Jones, urged employers to reposition their L&D strategy towards the collection and transfer of knowledge via electronic social networks; otherwise, they would face obsolescence (*People Management*, 2009).

TASK: In your view, was he right? Why?/Why not?

LEARNING EFFECTIVENESS

The list of factors that impact on the effectiveness of the learning intervention is countless. Here, we examine (1) motivation to learn, (2) individual differences and (3) learning culture as learner- and organisation-related indicative factors.

MOTIVATION TO LEARN

Motivation plays a significant role in adult learning (Mankin, 2009). Employees exhibit different individual characteristics (Noe and Tews, 2009) which have to be taken into consideration when designing training interventions. For instance, one individual may find it easier to obey certain rules or procedures while another may prefer to reflect on and understand the justification for the procedures.

As discussed above, Bandura (1977) indicated that in order to successfully implement learning it is important to ensure that the learner is interested in what he or she is being taught. Thus, in order to motivate an adult to accept learning, it is necessary to show that the intervention offers learning relevant to his or her needs. In addition, Blanchard and Thacker (2013) refer to the 'readiness' of the employee, that is, the learner's belief that he or she possesses substantial knowledge for a successful participation in the intervention. Further, the training intervention needs to incorporate customised features that enable the learner to maintain control and get involved in the learning process. Tai's (2006) study of 126 employees revealed that the framework for the training interventions influences employees' self-efficacy and motivation to learn, which ultimately affects training outcomes. Tai concluded that in order to build motivation, it is necessary to highlight the importance of the training intervention to the participants.

INDIVIDUAL DIFFERENCES

Individuals acquire different mental schemata, have diverse experiences and interact with various people; similarly, they have different learning styles, that is, the way in which they prefer to learn. Consequently, an L&D practitioner needs to take into consideration the prominent learning styles, in order to offer a more customised learning experience and thus a more effective intervention. The most popular taxonomy is Honey and Mumford's (2002) four learning styles:

- The activists (who learn by experiencing, e.g. tasks or assignments).
- The reflectors (who learn by looking back on what has happened and considering the diverse implications).
- The theorists (who learn by transforming their observations and thoughts into theories).
- The pragmatists (who learn by experimenting with new theoretical concepts and practices in order to verify their validity).

ORGANISATIONAL CLIMATE AND CULTURE

Noe and Tews (2009) argue that organisational climate and culture impact on the transferability of the acquired knowledge to the workplace. They indicate that when the climate within an organisation facilitates the use of the knowledge gained in a learning intervention, for example through providing appropriate feedback, reward or guidance, the learning effectiveness of the intervention is increased. Another way to facilitate learning is to highlight its importance by delivering all planned learning interventions during normal office hours. Otherwise, as a study with professionals in China showed, training during non-work time creates work–life conflicts (Xiao and Cooke, 2012) and, hence, may send the wrong message that learning is not that significant. Further, the learning effectiveness is improved within an organisation that adopts a continuous learning culture that praises the ongoing development of the employees and in which the individuals interact and interchange knowledge and ideas freely (Noe and Tews, 2009). 'Learning culture' is preferred, as a term, to 'learning organisation', which could be defined as an organisation 'in which employees are empowered to continuously learn and develop in a way that promotes collective capacity and therefore, helps the organisation incessantly reinvent itself' (Nyfoudi, 2016b: 258).

According to Shipton's (2006) framework, learning organisation research is categorised as prescriptive; it suggests more effective activities but lacks an empirical basis. Harrison (2009) indicates that the term 'learning organisation' should not be used interchangeably with 'organisational learning', which is defined as 'the study of the learning processes of and within organisations' (Easterby-Smith and Lyles, 2011: 3). On the contrary, a learning organisation should be viewed as 'an ideal type of an organisation' (Easterby-Smith and Lyles, 2011: 3), where individual learning is facilitated by an appropriate workplace setting and by HR systems such as team working (Shipton, 2006). Sloman (2007) argues that learning organisation research contributes to a better understanding of the L&D role.

Learning effectiveness

- Think about any barriers to learning you have personally experienced in the past.
- TASK: How could they have been overcome?

ONLINE STUDY TOOLS

Video Case Study: The importance of learning in organisations

Solidify your understanding of this topics by watching an interesting discussion on the concept of the Learning Organisation between Professor David Garvin and Professor Amy Edmondson, Harvard Business School.

https://edge.sagepub.com/crawshaw2e > **Student Resources** > **Chapter 9** > **Videos**

THE SYSTEMATIC TRAINING CYCLE

Increasing appreciation of the benefits of workplace-based interventions has shifted the attention towards a more informal, naturally occurring learning; yet managers continue to use formal interventions in order to satisfy the strategic L&D requirements (Mankin, 2009). According to the CIPD's Annual Learning and Talent Development Survey (2015), in-house developmental programmes are considered to be the second most used intervention (46 per cent of the respondents), followed by internal coaching (32 per cent) and e-learning courses (29 per cent). The most widespread framework that is used to design and implement such interventions is the systematic training cycle (STC). It originated in the US army in the 1960s (Fabac, 2006) as the ADDIE (Analyse, Design, Develop, Implement and Evaluate) model and, since then, different versions have emerged in order to satisfy the needs of the various users. For example, Harrison's (2009) eight-stage model offers a detailed step-by-step process for HR specialists in the L&D area, while Tannenbaum's (2002) strategic training and development process emphasises the contribution of the training interventions in the accomplishment of the strategic organisational objectives.

Traditionally, the model consists of four stages (Blanchard and Thacker, 2013; Mankin, 2009), but has evolved to reflect the contemporary trends as regards formal training. At present, as discussed above, there is an emphasis on learning over training, and thus the STC has been adapted accordingly. The model is constituted of: training and learning needs analysis; design; delivery; and evaluation of L&D interventions. It is worth mentioning that the learner, the L&D practitioner and the line manager are positioned at the centre of the cycle (Mankin, 2009). This corresponds with current thinking according to which the learner assumes responsibility for his or her own learning (Mankin, 2009), the line manager plays a key role in the facilitation of the learning process (Bednall et al., 2014) and the HR practitioner works closely with the latter in order to produce effective interventions and achieve vertical integration. The following sections examine these four stages.

STAGE 1: TRAINING AND LEARNING NEEDS ANALYSIS

The first stage of the STC is the training and learning needs analysis (TLNA). In the past, the term did not include the word 'learning'; thus, Mathews (1997: 10) defined the stage as:

> The structured process carried out by a variety of different methods by which information about an organisation's development and training needs is gathered, then reviewed and codified as the basis for [a] development plan.

Nevertheless, at present it is essential to highlight not only the identification of an organisation's developmental and training needs, but also the detection of an individual's learning needs. In addition, a TLNA should stem from the business strategy and aim at sustaining or improving business performance (see Chapter 2).

Further, according to Blanchard and Thacker (2013), needs analysis is a methodological procedure consisting of three phases: input, process and output. The input phase is concerned with the analysis of information regarding the individual, the department and the organisation (Goldstein and Ford, 2001); the process phase involves the identification of the causes of any performance gaps (Blanchard and Thacker, 2013); and the output phase determines whether training or non-training needs exist (Blanchard and Thacker, 2013). Thus, TLNA could be defined as the systematic process by which information is collected and analysed at strategic, operational and individual levels in order to identify training and non-training needs and draw up a developmental plan that corresponds to the strategic objectives of the organisation.

In the third phase of the TLNA, the identified needs are categorised into training and non-training. According to Blanchard and Thacker (2013), training needs correspond to performance gaps caused by employees' inadequate knowledge, skills or attitudes (KSAs), whereas non-training needs refer to performance gaps caused by other factors, such as low levels of motivation and time restrictions. Further, Sloman (1999) acknowledges two different types of training needs: the supply-led, that is, needs that are implemented in order to ensure the attainment of the strategic goals of the organisation; and the demand-driven, that is, needs that have arisen from a performance or development appraisal and refer to an employee's performance or development gaps. In other words, training needs could be either pushed by the senior management or arise from the incumbents. For instance, if an acquisition has recently been made, the management may push cultural training for the employees of the acquired organisation in order to facilitate the merger. However, at the same time, a need for presentation skills may be picked up from the annual developmental appraisals of the employees.

STAGE 2: DESIGN AND DEVELOPMENT OF L&D INTERVENTIONS

First and foremost, this stage involves the development of learning objectives. A good objective contains specific information regarding the desired outcome, the conditions under which the outcome will occur and the standards according to which it will be benchmarked (Blanchard and Thacker, 2013). It is imperative to produce objectives effectively in order to guide the L&D practitioner and the trainer through the next stages of the STC. Further, after a thorough consideration of the different alternatives, the L&D practitioner needs to select a suitable learning strategy. Will the learning intervention be developed and implemented on-site or off-site? Will it constitute a one-piece undertaking or be divided into small chunks? Will the learner be able to choose among different training methods or will only one method be provided? The answers to these questions will constitute the learning strategy of the intervention.

Moreover, the L&D practitioner needs to select an appropriate instructional strategy, which is concerned with the way an intervention is delivered. A useful tool for this process is the learning plan, that is, a list that contains all the necessary elements for the delivery of the intervention, such as content, training methods, media, venue, group size, duration, prior knowledge, learning objectives, participants' education and cultural background. The involvement of the line manager of the learner (employee) is crucial, since in this way it is more likely that he or she will support the intervention and encourage his or her direct report to participate.

In addition, at this stage, the L&D practitioner needs to reflect on the procedure and how various potential problems may be overcome. For instance, an intervention that incorporates traditional classroom-based training necessitates the existence of classrooms/instructors/blackboards or, alternatively, substantial financial provision to acquire these resources.

Finally, the L&D practitioner needs to design the evaluation stage and decide upon issues such as evaluation budget and time required. The earlier in the process the L&D practitioner decides upon provisions for the evaluation procedure, the smoother will the evaluation stage be executed.

STAGE 3: DELIVERY OF L&D INTERVENTIONS

This part of the STC uses the outputs from the design and development phase as inputs for implementing the training plan. Before initialising the actual intervention, a dry run and a pilot programme should take place. The first refers to an initial test of the software and hardware of training to ensure that everything is properly working. After any potential corrections are made, the pilot programme is executed. This constitutes a simulation which assists in assessing whether the intervention delivers the desired learning to the participants.

Following the refinements made according to the information collected on the pilot programme, the actual delivery process begins. In this phase, the trainer needs to be cautious about time, make a good first impression and keep learners interested (Blanchard and Thacker, 2013). To achieve these, the trainer needs to be very well prepared, pay attention to his or her appearance and aim for an interactive session with ice-breakers, exercises, pauses for breaks and group activities (Blanchard and Thacker, 2013).

Delivering training

- Thinking back on your past experience as a learner, consider a time that the delivery of an intervention went terribly wrong. What could have been done better?

- TASK: Reflect on the actions required for both the design and delivery stage of the systematic training cycle.

STAGE 4: EVALUATION OF L&D INTERVENTIONS

The evaluation stage is a vital part of the STC, since the L&D practitioner is able to tangibly showcase the contribution of L&D to the attainment of strategic goals. Easterby-Smith (1994) identifies four main purposes that the evaluation stage serves: (1) proving that the training was efficient; (2) controlling the procedural elements, that is, time limits, requirements and costs; (3) improving components, or the whole training process; and (4) reinforcing the correct behaviour and attitude towards learning with use of the evaluation results.

The most popular model that has been developed for the evaluation stage is Kirkpatrick's (1959) Four Level Training Evaluation model. According to this model, evaluation may be implemented at four levels, measuring: (1) reactions, that is, learner satisfaction; (2) the knowledge, skills, attitudes (KSAs) and competencies learned; (3) changes in behaviour at the workplace; and (4) changes in performance at the workplace. Yet, despite its popularity, Kirkpatrick's model has received extensive criticism (e.g. Alliger and Janak, 1989); thus, alternative methods have been developed, such as models that focus on return on investment (ROI) (Mathieu and Leonard, 1987) or on the holistic appreciation of performance improvement (Guzzo and Gannet, 1989).

LEARNING AND DEVELOPMENT STRATEGY

By now, the novice reader has acquired an understanding of L&D and conclusions can easily be drawn about its contribution to HR and organisational objectives. This part of the chapter links the L&D strategy with overall business strategy and highlights the strategic role L&D plays in creating value. In doing so, it builds upon Tannenbaum's (2002) strategic L&D process model.

HRM IN PRACTICE

Talent management in Brazil

The Alpargatas Group, the largest footwear manufacturing company in Latin America, has seen enormous growth in recent years. In line with its values, the group offers a range of development opportunities to its 18,400 employees (Alpargatas S.A., 2013). Specifically, in 2012 alone the group invested 33,000 working hours in employees' training, development and education. The company insists that thanks to its employees' talents the group's net sales revenue increased by 16.8 per cent in 2012, reaching over R$3 billion of Brazilian reals (Alpargatas S.A., 2013). Moreover, Alpargatas has founded the Alpargatas Institute, which offers customised training and education to employees. Performance improvement is always the focus of these initiatives, yet the benefits expand beyond this. Particularly, employees are offered and have completed primary and secondary education classes within the factories; while they are encouraged to undertake higher education and language courses as well (Alpargatas S.A., 2006). Furthermore, the institute has created the 'Ciranda de Ideas' programme to promote a culture of innovation within the group. In 2006 alone, the programme received 5543 improvement suggestions, 646 of which were adopted and saved about R$4.3 million. Finally, the Alpargatas Institute also offers development opportunities for its executives (Alpargatas S.A., 2006). For instance, the Alpargatas Integrated Management System criteria have been developed to identify any potential shortages of skills or talents that are crucial for an increasingly globalised company such as the Alpargatas Group.

Specifically, after establishing the vision and mission of the organisation, both the external and internal environments are scanned. In this way it is possible to detect the strategic factors that form the items of the so-called SWOT analysis; that is, Strengths, Weaknesses, Opportunities and Threats (Bratton and Gold, 2007). Thereafter, the business strategy is formulated and the sources of existing and potential competitive advantage identified (Mankin, 2009). According to the resource-based view of the firm (Barney, 1991; see also Chapter 2), in order for a resource to offer competitive advantage to the organisation, it needs to be valuable, rare and difficult to imitate or replace. Among the numerous sources, such as premium quality and cost leadership (Porter, 1985), 'knowledge and the sharing and the creation of knowledge are increasingly believed to be key sources of competitive advantage' (Noe and Tews, 2009: 268). Knowledge consists of explicit and tacit knowledge (Nonaka and Takeuchi, 1995), that is, the 'know-what' and 'know-how' (Mankin, 2009) of a specific process, theory or application respectively. Thus, since knowledge is captured, developed and transferred by individuals, intellectual capital is of great importance for the organisation.

The next stage constitutes one of the key steps that determine the contribution of the L&D to the business effectiveness and is concerned with the strategic vertical fit of the L&D division: through a strategic needs assessment, the objectives of the L&D division are specified and linked with the business strategy (Noe and Tews, 2009). Here, needs assessment is characterised as strategic due to the fact that it is used to assess the L&D needs of the whole organisation and not only the needs of a single employee or department. The strategic alignment of the L&D division, that is, the process by which L&D 'strategy, policies, and plans are aligned with an organisation's strategic goals and objectives' (Mankin, 2009: 55), is critical, if it is to add value to the organisation. This vertical fit enables the L&D manager to acquire a business partner

Vertical fit Through a strategic needs assessment, the objectives of the L&D division are specified and linked with business strategy.

role (Ulrich and Brockbank, 2009) and be occupied with more strategic issues, as discussed in the first chapter of this book.

The third step of the process is concerned with the actual implementation of the L&D strategy though the diverse L&D activities. In this part, the line manager plays an important role in the development and facilitation of the interventions, since the L&D practitioner is engaged with more strategic issues (Beattie, 2006; Bowen and Ostroff, 2004). Further, this is of great significance to achieve horizontal integration or fit, that is, the horizontal strategic alignment of the L&D discipline with the other HR areas. Thus, for instance, an L&D manager needs to ensure that an employee is provided with training that corresponds to any weaknesses traced in the performance appraisal.

The final step of the strategic L&D process involves the evaluation of the contribution of L&D to business objectives. Systematic evaluation is essential to demonstrate the value added and assists in building a robust basis/argument for HR. For this reason, a need exists to identify the appropriate metrics for evaluation, such as measures of intellectual, human or social capital (e.g. Bassi and McMurrer, 2004) and high-performance work practices (e.g. Huselid, 1995). According to Mankin (2009: 97), 'evaluation acts as a feedback loop' and thus the whole process is of an iterative nature.

Assessing the value of L&D

- Do a brief internet search to identify organisations in which L&D plays a strategic role.

- TASK: Identify factors revealing that organisations value L&D.

FUTURE CHALLENGES

The foregoing issues imply certain key challenges that need to be tackled by the L&D practitioner in the near future. Specifically, while moving towards a more self-directed learning process in an interconnected world, the L&D practitioner acquires the role of the consultant or facilitator of learning. At the same time, the line manager obtains further responsibilities by getting involved in the process of developing and conducting a learning intervention. Thus, both the L&D practitioner and the line manager need to acquire additional skills for the successful completion of their new roles.

Moreover, the information age offers potential for improvement in all aspects of human life. L&D practitioners need to support the emergence of intellectual capital, since it is a source of sustainable competitive advantage, while at the same time ensure that they meet the learning needs of an ever-growing multinational workforce. For instance, they need to provide a setting that facilitates and promotes communities of practice (social capital) and coaching (human capital), while at the same time offer intercultural awareness classes in order to promote inclusivity in the workplace. In doing so, both formal and informal interventions need to be utilised, so as to maximise the benefits of adopting blended learning methods.

GRADUATE INSIGHTS

L&D manager at PUBLICO

The following is taken from a conversation held with Rita (real name withheld), a recent Aston University graduate of the MSc HRM and Business course. Rita has risen quickly in her career and is currently L&D Manager at PUBLICO, a large organisation within the UK Civil Service.

Author: So, what does an L&D Manager do?

Rita: Well, I oversee and advise on training and development needs and activities for all our staff – from core employees through to our most senior managers. In this regard I report directly to the Head of Personnel and Development.

Author: Can you outline in more detail your day-to-day responsibilities?

Rita: OK, so learning and development covers everything from inductions, hard and soft skills training through to talent management and management development. I will work closely with team leaders and managers to identify training needs and also any trends that may affect the business units and business as a whole. Whilst some of my job will be to identify and source outside providers for training I will also get involved in directly delivering training – although this tends to be mainly for managers and mainly in softer skills. I have a very small team that I manage and of course I have to effectively manage and set out the training budget each year.

Author: How is your performance measured? How do you know whether your L&D strategy is effective or successful?

Rita: I obviously have an appraisal like everyone else and during these annual appraisals I will have personal and team targets set. External pressures – like funding for example – put different pressures on us at different times and my specific targets and goals obviously change. Unfortunately, training budgets do tend to suffer when money gets tighter. In short my job is to effectively, and perhaps more importantly efficiently, deliver the learning and development that we need to deliver (cost effectively) our services.

   In relation to specific training interventions we obviously seek feedback from those who have attended these sessions. We take this feedback very seriously and will obviously react to negative comments – whether that is in relation to training delivered internally or by external providers. At a broader level, we will also look to collect information and feedback, mainly from managers and team leaders from different parts of the organisation, on potential skills shortages, surpluses, team and individual performance so we can get a good idea on whether we are delivering effective learning and development to the organisation as a whole.

Author: How did you come to specialise in L&D? What advice would you give to others wanting to specialise in this field of HR?

Rita: It was pretty much by accident I have to say. On graduation I started my career in a fairly generalist HR role and I must say, despite my job title, I still deliver a generalist role. I would say my L&D role takes up around 50 per cent of my time, with the other 50 per cent still given to providing generalist HR support to the organisation and managers. Quite simply, an opportunity for promotion came up in the L&D team and, I was always kind of interested in this stuff, and I thought the job would be interesting. That role – the L&D

(Continued)

(Continued)

coordinator role – supports, and reports to, the L&D manager. The previous L&D manager eventually moved on and I successfully applied for this role around 12 months ago. Having been in L&D roles now for around three years – what I would say is that it is a very specific part of HR, with its own rather unique challenges. Consequently, if someone was thinking about specialising in L&D I would recommend that they do a bit more research on this than perhaps I did. It would make the transition a little smoother.

Author: What skills do you think a successful L&D manager should possess?

Rita: Well of course that will depend on the nature of that role in whatever organisation you look at. That's the problem sometimes with HR roles – a L&D manager may have very different roles and responsibilities in different organisations. Here, I would say you've got to have plenty of experience of delivering training but also of liaising with external providers of training. You got to be pretty strong numerically and be good at managing budgets. Like I said before, my experience is that you never have enough money but you have to be able to manage that budget well and be able to defend it if needs be. Finally, I suppose you need those general managerial skills – good communication, leadership, being confident and articulate. It's important to get people to buy into the importance of training and development and learning overall so it's partly my job to champion our function and get people to engage with learning and development.

Further, although substantial progress has been made in recognising the added value to business objectives, an L&D practitioner needs to continue enhancing the contribution of the L&D division. This may be achieved first by introducing innovative ways to support knowledge creation and sharing; second by adjusting rapidly to organisational changes and needs; and finally by delivering learning interventions quickly and effectively. Moreover, the practitioner needs to ensure that the L&D objectives are aligned with the overall HR objectives in order to achieve integration; at the same time, he or she should pursue a central role in the design of procedures that facilitate LLL and CPD. These objectives may only be achieved through the explicit acknowledgement of the added value that is offered by the L&D function, ensuring in this way that the L&D practitioner has become, indeed, a business partner.

CASE STUDY

L&D in Thailand

Thailand, a middle-income economy (United Nations, 2016), is located in South East Asia. The majority of the 64 million people are Buddhists and speak Thai as the official language. According to Hofstede et al.'s (2010) cultural dimensions, Thai society is highly hierarchical and collectivist.

Within the past 20 years, the country has made impressive progress with regard to poverty reduction, education and health. One of the main reasons for Thailand's success was public investment in social services (United Nations, 2016). Specifically regarding L&D, in 2002 the government put in force the Skills Development Promotion Act (SDPA), which replaced the Vocational Training Promotion Act (Division of Skill Development Promotion, Department of Skill Development, 2002). The SDPA promotes lifelong and workplace learning by offering a 200 per cent tax reduction on training costs to those organisations that establish and register training centres for their employees. In addition, the SDPA provides tax incentives for the purchase of training equipment and the employment of trainers. Further, companies of more than 100 employees have to train at least half of their staff each year; alternatively, they must pay a fee per untrained employee. Skills development and renewal are considered so important in Thailand that an annual Prime Minister's award is given by the Ministry of Industry for HRD excellence.

Unemployment is relatively low in Thailand. According to the latest labour force survey (National Statistical Office, 2016), the total number of unemployed people is 0.25 million, which corresponds to 0.7 per cent of the population. Yet more than half of the population (62.6 per cent) is occupied in informal employment (National Statistical Office, 2012). This type of employment does not protect employees or provide them with social security. As a result, they are underpaid, working under poor conditions with no safety measures. The low level of education of the majority of these employees has been recognised as a determinant factor for their welfare, and thus the latest Informal Employed Persons Survey (National Statistical Office, 2012) proposed the encourage-ment of agencies to support the education of workers in informal employment.

Summarising, Thailand is a fast-developing country with a relatively large popu-lation. The government places a lot of importance on the development of skills, and thus it provides various incentives to organisations in order to ensure the continuous personal development of the workforce. Notwithstanding government efforts, the majority of the Thai workforce is informally employed, and thus the employees are not able to benefit from the government initiatives.

CASE STUDY QUESTIONS

1 Reflect on the Thai Skills Development Promotion Act. What benefits may such an Act create for Thailand's economy in the short and long term?

2 If you were an HRD manager in Thailand, what type of training would you choose for the employees of the company? Why?

3 Do a brief internet search regarding informal employment in Thailand. Do you agree that educating the workers would help improve their working conditions? If you agree, how could education help? If you disagree, could you suggest any other solution?

CHAPTER SUMMARY

The key points that we have identified in this chapter are the following:

- The promotion of self-directed and lifelong learning has contributed to the shift from training to learning. It is increasingly recognised that control of the learning process lies with the learner.
- Intellectual capital, which is the combination of human and social capital, has emerged as a significant source of competitive advantage.
- The main learning theories encompass behaviourism, cognitivism, experiential learning and social learning. An employee may learn from past experiences, through accommodation or assimilation, by reflection and by social interaction.
- An organisation may initiate formal learning interventions such as coaching, mentoring, e-learning, job shadowing and job rotation, and/or they may provide an environment that facilitates informal learning, such as communities of practice (CoPs) and social networks.
- Adopting a learning culture accommodates the learning process by providing employees with both the opportunity and the facilities to participate in an intervention.
- The systematic training cycle (STC) is a framework for the implementation of formal learning interventions. It comprises four stages: training and learning needs analysis; design and development; delivery; and evaluation.
- The L&D practitioner may add value to an organisation by developing and implementing interventions that are strategically aligned with the organisational goals (vertical fit) and the other HR areas (horizontal integration).

REVIEW QUESTIONS AND EXERCISES

1. Explain the role and the importance of L&D in an organisation.
2. Define and explain the differences between the terms learning, training, education and development.
3. Critically evaluate the experiential learning theory.
4. Discuss the theoretical underpinning of coaching as a learning intervention.
5. Conduct a training and learning needs analysis for an IT graduate in a telecommunications organisation.
6. Critically assess Tannenbaum's (2002) model of the strategic L&D processes.
7. Examine and evaluate the future challenges for the L&D division.

EXPLORE FURTHER

Bednall, T.C., Sanders, K. and Runhaar, P. (2014) Stimulating informal learning activities through perceptions of performance appraisal quality and human resource management system strength: A two-wave study. *Academy of Management Learning and Education*, 13(1): 45–61. This article looks at the key role of line managers in workplace learning. The *Academy of Management Learning and Education* journal is an important source of up-to-date academic research in the field of learning and development.

Salas, E., Tannenbaum, S., Kraiger, K. and Smith-Jentsch, K. (2012) The science of training and development in organizations: What matters in practice. *Psychological Science in the Public Interest*, 13(2): 74–101. An article for more experienced learners that examines in detail the significance of training for organisations.

Shipton, H. and Zhou, Q. (2008) Learning and development in organisations, in Aston Centre for Human Resources (ed.) *Strategic HRM: Building Research-based Practice*. London: CIPD, pp. 159–188. Provides an alternative and similarly comprehensive and strategic examination of L&D.

GO ONLINE

Visit the companion website for **interactive quizzes**, explanatory **videos** and **podcasts**, **journal articles** to use in your essays, and **weblinks** to useful resources.

https://edge.sagepub.com/crawshaw2e

CHAPTER 10

REWARD STRATEGIES AND SYSTEMS

Ann Davis
Vidu Badigannavar

CHAPTER KNOWLEDGE OBJECTIVES

- To explore the broad context of pay policy.
- To identify the purposes of reward systems for key stakeholders.
- To evaluate what is meant by 'fairness' in reward.
- To identify what is rewarded in organisations.
- To recognise the range of available reward options.
- To understand the basis for determining fair reward systems.
- To critically evaluate recent developments in reward strategy.

KEY SKILLS OBJECTIVES

- To understand and recognise the importance of unit labour cost.
- To recognise what you value in work.
- To distinguish between the core components of a reward system.
- To explore and describe the process of job evaluation.
- To make recommendations on performance-related reward.

This chapter also provides indicative content for the following CIPD Intermediate and Advanced level modules:

CIPD INTERMEDIATE LEVEL MODULE

5RMT Reward management

CIPD ADVANCED LEVEL MODULE

7RWM Reward management

GO ONLINE

This chapter comes with loads of online tools to help you to go that extra mile in your studies!

- **Multiple choice questions** to help you test your knowledge and revise for exams
- **Journal articles** so you can read further for assignments and essays
- **Videos** and **podcasts** to help you to understand how complex concepts work in the real world

Visit **https://edge.sagepub.com/crawshaw2e** to access these resources for this topic.

INTRODUCTION

This chapter will introduce students to some of the challenges in developing and managing reward. Pay, or compensation (Martocchio, 2011) as it is sometimes called, is the most tangible component of the economic exchange between an employer and an employee. More broadly, reward is central to the social exchange relationship between employees and employers, both in contractual and in psychological terms (Rousseau and Greller, 1994; see also Chapters 2 and 12). It demonstrates what employers value and what employees desire, but can cause great dissatisfaction if inappropriately managed.

What reward systems represent and how reward strategies are developed is the main focus of this chapter. First, though, it will identify the significance of pay policy within organisations. It then examines the purposes of reward systems for key stakeholders. Within this framework, issues of fairness and equity are explored. Discussions of reward have generally focused on the idea of 'a fair day's wages for a fair day's work', a phrase that can be traced back to the Scottish essayist Thomas Carlyle in 1843, but what do we really mean by that? The chapter will further examine what is meant by reward in a broad sense, and what we actually do reward in organisations. It will outline some tools and techniques underpinning reward system design. Finally, it explores more critical arguments about how people should be rewarded, drawing on recent challenges to reward management.

THE SIGNIFICANCE OF PAY POLICY TO HRM

There is a plethora of mainstream HRM literature that deals with pay and rewards policies (e.g. Armstrong and Murlis, 2004; Hutchinson, 2013; Shields, 2016). Here however we will begin by exploring the labour economics literature to identify the significance of pay policy within the wider range of policy instruments available to HR analysts and practitioners (see e.g. Lazear and Gibbs, 2014; Marsden and Richardson, 1994; Sloane et al., 2013).

If you were to closely examine the balance sheet and the cost expenditure accounts of any organisation, you will soon realise that wage or pay bill constitutes one of the largest chunks of the firm's total operational costs. Typically in a manufacturing sector firm, the labour costs could be 20–30 per cent of the total operational costs. For a service sector firm such as a bank or an insurance firm or an educational institution, for instance, the labour costs could be as high as 50–70 per cent of the total operational

Compensation 'All forms of financial returns and tangible services and benefits employees receive as part of an employment relationship' (Milkovich et al., 2011: 10).

Reward system The policies, practices, processes, procedures and structures that govern rewards in an organisation. The approach taken by the organisation to fulfil its reward strategy.

Reward strategy The alignment of the reward policies and practices with the business and human resource strategies of the organisation, its culture and its environment, providing a set of goals and declaration of intent as to what the organisation wants to reward, and how critical reward issues will be addressed. A pathway linking the needs of the business and the staff with reward policies and practices in the organisation.

costs. This is one very good reason why managers should seek to understand pay policy. A second reason for attending to pay policy is that labour costs are relatively more controllable than other costs within a business. Employers typically do not have much control over the cost of raw materials, technology or the cost of raising capital to run their business, these being largely determined by the external market. They do however have some control of their wage bill because they can decide how many people they wish to employ, what type of people they wish to employ (i.e. skill mix), how much and how they wish to pay their employees. While these decisions are influenced to an extent by external market conditions (such as pay offered by rival firms within the sector, levels of unemployment in the labour market, etc., of which more later), the individual firm retains more influence over labour costs than over costs of raw materials or technology. A third reason why pay policy is of significance to employers is that it can provide a source of competitive advantage over and above the rival firms in the market (Felipe and Kumar, 2011).

It is worth noting here that most firms that go bust do not do so because they are not profitable enough. Firms are more likely to go bust if they are unable to control their costs. It is here that labour cost, which is a large proportion of the total operational cost, becomes the centre of attention (Felipe and Kumar, 2011). Human resource management can help firms control their labour costs – more precisely the unit labour cost (ULC), which is the average cost of labour per unit of output.

From an economic perspective, the aim of management, and a core component of the HR role, is to reduce this ULC to generate competitive advantage. In considering the task above you may have identified several options to achieve a reduction in ULC. Increasing the value of Q could be achieved by asking employees to work longer, harder, smarter or a combination of all three. Most workers however would be unwilling to work longer or harder without

Understanding unit labour cost

Let us assume a firm manufactures 10,000 widgets every week. A widget could be anything from computers to crayons. Let us call this total output 'Q'. The firm employs 100 employees, which we will call 'E'. Thus, the output per employee or labour productivity for the firm will be Q/E which is 10,000/100 = 100. Now let us assume that the firm pays a basic wage of £400 per worker per week. This we will call 'w'. In addition to the basic wage, this firm also incurs an additional expenditure of say £50 per week per worker on additional benefits such as a subsidised canteen, child care vouchers or private health insurance. We will call these fringe benefits 'f'. The total weekly labour cost for this firm will be the wage cost (w) plus the cost of additional benefits (f) multiplied by the number of employees (E), which in this case will be (£400 + £50) × 100 = £45,000. Therefore, unit labour cost, that is the labour cost of producing one widget, will be £45,000/10,000 (Q) = £4.50. Thus, we can calculate the ULC using a simple formula which is: $ULC = E (w + f)/Q$.

What then are the options available to management to reduce ULC and thus increase competitive advantage? Using our equation above, the options available are to increase the value of 'Q', or reduce the values of E, w or f. That is, produce more widgets over a given period of time, or reduce the cost of wages or fringe benefits, or reduce the number of employees, perhaps by replacing them with technology or higher skilled workers, or some combination of all four of these interventions.

- TASK: In groups, consider how as an employer you might seek to influence these values of E, w, f and Q. What actions might you take?

- What would these mean in practice to the people who actually produce the widgets? What difficulties might you face as an HR manager?

receiving some additional reward or compensation, and goodwill alone, i.e. the gratitude of the company, is unlikely to be a sufficient reward. Another is to reduce the total number of employees (E) perhaps by replacing labour with technology. However, advanced technology may need a different and higher skills set of employees to operate that technology. The firm would therefore either have to invest in skill training for existing employees or hire a more skilled workforce who may reasonably demand higher wagers.

A firm could directly target wages and fringe benefits (w) by, for example, slowing wage rises or imposing a pay freeze for a few years. Alternatively, the number and type of fringe benefits offered to its employees might be reduced. While plausible, these options may not be practical. Over time a pay freeze amounts to a pay cut if the cost of living keeps rising. Rival firms may become more attractive, resulting in higher labour turnover. Outsourcing or offshoring some functions may also help to reduce direct wage costs. The firm could buy in accounting, IT or HR services, or relocate production to low-wage countries in South Asia or Eastern Europe. However, this may increase the cost of monitoring and quality control, which can be difficult with distant locations.

Management could decide to reduce its fixed wage cost by splitting the total pay into a basic wage topped up with some element of variable pay such as individual performance-related pay, or perhaps offering share options to its employees. This not only reduces its fixed wage costs but also transfers some of the financial risk to the firm from employers onto the employees. This is a major theme in current reward management literature and will be returned to later in this chapter. The important point to note here is that irrespective of which policy options the firm chooses to reduce its labour costs, there are costs and risks attached. Management then has to carefully consider how best to manage those risks and reduce its costs.

THE PURPOSES OF REWARD

The preceding discussion outlines why it is important to understand pay policy. From a labour economics perspective, the aim of management is to reduce unit labour cost; that is, to reduce the cost incurred to produce a unit of output. In considering the purpose of reward systems, however, one question we need to ask is 'purpose for whom?' Different stakeholders in the employment relationship all have an interest in reward systems, but their interests will vary. Employers need to ensure that they can *attract*, *retain* and *motivate* employees as well as operate within their means, and use rewards to do so in accordance with their HR strategy (see Chapter 2). For employees, rewards enable them to maintain an appropriate lifestyle, but are also potent symbols of personal status and achievement. For society, reward systems are symbolic of core values, for example equality or fairness, of social justice or individual achievement. These outcomes are broader than a simple economic exchange. They imply meaning beyond the cash value of the pay package. So, while employers may be primarily concerned with reducing ULC, this cannot be their sole concern and is unlikely to even be a main concern of the employee. We need therefore to ensure we take a broader view of the purpose of reward than simply reducing ULC.

Stakeholders People, bodies and institutions with a legitimate stake in the organisation.

ATTRACTION

Job seekers are attracted by the headline salary that potential employers offer; however, opportunities for personal career development, the ability to balance work and home life, or the contribution that the organisation makes to creating a sustainable community may also influence job choice. Different generations, from baby boomers born in the 1950s and 1960s to generations X and Y through to millennials, seem to vary in the extent to which they see civic values or extrinsic rewards as important in their overall value structures (Strauss and Howe, 2000). Depending on candidates' value orientation, highly prestigious organisations, or those with a unique reputation, may offer lower salaries than others but still be attractive to quality applicants.

Employers making decisions about how to attract potential employees also have a range of factors to consider. What they can afford to pay, and how much other employees, both within the company and in the wider labour market, are paid for similar jobs – the 'market rate' or 'going rate' – will be critical. They will consider what the individual job holder is worth, and what they might contribute to achieving business strategy. At a strategic level, employers are concerned with the message their reward systems send about them as an employer. Do they pay more than the competition? A firm may decide to do this in order to attract and retain better quality candidates or those employees whose skills are in high demand. Netflix, for example, is less concerned with overall labour market rates than with the market compensation rate for each individual employee at all times. It has a reputation for paying at the top of the personal market for that employee as defined by three questions: what the employee could earn elsewhere, what Netflix would have to pay a replacement for that employee, and what they would pay to keep that person. If the individual was valuable to Netflix, they would be paid what they could earn elsewhere, at least what a replacement for them would earn at Netflix, and however much more Netflix would consider paying to keep that employee if they received a higher offer from another company. Paying above market rates may also dissuade employees from joining trade unions, therefore retaining greater flexibility in other aspects of employment practice. The organisational culture or core values may in some circumstances be substitutable for high pay. Either long-term prospects and security or short-term high risk for high return may be more or less attractive to potential and current employees and influenced by company strategy. Even within a cost leadership strategy (Porter, 1985), employers could choose to pay low wages to low-skilled employees, or pay higher wages for high levels of efficiency and skill.

GRADUATE INSIGHTS

Rewarding work?

Each year we ask both our undergraduate and postgraduate HRM students what they are looking for in work after graduation – that is, what they would find rewarding at work. The range of rewarding features of work they generate is quite extensive. There is a cluster of issues around recognition, both of behaviours and outputs, which differentiate them from other employees. Recognition was also felt to result in job satisfaction and the ability to raise personal standards and improve self-esteem. Goals were felt to be important, along with fairness and a sense that there was a fit between personal and organisational values. For example, increasingly we hear of students wanting to develop social enterprises which contribute to their community rather than simply seeking to make profit, or a public service orientation and making a difference to society as a whole. Personal development, meeting basic existence needs, along with specific personal expectations regarding work–life balance, all come into play. Some students explicitly recognise that they want and will strive for status and power, both of themselves and through explicit signifiers. There is a wide range of desires here, many of which are unrelated to the pay packet. Thinking of reward solely in terms of wage or salary therefore fails to recognise much of what is at the heart of a motivational and desirable job.

RETENTION

Rewards can encourage retention within the organisation. The broader employment relationship and social exchange play a significant role here. While most people are more likely to stay in the organisation if they consider their financial rewards are adequate (Rynes et al., 2004), other forms of reward can also be highly influential.

From a psychological perspective, rewards can be divided into those which are extrinsic and those which are intrinsic. Extrinsic rewards are tangible, external to the work itself and typically controlled by others, both in terms of their size and how they are distributed. Financial or monetary compensation is an extrinsic reward. This will comprise a basic salary, perhaps additional bonuses or the potential for additional payments based on performance, and further allowances or benefits to compensate for the disagreeable or dangerous nature of some jobs, or where the job itself is not sufficiently enticing.

Intrinsic rewards contribute more to our sense of self and are not directly controlled by external agents. They are intangible or relational returns (Milkovich et al., 2011). If we can develop a sense of meaningfulness or purpose in our work, if we feel competent and that we are enjoying our work, then we are experiencing intrinsic reward. These rewards meet our psychological needs. Flexible working arrangements, positive feedback, recognition, along with autonomy, interest and enjoyment can all enhance our sense of well-being or satisfaction and may not cost the organisation anything beyond how they choose to organise. The Great Place to Work® organisation emphasises that what makes great workplaces for employees are day-to-day relationships and in particular trust, pride and enjoyment, including the extent to which people feel they are treated fairly (www.greatplacetowork.co.uk/).

If the organisation has attracted an employee on a promise of a good salary, autonomy and career development, and then fails to deliver, the employee is likely to be disaffected and the psychological contract will have been breached (Robinson and Morrison, 1995; Rousseau, 1995), leading to an intention to leave the organisation. Maintaining individuals' interest in the organisation and their role through the effective management of both intrinsic and extrinsic rewards is a key facet of a line manager's role.

Extrinsic reward Rewards which are tangible, external transactional rewards for undertaking work. Typically these rewards are financial or confer financial benefit, and are under the control of an 'other'.

Intrinsic reward Intangible rewards derived from work and employment, which contribute towards feelings of competence, relatedness and autonomy.

DEBATING HRM

Intrinsic motivation: psychological reward or exploitation?

In recent years increasing attention has been paid to intrinsic motivation and employee engagement. Self-determination theory (SDT; Ryan and Deci, 2000) identifies that people have inherent psychological needs for a sense of competence, relatedness and autonomy, and where work design captures these conditions, people will strive to perform because they want to rather than simply because they are paid to. In a similar vein, Jeffrey Pfeffer, in his influential 1998 article 'Six dangerous myths about pay', highlights the motivational importance of stability, engaging work and fun in a suitable work environment as a counterpoint to the 'myth' that the most effective way to motivate people is through individual incentive compensation. In that article he cites Herbert Simon (1991), who noted that 'Although economic rewards play an important part in securing adherence to organisational goals and management authority, they are limited in their effectiveness. Organisations would be far less effective systems than they are if such reward were the only means, or even the principal means of motivation available' (Simon, 1991: 34).

Increasingly, organisations are seeking to develop an 'engaged' workforce. While a precise definition of this term remains elusive, it appears to rest on the type of autonomous, self-regulated and intrinsically motivated behaviour that SDT describes. In sum, if organisations can design work which encourages such autonomous and engaged operations, then all parties should benefit. The employee will benefit through a heightened sense of self-efficacy, the organisation will have a motivated workforce and the shareholders will not have to support high performance-related rewards.

TASKS: *In small groups, discuss the following:*

1   To what extent do you think the discussion about self-regulation and intrinsic reward is sustainable in contemporary business?

2   Do the demands of the workplace inevitably override the aspiration of autonomous, self-regulated working for most people?

3   Does SDT apply more to certain workers than to others?

4   Is employee engagement, whereby employees 'go the extra mile' for their employer, a positive outcome of an engaged workforce or a means through which employers seek to exploit their employees at no additional cost to themselves?

MOTIVATION

Motivation has become increasingly salient in the strategic reward literature. The selective provision or withholding of reward is viewed as a lever to motivate people to behave in particular ways. Setting standards and objectives for performance and offering rewards for their achievement is increasingly widespread and a core feature of high-performance work systems. In this regard, performance management systems have taken on great significance. A goal- or target-based approach to reward is founded in process approaches to motivation, particularly expectancy theory (Vroom, 1964) and goal setting theory (Locke, 1968). Taking these approaches together, they suggest that when people have a clear idea of what goals they are expected to achieve, and recognise that the achievement of those goals will result in their obtaining something they value (whether of intrinsic or extrinsic value), they are more likely to work hard in pursuit of those goals.

This entire process, however, has to come with something of a 'health warning'. The processes of identifying appropriate targets and linking them to appropriate rewards pose challenges to management, and will be discussed further later in this chapter and in Chapter 11.

FAIRNESS IN REWARD

It is generally agreed that whatever forms of reward are available, they should be allocated fairly. Fairness at work, and the positive and negative outcomes arising from it, was identified in Chapter 4 under the heading of organisational justice. Here we will consider what might be the key issues in relation to fairness or justice in relation to reward strategies and systems. First, we will consider the role of the state in this discussion and then we will consider individual-level concerns around judgements of fairness in reward.

The state has a variety of concerns regarding fairness in reward. First, it may wish to ensure that employers are not unfairly exploiting employees. Minimum wage or living wage legislation would be an example of such an approach. However, ensuring that workers are paid a fair wage given the cost of living in one country may make wages uncompetitive with workers' wages in other parts of the world, or may impose an unacceptable burden on employers. Globalisation has made it increasingly easy for employers to relocate their activities to parts of the world where labour costs are cheaper, allowing employers to reduce ULC but also threatening investment and jobs in their home country. Therefore, attempts to regulate wages may have the unwanted side-effect of eliminating jobs entirely, or indirectly encouraging the exploitation of workers elsewhere in the world.

The state may also seek to limit the discretion of management to set wages freely in order to ensure fair treatment of those who are perhaps disadvantaged in the workplace, for instance women, part-time workers or other groups who are systematically disadvantaged in the employment market (see Chapters 8 and 12). Finally, the state has a general interest in pay levels; in part because it gains much of its income through taxation of pay and company profits, but also because the state is typically a major employer and therefore it constitutes a major cost to government to reward employees in public sector jobs and state-owned enterprises.

At the individual level, what constitutes fairness in reward is difficult to evaluate. There are many possible lenses through which we can view fairness in reward allocation:

- We may argue that all employees should be paid an equal amount; presumably all roles in an organisation are necessary so why should there be any differentiation in reward? Cooperative organisations may operate in this way.

- We could suggest that people should be paid in relation to their needs; those supporting an extended family should be paid more than a single person living alone. Some state benefits apply this logic and it is implied in the living wage argument and in weightings on salary to accommodate the cost of living in expensive cities.

- We could choose to reward people for their commitment to the organisation, linking reward to organisational tenure. This is the basis of many incremental grading structures and has been a dominant feature of Japanese employment practices.

- We tend to assume that more senior people should be rewarded more highly than more junior colleagues as they shoulder more responsibility.

- We could argue that jobs which provide the greatest good to the greatest number of people should be the most highly rewarded. From such a viewpoint, doctors, teachers, care workers and refuse collectors should be rewarded more highly than supermodels, hedge fund managers and sports stars.

- We have already recognised that roles which are particularly disagreeable or particularly undesirable could be furnished with different extrinsic rewards to balance the intrinsic challenges or opportunities they offer. People who put themselves at risk, for example in the military or emergency services, might expect that that risk is 'compensated' for, although the excitement and personal challenge that such roles offer may, for some, provide sufficient 'psychic income' to counterbalance this threat to cost (Mitchell and Mickel, 1999).

- Dominant in the SHRM literature is the view that people should be rewarded on their merit; those who perform better are rewarded more highly.

Each of these arguments (and a number of others that you might like to consider) has something to commend it; however, there is no simple answer to the question of 'what is fair' in reward. Fairness is socially constructed; what most people believe to be fair is de facto 'what is fair', but this leaves room for much debate and disagreement. Moreover, different cultures (both national and organisational) will emphasise different elements of the 'fairness' agenda. Highly individualist cultures like the USA are likely to argue that rewarding on merit is fairest, and accept large discrepancies between the highest and lowest earners. More collectivist cultures, such as those in Japan or Thailand, are more likely to emphasise communal benefit, perhaps with less variation in reward and a greater proportion of reward based on seniority, collective achievement and organisational performance.

STRATEGIC AND TOTAL REWARD

It is apparent then that there is a range of purposes that a reward system serves, that there are many aspects of work that can be considered rewarding and that the composition of the reward system will be subject to critical scrutiny by those with a stake in it. As we saw in Chapter 2, strategic HRM models include reward as a key HR practice (Armstrong, 2006; Boselie et al., 2001; Delery and Shaw, 2001; Gomez-Mejia et al., 2004; Schuler and Jackson, 1987). The priorities for reward policy will depend on what the business and HR strategy are seeking to achieve in the context of what the company can afford and the nature of the environment in which it is operating.

DEBATING HRM

Pay inequality: how much are you worth?

Over recent years, disquiet has developed over the earnings of the wealthiest in society. Equilar reported that in 2015 David Zaslav, Chief Executive of Discovery Communications, earned over US$11 million in cash compensation with a further US$144 million in stocks and options, giving a total compensation package for the year of US$155 million, or over £100 million. Mark Hurd, CEO of Oracle Group, was paid a salary of US$53 million in 2016, similar to footballer Cristiano Ronaldo's US$53 million salary from Real Madrid. Factoring in Ronaldo's sponsorship arrangements, his annual income rounds out at around US$82 million or £55 million. What is it about these men (only nine of Equilar's top 200 earners in the USA in 2015 were women) and what they do that makes them worth so much?

In comparison with these figures, heads of state earn relatively little. The President of the United States of America (population approximately 319 million) earns a salary of just US$400,000 (around £270,000) per year; a figure unchanged since 2001. The Prime Minister of the UK (population approximately 64 million) earns around £143,500 (around US$210,000), which works out more per head of population. Estimates of the official salary of the current General Secretary of the Communist Party of China (population 1.35 billion) run at approximately US$40,000 (£27,000) per year.

A report by the BBC from the World Economic Forum in Davos in January 2015 identified that the richest 1 per cent in the world owns half of the world's wealth, while the world's 85 richest people have as much money as the poorest 3.6 billion. This income inequality was identified by participants at the World Economic Forum (80 of whom were billionaires) as the number 1 risk to the world as such inequality leads to the disintegration of societies (www.bbc.co.uk/news/business-30908234). The extent of the inequality in the distribution of wealth is graphically illustrated by the video clip Wealth Inequality in America (www.youtube.com/watch?v=QPKKQnijnsM). It claims that 1 per cent of the population of America has 40 per cent of the nation's wealth, while the bottom 70 per cent of the population has only 7 per cent of the wealth between them. However, the hourly compensation costs around the world seem to suggest that US citizens are perhaps not too badly off.

TASK: First, in small groups, discuss whether such inequality is morally defensible. Then, divide into two teams. One team should outline a case that supports such unequal distribution of wealth, while the other team should develop a case arguing for greater equality.

The recognition of a variety of different forms of reward (intrinsic and extrinsic) and the strategic options for reward systems have led to the development of the Total Reward Model (TRM). This model takes a variety of forms, though one of the more comprehensive of these is from WorldatWork. Its total reward model retains attraction, retention, motivation and engagement as the proximal objectives of a reward system. These outcomes can be achieved by the organisation offering desired and valued rewards in exchange for the employee's time, talent and efforts. This is referred to as the 'Employee Value Proposition' (EVP), 'the collective array of programs that an organization offers in exchange for employment … encompassing every aspect of the employment experience – from the organisation's mission and values; to jobs, culture and colleagues; to the full portfolio of total rewards programs' (Towers-Watson, 2012: 24). An effective reward strategy would result in both satisfied and engaged employees and an effective, high-performing organisation (see Figure 10.1; WorldatWork, 2015).

The contextual variables at the top of the model provide a backdrop to organisations' reward strategies. Concern about business strategy, HR strategy and company culture will shape what reward options are appropriate, desirable and available to the

Total reward All of the tools available to the employer that may be used to attract, motivate and retain employees. Total rewards include everything the employee perceives to be of value resulting from the employment relationship.

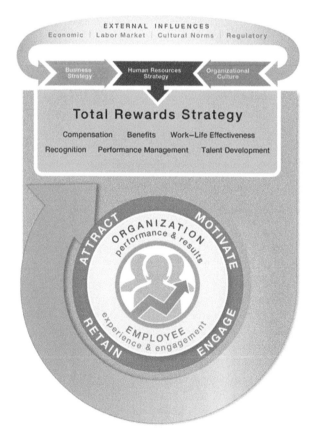

FIGURE 10.1 Total reward model

Reproduced with permission from WorldatWork.com

organisation. These, as we have seen, are influenced by broader institutional concerns and markets in which the company operates, along with labour market issues and cultural norms which may constrain or enhance its room for manoeuvre.

The key levers available to the organisation in order to achieve these outcomes are the six components of the Total Reward Strategy. We will examine these in turn.

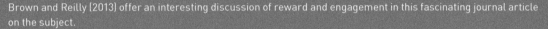

ONLINE STUDY TOOLS

Writing an essay? Expand your knowledge.

Brown and Reilly (2013) offer an interesting discussion of reward and engagement in this fascinating journal article on the subject.

https://edge.sagepub.com/crawshaw2e > **Student Resources** > **Chapter 10** > **Journal Articles**

COMPENSATION

Compensation refers to the monetary reward given to an employee for the service he or she provides. This may include a fixed base rate, the irreducible minimum that the organisation is contractually obliged to pay its employee for the time worked. There may be variable components on top of this, some of which may be regular and predictable and others more discretionary or dependent on circumstance. These rewards, sometimes known as 'plussage', may be offered for possessing specific qualifications, or in recognition of working in dangerous conditions, spending time away from home, working shifts, unsociable hours or overtime. Employers may pay 'time and a half' or 'double time' for working beyond contracted hours or working on public holidays, or offer a fixed additional amount.

There is also a range of non-contractual bonus payments which may be accrued but are not guaranteed. Incentive payments may be offered subject to the achievement of a particular level or standard of output or performance. Profit-sharing schemes similarly can provide employees with a significant uplift in their overall remuneration when a company performs at a sufficient level.

BENEFITS

Benefits are the additional non-cash items or services that nonetheless have financial value and therefore are sometimes referred to as indirect pay. Examples include pension contributions, health insurance, child care facilities, subsidised meals, company housing or paying for relocation. Discounts against goods and services provided by the company may also apply, such as subsidised mortgage rates for bank employees or company discounts in supermarkets. These serve to make the employee's salary go further. Sick pay and holiday pay are often legally mandated, whereas other benefits are discretionary.

WORK–LIFE EFFECTIVENESS

Work–life effectiveness refers to organisational practices, policies and programmes which actively seek to support employee efforts to achieve success both at work and at home – rewards that enhance employees' ability to balance the demands and expectations of work with those from life outside work. How work is organised (working from home, working flexible hours), designing jobs to make them interesting and satisfying and encouraging activities of benefit to the external community could all fall into this domain.

RECOGNITION

The earlier Graduate Insights box identified the importance of recognition at work. Here, as part of the total rewards model, this refers to formal and informal practices that pay special attention to employee efforts, behaviours or actions, typically, although not necessarily, in support of business strategy. These may range from simply thanking colleagues for their special efforts through to large-scale ceremonies highlighting individual or team contributions to organisational success. Mechanisms through which employee voice is heard at organisational level can also be considered as forms of recognition.

PERFORMANCE MANAGEMENT

Performance management is discussed in more detail in Chapter 11, however here the value it adds is through aligning individual and team efforts with the achievement of organisational goals. Understanding the expectations and behaviours required to succeed at work allows for the achievement of both intrinsic and extrinsic reward. Providing feedback on performance to enable continuous improvement enhances both individual and organisational capability and achievement. This may lead to the award of performance-related pay, applied retrospectively. We will return to this topic later in the chapter.

TALENT DEVELOPMENT

The provision of learning and development activities and courses is but a small subset of the developmental opportunities that employees might find rewarding (see Chapter 9). Wider support for learning and continuous development, through, for example, coaching and mentoring, supported by workforce intelligence planning (see Chapter 6), all contribute to the formal and informal mechanisms that support development. As personal development is widely viewed as a core responsibility for the individual (see Chapter 9), an environment rich in development opportunities enhances an employee's employability and value and therefore career, as well as being intrinsically motivating.

A Total Reward Strategy (TRS) seeks to combine and balance these components into an attractive EVP that achieves the desired individual and organisational outcomes. Thus flexible employment practices may encourage individuals to stay in an organisation which offers fewer developmental opportunities. The prospect of higher discretionary rewards for high performance may be attractive to some even though those earnings are not guaranteed, while others may prefer the security of a lower but predictable basic wage. The reward strategy chosen reflects organisational priorities and strategy. If we want a stable workforce which we can shape to our own organisational culture and which allows us to grow over the long term, we might emphasise a decent basic rate of pay with regular increments, good development opportunities, internal promotions and an attractive pension. If we are looking for rapid growth in a competitive market, we might offer lower base pay but high rates of discretionary pay tied to performance. This could result in high staff turnover, but star performers would stay long enough to make it worthwhile both for them and for the organisation. A successful reward strategy will then seek to combine the available rewards in a way which best achieves the organisational strategy while also addressing the motivational needs of our employees.

Of course, a total rewards approach should not be seen solely as a way of reducing ULC and recent research by the CIPD (2012) highlights that HR managers can find it difficult to convince employees of the value of the total reward offering. WorldatWork proposes that employers treat employees as customers ('Total Rewards is a product and employees are the consumers', www.worldatwork.org/waw/adimLink?id=78516). Within this view, it becomes a core role of the HR manager to identify what is important to those customers (employees) and construct their overall EVP around this.

We can see that reward is a broadly constructed term, and that what individuals find rewarding and what rewards an organisation can offer vary. Next we will focus on that most tangible component of reward, compensation. This is not to suggest that you should view pay separately from other aspects of reward. Rather, it allows us to consider more clearly what it is we actually reward.

WHAT DO WE PAY FOR?

This at first may appear a very straightforward question: we pay for people to work. Setting aside for a moment work for which there is no financial reward (voluntary or domestic work, for example), what exactly is it that is being bought? Compensation is defined by Milkovich et al. (2011: 10) as 'all forms of financial returns and tangible services and benefits employees receive as part of an employment relationship', but what is it exchanged for?

First, we are paying for a *job* to be done, so we need to know the value of that job to the organisation in order to establish a fair level of payment for the job holder. We would not want to pay either too much or too little for a role and we need to be aware of ULC. The process through which the value of a job is determined is called job evaluation. Base pay is usually expressed either as an hourly wage or as an annual salary and will be a function of the value of the job to the organisation, the market rate for that job, the total reward proposition adopted by the organisation, any influence of agreements between employers and employee representatives and any legal requirements such as minimum wage rates.

What do you value in work?

Work is more than just an exchange of effort for financial compensation. The preceding sections have identified intrinsic and extrinsic reward, and the total reward model further elaborates on a range of different sources of reward at work.

TASK: Go to the WorldatWork website and read the factsheet summarising the total rewards model (www.worldatwork.org/waw/adimLink?id=28330&nonav=y). Work through the Total Rewards Inventory and see which of the components are particularly important to you, and which are particularly unattractive. Does this affect your view of what you might look for in your next job?

Second, we are paying for the particular *person* to carry out the job. So, if we have someone with extensive relevant experience and qualifications, specific knowledge in the job domain or particular competencies, then we would be willing to pay more than we would to someone less skilled. As such, our base pay for a job will not be a single fixed amount, but may be represented by a range of values to account for these personal differences.

Finally, we may decide that we only want to pay for, or are willing to pay more for, people who *perform* well. This aligns with the 'performance and recognition' component of the total reward model above and is sometimes referred to as contingent or variable pay. Unlike the two elements above, contingent pay is not guaranteed; it is dependent on the employee, or group of employees, achieving the objectives that have been set.

Distinguishing between the core components of a reward system

Reward strategy is in part driven by organisational strategy. Different approaches to reward will, we hope, result in behaviours and outcomes that enable overall strategy to be achieved. Below is a selection of HR outcomes that we might be able to influence through our choice of reward strategy:

- Attraction of new staff
- Retention and stability of existing workforce
- Creativity and innovation
- Team working
- Conformity and reliability
- Quality of output
- Continual learning.

TASK: For each of the above objectives, construct a total reward package that you think would encourage each specific outcome.

We will explore each of these components in turn, addressing the HR considerations which inform decision making in the design of reward systems.

PAYING FOR THE JOB

In order to decide what a *job* is worth, we first need to know what the job entails and what it contributes to the organisation as a whole. From that we can make evaluations of the relative worth of different jobs within the organisation and allocate rewards accordingly. Chapter 7 introduced job analysis as a systematic process for identifying what a job entails and as a fundamental area of HR activity. In relation to designing a reward system, it is often the building block from which reward allocation decisions can be made, informed by the process of job evaluation which allows the organisation to recognise and reward those behaviours or competencies which it most values.

Job evaluation A systematic process for defining the relative worth or size of jobs within an organisation in order to establish internal relativities and provide the basis for an equitable grading structure.

Analytic approaches to job evaluation seek to break jobs down into important components (either factors of the role or competencies required of the role holder), which are pre-defined but common across all jobs, and can therefore be applied consistently across the range of jobs being considered. Typically, each factor or competency is allocated a point score for each job being evaluated. This rating indicates how significant that particular factor or competency is for effective job performance. The point scores can then be combined and compared directly across different jobs, to indicate which jobs are more demanding and valuable to the firm, and therefore more highly rewarded.

Clearly this is a complex and skilled process, often beyond the capabilities of an average organisation's HR department. A number of commercial and generic schemes have emerged over time, the most popular being the Hay system (HayGroup®, 2005). This analyses all jobs against three factors: know-how, problem solving and accountability. Other classification systems, for example the Position Analysis Questionnaire (McCormick et al., 1972, 1989) and O*Net (www.onetonline.org) share similar features.

It is important to note two features about such approaches. First, detail about what a job holder actually does is not included; it is not a job description. However, as the same factors are applied to jobs across the organisation, jobs which emerge with equal point scores are deemed to have equivalent levels of knowledge or skill requirements, and therefore are of equal value.

Second, the process is independent of the job holder. It does not take account of different levels of performance on the job by the more or less skilled job holder; it simply describes what is required by the job role and therefore the value of the job (Welbourne and Trevor, 2000).

Applying this approach to roles across the organisation provides an evaluation of the relative demands or requirements of each job and the level of competence and proficiency which is required of the job holder. Moreover, the points score approach actually indicates how much more demanding different jobs are.

Such analytical systems are very attractive to HR professionals. They establish a visible and shared set of evaluation dimensions which are applied impartially to all jobs. As such they are perceived by employees, and by employment tribunals, as fair. They are independent of the job holder, and therefore continue to be applicable beyond the tenure of any one individual. They ensure that all key attributes of the jobs are considered, and where new jobs are created, these can be rated against the same criteria.

Analytical approaches can however be difficult and expensive to administer, so for smaller or less well-resourced organisations a non-analytical approach is often adopted. Rather than break jobs down into their common underlying components, non-analytical approaches deal with jobs as a whole.

A 'job ranking' approach involves ranking all jobs in the organisation into a hierarchy, from the most complicated and demanding down to the least so. This may sometimes be carried out on the basis of a job title or a simple job description. Thus a 'Marketing Manager' would be ranked higher than a 'Marketing Assistant', but would probably be ranked equally with a 'Sales Manager'. A 'paired comparison' approach extends this process a little more systematically by comparing each job to each other job and allocating points according to whether the role demands greater, lesser or similar skills and abilities than the other roles. Again, however, jobs are treated as whole entities rather than as component skills or competencies.

Such approaches benefit from practical and conceptual simplicity. New jobs can be fitted into an existing structure easily without having to go through a complex analysis process. Similarly, when existing roles change, the new description for that position is incorporated into the overall framework. These approaches are particularly attractive to smaller businesses where there is a relatively small number of roles (and therefore fewer comparative judgements to make) and probably fewer resources available to support a more thorough and analytical evaluation. However, where there are a lot of different jobs in an organisation, systematically rank ordering all jobs, or comparing each job against each other job, is extremely complicated and quickly becomes unreliable. As the judgements being made risk being subjective and based on limited information, it is also likely to result in perceived unfairness as we risk missing out on crucial demands and skills that are fundamental, although not obvious, to the effective performance of that role.

Finally, judgements about the relative significance of roles within an organisation on the basis of incomplete information carried out in an unreliable manner are likely to perpetuate the existing stereotypes, prejudices and biases of the assessor. What he or she believes to be important becomes the basis for what is decided to be important in the organisation. Therefore, existing discriminatory practices are reaffirmed. For example, technical work is often assumed to be worth less than managerial work, although the level of knowledge and training and its contribution to organisational performance may be comparable. Where roles are gender-stereotyped, biases are even more likely to be evidenced (McShane, 1990; see also Chapter 8). Such limitations mean non-analytical approaches are not looked upon favourably in a legal context where cases for equal pay for work of equal value may arise (see Chapter 12).

Figure 10.2 gives an overview of the pros and cons of analytical and non-analytical approaches to job evaluation.

Whichever approach is used, what emerges is a hierarchy of roles, either a direct ordering of roles from the non-analytical approaches or a more comprehensive points score from the more structured analytical approaches. This provides a clear view of the relative importance or significance of the different roles. The next task is to put a financial or monetary value on the jobs within the structure or hierarchy.

Taking the analytical approach first, if we were simply to allocate a cash value to each point, we would end up with a system whereby each role had its own unique value. While this may make logical sense, it is unlikely to be the outcome of a job evaluation process. Having a single cash value on each role provides no opportunity for rewards to act as an incentive or motivator for anyone. No matter how long you have been doing the job, how well or how badly you do it, there is no opportunity to have your level of performance, your skills or your experience recognised. This would rightly be perceived as unfair or inequitable.

VALUING THE PERSON

We noted earlier that it is important to have ranges of values for jobs in order to reflect what the role holder brings to it. Identifying and recognising the individual

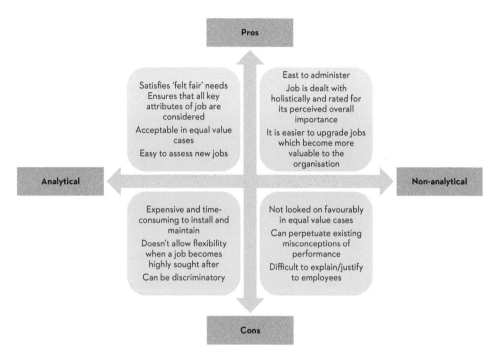

FIGURE 10.2 Comparison of analytical and non-analytical approaches to job evaluation

worth of job holders therefore comes into play. Typically this is achieved through grading structures. Jobs can be clustered into groups of jobs of similar value and these groups are allocated to grades or pay bands (or pay spines or job families). A range of values or pay levels is assigned to that grade. Individual attributes, qualities, achievements and competencies are recognised by where a job holder is located within the pay band.

The actual location of any individual on a pay grade may be a matter for negotiation between the employee and the organisation, or may simply be decided by management, taking account of personal skills, abilities and experience. This approach maintains a relatively simple overall structure while allowing for the recognition of individual differences in what people bring to the jobs they do. It also provides opportunities for improvements in performance, investment in skill or knowledge development, or even tenure, to be recognised by increases in pay within a grade.

The bands may be narrow or broad, flexible or fixed. There may be a single unified pay spine for all employees within an organisation, or there may be many different pay spines for different groups or skills. In some organisations, pay rates are more flexibly determined, based on individual negotiations, market rates and affordability. Where individuals have, for example, invested more in their education and training one would expect to see higher wages compared to those with lower qualifications

Exploring job evaluation

- Job evaluation is a systematic process which seeks to identify the value of job roles, rather than job holders, to the organisation as a whole. Identify an organisation that you might be interested in working for (your careers centre may be able to help with this). Go to the company's website and choose six jobs which are currently vacant. From the job description/person specification information included, rank these jobs from the most senior to the most junior.

- Now watch the video 'A Question of Job Evaluation' which can be found at www.haygroup.com/en/our-library/videos/hay-group-job-evaluation/#.VOHKVyFjbpl

- TASK: Reconsider the jobs you ranked along the three core factors that Hay identifies (accountability, know-how, problem solving). Evaluate the proportions of accountability, know-how and problem solving that each job requires. Hay suggests that more senior roles include more responsibility, while lower-level roles typically focus on know-how:

    1. Does the shape of the jobs you have identified change your initial subjective ranking from the first part of this task?

    2. Do you have enough information available to make accurate judgements of the three factors for each of the roles, given the information you have?

    Now look on O*Net for the generic descriptions of these jobs.

    3. Does this information enable you to make a more accurate assessment?

or skills. This human capital investment argument is one way of differentiating between individual role holders. If it is the firm which has paid for this investment, then it is clearly in the firm's interest to ensure that those employees have long-term career prospects in order that the firm can recoup on those costs.

So far our reward system design has considered only factors internal to the organisation. We discussed earlier the significance of external features which impact on absolute levels of pay beyond internal value benchmarks and now look at these in a little more detail.

Market conditions may mean that certain roles are more difficult to fill, either because they are particularly specialised, in short supply or where they are simply essential, irrespective of the skill components. Some IT roles arguably fall into this category as companies are dependent on a functioning IT infrastructure. There will be a premium to be paid for these skills, even if they are of only moderate value within the organisation's evaluation system. Employers may have little choice but to acquiesce to pay demands from these key performers. This argument is regularly used to justify executive pay decisions, discussed elsewhere in this chapter. Organisational remuneration committees, typically made up of a small group of independent non-executive directors or external remuneration consultants, may advise on appropriate rates and reward packages for senior posts on the basis of their broad knowledge of the market but where there is not a large pool of data available. However, such flexibility poses a challenge to some of our fairness lenses.

On a global scale, labour market rates differ significantly, and this has resulted in the offshoring of work from high-cost economies to those where local rates are much cheaper (see Figure 10.3). However, even within a single country it is common that some regions attract premium rates due to local living costs, again distorting internal relativities.

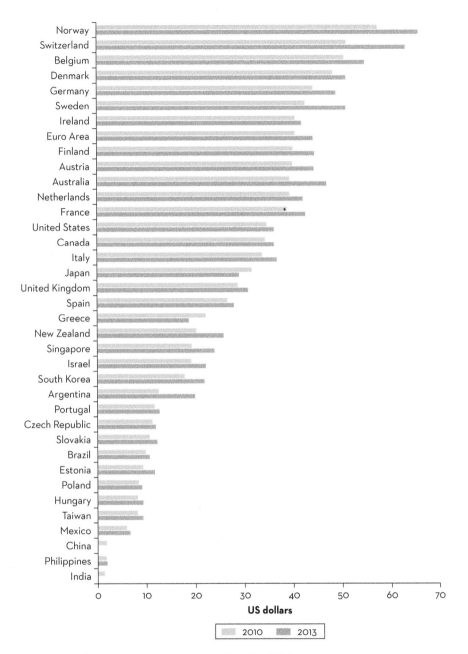

FIGURE 10.3 Hourly compensation costs in manufacturing (US$) 2013

Note: Compensation costs include direct pay, social insurance expenditures and labor-related taxes. Data for China and India are not strictly comparable with each other or with data for other countries. For complete definitions, country information and a description of data limitations associated with estimates for China and India, see the Technical Notes and Country Notes supplementing this report.

Source: The Conference Board, International Labor Comparisons program

Negotiated agreements with unions or employee representatives may influence pay rates, although such arrangements are becoming less common in the UK. Between 2012 and 2014 the CIPD's annual Reward Survey reported that the proportion of employers for whom collective bargaining was the major determinant of pay fell from 24 per cent to just 7 per cent (CIPD, 2015). Still, the Trades Union Congress (2013), which is the apex body representing about 6.5 million workers in Britain, claims that the union wage mark-up is about 7 per cent. In other words, a unionised firm in the UK would pay about 7 per cent higher wages compared to a similar non-union firm.

All these factors will to some extent distort the broadly objective values of jobs calculated through systematic job evaluation. Such variation challenges the sense of pay equity and fairness within the organisation. Some of these distortions may be overcome through the creative development of a TRS; however, such inconsistencies typically remain contentious.

In summary, a systematic approach to job evaluation and the development of reward structures emerging from it have been the dominant framework for reward system design. It is a systematic (rather than scientific) process which seeks to ensure that people are rewarded appropriately and equitably on the basis of the value of the job, adjusted for the characteristics and skills that a person brings to it. The absolute rates of pay bring in considerations of what the employer is able and willing to pay, and how they want to be seen in the broader labour market. Systematic job evaluation systems have much to recommend them. They are comprehensive, relatively transparent and open to challenge and rebuttal through appeal if necessary. They are also, crucially, recognised by employment tribunals as a defence against claims of unfairness. If the employer can demonstrate that an appropriate analytical job evaluation process has taken place, the employer is unlikely to lose a case. However recent trends seem to indicate a move away from such structures towards an increased use of individualised pay arrangements and 'spot rates' to recognise individual skills and competencies. Some of the challenges to these structured approaches are discussed in the next section.

HRM IN PRACTICE

The executive pay gap

In the USA in 2015, Glassdoor reported that the average CEO pay was 204 times the average employee's pay (Dishman, 2015). While these data are not collected systematically and may exaggerate the differences, they do highlight an argument that has led to increasing debate around the world. How much more than the average employee is a CEO worth? David Zaslav, who we saw earlier was the highest paid CEO, earns 1950 times Discovery Communications' median employee salary (US$156 million versus US$80,000 in 2014). The CEO of Fossil by comparison, Kosta Kartsotis, reported US$0 compensation in 2014. According to the filing that all US corporations are required to make to the Securities and Exchange Commission (SEC), 'Mr. Kartsotis again refused all forms of compensation for fiscal 2014. Mr. Kartsotis is one of the initial investors in our company and expressed his belief that his primary compensation is met by continuing to drive stock price growth.' At Google, CEO and co-founder Larry Page took only US$1 in pay, although with a personal wealth of US$38 billion one might suggest this is not too great a loss. From August 2015 the SEC has adopted a rule requiring a public company to disclose the ratio of the compensation of its CEO to the median compensation of its employees (SEC, 2015). In the UK, where equivalent comparison statistics are harder to come by, the High Pay Centre estimates that in 2014 the average pay ratio between UK FTSE 100 CEOs and the average wage of their employees was between 113:1 and 150:1, depending on the measure of CEO remuneration used (Marsland, 2015), and between 276 and 366 times the current National Living Wage of £7.20 per hour. The Trades Union Congress has called for a pay ratio of no more than 20:1.

Job evaluation has been criticised on a number of levels. First, the objectivity or accuracy of the process can be questioned, particularly but not exclusively where non-analytical methods are used (Collins and Muchinsky, 1993). Second, the increased flexibility in employment and the rate at which work roles change lead to accusations of unresponsiveness. Having to repeatedly re-evaluate jobs every time changes are made is prohibitive. Third, employees themselves are better informed about their market value and may choose to challenge salary decisions based more on external than internal relativities.

As individual employment situations have become more flexible, the straightjacket of systematic job evaluation systems has become increasingly challenged. Increases in part-time working, portfolio careers and flexible work roles, or an individual's desire to achieve a work–life balance, may all be difficult to reflect within traditional pay frameworks. At the same time, employers want the opportunity to recognise excellence, creativity or great teamwork wherever it occurs, leading to a greater call for flexibility in rewards to better fit company strategy, employee desires and customer needs. This leads on to the final component of the reward package noted earlier, that of paying for performance.

PAYING FOR PERFORMANCE

Paying for performance is by no means a new development. Piece-rate systems derived from the work of F.W. Taylor and Scientific Management rely on exactly that principle. In contemporary organisations simple piece-rate systems are relatively uncommon; however, identifying what behaviours or outcomes are required and linking their achievement directly to reward serve the same purpose. The assumption is that people will grasp the opportunity to obtain desired rewards through behaving in ways that are explicitly linked to the achievement of those rewards. If the behavioural or performance objectives are linked to organisational strategy, then we have a direct link between strategy and performance through the management of reward. This approach also encourages people to regulate their own behaviours, thus reducing the need for direct managerial control and supervision.

Paying for performance is a very attractive proposition and conforms to one of our fairness lenses. Rewarding better performers more generously than poorer performers feels fair, and the offer of desired reward should be both motivational and personally satisfying, resulting in benefits for both employer and employee.

However, we should beware of turning the entire employment relationship into one based solely on economic exchange. As Slater (1980: 127) concludes, 'Getting people to chase money … produces nothing but people chasing money.' This can result in a joyless and divisive work environment where every act has significance only in terms of how it affects personal interests – not a great place to work. Still, performance-related reward remains an intuitively attractive proposition. Remember the TRM: a valued reward does not have to be money.

A key challenge of performance-based reward systems is to identify what performance to reward. By specifying certain performance objectives, we inevitably downplay other behaviours or outcomes. The car salesperson above could reasonably be rewarded for the number or value of cars sold. However, if that were to result in pressure selling tactics being employed, encouraging customers to spend more than they can afford so that the salesperson achieves his or her target, it may result in subsequent defaults on finance agreements or a lack of repeat business from pressurised customers. For a high school teacher, student grades may be taken as indicators of good performance, so teachers may decide to grade their students more generously than perhaps they deserve. In both these cases, the outcomes we see (high sales and good results) may have been achieved through behaviours that we do not want (pressure selling and grade inflation).

It also can be difficult to attribute desired outcomes to particular behaviours. Student performance is not solely the result of the teacher's efforts. How able and motivated the students are and how effectively their parents support their learning and the resources available to them will all affect their level of achievement. Teacher performance will play some part here, but how much value they add is questionable.

For the emergency room nurse, the desired outcomes themselves are difficult to identify. The number of patients treated over a shift, or patient satisfaction, could be useful indicators of

Making recommendations on performance-related reward

Performance-related reward systems require that we can identify appropriate performance and recognise its achievement through the reward system.

TASK: For the following jobs, what performance would you want to reward and what form would that performance-related reward take?

- A car salesperson
- A high school teacher
- An emergency room nurse
- An expatriate production manager working to set up a new joint venture plant in Malaysia.

performance, but do not seem to capture the essence of what it is to be a 'good nurse'. An important feature might be whether the nurse demonstrated care and empathy with patients. Here we might shift our focus to identifying and evaluating appropriate or desired behaviours rather than outcomes or achievements.

The behaviours of other staff in the emergency room, as well as the resources available and events on the day, will also influence what is done and what is achieved. Any individual nurse has only partial control over his or her performance and the outcomes achieved. This reminds us of the AMO model discussed in Chapter 2. If employees have no opportunity to perform, is it reasonable to put a component of their reward package at risk depending on how well they perform? Perhaps performance should be assessed at the team level, but what is the 'team'? The nurses working that shift, the entire ER team, or the hospital as a whole?

A similar challenge is faced in assessing the performance of the expatriate production manager, where the success of the business unit may be the key consideration. Here time will also play a part. Medium- or long-term performance of the joint venture may be the best indication, but how long would you need or want to wait to evaluate that success?

There are therefore challenges to identifying what we mean by performance, what performance is desired, how to measure it and the extent to which it is under the control of the individual or team being evaluated. Behaviours typically are more under personal control than are outcomes, but tend to be difficult to observe, measure or assess, leading to fears of subjectivity and bias. Outcomes may be easier to define, but are rarely under individual control and may only be measurable a considerable time after the event. Team performance can be important, but leaves open the opportunity for social loafing, whereby team members rely on the efforts of others rather than taking personal responsibility for the common task. The issue of what performance to measure and at what level is a theme that will be picked up in the next chapter.

Much of the debate about what types of performance behaviour or outcome to reward stems from corporate, business and HR strategy. For a team-based organisation, individually-based reward systems could be divisive and set one colleague in competition with another. Value-based organisations are likely to want to encourage behaviours that are in accordance with the aspirations of the organisation. For example, are they ethical, supportive, reliable, efficient, innovative, and so on? These qualities, however, can be difficult to measure reliably, leading to suspicions of bias and favouritism.

Finally, the nature of the link between performance and reward needs to be considered. Should this be an automatic link whereby hitting performance goals automatically triggers a specific pay increase or a performance bonus, or should there be some variability to recognise unanticipated exceptional performance, or just missing out on some goals while exceeding on others? Again, this can only be decided within the overall context of the organisation. Can we afford the potential cost of all employees hitting or exceeding their targets? Might we impose a certain limit on the rewards available, either through restricting how many staff can gain, or through capping the amount available? Forced distribution performance ratings allow only the top performers, often the top 10 or 15 per cent, to be eligible for performance-related pay. However this is dependent on the accurate assessment of performance and can be divisive if the assessment is not trusted. The organisation also needs to standardise or moderate the ratings of different managers, a process which can be elaborate and time-consuming. In the CIPD (2015) reward survey respondents were unconvinced that this overall represented a valuable and worthwhile use of time given the questionable organisational benefit of many of the performance awards under discussion. Limiting the overall pot of performance bonus available is another route to balance cost control and reward. However, if there are a lot of people performing at a high level the actual value of the performance bonus will be so diluted as to be negligible, again leading to dissatisfaction rather than motivation.

To summarise, linking performance and reward is an attractive proposition and appears to be fair. However, its superficial attractiveness disguises a number of challenges in designing and operating such a system, which may undermine the fairness objectives that we seek to achieve. For an engaging exploration of this see Dan Pink's TED talk, 'The puzzle of motivation' (www.ted.com/talks/dan_pink_on_motivation). The final section of this chapter will explore some current issues in the reward field.

MINI CASE STUDY

Handelsbanken

Handelsbanken is one of Sweden's leading banks, with over 700 branches in 24 countries. Its goal is to have higher profitability than the average for its competitors, which it has achieved for the last 40 years. It also has exceptionally high levels of customer satisfaction: unusually in modern banking, branch employees are given extensive autonomy where the guiding principle is to fulfil the customers' requirements, rather than sell particular products or achieve pre-set targets. Handelsbanken believes that staff engagement is core to achieving the bank's goals. Its approach to risk is more long-term than is typical in the sector, and this carries over to the long-term perspective it adopts on rewarding its employees.

Handelsbanken operates a long-term profit-sharing scheme called Oktogonen. If the bank meets its goals then an allocation is made to the Oktogonen Foundation. All employees are allocated an equal investment in the fund, dependent only on hours worked, not on seniority or individual achievement. Individual performance is reflected separately in the company's pay policy.

As the large part of Oktogonen is invested in Handelsbanken itself, this approach encourages responsible action by employees – risking the bank's profitability risks their own long-term benefits through Oktogonen. As individuals can withdraw their share of Oktogonen only from age 60, it also fosters a long-term relationship. Staff turnover at Handelsbanken is low and employees have a genuine stake and sense of trust in the bank.

TASK: Compare this approach to more standard models of reward in the financial sector discussed elsewhere in this chapter.

1   What are the key characteristics of Handelsbanken's approach?

2   Identify the benefits and possible shortcomings of this system.

3   Would you find this approach to performance and reward attractive? Why, or why not?

RECENT AND CURRENT ISSUES FOR REWARD

Strategic HRM has at its heart concerns about employee reward (see Chapter 2) and yet reward systems seem strangely resistant to change. Indeed, it has been suggested that the 'rhetoric–reality' gap in HR is widest in the field of rewards (Bevan, 2013). In part this may arise from the outdated underpinning assumption of a direct link between 'at risk' reward and performance that Dan Pink explores in his TED talk. Here we will address three concerns around changes to reward systems and the challenges they pose for the HR manager. The first, New Pay, largely accepts the effort–reward assumption and tries to put it into practice. This shifts into the recent call for 'smart rewards', wherein core values are the strategic driving force for reward strategy. Finally we will consider the importance of transparency in reward.

NEW PAY

While New Pay is no longer so new, the agenda behind it highlights a number of the tensions in the design and development of reward systems. Led by Lawler (1990, 1995), the New Pay argument emphasises the need for flexible alignment between business strategy, organisational design and reward strategy within a dynamic organisational environment. Lawler's approach draws upon four principles:

New Pay   Identifying pay practices that enhance the organisation's strategic effectiveness. Typified by a strategic, flexible approach, incorporating payment for performance within a unitarist frame of reference.

- A strategic orientation to pay

- Flexible pay, responsive to market conditions

- Variable pay, and in particular pay related to performance

- Unitarism, a fundamental assumption that organisations and those within them share a common set of goals in the pursuit of mutual gain.

If, as contingent and configurational models of HRM suggest, different business strategies require different approaches to pay in order to support and secure them, then we should see greater variation in the nature of pay systems, determined by the choice of strategy. Typically this is interpreted as a shift of emphasis from paying primarily for the job towards paying primarily for performance, 'performance' being whatever the business identifies as 'strategic' and contributing to the achievement of business objectives. Given the underlying assumption of a unitarist perspective on the employment relationship (see Chapter 12), this is predicted to increase the exercise of discretionary effort by employees, who will align their activities with the needs of the organisation. The reward system underpinning this is characterised by individual flexibility and, crucially, increased use of contingent, performance-related or 'at risk' pay. That way businesses don't pay if they don't get the performance they want, and individuals are incentivised to work towards strategic performance goals which ultimately benefit both employer and employee. Behaviour not aligned to business strategy and objectives is not rewarded. The proportion of compensation which is dependent on performance (i.e. contingent reward) should increase (Lawler [1995] suggests that 10–15 per cent of 'at risk' pay is necessary to impact behaviour) while consolidated remuneration (that which is guaranteed) proportionately decreases.

While the attractiveness of this approach is clear, its effectiveness and impact on the employment relationship can be and has been questioned. The evidence for the effectiveness of such an approach we know is equivocal. Gerhart and Milkovich (1990), Abowd (1990) and Marsden (2009) all report positive associations between contingent reward and performance, while Bloom and Milkovich (1998) and Bloom (1999) showed that high levels of 'at risk' pay tend to be associated with lower levels of performance. Moreover, individualised pay for performance undermines collective and collaborative efforts and thus can have a negative effect upon organisational performance.

Edmund Heery has been particularly critical of this ideology. He highlights two particularly problematic concepts – those of risk and representation (Heery, 1996). The risk critique argues that a performance-dominated reward system shifts risk away from the employer onto the employee, which undermines their economic and psychological need for stability. In the meantime, the risk to the organisation and its shareholders is diminished but they continue to reap guaranteed rewards: if the expected performance (assuming it can be accurately measured) is not achieved, they do not lose; if expected performance is exceeded, they benefit.

Heery's representation critique argues that employee interests, both in strategy overall and reward strategy in particular, are unrepresented and that New Pay is therefore undemocratic. Employees ought to have a right to representation in matters that influence their conditions of employment. New Pay therefore is construed as a vehicle for managerial control and employee compliance.

SMART REWARDS

More recently, Lawler (2011) has revisited the field, basing his argument on workforce diversity and generational changes in expectations (see Chapter 8). Increasingly diverse workforces require diverse reward options. Treating everyone the same, while administratively straightforward, results in most people not being treated optimally – they will be treated either better or worse than they deserve. A positive stand on diversity and more individualised employment strategies will therefore have a number of practical advantages. The workforce will be more creative and innovative and will better represent potential customers. The organisation will find it easier to identify and retain talent and will generate a more responsive and agile organisation, and employees' interests are better represented. Somewhat in contrast, Brown (2014) suggests that such a potentially complex system would be more effective if reward strategy is more clearly linked to core values. Knowing what the core values and principles of the company are (e.g. innovation, engagement, achievement, teamwork) allows the firm to construct a reward strategy that recognises these values. The Netflix and Handelsbanken examples discussed earlier represent contrasting values but a similar alignment of reward strategy to values. Decisions on reward should be based on clear evidence about their effectiveness. Data on the costs and benefits of reward changes in relation to these core values should be collected and inform future reward strategy change. This includes engaging with employees to find out what they think about the firm's reward strategy and acting on that information, either through changing strategy or clarifying the link between values and strategy. This results in a greater emphasis on communication and delivery, or transparency within a values-aligned strategy, rather than endless complication and opacity until the employee has no idea what the reward objectives of the firm are.

TRANSPARENCY

As indicated in the previous section, transparency is a theme which has come more to the fore in recent years. The tendency for firms to maintain secrecy in their reward strategies and allocation is becoming increasingly untenable. The wide availability of salary information through online tools such as Glassdoor, bodies such as Incomes Data Services (www.incomesdata.co.uk), which provides regular updates on average pay rates for different jobs, and other published data from proprietary job evaluation systems like Hay, gives rise to a high level of familiarity with market rates and market value. We have seen elements of transparency become enacted in the USA through the SEC's rules for pay disclosure, and pressures more widely seem to be heading in the same direction (Risher, 2014). Reward transparency achieves a number of ends; for employees it allows them to identify where unfairness may exist, for example in relation to gender equality (see also Chapter 8 on diversity in organisations). Global comparisons continue to highlight the disparity in earnings between men and women. South Korea has a gender pay gap of over 36 per cent, while in New Zealand, the most 'equal' society on the OECD's evaluations from 2014, this gap is just 5.6 per cent (OECD, 2015). Where employees are unaware of co-workers' rewards and the firm's reward strategy, speculation arises, typically inaccurate speculation. Lawler (2012) claims that 'when employees do not know what other people earn, they overestimate what their coworkers earn and end up being more dissatisfied than they would be if they had accurate pay information'.

Non-disclosure of reward information undermines trust, leading to challenges in building employee engagement. Equity (see Chapter 4) and expectancy theories of motivation both require transparency in the allocation process and level of reward in order to impact motivation. Lack of transparency therefore undermines percep-tions of fairness and the motivational intentions of reward strategy. In some domains transparency already exists, for example public sector organisations, or where union negotiations are involved. A recent (non-scientific) survey by Glassdoor (2016) sug-gested 70 per cent of employee respondents believed that salary transparency had a positive impact both on employee satisfaction and on the business as a whole. Some firms, for example Whole Foods, already share all employees' salaries; and the

Glassdoor survey identified that over one-third of employers already disclose salaries internally. So why is pay secrecy still so widespread? The obvious (although not necessarily accurate) conclusion would seem to be that there is something to hide. Curtailing reward secrecy is likely to have a fairly dramatic impact in the short term, particularly where it highlights inequalities; Salesforce's internal audit in 2015 resulted in a spend of nearly US$3 million to eliminate statistically significant differences in pay. This discussion may remind you of an issue we addressed earlier in the chapter: the need for effective, systematic and open job evaluation processes. The increasing pressure to disclose, along with the perceived benefits of transparency, may encourage firms to clean up their act sooner, before possible legislation requires them to do so.

CASE STUDY

Recruitment, retention and reward in China

In the past two decades, China has been a magnet for inward investment, largely due to the low unit labour cost the region offers. China has moved rapidly away from state regulation of wages and, in association with the marketisation of the economy and the influence of increased foreign direct investment, has sought increasingly to implement performance-based payment systems (Huang and Brown, 2007). Increasingly, however, recruitment and retention is a major problem, in particular that of attracting and retaining high-quality talent (Lin et al., 2011). Meanwhile in recent years, against the background of China's development, other countries in the region, particularly Vietnam and the Philippines, are becoming much cheaper for multinational companies who want to reduce their unit labour costs through a focus on wages. Still, and despite a culture of job hopping, with turnover rates double or triple those in mature Western markets, wage inflation continues in China: the 2016 Hays Asia Salary Guide (2016) reports an average of 6 per cent wage inflation per year, and 70 per cent of employers intending to increase pay packages by at least 6 per cent in 2016 against only 30 per cent of employers in other Asian countries reporting similar intentions. Adam and Chen (2013) report average remuneration in China more than tripling between 2000 and 2011.

At the same time, Brown (2013) reports that workers in Asia–Pacific are disengaged, struggling to cope with their work situation and anxious about their financial future. According to Hays, the main reasons employees stay with a current employer in China is work–life balance (49 per cent), while in Japan, the dominant driver for retention is career progression (43 per cent), and in Malaysia, salary (42 per cent). In contrast, the main reason people report looking for other jobs in China was to obtain better salary and benefits (41 per cent).

Brown speculates that total rewards are not well recognised within this workforce. It is not that total rewards are not available, rather that employees focus primarily on pay and monetary compensation when evaluating reward equity rather than on a broader employee value proposition (EVP). Hays' more recent data may cast some doubt on this, with career progression, management style and company culture, and job security all reported to be more influential in Chinese employees' decisions to stay with their current employer than pay.

Perceptions of pay equity in particular are reported to be low. For example, it is widely known that foreign workers in China typically earn considerably more than local staff, and their numbers continue to rise as more companies relocate to or open joint ventures in China. This further stokes a sense of inequity among local workers.

TASKS: On the basis of the description above, identify the key challenges facing a privately owned European manufacturing business considering setting up a joint venture in China:

1   How do these challenges impact on the reward strategy that such a business might adopt?

2   Considering the concepts discussed within the chapter, particularly the total reward model, identify an original EVP for such an organisation which would serve to attract and retain talent in the organisation.

3   What steps would you take to ensure that your EVP is acceptable, valued and recognised by employees?

4   What might be the possible drawbacks of your proposal?

CHAPTER SUMMARY

The key points that we have identified in this chapter are the following:

*   Reward strategies exist within a broad context of pay policy, an important but sometimes overlooked area of HRM.

*   Reward systems serve to attract employees to an organisation, retain them within the organisation and motivate them to perform effectively while employed, taking account of affordability.

*   They also serve symbolic purposes for the employer and employee, signifying what the organisation values and how it positions itself in the wider labour market.

*   Perceptions of fairness in reward are extremely important, particularly for employees. However, as fairness is a socially constructed phenomenon it is very difficult to meet all expectations of fairness for all the key stakeholders.

*   The notion of reward goes beyond simply how much people are paid. Total reward models emphasise both tangible and intangible benefits which individuals may accrue in the course of their employment.

*   Reward strategy seeks to align reward choices to the strategic goals of the organisation. Reward systems therefore are constructed to recognise the value of the job to the organisation, the value of the person performing that job and the value of the behaviours displayed to the overall organisational strategy.

- Job evaluation represents a systematic approach to the determination of the relative values of jobs within an organisation.

- Performance-based reward is presented as a strategy to achieve the motivational aims of reward. It seeks to encourage specific behaviours which are judged to be particularly relevant to achieving organisational strategy.

- There are concerns around performance-based reward which risk undermining its effectiveness. These concerns centre around identifying what aspects of performance should be rewarded and whether they can be adequately assessed.

- Recent trends in discussions around reward arise from changes in the business environment. These have included increased individualisation of reward coupled with concern for transparency in reward, two pressures which may not always sit easily together.

REVIEW QUESTIONS AND EXERCISES

1. Can a reward system ever be fair? Why?

2. Total reward models can be taken to imply that intrinsic reward can serve as a substitute for compensation. To what extent do you believe this is a reasonable interpretation of TRM?

3. What are the key differences between analytical and non-analytical approaches to job evaluation? How might these affect the acceptability of the different approaches within organisations?

4. Compare and contrast the advantages and disadvantages of rewarding behaviour versus rewarding outcomes. In what circumstances would each approach be more or less appropriate?

5. Identify four current job advertisements. What do they say about the rewards on offer? Consider this in light of the total rewards model. What intrinsic and extrinsic rewards are on offer? To what extent do they link pay to performance?

6. Identify a case organisation. To what extent is its reward strategy aligned with its business strategy? What recommendations would you make to improve the fit?

7. What employee value proposition would be most attractive to you? How much would you have to be paid to continue in a job you did not enjoy?

EXPLORE FURTHER

Armstrong, M. (2015) *Armstrong's Handbook of Reward Management Practice: Improving Performance through Reward*, 5th edn. London: Kogan Page. Michael Armstrong is probably the pre-eminent UK writer on reward. This latest edition of his definitive text provides detail on reward strategy and systems beyond the scope of the current text.

Rynes, S.L., Gerhart, B. and Parks, L. (2005) Personnel psychology: Performance evaluation and pay for performance. *Annual Review of Psychology*, 56: 571–600. While this chapter has taken a somewhat sceptical approach to pay for performance, it is important to recognise that there is some strong evidence in its favour. This review article provides a comprehensive overview of the literature in the field.

The WorldatWork website at www.worldatwork.org. For more information on total reward, including case studies, tools and research reports.

GO ONLINE

Visit the companion website for **interactive quizzes**, explanatory **videos** and **podcasts**, **journal articles** to use in your essays, and **weblinks** to useful resources.

https://edge.sagepub.com/crawshaw2e

CHAPTER 11

PERFORMANCE MANAGEMENT AND MOTIVATION

Arup Varma

Pawan Budhwar

Peter Norlander

CHAPTER KNOWLEDGE OBJECTIVES

- Identify key components of effective performance management systems.
- Understand the role of motivation in performance.
- Explore the different types of motivating tools and understand why people are motivated differently.
- Understand why a performance management system developed for domestic purposes does not automatically work for international operations.

KEY SKILLS OBJECTIVES

- Learn how to set goals for subordinates and/or team-mates.
- Learn how to give effective feedback to subordinates.
- Learn how to avoid creating in-groups and out-groups.
- Learn how to manage differently in different cultures.

This chapter also provides indicative content for the following CIPD Intermediate and Advanced level modules:

CIPD INTERMEDIATE LEVEL MODULES

5ENG Employee engagement

5IVP Improving organisational performance

CIPD ADVANCED LEVEL MODULES

7LMP Leading, managing and developing people

7PFM Performance management

7EEG Employee engagement

GO ONLINE

This chapter comes with loads of online tools to help you to go that extra mile in your studies!

- **Multiple choice questions** to help you test your knowledge and revise for exams
- **Journal articles** so you can read further for assignments and essays
- **Videos** and **podcasts** help you to understand how complex concepts work in the real world

Visit **https://edge.sagepub.com/crawshaw2e** to access these resources for this topic.

INTRODUCTION

In order to achieve their strategic goals, organisations need to capitalise on a number of critical resources, including financial, material, technical and human resources. In this connection, scholars (e.g. Stroh and Caligiuri, 1998; Varma et al., 2015) have argued that the human resources of an organisation are often its chief source of sustainable competitive advantage (Aguinis, 2013), especially in the global arena. However, in order to ensure that employees are able to perform their tasks at optimal levels, organisations need to manage their performance in a systematic fashion, using appropriate human resource strategies (Schuler, 1992).

Performance management is the process through which organisations can ensure that individual employees are working towards organisational goals, by monitoring and guiding their performance. This includes several critical components, namely (1) job assignment, (2) goal setting, (3) establishing performance standards, (4) providing feedback, (5) performance appraisal (including documentation) and (6) distributing/allocating outcomes (rewards/punishment). As we can see, while the concepts of performance management and performance appraisal are often used interchangeably, essentially the performance appraisal is just one piece (albeit an important one) of the overall performance management process. We discuss each of these components in detail below, while also examining the importance of two intervening (often overlooked) variables that may have a significant impact on the performance management process, namely (1) employee motivation and (2) supervisor–subordinate relationships.

Sidebar definitions

Performance management
The process by which organisations ensure that employees are working towards achieving a company's strategic objectives. This includes job assignment, goal setting, coaching, feedback, rewards/punishments and performance appraisal.

Job assignment
The process of matching individuals' competencies with job requirements, so as to achieve the best fit.

Performance standards
Specific performance expectations and levels against which an employee's performance will be judged – thus, it should be clear to the employee what level(s) of performance would be deemed unacceptable, acceptable and surpassing expectations.

Feedback The process by which individuals are informed of the degree to which they are meeting desired or expected levels of performance.

Performance appraisal
The process of evaluating an individual's past performance for a specific period, usually one year.

HRM IN PRACTICE

A consultant's view

Performance management in its most effective form occurs when there is a clear connection between organizational strategic goals and every individual in the company. Once the strategic goals are clearly established, we identify the tactical steps, processes, or practices needed to achieve those goals. We continue to break out the tactical actions until we are able to establish how every person in the organization contributes to the company achievement of its goals.

(Continued)

(Continued)

The details of each person's actions which contribute to the organization's success are best defined in a measureable way. As a result, we create measureable criteria job descriptions as a first step. In the early days of working in HR in healthcare, exposure to criteria-based job descriptions and performance evaluation processes showed the effectiveness of the connection. The measureable tasks made the performance management conversation easy and far less subjective.

The resulting measureable job criteria become 1/3 of the performance management conversation. Another 1/3 of the performance management conversation covers an employee's performance in light of the company's values, policies and procedures. The final 1/3 of the performance management conversation is in the form of establishing measurable SMART goals for the next performance management period. As a practical matter, we use the performance deficiencies of the first two elements of the performance management conversation and use them as criteria for goal setting for the next period.

When we create a fully integrated performance management process that connects every employee to the organization's strategic goals, we find a much more highly motivated workforce is the result. We find this process especially appealing to millennials. Given our work with large and small companies, manufacturing and professional services, startups and mature organizations, most organizations discover a much more engaged and motivated workforce with this process.

We recommend quarterly formal performance review conversations. In many organizations, we see combinations of performance management tools utilized with great effectiveness. For example, a daily 'huddle' at the start of a shift or work day. These daily huddles ask each person four simple questions: 'What are you working on today? What are your priorities? What problems do you anticipate? How can I help?' These simple performance management tools help keep supervisors informed of activities while at the same time providing coaching and collaborating opportunities for employees.

This cycle of goal setting, measurement, and continuous improvement measurement, combined with a measurement of the job specific tasks aligned with the business objectives, makes for an effective performance management system that produces a more highly engaged employee population. The key to creating a motivated workforce is to have a fundamentally sound performance management process that ties individual job related activities to organizational goals; and that the connection is real and equally impactful to the employee as to the organization towards the achievement of company goals. When this occurs, organizations – as well as employees – are far more likely to reach their full potential.

Source: Interview with John Petrusa, Organisation Development Consultant, Chicago

PERFORMANCE MANAGEMENT: PURPOSES AND PROCESSES

As Fletcher (2001) has noted, performance management systems (PMSs) are the primary vehicle through which organisations (1) assign work, (2) set goals, (3) determine standards, (4) evaluate performance and (5) distribute rewards or punishments. Further, PMSs can help organisations successfully implement their business strategy (Schuler and Jackson, 1987). In other words, organisations need to design and implement sophisticated PMSs in order to be able to get optimal performance from all employees. To do this, they need to ensure that the key stages/components of PMSs listed above are put in place, implemented and reviewed on a regular basis. Each of these components of a PMS is discussed below.

WORK ASSIGNMENT

Although recruitment and selection have been discussed in Chapter 7, we touch upon it again here, since it has a critical relationship with the performance management process. Organisations need to be diligent and vigilant in hiring employees. This involves making sure that the individual is a good fit with the organisation and the job. However, as we saw in Chapter 7, this is easier said than done, since it involves a whole series of activities, including identifying the appropriate criteria and testing each through a matching predictor. HR managers may pick the best applicant from those that apply for any position – someone who meets most, but not all, of the requirements of the job in question. Right away we can see that such an individual is at a disadvantage and will need training and/or guidance to cover the skills/abilities gap (Chapter 9). Even in cases where the organisation has hired an individual who is a perfect fit for the job, the organisation needs to be cognisant of the fact that both individuals and jobs evolve. In other words, someone who was a perfect fit at the time of hiring may not be such a good fit a few months later since the job's demands may have changed and/or the individual's skills and abilities may fall short of the requisite level. Clearly, the bigger the gap between the individual's skills/abilities and the job requirements, the greater is the need for performance management. Goal setting, feedback/coaching and other developmental activities are all components or outcomes of the performance management process, which seeks to bridge the gap between achieved and desired performance.

Goal setting The process of assigning work tasks to individuals so that they are clear on what is expected of them. To be effective, the goals should be specific, measurable, attainable, realistic and time-bound.

GOAL SETTING

In order for individual employees to know what is expected of them, it is critical that they are set clear and unambiguous goals. It is well documented that individuals who have been provided goals are able to work more efficiently and are also more effective at their assignments than those who are not given goals and

Goal setting

Goal setting is the process of establishing targets for subordinates and/or team members, so that they are aware of what is expected of them. However, in order for goal setting to be efficient and effective, the goals should be specific, measurable, achievable, realistic and time-bound. General or ambiguous goals (e.g. 'do your best', or 'make sure revenues increase') can be confusing and, most often, do not achieve desired results.

TASK: For this task we suggest you work with a couple of classmates (or co-workers). Assign them either a task that you are familiar with or something straightforward like preparing a speech. Talking to them individually, tell one of them simply to 'do a good job'. Next, tell the other individual exactly what you want him or her to do, how, and by when. Have them both complete the task, and then evaluate how well they did. You should find that the individual who received specific detailed instructions does a much better job than the one who was simply told to do their best. Next, talk to them about how they went about completing the tasks, and let them compare how they felt about the instructions they each received.

must figure these out from their own understanding of the job (Locke, 1968; Shantz and Latham, 2011). Having goals that are clearly defined helps employees understand what is expected of them, and assists them in planning and prioritising their work accordingly. However, in order for goal setting to be effective and for the individual to be able to use the goals in accomplishing his or her work, these goals should be (1) specific, (2) measurable, (3) attainable, (4) relevant and realistic and (5) time-bound. Thus, for example, a goal that states 'reduce shipping costs by 3 per cent over the next six months' is likely to be more helpful to an individual than simply 'cost reduction'.

ESTABLISHING PERFORMANCE STANDARDS

Once clear goals have been set, it is essential that clear performance standards are established so that the employee is aware of how his or her performance will be judged and rated. Each employee can then be measured, during the performance review, against these established standards (see also Bobko and Colella, 1994). For example, let us say it is established that a rating of 5 on the dimension 'quantity of sales' (on a five-point scale, with 5 being the highest possible level of performance and 1 being the lowest possible level) can only be obtained by individuals who have sold a minimum of 100 units of whatever the company is selling. By this measure, individuals who have sold 97, 98 or even 99 units will receive a rating of 4 on this dimension. One of the biggest advantages of providing clear standards is that it reduces unnecessary and unpleasant surprises and makes it easier for employees to keep track of how they are performing by regularly assessing their achievements against the established standards. In addition, this practice can motivate employees to be more proactive and seek out feedback (discussed below), so they know more about how they could improve their performance and earn the desired rating level.

PROVIDING FEEDBACK

Feedback is the mechanism through which an individual can be informed of how he or she is doing on the job. As one might expect, this process is rather complicated and is often avoided by both supervisors and subordinates, especially in cases where the supervisor is required to share feedback that is negative, as it is likely to be an unpleasant exchange. However, it is critical that supervisors provide regular feedback to employees (see Murphy and Cleveland, 1995), since timely and directed feedback can help employees correct performance deficiencies and prevent future errors. Further, it is clear that, in spite of some reluctance, it is very important that managers provide feedback on a consistent basis and deliver it with a view to helping the subordinate improve his or her performance, and do not use the feedback session as an opportunity to 'punish' the subordinate and/or make him or her look bad (see also Chapter 10). Feedback delivered in a spirit of fairness is likely to be accepted by the subordinate, whereas in situations where the subordinate feels that the feedback is insincere, or designed as an excuse to punish him or her, the subordinate is likely to reject it, thus defeating its very purpose (Leung et al., 2001).

Clearly, organisations need to create a culture where feedback is easily accepted by all people concerned and is seen as a critical part of the performance management process. In cases where managers deliver insufficient feedback, human resource

departments may need to institute policies that mandate feedback giving for
managers, perhaps by requiring documentation of their feedback meetings
and following up with subordinates to
make sure they have received timely and
useful feedback.

PERFORMANCE APPRAISAL

Performance appraisal refers to the formal evaluation of employees, conducted
to determine the degree to which they
are meeting specified objectives. The primary purpose of performance appraisals
tends to be administrative – determining merit raises, promotions and so on.
There is, however, another purpose for
which some organisations use performance appraisals: to determine the developmental needs of individual employees.
A developmental approach to appraisal
is particularly important as it holds out
the prospect of improving future performance rather than simply measuring
past performance.

In either case, for the performance
appraisal process to proceed smoothly
and to serve the desired purpose, it is
essential that the organisation design
and implement comprehensive, fair and
transparent systems and processes that
are explicitly shared with both supervisors and subordinates. All employees, both appraisers and appraisees, should
be familiar with the appraisal purpose
and process, the appraisal documenta-
tion, the relevant dimensions of evaluation and the standards that will be used to
rate performance. This way, all parties know what to expect and when to expect
it. Communicating the purpose and process of appraisal is an important aspect of
performance management, and comprehensive guidance is needed to spell out the
key features of the process.

The following subsections should be treated separately rather than just as issues to consider in relation to providing appropriate documentation. This is the heart of appraisal,
which is intrinsic to performance management and should be treated as such.

Providing feedback

Feedback is a process designed to provide information to individuals about how they are doing (or have done) on tasks. In
order for feedback to be effective, it should be provided as soon
as possible after the occurrence, and should provide specifics on
what an individual did well and what he or she could improve. It
is important to remember that feedback should always be about
the task (e.g. 'your reports are very succinct, but could use more
data on the gap analysis') and never about the person (e.g. 'you
are a great employee', or 'you will never amount to anything'!).
Timely and specific feedback, provided in a spirit of helping, is
likely to help the individual improve his or her performance,
whereas ambiguous feedback or personal comments are likely
to make the individual defensive.

TASK: For this task, we suggest you work with a couple of classmates (or co-workers). Assign them a task that both are familiar
with, or something straightforward like preparing a speech. After
they have completed the task, talking to them individually, tell
one of them how they might improve what they did on the task,
and provide specifics on how they might do better. Next, tell the
other individual that he or she did a good job (or bad job), but
provide no specifics. Later, talk to them together and ask how
they felt when you gave them the feedback, and how they would
go about changing what they had done. You should find that the
individual who received specific and timely feedback would be
able to give specifics on how he or she would improve on the
task, whereas the other individual would be at a loss for how
to improve or may simply come up with generalities. Next, ask
them specifically about how they felt when you gave them the
feedback – watch the reactions of the person who was simply
told 'good job' or 'bad job'.

Appraiser The individual
charged with evaluating
or assessing another
individual's performance.

Appraisee The individual
whose performance is
being evaluated.

The evaluation process

This should be clearly explained, with the appraiser's and appraisee's roles laid out clearly. Thus, for example, if the employee is expected to fill out a self-evaluation questionnaire or provide documentation to support his or her actions and behaviours, he or she can prepare well in advance of the meeting and keep records of achievements throughout the appraisal period. Similarly, the appraiser should be aware of how she or he is expected to document information related to the appraisee's performance and how to evaluate performance against established standards. Further, mechanisms should be developed to record performance-related information in an easily accessible format (for suggestions on diary keeping, see Varma et al., 1996). In recent times, several providers have started offering 'off-the-shelf' software programmes designed to assist appraisers in recording appraisee performance. However, organisations should check the reputation of the providers and, of course, whether such generic software is suitable for their specific purposes.

Scheduling the evaluation

While most organisations conduct annual evaluations, there are several variations in practice – including quarterly and biannual evaluations. Evaluations could also be conducted at the conclusion of a project. Even the annual evaluation may vary in its scheduling, taking place either on the anniversary of the individual joining the organisation or around the same date for everyone each year. Irrespective of the version adopted, it is critical that all parties are clearly informed of the timing and stick to the required schedule. This may be particularly important if evaluations are linked to performance-based rewards. Employees are generally keen to learn the details of any such changes to their reward package so they may plan for the year ahead. Thus it is important that the specific date and time of when the meeting is to be held should be announced well in advance, thus allowing both parties to be well prepared.

The appraiser

It is essential that whoever has responsibility for carrying out the appraisal is clearly articulated. It is most common for the appraiser to be the appraisee's immediate supervisor, although this is not always the case. The advantages of such a choice are that the appraiser will be most familiar with the appraisee's work and will already have a working relationship with that individual. It also enables feedback and coaching, provided throughout the review period, to be consistent and in line with objectives that have been set. Another approach to appraisal that has often been touted as an alternative to single-source evaluation and feedback is known as 360-degree or multisource feedback (London and Beatty, 1993; London and Smither, 1995). Under this method, information about an appraisee's performance is collected from several sources – the immediate supervisor, the appraisee's subordinate(s), peers and clients and/or customers. It is expected that multisource evaluations will provide a more realistic picture of the appraisee's performance because the appraiser can compare the information received from various sources to identify convergence and divergence.

Multisource feedback Involves collecting information about an individual's performance from several sources, such as the employee's supervisor, peers, subordinates, clients and/or customers.

There are, however, some problems with this method. First, different sources see different aspects of an individual's performance, thus making it difficult to compare their perspectives/evaluations. Further, scholars have also argued that multisource information is best used for developmental purposes, and not for administrative decisions such as merit raises.

MINI CASE STUDY

The end of the performance review at GE?

In 2015, GE abandoned its annual performance review, joining Microsoft, Accenture and Adobe and other leading companies that are looking for alternatives to the traditional performance management system. Famous for use of a forced ranking system (see 'Debating HRM: The bell curve rating method' later in this chapter), the hard-driven style of performance management at GE and elsewhere has been criticised by academics, HR practitioners, managers and employees. The recent turn of events at GE led some to call into question the future of performance management. A recent article in *Fast Company* predicted that 'half of Fortune 1000 companies will drop stack rankings and numeric rankings as a basis for annual performance reviews'. But media reports on the death of performance management may be greatly exaggerated.

Instead, performance management at GE is becoming more continuous, less formal, more development oriented, and less quantitatively driven. With regard to the frequency of appraisal, 'the world isn't really on an annual cycle any more for anything', said GE's Head of Human Resources Susan Peters. The annual appraisal, according to Peters, 'had become more a ritual than moving the company upwards and forwards'. Instead, in part due to generational preferences, the company is adopting an instantaneous feedback model, which Peters says is 'more frequent, faster, mobile-enabled'. The programme called 'PD@GE' or 'performance development at GE' assigns each employee short-term goals. Rather than annual reviews or quantitative rankings, managers are expected to frequently monitor progress towards the completion of priorities following a philosophy of continuous improvement rather than ranking. An app serves as a central note-taking repository for managers and employees, who can also request to receive, or give, feedback at any point. The language has also changed: goals are 'priorities', performance conversations are 'touchpoints' and feedback is give through 'insights'. Coaching has replaced ranking as the operative verb in the process.

And the annual performance review? It's still in place at GE, although now it's a summary conversation held in December, in which managers and employees can look back with the benefit of data gathered throughout the year and set goals for the future without the fear and stress of having a once-a-year appraisal that determines a person's career prospects or future pay. GE still rewards performance through pay,

(Continued)

(Continued)

a process it refers to as 'differentiation'. As Peters put it, 'One thing we do know is that we will maintain our culture of meritocracy and differentiation. ... We're trying to figure this out and keep some of the fundamentals of the culture and also move to a place where it's more contemporary. I don't know what the answer on that's going to be yet.'

CASE STUDY QUESTIONS

1   What do you think of organisations doing away with numeric ratings? Will it help boost morale and productivity, or cause ambiguity and confusion?

2   If you were managing a team, how would you compare team-member performance, when necessary, without using numbers?

Sources: 'Why the annual performance review is going extinct', *Fast Company*, 21 October 2015; and 'Why GE had to kill its annual performance reviews after more than three decades', *Quartz*, 13 August 2015.

Evaluating performance

The task of evaluating performance is itself a difficult one and consideration should be given to training for appraisers and appraisees. Given that performance management systems are designed to evaluate and guide individuals' careers, letting untrained individuals operate the system is essentially a recipe for disaster. After all, no organisation would let an individual operate a fork lift, or a computer for that matter, without proper training. If PMSs are truly to be effective, all parties need to be trained in the specifics of the system. Such training should include, but not be limited to, the following critical components:

- The organisation's philosophy regarding PMSs
- The primary purpose of appraisals (developmental or administrative)
- The organisation's performance appraisal process
- Performance standards established by the organisation
- Appraisal forms
- The feedback process
- The impact of evaluation on the subordinate's compensation and career with the organisation.

It is also important to note that a wide range of biases in decision making (Kahneman, 2011), including all the biases identified in Chapter 7 in relation to selection processes, are just as likely to arise in appraisal interviewing. Further, a belief in the high prevalence of these biases risks creating a social norm that biased judgements are acceptable (Duguid and Thomas-Hunt, 2015). Therefore, appraisers in particular should be trained that biases are uncommon, undesirable, and given instruction to avoid biases such as **central tendency error**, **severity/leniency error(s)** and **recency error**.

What will be evaluated (traits, behaviours, outcomes)?

This is an issue that was also raised in Chapter 10. While organisations may decide to evaluate different aspects of an individual's job performance, there are three broad categories of criteria that have been most commonly used – traits, behaviours and outcomes – though there is no agreement among practitioners or researchers as to which of these three should be used (see DeNisi [1996] for a comprehensive discussion). Not surprisingly, those who favour evaluating traits argue that if an individual has the right traits (e.g. conscientiousness) she or he will perform as expected. Those that are in favour of evaluating behaviours (e.g. quantity of work) argue that possessing the right traits does not guarantee that the individual will perform at the expected level, and that as long as the individual engages in the right behaviours, the desired results will follow. The third option, outcomes, may be the easiest to measure but may not be the most useful. If results are all that will get measured, employees will

TABLE 11.1 Common evaluation errors in performance appraisal

Central tendency error	Often, supervisors take the easy way out by rating their subordinates around the middle of a scale. This helps them avoid explaining extreme ratings to the organisation.
Halo/Horns error	Sometimes, an individual's outstanding or poor performance on one dimension causes the supervisor to rate the subordinate outstanding/poor on all other dimensions.
Severity/Leniency error	Some supervisors believe that they need to project an image of being tough/easy, so they rate subordinates lower/higher than their performance objectively deserves.
Recency error	In many organisations, especially where the appraisal is done once a year, individuals have been known to change their behaviour a month or two before the appraisal is due. So they start working much harder, and make sure they inform the supervisor of their achievements. Since supervisors can't remember what a subordinate has done for the past 12 months, they tend to use the new information in making their evaluations.

be tempted to get the desired results by hook or by crook, without any concern for drawing upon the right traits or demonstrating the right behaviours. The folly of this approach should by now be obvious: when driven simply by the desire to achieve certain results, some individuals may cut corners and engage in unethical or unacceptable behaviours. What combination of these three categories an organisation chooses to include in its appraisal system will ultimately depend on its culture and values, its objectives, and its management philosophy. However, no matter what the company decides to evaluate, it is essential that the information is shared with the employees.

DEBATING HRM

Traits, behaviours or outcomes

Almost since the first research paper on performance appraisal was published, the debate over what should be measured has continued. So many scholars and appraisers argue that individual traits are all that matter – in other words, if an individual has the right traits (e.g. sincerity), his or her work will reflect this. As such, there is no need to worry about measuring actual behaviour, since this 'sincere' employee would finish all tasks assigned to him or her.

The second group argues that individual traits do not guarantee desired levels of performance. So it is possible that someone may be very loyal to the organisation, and thus show up every day and try to work hard. But if this individual does not understand the job or works very slowly, he or she will not be able to achieve the set objectives. As such, this second group of scholars/practitioners argues that we should only be concerned with measuring work behaviours (e.g. quality and/or quantity of work). As long as someone is doing the right things, why worry about traits?

The third group believes that neither traits nor behaviours really guarantee the right outcomes. As such, they argue that the only thing that really matters is the outcome. So, as long as employees deliver on targets, their traits or behaviours do not matter, and thus we should only measure results.

TASK: Working in groups, use appropriate theory to discuss which of these three – traits, behaviours, outcomes – should really be measured in appraising an individual's performance. Why?

Performance-related information

One issue that is often ignored relates to the information to be used by the supervisor in evaluating the subordinate's performance. Given that the performance appraisal process is designed to allow the supervisor to rate an individual's performance achievements and potential, it is critical that the organisation design mechanisms to collect relevant information. After all, what should be avoided at all costs is the supervisor making a global evaluation of the subordinate (e.g. the subordinate is a great performer, or is not up to the mark). By establishing information collection protocols, the organisation can ensure that the PMS is objective and unbiased. Furthermore, such protocol can help a supervisor know where to track relevant information about subordinate performance, and ensure that such information is collected and documented in a systematic fashion, on a regular basis. This will also help avoid situations where the supervisor ends up using irrelevant information in conducting a subordinate's appraisal. In addition, by deciding and sharing what information is to be collected and used for the evaluation, the organisation can also help the subordinate become aware of what she or he will be evaluated on.

HRM IN PRACTICE

Performance appraisal – a practitioner's guide

The following is from Abhijit Bhaduri, Chief Learning Officer, Wipro Ltd.

Why is it so hard?

Ask a group of employees how many of them would rate their performance and skills in the 90th percentile or more. Even though statisticians will tell you that only ten per cent of people should see themselves in the top performer category, whenever I have done this exercise with groups of executives, the overwhelming majority rates itself at the top. Now imagine the plight of the manager who has to appraise the performance of such a group of employees and you know that such a conversation is not going to be easy.

A lot at stake

Performance appraisals are, perhaps, the most controversial of all processes. Not only is it a time when someone sits in judgement about the quality of your work, but eventually, reward and recognition get linked to it, and so does the development effort that companies are willing to invest. No one likes to be left out of the room when money is being counted. Appraisals are not just an exercise in data and evidence, but are largely about the soft skills of the manager. Appraisals are opportunities to have ongoing conversations between the manager and the employee. Unless there is trust in the relationship, the conversation lacks honesty and sensitivity.

Setting goals

The goals that we set are also meant to inspire and motivate action. So the foundation for good performance appraisals lies in setting the right number of goals. I have seen most leaders tend to focus best when they have four to five well-articulated goals.

What I have learnt about goals

Slightly difficult goals tend to motivate people more than easy goals. A stretch goal combined with ongoing coaching conversations with the manager is the best development tool possible. Also, ensure that critical goals are aligned with what we are naturally inspired to do. Ask if the goal will leverage the strength of the individual. Finally, along with the goals, if the manager and the employee agree on a monthly schedule to review progress, it is a great way to ensure that the employee and the organization get the best out of the experience.

Performance appraisals in the digital age

Most performance appraisal systems were developed when the world was relatively stable. So a goal was set and performance was measured against that at the end of

(Continued)

(Continued)

a year. The manager would be expected to spend time twice a year giving feedback to the employee that would serve to do the course corrections as needed.

Not so in the digital age. When we use Uber to hail a cab, we get a chance to evaluate the service as soon as we get off the cab. If the service is rated less than four on a five point scale, we have to explain why we were unhappy with the service. In the same vein, the driver also evaluates us. Did we pass muster as the kind of customers Uber would like to nurture? This two-way evaluation is going to be the norm. The advantage of this model is that feedback is provided as soon as the service has been provided. Digital organizations compete on data generated by each interaction with the customer. The same will also seep into the way employees are appraised.

The business environment is constantly shifting with new competitors emerging with innovative offerings at radically different price points. While GM and Ford may have always viewed companies like Toyota, Volvo, etc. as their competitors, they would have never imagined that they would have to compete with a search engine. Google's driverless cars changed the competitive scenario for automobile companies. Tesla has proved that automobiles are simply platforms to deliver technology. In this scenario, it is necessary to do frequent course corrections to stay competitive. So the Uber model of frequent feedback and course correction will become the norm.

New roles to manage performance

The digital age will demand more nuanced handling of performance. The Deloitte Human Capital Trends of 2015 says that more than twice as many employees are motivated by work passion than career ambition. Yet we know that motivation is a deeply personal process. Two people doing the same job could be motivated by two different needs. We may need Talent Sherpas and Motivational Insights Analysts to support the employee's performance.

The Talent Sherpas will have a way of understanding the skills and learning capabilities of people and can suggest roles that help the candidate to realize their potential. The Motivational Insights Analysts will be able to shape the role, the total rewards system and the feedback process in a manner that makes it meaningful to the employee. It is surprising that we have left the important business of motivating employees to people who usually have no special training in this field. And yet we expect people to stay motivated and engaged.

In conclusion

The performance appraisal is a tool. The skill of the manager determines the quality of the outcome. The ability of a manager to set goals that are meaningful is a skill. If the manager and employee have monthly reviews of progress, any deviations from the expected results are detected early. If the appraisal discussion generates more heat than light, then it may indicate that the appraiser has not tracked feedback throughout the year and shared it with the appraisee. The intent behind the appraisal is to foster more frequent conversations between the manager and the employee. Without frequent discussions on the what, why and how of work, it can never be motivating enough. Appraisals are not just about receiving judgement on the final output – they are about getting feedback and jointly working to improve each step along the way.

Source: www.abhijitbhaduri.com/index.php/2016/01/6-future-hr-roles/

DISTRIBUTING/ALLOCATING OUTCOMES (REWARDS/PUNISHMENT)

As we noted in the introduction, individuals work for organisations in exchange for appropriate compensation and rewards. Thus, an individual who performs better than a colleague should have a reasonable expectation that she or he will get rewarded at a higher level than the said colleague. Indeed, the performance appraisal process plays a critical role in this determination. However, it is important that the organisation has fair and transparent procedures so that employees have a clear understanding of what kinds of reward are likely to be associated with the relevant level of performance. It is also important that the organisation adhere to the stated policies and procedures. This issue was discussed more extensively in Chapter 10.

PERFORMANCE MANAGEMENT AND EMPLOYEE MOTIVATION

According to Pritchard and Ashwood (2008: 6), motivation is the 'process used to allocate energy to maximize the satisfaction of needs'. Indeed, almost all scholars agree that motivation is guided by individual needs. So, when someone is hungry, they need food to satisfy that hunger, and are thus motivated to find food. On the other hand, if someone believes they need a bigger house than their current residence, they will be motivated to find ways to earn enough money to buy a bigger house. Of course, one might argue that often what motivates people are their wants (e.g. luxury items) and not their needs (basic necessities like food and clothing). Nonetheless, people are driven to achieve whatever they believe they need, and not everyone is motivated by the same things.

Thus, supervisors who understand what motivates their subordinates will be better able to manage their performance by addressing those needs. Of course, not all employee needs can be easily fulfilled by organisations, and, as we note above, not all employees have the same needs. Take, for example, two employees – the first needs a half-day off to take care of family business, while the second wants (of course believes she or he needs) promotions every year. In both cases, performance will begin to suffer if the needs are not met. However, while the organisation may be able to fulfil the first employee's need without much trouble, the second employee's need may be impossible to meet.

FIGURE 11.1 Summary of Pritchard and DiazGranados's (2008) performance management and motivation model

Pritchard and DiazGranados (2008) present a useful model that summarises the potential connection between performance management and employee motivation (or need satisfaction) (see Figure 11.1). Essentially, their model mirrors Vroom's (1964) expectancy theory, inasmuch as motivation is viewed as a 'future-oriented concept' where individual behaviour is driven by the expected receipt of desirable rewards (see also Latham, 2007). We next look at each link individually:

PERFORMANCE → RESULTS

It is critical that individuals perceive the match between their abilities and the results expected of them. Perhaps an example would help illustrate this best. Several years ago, the first author of this chapter was asked to teach a graduate-level course in accounting and finance, and he was to start almost immediately since the previous instructor had suddenly left. Since he had just completed his doctoral thesis in human resources and industrial relations, and had almost no background in accounting or finance (having taken just two courses on these subjects in over 20 years of school), he perceived this link to be very weak, and thus had no motivation to take on this assignment.[1] In other words, he believed that no matter how hard he worked, he would not be able to achieve the desired results in the time frame specified. If individuals perceive that they have the abilities, and that their performance will lead to the desired results, they will be motivated.

RESULTS → APPRAISAL

Once individuals have achieved the desired results, it is essential that a formal, structured evaluation is conducted at the appropriate time, and that detailed descriptive feedback is provided to the individuals. In other words, it is critical that once the results have been achieved the supervisor explain to the subordinate in detail, supported by facts and figures, why his or her performance exceeds expectations on some dimensions, meets expectations on others, and is perhaps below expectations on yet others, as the case may be. Such feedback will allow the subordinate to improve his or her abilities and/or acquire or request relevant guidance and/or training, where necessary. The critical issue here is: subordinates must believe that their achievements and related results will be fairly and accurately appraised.

APPRAISAL → OUTCOMES

Once the appraisal is done, another important link (appraisal to outcomes) must be seen by subordinates as real and valid. In other words, if the subordinate has been rated as someone who has exceeded expectations and yet receives an average reward (i.e. merit raise and/or bonus), the subordinate is likely to see this link as broken. Thus it is absolutely critical that an organisation follow fair and transparent procedures when deciding raises/bonuses, and these should mirror the appraisal ratings. Too often, supervisors are tempted to reward subordinates they like by awarding them higher than deserved raises, or awarding lower than deserved raises to subordinates they don't like. Once information on this anomaly gets out, the employees' trust in the performance appraisal system is likely to take a severe hit and they will see this link as broken, which will have a negative impact on motivation.

DEBATING HRM

The bell curve rating method

Over the last two decades, many organisations have begun to use the **forced distribution method**, also known as the 'bell curve'. Under this system, supervisors are required to rate no more than a certain percentage of their subordinates at the high end of the scale (so, usually about 10 per cent will get a 5 on a five-point scale), and at least the same percentage at the low end of the scale (1). The remaining subordinates are then to be awarded ratings in the middle of the scale. As is obvious, it is rare that the true performance of any group of employees would mirror this distribution. This forces supervisors to distort ratings and award 4s to some individuals who may truly deserve a 5, and 1s to some individuals who might have truly earned a 2. As a result, an employee who has truly earned a 5 but was awarded a 4 due to limitations of the bell curve is often told to work even harder so that he or she may be awarded the 5 the following year. What often ends up happening is that, over a period of time, they reduce their efforts and end up working just hard enough not to get fired (a phenomenon known as regression to the mean).

TASK: Working in groups, use appropriate theory to outline an ethical case for and against using the bell curve to force appraisers to rate appraisees.

OUTCOMES → NEEDS SATISFACTION

The final link, outcomes to needs, is perhaps the most important of the four in this motivation process model. No matter what outcomes the organisation offers, if those outcomes do not meet the employees' needs they will not be motivated. Of course, as we have noted earlier, not all individuals are satisfied by the same needs. We realise the dilemma this poses for an organisation – how do you come up with a reward system that can satisfy each individual employee's needs? Further, as many executives have pointed out to us, sometimes employees' needs are beyond the organisation's capacity to meet. While this might indeed be true in some cases, the fact remains that effective performance management requires that organisations try to meet as many of their employees' needs as is practical.

This requires HR departments to survey employees and learn their needs, and then work within organisational boundaries to try and find ways to meet as many of the needs as they reasonably can. Of course, individual supervisors have the primary responsibility of learning about their subordinates' needs, and what motivates them, if they want to be effective performance managers.

Overall, the above model presents one of the clearest representations of motivation at work. Organisations and supervisors that truly care about performance management would do well to understand the individual components and work on ensuring that the links are seen as real and valid. To be sure, we are not suggesting that supervisors simply work at making the links seem real – instead, they should ensure that the links work.

GRADUATE INSIGHTS

Employee retention and growth in China

The following is a conversation with Daisy, an MBA graduate (2006) and now a marketing professional in China:

AV: Daisy, thanks for agreeing to speak with me again for this edition of the book. I can't believe it has been over 10 years since you took my course!

Daisy: I still remember your course fondly. Even though most of us were not interested in pursuing careers in HR, once we started working after graduation, it became clear how HR affects our lives on a day-to-day basis.

AV: Thank you. I am interested in hearing more about your experience, especially how HR has impacted your career.

Daisy: I have been working for MNCs for almost 10 years in China. Every company I've worked for has been growing at tremendous rates – not surprising, given the rate of growth of the Chinese economy. In such a situation, we are all expected to take on tremendous amounts of work, and my colleagues and I feel the pressure. Of course, in return for working under such heavy load and high pressure, people have certain expectations from the organisation, in terms of compensation and other benefits. I mean, if I am taking on the work of two people, shouldn't I be paid twice as much *(chuckles!)*. But, on a serious note, I have seen several positive changes since we last spoke, especially in terms of performance management.

AV: I am curious to hear your experience with PMS!

Daisy: In my current company, the HR department has designed quite a few training and development pro-grammes for all categories of employees. For example, we have a programme called the Future Leader Programme (FLP), wherein fresh college graduates with bachelor's or master's degrees are hired and rotated through three different departments of their choice. They spend one year in each of these depart-ments, and are then assigned to the department/position for which they are deemed most suitable. This programme has been reported to be quite successful, and many of the FLPs have gone on to acquire key positions of leadership. Indeed, the FLP programme is proving to be a great recruitment tool for the company. In addition, the company offers employees like me the opportunity to take two leadership skills courses from [the] American Management Association (AMA) every year, on topics such as communication skills, strategic planning, etc. Overall, it is clear that the emphasis has shifted from hiring to retention and performance management.

THE SUPERVISOR–SUBORDINATE RELATIONSHIP

Along with motivation, another topic that is often overlooked in discussions of performance appraisals is the role played by the type of relationship an individual shares with his or her supervisor. Clearly, in the context of performance management and the primacy of the supervisor's role, this relationship is crucial. Graen and Cashman (1975) first proposed the leader–member exchange (LMX) theory which argues that supervisors do not treat all their subordinates equally – instead, consciously or subconsciously, supervisors create in-groups and out-groups among their direct reports. While there are a number of factors that determine who gets into the in-group and who remains in the supervisor's out-group, overall it can be said that subordinates in a supervisor's in-group are people she or he likes, and those in the out-group are individuals the supervisor does not like (or likes less). Indeed, as Pichler et al. (2008) argue, liking is very closely related to the quality of the supervisor's relationship with his or her subordinates. In this connection, research has consistently shown that subordinates in their supervisor's in-groups receive significantly higher performance ratings than those in the out-groups, controlling for performance (e.g. Varma and Stroh, 2001).

Clearly, this is a critical issue as the in-group/out-group categorisation introduces bias into the appraisal process which, in addition to being unfair, is often illegal. Thus, it is important that supervisors receive training on performance management, specifically as it relates to the potential for forming such groups. Such training should include information on (1) the possibility that they might be creating in-groups and out-groups, (2) suggestions on how to avoid creating such groups and (3) ensuring that evaluations are based on objective data and are not biased by supervisors' relationships with their subordinates.

PERFORMANCE MANAGEMENT SYSTEMS FOR GLOBAL ORGANISATIONS

Over the last 20 years the world economy has seen a major shift as more and more organisations are establishing operations in different countries (see Chapter 5 for a detailed discussion of globalisation). From an HR perspective, the advent of the new MNEs requires a close look at existing PMSs. So, for example, PMSs developed for the Indian

Avoiding the creation of in-groups and out-groups

As we note above, research shows that most individuals tend to create in-groups and out-groups among people they know, including those that we call friends. This practice extends to the workplace, where supervisors often create in-groups and out-groups. This can lead to problems, as those cast in the out-group can feel demotivated and reduce efforts at work, doing just enough to get by. Often, this might even be illegal, especially if those cast into the out-group mostly belong to a particular group (e.g. men/women).

TASK: Think about whom you like spending time with – especially after class or outside the workplace. Do they mostly belong to a particular group? When opportunities arise to offer leadership roles or include others, do you first (or often, or always) think of someone who is similar to you? Talk to people who are currently working, and ask them if they feel that their supervisors have created such groups. Ask them which group they belong to, and how this makes them feel. Then think about how individuals could go about being more inclusive, especially in the workplace.

market cannot automatically be transferred to the company's operations in the UK. In addition to the obvious difference in culture and language, the notions of work and performance are likely to be significantly different.

Ironically, the issue of PMSs in global organisations has received limited attention in the literature (Varma et al., 2008). In order to address this lacuna, we should first note that PMSs typically have two purposes: (1) administrative decisions, such as merit raises; and (2) developmental goals, such as feedback and training (Murphy and Cleveland, 1995). It would seem that most organisations, especially MNEs, would be able to achieve these goals with ease by setting up appropriate systems that specify the link between performance and outcomes, keeping the relevant context in mind. However, often organisations simply transfer systems developed for the home office to other locations without adapting them (Tung and Varma, 2008). It should be noted here that performance cannot be defined in isolation – we must take the relevant culture into account (Aycan, 2005).

Next, it should be obvious that the goals of performance management systems can vary widely between locations of firms, resulting in key differences in how individuals in different cultures view performance. For example, in the USA performance appraisals are primarily designed to evaluate individuals' performance and award appropriate rewards (Cardy and Dobbins, 1986). On the other hand, in collectivist cultures like Japan, performance appraisals are more concerned with evaluating employees' long-term potential (Pucik, 1987), thus encouraging individuals to develop their skills and competencies. Clearly, performance management systems must be based on context, to make allowances for the unique circumstances and cultural norms of the location.

However, too often global organisations treat performance management systems for their international operations as a mere extension of domestic evaluation systems (Shih et al., 2005), thereby using forms and criteria developed for domestic purposes in their international operations. Given that the culture and context of work can vary significantly from country to country, it is clear that PMSs and the related appraisal mechanisms should be tailored to the unique realities of the country. This makes it important that HR practitioners everywhere critically evaluate the PMS before adopting it – systems developed in any country may not be automatically appropriate for implementation in other locations, and should be adapted or modified as necessary.

Managing in different cultures

People of different cultures have different ways of living their lives, and may define performance and work differently (Hofstede, 1980). The context-specific nature of work makes it critical that managers adapt their management styles to the realities of the culture wherein they operate.

TASK: Go to https://geert-hofstede.com/countries.html. Click on country comparisons and pick any two countries and look at their scores on the various dimensions. Then pick the dimension (e.g. power distance) on which the two countries are at opposite ends. Next, using the definitions provided, try to come up with a list of specific changes you would need to make in your management style if you were managing employees in these countries. Do this for all the dimensions. Finally, try to find people who are from the countries you used for your comparative analyses (or people who have worked or managed in those countries), and see if your lists match up with their experiences.

CASE STUDY

Bias in performance appraisals

Gypsy Tigers is a medium-sized manufacturing company, located near Goshoura, India. The company manufactures consumer products for numerous well-known global brands. The company grew out of a small family business, and has been slow to modernise and/or adopt formal HR systems. The owners believe that good human relations are critical, and thus their emphasis has been on treating all their employees like family members, with little emphasis paid to establishing formal systems. However, the global brands that Gypsy Tigers serves have been doing very well, thus putting pressure on the company to modernise its systems.

At the clients' insistence, the owners recently brought in a consultant, Miss Rita Kohli, to help with establishing selection and performance management systems. Miss Kohli is a graduate of the top business school in India, and has worked with several MNCs – her specialty being performance management systems. Among the first tasks she was assigned by the CEO, Mr Ajay Srivastava, was to establish a performance management system, whereby formal appraisals are conducted once a year. However, Mr Srivastava also let Miss Kohli know that the company would like to keep the results of the evaluations confidential. In other words, the plant managers and other supervisors would evaluate each of their direct reports once a year, and the completed appraisal forms would be placed in the employee's personnel file, but not discussed or shared with the individual employee. When Miss Kohli enquired why the appraisals were to be kept confidential, Mr Srivastava told her that they had always treated all their employees as family members, and sharing 'report cards' with them would create tension among the workforce and lead to unhealthy competition between employees, instead of the cooperation that the employees have been demonstrating all these years.

Miss Kohli was somewhat taken aback, though not surprised, at the owners' thought process. She was well aware that many companies in India (and elsewhere in Asia and Latin America) follow the paternalistic model, whereby employees are treated like family members and are protected by the company. At the same time, the professors in her business school had continuously reinforced the importance of transparency and providing feedback to individuals. Indeed, in her work with other companies, she had found that global companies often had open systems, whereby each manager/supervisor discussed their subordinate's evaluation with them and explained each rating.

Indeed, as part of her climate survey, Miss Kohli spoke to several employees and asked how they felt about not being evaluated formally, and almost all of them said that they would like to know how they were doing, so they could improve where necessary. Many employees also noted that almost all their colleagues got the same (or very similar) raises, even though they knew that many of their colleagues did not work as hard.

(Continued)

(Continued)

When Miss Kohli approached Mr Srivastava with the feedback she had gathered from the employees, he seemed unhappy and asked her to simply concentrate on the task she was given, instead of starting trouble.

CASE STUDY QUESTIONS

1   What do you think of Mr Srivastava's argument that 'sharing "report cards" with them would create tension among the workforce and lead to unhealthy competition between employees'?

2   If you were Miss Kohli, how would you convince Mr Srivastava that individual performance improves when people know how they are doing?

3   In your opinion, what are the benefits of keeping performance appraisals confidential? It may be difficult at first, but try to force yourself to think of some! Next, discuss the advantages of sharing the information with the individual subordinate.

4   Many corporations around the world practise the 'family' type culture of Gypsy Tigers, whereby employees are not pressured to perform at very high levels – instead, moderate performance is accepted as the norm. From a performance management perspective, what are the advantages/disadvantages of such practices?

(Note: This case is based on the first author's personal experience, as part of his consulting practice. However, the names of the company and the main characters have been changed.)

CHAPTER SUMMARY

The key points that we have identified in this chapter are the following:

- Performance management systems are critical to successful performance management.
- Performance appraisals are an integral part of PMSs, but, necessary as they are, they are not sufficient. Organisations need to address all the other components of performance management, including job assignment, goal setting, establishing performance standards and providing feedback.
- Intervening factors such as employee motivation and supervisor–subordinate relationships have significant impact on the performance management process, and HR executives as well as line managers need to be cognisant of these and address them appropriately.
- Supervisors need to be trained in all aspects of the PMS process, including how to conduct goal setting, give feedback and evaluate employee performance.

- Employee motivation plays a big role in determining what kind of effort the employee will exert, and the resultant performance levels.

- The type of relationship a supervisor develops with his or her subordinate has been shown to impact the subordinate's rating, controlling for performance. Thus, supervisors need to be trained to treat all subordinates fairly, irrespective of their personal characteristics and whether or not the supervisor likes a particular subordinate.

- PMSs developed for a particular country cannot automatically be transferred to the global units of any organisation. These need to be adapted, keeping in mind the culture of the other nations.

REVIEW QUESTIONS AND EXERCISES

1. Discuss the key components of PMSs.

2. What are key differences between PMS and performance appraisal?

3. What impact do goal setting and feedback have on an individual's ability to do his or her job?

4. Why does motivation play such a critical role in the performance management process? How can supervisors improve employee motivation?

5. Explain how supervisor–subordinate relationships can impact subordinate performance appraisals. How can supervisors prevent themselves from creating in-groups and out-groups among their subordinates?

6. Identify a case organisation. Research its PMS, and compare its components and the organisation's practices with what we have discussed above. How might the organisation modify its PMS? What likely impact would that have on organisational performance?

7. Reflect upon your own experience with performance management systems – this could be paid or unpaid, or an internship/placement experience. Were you given goals? If yes, what impact did this have on your ability to do your job? If not, what impact did this have? Did the environment help or hinder your motivation? Specifically, what was it about the environment or your supervisor that caused your motivation to increase or decrease? What could the organisation or your supervisor have done to help address this (or, what did they do)?

EXPLORE FURTHER

Varma, A., Budhwar, P.S. and DeNisi, A. (eds) (2008) *Performance Management Systems: A Global Perspective*. Global HRM Series. London: Routledge. This edited volume takes a look at PMS in 11 countries around the world. The initial chapters discuss issues such as motivation, compensation and rater–ratee relationships. The book also presents a comprehensive model of PMSs.

DeNisi, A.S. and Pritchard, R.D. (2006) Performance appraisal, performance management and improving individual performance: A motivational framework. *Management and Organization Review*, 2(2): 253–277. An excellent review and theory paper that proposes an interesting motivational theoretical perspective on performance management and performance appraisals.

The Society for Human Resource Management (SHRM) at: www.shrm.org. The SHRM is the largest global professional association for human resources professionals, with 275,000 members in 140 countries, and subsidiary offices in China, India and the United Arab Emirates. The website provides links to a whole array of resources, including articles on the latest topics and trends in HR.

NOTE

1. I did agree to take on this assignment, as a challenge, but with the caveat that I would need a minimum of six months to prepare the graduate-level course. I ended up teaching it for the next 10 years, and really enjoyed the classes. Apparently, so did the students – at least that's what was reflected in their evaluations!

GO ONLINE

Visit the companion website for **interactive quizzes**, explanatory **videos** and **podcasts**, **journal articles** to use in your essays, and **weblinks** to useful resources.

https://edge.sagepub.com/crawshaw2e

CHAPTER 12

WORKPLACE RELATIONS AND REGULATIONS
Kathy Daniels

CHAPTER KNOWLEDGE OBJECTIVES

- To explore the growth of employment legislation over recent years.
- To evaluate the impact that employment legislation has on both sides of the employment relationship.
- To understand the changing balance of power in the employment relationship and how this impacts on both the employer and the employee attitudes.
- To be aware of specific legislation relating to employee relations and its impact on bargaining and negotiation.
- To understand how legislation is used to encourage participation and involvement.
- To critically evaluate the role of the Employment Tribunal in applying regulation.

KEY SKILLS OBJECTIVES

- To understand the skills required for effective negotiation.
- To explain employment legislation succinctly and effectively.
- To understand the skills required to encourage participation.
- To understand the process for defending a claim in the Employment Tribunal.

This chapter also provides indicative content for the following Intermediate and Advanced level CIPD modules:

CIPD INTERMEDIATE LEVEL MODULES

5EML Employment law

5DER Contemporary developments in employment relations

CIPD ADVANCED LEVEL MODULES

7ELW Employment law

7MER Managing employment relations

GO ONLINE

This chapter comes with loads of online tools to help you to go that extra mile in your studies!

- **Multiple choice questions** to help you test your knowledge and revise for exams
- **Journal articles** so you can read further for assignments and essays
- **Videos** and **podcasts** to help you to understand how complex concepts work in the real world

Visit **https://edge.sagepub.com/crawshaw2e** to access these resources for this topic.

INTRODUCTION

The employment relationship is the fundamental basis of all interactions in the workplace. Research has shown that motivation, productivity, job satisfaction and many other factors are positively linked to the health of the employment relationship.

As with any relationship, each side has some power. At a basic level, the employer has the power to terminate the employment of the employee and the employee has the power to resign and leave the employer. However, the power within the relationship is used in many more ways than determining whether or not the relationship will end. For example, the determination of a level of pay often involves each side exercising some level of power to reach an amount of pay that satisfies them (see also Chapter 10).

In this chapter we will be exploring this concept of the balance of power by looking at some of the factors that impact on it. The chapter will look in particular at the impact of growing legislation on the employment relationship. We will look at some specific areas of employment law (it is beyond the scope of this chapter to look at legislation in detail) and consider how they have impacted on the employment relationship and how the change in legislation might have changed the balance of power.

We will start by considering the nature of the employment relationship, and how and why employment legislation has grown. We will then consider how some of these changes in employment legislation have also changed the balance of power in the relationship. We will then move on to look at the role of trade unions and how they contribute to the employment relationship, and we will look at how the legislation relating to bargaining and negotiation has regulated the power in the relationship. We will then move on to look at employee involvement and participation, and again consider the contribution of the law to this aspect of the employment relationship.

Finally, we will look at the role of the Employment Tribunal – the place where employment relationships can end up when they are damaged. We will also look at concerns about the current tribunal system and consider how proposals to change the system will impact on the balance of power in the employment relationship.

WHAT IS THE EMPLOYMENT RELATIONSHIP?

Before we examine the balance of power within the employment relationship, we need to understand the nature of the relationship itself. At its simplest, the employment relationship is simply the interaction between the employer and the employee. Two theories have tried to explain that interaction more clearly. Fox (1966) put forward the theories of 'unitarism' and 'pluralism'. These perspectives were identified in Chapter 1 and are elaborated upon here.

The key theme of unitarism is that there is harmony between the employer and the employee. There is effective teamwork, with management as the single source of authority. It is expected that there will be harmony, and conflict does not occur because everyone is working towards the same goals. If conflict ever does occur, then it will be because there is some misunderstanding, poor communication or a troublemaker in the team. There is no need for a trade union because there is harmony and no conflicts.

The weakness of this theory is that it presumes that the employer and the employee have common goals. It is certainly true that the employer and the employee might both have the goal of the organisation being a success. However, they might have different ideas about how this can be achieved.

It is also interesting to note that the theory suggests that a lack of harmony can be the result of a troublemaker. Palmer (1983) refers to the need to remove deviancy. In 1984–5 the then UK Conservative government announced a programme of pit closures that would result in thousands of miners losing their jobs. The response was industrial action that lasted for nearly nine months. The National Union of Mineworkers (NUM) was unsuccessful in persuading the government to change the pit closure plan. The NUM leader was Arthur Scargill, a strong and charismatic leader. Some would argue that, if there had not been a leader of the NUM that was so strong, then this conflict would never have lasted so long. Could it be argued that removing Scargill would have resulted in more harmony? Pluralism tried to address some of the weaknesses that we have already identified in the definition of unitarism. Pluralism identifies that there are a number of groups within an organisation, which have different interests. There is a central body that tries to get these groups together to achieve a common goal.

HRM IN PRACTICE

The PCS, Unison and austerity Britain

To understand unitarism, let us consider the government and the members of the Unison and PCS (Public and Commercial Services) trade unions. Following the introduction of austerity measures and cost cutting by the government, wages for all public sector workers earning more than £21,000 were frozen in 2011–12. That pay freeze was then continued for 2012–13. A 1 per cent increase was then imposed for 2013–14 and for each subsequent year up to 2016–17. Both the government and the members of the trade unions want to provide excellent public services – they have a common goal. However, they do not agree on the way that this can be achieved. The government says that it has to be achieved through improved efficiency and cost cutting, whereas the trade unions say that this is not fair on their members. This example helps us to understand unitarism more – and also helps us to see the weakness of presuming that there will be harmony if there is a common goal.

This theory does seem to be more effective in describing the nature of relationships in organisations today. Many organisations are large and fragmented, and it is not realistic to presume that all groups have common interests. This can be seen by considering some of the large banks, such as the Royal Bank of Scotland or Lloyds TSB. They have a number of different divisions (e.g. commercial, retail, investment), which have different customer bases and different products. It would be fair to presume, therefore, that they have some common interests (e.g. the overall success of the bank) but also some very different interests due to the different nature of the divisions.

Another approach to looking at the employment relationship is to consider the construct of psychological contract.

THE PSYCHOLOGICAL CONTRACT

Schein (1988) defined the psychological contract as the unwritten expectations of the employer and the employee. He further suggested that employees have three areas of individual expectation:

1. The need to be treated fairly;

2. In return for loyalty to their employer, employees seek some level of security; and

3. A need for fulfilment, satisfaction and progression.

The theory of the psychological contract (identified in both Chapters 4 and 10) is useful in identifying that the employment relationship is an individual relationship between the employer and the employee, and that there are aspects of that relationship that are specific to the individual. However, it is wrong to presume that a breach of the psychological contract will always lead to the employment relationship breaking down.

It could certainly be argued that the members of the PCS and Unison trade unions that we referred to above have a fractured employment relationship due to their fury over the pay freezes that have been imposed (and also changes to pensions). If we look at the definition of the psychological contract we could argue that the contract has been breached because they do not consider that they have been treated fairly. However, just because there has been a breach of expectations it does not mean that the employment relationship has to break down.

Back in 2008, when the Global Financial Crisis first developed, the construction equipment manufacturer JCB was struggling. It put in place pay cuts, as well as some redundancies. This was achieved with no conflict. Although no employees wanted a pay cut and there was a lack of job security, the situation was managed without significant damage to the relationship. How did the organisation manage this? Partly because the pay cuts were applied at all levels of the organisation, including senior management. Partly because there was trust between the employer and the employees. The employer promised that pay would be restored, and as many people re-employed as possible, when the situation eased. This did happen. So, not only did the employees trust the employer but this trust was shown to be well founded.

THE CHANGING EMPLOYMENT RELATIONSHIP

Another issue that we must remember when considering the employment relationship is that it is not static. For example, a change in chief executive can have a significant impact on the nature of the employment relationship, or a change in circumstances can change the ethos of the organisation. In addition, a change in legislation can have a significant impact on the basis on which the employment relationship is managed. To understand this, we will look at some of the significant changes that have occurred in recent times.

THE GROWTH OF LEGISLATION

In today's workplace in the UK, we are used to having a well-regulated employment relationship. Much of the legislation that regulates the employment relationship has been introduced in the last few decades. The first legislation regulating dismissal was only introduced in 1971 by the Industrial Relations Act 1971. The first discrimination legislation addressed only the differences in the terms and conditions of employment between men and women and was addressed by the Equal Pay Act 1970 (which has since been repealed and replaced by the Equality Act 2010). This means, therefore, that as recently as the 1970s there was only very basic and limited legislation in place.

Indeed, discrimination legislation is an interesting area to look at, especially the growth of the legislation. As noted above, the Equal Pay Act 1970 was the first discrimination legislation. This was followed quite quickly by the Sex Discrimination Act 1975 and the Race Relations Act 1976 (note that all the legislation relating to discrimination which is referenced here has been repealed and replaced by the Equality Act 2010).

However, there were no additions to the list of discrimination legislation until 1995. Hence, up to 1995 it was not unlawful to treat someone less favourably because of their age, disability, sexual orientation, etc. It is important to reflect on this for a moment. Today we live in a well-regulated society, and it is sometimes easy to forget how recent much of this regulation is.

In 1995 the Disability Discrimination Act was introduced, followed by the Sex Discrimination (Gender Reassignment) Regulations 1999, which made it unlawful to discriminate against individuals who had undergone or were undergoing gender reassignment.

To continue our reflections, it is important to note that by the turn of the century it was still not unlawful to discriminate against an individual on the grounds of such factors as religion, age or sexual orientation.

This changed in 2003 when the Employment Equality (Sexual Orientation) Regulations 2003 and the Employment Equality (Religion and Belief) Regulations 2003 were introduced. The final area of discrimination to be covered was age, by the Employment Equality (Age) Regulations 2006.

The replacement of all this discrimination legislation by the Equality Act 2010 did not add to, or subtract from, the characteristics that are protected. The purpose of the Equality Act 2010 was to 'tidy up' the many anomalies and confusions that resulted from having nine major pieces of discrimination legislation and over 100 smaller pieces of legislation.

Just by taking discrimination as a topic, we can see how employment law has developed. However, we also need to remember that law alone does not dictate the balance of power in the employment relationship. We have extensive discrimination legislation, but we still have discrimination occurring in the workplace (Chapter 8). Legislation puts in place a penalty for not complying with the standards set by the law makers. However, it does not mean that the behaviour necessarily stops.

Even though law has limited power it is still important. It will not stop all behaviour that is unwanted, but it will certainly deter the behaviour. We need to understand how and why law develops. Legislation develops for different reasons. Three primary ones are political and social reasons, and being a member of the European Union.

POLITICAL

Different governments have different political agendas. This is illustrated effectively by returning to the Equality Act 2010. This legislation was introduced right at the end of the time of the Labour government (1997–2010) term of office. Addressing equality and discrimination had been a key aim for this government. However, the Coalition government did not support all the measures in the Act (such as the introduction of compulsory pay audits) and the Act was not introduced in its entirety.

An interesting example of different political agendas comes from France. In the 1990s the Socialist government of the time introduced a 35-hour limit on the working week. If an organisation wants employees to work longer than 35 hours it has to pay between 10 and 50 per cent extra. However, more recently there has been concern expressed about this and the restrictions that it places on businesses. So, at the start of 2016 the French government started to change this situation and is giving organisations the right to renegotiate longer working hours and reduced overtime payments with their staff. The 35-hour week will remain, but employees will receive less pay for working longer than this. These proposals have caused considerable disquiet and there has been industrial action across the country.

Here we have different political agendas, and also a need seen by the government of the day to respond differently to the challenges that both the employer and the employee are facing.

SOCIAL

A significant change in society over recent years has been the growing number of families where both parents are working. There are concerns about the impact that this might be having on young children. To respond to such social needs, the Labour government of 1997–2010 introduced the Work and Families Act 2006, giving new rights to parents, and making it easier (from a legal perspective) for them to balance work and family responsibilities. The current Conservative government (in office since 2015) also has concerns about families, and is currently consulting about the introduction of Shared Grandparental Leave (due to be introduced in 2018) to further help families to manage child care.

EUROPEAN UNION

On 23 June 2016 the UK voted to leave the European Union. At the time of writing formal notification (triggering Article 50 of the Lisbon Treaty) has not been given to the EU of the intention to leave. Once notification is given to leave it is expected that negotiations will take at least two years to complete. At present it is not possible to say what the impact will be of this on employment law. However, we do know that the UK will remain part of the EU for some time to come, and hence it is important that we understand the way that the EU affects our law making. It is also important to understand this so that we understand the implications of leaving the EU when it occurs.

There are many examples of legislation that the UK has had to introduce because of its membership of the European Union. For example, there are the Working Time Regulations 1998, that regulate the hours that can be worked in a day, rest breaks, holidays and night work. Another example is the Agency Workers Regulations 2010, which gives agency workers parity of terms with permanent employees (although the UK has negotiated an agreement that this applies in the UK only after an agency worker has been placed in the organisation for 12 weeks). This law will not automatically be removed when the UK leaves the EU. All law that has been introduced as a result of EU membership has become part of UK law, and for it to be removed it would have to be formally repealed.

THE IMPACT OF GROWING LEGISLATION

We have seen that employment law has developed rapidly. We are now going to turn back to the employment relationship and consider what impact the growth in employment law has had on that relationship.

Let us start this review by thinking about the agenda of the Coalition government which held office from 2010 to 2015. The Coalition government took office during one of the worst recessions that the world has ever known. A key part of its manifesto was to support growth in businesses. Indeed, there was an emphasis on the need to provide support to small and medium-sized businesses in particular, because the government saw these businesses as providing particular growth opportunities.

A number of measures were taken to try to increase support to businesses, such as an ongoing battle to get banks to lend more. However, our interest here is in the changes to employment law. The government was concerned that employment law is stifling the growth of businesses. Hence, it tried to reduce some of the red tape surrounding employment.

Explaining employment legislation succinctly and effectively

As we have already noted, it is not possible to cover the huge range of employment legislation in one chapter. However, it is possible for you to understand the key principles, and have an overview of the main legislation.

TASK: Go to www.acas.org.uk – the website of the UK's Advisory, Conciliation and Arbitration Service. This organisation provides advice to employers and employees on all employment matters. Choose one topic (e.g. equality, dismissals, redundancy) and read the Acas advice about this. This will help you to develop your knowledge of employment law.

Maybe the most notable area of change was to the Employment Tribunal system, which we will look at in detail at the end of this chapter.

However, there were also a number of other changes that the government made, such as:

- Any employee who starts work on or after 6 April 2012 is required to have two years' service before being eligible to bring a claim of unfair dismissal. This has been increased from one year. This will reduce the number of employees who have the right to bring a claim and hence reduce the burden on businesses of addressing such claims.

- The maximum compensatory award that can be awarded following a successful claim of unfair dismissal is reviewed each year (it was last reviewed in April 2016 when it increased to £78,962). However, the Coalition government also altered the cap so that it is this amount or the claimant's annual salary, whichever is lower. This change was made to encourage claimants to think more reasonably when making claims and considering offers of settlement made by their employer.

- Prior to 6 April 2013 there was a requirement to consult for 90 days if 100 or more jobs were being made redundant. This was reduced to 45 days to enable employers to act more quickly when there is a need to cut costs.

- Third-party harassment was removed from the Equality Act 2010 on 1 October 2013. Prior to this, an employer could be liable for harassment to an employee from a customer or other external body if it had happened at least twice, the employer knew about it and had done nothing to stop it. The government thought that this put an impossible burden on employers.

The changes listed here are just a few of the many that were made. However, by just looking at these examples we can see the purpose of the changes, and the impact that the changes had on the balance of power in the employment relationship.

LEGISLATION AND THE BALANCE OF POWER

All of the changes to employment legislation that we have just listed give more power to the employer. Read through them again – do you see how they are taking rights away from employees, reducing compensation or making it easier for the employer to manage difficult situations? If we go back to the 1960s the balance of power was firmly balanced in favour of the employer. The employer could pay the employees what it wanted (there was no national minimum wage), could dismiss the employee without good reason and could discriminate against employees of certain religions, races and gender, etc. In thinking about the balance of power it would be wrong to presume that every addition to employment legislation is good for the employee and bad for the employer. To illustrate this let us consider the introduction of the National Minimum Wage (NMW) as a result of the National Minimum Wage Act 1998.

Introducing the NMW was a key part of the Labour Party's manifesto leading up to the 1997 general election. The Conservative Party, which had been in office from 1979 to 1997, had distanced itself somewhat from the European Union and, importantly, had refused to sign the Social Chapter of the Maastricht Treaty 1992. This treaty set out basic rights relating to a number of areas such as housing, education and employment. Within this was the right of all EU citizens to a minimum wage. The Labour Party promised that it would sign the Social Chapter, which the government did soon after election. As a result, the NMW had to be introduced.

Maastricht Treaty 1992
A European treaty setting out the right to enjoy basic rights in areas such as employment, education and housing.

DEBATING HRM

The balance of power in the employment relationship

Another example of the changing balance of power was the introduction of the National Living Wage in April 2016. Introduced at the rate of £7.20 per hour this applied to those aged 25 years and above. A number of organisations have said that this has resulted in additional costs, and they have cut other benefits (often benefits that applied to all employees, regardless of age) to compensate for this.

TASK: Working in small groups, research some of the actions that organisations have taken in response to the introduction of the National Living Wage. Then, consider whether these actions mean that the balance of power has been altered in favour of the employees or the employer.

THE ROLE OF THE TRADE UNIONS IN REGULATING THE EMPLOYMENT RELATIONSHIP

In considering the employment relationship and the balance of power so far, we have been focusing on the individual relationship between the employee and the employer. However, it is important to note that there are trade unions and around 7 million people (www.certificationofficer.org) in the UK belong to a trade union. Although this is considerably less than the 12.6 million members recorded in 1980, it is still a sizeable number.

To understand the role of the trade union we need to start by considering its purpose. Salamon (2000) suggests that there are six distinct roles of the trade union:

- Power – to act as protection and support for the individual and employee, and to create a force of persuasion.
- Economic regulation – to ensure that members receive the best pay and benefits possible.
- Job regulation – to ensure that decisions made about daily working are fair and that employees are allowed to participate in decision making.
- Social change – to help to develop a society that reflects the social cohesion, aspirations and political ideology of the members.
- Member services – to provide relevant and appropriate services for members.

- Self-fulfilment – to allow members to do more than just work within the confines of their job role and to be involved in the decision-making process.

Gennard and Judge (2010) are more succinct and see there being one key primary purpose of trade unions, that of protecting and enhancing the living standards of its members.

The common theme that we see in the various definitions of the trade union that have been put forward is that the trade union is there to regulate the employment relationship and to protect the interests of its members. It is important to remember that trade unions were first legalised back in 1871, when there was no specific employment legislation to protect their members. Hence, the roots of the trade union movement are in a time when they were the only source of protection for employees.

Just as we have looked at the sources of power for the employer and the employee, it is also interesting to consider the source of power for the trade union. Metcalf and Barber (2005) suggest that the primary sources of power were the closed shop and the power to strike. A 'closed shop', which is no longer lawful, was when employees who entered a certain job or profession were required to join the associated trade union. This was made unlawful by the Trade Union and Labour Relations (Consolidation) Act 1992 (TULRCA). Hence, if we agree with Metcalf and Barber, the only source of power remaining for the trade union is the power to take strike action. This is certainly an interesting point to consider, and it was a concern for the Conservative government of 1979–97, and is still a concern for today's Conservative government.

Closed shop When employees had to join a trade union if they joined a certain profession. This is no longer lawful.

When the Conservatives took office it was just following the 'Winter of Discontent' of 1978–79. This was a period of time when there was widespread industrial action from local authority workers, following the imposition of a pay freeze. The 1970s had also seen a significant amount of industrial action in UK manufacturing, particularly in the car industry. The Conservative government saw the need to address the problem of conflict and industrial action, concerned that it was having a negative impact on the UK economy. The Conservative government acted by putting in place strict rules about ballots that must be carried out before industrial action can take place. In brief, a trade union must give the employer seven days' notice that there is to be a ballot, it must then hold the ballot, and then it must give seven days' notice of any industrial action that is to be taken.

Pay freeze A decision not to increase pay at the annual review time.

The current Conservative government is concerned that the existing ballot rules do not do enough to protect the employer. In particular, they are concerned about the rule that only a majority of those who vote have to be in favour for industrial action to go ahead. For example, there could be 1000 employees balloted, but only 10 vote. If 6 of those are in favour the industrial action would be lawful. This would be so, even though 994 employees had not voted in favour. The government sees this as unfair for employers.

As a result of this the UK government has introduced the Trade Union Act 2016. This has now received Royal Assent, which means that it is law, but it has not been implemented. No implementation date has been set, but it is expected to be in place by the end of 2016. As a result of this Act it will be a requirement to have a minimum turnout of 50 per cent of those eligible to vote at any ballot for industrial action. Then, a majority of those who vote must be in favour for industrial action to go ahead. In addition, the government is planning that in essential public services (defined as health, education, fire, transport, border security and nuclear decommissioning) at least 40 per cent of those entitled to vote must be in favour of industrial action for it to go ahead. There are also a number of changes to other rules, including those relating to picketing. As a whole, this change to the law will make it more difficult for employees to take industrial action. Hence, this is clearly altering the balance of power in favour of the employer.

BARGAINING AND NEGOTIATION

So far, we have looked in some detail at how the employment relationship is regulated. However, in many ways the legislation just gives a framework, and within that framework the employer and the employee have to discuss issues and reach their own agreements. For example, the National Minimum Wage Act 1998 sets out a minimum wage, but it does not tell an employer what all employees should be paid. To determine this, the employer and the employee have to talk to each other and reach an agreement. To understand this process we need to consider the processes of collective bargaining and negotiation.

Collective bargaining
A process of discussion and negotiation which takes place between an employer and a recognised trade union.

Recognition process
A formal process of agreeing a relationship between a trade union and an employer.

If an organisation recognises a trade union (i.e. has an agreement with the trade union that it will talk to it about issues affecting its members), then it has to engage in collective bargaining. Part of the recognition process is to agree the approach that will be taken to collective bargaining. Collective bargaining typically covers pay, other benefits and maybe procedures such as discipline and grievance.

The first theoretical reference to collective bargaining comes from Webb and Webb (1902). At this time the role of the trade union was developing, and they observed a process in which the trade union was both seeking to improve benefits for its members and lobbying for improvements in the overall legislation that protected the members.

In their analysis, Webb and Webb saw a clear parallel between the approaches of individual bargaining and collective bargaining, that there is a proposal, a discussion and then a decision to accept or reject the proposal.

However, Blyton and Turnbull (2004) take a more complex view of collective bargaining. They suggest that it is actually a form of management control. If the employees refuse to engage in collective bargaining, then the employer will simply impose the terms of employment. Hence, there is no real freedom to decide whether or not to engage with the process.

This is an interesting point, because it emphasises the difference between bargaining and negotiation in the employment relationship and in other relationships. As Daniels (2006) notes, in a commercial relationship there is the opportunity to conclude that no agreement can be reached and to walk away. For example, if you are buying a car and you are not happy with the price that is being suggested you can walk away from the negotiations and look for another car to buy. However, in employment there are some significant differences. If the employee walks away from the employer she or he no longer has employment, hence the consequences are severe.

It could be argued, therefore, that Blyton and Turnbull have an important point. If the trade union is not happy with the negotiations it cannot simply go and conduct negotiations with another employer. It has a relationship with that employer which has to be maintained. It can try and exercise persuasion through the threat or carrying out of industrial action, but there is no guarantee that the employer will give in (indeed, as we have seen through looking at the example of the miners' strike, it is quite possible that the employer does not give in).

Although there are some complexities associated with collective bargaining, both parties will typically enter the bargaining with the desire to reach agreement. It is to the benefit of both parties not to have prolonged and aggressive discussions. To achieve this, there is a need to have the skills of negotiation.

As Gennard and Judge (2010) note, the purpose of negotiation is constructive compromise and peaceful persuasion. To understand this it might be easiest to think of a negotiation that you might well have engaged in at some time as a teenager. You wanted to stay out late, and you needed to agree with your parents on a time to return. You might have asked to stay out until midnight, hoping that you would be allowed to stay out until 11 p.m. Your parents said that you had to be home by 10 p.m. (although they were really quite happy for you to stay out until 11 p.m.). There was some discussion, and it was finally agreed that you would be home by 11 p.m. Both you and your parents were happy with the outcome.

It is this approach that is often used in employment negotiations. The employee asks for more than she or he expects to receive, the employer offers less than it is prepared to give and there is some discussion leading to a constructive compromise. As part of the negotiation process each side tries to persuade the other why it should change its stance.

It is when this peaceful process breaks down that the exercise of power becomes relevant. For example, the threat of industrial action is one way in which the employee side can take a more aggressive stance.

To be a successful negotiator there is a need to develop appropriate skills. These skills are developed through experiencing negotiations. However, there are also some practical steps that can be taken to ensure effective negotiations. Gennard and Judge (2010) summarise these as being:

- Ensure that there is effective preparation and analysis of the facts.
- Prepare a presentation setting out the stance that is being taken.
- In discussing the issues search for common ground, and ensure that there is agreement when areas of common ground have been reached.

- Identify the point at which it is appropriate to determine that the negotiations are concluded.
- Ensure that any agreement is recorded in writing.

MINI CASE STUDY

Pay negotiations with the Fire Brigades Union

An interesting example of how negotiations can lead to compromise comes from the pay negotiations with the UK Fire Brigades Union in 2002–3. The FBU put in a pay claim of 40 per cent. Clearly the cost of such an increase would be huge, and the claim was rejected. Negotiations followed, which broke down and led to the FBU taking industrial action. The matter was finally resolved with a 14 per cent pay increase in stages over three years. However, in return for this the FBU had to agree to the modernisation of working practices. The final solution was a compromise of the employer paying more than it might have hoped, but getting improved working practices in return. Although agreement was reached, the issues were not resolved for some years. There was further conflict over the terms of the agreement, with both sides arguing at some point that the other had not met the agreed terms at the agreed dates.

CASE STUDY QUESTIONS

1   Was a pay claim of 40 per cent ever realistic? Why do you think that the FBU made such a large claim?

2   What were the advantages and disadvantages of linking the pay increases to the modernisation of working practices?

PARTICIPATION AND INVOLVEMENT

When we looked at the role of trade unions as defined by Salamon (2000), we noted that one role was to ensure that their members were involved in decision making. In this section we are going to look in more detail at how employees can get involved in decision making, and the impact that this has on the employment relationship.

Employee involvement
The joint activity of the employer and individual employees in developing business initiatives.

Employee involvement grew in the UK in the 1980s. Much of the impetus for the involvement of employees came from the work of people such as W. Edwards Deming (1900–1993). Deming, among others, identified that one reason for the decline of British management was the poor quality of products compared with those being produced in the Far East. Much of Deming's work focused on variation in processes, but he also produced a 14-point plan to achieve higher levels of quality. These included such points as 'breaking down barriers' and 'driving out fear'. Indeed, what Deming was promoting was a culture where the involvement of employees was possible.

It is important to note the emphasis on the need for there to be a culture where employee involvement is possible. Daft (2009) identified four different types of culture within organisations. One of these is the 'clan culture', where involvement and participation is the key to success. However, Daft notes that this culture does not suit all employees. He suggests that it is most effective in cultures where change is encouraged and there are high levels of trust between the employer and the employee. This suggests that employee involvement will not be successful in all organisations. Indeed, Marchington and Cox (2007) make some interesting points about employee involvement schemes:

Effective negotiation

It takes time to develop effective negotiation skills. Try now by planning out a negotiation.

TASK: Go to www.bbc.co.uk/news and read about the dispute between the Junior Doctors and the UK government in 2016. As you will read, the UK government wanted to introduce a new contract, there was industrial action following a breakdown in negotiations, and then it was thought that there was agreement reached. However, the Junior Doctors voted against the introduction of the new contract and then the new contract was imposed. At the time of writing we are waiting to see if further industrial action will take place. Write a short negotiation brief for both the employer and the employee, explaining what they need to consider to try to resolve the dispute.

- They are primarily instigated by management.
- It is assumed that employees want to have more involvement, irrespective of the form that it might take.
- It is presumed that it is possible to achieve unity between management and employees.
- It is expected that a greater level of commitment and productivity will result from employee involvement.

The authors comments are made in relation to specific employee involvement schemes, for example the use of suggestion schemes or quality circles (where groups of employees select an issue in the organisation to resolve and seek a resolution without management interference). However, it could be argued that organisations that need to have formal employee involvement schemes do not have true employee involvement, because they have to 'force' it through the operation of schemes. If organisations have involvement as part of their culture then it happens as part of daily activity, rather than through some form of structured activity. To explore the question of whether employee involvement should be through structured activities, let us look at the HRM in Practice example overleaf.

However, also read the insight overleaf from an undergraduate student returning from a year's placement in industry.

The example from BMW and the experiences of the undergraduate suggest that employee involvement can be both a success and a failure. Indeed, it is interesting to note that the undergraduate suggested that the approach to employee involvement in the organisation where she had worked had actually damaged the enthusiasm of employees.

HRM IN PRACTICE

The BMW suggestion scheme

In 2002 BMW in Oxford put in place a suggestion scheme. During that year they received 10,339 suggestions from employees, which equated to more than two per employee. As a result of these suggestions savings of more than £6 million were made. All those who made a suggestion received a cash reward. In 2003 the scheme ran again, but with some changes. This time all employees were entitled to a bonus of £260 if, in addition to meeting quality and output targets, they came up with an average of three ideas bringing savings of £800. This structured approach to employee involvement resulted in positive results for the organisation, and increased the commitment of employees.

GRADUATE INSIGHTS

Employee involvement

The organisation where I worked had an employee involvement scheme, which required all employees to get together into groups, choose some aspect of the business that needed improving and to improve it. When I first arrived at the organisation I thought that this sounded like a brilliant idea. However, it did not work.

The first problem was that we were given no extra time to attend the meetings. So, that often meant that on the day that we had a meeting we all had to work late to complete our day's work. There was no extra pay or recognition for this, and this meant that employees started to resent attending the meetings. It also meant that a lot of people were often finding excuses not to attend meetings, and nothing ever got agreed – it was always deferred.

The other big problem was that management retained the right to veto any ideas. In the time that I was with the organisation my group came up with three ideas, all of which we developed in some detail. Each one was presented to management before implementation, and for each one we were told that it could not go ahead. When I left my placement to return to university 'employee involvement' had become something that was mocked in the organisation. If anything, introducing employee involvement actually reduced the enthusiasm of employees to get involved.

As we have already noted, it could be argued that organisations that have to 'force' employee involvement through formal schemes might not have the real involvement and commitment of employees. This view appears to be supported by a joint CIPD/DTI (Department of Trade and Industry) research document (2004). This document looked at 'high-performance work practices', focusing on organisations that were particularly successful. It found that successful organisations did not focus on employee involvement individually, but that employee involvement was part of an approach to managing employees, which had three broad areas:

- High employee involvement
- Sophisticated human resource practices (e.g. recruitment, performance management)
- Comprehensive reward and commitment practices.

This suggests, therefore, that for employee involvement to be effective there is a need for it to be part of the ethos of the organisation, part of the way that employees are treated.

Encouraging employee participation

As we have seen, different organisations have different experiences of involving employees. Learn more about what is effective and ineffective in encouraging involvement and participation.

TASK: Go to: www.cipd.co.uk/binaries/dtihpwprac.pdf and read the CIPD/DTI report that has just been referenced. Use this report to understand more about the effective involvement of employees.

Despite the questions that might be raised about the effectiveness of involving employees, this is still promoted by many bodies and by legislation. Of course, we have trade unions and their role in representing the voice of employees in the workplace. However, they do not tend to be involved at a group level in organisations that are operating internationally and clearly are not involved in organisations that do not recognise a trade union. Two different pieces of legislation have addressed these areas.

The Transnational Information and Consultation of Employees Regulations 1999 set out the rules relating to a European Works Council (EWC). An EWC can be set up if an organisation has at least 1000 employees working in the European Union, and at least 150 members in each of at least two member states (i.e. countries within the EU).

European Works Council A consultation body that has to be set up following a valid request from employees when there are at least 1000 employees in the EU and at least 150 employees in at least two member states.

If the organisation meets the criteria set out above, then it has to set up an EWC if a valid request is received. A valid request is one that must include at least 100 employees from at least two member states.

An EWC must have between three and 30 members, and its remit is for employees to receive information about, and to consult on, anything that interests the organisation as a whole. So, this might be mergers, cutbacks, redundancies, etc. There is some general concern that the EWC has little impact, due to the differences in legislation and approaches in different countries within the EU. Some amendments were made to the legislation in 2011, which it is hoped will address some of these concerns.

Clearly, an EWC is only relevant if the organisation is operating on an international basis. That still leaves many organisations in the UK that do not recognise a trade union, and that do not come under the remit of setting up an EWC. This is addressed through the Information and Consultation of Employees Regulations 2004, although they only apply to organisations with 50 or more employees.

If a valid request is received, an organisation is required to set up an information and consultation body. A valid request is one that comes from at least 10 per cent of the employees (or at least 15 employees if the workforce comprises fewer than 150 staff, or at least 2000 employees if it comprises more than 25,000 staff). If the organisation considers that it already has a pre-existing arrangement in place that meets the requirements of providing information and consulting with employees, then it can arrange a ballot to endorse those arrangements.

The effect of both pieces of legislation is to give support to the involvement of employees and to provide a mechanism for it to happen. However, going back to our question of whether there has to be a certain culture and ethos in an organisation for involvement to be successful, it has to be questioned whether it will be successful if involvement is introduced as a result of legislation.

Before we leave the topic of employee involvement, it is interesting to return to the question of the balance of power. Does allowing the involvement of employees take power away from the employer? If involvement is successful, and employees and the employer are working together effectively, it could be argued that there *is* a balance of power – that no side of the relationship is more powerful than the other. However, if the approach to employee involvement is as described by the undergraduate quoted above, then employees might have been given a little more power through being allowed to present ideas but the degree of power given is very minimal if the ideas can ultimately be vetoed.

THE EMPLOYMENT TRIBUNAL

Employment Tribunal
A court that hears disputes relating to employment issues.

Employment Tribunals were created as a result of the Industrial Training Act 1964. The original remit was to address the assessment of training levies. However, following a review into employment relations known as the Donovan Report in the mid-1960s (see 'Explore Further' section at the end of this chapter), the remit was extended in 1968 to include issues relating to employment. The remit of the Employment Tribunal has now grown, and most disputes relating to employment are now addressed within the Employment Tribunal system.

When Donovan first proposed that the industrial tribunal (as it was then known) system should be created, he had four criteria that he saw as essential for the underpinning of a successful system. These were:

- **Easily accessible**. Donovan envisaged a system that the worker could easily access, both through the process of making a claim and through attending a hearing that was held locally.
- **Informal.** Donovan wanted a system whereby the worker could seek an outside opinion about a dispute. He did not envisage a system with lawyers and formal courtrooms, rather an experienced third party who could give advice about how a dispute could be resolved.
- **Speedy.** Donovan, in carrying out research for the report, had noticed that disputes tended to become more serious if they were not dealt with quickly. Hence, he saw the speedy resolution of problems as essential.
- **Inexpensive.** Donovan wanted a system that anyone could access without great expense.

The process of bringing a claim to the Employment Tribunal, and defending it, has not altered significantly since the creation of the system. However, every time that new employment legislation is introduced there are new claims that can be brought to the tribunal. In the late 1960s there were around 9500 claims to the Employment Tribunal each year. The figure peaked at well over 100,000 by the early 2010s, but has now reduced by about 87 per cent. This is following the introduction of a fee to bring a claim to the Employment Tribunal in July 2013 – we will explore that in more detail shortly.

As already noted, the Employment Tribunal system was considerably altered by the Coalition government. The reason for this was to allow employers to manage more effectively, without the worry of the cost and time that tribunals take to manage. The cost comes from management time and from seeking legal advice (which is not essential, but as the law becomes more complex so there is more need for legal support). Adam Marshall, Director of Policy for the British Chamber of Commerce, commented in December 2011 in a press release that the average cost for an employer of defending a tribunal claim was £8500.

Another concern that employers had is that an employee would put in a weak claim, expecting that the employer would be willing to pay him or her some money in the form of settlement rather than experience the cost of defending the claim.

These concerns about the Employment Tribunal led to a full review of the system. A number of minor changes were made, but the most significant was the introduction of a fee to bring a claim.

The introduction of fees was probably the most controversial of all the changes to the tribunal system, and was introduced on 29 July 2013. For claims that are relatively quick to hear, the level of fee is £160 when making the claim and £230 when the claim is heard; for more complex claims such as unfair dismissal and discrimination, the fee is £250 when making the claim and £950 when the claim is heard.

An Employment Tribunal has the discretion to order the losing party to pay the fee, but this does not happen automatically. Those who struggle to meet the cost and meet certain criteria have the fee reduced, or do not have to pay any fee.

Clearly, the introduction of fees has a real impact on the balance of power within the employment relationship. Previously, many would have argued that the system operated in favour of the employee. There was no cost to bring a claim, and an employee would often manage to get some money from an employer in the form of a settlement payment even if the case did not go to a hearing. But a fee deters employees from making a claim, particularly if the claim is of low value. The fees have been challenged by the trade union Unison, and the government has said that it is currently reviewing the fees – however, for now, they remain.

The government does not want the changes to increase the opportunity for bad employers to treat employees badly. Alongside the compensation that can be awarded to an employee a penalty has been introduced that can be imposed on employers of 50 per cent of any financial award that is imposed in a tribunal, with a minimum of

£100 and a maximum of £5000, where there are 'aggravated features'. There is a 50 per cent discount if the employer pays within 21 days.

In addition to putting a fee in place, there is now an Early Conciliation process which must be engaged with before the claimant can bring a claim to the Employment Tribunal. To trigger this process the claimant must go online, or phone, and give their name and contact details and the name and contact details of the employer. An Early Conciliation Officer from Acas will then contact the claimant to discuss the conciliation process and to get more details about the claim.

At this stage the claimant can say that she or he does not want to progress with the conciliation process. In this situation the claimant is given an Early Conciliation number and can proceed with making a claim to the Employment Tribunal. If the claimant does want to engage in conciliation, Acas contacts the employer and tries to facilitate a settlement between the individual and the employer. This process lasts for one month, but can be extended by a further two weeks if both the individual and the employer agree.

If the conciliation is successful the claim is settled and it does not proceed to an Employment Tribunal. If the conciliation is not successful the claimant is given an Early Conciliation number and can proceed to make a claim to the Employment Tribunal. This process is free. Given that the process is free, it can be argued that the employees who would previously have a try at bringing a weak claim simply have a new route by which they can do this. However, an employer can refuse to engage in conciliation and wait to see if an employee does go ahead with a claim in the Employment Tribunal.

Here we see an interesting balance of power between the employer and the employee. It can certainly be argued that introducing the fees has given more power to the employer, because the employee will be less ready to take a claim to the Employment Tribunal. However, the Early Conciliation scheme means that the employee could still have a go at seeking some recompense for whatever has happened, without any cost, and then decide not to take the case any further if a settlement is not achieved.

Defending a claim in the Employment Tribunal

- To ensure that you have an understanding of the Early Conciliation process, research it further, considering: the way in which the process regulates the relationship between the employer and the employee; the power that the employee has in using the system; and the power that the employer has in using the system.

- TASK: Go to www.acas.org.uk/index.aspx?articleid=4028, which is a useful start.

The Early Conciliation scheme certainly gives the opportunity for settlement without recourse to legislation, but does it actually encourage some sort of 'game playing' rather than genuinely seeking the opportunity to resolve the situation? For example, will an employer refuse to engage with early conciliation and wait to see if the employee is prepared to meet the cost of the Employment Tribunal? Is this a form of strategic game playing, rather than carefully thinking about whether the employee has a case and evaluating whether a settlement would be fair?

DEBATING HRM

The role of Employment Tribunals

As we have seen above, there have been many more changes to the Employment Tribunal system. Do you think that there is a place today for such a system?

TASK: Identify any additional changes that you think should be made to the system. Then discuss these with colleagues or friends. Try to reach an agreement about the changes that are needed most urgently.

CASE STUDY

The Junior Doctors

We have already made brief reference to the tensions between the Junior Doctors and the government, which has been evident throughout 2015 and 2016; let us now look at this in more detail.

The dispute occurred due to the government's plans to introduce a National Health Service which is open 24 hours a day, 7 days a week. Of course, to some extent the NHS is already open all hours, but many routine services are not available at weekends and in the evening. The NHS is struggling to cope with demand, and the government sees the extension of services to be the answer to this problem.

The concern comes about pay. Prior to the dispute Junior Doctors received additional pay for work between 7 p.m. and 7 a.m. and at weekends. The government wanted to change this so that additional pay does not start until 9 p.m. on weekdays, and it also wanted to change the rates of pay at the weekend. This would mean that the additional rates of pay were lower, but in return the government proposed to increase the base pay of Junior Doctors. The British Medical Association (the trade union representing the doctors) put in place counter-proposals.

There were extensive negotiations, which collapsed and industrial action took place. When further negotiations broke down in February 2016, the government announced that it would impose the changes. There was then further industrial action, talks resumed and it looked as if a solution had been reached. However, when this was put to the members they rejected the offer (note that the representatives can reach an agreement during negotiations, but the final offer still has to be put to members to accept or reject. It is usual for the members to go with the recommendations of the representatives, but on this occasion that did not happen). So, in July 2016 it was announced that the new contract would be imposed. At the time of writing we are still waiting to see if this will result in further industrial action occurring.

(Continued)

(Continued)

CASE STUDY QUESTIONS

1   Where does the balance of power lie in this situation? If the employer (the government) can impose the new terms then do the doctors have any power at all?

2   Is it reasonable to allow Junior Doctors to take industrial action? Should the law prohibit industrial action among key service providers?

3   The Trade Union Act 2016 will change the rules relating to a ballot for industrial action. If the individuals work in essential public services, as with Junior Doctors, at least 40 per cent of those who are eligible to vote must be in favour of the industrial action for it to go ahead. This will stop situations where industrial action is legally allowed, even though a small percentage of those involved actually vote in favour of it taking place. Does this seem fair? Should those working in essential public services be treated differently to employees working in other types of organisations? Should they, in effect, have different rights?

CHAPTER SUMMARY

The key points that we have identified in this chapter are:

- There are various factors impacting on the employment relationship that result in it changing.

- Employment legislation has grown significantly in the UK from a point in the 1970s when legislation first started to be introduced.

- The introduction of legislation impacts on the balance of power in the employment relationship, and the UK government is currently reviewing some legislation to review this balance.

- Trade unions have a significant role to play in the regulation of the employment relationship.

- Bargaining and negotiation are used to try to reach agreement between the employer and the employee.

- Involving employees can be an effective way of gaining commitment, but there has to be an appropriate culture and ethos within the organisation.

- The Employment Tribunal system was set up with the aim of providing support to the employee, but is currently under review.

KEY STATUTES

Trade Union Act 2016

Agency Workers Regulations 2010

Equality Act 2010

Industrial Relations Act 1971

Information and Consultation of Employees Regulations 2004

National Minimum Wage Act 1998

Trade Union and Labour Relations (Consolidation) Act 1992

Transnational Information and Consultation of Employees Regulations 1999

Working Time Regulations 1998

REVIEW QUESTIONS AND EXERCISES

1   What factors are most likely to result in the employment relationship changing?

2   Choose any piece of employment legislation. How did the introduction of this legislation impact on the balance of power in the employment relationship?

3   What is the purpose of trade unions in today's organisations?

4   Evaluate the impact of the Employment Tribunal system on the balance of power in the employment relationship.

5   Choose a trade union. Find out more about its current objectives and how it is trying to achieve them.

6   Research the current proposals for reforming the Employment Tribunal system. Find out the reasoning underpinning each proposal.

7   Find out where your nearest Employment Tribunal is (all addresses are available at www.justice.gov.uk). Attend a tribunal (just turn up on the day, be there by 9.45 a.m.) and see it in action. Think about the case you observed. How did having access to the Employment Tribunal assist both the employer and the employee in resolving the issue?

EXPLORE FURTHER

www.channel4.com/programmes/when-britain-went-to-war/episode-guide/series-1/episode-1. In this chapter we have looked briefly at the miners' strike of 1984–5. Although that is now a long time ago, there are many principles of employment relations to be addressed through thinking about that strike. There is an excellent documentary that sets out the key events, and also puts them into the social, economic and political context.

The Donovan Report at: www.erudit.org/revue/ri/1969/v24/n2/028022ar.pdf. The Donovan Report resulted in the setting up of the Employment Tribunal system.

The Gibbons Report at: webarchive.nationalarchives.gov.uk/+/http://www.berr.gov.uk/employment/Resolving_disputes/gibbons-review/index.html The Gibbons Report was written in 2007, reviewing the state of dispute resolution

GO ONLINE

Visit the companion website for **interactive quizzes**, explanatory **videos** and **podcasts**, **journal articles** to use in your essays, and **weblinks** to useful resources.

https://edge.sagepub.com/crawshaw2e

PART THREE

HRM IN CONTEXT

CHAPTER 13

HRM IN SMALL AND MEDIUM SIZED ENTERPRISES (SMES)

Nicholas Theodorakopoulos
Safa Arslan

CHAPTER KNOWLEDGE OBJECTIVES

- To appreciate the role of small and medium sized enterprises (SMEs) as employers in the UK and other countries.
- To understand the nature and form of HR practices in SMEs.
- To assess the usefulness of different accounts of people management in SMEs.

KEY SKILLS OBJECTIVES

- To be able to evaluate labour management practices in SMEs.
- To be able to develop HRM policies and apply practices appropriate for SMEs.
- To be able to assess the relevance of European and national government policy relating to the employment relationship in SMEs.

This chapter also provides indicative content for the following CIPD Intermediate and Advanced level modules:

CIPD INTERMEDIATE LEVEL MODULES

5CHR Business issues and the context of human resources

5HRF Managing and coordinating the human resources function

CIPD ADVANCED LEVEL MODULES

7HRC Human resource management in context

7SBL Developing skills for business leadership

GO ONLINE

This chapter comes with loads of online tools to help you to go that extra mile in your studies!

- **Multiple choice questions** to help you test your knowledge and revise for exams
- **Journal articles** so you can read further for assignments and essays
- **Videos** and **podcasts** to help you to understand how complex concepts work in the real world

Visit **https://edge.sagepub.com/crawshaw2e** to access these resources for this topic.

ONLINE STUDY TOOLS

Test yourself by reading the document 'Achieving excellence: HR and people management in Singapore SMEs' hosted on the CIPD website, and consider the feasibility and appropriateness of a stages framework such as the one suggested in the document.

https://edge.sagepub.com/crawshaw2e > **Student Resources** > **Chapter 12** > **Web Links**

INTRODUCTION

Given their paramount socio-economic significance, a great deal is written on small and medium sized enterprises (SMEs), with several academic and practitioner journals focused on them. Employing fewer than 250 employees, SMEs are considered the driving engine of economic growth, employment generation and innovation in most economies. Moreover, the current trend towards knowledge-intensive industries means that competitiveness increasingly depends on the management of the relational bases of employees. Work culture, engagement and commitment of employees become ever-important to the success of all organisations, regardless of size. This, within the context of the complexity of an international business environment, which is not only a concern for multinational enterprises (MNEs) but also for SMEs (Brewster et al., 2011), brings the need for developing human capital and effective human resource management in SMEs to centre stage. Human capital is the knowledge, skills and abilities of employees while HRM includes all activities related to the management of employment relationships in the firm (Hayton, 2005). Examples of these policies and practices are recruitment and selection, training and development and reward systems, along with business strategies. Yet a defining characteristic of the sector is its heterogeneity. SMEs, in particular, tend to lack formal HR systems and where such systems are present they vary in their extent. Notably, the likelihood of the presence of HR systems increases with size, and this seems to be a cross-national fact (Edwards and Ram, 2009).

However, there are a variety of approaches to people management and employment relations within the SME sector and it has to be acknowledged that HR practices tend to vary according to sectoral conditions and prevailing supply chain relationships, which can affect the nature of such practices. From the growing base of research on HRM in SMEs, it would appear that firm size alone does not determine a specific type of people management. As Marlow (2006: 385) points out, 'Whilst there are some qualified generalisations that can be applied, it is recognised that there are a variety of policies and practices that firm owners utilise to manage their employees; moreover, it is essential to place these practices into the wider context of the market.' This is something to be borne in mind when considering HRM practices in SMEs.

For this chapter, we consider HRM in its broad sense, that is, labour management in SMEs. The chapter is organised as follows. The next section provides a background of the sector, highlighting its socio-economic significance. After this, we discuss the nature of HRM in SMEs. We then deal with the way HR functions are performed in SMEs. The following section highlights the main challenges related to managing

Small and medium sized enterprises (SMEs) Under the EC definition, SMEs are firms with fewer than 250 employees, a turnover of less than or equal to €50 million and a balance sheet total of less than or equal to €43 million.

people in SMEs, referring specifically to regulatory demands and the increasing diversity of the workforce. This is followed by an end of chapter case study and a summary of the chapter. The final sections posit review questions and signposts to material for further exploration.

SIGNIFICANCE OF THE SME SECTOR

> By any measure, the small business is clearly a vital component of a competitive and dynamic market-based economy. (Worthington et al., 2001: 356)

There is a multitude of reasons for the above assertion. Since the end of the 1970s, especially after Birch's (1979) seminal work, SMEs have increasingly attracted the attention of scholars and policy makers at local, national and supra-national levels. SMEs, and in particular the small business sector, are considered as significant contributors to employment generation, innovation, competitiveness, productivity, economic growth and social progress (European Commission, 2014; NESTA, 2009; Storey and Greene, 2010). The fact that small-firm policy has shifted from the periphery of the socio-economic policy-making framework to centre stage in the last decade in the UK and the EU attests to the importance attached to this sector.

The heterogeneity of the small business sector renders defining the small enterprise an extremely demanding exercise in measurement and judgement. A natural corollary of this is the absence of a single and uniform definition of a small firm. Objective measures used as a basis for defining the small business, such as turnover, capitalisation, profitability and employment, differ considerably across different industry sectors and countries. For instance, in the United States, the number of employees and annual firm revenue are used as basic classification criteria for the firms in the manufacturing, agricultural and service sectors by Small Business Administration and the US Department of Commerce. The classification standards for SMEs in the following industries are: manufacturing and non-exporting services firms fewer than 500 employees, revenue is not applicable; exporting services firms fewer than 500 employees and revenue less than US$25 million (USITC, 2010). In China, SMEs are classified according to their number of employees; operating revenue and total assets and thresholds differ by sector. For instance, the classification standards for SMEs in industrial and construction sectors are fewer than 1000 employees, revenue not exceeding Rmb400 million, whereas retail SMEs have fewer than 300 employees or revenue less than Rmb200 million. Notably, an SME in the USA or in China may be quite large relative to SMEs in other countries, such as EU countries, where the most common upper limit for an SME is 249 employees. As Deakins and Freel (2003: 36) point out, 'a clothing sector firm employing less than 50 employees will be relatively much smaller than, say, an information technology firm employing less than 50 and there will be little comparison between their respective turnovers'.

European Commission
The executive body of the European Union, which initiates action in the EU and mediates between member governments.

Under the current European Commission (EC) definition of SMEs, the sector is disaggregated into three components, taking into account employment size, annual turnover or balance sheet and independence. This is summarised in Table 13.1.

A firm must meet both the employee and the independence criteria and either the turnover or the balance sheet criterion to qualify as an SME. Applying the same rationale for statistical purposes, the Department for Business, Innovation and Skills (BIS) adopts the employment size criterion of the EC definition. Notably, the problem is that the EC definition is all-inclusive, treating small firms as a homogeneous cohort. In practice, schemes and research projects, which are nominally targeted at small firms, adopt a variety of working definitions, depending on their particular objectives (see Curran and Blackburn, 2001). However, it is noteworthy that often when we refer to small firms in Europe, as in this chapter, we mean firms employing fewer than 50 workers, including micro-firms.

Despite the fact that the small-firm sector had been largely dismissed as anachronistic or irrelevant to economic development by economists and management authorities in the 1950s and 1960s, it has grown conspicuously over the last 30 years. In the UK, at the start of 2012, SMEs accounted for 99.9 per cent of all private sector businesses, representing no change since 2011 and almost unchanged since 2000 (BIS, 2015). According to EC growth, SMEs constitute the backbone of the EU economy – accounting for 99 per cent of non-financial enterprises in 2013, which is over 21 million businesses. In employment terms, SMEs provide 88.8 million jobs throughout the EU, which means two jobs are created by SMEs out of every three jobs. Similarly, in the USA, less than 2 per cent of the total stock of enterprises employ more than 100 employees and so the socio-economic significance of firms with fewer than 250 workers is paramount. This is in stark contrast to the scepticism expressed by the Bolton Committee (1971), which found it extremely difficult to identify any factors working strongly in favour of the small firm. Figure 13.1 depicts the share of enterprises, employment and turnover by the size of business in the UK private sector.

There are several well-documented, often interdependent and complementary reasons for the revival of the small business sector. These include the structural changes and the growth of the services sector during the last 30 years – where the 'optimal' size is lower, and we find liberalisation, privatisation and enterprise-focused government policy at national, regional and local levels, plus outsourcing trends and the demand for flexible specialisation.

Moreover, it is noteworthy that small-firm growth, in employment terms or otherwise, is a complex and multifaceted concept (Davidsson et al., 2002). Yet, notwithstanding the stunning revival of the smaller business over the last three decades, it is well documented on both sides of the Atlantic that it is only a very small proportion of small firms that make the most significant contribution to employment generation

Department for Business, Innovation and Skills (BIS)   The department for economic growth in the UK. The department invests in skills and education to promote trade, boost innovation and help people to start and grow a business. BIS also protects consumers and reduces the impact of regulation.

TABLE 13.1 EC definition of SMEs (European Commission, 2014)

Criteria	Micro-enterprise	Small	Medium
• Number of employees	• 0–9	• 10–49	• 50–249
• Annual turnover	• ≤ €2 m	• ≤ €10 m	• ≤ €50 m
• Balance sheet	• ≤ €2 m	• ≤ €10 m	• ≤ €43 m
• Independence	• No more than 25 per cent of the capital or voting rights held by one or more enterprises which are not themselves SMEs		

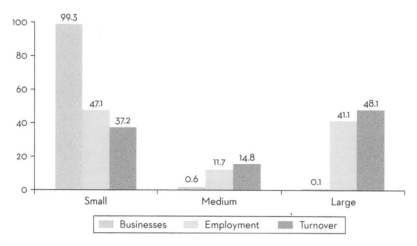

FIGURE 13.1 Percentage of enterprises, employment and turnover by size-band in the UK (start of 2012)

Source: Department of Business, Innovation and Skills (2012).

and economic growth (Acs and Armington, 2006; Anyadike-Danes et al., 2009; Storey and Greene, 2010). This disproportionate share of gross and net new jobs has led to a tendency in academic and policy-making circles to focus on high growth or 'high growth potential' firms. The latter are those enterprises believed to create most of the jobs and contribute significantly towards economic development.

It has to be noted, though, that very few owner-managers have the inclination, resources or expertise to achieve growth (employment or otherwise). Those with a growth orientation tendency have been termed 'entrepreneurs', to be distinguished from their 'lifestyle' counterparts who are more concerned with achieving a comfortable income and/or addressing non-business issues and would rate growth as one of the least important objectives (Stanworth and Curran, 1986). Indeed, growth orientation in its own right is of major significance, as it appears to improve the probability of survival and growth (Storey and Greene, 2010). Further, distinguishing SMEs between 'fliers'/'high growth', 'trundlers' and 'failures' appears to be analytically helpful in identifying those enterprises that outperform their counterparts and account for the bulk of net job creation. This is a very small proportion of small firms; recent evidence in the UK indicates a crucial 6 per cent (Anyadike-Danes et al., 2009).

Critical thinking

Consider the importance of SMEs for employment generation at different levels – that is local, regional and national levels.

TASK: Access the EC, BIS or any other credible website of your choice and identify content relating to employment by sector and firm-size in different countries/regions. Are there any significant differences? What could be the reasons for these?

THE NATURE OF HRM IN SMES

The above section highlights the fact that SMEs make an 'increasingly important contribution to national economic performance' (Bacon and Hoque, 2005: 1976). Arguably, the ability of an SME to survive and grow depends on the quality of its human resources and its approach to managing people. Due to the impact of SMEs on the growth of most economies, and the putative link between managing employment relationships and SME performance, there has been a substantial surge of interest in this area, especially over the last two decades. Notwithstanding the surge of interest in HR management practices in SMEs, as Huselid (2003: 297) points out, 'We actually know very little about the science and practice of HR in small firms.' Specifically, knowledge of how HR strategy as discussed in Chapter 2 is developed and implemented in SMEs, and whether HR practices designed for larger organisations actually work in these smaller environments, is scant and fragmented (Karami et al., 2008; Mayson and Barrett, 2006). It is noteworthy that even large-company studies, however useful in identifying the potential value of HRM they may be, provide little evidence regarding the processes through which this value is created. Therefore, further research is needed in this area (Guest, 2011).

HRM in SMEs is characterised by informality. It has been widely acknowledged that reluctance to delegate authority within such firms appears to be a contributing factor to an absence of professionally managed HRM policy and practice (Atkinson and Curtis, 2004; Marlow, 2002; Ram et al., 2001). In addition, this lack of formalisation of HRM practices is often attributed to the spatial and social proximity between owners, managers and labour and lack of resources (Edwards and Ram, 2009; McEvoy, 1984; Marlow et al., 2005). Formalised HRM practices require considerable development costs and, due to the tight supply of resources, SMEs often fear that this is a cost disadvantage (Klaas et al., 2000). This highlights the argument for taking into account the embeddedness of SMEs in enabling and constraining socio-economic contexts (Edwards et al., 2003; Harney and Dundon, 2006). Smaller organisations lack the resources they need to develop and implement their strategy in the classicist sense and are likely to take a more emergent approach. Marlow's (2000) study of emergent HRM strategy in 64 small firms is a case in point, indicating 'a clear recognition of the need for strategic awareness to support durability and growth' (p. 146), but with little evidence that this was actually implemented.

Nevertheless, based on the orthodox views on strategic HRM (Boxall, 1996; Delaney and Huselid, 1996), discussed in Chapter 2, it has been suggested that SMEs seeking growth should reconsider their HRM practices in light of their business strategy to ensure that there is a good fit between unique bundles of interlinked HRM practices and their business strategy. Thus, it has been postulated that strategic HRM can provide SMEs with the internal capacity to adapt and adjust to their competitive environments by aligning HRM policies and practices (Kidwell and Fish, 2007). The firm's ability to develop HRM practices aligned with its business strategy is seen as instrumental to building competitive advantage. Notably, research on the nature of HRM within SMEs paints a variegated picture, with certain studies finding a greater level of sophistication in HRM practices than expected (De Kok and Uhlaner, 2001; Duberley and Walley, 1995).

Storey (1994) described HRM practices as one of a series of factors common to start-up companies that successfully achieve growth, as they are able to link different parts of the small firm and encourage team working practices and flexible management systems. On this point, Bacon and Hoque (2005: 1976) suggest that although SMEs may 'lack the capability to develop HRM practices', if they employ highly skilled individuals and are networked with other organisations then they are more likely to adopt more formal processes. Kerr et al.'s (2007) study of small businesses in Canada suggests that having an HR manager positively correlated with the development of high-performance work systems, as mentioned in Chapter 2, can enhance employee and organisational performance. Moreover, Ferligoj et al.'s (1997) findings indicate that systematic HRM efforts in SMEs contribute to gaining competitive advantage to a certain degree, which fuels business growth. In the same line, Way's (2002) and Hayton's (2003) findings suggest that SMEs that adopt more sophisticated HRM practices report superior performance. However, their research includes firms employing up to 500 workers. Moreover, systematic HRM practices are found to contribute to the survival of new ventures and the impact of resource acquisition, allocation and development on the speed and direction of growth in rapidly expanding firms (Heneman et al., 2000; Katz et al., 2000).

Indicatively, Hornsby and Kurato (1990), having examined HRM practices within three US organisations, found that as these grew, so did the level of sophistication of HRM practices. In the same line, Barrett and Mayson's (2007) analysis shows that growth-oriented small firms are more likely than non-growing ones to use formal HRM practices, where that means that they are written down, regularly applied or assured to take place. However, their research was based on Australian organisations, which, as the authors note, tend to be far smaller than their European counterparts. Nevertheless, their study lends support to Nguyen and Bryant (2004), who suggest that firm size is positively related to HR formality and that formality is positively related to firm performance. Kotey and Slade's (2005) study of 1330 SMEs within South Queensland, Australia, also suggests that the adoption of formal HR practices increases with firm size. However, the authors acknowledge the diversity of HRM practices within SMEs.

The most commonly found HR practices in smaller firms tend to be those associated with organisational necessity such as recruitment and selection (Chapter 7), rather than as a result of a 'best practice' or 'best fit' approach (Boxall and Purcell, 2000). Even then, research indicates that SMEs are 'less likely to have adopted sophisticated practices for recruitment' (Carroll et al., 1999: 238). This preference for informal practices, attributable to resource constraints (Marlow and Patton, 1993), has led commentators to characterise HRM within such firms as 'bleak house' (Bacon and Hoque, 2005). Notably, this is somewhat at odds with the conventional wisdom of 'small is beautiful'. The latter assumes harmonious employment relations in SMEs. However, as Harney and Dundon's (2006) analysis of HRM in SMEs in Ireland illustrates, such a dualism is simplistic and HRM practices in such firms, shaped by individual, economic and social considerations, are neither beautiful nor bleak, just complex. Moreover, along this line, they argue that the two normative models of HRM which have been central to theoretical debate, 'best fit' and 'best practice', do not consider the wider complexities of SMEs adequately. As Barrett and Mayson (2007) argue, strategic HRM literature has commonly centred on the study of large and well-resourced firms and therefore future research needs to address the distinctiveness and heterogeneity of SMEs in order to gain a deeper understanding of the role of HRM.

In fact, recent thinking suggests that informality and formality should be seen as a dualism rather than a dichotomy, and challenges the notion that small firms always move from informality to formality. Marlow et al. (2010) examine the presence of formal HRM practices in SMEs. They challenge the overall notion 'that small firms must, should, or inevitably do, move from informality to formality'. Through their study of six growing medium sized organisations, they find that although there has been some adoption of HR policies and some professionalisation of the HR function, there is still a desire by 'managers and owners to retain informal control over the employment relationship' (Marlow et al., 2010: 964). Moreover, as Marchington et al. (2003) suggest, informality should not be dismissed altogether as ineffective, as it can be appropriate to the organisational context. Therefore, it is worth exploring when formal policy is acknowledged and adopted as a legitimate response to managing employment relationships.

The above becomes even more complicated when considering different locales and cultures and organisational forms. For instance, the findings of Saini and Budhwar's (2008) study, examining HRM in Indian SMEs, indicates that in the sphere of people management in such firms, the willingness to innovate and formalise the HR systems is constrained by a kind of bounded rationality – in their study the owners of SMEs believe that they are already doing what is humanly possible in this regard.

Moreover, across the EU and elsewhere, there has been an increasing use of third sector organisations to deliver public services over the last two decades. Evidence from Europe and the USA seems to show some variation in the role that the third sector plays in delivering public services, according to the existing arrangements and social politics in individual countries. However, as Carmel and Harlock (2008) point out, there are some markedly similar trends, with significance for both states and the third sector. The latter is being seen as a generator of employment growth and competition, as well as a source of public service modernisation. Across Europe, this approach has led to the emergence of a wide and highly variable range of organisations being involved in public and welfare service delivery via a variety of arrangements, at local, regional and national levels. Furthermore, the blurring of organisational boundaries between state and non-state actors and pressure on third sector organisations to change their organisational forms and even goals as a result of their involvement in public service delivery have implications for the management of their human resources. Notably, a large number of third sector organisations are small or medium sized. In addition, with many of the services provided by such organisations being labour-intensive, the management of human resources is likely to be a key area of management. Notwithstanding their socio-economic significance, relatively little is known about the way in which human resources are managed in these organisations.

As Parry et al. (2005) point out, this is surprising given the sector's growing significance as an employer and provider of public sector services.

It is therefore clear that despite the increased study of HRM in SMEs there are still many unanswered questions, and much of the prescriptions suggested are based on research in larger organisations. Despite the dearth of conclusive evidence-based prescriptions, a strategic approach to managing human resource is often seen as vital to the success of SMEs (Brand and Bax, 2002; Hornsby and Kurato, 2003; Mazzarol, 2005). The following section deals with the activities comprising the HRM function in SMEs, highlighting some of the key characteristics of smaller firms which distinguish them from large organisations in this domain.

HRM IN PRACTICE

Formalising the HR function at Omicron-Care

Omicron-Care is a growth-oriented SME operating in the social care sector. The firm has experienced rapid growth over the last five years and currently employs more than 200 people. This rapid growth period was concomitant with formalising the HR function. One of the challenges related to formalising HRM in the firm during the growth period was 'resistance to change' and getting 'conflicting messages from the top'. Receiving mixed messages lessened efficiency for some time during this period. Change is often met with some resistance, but again it would appear that organisational objectives may not have been as clear and consistent as they could have been. Formalising HRM successfully consisted of effectively addressing challenges related to:

- Gaining a deep understanding of the organisation's context and strategy in order to shape appropriately the HR strategy and practices in the organisation during transition.
- Engraining the entrepreneurial values and vision in the organisation's HRM functions.
- Using insight into people management issues and future challenges to fine-tuned formalisation.
- Striking the balance between structure and flexibility to preserve responsiveness and innovation.
- Getting rid of organisational processes and cultural elements that no longer support strategic vision and priorities.
- Looking beyond immediate operational necessities and using the challenges presented by the growth process as an opportunity for laying cultural foundations that support future entrepreneurial performance.

These key elements are echoed in a recent CIPD report titled 'Sustainable Organisation Performance through HR', which identifies vital insights for HR practice and strategy for driving long-term performance in SMEs. This CIPD report can be accessed via www.cipd.co.uk/hr-resources/research/achieving-performance-hr-sme.aspx

THE HR FUNCTION IN SMES

RECRUITMENT AND SELECTION

Despite its significance, recruitment and selection of capable employees is often problematic in SMEs, especially smaller ones, due to limited financial resources, lack of related expertise and lack of appeal in the labour market (Hornsby and Kuratko, 1990), as employees typically perform multiple roles with unclear boundaries, job responsibilities and career paths. As a result, recruiting approaches are often ad hoc, in contrast to the strategic, systematic, evidence-based approach advocated in Chapter 7. To avoid the costs related to hiring trained HR professionals, HR activities often become the responsibility of general managers, who are less likely to develop the skills and tacit knowledge required to perform needed HR activities well (Klaas et al., 2000). Generally, recruiting in smaller firms mainly involves approaches that are convenient, inexpensive and directly controllable by the firm, such as direct applicants, personal and employee referrals and newspaper advertisements (Hornsby and Kuratko, 1990; McEvoy, 1984). Selection is based mostly on interviews, training experience and education requirements for jobs, plus reference and background checks, and is often done in consultation with supervisors and employees of the vacancy domain. SMEs also place much emphasis on the compatibility between organisational norms and values and the applicants. Moreover, the focus is on the match of applicant competencies to general organisation needs rather than to specific job requirements (Heneman et al., 2000).

In addition to 'muddling through', several approaches have been suggested to SMEs for effective recruitment and selection. One of these is to increase their appeal as employers in the labour market by adopting recruiting practices that reflect industry norms. This involves imitating standard forms of job advertisement and providing recruitment brochures similar to those of larger competitors. Employing common approaches, such as placing advertisements in newspapers, attending recruitment events and having in place well-defined job positions, may help SMEs attract and retain a quality workforce. In sharp contrast, another approach is to adopt practices that constitute a radical departure from industry norms, aiming for uniqueness rather than imitation. For instance, many SMEs pride themselves on not being bureaucratic and offering a place where employees are not just a cog in the machine, but can see their contribution to the development and growth of the business. Free of bureaucratic procedures and based on their informal and empowered approach to work, such SMEs are able to successfully recruit and retain valuable employees. This begs the question of whether and under what conditions imitation is more effective than uniqueness in attracting and retaining talent in smaller firms (Cardon and Stevens, 2004). Moreover, SMEs are increasingly outsourcing HR services such as the development of employment policies, job design, payroll, health and safety, performance evaluations, disciplinary processes and training and development (Klaas et al., 2000). SMEs can also recruit the necessary skills through temporary workers, independent contractors, interns and consultants. Using these sorts of HR outsourcing approaches along their growth path enables smaller firms not only to lower their cost structure but also to be responsive to changing market conditions.

TRAINING AND DEVELOPMENT

Employees in SMEs, especially in smaller firms, receive less formal, off-the-job training than employees in large firms. Moreover, training that leads to a formal qualification tends to be less prevalent. One of the reasons for this is that smaller firms do not have the economies of scale to provide large formal programmes of training based on needs analysis as described in Chapter 9. Given that SMEs usually operate with significantly fewer resources than their larger counterparts, releasing employees for training is particularly challenging for them. Furthermore, management development is often neglected in SMEs. This is particularly important, given that the organisational strategy, structure and culture of such enterprises are often a reflection of the motivations, attitudes, values and competences of the owner-manager (Wyer et al., 2000). There are certain SMEs which adopt a strategic approach to human resource development (HRD), placing emphasis on integrating their learning activities with their business strategy, reviewing and addressing their learning needs according to their business plan (Kerr and McDougall, 1999). The fact is that business planning itself is absent in many SMEs, especially in smaller firms, let alone strategic HRD. However, in smaller firms, informal, on-the-job training is prevalent, which is hard to measure (Patton et al., 2000). In the UK, the Federation of Small Business Barriers Survey lends support to this, with almost one-third of the firms surveyed reporting that training is delivered by staff members in the workplace. In fact, many small firms pride themselves on providing workers with more hands-on, practice-based learning opportunities and avoiding formalised systems and bureaucratic procedures such as are often found in large organisations. Despite a general lack of formally codifying and documenting knowledge advancements in smaller organisations, training and learning are occurring.

One form of employee learning and development that has been examined recently is the process of socialisation, where new employees learn their roles within the organisation and adjust to job demands, skill requirements and organisational culture (Cardon and Stevens, 2004). Socialisation includes both formal and informal on-the-job training and influences learning and development regardless of organisational size. However, the process of socialisation may occur more rapidly in smaller organisations, as new employees are more readily integrated into formal and informal organisational events, have access to old-timers and senior managers and see how their work contributes to fulfilling the end purpose. This perhaps explains to a certain extent job satisfaction in smaller enterprises, where remuneration, benefits and career paths in general are less appealing than in their large counterparts.

With regard to policy making in this field, there are questions over the potential of government initiatives that aim to increase the take-up of employee training and development in small firms. An example of this is the 'Train to Gain' scheme in the UK. While there may be a commitment from some areas of government to work with smaller employers, target-driven policy initiatives are more likely to push government agents to work with large employers as the numbers trained can be increased more easily. Even when considering employers regardless of size, concerns about the usefulness of such initiatives are reflected in the findings of the CIPD's Labour Market Outlook surveys,

Human resource development (HRD) Is 'the study and practice of increasing the learning capacity of individuals, groups, collectives and organizations through the development and application of learning based intervention for the purpose of optimizing human and organizational growth and effectiveness' (Chalofsky, 1992: 179).

which suggest that more than 40 per cent of the employers would not consider signing up to training services, citing the costs of training and the lack of evidence of a business case in their particular sector. To a large extent this relates to a credibility problem that government has in delivering training programmes (Storey and Greene, 2010).

APPRAISAL AND REWARD

The extent to which SME managers take a systematic and rational approach to compensation, appraisal and reward, as HRM orthodoxy suggests (see Chapters 10 and 11), is questionable. Formal appraisals are usually absent and the compensation practices (especially in smaller firms) are often uncoordinated and ad hoc, which arguably impacts employee behaviour and performance. Moreover, pay structures differ between SMEs and large firms, as the latter tend to have flat organisational structures, with few levels of management, which translates into a uniform approach to compensation and rewards (Graham et al., 2002). Especially in small firms, traditional hierarchical distinctions are rare and so rewards are not indicative of status differences among employees. Also, automatic annual salary increases, which are common in large organisations, are not affordable to small ones. However, it has been suggested that compensation practices should be considered from a total rewards perspective, where compensation includes psychological rewards, learning opportunities and recognition in addition to monetary rewards in the form of base pay and incentives (Graham et al., 2002; Heneman et al., 2000). As Cardon and Stevens (2004: 307–308) put it,

> The rewards of employment with an entrepreneurial firm are multidimensional, including the risk and potential payoff from gambling on an innovation, invention, or business prospect and the satisfaction of ownership (even if only partial), experienced responsibility of having a tangible stake in the business, or the opportunity to work in an environment unencumbered by traditional constraints of bureaucracy.

Moreover, formalised procedures for managing performance reviews, disciplinary processes or dismissals of workers are rare in smaller firms. This could also be because of lack of expertise but also because SME managers and employees have informal ongoing communication and feedback, which they may prefer to highly formalised processes. However, given that tacit knowledge in entrepreneurial firms resides with employees, turnover of key staff without institutionalising their knowledge, or even knowledge leakages to competitors, are problematic. High levels of turnover especially can be detrimental to firm success, particularly in knowledge-intensive/high-technology sectors.

As mentioned earlier, SMEs constitute a heterogeneous cohort and so one has to be mindful of sweeping generalisations that are not appropriate. A lot depends on the age and stage of development of the firm and the sector within which it operates. The latter determines industry characteristics, skills requirements, labour market conditions and management style, to name just a few of the factors that shape HRM in SMEs. Therefore, it has to be borne in mind that there is considerable variation in undertaking recruitment and selection, training and development and appraisal and reward in SMEs, and that toolkits and 'recipes' for effective HRM that have been developed by studying large organisations may not directly be applicable to SMEs. For instance, informality to some extent and possibly in conjunction with a formalisation of practices may constitute a strategic advantage for such firms, enabling them to identify and successfully exploit entrepreneurial opportunities. Evidence suggests that SMEs are important for innovation in manufacturing and services. It further points out the flexibility of SMEs, their simple organisational structure and their receptivity, characterised by informal processes, as the essential features that enable them to be innovative (European Commission, 2014).

HRM IN PRACTICE

Insights from Singapore SMEs

The CIPD has recently conducted research into the vital role of HRM and the importance of good people management practices in Singapore SMEs. In particular, this research draws on prior work in the UK to look at how good people management drives sustainable organisation performance through different stages of organisational transition. The findings of this research offer useful insights to HR professionals and others responsible for people management in growth-oriented SMEs. These are summarised as follows:

- Anticipation is the key: readiness and relevance will determine success. Anticipation of the next stage of organisation transition, through having a deep understanding of your organisation's context, strategy, vision and values, is needed.

- Organisation values and purpose need to be the constant bedrock of the business. Clearly articulated organisation purpose and values set direction and steer the organisation. Relentless reinforcement is required to preserve the owner/leader's founding vision and values. Skilful alignment of people management insight with leaders' aspirations is a critical HR challenge. A deep understanding of the owner/founder's vision and their expectations of HR's role needs to be coupled with HR's detailed diagnosis of both current people management issues and future challenges.

- Simplicity of structure and purity of process preserve innovation and entrepreneurship. Finding the right balance between structure and fluidity at each stage of organisation transition is the key.

- Sustainable growth involves striking a balance between preservation and evolution. It is important that attention is dedicated to identifying the aspects of your organisation that need to be retained as the organisation grows.

- Look beyond immediate operational issues and take the opportunity to lay the organisation's cultural foundations for the future. With each presenting issue there is an opportunity to look beyond immediate solutions and build on the organisation's cultural foundations.

Source: CIPD (2013) *Achieving Excellence: HR and People Management in Singapore SMEs*. Research Report. Accessed online at: www.cipd.co.uk/hr-resources/research/achieving-excellence-hr-singapore.aspx (accessed 18 April 2016).

Developing HR policy in SMEs

- Consider a mix of approaches for developing HRM practices in a small firm operating in a knowledge-based industry, for example in electronic engineering.
- TASK: Consider the critical success factors in an industry of your choice and think about what sort of HRM practices would help address these factors.

DEBATING HRM

Formalising HRM in SMEs

Consider a mix of approaches for developing HRM practices in a small firm operating in a knowledge-based industry, for example in electronic engineering.

TASK: In small groups, debate in favour of and against formalising HRM in SMEs.

GRADUATE INSIGHTS

Challenges of formalising the HR function at Omicron-Care

Corina is a graduate of the MSc HRM and Business course. During the last five years she has been working in the HR department of Omicron-Care, the growth-oriented SME in the social care sector, which was presented in an 'HRM in Practice' feature earlier in this chapter. Corina has contributed to Omicron-Care's growth from the HR front and is now the HR Director in the firm. One of her challenges related to formalising HRM in Omicron-Care during the growth period:

I did a research project on the changes that took place during the growth period in Omicron-Care. Apart from my own reflection I took into consideration other people's views, including senior management. Having considered the changes in more detail, it was important to look at the sort of challenges that were faced as a result, and how the formalisation of HR impacted on the employee relationship. … It became evident that it has been challenging to get middle management to take 'ownership' and 'responsibility' for the new HRM practices. It has been too easy for managers to think that because we have a HR department they can give all staff issues to HR to deal with and perhaps allow some of the managers to dissolve [sic] themselves of accountability. Therefore, although one would think that the implementation of more formal HRM practices can impact positively on organisational performance, it would appear that without strong leadership and management, the impact of this can be diluted.

MINI CASE STUDY

Learning and development opportunities at Alpha-Soft

Alpha-Soft is an internationalised small software developer specialising in secure messaging, mainly for the military. Its home office is in the UK, with subsidiaries in Canada, the USA and Australia. Overall, it employs 48 people, of which 70 per cent are technical staff. Its customer base includes the UK Ministry of Defence (MoD), the Australian, Canadian and Luxembourg Departments of Defence, the National Security Agency, the US Navy and the North Atlantic Treaty Organisation (NATO).

The management team promotes a culture of continuous development. Central to this are efforts to recognise and build on each individual's talents so that employees find enjoyment and satisfaction in their work. The firm is recognised as an Investor in People (IiP) and is accredited to ISO 9001/TickIT and BS 7799. Staff learning and development is regarded as crucial for its competitive performance and all employees are encouraged to pursue training, qualifications and further education opportunities. Beyond formal training, as Brian, the Managing Director, explains, 'Alpha-Soft participates in and monitors the work of organisations like the Armed Forces Communications and Electronics Association (AFCEA), Communications-Electronics Security Department (CESG), European Electronic Messaging Association (EEMA). ... Conferences and exhibitions organised by them are key industry forums for learning and coming up with new ideas.'

Informal learning through such events and generally close relationships with the end customers (military organisations), system integrators, collaborators and advisory boards are viewed as most significant for identifying entrepreneurial opportunities and to hone skills and capabilities in the firm. Tony, who is a Senior Technical Architect, remarks on this point: 'We got to work in that environment and look out what the opportunities are for us and what capabilities we need to exploit these. These come from customer requirements, from influential focus groups in the industry – our advisory boards, or standards boards to collaborators in projects.'

Identifying entrepreneurial opportunities and developing existing and new competences that enhance human capital in Alpha-Soft are often enabled by participation in 'boundary processes'. These take place during events where systems integrators, collaborating software developers and military procurers meet to put together and test systems. These events offer interfaces through which information/knowledge is gleaned, which helps Alpha-Soft innovate with new products/services. Interestingly, system integrators and collaborators who work with Alpha-Soft on a given project may be competitors in another tender.

CASE STUDY QUESTIONS

1   What learning and development opportunities are available to employees at Alpha-Soft?

2   What HR practices would help Alpha-Soft generate new knowledge about opportunities for new product/service development?

3   What is the risk for knowledge outflows to competitors involved in the events described above, and what sort of HR practices would mitigate such risk?

DEBATING HRM

Disseminating crucial knowledge within the firm

Consider Alpha-Soft as a knowledge-based professional firm, where knowledge is power.

TASK: Working in groups, use appropriate theory to discuss the extent to which Alpha-Soft should employ cultural control and HRM practices that prevent hoarding knowledge, such as assessing in performance appraisal the degree to which employees communicate the knowledge they have to their colleagues and superiors.

This section has discussed some of the challenges and approaches related to undertaking the core HRM activities in SMEs, putting emphasis on the internal context and resource considerations. The next section deals specifically with two of the main challenges in managing people in SMEs that stem from the operating environment: coping with regulation and dealing with employee diversity.

ONLINE STUDY TOOLS

Writing an essay? Expand your knowledge.

Kerr and McDougall (1999) provide a seminal article on SMEs titled 'The small business of developing people'.

https://edge.sagepub.com/crawshaw2e > Student Resources > Chapter 13 > Journal Articles

OTHER CHALLENGES IN MANAGING PEOPLE IN SMES

All organisations face several challenges stemming from both their external environment and their internal context. Given the fact that small firms often have to operate under-resourced in terms of human and financial capital, these challenges are particularly acute for such firms. It is well documented that small firms bear a disproportionate burden of any costs associated with the introduction of new regulations (Chapter 12), given the large fixed costs of compliance. For instance, Crain and Crain (2010) found that adopting new regulations puts small businesses at a greater competitive disadvantage than larger firms in the USA. The Department for Business, Enterprise and Regulatory Reform (BERR, 2008) report also concluded that small businesses are less able or motivated to adapt their enterprises to regulation than larger firms. Increasing regulatory concerns relating to dismissal and minimum wage, as well as a host of acts relating to equality at work and health and safety, are all important aspects, which add to the complexity of managing people in small firms.

INCREASING REGULATORY CONCERNS

The evidence gleaned from a range of studies that examine the impact of regulation on small firms is somewhat mixed. There seems to be some evidence that the complexity of regulation is an issue for many small firms, but another stream of research suggests that regulation is not a burden. Also, the impact of regulation on employment relationships in small firms can be a mixed blessing and may instigate different approaches. Ram et al. (2001), for instance, find in their study that the regulatory shock of the National Minimum Wage (NMW) had varying effects, as some firms moved up-market and others were pressed to the edges of the legitimate market and in some cases went out of business altogether. In the small firms moving up-market, informality was redefined into a more disciplined and formalised approach, while those going down-market relied even more heavily on family and other ties to survive. The NMW led to some improved wages, though there was also evasion, and it has sharpened the divide between the legitimate and illicit areas of business.

At an international level, again it is difficult to appreciate the full impact of regulation, and comparisons across countries are difficult. Reasons for this include the fact that the indicators used disregard many aspects of the regulatory environment, that different methods are employed and that the extent to which any regulation is implemented varies greatly between countries.

Previous research findings have also presented the idea that there is a general belief in SMEs that employment regulations are an obstacle to their success (Bacon and Hoque, 2005). Atkinson and Curtis (2004: 486) comment that this may be to the extent that 'small companies may not be granting their employees all their statutory rights'; however, it is unclear whether this is a 'deliberate strategy' or due to 'ignorance'. With research findings supporting the idea that SME strategy is often emergent (Brand and Bax, 2002), it would seem more likely to be the latter. Interestingly, SMEs have been found to be the principal source of unfair dismissal claims to UK employment tribunals (Bacon and Hoque, 2005; Earnshaw et al., 2000), and therefore it would seem that SMEs do need to start recognising the value of investing in HRM practices. This is particularly relevant in growing SMEs, as employees within larger and more economically stable organisations tend to have greater awareness of legal entitlements and are more likely to exercise their rights (Marlow, 2002).

WORKFORCE DIVERSITY

Small firms are more likely to be employing a higher percentage of employees from a range of groups that have traditionally faced some form of disadvantage in the labour market. Older workers and women constitute a large proportion of employees in small firms, and while this may be attributable to a host of factors, the high proportion of part-time working in such firms indicates flexible labour management practices. Some of these flexible arrangements are usually considered within the domain of work–life balance.

Moreover, there seems to be a tendency for ethnic minorities as a whole to make up a large proportion of the self-employed, and of employees in the largest of firms. Yet, as Urwin et al. (2008: 20) note, 'this overall picture obscures very different profiles for Asian/Asian British and Black/Black British groups; with the former making up a much higher proportion of employees in both the largest (4.8 [per cent]) and smallest (4.6 [per cent]) of firms, and the latter making up a growing proportion of employees as we consider larger and larger categories of business'. Contrast this with the discussion of diversity presented in Chapter 8. Developing inclusive practices and managing diversity however may be particularly challenging for SMEs and especially smaller firms, which usually lack the expertise to deal with such important considerations.

Reflecting on the role of government

- Consider government policy relating to the employment relationship in SMEs in general and small firms in particular. Access the announcement of the UK government to reform employment relations for SMEs via www.gov.uk/government/speeches/reforming-employment-relations and consider the impact that reforming policies may have on different stakeholders, including the owner/management team, the employees of the firm and the local community. Go to www.eurofound.europa.eu/observatories/eurwork/comparative-information/smes-in-the-crisis-employment-industrial-relations-and-local-partnership and read the article 'SMEs in the crisis: Employment, industrial relations and local partnership'.

- TASK: Consider the impact of the economic crisis on European SME employment relations. To what extent does this differ across different countries?

CASE STUDY

Innovative HRM and challenges for SMEs

XYZ is a three-year-old telecommunication company with 52 employees and is located in Istanbul, Turkey. The firm has a good reputation for providing high-quality telecommunication and security consultancy services. The management of the firm tries to build high-quality human capital as it deems human capital key to success in the information and telecommunication industry. The company recognises the importance of HRM practices to develop human capital and enhance the performance of the firm. HRM is seen as a strategic partner for the business, and investment in HRM practices has taken place at an early stage. The CEO of XYZ, Mr Beyaz, also the owner of the firm, underlined the importance of HRM as follows:

> We want HRM to be a strategic partner for the company. It is evident that well-established HR practices enhance human capital which is the most critical factor in this particular industry. Our employees are the most valuable asset at the firm, and they just walk away every night. It has been two years since we have introduced a dedicated HRM department and hired an HR professional. However, our HR department is not at the level we want now. There is a great need for more formal policies and defined procedures for HR practices.

(Continued)

(Continued)

HRM in SMEs is less sophisticated and contains both formal and informal structure. Size and industry are the most important factors that affect the adaptations of HRM in such firms. However, HRM practices can help SMEs to increase performance. XYZ Telecommunication has initiated a drastic investment in HRM and practices to enhance its human capital. Mr Beyaz stated that they were particularly interested in the pooling and developing of high-quality human capital to increase their innovative performance. As noted, XYZ hired an HR professional two years ago to establish an HR department. The firm has set two important targets to achieve, first to recruit the best candidates with required KSAOs and experience. The second is to enhance innovation at the firm via encouraging employee creativity and participation.

Recruiting talent in the industry is one of the significant challenges. XYZ faced difficulties in reaching out to the best people. To overcome this challenge, the management introduced a referral system to reach qualified candidates. It is a straightforward system. If the company recruits an employee's referral, the employee will receive a monetary reward. According to Mr Beyaz, this system has worked very well for them as they were able to hire not only the best people in terms of skills, but people who fit the work culture.

The management of XYZ Telecommunication has given great importance to developing such a work environment to enhance employee effectiveness. The CEO says that the IT industry is very dynamic, and customers are demanding:

> There are always emerging problems and issues that need to be solved immediately. We just have to be quick and efficient to solve the problems and meet the customer needs.

The value room is an excellent example of a useful, less formal practice to generate quick solutions. The firm dedicated a small room with furniture (table, chairs, whiteboard) and technological infrastructure for immediate meetings for employees, managers, etc. If an employee or a manager needs to receive the support of one of their colleagues or a little discussion, the value room is available for them to hold an intuitive meeting. The room has rules similar to Chatham House rules. They can discuss anything related to job issues.

According to the HRM manager, Mrs Oztel, with the firm for two years, the firm is already giving importance to managing information and knowledge across the firm. There are various activities for effective information and knowledge sharing among the employees. One of them is the XYZ Academy initiative. XYZ Academy enables employees to share their knowledge and experience with their colleagues and students who are prospective colleagues. The company has appeared in the national press and won an award at the Best of IT Industry competition. Mrs Oztel stated that employees' reaction to the Academy was very good:

> They like to share their experience and knowledge. You can see the satisfaction on their faces.

One of the employees who gave a presentation at XYZ Academy stated the following:

> I was happy to share my experience with friends and students who can make use out of it. It was also a recognition of my contribution to the firm as I shared the project I run here.

Not everything goes well at XYZ Telecommunication regarding HRM, of course. The CEO of XYZ stated that they wanted to enhance employee creativity and participation by introducing a reward system. The system looks simple but requires some effort from employees. Individuals, or a group of employees, are required to prepare a formal application ready to submit to the Patent Agency with an executive report about a noble and creative idea. If the application is accepted by the firm, the employee receives 5000 TL. If the patent application is accepted by the agency, the rights are shared by the employees and the firm. It was a big initiative for an SME. However, the firm did not receive as many applications as expected. The CEO of XYZ put it this way:

> Our employees are developers and engineers who are already occupied with their jobs, tasks and duties. Furthermore, the process has been too formal for them as they do not like paperwork at all. It has been a very formalised and structured process for them. It would be easier if the HR department could have helped us when we introduced the application system by training employees to make a formal application. The HR department has not reached that level yet – the HR department lacks strategic orientation to identify the need. Once we get there, I assume HR becomes [a] strategic partner.

On the other hand, Mrs Oztel states that the HR department is also responsible for the quality assurance policies and project applications to the Patent Agency on behalf of their clients. She complains about the workload as follows:

> It just requires a number of procedures to go through and prepare paper work. There is almost no time to focus on our core job as HR department at the firm.

The balance between formal and informal practices is important for the success of an HRM practice in SMEs. In the flat and less hierarchical organisational structure of SMEs, employees need simple, useful and less formal practices. The rapid growth of SMEs causes top executives to make wrong investment decisions. The growth in SMEs also brings an extra workload to the HR department, which inhibits the effectiveness of the HRM.

XYZ has since become a publicly traded company after experiencing a great deal of growth. The management of the company initially decided to replace the HR manager and later outsourced most HR functions.

(Continued)

(Continued)

CASE STUDY QUESTIONS

1 How would you rate the management approach of XYZ to HRM in developing HR practices?
2 Would such an approach to HRM be feasible or appropriate in other firms, operating in different sectors?
3 What sorts of challenges are involved in the HRM activities of firms such as XYZ with regard to people management?
4 How can employees in smaller firms be participative and creative?
5 In your view, what sort of people management policies and practices can help SMEs in increasing their intellectual property?
6 In your view, how can HRM become a strategic partner? What critical factors affect the strategic orientation of HRM?

CHAPTER SUMMARY

The key points that were identified in this chapter are as follows:

- Given the importance of the SME sector for innovation, economic growth and employment generation, its socio-economic role is paramount in economies throughout the world.

- The current trend towards knowledge-intensive industries means that competitiveness increasingly depends on the management of the relational bases of employees.

- A defining characteristic of the SME sector is its heterogeneity. SMEs, and in particular small firms, tend to lack formal HR systems and where such systems are present they vary in their extent. Notably, the likelihood of the presence of HR systems increases by size and this seems to hold cross-nationally.

- However, from the growing base of research on HRM in SMEs, it would appear that firm size alone does not determine a specific type of people management. There are a variety of approaches within the SME sector and it has to be acknowledged that HR practices tend to vary according to industry conditions and prevailing supply chain relationships, which can affect the nature of such practices.

- Despite the dearth of conclusive evidence-based prescriptions, a strategic approach to managing human resource is often seen as vital to the success of SMEs.

- Entrepreneurial SMEs have discovered synergistic HR practices, where informality and formality can coexist. This is not to say that SMEs do not need to view HR practices as choices of strategic importance. Yet this may take a combination of strategic thinking and formalisation with 'gut feeling' and informal practices.

- SMEs face a host of challenges stemming from both their external environment and their internal context. Given the fact that they often have to operate under-resourced in terms of human and financial capital, these challenges are particularly acute for such firms.

- With regard to policy making, an examination of 'what works' should provide solid evidence to inform the formulation of support programmes and regulative measures that serve all SME stakeholders.

REVIEW QUESTIONS AND EXERCISES

1 How important are SMEs for socio-economic development at local, regional, national and international levels?

2 SMEs have a harder time coping with economic downturns than do large firms. What are the key transition points in emerging HR systems?

3 SMEs experience a lot of change. How should HR practices in SMEs change as the organisation grows?

4 Changes in organisations, including HRM practices, are often destabilising to SMEs. Do changes in HRM practices follow typical lifecycle models, moving necessarily from informal to formal practices?

5 Employee issues are often handled arbitrarily in SMEs. What equity, fairness, justice or work–life balance issues are relevant in SMEs, and how do these impact employee or organisational performance?

EXPLORE FURTHER

Edwards, P. and Ram, M. (2009) HRM in small firms: Respecting and regulating informality, in A. Wilkinson, N. Bacon, T. Redman and S. Snell (eds) *The Sage Handbook of Human Resource Management*. London: Sage, pp. 524–540. An excellent chapter in this edited book summarising the key themes and issues of HRM in small firms.

Saini, D.S. and Budhwar, P.S. (2008) Managing the human resource in Indian SMEs: The role of indigenous realities. *Journal of World Business*, 43: 417–434. An excellent article providing a specific Indian perspective on, and examples of, HRM in SMEs.

'Small and medium-sized enterprises (SMEs): Management skills for SMEs' on the European Commission website, at: http://ec.europa.eu/DocsRoom/documents/2266/attachments/1/translations/en/renditions/pdf. This is the final report of the expert group on 'Management Capacity Building'. The report highlights the role of management capacity building to support the creation and growth of SMEs. It provides 15 examples of 'good practice' cases, illustrating different successful ways of supporting management capacity building in SMEs.

GO ONLINE

Visit the companion website for **interactive quizzes**, explanatory **videos** and **podcasts**, **journal articles** to use in your essays, and **weblinks** to useful resources.

https://edge.sagepub.com/crawshaw2e

CHAPTER 14

HRM IN THE NOT-FOR-PROFIT SECTORS*

Jennifer Surtees

Karin Sanders

Helen Shipton

Louise Knight

CHAPTER KNOWLEDGE OBJECTIVES

- To understand and appreciate the differences in environment, strategy, employees and culture which apply within public versus private sector organisations.
- To understand the different roles that HRM may play within public versus private sector organisations.
- To understand why people choose to work in the public sector and to recognise the distinctive challenges of managing the work of employees within this sector.
- To understand the differences in HRM in public and private sector organisations.
- To be able to discuss critically why HRM in the public sector may, or may not, differ from HRM in business (for-profit) organisations.

KEY SKILLS OBJECTIVES

- To be able to design a strong HRM system for both public and private organisations.
- To be better equipped to develop, implement and manage HRM systems by taking into account differences across public and private sector organisations as well as the salient contemporary issues.
- To improve the effects of HRM in public, voluntary and private organisations.
- To be able to design an HR approach tailored to the special features and challenges of public sector and voluntary sector work, as well as the internal and external cultural and political climates.

This chapter also provides indicative content for the following Intermediate and Advanced level CIPD modules:

CIPD INTERMEDIATE LEVEL MODULES

5CHR Business issues and the context of human resources

5HRF Managing and coordinating the human resources function

CIPD ADVANCED LEVEL MODULE

7HRC HRM in context

---

*With special thanks and acknowledgements to Leon Neil (HR Professional and Aston Business School MSc Graduate) and Indrayanti (Lecturer and Researcher at the Faculty of Psychology, Gadjah Mada University, Indonesia).

GO ONLINE

This chapter comes with loads of online tools to help you to go that extra mile in your studies!

- **Multiple choice questions** to help you test your knowledge and revise for exams
- **Journal articles** so you can read further for assignments and essays
- **Videos** and **podcasts** to help you to understand how complex concepts work in the real world

Visit **https://edge.sagepub.com/crawshaw2e** to access these resources for this topic.

INTRODUCTION

This chapter focuses on the similarities and differences between profit and not-for-profit sectors and the consequences of these similarities and differences in terms of their human resource management (HRM). In addition to the not-for-profit sector we pay attention to a 'third' sector, the voluntary, community or charity sector. After defining the three sectors and elaborating on the differences and similarities between them, we explore their HRM. We will unpick the differences and similarities with regard to HRM within these sectors, and the implications that these differences and similarities have. We then explore industrial examples of the not-for-profit sector and the challenges common to the sector.

The objective of this chapter is to demonstrate that the core tasks of HRM departments are the same across the three sectors, enabling their organisation to draw in, develop, motivate and retain top talent. However, due to differences in tasks, objectives, values, processes of decision making and their environment (stakeholders), there are differences in the way in which HRM is perceived and enacted in the public versus the private sector. We will be discussing HRM within organisations which are 'not-for-profit', that is, with objectives that do not include those of private companies, which are to increase profit and market share. The chapter will mainly focus on the public sector but will also include those companies described as 'third sector'.

DEFINING THE PRIVATE, PUBLIC AND NOT-FOR-PROFIT SECTORS

A common feature of privately owned companies, regardless of the sector into which they are classified, is that they seek to achieve similar objectives: to generate a profit, to obtain competitive advantage over companies selling similar goods or services and so to gain an increase in their share of the market. This way of working is usually found in the private sector.

There are organisations that exist for reasons other than profit making and generating competitive advantage. This is known as the not-for-profit sector. There are several subdivisions within this sector, one of which is the public sector. The public sector organisations run on public (tax) funding from either national or local government, with the remit to offer services for free or at a subsidised cost. Examples from the UK public sector are the National Health Service (NHS), schools and local education authorities and the Civil Service. Examples from the EU include SNCF (Société Nationale des Chemins de Fer Français, the French National Railway Corporation) and La Poste. International examples include semi-privatised Telkom SA (the South African national fixed line telephone

Private sector
Organisations privately owned which operate in order to achieve competitive advantage or earn profit through either selling products, manufacturing, or providing a service and hospitality.

Not-for-profit sector
A term that describes the different types of organisations which operate with objectives that go beyond achieving market advantage and profit. This includes the public and third sectors.

Public sector
Organisations operating in order to provide a public or community-based service, funded by the taxpayer and under government jurisdiction. Organisations in the UK include the National Health Service, emergency services and the education system.

Third sector The sector of organisations operating not-for-profit, with no government funding, for charitable reasons; they include the charity and voluntary sectors.

network) with 38 per cent state ownership, the Indian Oil Corporation and the Afghan Public Protection Force (APPF, a public security company in Afghanistan). Commonly the public sector is positioned as significantly distinct from the private sector.

There is also a 'third' sector which is encompassed in the 'not-for-profit' category alongside the public sector. This third sector is often referred to as the voluntary, community or charity sector. These are social enterprises with the aim of generating funds or providing manpower to donate to social causes. Examples from the UK include the Royal Society for the Prevention of Cruelty to Animals (RSPCA), the National Society for the Prevention of Cruelty to Children (NSPCC) and the National Council for Voluntary Organisations (NCVO). Examples from outside the UK include United Hatzalah for emergency medical first response and the Volnoe Delo Foundation in Russia.

PRIVATE AND PUBLIC SECTORS: SIMILARITIES AND DIFFERENCES

Mullins (1999) claims that the polar objectives confirm obvious differences. Private sector organisations exist to achieve profit, competitive advantage, market share and efficiency. Public sector organisations by contrast are concerned with service provision, budget spending, quality of care and delivery (Sparrow and Cooper, 2012; Tsui and Lai, 2009). According to Sims and Slack (2007), there are some structural and organisational factors that are common to both sectors, as well as distinct differences:

- **Values and structures:** The top echelon of directors is selected; they then select a senior management team. This is the typical structuring of the public as well as the private sector. In the public sector, management and those below are under implementation instructions from an external elected body. The structure of the public sector echoes the private sector but the values differ subtly. In the public sector the values are in response to the needs and demands of the public, affecting the way in which the service is run by those elected representatives. In the private sector, the values of the organisation are chosen by how the organisation wishes to be perceived to the outside world, and to its customers (see also Chapters 4 and 13).

- **Decision makers:** Sims and Slack (2007) suggest that in the public sector there are many dispersed decision makers, so that accountability and responsibility are less clear than in the private sector. The decision-making process in the private sector runs smoothly compared to the sometimes drawn-out decision making in the public sector, conflict-ridden as a result of the role played by multiple parties (Rodriguez and Hickson, 1995; Schwenk, 1990).

- **Stakeholder diversity:** This varies within the public sector; for example, patients, doctors, inventors and the public as well as government officials could all be considered stakeholders in a hospital trust. However, this could be perceived as parallel with the private sector as here there is also an array of stakeholders reliant on the organisation (i.e. suppliers, contractors, consultants, customers, etc.) (see Chapter 13). This diversity affects the accountability and decision making of the individuals holding responsibility.

As with the example above, during recruitment of nursing staff there may need to be several different people involved in assessing applicants for the position of nurse, including the hospital executives (justifying the new position), HR, those responsible for financing the position, as well as employees that may work alongside or manage the nurse. HR must oversee a process which involves many different stakeholders. Patients and service users could also be considered stakeholders as certainly their satisfaction with the nurse's treatment of them is ultimately the result of good performance.

- **Access by the public:** This is a key area which demonstrates the differences between the public and private sectors. Users and customers have access to and can affect the running of public organisations, which is not present to the same degree in the private sector. Most information must be made as accessible and available to the public as possible (within reason for confidential and personal information). The organisation is always accountable for how funding budgets are spent. There must be a transparent customer/user process for complaints and these must be seen to be dealt with officially and efficiently.

More recently it has emerged that the fallout from the recession and market downturn have had a divergent effect on the budget, focus and priorities of the two sectors (Faragher, 2014). Faragher reports that the recovery from the recession has resulted in XpertHR's 2014 finding of an increased budget for private sector HR activity; while there has been budgetary reduction for these activities in the public sector (Geldman, 2014, in Faragher, 2014). Moreover, there is a greater focus on priorities relating to attrition and retention for the private sector at present, while redundancies and restructuring remain at the forefront of HR activity in the public sector. Conversely, a comparison between public and private sector banks in India found no differences in their HR practices (Kalidoss and Vijayalakshmi, 2016). Thus differences in the public and private sector may not always result in differences in HRM practices.

Indeed, the differences in HRM practices are more likely to be keenly felt within the third sector since demonstrating the value of investment within the constraints of extremely tight budgets is most common. Leadership development has been seen as lacking in particular within this sector (Woods, 2010) and leadership effectiveness is a fundamentally critical requirement for managing the difficulties in service delivery within the sector. However, this is an area of literature that requires extensive further research, particularly focusing on values-based HR systems, the effect of high-performance work systems (HPWS; see Chapter 2) and the impact that HRM has on person–role fit, engagement and retention in this sector (Baluch, 2016; Kellner et al., 2016).

Designing HRM in the public sector

- Go to the following webpage and read the blog about the decentralisation of the public sector: www.conservativehome.com/platform/2012/12/from-gregclarkmp-this-government-is-decentralising-the-public-sector-for-the-first-time-in-more-than.html

- TASK: Discuss in groups the impact this could have (and has had where possible) upon the HRM approach and organisation in the public sector. Also consider the potential effects on a private sector business.

HRM IN THE PUBLIC AND PRIVATE SECTORS

A study by Guest et al. (2000) exemplifies the key comparisons and differences in the use of high-commitment HRM practices (see Chapter 2) between the private and public sectors. In this research Guest et al. (2000) used information taken from the 1998 UK Workplace Employment Relations Study (WERS) to explore the different usage of high-commitment HRM practices (see Chapter 2), defined by the authors as those typified by: (1) high levels of employee involvement, (2) firm-level investment in employees (e.g. training, promotion, and sharing firm profits) and (3) a concern with finding employees who will fit within the organisation (see also Burton and O'Reilly, 2004).

The reported findings show that some HR practices are commonly performed by both public and private sectors, such as induction programmes, grievance procedures and formal appraisals. However, their analysis also showed that:

- More public sector organisations devote meeting time to employee questions, which may be related to the structure of the organisation and its line management systems.

- There is a higher number of public sector organisations ensuring on-the-job training is current and available to employees.

- Job security guarantee is low in both sectors; however, employees' perceptions of job security are reported to be significantly higher in the public sector despite a greater use of fixed-term contracts in those organisations (Sparrow and Cooper, 2012). (For an alternative perspective on this issue see the 'Graduate Insights' section later.)

- There are four practices engaged in by a high number of private sector organisations: (1) internal candidate selection preferences, (2) formal appraisals, (3) performance-related pay and (4) shared ownership schemes (which of course are only really relevant for the profit-making sector).

Overall, therefore, the findings suggest a higher frequency of public sector organisations engaging in high-commitment HR practices, which indicates an overall difference in the perceived high-commitment HRM approach, or perhaps a more suitable environment to put them into practice. It is clear that the organisational goals not only differentiate between the two sectors, but also shape the different HRM practices.

Stanton and Manning (2013) suggest the characteristics of the public sector which are seen to impact on employees and thus affect the management of high-performance work systems in the sector. These include the context associated with policy making, the diversity of the incumbent workforce, the variety of the work and the 'scope of the public sector in relation to employment status of its employees' (Stanton and Manning, 2013: 265). All of these must be negotiated in order to perform HRM efficiently and adequately while promoting employee well-being and performance.

Farnham and Horton (1996) propose four key characteristics of HRM in the public sector: paternalistic management style, standardised employment practices, collectivism (see Chapter 10) and aspiration to be 'model' employers of staff. This analysis suggests that the HR function in public sector organisations is concerned with promoting and protecting employee well-being and staff performance, which has implications for

HRM alignment and emphasis. Compared to private sector organisations, public sector entities are concerned about achieving balance between employee well-being and organisational performance. Remembering that the public sector usually involves provision of a service, resulting in different job performance outcomes and employee motivators, this impacts HRM.

Boyne et al. (1999) suggest that the characteristics of HRM in the public sector have been diminished by political policies that encourage public sector organisations to take on many private sector characteristics. As in the private sector, there has been a devolution of power to line managers, flexibility and differentiation in employment practices, more individualistic approaches to employee relations and modelling on the private sector rather than striving to set the bar as a model employer (Boyne et al., 1999). Some trade unions specifically represent public service employees (e.g. Unison), highlighting this move (see Chapter 12 on employee relations for further discussion on trade unions). Although there has been and is pressure on the public sector to adopt private sector approaches to HRM, it is argued that this does not always translate to different contexts (Boyne et al., 1999; Storey, 1992).

> **Pay in the public and private sectors**
>
> Some differences in pay in the public and private sectors are discussed in the following article: www.telegraph.co.uk/finance/personalfinance/pensions/11152840/Public-vs-private-sector-pay-gap-is-5000-or-a-fifth-of-earnings.html
>
> TASK: What are the considerations that must be made when attracting, retaining and motivating employees in the two sectors? Do you think this will have an impact on the wider HR approaches in the two sectors? Why? How do you think they will differ in the HRM practices?

CHALLENGES FACING DIFFERENT PUBLIC SECTOR ORGANISATIONS

This section explores four distinct types of public sector organisations, each illustrated with some contemporary examples of research.

HEALTHCARE

Building and sustaining health services that reflect the aspirations of the communities they serve has proved a major challenge throughout the developed world, especially in the UK, where such provision is notionally 'free' at the point of delivery. If healthcare organisations want to accomplish their goals of high-quality patient care, safety care and to reduce costs, HRM is important, with the link between strategic HRM (SHRM) practices and organisational performance replicated in the healthcare sector (e.g. Bartram et al., 2007). West et al. (2002) reported that where healthcare organisations have integrated and strategically focused HRM practices, patient mortality is likely to be lower than in those where there is less commitment to effective people management.

HRM continues to be relatively low profile in most healthcare systems around the world. HRM specialists are frequently under-represented in top management teams and often have a muted input into strategic decision making (Khatri et al., 2006). This may be partly because healthcare organisations are by tradition led by clinicians and specialist medical staff, who often dominate even in matters outside their areas of specialist expertise (Khatri et al., 2006). Employees in support functions may have a low status relative to employees who provide patient care, despite the potential contribution that effective HRM can offer (Khatri et al., 2006). A leadership team which is transformational rather than transactional (Burns, 1978) is associated with a workplace climate that emphasises patient care (Shipton et al., 2008) – probably by implementing mechanisms such as performance management to this end. Such leaders are also likely to rely upon informal HRM practices such as knowledge sharing that in turn may elicit innovative behaviours (see the Case Study below).

Sanders and Shipton (2012) showed that the relationship between transformational leaders and employees' innovative behaviour in Dutch healthcare organisations could be explained by team learning. Pei et al. (2004) researched the increased responsibilities of managers of Chinese hospitals in staff management, finding that a barrier to management was a lack of local decision-making ability on wage and recruitment policy.

MINI CASE STUDY

Leadership development in UK healthcare

Taking a sample of 86 hospital trusts in the UK, a group of researchers from Aston Business School examined the relationship between perceptions of leadership effectiveness and healthcare performance. They drew on measures arising from the Commission for Health Improvement star-rating system (now the 'Annual Health Check'), the Clinical Governance Review ratings of hospital trust performance, and also focused on a novel aspect of service quality: patient complaints as a proportion of patients treated. They worked on the basis that leaders influence performance outcomes to the extent that they shape employees' collective belief that patient needs come first; in other words, there is some factor of climate that reflects a common determination to achieve high standards of patient care. The research concluded that transformational leaders are called for, that is, those who create a vision of where the organisation is going and implement initiatives to achieve the vision. Such leaders generate enthusiasm for goal achievement and communicate employees' roles in contributing to the organisation's strategy. They also engage with the external environment, building collaborative relationships within the wider community to promote the necessary change orientation across the organisation.

Source: Shipton, H., Armstrong, C., West, M. and Dawson, J.F. (2008) The impact of leadership and quality climate on hospital performance. *International Journal for Quality in Healthcare*, 20(6): 439–445. Reproduced with the permission of the *International Journal for Quality in Health Care*.

CASE STUDY QUESTIONS

1   To what extent do you think transformational leaders rely on HRM practices to deliver the performance outcomes suggested in the above case?

2   What HRM practices or combinations of practices are likely to be most salient in delivering the strategic outcomes required?

3   What role, if any, might those with HRM responsibility play in developing leaders with the capabilities described above? What developmental initiatives could be put in place to nurture future leaders?

DEBATING HRM

NHS weekend working

A recent announcement in the NHS reforms suggested that routine NHS service provisions should be made available seven days a week. Currently services are available on weekdays, with some surgeries opening for a few hours during the weekend. However, there have been warnings that seven-day working will overstretch staff and lead to overworked and under-motivated employees (Pil and Leana, 2009).

TASK: In groups, discuss the case for and against this reform. Consider some of the HR practices and employee behaviours that may need to be dealt with and how you may go about doing so.

EDUCATION

Despite less attention in the literature, schools' relatively homogeneous set of activities, work structures and policy guidelines make them a viable and insightful context for research.

In this sector, union membership is strong and professional bodies such as the National Union of Teachers (NUT) and National Association of Schoolmasters Union of Women Teachers (NASUWT) directly influence teachers' terms and conditions of employment. There is a stringent process for discipline and scope for and often willingness to take industrial action when it comes to pay and pension negotiations. This is a focus for HR (managed within the local education authorities in the UK) and a concern of the manager within the school (Blandford, 2012). Staff must feel safeguarded and not overworked in response to the demands of their job.

Runhaar and Sanders (2013) offered insight into the causes of the stagnation of HRM implementation in schools for vocational education and training (VET schools). These schools face serious challenges worldwide which require them to implement HRM:

1   Due to the increased expectations of employers regarding employees' lifelong learning skills and their contribution to organisational development, the emphasis in vocational educational programmes has shifted from pure knowledge acquisition to career guidance.

2   The educational sectors of most Western societies face considerable teacher shortages as a result of the poorer image and reduced status of the teaching profession and the ageing of the teaching workforce (OECD, 2011). As a result schools must refine and professionalise their recruitment and selection practices (Grieves and Hanafin, 2005).

3   Schools and teachers are increasingly held responsible for students' achievement (OECD, 2011). Performance appraisal systems need to be implemented in order to systematically evaluate and improve teachers' performance (e.g. Cousins, 1995).

Using a qualitative study in which 30 respondents of five Dutch VET colleges participated, Runhaar and Sanders (2013) asked the following research question: 'What factors impede and promote the implementation of HRM, in the view of policymakers and executives of HRM policy?' In response to the question 'What impedes the implementation of HRM within school?':

- 82 per cent referred to soft factors (e.g. resistance, culture within the school)

- 18 per cent of the answers were related to hard factors (i.e. lack of time and money).

More or less the same numbers were found for the question 'What are the factors that promote the implementation of HRM?':

- 78 per cent of the answers were related to soft factors (i.e. improved communications, creation of a sense of urgency)

- seven answers were related to hard factors.

Research on HRM system impact on performance outcomes within schools is increasingly on the research agenda. In a recent study, Bednall et al. (2014) investigated the effects of perceptions of performance appraisal quality and HRM system strength on three informal learning activities: reflection on daily activities, knowledge sharing with colleagues and innovative behaviour, in six Dutch vocational and further educational training establishments. Using a sample of 238 employees from 54 work teams, performance appraisal quality was found to be positively associated with increased participation in each activity over time, and HRM system strength augmented these relationships. Moreover, participation in informal learning activities was positively related to organisational performance.

Benitez et al. (2016) performed a comparison on 16 regional universities across two regions of Spain. The higher education policies were found to have been interpreted and adopted in different ways across the two regions, leading to one more traditional and one more transformational approach to HRM in the higher educational sector, resulting in different priorities. This is an important finding as it demonstrates that even with policies and regulations, the public sector has flexibility; however the room for interpretation and more piecemeal approach to policy results in a reduction in consistency. This is exacerbated compared to the private sector where senior leadership teams oversee and report to an overarching hierarchy despite regional distribution.

POLICE

Employee protection is of paramount importance for those with responsibility for HRM within the police force, due to the physically demanding and unsafe nature of the job.

The perceived benefit of doing the job must be inherent in all HRM practices, ensuring that employees remain committed and do not feel disillusioned with their job. Employee commitment is vital in ensuring that performance remains high (Metcalfe and Dick, 2000). Personnel practices and limitations in management have been found to seriously affect commitment in the police, as has gender. Links between SHRM and organisational commitment within the context of the police have also been found (Dick and Metcalfe, 2001). The police force has previously attracted certain types of people to join, and in recent years the effort has been made to ensure that the police force is as inclusive and diverse as possible. This ensures that all individuals remain closely identified with the police but allows the option for diverse approaches to situations and individuals.

Talent management must be effectively managed so that strengths are identified through appraisals and developed. The crime control performance of US municipal police officers is significantly affected by the job task description, and by participation in a variety of tasks (Hur, 2007). Moreover, Hur (2007) indicates that there is constant pressure on state police departments to prove that their cities are safer than others, impacting on the department strategy in order to justify spending and budget.

VOLUNTARY AND CHARITY ORGANISATIONS

The not-for-profit sector includes charities and voluntary organisations working either to provide free services or to raise money for particular causes. There has been a considerable influence on the voluntary sector from the government, leading to an increase in performance-oriented HR practices, communication and involvement schemes and welfare-oriented practices (Kelliher and Parry, 2011). This mirrors the public sector move from simplistic and traditional HRM practices to an HRM approach mirroring that of the private sector (Mullins, 1999). This is due to a more businesslike approach and the influence of HRM practice standards.

A recent report, examining 71 third-sector organisations (including 62,000 employees and 107,000 volunteers), found that the sector has been experiencing a 'vibrant' phase in terms of the recruitment of new staff, with significantly more job opportunities existing across the charity sector in 2014 than has been the case in the preceding years. Because most of the vacancies for the sector are in London and the South East, turnover is a challenge, averaging 22 per cent. The survey also found that absence levels tended to be higher in the voluntary sector than the overall UK average, with employees taking an average of 8.4 sick days, costing employers around £622 per employee. This was also an increase relative to 2013, when sick pay cost third sector employers £587 per person, per year. Investment in learning in third sector employers increased slightly, with a median spending rise of £20 per person per year to £344. This was still lower than the average UK L&D spending figure of £513, however; suggesting that the sector may be more reliant on employees learning informally, on the job, rather than experiencing paid training that diverts resources from the disadvantaged groups whose needs they exist to serve.

Hence, retention and extrinsic motivation are as important in the not-for-profit as in other sectors. These organisations operate on the lowest overheads that they can, and cannot afford absences or potential wasted training. HRM practices must focus on these aspects of employee well-being and build extrinsic as well as intrinsic motivation (Deci et al., 1999). One might reasonably expect that intrinsic motivation (derived from qualities inherent in the job) would be higher for this in comparison with other organisational types. Indeed Miao et al. (2013) found that intrinsic motivators and social rewards had a strong relationship with organisational commitment in the public sector in China, when compared to extrinsic rewards.

Although, as the above sections show, the public sector is by no means a homogeneous group, there are areas of commonality that enable points of comparison across the sector.

HRM IN PRACTICE

Safety training in the public sector

Following an increase in health and safety compensation claims in the public sector workplace, and managers accepting that it is nearly impossible to train all staff in all required health and safety information, Simon Lowe has produced a special report for publicservice.co.uk identifying a need for change in training within the public sector. Lowe ascertains that there are a number of issues related to health and safety training, including identifying which levels of training are required by different employees, and ensuring that the e-training that is available is suitable for these levels. There are many associated issues in providing only e-training for staff and these include the lack of face-to-face observation by trainers as to whether a member of staff has engaged with the training as well as being able to observe the training being put into practice. Lowe suggests a blended approach to health and safety training which incorporates e-training.

Source: Simon Lowe (30 May 2013) *Special report: E-training vital for the public sector.* http://handsam.co.uk/public-service-article-e-training-vital-for-the-public-sector/

NEGOTIATING THE POLITICAL AND ECONOMIC ENVIRONMENT

A complex and dynamic external context characterises the public and third sectors. Tensions surround the need to demonstrate value for money while at the same time offering a high quality provision to meet the expectations of service users. The issue is compounded by the fluctuating priorities of those resourcing the public sector, where one initiative sometimes follows another in close succession. Sometimes organisations on the receiving end experience a sense of powerlessness and 'change fatigue' (schools are often cited as an example), while at other times public sector entities are seen as bureaucratic and lacking capability to change. The British NHS, for example, has been criticised for its lack of responsiveness to local need.

Such pressures present challenges for those with HRM responsibility. On the one hand, there may be requirements to cut costs by employing fewer staff or even making redundancies. On the other hand, HRM specialists must build on the expectations of staff (and service users) that are likely to envisage a high-quality provision that is objectively distributed in line with need rather than ability to pay. Because the political and economic landscape is changeable, developing a clear vision to bring together employees and focus on a future that reconciles such tensions may be problematic.

Boosting HR performance in the public sector

- Read the policy report from the CIPD on personnel management in the Irish public sector: www.cipd.co.uk/publicpolicy/policy-reports/boosting-hr-performance-irish-public-sector.aspx

- TASK: Consider the approach you might take as an HR manager in a large multinational manufacturing firm in the private sector if tasked with making large budget cuts and improvements. Using the report above, identify which aspects you would need to keep the same and with which you would have to take a different course of action due to the context.

Those with responsibility for HRM within this dynamic landscape also have to deal with the different contractual arrangements that are a feature of services where state and private sectors operate in tandem. In the UK, the outsourcing and contracting out of ancillary services has become widespread to curb costs and/or to offer better quality customer provision (Broaden et al., 2008). Here HR specialists need to consider a number of factors, such as pay (see Chapter 10) and other terms and conditions of employment, as well as performance measures and maintaining a constructive line of communication with outsourcers. Such arrangements work well where HR specialists offer long-term and repeat contacts, with regular meetings between managers and partners, and demonstrate joint commitment to embedding good employment practice (Broaden et al., 2008).

DEBATING HRM

Public sector pressure

The 2015 Autumn Statement from the Conservative government indicated that there could be at least 100,000 jobs cut in the public sector during the course of the coming parliament. This means that public sector employees will comprise less than 17.2 per cent of the workforce and the Civil Service is its smallest since the Second World War. (Read in full at www.cipd.co.uk/pm/peoplemanagement/b/weblog/archive/2015/11/27/large-scale-job-losses-in-public-sector-still-to-come-warn-employment-experts.aspx)

TASK: In groups, discuss what your priorities would be in a local authority HRM position. How would you address the demands for higher performance while also juggling the cuts in jobs, pay rises and budget?

Insights elsewhere suggest that the high-performing public sector entities (e.g. a cadre of UK hospitals) have management teams with vibrant external networks (Mannion et al., 2005). Engaging externally is likely to be important for other public sector organisations outside healthcare. HRM professionals and implementers (e.g. line managers) who forge allegiances with other providers, support groups and policy bodies are likely not just to keep abreast of developments in the political and economic landscape but also to influence these groups. This external orientation may enable public sector entities to achieve the change orientation typical of high-performing private sector organisations (Shipton et al., 2012).

The political nature of the environment within the public sector influences how the organisation aligns itself and adapts to the political landscape. The effect on an organisation mirrors the changes in the external environment that private sector organisations must deal with. A key difference is that it is the external environment that is likely to change and enforce a change in private sector organisations. The public sector is influenced more by the electorate's voting patterns and governmental transition. Incumbent governmental changes impact on the appointed professionals and advisors at a national and local level as parties gain or lose power depending on the outcome of elections. In turn this influences which initiatives are prioritised and how budget is allocated to new or existing projects.

Recent cuts to public sector budgets and UK government policies of reform to the NHS (despite a no-change manifesto) have had a significant impact on HR strategy direction. The political climate can change drastically, and a skill of HRM in the public sector is to predict and plan for this change and to be ready for it to happen quickly.

Some examples from the Middle East and the Republic of Georgia public sectors offer excellent illustrations of the extent to which political climate can influence HR policy and practice. Iles et al. (2012) present a cohesive representation of the influences affecting HRM in the Middle East: strong culture, religion and influence held by connections ('*wasta*'/'*piston*') have a huge impact on how HRM is conducted, coupled with global and international politics. Iles et al. (2012) argue that the intense conflicts of influence create an absence of fair, equal and overall policies for dealing with staff. This presents challenges for HRM.

In the public sector HRM is not yet an equal business partner and the key role that HRM has to play in achieving organisational objectives has not yet been accepted. HR professionals do not yet have a strong identity in the Middle East (Iles et al., 2012) and workforce diversity and inclusivity are a challenge (for more information see Chapter 8). The role politics plays in HRM policies is also found in the Republic of Georgia (Common, 2011), where administrative system politics were found to act as a barrier to HRM-based reform.

ONLINE STUDY TOOLS

Writing an essay? Expand your knowledge

Purohit and Verma (2013) provide a fascinating study of Human Resource Development in government health centres in India.

https://edge.sagepub.com/crawshaw2e > **Student Resources** > **Chapter 14** > **Journal Articles**

ACHIEVING STRATEGIC INTEGRATION

The challenge to achieve a strategic profile facing those with responsibility for HRM is well documented (see Shipton and Davis [2008] for a review). In the public sector, there are particular barriers to overcome. HR specialists must deal with powerful interest groups (i.e. clinicians in healthcare organisations, teachers within schools); they are also faced with what some have described as institutional isomorphism – a phenomenon that occurs when one particular organisation becomes a leader in the market and other organisations in the competing field seek to adopt a similarity of structure and processes in order to mimic similar success (DiMaggio, 1998; DiMaggio and Powell, 1983). This factor both limits and constrains the variety of strategic options available. In the UK and Ireland, HR policy is determined at national level. Public sector organisations have little say over whether or not a particular initiative should be employed. In the UK, whether or not there is a staff appraisal scheme and opportunities for staff involvement are taken into account by auditors when assessing the performance of healthcare trusts.

> **Institutional isomorphism**
> The phenomenon that occurs when one particular organisation becomes a leader in the market and other organisations in the competing field seek to adopt a similarity of structure and processes in order to mimic similar success (DiMaggio and Powell, 1983). This becomes an entrenched way of doing things.

The provision for financial reward is closely prescribed within the public sector in the UK and Ireland. In the People's Republic of China, public sector organisations were once wholly owned by the central state, have now been made public and are governed by both local and central government structures. In 2011, profits of 43 per cent were made in state-owned organisations. This has an impact on the historical organisational culture and mirrors the findings discussed above for the UK and Ireland.

Paauwe and Boselie (2003) suggested that public sector employees have certain expectations of the opportunities they will be offered and the career aspirations that they will achieve. This so-called normative institutionalism makes it problematic for HR professionals to offer an employment package that makes their organisation

> **Normative institutionalism**
> Sees actors within the organisation utilising learned social norms and behaviours in order to guide their behaviour and actions (March, 1994). Processes, practices and policies are similar to those in other organisations, making it difficult to stand out.

stand out as an employer of choice – many others will have in place the same processes and practices.

In China, there is still tremendous respect for the role of civil servant; employees in the civil service are expected to work hard in return for a perceived higher-than-average salary (Han et al., 2013), despite HR managers in the civil service attempting to introduce electronic HRM practices in line with private sector organisations. By offering an employment package that helps their institution to be more prominent and that aims to rival private sector organisations, public sector organisations can meet the work-related expectations of a similar group of professionals (Paauwe and Boselie, 2003).

In Western contexts, European-level stipulations surrounding pay and collective bargaining, procedures for dealing with disputes, unfair dismissal, working time and many other factors shape the variety and scope of HR initiatives that can be implemented. Public sector organisations are expected to be exemplars of good practice in these areas. This could suppress novel and innovative practices that may have served as devices for those with HRM responsibility in their quest to attract and retain the best talent. In the Eastern context, the public sector is held in high regard and is therefore also considered as setting an exemplar as an employer.

Nonetheless, there is scope for those with responsibility for HRM to enhance their strategic profile. Research suggests that line managers frequently experience stress and confusion when they are made responsible for HR matters (McConville, 2006). Basing her findings on qualitative evidence derived from middle line managers in NHS hospital trusts, McConville found that taking responsibility for HR exacerbated the tensions in their roles. The managers felt ill-equipped to deal with many of the issues with which they were presented, and unsure of where to go for support. Studies in a healthcare context have found that HR initiatives (i.e. performance management, training and development) have a stronger resonance when they are embraced by line managers (Currie and Procter, 2001). HR may achieve strategic integration where a strong supportive profile exists for HR managers working with their line colleagues, communicating where priorities lie and emphasising the relationship between individual and organisational capability (Purcell et al., 2003).

Another factor concerns the skills and knowledge of the HR specialists. Truss et al. (2002) compared and contrasted the activities of HR specialists in two case study organisations. In the first, a healthcare trust, HR had gradually achieved a degree of ascendancy over the eight-year period of the study, and was felt to be playing a valuable role driving through change. One line manager stated that HR policies 'are the strongest and probably the most pertinent and up-to-date' of any encountered elsewhere; another that 'I feel that they are in touch with the direction of the trust, especially the director of HR'. In the second organisation, a financial services operation, the converse was the case. HR appeared to have become more 'transactional' in orientation, engaging in reactive 'fire-fighting' tactics in order to respond to the requirements of internal customers.

Conclusions suggest that in both cases there were constraining factors that could potentially have inhibited HR strategic integration and are relevant for each of the national contexts considered here. Both organisations were part of much larger operations with clear HR strategic agendas stipulated elsewhere (by national or international bodies), and both had to deal with some lack of understanding from line managers about the HR role and contribution. Two factors seemed to distinguish the strategic from the transactional HR function. In the NHS trust, there was an expectation among all stakeholders that HR strategy laid down at national level would be interpreted and communicated by the HR team at local level. The HR team was therefore seen as part of the decision-making process, although it was frequently following instructions for implementing national-level initiatives. In the financial services operation, head office seemed to dominate the HR agenda, leaving more ad hoc, transactional arrangements to the local HR team. Although this variable was (arguably) outside the control of the HR departments examined, a second factor may be more salient. The HR director in the NHS trust worked to increase the visibility and credibility of the department. Choosing to focus on high-profile interventions enabled her department to play a long-term, strategic role. This did not appear to be replicated in the financial services operation. From the evidence it was concluded that HR's perceived poor performance on lower level, administrative tasks in this organisation was an inhibitor for greater 'strategic' involvement.

In a study of 137 large manufacturing firms from both the Indian public and private sectors, the perceived gap between HR practices in the two sectors was found to be not significant, although there were a number of similarities and differences reported (Budhwar and Boyne, 2004). It was found that the private sector firms had adopted a more rational strategy for HR policies in a range of areas including training and development and compensation, compared to public sector organisations. This indicates that there is freedom for Indian public sector organisations to engage in less rational and more innovative, flexible HR strategies.

The idea that organisations operating in the public sector have a choice, like any other, to develop a strategic role for HR is to some extent borne out by Valverde et al. (2006), who investigated the extent to which HRM roles vary across sectors. In their survey of 230 Spanish organisations (employing fewer than 200 employees), they identified seven 'agency mix' statistical models. One model featured HR taking full responsibility for HR activity along a continuum; another saw HR working in conjunction with line managers; and another modelled situations where HR activity is totally outsourced. The authors' hypothesis that the agency mix model would vary depending upon sector, size, employee characteristics and a variety of other factors was unsupported. They concluded that HR activity mix may be more a matter of corporate choice than a factor of contextual variables.

DEVELOPING A SERVICE ORIENTATION

Evidence demonstrates a growing interest in how the public sector organisations profiled here are recognising and responding to the needs of service users. The Care

Quality Commission in the UK runs an annual patient survey which captures, among other factors, the extent to which employees put patient needs first. Furthermore, in the UK, the 'Annual Health Check' attaches sizeable weighting to perceptions of service users and their families, which alongside clinical and financial factors are taken into account in determining the relative performance of UK healthcare provision. In the Netherlands, within the last two years a nationally sponsored Centre for Consumer Experience has evolved to capture patient experiences on healthcare issues and measure experiences in a systematic and reliable way. The so-called Consumer Quality Index offers insight into patient priorities in healthcare as well as experiences of patients and their families. Ireland has four regional health forums, established in 2006, with a brief to focus on patient perceptions of care, and a system to respond appropriately to customer complaints by overseeing procedures and following up on unresolved issues.

There is growing interest in the HRM literature outside the public sector in the implications of developing a service user orientation. Batt (2002) showed, in a study focusing on the financial services industry, that HR practices influenced performance outcomes (measured in productivity and profitability terms) to the extent that such practices created a climate which put the customer first. In a series of studies, Schneider (2008) demonstrated that there was a positive and significant relationship between customer and employee satisfaction, as well as organisational performance for the companies analysed. Mannion et al. (2005) compared UK and Canadian hospitals and found that those judged most successful (in the eyes of external auditors) were clear about their strategic priorities and had developed a culture to reinforce the focus that they had identified. Those with responsibility for HRM would have a role in creating a collective consensus around key strategic goals, that is, putting the patient first (see also Shipton et al., 2008).

There are three factors to consider as those with responsibility for HRM develop a culture or climate to reinforce a 'service user' orientation:

1 Well-articulated HR strategy conveys the envisaged sense of direction linked with service user satisfaction. In reference to a UK hospital trust that scaled rankings in preceding years, Broaden et al. (2008) reported that its HR role was 'to ensure that our patients receive the best care that our workforce can provide and they don't feel let down by the service we provide'.

2 HR practitioners could focus on communication and training to reinforce the messages they have identified. This might involve coaching staff to offer support in day-to-day interaction with patients, or offering training to help recognise how to sustain a service user orientation.

3 Another role would be in performance management and appraisal. Working with line managers, this involves setting targets aligned with strategic objectives, measuring performance and offering appropriate reward and recognition.

GRADUATE INSIGHTS

HR in a city council

Leon Neil (MSc) graduated from Aston Business School in 2010 obtaining an MSc in Work Psychology and Business. Leon worked as an HR advisor in the HR department at a Central London (UK) council for three years. City councils are responsible for providing a large range of services to residents, businesses, visitors and service users within their area. Services range from culture and entertainment to essential community services (e.g. housing, education, welfare, environmental services). These services are maintained through public funds, so council activities are accountable to central and local government whose duty it is to appropriately allocate the use of funds raised from the UK taxpayer. Local and central government policies and directives determine how public funding is allocated and used, and also influence the direction of councils' priorities.

Author: In your time at XCC, what have you found the key challenges faced by HRM in the public sector to be?

Leon: A continual challenge for councils is the need to adapt to a changing political landscape. This could be at a national level (changes in central government policy), or at a local level (changes to the political party majority within local constituencies). Often it involves both. As councils are run by their elected councillors, their wishes can directly affect how services are run and which services or projects are prioritised. HR plays a fundamental part in enabling organisations to achieve their objectives through their workforce, so HR must continually adapt to changing requirements to ensure that council objectives can be delivered to the expectations of the voting public.

Author: What impact have you seen of this political influence on HRM?

Leon: Councils tend to be quite hierarchical with several levels of seniority. Typical impacts can include extended times for decisions to be taken – for a project to be initiated, they often require support and agreement of team leaders, department heads or higher, depending on project scope and significance on the prevailing political agenda. This can be magnified particularly around election times when it is not necessarily known which political party will win the majority. As different parties have different priorities, this can have direct impact on delivery and future of existing projects and planned ones.

Author: Have you seen the recent efficiency savings and 'frugal' approaches have an impact on HRM?

Leon: Arguably the greatest challenge over the last five years has been the current financial climate, which has made huge demands on organisation efficiency in service delivery and delivering significant savings. HR functions are playing a critical role in supporting organisations to deliver these efficiencies. The most direct impacts within HR are likely in organisational change (restructuring teams, departments and services to increase efficiency and deliver savings to the taxpayer), as well as recruitment (meeting the challenge of bringing new expertise in under significant budget restrictions and conditions such as pay or recruitment freezes imposed by the government). Much of my work involved recruitment, organisational change and redeployment of employees who were at risk of redundancy as a result of their departments undergoing restructures. I observed recruitment trends within the public sector shift towards favouring fixed-term assignments over permanent roles. My own role was a series of fixed-term assignments, lasting a few months at a time. Organisational change projects often lead to redundancies, and significant efforts were

(Continued)

(Continued)

made to avoid redundancies through redeploying as many people as possible. In reality there were increasingly fewer roles available – a situation mirrored in councils and organisations across the country. It is worth noting that HR can be pivotal in devising and implementing effective and innovative ways forward for organisations during such difficult times. A key concern is how to implement efficiencies whilst managing the fears and expectations of the workforce – particularly during times where job security is probably lower amongst staff at all levels.

Author: When reflecting on what you learned about HRM on your MSc course, what would you advise a current student?

Leon: The course gave a good grounding in the types of things you can expect to see, hear or encounter within an organisation, that is, potential structures, policies and procedures. It also familiarised me with the concept and some proposed methods of best practice. What the course can't effectively give you is the feeling of actually being involved in implementing or designing these. Nor can it provide a live-action perspective as, in practice, organisations exist in various states of transition; either of leadership, structure or process. It will be down to the individual to take the initiative to add value and deliver best practice solutions tailored to the unique situations that they will encounter and be required to navigate as an HR practitioner.

HRM IN PRACTICE

Stress management among NHS staff

Recently, the UK Health Minister, Dr Dan Poulter, has announced the expansion of the 'Schwartz Centre Rounds' scheme aimed at encouraging a culture of compassionate patient care among NHS staff. This comes in light of one or two very high-profile cases of poor patient care in NHS trusts around the UK. Over the next two years, £650,000 of additional funding is being released to the Point of Care Foundation (PCF) to extend this culture change programme.

The scheme, pioneered originally in the USA, provides NHS staff with the opportunity, through monthly get togethers, to communicate and reflect upon the day-to-day problems and stresses they face while caring for patients. The sessions are currently run by 15 NHS trusts, and employees who have used them have reported a number of benefits, including (1) better communication with patients and colleagues, (2) more support and less isolation, (3) a better ability to cope with the emotional pressures of work, and finally (4) a better understanding of how their colleagues think.

(Read more about the evaluation of the UK pilot rounds at www.kingsfund.org.uk/sites/files/kf/field/field_publication_file/schwartz-center-rounds-pilot-evaluation-jun11.pdf; and read more about the stress levels within the UK NHS at www.publicworld.org/blog/time_to_insist_nhs_employers_talk_about_staff_stress)

MEETING EMPLOYEE EXPECTATIONS

Employee expectations shape the psychological contract, determining how the employment relationship unfolds and the extent of commitment that employees exhibit (Rousseau, 2004). Public sector employees are a heterogeneous group, with each group, from senior service providers to administrative assistants, likely to have a different set of expectations about what work can deliver and the contribution they can offer.

There may be some points of commonality. Public sector organisations are 'professional' organisations characterised by high levels of professional autonomy (Buchanan et al., 2007). Employees here feel strong loyalty to professional standards and clients rather than to the employing organisation, and are correspondingly disenchanted with initiatives perceived to dilute the service quality they are able to offer to the end-user. Managers in HR and elsewhere must persuade and influence professionals to gain their commitment to policy initiatives rather than acting arbitrarily (Buchanan et al., 2007).

Motivating in difficult times

- Read the following articles: www.bbc.co.uk/news/uk-politics-32694166 and www.theguardian.com/uk/2010/may/16/civilian-staff-outnumber-police-officers
- TASKS:

  1 As an HR manager, how might you motivate your staff in light of this announcement, and what other HR practices may you wish to consider revising?

  2 Consider the impact the issues in these articles may present for teamwork, well-being and morale. Are there any other areas you may expect to see an effect?

  3 Discuss the initiatives that you would put in place to tackle these areas, and how feasible these would be with budgetary constraints and efficiency targets.

CONCLUSION

Public sector organisations frequently exist in a state of flux, while funding providers, politicians, policy bodies and stakeholders try to maximise the influence they have over scarce resources. Issues of professional identity and the role of service and specialist staff are fundamental to many dilemmas facing HR and other managers. These are common to each sector considered here. There are also substantial differences, most notably in the extent to which decision making is decentralised as opposed to closely prescribed, and in overall funding for the provision of service. According to our analysis, turnover and retention of key front-line workers – those delivering services and care – vary considerably across the types of public sector entities, as do arrangements for involving staff in decision making and implementing high-performance work systems.

There are challenges for those with responsibility for HRM in the public sector. Perhaps three stand out. First, to engage with the fluctuating external context, those managing HRM in public sector organisations need to develop networks externally. They can both bring in knowledge to influence strategic decision making in their organisations and exert an influence on policy formulation. Second, such expert people managers must recognise and understand the perspectives of two key

Front-line workers Employees working on the interface of the workforce, dealing directly with customers or service users. For example, in the NHS front-line workers would be nurses and consultants.

stakeholders: service users and employees. This will facilitate the development of a customer-focused orientation, leading to staff who are committed to putting client needs first and who appreciate the value of mechanisms intended to heighten organisational capability in this area. Finally, those with responsibility for HRM in a public sector must strive to demonstrate their strategic contribution, perhaps more than most. In a Western European setting, institutional isomorphism combined with the hegemony of knowledge workers and clinicians underscores the importance for HR professionals of being proactive in developing HR strategy in line with the goals of the organisation and actively marketing what they are able to deliver. Evidence suggests that effective HRM has the potential to address the fundamental dichotomy of public sector service provision and offer a high-quality service, while at the same time maximising the value that is delivered.

CASE STUDY

HRM in Indonesia's public sector

Culturally, Indonesia is a nation with a large power distance, highly collectivist orientation, slightly weak uncertainty avoidance, and slightly feminine dominance (Hofstede and Hofstede, 2005). After over 300 years of colonisation, the country now has political and economic freedom and has increasingly adopted international concepts of HRM, ranging from attracting (recruiting) through to terminating (pension), in all sectors. Generally, HRM practices within Indonesian organisations lead to employee development by using basic principles along five dimensions: emphasis on people; participative leadership; innovative work styles; strong client orientation; and a mindset that seeks optimum performance (Wright and Rudolph, 1994). It has been argued that national culture influences career development and compensation, while organisational culture influences staffing and participative management (Suharnomo, 2009). There are enormous variations across the public and private sectors in the extent to which HRM is adopted, embraced and implemented. This case gives a flavour of overall trends.

Traditionally, the recruitment process in the Indonesian public sector has been internally focused, using within-company channels (i.e. word-of-mouth recommendations) and not especially demanding selection tests. As a consequence, there are now many employees who are less capable of dealing with demands for continuous improvement. Furthermore, in developing skills and capabilities, public sector organisations have often provided training that is based on *tenure*, not the specific skills needed. Consequently, the professionalism and capabilities of employees in doing the tasks have not been improved as much as they could have. Bennington and Habir (2003) reported that training in the Indonesian public sector is more likely to be a means for additional income and securing 'moonlighting' opportunities, that is, taking on additional jobs. These are two key areas for improvement in HRM practice (in some but by no means all public sector organisations).

Generally, performance management is taken seriously. Every year employees have an appraisal from their supervisor about their performance, including loyalty, work achievement, responsibility, fidelity, honesty, cooperation, initiative and leadership (Rohdewohld, 1995), a process known as 'DP3'. The criteria for each element consist of five grades: very good (91–100), good (76–90), average (61–75), below average (51–60) and fair (under 50) (National Civil Service Agency website, 2007). Most public sector organisations implement a three-way leadership relationship structure involving a leader (*pimpinan*), the assistant to the leader (*wakil pimpinan*) and the implementer (*pelaksana*). The line of command corresponds closely to the Western concept of the line of responsibility, with the subordinate being responsible to the superior officer who is responsible for the junior (Freeman, 1993).

HRM in the public sector experienced a turning point after the economic, social and political crisis at the end of the 1990s. Strategically, HRM has been influenced by national political reform, which strengthened local government and emphasised local over national culture (Hartono, 2010). Simultaneously, the government has become more active in regulating HRM and in issuing laws and governmental protocols to guide practice. Coupled with the emergence of the so-called 'grand design' of bureaucracy reform 2010–25, there is now a clear strategic framework for HRM in public sector institutions in Indonesia (Sekretariat Wakil Presiden Republik Indonesia, 2012). Thus, there are changes in the implementation of HR practices from recruitment to retirement. HR practices have become more transparent and accountable. Recruitment is more objective and focused on quality of character and capability. Some public sector institutions such as banks and hospitals have used employee assessment to map needs like improving skills and competencies. Employees have more opportunities to get training and education to improve their skills and capability, based on need assessment and performance appraisal. Performance appraisal has adopted Key Performance Indicators (KPIs) and balanced the scorecard in some public institutions.

Moreover, 16 agencies have obtained new performance allowances based on the promise of future reform in order to achieve several aims: realising an administration that is free from corruption, collusion and nepotism, improving public service quality and improving capacity and accountability or bureaucracy performance (KemenPAN and RB website, www.menpan.go.id).

Overall, Indonesian public sector organisations have gradually improved the quality of HRM, moving from simple to complex HR practices in response to national and international influences and pressures. There are still weaknesses in some areas (balancing supply and demand, managing performance, demonstrating a clear contribution to the nation, managing corruption and so forth). Recently, shifting political parameters have further influenced HRM, emphasising the roles of leadership, commitment and organisational culture. To realise its vision of excellent public sector performance, Indonesia needs strong leadership, commitment from employees and an appropriate organisational culture. HRM therefore has a vital role to play.

(Continued)

(Continued)

(With special thanks and acknowledgements to Indrayanti, lecturer and researcher at the Faculty of Psychology, Gadjah Mada University, Indonesia and doctoral student at the Nottingham Business School, Nottingham Trent University, Nottingham, UK.)

CASE STUDY QUESTIONS

1 Consider the reasons for the assertion that 'national culture influences career development and compensation, organisational culture influences staffing and participative management' (Suharnomo, 2009). How might you attempt to harness these influences as an HRM practitioner in Indonesia?

2 Can you see any key differences between the Indonesian examples outlined here and the approach to HRM within a different country of your choice?

3 In the last few sentences, the case study outlines the key areas and weaknesses that need to be realised and addressed in order to deliver the desire for excellent public sector performance. Consider the HRM strategies, policies and practices which would need to be put in place in order to achieve the desired result.

CHAPTER SUMMARY

The chapter has identified the following key points:

- The not-for-profit sectors encompass many different types of organisation (public, voluntary and third sector); however, collectively they differ from the private sector as they exist for reasons other than profit making. There are differences between the private and public sectors – categorised by the values and structures, decision makers, stakeholder diversity and access by the public.

- Although some HR practices are performed by both public and private sector organisations, more public sector organisations have been found to engage in high-commitment HR approaches, perhaps due to a more favourable context.

- HRM must work alongside a changeable external environment. This is true across international boundaries, and an area of interest is the ways in which different countries' political regimes affect public sector HRM practices.

- We must consider the different types of services and organisations that make up the public sector and not-for-profit sectors – each with their own impacts and challenges for HRM to negotiate.

- The complex economic and political environment is characteristic of the public sector, with tight budgets and political pressures. HRM must be aware of and understand the environment and also reflect and manage the issues within the HRM approach.

- Public sector organisations in any of the national contexts profiled may make choices about how to organise the HR function, which may, in turn, influence the extent of strategic integration.

- There are barriers within the public sector to overcome before achieving strategic integration of HRM; these are particularly found in organisational cultures, staff expectations and political pressures.

- To achieve a service user orientation and satisfaction there are three factors that those with HRM responsibility must consider: a well-articulated HR strategy; a focus on communication and training; and performance management and appraisal.

- The 'professional' perceptions of public sector workers give rise to staff portraying greater loyalty to professional standards and clients than to the employer, and showing disenchantment with initiatives that detract from this. As a successful employer in the public sector, HR managers must be mindful of the intrinsic rewards staff receive, and protect them.

REVIEW QUESTIONS AND EXERCISES

1. One of the challenges facing those responsible for HRM in the public sector is to achieve strategic integration, that is, implement HR practices to achieve outcomes that are strategically valuable for the organisation. To what extent does adopting the 'employee champion' role described above enable or impede this outcome?

2. What do you think employees expect of HR professionals? Is there a difference in employee perceptions in the public relative to the private sector?

3. HRM is defined in its broadest sense, throughout this chapter, as a set of best practice indicators that together engage employees and enhance performance outcomes. What do you think might be the role of:

   i. the HRM specialist, and

   ii. the line manager in actually implementing these practices?

   Is there a difference in the HR role for public versus private sector?

4. A strategic approach to HRM in the public sector is one of the most important issues to address and is vital to organisational performance in the sector. Giving justification, how far do you agree with this statement? Would you feel the same if the statement were about the voluntary/third sector?

5. In order to properly implement a strategic HRM approach, one of the first stages is to scan the environment. Research and identify some salient contemporary environmental and contextual factors affecting SHRM in the public sector; also consider the ways to manage for them. Do this for a UK context and an international country of your choice.

6. Discuss the ways in which internal and external factors can affect recruitment, HR planning, job analysis and selection processes in a public sector organisation.

7. You are an HRM practitioner responsible for adopting and implementing the latest strategies. In this role you must consider all of the different aspects of HRM. Carry out the following task, imagining that you are working in (a) a local government office in India, (b) a healthcare authority in the UK and (c) the head office for an international charity.

    i.   Consider the general policies that you would expect to find in the organisation.

    ii. The incumbent political parties change in the country. How might this affect your policies?

    iii. Budget and funding is cut as a result of the political change. Identify the priority areas and the areas that could be subject to change.

    iv. Downsizing and redundancies become a necessity. Create a plan to reduce the cost of staffing but also to ensure you do not lose good staff. Could pay cuts be implemented? Which staff members should be made redundant first? How might you ensure job security and motivation in those remaining?

EXPLORE FURTHER

Burke, R.J., Noblet, A.J. and Cooper, C.L. (eds) (2013) *Human Resource Management in the Public Sector.* Cheltenham: Edward Elgar. An excellent edited collection of papers discussing various issues/aspects of HRM in the public sector.

Gatenby, M., Rees, C., Truss, C., Alfes, K. and Soane, E. (2015) Managing change, or changing managers? The role of middle managers in UK public service reform. *Public Management Review*, 17(8): 1124–1145. Explores the role of line managers during change and reform of the UK public sector.

Kinemo, S., Ndikumana, E., Kiyabo, H., Shillingi, V., Kwayu, M.D. and Andrea, P.T. (2015) Human resource management in a decentralized context: Case of Dodoma Municipal and Chamwino District Councils. Available at SSRN 2564984. A research report exploring the impact of reforms in Tanzania, particularly focusing on the positive and negative impacts that HRM decentralisation has had in this international contextual setting.

Paauwe, J. and Boselie, P. (2003) Challenging 'strategic' human resource management and the relevance of institutional setting. *Human Resource Management Journal*, 13(3): 56–70. An important piece of work exploring the links between strategic HRM and institutional context.

www.publicsectorexecutive.com/ Excellent source of information on news, change and management in the public sector.

GO ONLINE

Visit the companion website for **interactive quizzes**, explanatory **videos** and **podcasts**, **journal articles** to use in your essays, and **weblinks** to useful resources.

https://edge.sagepub.com/crawshaw2e

GLOSSARY OF TERMS

Adverse impact A potential outcome of a selection process in which a minority social group is disadvantaged compared to the majority group. Most commonly assessed through the comparison of selection ratios between social groups.

AMO model This approach argues that organisational performance is best served by employees who have the ability to do the work, possessing the necessary skills and knowledge, who are motivated to work appropriately, and who have the opportunity to arrange their skills in doing their work.

Appraisee The individual whose performance is being evaluated.

Appraiser The individual charged with evaluating or assessing another individual's performance.

ASA model A model that describes the creation and maintenance of organisational culture through the cycle of attraction, selection and attrition (leaving the organisation).

Assessment centres A series of assessment methods spread over one or a number of days, designed to assess candidates many times on many traits at once.

Behavioural change Transformation and/or modification of an individual's routine, habits and ways of working.

Behaviours The specific actions of an individual geared towards achievement of specified objectives, e.g. quantity of work, and quality of work.

Black box The unknown mechanism that is supposed to explain the influence of HR practices on business performance.

Broaden-and-build theory The broaden-and-build theory suggests that positive emotions broaden an individual's awareness and encourage novel, varied and exploratory thoughts and actions.

Business ethics The study of the moral challenges, dilemmas and responsibilities of business organisations, and their potential evaluation of, and responses to, these challenges.

Business plan This involves the organisation's plan of future strategy. The plan generally sets out the future strategy and financial development of a business, usually covering a period of several years. It includes a formal statement of a set of business goals as well as the rationale for making them achievable. The plan will map out the route and risks for reaching those goals. It may also contain background information about the organisation and who is involved in implementing the business plan.

Central tendency error Often, supervisors take the easy way out by rating their subordinates around the middle of a scale. This helps them avoid explaining extreme ratings to the organisation.

Change agent   A person who indirectly or directly initiates change and assists others in understanding and implementing changes. Change agents are often referred to as catalysts for change.

Change content   Content of the change effort refers to the type of change implemented.

Change context   The external and internal circumstances in which change occurs.

Change process   The way in which a specific change is implemented.

Change vision   Describes the desired future state after the changes have been implemented and thus provides direction throughout the change process.

Closed shop   When employees had to join a trade union if they joined a certain profession. This is no longer lawful.

Coaching   Is usually a one-on-one intervention between the employee (coachee) and the coach (peer, manager or external practitioner) that involves a set of techniques (questioning, active listening, reflection, goal setting and feedback) with the intention to help the former achieve a personal, professional or performance-related goal that is specific and time-bound (Nyfoudi, 2016).

Coefficient   A number between 0 and 1 used as a measure of the reliability or validity of a selection method. The closer to 1 a coefficient is, the higher the reliability or validity.

Collective bargaining   A process of discussion and negotiation which takes place between an employer and a recognised trade union.

Common method bias   The methodological problem arising from the fact that in surveys exploring the HR–performance relationship single respondents provide the measures of both HR practices and performance.

Comparative HRM   Focuses specifically on the way that people work and explores the differences between nations in the way organisations manage their human resource processes.

Compensation   'All forms of financial returns and tangible services and benefits employees receive as part of an employment relationship' (Milkovich et al., 2011: 10).

Competency   A class of behaviour that is specific, measureable, observable and related to performance in a job.

Configurational model of HRM   An approach that suggests higher business performance is predicted by specific combinations or bundles of HR practices that best reflect the specific organisational context.

Consolidation of change   To strengthen and continuously reinforce the desired changes and provide a supportive organisational context.

Contingency model of HRM   A view arguing that the organisation is developing a range of HR practices that fit the organisation's strategies outside the area of HRM in order to improve performance.

Corporate social responsibility (CSR)   Refers to the responsibility of organisations for their impact upon society – both locally and globally.

Cross-cultural management   Is rooted in the ideology that every nation has its unique sets of deep-lying values and beliefs, and that these are reflected in the ways societies operate and in the ways that the economy operates and people work and are managed at work.

Department for Business, Innovation and Skills (BIS)   The department for economic growth in the UK. The department invests in skills and education to promote trade, boost innovation and help people to start and grow a business. BIS also protects consumers and reduces the impact of regulation.

Development   Refers to the acquisition or improvement of a portfolio of knowledge, skills or attitudes in a specific area of interest. It 'involves preparing someone to be something' (Matthews et al., 2004: 93).

Discrimination   Workplace discrimination can be overt or hidden and subtle but manifests itself when one social category is given preferable treatment, and/or another is disadvantaged, in relation to access to jobs, promotion, training or better terms and conditions in employment (formal) or is subjected to verbal and non-verbal behaviours limiting the respect, credibility and psychological well-being of individuals (informal discrimination).

Distributive justice   Refers to the fairness of outcomes one receives from one's employer.

Diversity   Used to refer to social categories such as gender, ethnicity, age, disability, religion and sexual orientation, which indicate groups who have been historically subjected to discrimination in society and work. Other dimensions such as social class and work or management status are often included when referring to diversity within organisational life. Diversity is, thus, generally applied to recognising group differences and seeks to move beyond traditional characterisations of difference.

Diversity management (DM)   Generally refers to the business need for more diverse workforces to compete in new global labour and consumer markets. Inherently linked to the business case and liberal approach to equality, most DM approaches are grounded in the economic imperative to increase the diversity of employees within organisations.

Education   A formal procedure led by one or more instructors with the purpose to achieve learning in one or more areas of interest.

eHR   Any HR activities that are carried out via, or utilise, electronic systems, i.e. web-based systems.

Employee involvement   The joint activity of the employer and individual employees in developing business initiatives.

Employee value proposition 'The collective array of programs that an organization offers in exchange for employment ... encompassing every aspect of the employment experience – from the organization's mission and values; to jobs, culture and colleagues; to the full portfolio of total rewards programs' (Towers-Watson, 2012: 24).

Employment Tribunal A court that hears disputes relating to employment issues.

Equifinality The principle arguing that there may be many combinations of HR practices that result in identical organisational outcomes.

Environmental sustainability Meeting the needs of the present without compromising the ability of future generations to meet their own needs.

Equal opportunity (EO) The term predates diversity management and is based on the principle of treating all people the same and not discriminating against people on the basis of particular characteristics, such as gender, race, ethnicity, sexual orientation, disability and age. In Western society EO approaches have become enshrined in employment law and reflected in policies of employment to prevent discrimination within the workforce.

ET1 The form used to bring a claim to the Employment Tribunal.

ET3 The form used to respond to a claim made to the Employment Tribunal.

Ethics in business Principles and standards that guide behaviour in the world of business (Ferrell et al., 2008).

Ethnocentric approach An approach taken when strategic decisions are made at headquarters and key positions in both the domestic and foreign operations of an MNE are mainly filled by personnel from the parent country (i.e. by PCNs), with zero or very limited autonomy delegated to the foreign subsidiaries; an MNE is said to be following an ethnocentric approach.

European Commission The executive body of the European Union, which initiates action in the EU and mediates between member governments.

European Union An economic and political union established in 1993 after the ratification of the Maastricht Treaty by members of the European Community. The establishment of the European Union expanded the political scope of its predecessor, the European Economic Community, and set the foundations for the creation of a Central European Bank and the adoption of a common currency, the euro.

European Works Council A consultation body that has to be set up following a valid request from employees when there are at least 1000 employees in the EU and at least 150 employees in at least two member states.

Expatriates Groups of managers/experts who are sent to local units to disseminate corporate strategy and culture and to transfer competence across borders.

External reasons for change Reasons for change that can be found outside of the organisation's boundaries and are usually situated within the macro-environment.

Extrinsic rewards   Rewards which are tangible, external transactional rewards for undertaking work. Typically these rewards are financial or confer financial benefit, and are under the control of an 'other'.

Feedback   The process by which individuals are informed of the degree to which they are meeting desired or expected levels of performance.

First-order change   Organisational adaptations or variations made within an existing system without changing the system itself (incremental change).

Fit   The extent to which a person perceives that they fit with their job, work environment, career or organisation.

Force field analysis   Provides an environmental scanning tool that answers the question whether or not organisational change is necessary by comparing driving and hindering forces for change.

Forced distribution method   A performance evaluation system whereby appraisers are allowed to rate no more than a certain percentage of appraisees at the higher end of the scale (usually 10–15 per cent), and must place a similar number (also 10–15 per cent) at the lower end of the scale, with the remaining 70–80 per cent rated at the middle of the rating scale.

Front-line workers   Employees working on the interface of the workforce dealing directly with customers or service users. For example, in the NHS front-line workers would be nurses and consultants.

General causal model   The model that explains the HRM–performance relationship, whereby the precise mediating mechanisms through which HR practices influence business performance are indicated.

Geocentric approach   Within a geocentric approach the MNE thinks more globally in terms of its operations, recognising that each part (subsidiaries and headquarters) makes a unique contribution with its unique competence. Nationality is ignored in favour of ability and all the aspects of business are integrated into one.

Global diversity management strategy   A global diversity strategy in MNCs is centrally controlled by the head office and can be equally adopted across all subsidiaries; alternatively, the policies and practices are adapted to different national contexts within which the organisation operates.

Goal setting   The process of assigning work tasks to individuals so that they are clear on what is expected of them. To be effective, the goals should be specific, measurable, attainable, realistic and time-bound.

Guiding coalition   A group of individuals who can actively guide the change and function as a team (also referred to as change team).

Hard HRM   Those HR policies and practices that enable the close control and coordination of employees – viewing employees as an organisational resource to be effectively utilised.

High-commitment work practices   Those policies and practices designed and implemented by organisations in order to elicit the affective commitment and engagement of some or all of their employees.

High-performance work systems (HPWS)   An approach to organisational design and management which aligns the organisation with the environmental context as well as the systems, structures and processes. The approach seeks to achieve organisational effectiveness and high levels of performance.

Horizon planning   Horizon planning is not just about looking within the organisation to understand the workforce skills and abilities, it is also about looking externally at the situational context to understand what trends are on the horizon. These can be a range of trends such as demographic, economic and political trends. Most government organisations provide information on workforce trends on websites that are used by horizon planners.

Horizontal fit   The horizontal strategic alignment of the learning and development discipline with the other HR areas. Thus, an L&D manager needs to ensure that an employee is provided with training that corresponds to weaknesses traced in the performance appraisal.

Host country nationals (HCNs)   Employees whose nationality is the same as that of the local subsidiary.

HR business partnering   HR business partners are key (potentially senior) HR professionals who are embedded within the various functions/departments within the organisation so that they may work closely with managers to influence, direct and implement business strategy.

HR centres of excellence   The core functional areas of HR practices and expertise, e.g. careers, reward, learning and development, talent management and engagement.

HR information systems   The technologies used to design, deliver and support one's HR strategies, policies and practices.

HR outsourcing   The use of a third party (organisation) to deliver all or part of the HR function and its services.

HR self-service systems   The devolvement or decentralisation of the HR function in order to empower or enable individual employees to access relevant HR services directly.

HR shared service   HR shared service centres often take the form of a call centre that is commonly geographically separate from the main organisation and its subsidiaries. The services they provide often (but not solely) focus on administrative activities associated with payroll, recruitment, the upkeep of personnel records and training procurement.

HR systems   Multiple conceptualisations of HR systems proliferate in the literature. An HR system refers to a high level of analysis and reflects a programme of many HR policies (delivered by a set of practices) that are espoused to be internally consistent and reinforcing in order to achieve certain overarching results.

HRM content   The individual HR policies and practices that make up an HRM system.

HRM process   The method by which HR policies and practices are communicated to employees.

Human capital   This approach advocates that when opportunities for any particular group to develop and progress are obstructed, the result will be the sub-optimal use of human resources. Adopting a resource-based view of the firm, the management of diversity is not concerned with inequality but with optimising the resource value of each employee.

Human resource development (HRD)   'The study and practice of increasing the learning capacity of individuals, groups, collectives and organizations through the development and application of learning based intervention for the purpose of optimizing human and organizational growth and effectiveness' (Chalofsky, 1992: 179).

Human resource management (HRM)   The organisational function that deals with issues related to its workforce. HRM may also be seen as a particular 'perspective' on people management – one that emphasises a strategic and integrated approach.

Human rights   Many ethical issues in HRM relate to issues of human rights. These include: freedom from discrimination, privacy, due process, participation and association, healthy and safe working conditions, fair wages, freedom of conscience and speech, work and dignity at work.

Idiosyncratic rating tendencies   Biases in perception that give rise to variation in assessors' subjective ratings of candidates. Examples of idiosyncratic rating tendencies are the halo effect, the similarity effect and the beautyism effect.

Inclusion   A state of being valued, respected and supported. It emphasises the respect of every employee's identity, ensuring that the right conditions are in place for each person to achieve their potential. Inclusion should be reflected in an organisation's culture, practices and relationships that are in place to support a diverse workforce.

Institutional isomorphism   The phenomenon that occurs when one particular organisation becomes a leader in the market and other organisations in the competing field seek to adopt similarity of structure and processes in order to mimic similar success (DiMaggio and Powell, 1983). This becomes an entrenched way of doing things.

Institutionalisation of change   The anchoring of changes in the organisational culture to avoid falling back on old routines and habits.

Integration approach   A theoretical framework whereby HRM strategy formulation focuses on the alignment of HR policies and practices with other business strategic objectives.

Interactional justice   Refers to the fairness of one's interactions with the decision maker – often one's direct line manager.

Internal reasons for change Organisational alterations in technology, primary task, people and administrative structures.

International HRM Focuses on the way in which organisations manage their people resources across different dimensions of national contexts, but typically within the same firm.

Intersectionality The study of overlapping or intersecting social identities and related systems of oppression, domination, or discrimination. The theory examines how social and cultural categories such as gender, race, class, ability, sexual orientation, religion, caste, age, nationality and other identities interact on multiple and often simultaneous levels, resulting in specific experiences of discrimination.

Intrinsic rewards Intangible rewards derived from work and employment, which contribute towards feelings of competence, relatedness and autonomy.

Job analysis A systematic process designed to determine what a job role involves and what makes for an effective worker in that role. It produces either a job description (work-oriented job analysis) or a person specification (worker-oriented analysis).

Job assignment The process of matching individuals' competencies with job requirements, so as to achieve the best fit.

Job evaluation A systematic process for defining the relative worth or size of jobs within an organisation in order to establish internal relativities and provide the basis for an equitable grading structure.

Kotter's eight-step change model Change model that describes eight stages of change a company must successfully complete to achieve sustainable change and business improvements.

KSAOs The knowledge, skills, abilities and other attributes/characteristics that make a worker effective in a particular role.

Learning A 'self-initiated, personal and intentional' process (Roberson, 2005: 29) that involves a change in cognition, action or interaction with others. This change may concern an individual's acquisition of a specific type of knowledge, skill or attitude.

Learning and development (L&D) A function that contributes to the attainment of strategic organisational objectives, providing the mechanisms for knowledge creation and exchange. L&D has been recognised as one of the core HR functions.

Lewin's change model A change model that describes a three-stage process of 'unfreezing', 'changing' and 'refreezing'.

Liberal approach to equal opportunity This approach suggests that equality of opportunities exists when individuals are enabled to freely compete for social rewards. Therefore the role of the policy maker is merely that of the referee, required to ensure that the rules of competition are not discriminatory and are fairly applied for all. The function of EO/DM policies is to devise fair procedures, avoiding direct and indirect discrimination.

Maastricht Treaty 1992   A European treaty setting out the right to enjoy basic rights in areas such as employment, education and housing.

Manpower planning   A centralised, number-crunching type of process that predicts the number and types of staff skills required for current and future organisational needs. The process was discredited in the 1980s for not predicting the economic downturn.

Mentoring   Involves a one-to-one relationship; yet it focuses more on the individual and on issues wider than those concerning the job role, such as the employee's personal development and career aspirations.

Motivation   A psychological drive to behave in a particular fashion, driven to achieve certain outcomes that are expected to fulfil certain needs.

Multinational diversity management strategy   Refers to an approach where policies and practices are developed by each national context (e.g. in each subsidiary) by local professionals with consideration for the national culture(s) and how these are shaped by political, social, historical, legal and religious norms.

Multinational enterprise (MNE)   MNEs or multinational corporations (MNCs) are those companies that are registered in more than one country and are involved in trade of products or services in various countries.

Multisource feedback   Involves collecting information about an individual's performance from several sources, such as the employee's supervisor, peers, subordinates, clients and/or customers.

NESTA   The National Endowment for Science, Technology and the Arts is an independent charity that works to increase the innovation capacity of the UK by providing investments and grants and mobilising research, networks and skills.

Neuroplasticity   Refers to the fact that our adult brain is constantly changing and generates new pathways and new neurons.

New Pay   Identifying pay practices that enhance the organisation's strategic effectiveness. Typified by a strategic, flexible approach, incorporating payment for performance within a unitarist frame of reference.

Normative institutionalism   Sees actors within the organisation utilising learned social norms and behaviours in order to guide their behaviour and actions (March, 1994). Processes, practices and policies are similar to those in other organisations, making it difficult to stand out.

Not-for-profit sector   A term that describes the different types of organisations which operate with objectives that go beyond achieving market advantage and profit. This includes the public and third sectors.

Organisational change   The process by which organisations transform their present state to some desired future state.

Organisational culture   A set of shared organisational beliefs and values, indicating what is important on the one hand, and practices and norms that express how one is supposed to react or behave on the other hand.

Organisational justice   The psychological concept of fairness as perceived by the employee.

Parent country nationals (PCNs)   Employees whose nationality is the same as that of the headquarters of the multinational firm.

Pay freeze   A decision not to increase pay at the annual review time.

Performance appraisal   The process of evaluating an individual's past performance for a specific period, usually one year.

Performance manag After ement   The process by which organisations ensure that employees are working towards achieving a company's strategic objectives. This includes job assignment, goal setting, coaching, feedback, rewards/punishments and performance appraisal.

Performance outcomes   The final and overall evaluation of the degree to which an employee has achieved specific targets set for him or her.

Performance standards   Specific performance expectations and levels against which an employee's performance will be judged – thus, it should be clear to the employee what level(s) of performance would be deemed unacceptable, acceptable and surpassing expectations.

PESTEL   The common acronym used for the political, economic, social, technological, environmental and legal factors that may influence strategy and affect the performance of an organisation.

Pluralistic   A perspective on the employment relationship that recognises the multiple (and often competing) goals of different stakeholders.

Polycentric approach   An approach adopted when an MNE treats each subsidiary as a distinct national entity. Typically, the host country operation will be allowed more decision-making autonomy, and will be staffed primarily by host country nationals (HCNs).

Positive action   An approach to increasing the representation of a particular group in an organisation that includes encouraging applications from members of this group and advertising in places that target this group. Distinct from positive discrimination.

Positive discrimination   The intentional treatment of a disadvantaged group in a more favourable way than other social groups, such as through use of quota systems.

Predictive validity   A form of criterion-related validity that measures the extent to which a selection method can accurately predict some important criterion in the future (most commonly future job performance) based on assessment scores in the present.

Private sector   Organisations privately owned which operate in order to achieve competitive advantage or earn profit through either selling products, manufacturing, or providing a service and hospitality.

Proactive change   Organisations are faced with driving forces that are foreseen in the future and thus haven't yet impacted organisational performance.

Procedural justice   Refers to the organisational procedures and processes followed to make decisions on reward or resource allocation.

Psychological contract   The unwritten expectations regarding terms and conditions of an exchange agreement between an employee and the employer.

Psychometrics   Standardised tests used in selection to measure hidden attributes of a candidate. Subdivided into ability tests and personality questionnaires.

Public sector   Organisations operating in order to provide a public or community-based service, funded by the taxpayer and under government jurisdiction. Organisations in the UK include the National Health Service, emergency services and the education system.

Radical approach to equal opportunity   The radical approach significantly differs from the liberal view in that it is more proactive in seeking intervention on workplace practices on the basis of moral value and social worthiness. The radical approach is concerned with the outcome of the contest and the distribution of rewards.

Reactive change   Organisations are faced with driving forces that exert so much pressure that change becomes obligatory.

Recency error   In many organisations, especially ones that have annual appraisal cycles, individuals have been known to change their behaviour (working harder and making sure that their supervisor knows of their achievements) a month or two before the appraisal is due. Since supervisors cannot possibly remember what a subordinate has done for the past 12 months, they tend to use the new (recent) information in making their evaluations.

Recognition process   A formal process of agreeing a relationship between a trade union and an employer.

Recruitment   The process of attracting people to join an organisation.

Regiocentric approach   Refers to a geographical strategy and structure that are based within a particular geographical region of the world.

Reliability   A measure of how accurate an assessment method is.

Repatriation   The process of reintegrating an employee into their home country organisation after a period of assignment in a foreign country.

Resistance to change   The refusal to accept or comply with organisational change.

Resource-based view   A theoretical framework whereby HRM influences performance according to the human capital held by the organisation.

Reward strategy   The alignment of the reward policies and practices with the business and human resource strategies of the organisation, its culture and its environment, providing a set of goals and declaration of intent as to what the organisation wants to reward, and how critical reward issues will be addressed. A pathway linking the needs of the business and the staff with reward policies and practices in the organisation.

Reward system   The policies, practices, processes, procedures and structures that govern rewards in an organisation. The approach taken by the organisation to fulfil its reward strategy.

Scenario planning   Encourages staff to think outside the box and conceptualise a 'what if' situation. It is used by some organisations to analyse future situations. It can be a valuable and complementary process to workforce planning. For example, staff might be considered to think about how an organisation might survive if there were serious behavioural problems in the workforce that impacted on their core service or product delivery. Scenario planning also enables the managers to visualise the impact of an ageing workforce, consider succession planning and balance skill levels to address potential skills gaps.

Second-order change   A change which breaks with the past basic assumptions and transforms fundamental characteristics and attributes of the organisation (discontinuous change).

See–feel–change   Individual change only appears if individuals first see and visualise the need for change (see), then understand and care about the change (feel), which finally leads to a change in behaviour.

Selection   The process of assessing people to determine their suitability to join an organisation.

Self-directed learning (SDL)   Highlights individuals' responsibility for their own learning and promotes the transfer of learning.

Service user orientation   The orientation of a system of management practices to ensure that the end-user is the focus and their satisfaction is the ultimate objective.

Severity/leniency error(s)   Some supervisors believe that they need to project an image of being tough/easy, so they rate subordinates lower/higher than their performance objectively deserves.

Situational judgement tests (SJTs)   Standardised tests used to assess a candidate's judgement in workplace situations based on hypothetical scenarios. Used to predict future behaviour or assess job knowledge.

Small and medium sized enterprises (SMEs)   Under the EC definition, SMEs are firms with fewer than 250 employees, a turnover of less than or equal to €50 million and a balance sheet total of less than or equal to €43 million.

Smart rewards   An approach to reward strategy based on the firm's core values, evidence-based decisions on reward effectiveness and engaging and communicating with employees in the design and operation of the strategy.

Social categories   Generally refers to gender, race or ethnicity, age, sexual orientation, religion, physical and mental ability. Categorisation, while it can be useful in understanding the specific needs of social groups, can also lead to the formation of stereotypes, as individuals are often perceived to belong to only one category rather than allowing for category fluidity, and to possess all the characteristics of that category.

Social justice   Located within the humanistic view of HRM, the social justice approach views diversity management from a moral and ethical perspective and focuses on the processes that determine injustice. A social justice approach seeks to address inequalities by promoting the understanding and integration of social differences. The emphasis is therefore on the promotion of equality as a social duty for the employer rather than as an economic imperative.

Soft HRM   Those HR policies and practices that aim to elicit the affective (emotional) commitment of employees to the organisation and its goals.

Stakeholder   People, bodies and institutions with a legitimate stake in the organisation.

Strategic HRM   The processes that link HRM policies and practices with the strategic objectives of the organisation in order to improve performance.

Strategic management   Denotes a pattern of managerial decisions and actions undertaken by senior managers in order to improve performance in an organisation.

Strategic workforce planning   The term is used in conjunction with workforce planning and workforce intelligence planning, and more commonly used in the USA and Europe. It signifies an HR system designed to have the right people in the right place at the right time, with the right behaviours (and at the right cost).

Supply and demand   In general this means the capacity supply of the workforce and demands placed upon the workforce. Various modelling techniques are used. For example, the Centre for Workforce Intelligence generates forecasts by considering factors affecting supply. To look at the supply of doctors to the specialist register this would include the number of doctors in training, future healthcare requirements, international recruitment and young leavers. This supply forecast represents all doctors eligible for entry to the specialist register, but does not mean that all these doctors will be employed. The supply forecast can then be compared with the Centre's view of workforce demand, which is the required workforce that the NHS can afford. Workforce demand is often confused with workforce need, which is the required workforce without any financial constraints to deliver the service.

Sustainability   The capacity for continuance into the long-term future, living within the constraints and limits of the biophysical world. Sustainable development is the *process* by which we move towards sustainability (Porritt, 2007).

Synergy   The concept explaining that the combined performance of a set of HR policies and practices is greater than the sum of their individual performances.

Talent management   The identification of either key positions or high-potential individuals with the intention of managing individuals into positions that contribute to the strategic goals of the organisation.

Tenure   The length of time a position has been held.

Third country nationals (TCNs)   Employees whose nationality is neither that of the headquarters nor of the local subsidiary – that is, a third separate country.

Third sector   The sector of organisations operating not-for-profit, with no government funding, for charitable reasons; they include the charity and voluntary sectors.

Total reward   All of the tools available to the employer that may be used to attract, motivate and retain employees. Total rewards include everything the employee perceives to be of value resulting from the employment relationship.

Training   May be defined as *'planned instruction'* (Armstrong, 2012: 296) with the purpose of achieving learning in order to improve performance (see Chapter 2) or satisfy development needs.

Trait   An individual's distinguishing characteristic, such as sensitivity or conscientiousness.

Transnational corporation (TNC)   This is an organisational form that is characterised by an interdependence of resources and responsibilities across all business units regardless of the organisation's national boundaries.

Unconscious bias   The associations we hold about people from different social categories, which exist outside our conscious awareness and have a significant influence on our attitudes and behaviour. In organisational diversity terms it is considered of particular relevance in recruitment and selection and performance appraisal, as unconscious bias means assessors can automatically respond positively or negatively to people irrespective of merit.

Unitaristic   A perspective on the employment relationship that assumes the commitment to a single set of (organisational) goals by all stakeholders.

Unit labour cost (ULC)   The average cost of labour per unit of output.

Universalistic or best practice model of HRM   An approach arguing that the organisation is developing a range of interconnected and mutually reinforcing HR practices that will always produce superior results whatever the accompanying circumstances.

Validity   A measure of the degree to which an assessment method measures what it is supposed to measure.

Values (individual and organisational)   Values have been defined as ideas or cognitions present in every group or society about desirable end states (Rokeach, 1973) and play an important role in driving individual behaviour within and outside the workplace (Schwartz, 1999).

Vertical fit   Through a strategic needs assessment, the objectives of the L&D division are specified and linked with business strategy.

Workforce agility   This is the organisation's human resource responsiveness that would allow it to deal with organisational change and adapt quickly to internal and external opportunities and challenges.

Workforce intelligence planning   'Workforce intelligence planning is all about matching need with the right number of employees with the right knowledge, skills and behaviours in the right place at the right time' (Department of Health, 2012).

Workforce plan   In general, workforce plans are designed for short term (one year) medium term (three years) and long term (five years plus). However, the more uncertain the situation, the more likely is the time plan to be shorter. It is also worthwhile being cautious for optimising such plans in organisations where planning can be regarded as continuously changing due to contextually specific external factors.

Workforce planning   'A core process of human resource management that is shaped by the organisational strategy and ensures the right number of people with the right skills in the right place at the right time to deliver short and long term organisation objectives' (Baron et al., 2010: 4). It can be described as 'an organisational attempt to estimate the demand for labour and evaluate the size, nature and sources of supply which will be required to meet that demand'.

REFERENCES

CHAPTER 1

Belcourt, M. (2006) Outsourcing – The benefits and the risks. *Human Resource Management Review*, 16: 269–279.

Blyton, P. and Turnbull (eds) (1992) *Reassessing Human Resource Management*. London: Sage.

Bowen, D.E., Galang, C. and Pillai, R. (2002) The role of human resource management: An exploratory study of cross-country variance. *Human Resource Management*, 41(1): 103–122.

Bramham, J. (1987) Manpower planning. *Personnel Management Handbook*. Aldershot: Gower.

Budhwar, P.S. (2000) Evaluating levels of strategic integration and devolvement of human resource management in the UK. *Personnel Review*, 29(2): 141–161.

Budhwar, P.S. (2012) Management of human resources in foreign firms operating in India: The role of HR in country-specific headquarters. *The International Journal of Human Resource Management*, 23(12): 2514–2531.

Burke, R. and Ng, E. (2006) The changing nature of work and organizations: Implications for human resource management. *Human Resource Management Review*, 16: 86–94.

Caldwell, R. (2003) The changing roles of personnel managers: Old ambiguities, new uncertainties. *Journal of Management Studies*, 40(4): 983–1004.

Caldwell, R. (2004) Rhetoric, facts and self-fulfilling prophecies: Exploring practitioners' perceptions of progress in implementing HRM. *Industrial Relations Journal*, 35(3): 196–215.

Caldwell, R. (2008) HR business partner competency models: Re-contextualising effectiveness. *Human Resource Management Journal*, 18(3): 275–294.

Caldwell, R. and Storey, J. (2007) The HR function: Integration or fragmentation, in J. Storey (ed.) *Human Resource Management: A Critical Text*, 3rd edn. London: Thomson Learning, pp. 21–38.

CIPD (2007) *Survey Report: The Changing HR Function*. London: Chartered Institute of Personnel and Development.

CIPD (2010) *Next Generation HR Asia*. Research Report. Accessed online at: www.cipd. co.uk/binaries/hr-strategies-for-growth-in-asia_2012-overview.pdf (accessed 16 April 2016).

CIPD (2011) *HR Outsourcing Factsheet*. London: Chartered Institute of Personnel and Development.

CIPD (2012a) *Absence Management Annual Survey Report*. London: Chartered Institute of Personnel and Development.

CIPD (2012b) *HR Business Partnering Factsheet.* London: Chartered Institute of Personnel and Development.

CIPD (2012c) *HR Shared Service Centres Factsheet.* London: Chartered Institute of Personnel and Development.

Coda, R., César, A.M.R.V.C., Bido, D. de S. and Louffat, E. (2009) Strategic HR? A study of the perceived role of HRM departments in Brazil and Peru. *Brazilian Administration Review*, 6(1): 15–33.

Connor, J. (2011) Eastern time. *People Management*, 27 January: 22–25.

Cooke, F.L. (2006) Modeling an HR shared services centre: Experience of an MNC in the United Kingdom. *Human Resource Management*, 45(2): 211–227.

Cooke, F.L., Shen, J. and McBride, A. (2005) Outsourcing HR as a competitive strategy? A literature review and an assessment of implications. *Human Resource Management*, 44(4): 413–432.

Elkington, J. (1999) *Cannibals with Forks: The Triple Bottom Line of 21st Century Business.* Oxford: Capstone Publishing.

Freitas, W.R. de S., Jabbour, C.J.C. and Santos, F.C.A. (2011) Continuing the evolution: Towards sustainable HRM and sustainable organizations. *Business Strategy Series*, 12(5): 226–234.

Gillan, A. (2005) Work until you drop: How the long-hours culture is killing us. *The Guardian*, 20 August.

Gratton, L. (2011) Workplace 2025 – What will it look like? *Organizational Dynamics*, 40: 246–254.

Greenwood, M.R. (2002) Ethics and HRM: A review and conceptual analysis. *Journal of Business Ethics*, 36: 261–278.

Gurchiek, K. (2005) Record growth in outsourcing of HR functions. *HR Magazine*, 50(6): 35–36.

Kaufman, B.E. (2014) The historical development of American HRM broadly viewed. *Human Resource Management Review*, 24(3): 196–218.

Keenoy, T. (1990) Human resource management: A case of wolf in sheep's clothing. *Personnel Review*, 19(2): 3–9.

Lai, Y., Saridakis, G., Blackburn, R. and Johnstone, S. (2016) Are the HR responses of small firms different from large firms in times of recession? *Journal of Business Venturing*, 31(1): 113–131.

Larsen, H.H. and Brewster, C. (2003) Line management responsibility for HRM: What is happening in Europe? *Employee Relations*, 25(3): 228–244.

Lawler III, E.E. (2011) Creating a new employment deal: Total rewards and the new workforce. *Organizational Dynamics*, 40: 302–309.

Lawler III, E.E. and Mohrman, S. (2003) HR as a strategic partner: What does it take to make it happen? *Human Resource Planning*, 26(3): 15–30.

Legge, K. (2005) *Human Resource Management: Rhetorics and Realities*, anniversary edn. Basingstoke: Palgrave Macmillan.

Leiserson, W. (1929) Contributions of personnel management to improved labor conditions. *Wertheim Lectures on Industrial Relations*. Cambridge, MA: Harvard University Press.

McGaughey, S.L. and De Cieri, H. (1999) Reassessment of convergence and divergence dynamics: Implications for international HRM. *The International Journal for Human Resource Management*, 10: 235–250.

Maatman, M., Bondarouk, T. and Looise, J.K. (2010) Conceptualising the capabilities and value creation of HRM shared service models. *Human Resource Management Review*, 20: 327–339.

Malik, A. (2013) Post-GFC people management challenges: A study of India's information technology sector. *Asia Pacific Business Review*, 19(2): 230–246.

Mayrhofer, W., Brewster, C. and Morley, M. (2000) The concept of strategic European human resource management, in C. Brewster, W. Mayrhofer and M. Morley (eds) *New Challenges for European Human Resource Management*. London: Macmillan, pp. 3–34.

Parkes, C. and Davis, A.J. (2013) Ethics and social responsibility – do HR professionals have the 'courage to challenge' or are they set to be permanent 'bystanders?'. *The International Journal of Human Resource Management*, 24(12): 2411–2434.

Personnel Today (2008) *HR Self-Service Emerges as a Key Weapon in the War for Talent*. Accessed online at: www.personneltoday.com/articles (accessed 15 January 2013).

Pryor, M.G., Humphreys, J.H., Taneja, S. and Toombs, L.A. (2011) Where are the new organizational theories? Evolution, development and theoretical debate. *International Journal of Management*, 28(3): 959–978.

Renwick, D. (2000) HR-line work relations: A review, pilot case and research agenda. *Employee Relations*, 22(2): 179–205.

Renwick, D. (2003) Line manager involvement in HRM: An inside view. *Employee Relations*, 25(3): 262–280.

Sako, M. and Tierney, A. (2007) *The Future of HR: How Human Resource Outsourcing is Transforming the HR Function (Executive Briefing)*. London: AIM Research.

Sheehan, C., Holland, P. and De Cirei, H. (2006) Current developments in HRM in Australian organisations. *Asia Pacific Journal of Human Resources*, 44(2): 132–152.

Shen, J. (2011) Developing the concept of socially responsible international human resource management. *The International Journal of Human Resource Management*, 22(6): 1351–1363.

Sparrow, P. (2000) New employee behaviours, work designs and forms of work organization: What is in store for the future of work? *Journal of Managerial Psychology*, 15(3): 202–218.

Sparrow, P., Brewster, C. and Harris, H. (2004) *Globalizing Human Resource Management*. London: Routledge.

Sparrow, P., Schuler, R.S. and Budhwar, P. (2009) Editors' introduction: Developments in cross-cultural HRM, in P. Budhwar, R. Schuler and P. Sparrow (eds) *Major Works in International Human Resource Management – Volume 3.* London: Sage, pp. vii–xviii.

Srimannarayana, M. (2010) Human resource roles in India. *Indian Journal of Industrial Relations*, 46(1): 88–99.

Storey, J. (1989) Introduction: From personnel management to human resource management, in J. Storey (ed.) *New Perspectives on Human Resource Management.* London: Routledge, pp. 1–18.

Storey, J. (1992) *Developments in the Management of Human Resources.* London: Blackwell Business.

Storey, J. (2007) Human resource management today: An assessment, in J. Storey (ed.) *Human Resource Management: A Critical Text*, 3rd edn. London: Routledge, pp 3–19.

Taylor, F.W. (1911) *The Principles of Scientific Management.* New York: Harper & Brothers.

Truss, C., Gratton, L., Hope-Hailey, V., McGovern, P. and Stiles, P. (1997) Soft and hard models of human resource management: A reappraisal. *Journal of Management Studies*, 34(1): 53–73.

Ulrich, D. (1997a) A new mandate for human resources. *Harvard Business Review*, January–February: 124–134.

Ulrich, D. (1997b) *Human Resource Champions: The Next Agenda for Adding Value and Delivering Results.* Boston, MA: Harvard Business School Press.

Ulrich, D. and Brockbank, W. (2005) *The HR Value Proposition.* Boston, MA: Harvard University Press.

Weber, M. (2009 [1946]) Characteristics of bureaucracy, in *From Max Weber: Essays in Sociology.* London: Routledge, pp. 196–198.

Whittaker, S. and Marchington, M. (2003) Devolving HR responsibility to the line: Threat, opportunity or partnership? *Employee Relations*, 25(3): 245–261.

Wood, S. and De Menezes, L. (1998) High commitment management in the UK: Evidence from the Workplace Industrial Relations Survey and the Employers' Manpower and Skills Practices Survey. *Human Relations*, 51(4): 485–515.

Woods, D. (2010a) Gap between pay rises in retail and the general market shows no sign of closing. *HR Magazine*, 3 November.

Woods, D. (2010b) Technology: Employee self-service – can HR keep up with the pace of self-service technology? *HR Magazine*, 23 February.

Woods, S. and West, M. (2010) *The Psychology of Work and Organizations.* Andover: Cengage Learning EMEA.

Zhu, C.J., Cooper, B., De Cieri, H. and Dowling, P.J. (2005) A problematic transition to a strategic role: Human resource management in industrial enterprises in China. *The International Journal of Human Resource Management*, 16(4): 513–531.

CHAPTER 2

Anthony, W.P., Perrewe, P.L. and Kacmar, K.M. (1996) *Strategic Human Resource Management.* Fort Worth, TX: The Dryden Press.

Appelbaum, E., Bailey, T., Berg, P. and Kalleberg, A.L. (2000) *Manufacturing Advantage: Why High-Performance Work Systems Pay Off.* Ithaca, NY: Economic Policy Institute, Cornell University Press.

Armstrong, M. (2006) *A Handbook of Personnel Management Practice.* London: Kogan Page.

Armstrong, M. and Long, P. (1994) *The Reality of Strategic HRM.* London: Institute of Personnel Development.

Barney, J (1991) Firm resources and sustained competitive advantage. *Journal of Management*, 17(1): 99–120.

Becker, B.E., Huselid, M.A., Pickus, P.S. and Spratt, M.F. (1997) HR as a source of shareholder value: Research and recommendations. *Human Resource Management*, 36(1): 39–47.

Bednall, T.C., Sanders, K. and Runhaar, P. (2014) Stimulating informal learning activities through perceptions of performance appraisal quality and HRM system strength: A two-wave study. *Academy of Management Learning and Education*, 13(1): 45–61.

Bontis, N., Dragonetti, N.C., Jacobsen, K. and Roos, G. (1999) The knowledge toolbox: A review of the tools available to measure and manage intangible resources. *European Management Journal*, 17(4): 391–402.

Boselie, P., Dietz, G. and Boon, C. (2005) Commonalities and contradictions in HRM and performance research. *Human Resource Management Journal*, 15(3): 67–94.

Bowen, D.E. and Ostroff, C. (2004) Understanding HRM–firm performance linkages: The role of the 'strength' of the HRM system. *Academy of Management Review*, 29(2): 203–221.

Boxall, L. and Purcell, J. (2003) *Strategy and Human Resource Management.* London: Palgrave.

Brewster, C. (1994) Human resource management in Europe: Reflection of, or challenge to, the American concept?, in P. Kirkbride (ed.) *Human Resource Management in the New Europe: Perspectives on the 1990s.* London: Routledge, pp. 56–92.

Budhwar, P. and Sparrow, P.R. (1997) Evaluating levels of strategic integration and devolvement of human resource management in India. *The International Journal of Human Resource Management*, 8(4): 476–494.

Budhwar, P. and Sparrow, P. (2002) An integrative framework for determining cross-national human resource management practices. *Human Resource Management Review*, 12(3): 377–403.

Camps, J. and Luna-Arocas, R. (2012) A matter of learning: How human resources affect organizational performance. *British Journal of Management*, 23(1): 1–21.

Chowhan, J. (2016) Unpacking the black box: Understanding the relationship between strategy, HRM practices, innovation and organizational performance. *Human Resource Management Journal*, 26(2): 112–133.

Combs, J., Liu, Y., Hall, A. and Ketchen, D. (2006) How much do high-performance work practices matter? A meta-analysis of their effects on organizational performance. *Personnel Psychology*, 59(3): 501–528.

Conway, N. and Briner, R.B. (2005) *Understanding Psychological Contracts at Work.* Oxford: Oxford University Press.

Delery, J. and Doty, D.H. (1996) Modes of theorizing in strategic human resource management: Test of universalistic, contingency and configurational performance predictions. *Academy of Management Journal*, 39(4): 802–835.

Delmotte, J., De Winne, S. and Sels, L. (2012) Toward an assessment of perceived HRM system strength: Scale development and validation. *International Journal of Human Resource Management*, 23(7): 1481–1506.

Doty, D.H., Glick, W.H. and Huber, G.P. (1993) Fit, equifinality, and organizational effectiveness: A test of two configurational theories. *Academy of Management Journal*, 36(6): 1198–1250.

Frenkel, S.J. and Yu, C. (2011) Managing coworker assistance through organizational identification. *Human Performance,* 24(5): 387–404.

Frenkel, S.J., Li, M. and Restubog, S.L.D. (2012) Management, organizational justice and emotional exhaustion among Chinese migrant workers: Evidence from two manufacturing firms. *British Journal of Industrial Relations,* 50(1): 121–147.

Gerhart, B. (2005) Human resources and business performance: Findings, unanswered questions, and an alternative approach. *Management Revue*, 16(2): 174–185.

Gerhart, B. (2007) Modeling HRM and performance linkages, in P. Boxall, J. Purcell and P. Wright (eds) *The Oxford Handbook of Human Resource Management.* Oxford: Oxford University Press, pp. 552–580.

Gomez-Mejia, L.R., Balkin, D.B. and Cardy, R.L. (2004) *Managing Human Resources,* 4th edn. Upper Saddle River, NJ: Pearson Education.

Guest, D.E. (1997) Human resource management and performance: A review and research agenda. *The International Journal of Human Resource Management*, 8(3): 263–276.

Guest, D.E. (2011) Human resource management and performance: Still searching for some answers. *Human Resource Management Journal*, 21(1): 3–13.

Harter, J.K., Schmidt, F.L. and Hayes, T.L. (2002) Business–unit level relationship between employee satisfaction, employee engagement, and business outcomes: A meta-analysis. *Journal of Applied Psychology*, 87(2): 268–279.

Hawkins, P. and Shohet, R. (2004) *Supervision in the Helping Professions.* Milton Keynes: Open University Press.

Huselid, M.A (1995) The impact of human resource management practices on turnover productivity and corporate financial performance. *Academy of Management Journal*, 38(3): 635–672.

Jiang, K., Lepak, D.P., Hu, J. and Baer, J.C. (2012) How does human resource management influence organizational outcomes? A meta-analytic investigation of mediating mechanisms. *Academy of Management Journal*, 55(6): 1264–1294.

Katou, A.A. (2012a) Investigating reverse causality between human resource management policies and organizational performance in small firms. *Management Research Review*, 35(2): 134–156.

Katou, A.A. (2012b) Justice, trust, and employee reactions: An empirical examination of the HRM system. *Management Research Review*, 36(7): 674–699.

Katou, A.A. and Budhwar, P.S. (2006) Human resource management systems and organizational performance: A test of a mediating model in the Greek manufacturing context. *The International Journal of Human Resource Management*, 17(7): 1223–1253.

Katou, A.A. and Budhwar, P.S. (2010) Testing competing HRM–performance linkage models: Evidence from the Greek manufacturing sector. *European Journal of International Management*, 4(5): 464–487.

Katou, A.A., Budhwar, P.S. and Patel, C. (2014) Content vs. process in the HRM–performance relationship: An empirical examination. *Human Resource Management*, 53(4): 527–544.

Kinnie, N., Hutchinson, S., Purcell, J., Rayton, B. and Swart, J. (2005) Satisfaction with HR practices and commitment to the organisation: Why one size does not fit all. *Human Resource Management Journal*, 15(4): 9–29.

Lepak, D.P., Liao, H., Yunhyung, C. and Harden, E.E. (2006) A conceptual review of human resource management systems in strategic human resource management research. *Research in Personnel and Human Resources Management*, 25: 217–271.

Levering, R. and Erb, M. (2011) Emerging trends in people management. *Outlook: Swiss Business*, January/February: 30–33.

MacDuffie, J.P. (1995) Human resource bundles and manufacturing performance: Flexible production systems in the world auto industry. *Industrial Relations and Labour Review*, 48(2): 197–221.

Marchington, M. and Cox, A. (2007) Employee involvement and participation: Structures, processes and outcomes, in J. Storey (ed.) *Human Resource Management: A Critical Text*, 3rd edn. London: Thomson Learning, pp. 177–194.

Marchington, M. and Grugulis, I. (2000) Best practice human resource management: Perfect opportunity or dangerous illusion? *The International Journal of Human Resource Management*, 16(11): 1104–1124.

Neal, A., West, M.A. and Patterson, M.G. (2005) Do organizational climate and competitive strategy moderate the relationship between human resource management and productivity? *Journal of Management,* 31(4): 492–512.

Organ, D.W. (1988) *Organizational Citizenship Behaviour: The Good Soldier Syndrome.* Lexington, MA: Lexington Books.

Osterman, P. (1994) How common is workplace transformation and how can we explain who does it? *Industrial and Labour Relations Review,* 47(2): 173–188.

Ostroff, C. and Bowen, D.E. (2016) Reflections on the 2014 decade award: Is there strength in the construct of HR system strength? *Academy of Management Review,* 41(2): 196–214.

Paauwe, J. (2004) *HRM and Performance: Achieving Long Term Viability.* Oxford: Oxford University Press.

Paauwe, J. (2009) HRM and performance: achievements, methodological issues and prospects. *Journal of Management Studies,* 46(1): 129–142.

Paauwe, J. and Richardson, R. (1997) Introduction special issue on HRM and performance. *The International Journal of Human Resource Management,* 8(3): 257–262.

Pfeffer, J. (1994) *Competitive Advantage through People.* Boston, MA: Harvard Business School Press.

Phillips, J.J. (2007) *Measuring ROI in Human Resources.* Chelsea, AL: ROI Institute.

Pil, F.K. and MacDuffie, J.P. (1996) The adoption of high-involvement work practices. *Industrial Relations,* 35(3): 423–455.

Purcell, J. and Kinnie, N. (2007) Human resource management and business performance, in P. Boxall, J. Purcell and P. Wright (eds) *The Oxford Handbook of Human Resource Management.* Oxford: Oxford University Press, pp. 533–551.

Purcell, J., Kinnie, N., Hutchinson, S., Rayton, B. and Swart, J. (2003) *Understanding the People and Performance Link: Unlocking the Black Box.* London: CIPD.

Richardson, R. and Thompson, M. (1999) *The Impact of People Management Practices on Business Performance: A Literature Review.* London: Institute of Personnel Development.

Ribeiro, T.R., Coelho, J.P. and Gomes, J.F.S. (2011) HRM strength, situation strength and improvisation behavior. *Management Research,* 9(2): 118–136.

Robinson, S.L. and Rousseau, D.M. (1994) Violating the psychological contract: Not the exception but the norm. *Journal of Organizational Behavior,* 15(3): 245–259.

Rousseau, D.M. (1990) New hire perceptions of their own and their employer's obligations: A study of psychological contracts. *Journal of Organizational Behavior,* 16(11): 389–400.

Rousseau, D.M. (1995) *Psychological Contracts in Organizations: Understanding the Written and Unwritten Agreements.* London: Sage.

Rousseau, D.M. and Greller, M.M. (1994) Human resource practices: Administrative contract makers. *Human Resource Management,* 33(3): 385–401.

Sanders, K., Dorenbosch, L. and de Reuver, R. (2008) The impact of individual and shared employee perceptions of HRM on affective commitment: Considering climate strength. *Personnel Review,* 37(4): 412–425.

Schuler, R.S. (1989) Strategic human resource management. *Human Relations*, 42(2): 157–184.

Schuler, R.S. and Jackson, S.E. (1987) Organisational strategy and organisational level as determinants of human resource management practices. *Human Resource Planning*, 10(3): 125–141.

Stevens, J. (1998) *High-Performance Working is for Everyone*. London: Institute of Personnel Development.

Subramony, M. (2009) A meta-analytic investigation of the relationship between HRM bundles and firm performance. *Human Resource Management*, 48(5): 745–768.

Wood, S. (1996) High commitment management and organization in the UK. *The International Journal of Human Resource Management*, 7(1): 41–58.

Wood, S. (1999) Human resource management and performance. *International Journal of Management Reviews*, 1(4): 367–413.

Wright, P.M. and Gardner, T.M. (2003) The human resource-firm performance relationship: Methodological and theoretical challenges, in D. Holman, T.D. Wall, C.W. Clegg, P. Sparrow and A. Howard (eds) *The New Workplace: A Guide to the Human Impact of Modern Working Practices*. London: John Wiley, pp. 311–328.

Wright, P.M. and Snell, S.A. (1989) Towards an integrative view of strategic human resource management. *Human Resource Management Review*, 1(3): 203–225.

Wright, P.M., McMahan, G.C. and McWilliams, A. (1994) Human resources and sustained competitive advantage: A resource-based perspective. *The International Journal of Human Resource Management*, 5(2): 301–326.

CHAPTER 3

Aguilar, F.J. (1967) *Scanning the Business Environment*. New York: Macmillan.

Beer, M. (1980) *Organization Change and Development: A Systems View*. Santa Monica, CA: Goodyear Publishing Company.

Bem, D.J. (1967) Self-perception: An alternative interpretation of cognitive dissonance phenomena. *Psychological Review*, 74(3): 183–200.

Ben-Shahar, T. (2009) *The Pursuit of Perfect: How to Stop Chasing Perfection and Start Living a Richer, Happier Life*. New York: McGraw-Hill Professional.

Branden, N. (1995) *The Six Pillars of Self-Esteem*. New York: Bantam Dell.

Bruch, H. and Ghoshal, S. (2004) *A Bias for Action: How Effective Managers Harness their Willpower, Achieve Results, and Stop Wasting Time*. Boston, MA: Harvard Business Press.

Cha, S.E. and Edmondson, A.C. (2006) When values backfire: Leadership, attribution, and disenchantment in a values-driven organization. *The Leadership Quarterly*, 17(1): 57–78.

Davidson, R.J., Jackson, D.C. and Kalin, N.H. (2000) Emotion, plasticity, context, and regulation: Perspectives from affective neuroscience. *Psychological Bulletin*, 126(6): 890–909.

Forsyth, D.R. (2009) *Group Dynamics*, 5th edn. Belmont, CA: Cengage Learning.

Fredrickson, B. (2009) *Positivity: Ground-Breaking Research Reveals How to Embrace the Hidden Strength of Positive Emotions, Overcome Negativity, and Thrive*. New York: Crown Publishing.

Johnson, G., Scholes, K. and Whittington, R. (2008) *Exploring Corporate Strategy*, 8th edn. Harlow: Prentice-Hall.

Kotter, J. (1995) Leading change: Why transformation efforts fail. *Harvard Business Review*, 73(2): 59–67.

Kotter, J. (1996) *Leading Change*. Boston, MA: Harvard Business School Press.

Kotter, J. and Cohen, D.S. (2002) *The Heart of Change: Real-Life Stories of How People Change their Organizations*. Boston, MA: Harvard Business Press.

Kotter, J. and Schlesinger, L.A. (2008) Choosing strategies for change. *Harvard Business Review*, 86(7/8): 1–13.

Leavitt, H.J. (1964) Applied organizational change in industry: Structural, technical, and human approaches, in W.W. Cooper, H.J. Leavitt and M.W. Shelley (eds) *New Perspectives in Organizational Research*. Chichester: Wiley, pp. 55–71.

Lewin, K. (1951) *Field Theory in Social Science: Selected Theoretical Papers*. New York: Harper & Brothers.

McCosker, P. (2003) *EasyJet – The Largest Low Cost Airline in Europe*. European Case Clearing House.

Nir, D. (2008) *The Negotiational Self: Identifying and Transforming Negotiation Outcomes within the Self*. PhD dissertation, Hebrew University, Jerusalem.

Quinn, J.B. (1978) Strategic change: Logical incrementalism. *Sloan Management Review*, 20(1): 7–19.

Quinn, R.E. (1996) *Deep Change: Discovering the Leader Within*. San Francisco, CA: Jossey-Bass.

Regani, S. and Dutta, S. (2003) *EasyJet – The 'Easy' Way to Succeed*. European Case Clearing House.

Romanelli, E. and Tushman, M.L. (1994) Organizational transformation as punctuated equilibrium: An empirical test. *Academy of Management Journal*, 37(5): 1141–1166.

Schein, E.H. (1984) Coming to a new awareness of organizational culture. *Sloan Management Review*, 25(2): 3–16.

Seligman, M.E.P. (1991) *Learned Optimism*. New York: A.A. Knopf.

Storey, J. (1992) *Developments in the Management of Human Resources*. London: Blackwell Business.

Strebel, P. (1994) Choosing the right change path. *California Management Review*, 36(2): 29–51.

Ulrich, D. and Brockbank, W. (2005) *The HR Value Proposition*. Boston, MA: Harvard University Press.

Vanette, D., Cameron, K.S. and Powley, E. (2006) *Implementing Positive Organizational Scholarship at Prudential*. William Davidson Institute, University of Michigan.

Watzlawick, P., Weakland, J.H. and Fisch, R. (1974) *Change: Principles of Problem Formation and Problem Resolution*, 1st edn. New York: Norton.

CHAPTER 4

Adams, J.S. (1965) Inequity in social exchange. *Advances in Experimental Social Psychology*, 62: 335–343.

American Heritage® (2007) *Dictionary of the English Language,* 4th edn. Boston, MA: Houghton Mifflin. Accessed online at: http://dictionary.reference.com/browse/Ethics (accessed 27 March 2007).

Baron, J. (1996) Do no harm, in D.M. Messick and A.E. Tenbrunsel (eds) *Codes of Conduct: Behavioral Research into Business Ethics*. New York: Russell Sage Foundation, pp. 197–213.

Bertolino, M. and Steiner, D.D. (2007) Fairness reactions to selection methods: An Italian study. *International Journal of Selection and Assessment*, 15(2): 197–205.

Blowfield, M. and Murray, A. (2008) *Corporate Responsibility: A Critical Introduction.* Oxford: Oxford University Press.

Borland, H. (2009) Conceptualising global strategic sustainability and corporate transformational change. *International Marketing Review*, 26(4/5): 554–572.

Borland, H. and Lindgreen, A. (2013) Sustainability, epistemology, ecocentric business and marketing strategy: Ideology, reality and vision. *Journal of Business Ethics*, 117(1): 173–187.

Borland, H., Ambrosini, V., Lindgreen, A. and Vanhamme, J. (2016) Building theory at the intersection of ecological sustainability and strategic management. *Journal of Business Ethics*, 135: 293–307.

Cadbury, E. (1912) *Experiments in Industrial Organisation*. London: Longmans, Green & Co.

Carroll, A.B. (1999) Corporate social responsibility: Evolution of a definitional construct. *Business and Society*, 38(3): 268–295.

CIPD (2009) *The HR Profession Map*. London: Chartered Institute of Personnel and Development.

CIPD (2010) *Creating an Engaged Workforce*. Research Report. London: Chartered Institute of Personnel and Development.

Colquitt, J.A., Conlon, D.E., Wesson, M.J., Porter, C.O. and Ng, K.Y. (2001) Justice at the millennium: A meta-analytic review of 25 years of organizational justice research. *Journal of Applied Psychology*, 86(3): 425–445.

Conlon, D.E., Meyer, C.J. and Nowakowski, J.M. (2005) How does organizational justice affect performance, withdrawal, and counterproductive behavior?, in J. Greenberg and J.A. Colquitt (eds) *The Handbook of Organizational Justice*. Mahwah, NJ: Lawrence Erlbaum, pp. 301–328.

Crane, A. and Matten, D. (2010) *Business Ethics: Managing Corporate Citizenship and Sustainability in the Age of Globalization*, 3rd edn. Oxford: Oxford University Press.

Crawshaw, J.R., Cropanzano, R., Bell, C.M. and Nadisic, T. (2013) Organizational justice: New insights from behavioural ethics. *Human Relations*, 66(7): 885–904.

Cropanzano, R. and Greenberg, J. (1997) Progress in organizational justice: Tunneling through the maze, in C. Cooper and I. Robertson (eds) *International Review of Industrial and Organizational Psychology*. New York: Wiley, pp. 317–372.

Cropanzano, R., Byrne, Z.S., Bobocel, D.R. and Rupp, D.E. (2001) Moral virtues, fairness heuristics, social entities, and other denizens of organizational justice. *Journal of Vocational Behavior*, 58(2): 164–209.

Cropanzano, R., Goldman, B. and Folger, R. (2005) What is self-interest? *Journal of Organizational Behavior*, 26: 985–991.

Edelman Trust Survey (2016) 2016 Edelman Trust Barometer. Accessed online at: www.edelman.com/insights/intellectual.../2016-edelman-trust-barometer/ (accessed 30 October 2016).

Elkington, J. (1999) *Cannibals with Forks: The Triple Bottom Line of the 21st Century*. Oxford: Capstone Publishing.

European Commission (2013) *Corporate Social Responsibility Strategy*. Accessed online at: http://ec.europa. eu/enterprise/policies/sustainable-business/corporate-social-responsibility/index_en.htm (accessed 1 June 2013).

Ferrell, O.C., Fraedrich, J. and Ferrell, L. (2008) *Business Ethics: Ethical Decision-Making and Cases*. Boston, MA: Houghton Mifflin.

Fisher, C.M. (2000) The ethics of inactivity: Quietism and human resource managers. *Business and Professional Ethics Journal*, 19(3): 55–72.

Folger, R. and Cropanzano, R. (2001) Fairness theory, in J. Greenberg and R. Cropanzano (eds) *Advances in Organizational Justice*. Stanford, CA: Stanford University Press, pp. 1–53.

Garriga, E. and Mele, D. (2004) Corporate social responsibility: Mapping the territory. *Journal of Business Ethics*, 53: 51–71.

Gilliland, S.W. (1993) The perceived fairness of selection systems: An organizational justice perspective. *The Academy of Management Review*, 18(4): 694–734.

Greenbaum, R.L., Mawritz, M.B., Mayer, D.M. and Priesemuth, M. (2013) To act out, to withdraw, or to constructively resist? Employee reactions to supervisor abuse of customers and the moderating role of employee moral identity. *Human Relations*, 66(7): 925–950.

HEA (2007) *Employable Graduates for Responsible Employers*. York: Higher Education Academy. Accessed online at: www.heacademy.ac.uk/ourwork/ teaching and learning/alldi splay?type=projects&newid=esd/esd_employable_graduates&site=york (accessed 7 January 2011).

Judge, A. (2002) *Psychology of Sustainability: Embodying Cyclic Environmental Processes*. UN World Summit on Sustainable Development (Johannesburg, 2002). Accessed online at: www.laetusinpraesens.org/ docs/psychsus.php

Leventhal, G.S. (1980) What should be done with equity theory? New approaches to the study of fairness in social relationship, in K. Gergen, M. Greenberg and R. Willis (eds) *Social Exchange: Advances in Theory and Research*. New York: Plenum Press, pp. 27–55.

Lind, E.A. (2001) Fairness heuristics theory: Justice judgments as pivotal cognitions in organizational relations, in J. Greenberg and R. Cropanzano (eds) *Advances in Organizational Justice*. Stanford, CA: Stanford University Press, pp. 56–88.

Lowry, D. (2006) HR managers as ethical decision-makers: Mapping the terrain. *Asia Pacific Journal of Human Resources*, 44(2): 171–183.

McWilliams, A., Siegel, D. and Wright, P. (2006) Corporate social responsibility: Strategic implications. *Journal of Management Studies*, 43(1): 1–18.

Martin, G. and Hetrick, S. (2006) *Corporate Reputations, Branding and Managing People: A Strategic Approach to HR*. Oxford: Butterworth-Heinemann.

Parkes, C. and Borland, H. (2012) Strategic HRM: Transforming its responsibilities towards ecological sustainability – the greatest global challenge facing organizations. *Thunderbird International Business Review*, 54(6): 811–824.

Parkes, C. and Davis, A.J. (2013) Ethics and social responsibility: Do HR professionals have the 'courage to challenge' or are they set to be permanent 'bystanders?' *The International Journal of Human Resource Management*, 24(12): 2411–2434.

Parkes, C. and Harris, M. (2008) Corporate responsibility, ethics and strategic HRM, in Aston Centre for Human Resources (ed.) *Human Resource Management: Building Research-Based Practice*. London: CIPD, pp. 296–326.

Porritt, J. (2007) *Capitalism as if the World Matters*. London: Earthscan.

Porter, M.E. (1980) *Competitive Strategy: Techniques for Analysing Industries and Competitors*. New York: The Free Press.

Porter, M.E. (1985) *Competitive Advantage: Creating and Sustaining Superior Performance*. New York: The Free Press.

Purser, R.E., Park, C. and Montuori, A. (1995) Limits to anthropocentrism: Toward an ecocentric organization paradigm? *Academy of Management Review*, 20: 1053–1089.

Ragodoo, N.J.F. (2009) CSR as a tool to fight against poverty: The case of Mauritius. *Social Responsibility Journal*, 5(1): 19–33.

Rokeach, M. (1973) *The Nature of Human Values*. New York: The Free Press.

Rolston, H. (1994) *Conserving Natural Values*. New York: Columbia University Press.

Schwartz, S.H. (1999) A theory of cultural values and some implications for work. *Applied Psychology: An International Review*, 48(1): 23–47.

SRSG (2011) Special Representative of the Secretary General 'Guiding Principles on Business and Human Rights: Implementing the United Nations "Protect, Respect and Remedy" Framework'. Advance Edited Version (21 March) UN Doc A/HRC/17/31. Accessed online at: www.business -humanrights.org/media/documents/ruggie/ruggie-guiding-principles-21-mar -2011.pdf (accessed 31 May 2016).

Stead, J.G. and Stead, W.E. (2010) Sustainability comes to management education and research: A story of co-evolution. *Academy of Management Learning and Education*, 9(3): 488–498.

Tajfel, H. and Turner, J.C. (1986) The social identity theory of intergroup behaviour, in S. Worchel and W.G. Austin (eds) *Psychology of Intergroup Relations*. Chicago, IL: Nelson-Hall, pp. 7–24.

Turban, D.B. and Greening, D.W. (1997) Corporate social performance and organizational attractiveness to prospective employees. *Academy of Management Journal*, 40: 658–672.

Turner, J. (2015) Tax avoidance. *The Times*, 18 November: 5.

UNDP (2015) Sustainable Development Goals. Accessed online at: www.undp.org/content/undp/en/home/sustainable-development-goals.html (accessed 3 February 2016).

United Nations Commission on Environment and Development (1987) *Our Common Future*. The Brundtland Report. New York: Oxford University Press.

United Nations Office of the High Commissioner for Human Rights (n.d.) Accessed online at: www.ohchr. org/ (accessed 25 June 2013).

Van den Bos, K. and Lind, E.A. (2002) Uncertainty management by means of fairness judgments. *Advances in Experimental Social Psychology*, 34: 1–60.

Verbos, A.K., Gerard, J.A., Forshey, P.R., Harding, C.S. and Miller, J.S. (2007) The positive ethical organization: Enacting a living code of ethics and ethical organizational identity. *Journal of Business Ethics*, 76: 17–33.

Visser, W. (2008) Corporate social responsibility in developing countries, in A. Crane, A. McWilliams, D. Matten, J. Moon and D. Siegel (eds) *The Oxford Handbook of Corporate Social Responsibility*. Oxford: Oxford University Press, pp. 473–479.

Webley, S. (2006) Making business ethics work: The foundations of effective embedding. *Institute of Business Ethics*. Accessed online at: www.ibe.org.uk (accessed 2 August 2013).

Wong, W., Albert, A., Huggett, M. and Sullivan, J. (2009) *Quality People Management for Quality Outcomes: The Future of HR – Review of Evidence on People Management*. London: The Work Foundation.

CHAPTER 5

Bartlett, C. and Ghoshal, S. (1998) *Managing Across Borders: The Transnational Solution*, 2nd edn. London: Random House.

Bartlett, C. and Ghoshal, S. (2004) *Transnational Management: Text, Cases, and Readings in Cross Border Management*. Boston, MA: Irwin.

Belizon, M.J., Gunnigle, P. and Morley, M. (2013) Determinants of central control and subsidiary autonomy in HRM: The case of foreign owned multinational companies in Spain. *Human Resource Management Journal*, 23: 262–278.

Black, J.S., Mendenhall, B. and Oddou, G. (1991) Toward a comprehensive model of international adjustment: An integration of multiple theoretical perspectives. *Academy of Management Review*, 16(2): 291–317.

Brewster, C., Sparrow, P., Vernon, G. and Houldsworth, L. (2011) *International Human Resource Management*. London: CIPD.

Briscoe, D.R., Schuler, R.S. and Tarique, I. (2011) *International Human Resource Management*. London: Routledge.

Budhwar, P. (2012) Management of human resources in foreign firms operating in India: The role of HR in country-specific headquarters. *International Journal of Human Resource Management*, 23(12): 2514–2531.

Budhwar, P. and Debrah, Y. (2001) Rethinking comparative and cross national human resource management research. *International Journal of Human Resource Management*, 12(3): 497–515.

Budhwar, P. and Sparrow, P. (2002) An integrative framework for determining cross-national human resource management practices. *Human Resource Management Review*, 12(3): 377–403.

Budhwar, P., Schuler, R. and Sparrow, P. (eds) (2009) *Major Works in International Human Resource Management*. London: Sage.

Caligiuri, P.M. and Cascio, W. (1998) Increasing global competitiveness through effective people management. *Journal of World Business*, 33(1): 1–16.

De Cieri, H. and Dowling, P.J. (1999) Strategic human resource management in multinational enterprises: Theoretical and empirical developments, in G.F. Ferris, P.M. Wright, L.J.W. Dyer, J.W. Boudreau and G.T. Milkovich (eds) *Research in Personnel and Human Resource Management, 4: Strategic Human Resources Management in the Twenty First Century*. London: JAI Press, pp. 305–327.

De Cieri, H. and Dowling, P. (2006) Strategic international human resource management in multinational enterprises: Developments and directions, in G.K. Stahl and I. Björkman (eds) *Handbook of Research in International Human Resource Management*. Cheltenham: Edward Elgar, pp. 15–35.

Dicken, P. (2007) *Global Shift: Mapping the Changing Contours of the World Economy*, 5th edn. London: Sage.

Dowling, P., Festing, M. and Engle, A. (2013) *International Human Resource Management*. London: Thomson.

Edwards, T. and Rees, C. (2011) *International Human Resource Management: Globalization, National Systems and Multinational Companies*, 2nd edn. Harlow: Pearson.

Evans, P., Pucik, V. and Björkman, I. (2011) *The Global Challenge: Frameworks for International Human Resource Management*. New York: McGraw-Hill.

Goldstein, A. and Pusterla, F. (2010) Emerging economies' multinationals: General features and specificities of the Brazilian and Chinese cases. *International Journal of Emerging Markets*, 5(4): 289–306.

Harris, H., Brewster, C. and Sparrow, P. (2003) *International Human Resource Management*. London: CIPD.

Johnson, R. (2006) The real deal. *People Management*. Accessed online at: www.cipd.co.uk/pm/peoplemanagement/b/weblog/archive/2013/01/29/therealdeal-2006-07.aspx (accessed 30 August 2013).

Morgan, P.V. (1986) International human resource management: Fact or fiction? *Personnel Administrator*, 31(9): 43–47.

Perlmutter, H.V. (1969) The tortuous evolution of the multinational corporation. *Columbia Journal of World Business*, 4(1): 9–18.

PricewaterhouseCoopers (2010) *Economic Views: Emerging Multinationals, the Rise of New Multinational Companies from Emerging Markets*. Accessed online at: http://kc3.pwc.es/local/es/kc3/publicaciones.nsf/V1/153A71BAD7E4F7D7C125771F002E4EB9/$FILE/Emerging%20 Multinationals.pdf (accessed 22 February 2013).

Reed, M. (1996) Organizational theorizing: A historically contested terrain, in S.R. Clegg, C. Hardy and W.R. Nord (eds) *Handbook of Organization Studies*. London: Sage, pp. 31–56.

Robinson, R.D. (1978) *International Business Management: A Guide to Decision Making*, 2nd edn. Hinsdale, IL: Dryden.

Rosenzweig, P.M. and Nohria, N. (1994) Influences on human resource management in multinational corporations. *Journal of International Business Studies*, 25(2): 229–251.

Schuler, R.S. and Jackson, S.E. (2005) A quarter-century review of human resource management in the U.S. *Management Revue*, 16(1): 1–25. Reprinted in: N. Anderson (ed.) *Fundamentals of Human Resource Management: Volume 1, HRM Defined and in Organizational Context*. London: Sage, 2007. Reprinted in: R.S. Schuler and S.E. Jackson, *Strategic Human Resource Management*, 2nd edn. London: Blackwell, 2007, pp. 214–240.

Schuler, R. and Tarique, I. (2005) Alliance forms and HR issues, implications and significance, in O. Shenkar and J. Reuer (eds) *Handbook of Strategic Alliances*. Thousand Oaks, CA: Sage, pp. 219–240.

Schuler, R.S., Fulkerson, J.R. and Dowling, P.J. (1991) Strategic performance measurement and management in MNCs: An example of Pepsi-Cola. *International Human Resource Management*, 30(3): 365–392.

Schuler, R.S., Dowling, P. and De Cieri, H. (1993) An integrative framework of strategic international human resource management. *Journal of Management*, 19: 419–459.

Schuler, R.S., Budhwar, P. and Florkowski, G.W. (2002) International human resource management: Review and critique. *International Journal of Management Reviews*, 4(1): 41–70.

Sparrow, P.R. (2007) Globalization of HR at function level: Four UK-based case studies of the international recruitment and selection process. *The International Journal of Human Resource Management*, 18(5): 845–867.

Sparrow, P.R., Brewster, C. and Harris, H. (2004) *Globalizing Human Resource Management*. London: Routledge.

Tarique, I., Schuler, R. and Gong, Y. (2006) A model of multinational enterprise subsidiary staffing composition. *International Journal of Human Resource Management*, 17: 207–224.

Tung, R.L. (1998) American expatriates abroad: From neophytes to cosmopolitans. *Journal of World Business*, 33: 125–144.

CHAPTER 6

Aston, D., Brown, P. and Lauder, H. (2009) Developing a theory of skills for global HR, in P. Sparrow (ed.) *Handbook of International Human Resource Management: Integrating People, Process and Context*. Chichester: Wiley, pp. 321–339.

Baron, A., Clarke, R., Pass, S. and Turner, P. (2010) *Workforce Planning: Right People, Right Time, Right Skills*. London: CIPD.

Bass, B.M. (1985) *Leadership and Performance Beyond Expectations*. New York: The Free Press.

Bass, B.M., Jung, I.J., Avoilio, B.J. and Benson, Y. (2003) Predicting unit performance by assessing transformational and transactional leadership. *Journal of Applied Psychology*, 88: 207–218.

Beynon, H. (1973) *Working for Ford*. London: Allen Lane Penguin Education.

Boxall, P.F. and Purcell, J. (2003) *Strategy and Human Resource Management*. New York: Palgrave Macmillan.

Boyatzis, R. (1982) *The Competent Manager: A Model for Effective Performance*. Chichester: Wiley.

Bradford Teaching Hospitals NHS Foundation Trust (2008) *The Right Staff, with the Right Training, in the Right Place, at the Right Time*. Accessed online at: www.bradfordhospitals.nhs.uk/

Bramham, J. (1975) *Practical Manpower Planning*. London: Institute of Personnel Management.

Bramham, J. (1989) *Human Resource Planning*. London: Institute of Personnel Management.

Bryman, A. (2001) *Social Research Methods*. Oxford: Oxford University Press.

Buahenee, A.K. (2009) Engaging a multigenerational workforce: The why and the how. Paper presented at the SHRM Conference, New Orleans.

Budhwar, P. and Sparrow, P.R. (2002) An integrative framework for determining cross-national human resource management practices. *Human Resource Management Review*, 12: 377–403.

Cappelli, P. (2009) A supply chain approach to workforce planning. *Organizational Dynamics*, 38(1): 8–15.

CFWI (Centre for Workforce Intelligence) Annual Conference (2012) contact: workforceintelligence@dh.gso.gov.uk

CIPD (2010) *Survey Report: Resourcing and Talent Planning*. London: Chartered Institute of Personnel and Development.

CIPD (2011) *Sustainable Organisation Performance: What Really Makes the Difference?* London: Chartered Institute of Personnel and Development.

CIPD (2012) *Workforce Planning Fact Sheet*. London: Chartered Institute of Personnel and Development.

Clegg, S., Kornberger, M. and Pitsis, T. (2005) *Managing and Organizations: An Introduction to Theory and Practice*. London: Sage.

Davis, A. and Scully, J. (2008) Strategic resourcing, in Aston Centre for Human Resources (ed.) *Strategic Human Resource Management: Building Research-Based Practice*. London: CIPD, pp. 95–128.

Delery, J. and Doty, D.H. (1996) Models of theorising in strategic human resource management: Test of universalistic, contingency and configurational performance predictions. *Academy of Management Journal*, 39: 802–835.

Deloitte (2011) *Workforce Analytics: Up the Ante Human Capital Trends; Creating a Business-Driven Workforce*. Accessed online at: http://talentsnapshot.com/wp-content/uploads/2012/11/DeloitteHumanCapitalTrends2011.pdf

Demerouti, E., Bakker, A.B., Nachreiner, F. and Schaufeli, W.B. (2001) The job demands–resources model of burnout. *Journal of Applied Psychology*, 86: 499–512.

Department of Health (2004) *The Emergency Care Practitioner Report: Right Skill, Right Time, Right Place*. London: Department of Health. Accessed online at: www.dh.gov.uk/en/Publicationsandstatistics/Publications/PublicationsPolicyAndGuidance/DH_4093086 (accessed 12 October 2009).

Department of Health (National Centre for Workforce Intelligence) (2012) *National Centre for Workforce Intelligence: Leadership Perspectives*. London: Department of Health. Accessed online at: www.cfwi.org.uk

Department of the Navy (2013) *Workforce Planning is Used as the Keystone to an Effective and Efficient Recruiting and Hiring Program*. Department of the Navy, Civilian Human Resources, 29 April.

Firth, S. (2012) HP Labs is reinventing workforce planning. *Innovation @ HP Labs, Insights on Research, Innovation, and Emerging Technology from HP Labs Researchers around the World*. Hewlett Packard. Accessed online at: http://innovation859.rssing.com/chan-7571993/all_p1.html

Freyens, B.P. (2010) Managing skill shortages in the Australian public sector: Issues and perspectives. *Asia Pacific Journal of Human Resources*, 48(3): 262–286.

Guest, D.E. (1997) Human resource management and performance: A review and research agenda. *International Journal of Human Resource Management*, 8: 263–276.

Guest, D.E. (2002) Human resource management, corporate performance and employee well-being: Building the worker into HRM. *Journal of Industrial Relations*, 44: 335–358.

Hackman, J.R. and Oldham, G.R. (1980) *Work Redesign*. Reading, MA: Addison-Wesley.

Henwood, K.L. and Pidgeon, N.F. (2013) *Risk and Identity Futures*. UK Foresight Future of Identities Project Report DR18. London: Department of Business, Innovation and Skills.

Huerta-Melchor, O. (2013) *The Government Workforce of the Future: Innovation in Strategic Workforce Planning in OECD Countries* (No. 21). Paris: OECD Publishing.

Huselid, M.A. (1995) The impact of human resource management practices on turnover productivity and corporate financial performance. *Academy of Management Journal*, 38: 635–672.

Huselid, M.A. and Becker, B.E. (1996) Methodological issues in cross-sectional and panel estimates of the human resource–firm performance link. *Industrial Relations*, 35(3): 400–422.

Katou, A.A. and Budhwar, P.S. (2006) Human resource management systems and organizational performance: A test of a mediating model in the Greek manufacturing context. *International Journal of Human Resource Management*, 17(7): 1223–1253.

Khatri, N. (2000) Managing human resource for competitive advantage: A study of companies in Singapore. *International Journal of Human Resource Management*, 11(2): 336–365.

Kelly, B. and All, L. (2013) *Workforce Planning: Starbucks Case Study*. Mercer Starbucks Webinar presented on 26 February 2013. Accessed online at: www.mercer.com/webcasts/workforce-planning-studystarbucks&idSession=15071500 (accessed 29 August 2013).

Klosk, R. (2013) Alignment A-Z at HP. Paper presented at the Workforce Planning and Analytics Conference, 5–7 February, Human Capital Institute, Atlanta, GA.

Kotter, J.P. (1995) Leading change: Why transformation efforts fail. *Harvard Business Review*, March–April: 59–67.

Laabs, J. (1996) Duke's newest power tool. *Personnel Journal*, 75(6): 102–116.

McKinsey & Co. (2012) *The State of Human Capital 2012*. A report by McKinsey and Company and the Conference Board.

Melchor, O.H. (2013) *The Government Workforce of the Future*. Accessed online at: OECD-library.org

Mintzberg, H. (2004) Enough leadership. *Harvard Business Review*, 82(11): 22–24.

Motion, R.D. (2013) It's not just data: Workforce planning and change management, in D.L. Ward and R. Tripp (eds) *Positioned: Strategic Workforce Planning that Gets the Right Person in the Right Job*. New York: AMACOM/American Management Association.

NHS Health Education England (2013) *Developing People for Health and Health CARE. Introducing Health Education England. Our Strategic Intent*. Accessed online at: www.hee.nhs.uk

Nutt, C. (2010) Why workforce planning is a strategic imperative, in CIPD (ed.) *Reflections on Workforce Planning*. London: Chartered Institute of Personnel and Development.

OECD (2011) *Public Servants as Partners for Growth: Toward a Stronger, Leaner and More Equitable Workforce*. Paris: OECD Publishing.

Peterson, D. and Krieger, T. (2013) Strategic workforce planning at Boeing, in D.L. Ward and R. Tripp (eds) *Positioned: Strategic Workforce Planning that Gets the Right Person in the Right Job*. New York: AMACOM/American Management Association.

Pfeffer, J. (1994) *Competitive Advantage Through People*. Boston, MA: Harvard Business School Review.

Pinnington, A. and Morris, T. (2003) Archetype change in professional organizations: Survey evidence from large law firms. *British Journal of Management*, 14(1): 85–99.

Pritchard, R.D. (1990) Organizational productivity, in M.D. Dunnette (ed.) *Handbook of Industrial and Organizational Psychology Vol. 4*, 2nd edn. Palo Alto, CA: Consulting Psychologists Press, pp. 443–471.

Purcell, J. and Ahlstrand, B. (1994) *Human Resource Management in the Multi-Divisional Company*. Oxford: Oxford University Press.

Purcell, J., Kinnie, N., Hutchinson, S., Rayton, B. and Swart, J. (2003) *Understanding the People and Performance Link: Unlocking the Black Box*. London: CIPD.

Reilly, P. (1996) *Human Resource Planning: An Introduction*. Institute for Employment Studies Report 312. Brighton: IES.

Schaufeli, W.B., Taris, T.W. and Van Rhenen, W. (2008) Workaholism, burnout, and work engagement: Three of a kind or three different kinds of employee well-being? *Applied Psychology: An International Review*, 57(2): 173–203.

Schuler, R.S. (1992) Strategic human resource management: Linking people with the needs of the business. *Organizational Dynamics*, 21(1): 18–32.

Schuler, R.S. and Jackson, S.E. (1987) Organisational strategy and organisational level as determinants of human resource management practices. *Human Resource Planning*, 10(3): 125–141.

Shapiro, J. and Davenport, T. (2013) The rise of talent analytics, in D.L. Ward and R. Tripp (ed.) *Positioned: Strategic Workforce Planning that Gets the Right Person in the Right Job*. New York: AMACOM/American Management Association.

Sinclair, A. (2004) *Workforce Planning: A Literature Review*. Brighton: Institute for Employment Studies.

Sparrow, P.R. and Brewster, C. (2006) Globalizing HRM: The growing revolution in managing employees internationally, in R.J. Burke and C.L. Cooper (eds) *The Human Resources Revolution: Why Putting People First Matters*. London, New York and Amsterdam: Elsevier, pp. 99–122.

Sparrow, P. and Hiltrop, J. (1994) *European Human Resource Management in Transition*. London: Prentice-Hall.

Stevens, M. (2010) Royal Navy faces workforce planning 'conundrum'. *People Management*, 18 June. Accessed online at: www.cipd.co.uk/pm/peoplemanagement/b/weblog/archive/2013/01/29/ royal-navy-faces-workforce-planning-conundrum-2010-06.aspx (accessed 29 August 2013).

Sullivan, T. (2002) Why workforce planning is hot, *Industry Trends*, 29 July.

Taylor, F.W. (1911) *The Principles of Scientific Management*. New York: Harper & Brothers.

The Times (2013) *The Times 100 Business Case Studies*. Accessed online at: http://businesscasestudies.co.uk/tesco/recruitment-and-selection/workforce-planning.html#axzz2dMTK9Sw4 (accessed 29 August 2013).

Trist, E.L. and Bamford, K.W. (1951) Some social and psychological consequences of the Longwell method of coal getting. *Human Relations*, 1: 3–38.

Turner, P. (2002) *HR Forecasting and Planning*. London: CIPD.

Turner, P. (2010) From manpower planning to capacity planning: Why we need workforce planning, in CIPD (ed.) *Reflections on Workforce Planning*. London: CIPD.

Ulrich, D. (1992) Strategic human resource planning: Linking customers and employees. *Human Resource Planning*, 15(4): 47–62.

Ulrich, D. (1997) *Human Resource Champions: The Next Agenda for Adding Value and Delivering Results*. Boston, MA: Harvard Business School Press.

Ulrich, D. (2013) The future targets or outcomes of HR work: Individuals, organizations and leadership, in D.L. Ward and R. Tripp (eds) *Positioned: Strategic Workforce Planning that Gets the Right Person in the Right Job*. New York: AMACOM/American Management Association.

Ulrich, D., Younger, J., Brockbank, W. and Ulrich, M. (2012) HR talent and the new HR competencies. *Strategic HR Review*, 11(4): 217–222.

US Department of the Interior (2001) *Workforce Planning Instruction Manual*. Washington, DC: Department of the Interior. Accessed online at: www.doi.gov/hrm/WFPImanual.pdf (accessed 12 October 2009).

Ward, D.L. (2013) How long has this been going on?, in D.L. Ward and R. Tripp (eds) *Positioned: Strategic Workforce Planning that Gets the Right Person in the Right Job*. New York: AMACOM/American Management Association.

West, M. (1994) *Effective Teamwork*. Leicester: British Psychological Society Books.

CHAPTER 7

Ackerman, P.L., Kanfer, R. and Goff, M. (1995) Cognitive and non-cognitive determinants and consequences of complex skill acquisition. *Journal of Experimental Psychology*, 1: 270–304.

Anderson, N. and Witvliet, C. (2008) Fairness reactions to personnel selection methods: An international comparison between the Netherlands, the United States, France, Spain, Portugal, and Singapore. *International Journal of Selection and Assessment*, 16(1): 1–13.

Anderson, N., Salgado, J.F. and Hülsheger, U.R. (2010) Applicant reactions in selection: Comprehensive meta-analysis into reaction generalization versus situational specificity. *International Journal of Selection and Assessment*, 18(3): 291–304.

Andrews, M.C., Baker, T. and Hunt, T.G. (2011) Values and person-organization fit: Does moral intensity strengthen outcomes? *Leadership and Organization Development Journal*, 32(1): 5–19.

Anseel, F. and Lievens, F. (2009) The mediating role of feedback acceptance in the relationship between feedback and attitudinal and performance outcomes. *International Journal of Selection and Assessment*, 17(4): 362–376.

Arthur, W., Day, E.A., McNelly, T.L. and Edens, P.S. (2006) A meta-analysis of the criterion-related validity of assessment centre dimensions. *Personnel Psychology*, 56(1): 125–153.

Arthur, W., Glaze, R.M., Villado, A.J. and Taylor, J.E. (2010) The magnitude and extent of cheating and response distortion effects on unproctored internet-based tests of cognitive ability and personality. *International Journal of Selection and Assessment*, 18(1): 1–16.

Barrick, M.R. and Mount, M.K. (1991) The big five personality dimensions and job performance: A meta-analysis. *Personnel Psychology*, 44(1): 1–26.

Bartram, D. (2005) The Great Eight competencies: A criterion-centric approach to validation. *Journal of Applied Psychology*, 90(6): 1185–1203.

Bauer, T.N., Truxillo, D.M., Sanchez, R.J., Craig, J.M., Ferrara, P. and Campion, M.A. (2001) Applicant reactions to selection: Development of the selection procedural justice scale (SPJS). *Personnel Psychology*, 54(2): 387–419.

Berry, C.M., Clark, M.A. and McClure, T.K. (2011) Racial/ethnic differences in the criterion-related validity of cognitive ability tests: A qualitative and quantitative review. *Journal of Applied Psychology*, 96(5): 881–906.

Berry, C.M., Cullen, M.J. and Meyer, J.M. (2014) Racial/ethnic subgroup differences in cognitive ability test range restriction: Implications for differential validity. *Journal of Applied Psychology*, 99(1): 21–37.

Bertua, C., Anderson, N. and Salgado, J.F. (2005) The predictive validity of cognitive ability tests: A UK meta-analysis. *Journal of Occupational and Organizational Psychology*, 78(3): 387–409.

Bobko, P. and Roth, P.L. (2010) An analysis of two methods for assessing and indexing adverse impact: A disconnect between the academic literature and some practice, in J.L. Outtz (ed.) *Adverse Impact: Implications for Organizational Staffing and High Stakes Selection*. New York: Routledge, pp. 29–49.

Breaugh, J.A. (2008) Employee recruitment: Current knowledge and important areas for future research. *Human Resource Management Review*, 18(3): 103–118.

Brown, V.R. and Vaughn, E.D. (2011) The writing on the (Facebook) wall: The use of social networking sites in hiring decisions. *Journal of Business and Psychology*, 26(2): 219–225.

Campion, M.A., Pursell, E.D. and Brown, B.K. (1988) Structured interviewing: Raising the psychometric properties of the employment interview. *Personnel Psychology*, 41(1): 25–42.

Campion, M.A., Palmer, D.K. and Campion, J.E. (1997) A review of structure in the selection interview. *Personnel Psychology*, 50(3): 655–702.

Campion, M.A., Fink, A.A., Ruggeberg, B.J., Carr, L., Phillips, G.M. and Odman, R.B. (2011) Doing competencies well: Best practices in competency modeling. *Personnel Psychology*, 64(1): 225–262.

Cascio, W.F. and Aguinis, H. (2008) 3 staffing twenty-first-century organizations. *The Academy of Management Annals*, 2(1): 133–165.

Chapman, D.S., Uggerslev, K.L., Carroll, S.A., Piasentin, K.A. and Jones, D.A. (2005) Applicant attraction to organizations and job choice: A meta-analytic review of the correlates of recruiting outcomes. *Journal of Applied Psychology*, 90(5): 928–944.

Christian, M., Edwards, B. and Bradley, J. (2010) Situational judgement tests: Constructs assessed and a meta-analysis of their criterion-related validities. *Personnel Psychology*, 63: 83–117.

Collings, D.G. and Mellahi, K. (2009) Strategic talent management: A review and research agenda. *Human Resource Management Review*, 19(4): 304–313.

Cooper, D. and Robertson, I. (1995) *The Psychology of Personnel Selection: A Quality Approach*. London: Routledge.

Doherty, R. (2010) Getting social with recruitment. *Strategic HR Review*, 9(6): 11–15.

Eckland, B.K. (1979) Genetic variance in the SES–IQ correlation. *Sociology of Education*, 52: 191–196.

Gale, T.C.E., Roberts, M.J., Sice, P.J., Langton, J.A., Patterson, F.C., Carr, A.S., Anderson, I.R. et al. (2010) Predictive validity of a selection centre testing non-technical skills for recruitment to training in anaesthesia. *British Journal of Anaesthesia*, 105(5): 603–609.

Galin, A. and Benoliel, B. (1990) Does the way you dress affect your performance rating? *Personnel*, August: 49–52.

Gaugler, B.B., Rosenthal, D.B., Thornton, G.C. and Bentson, C. (1987) Meta-analysis of assessment center validity. *Journal of Applied Psychology*, 72(3): 493–511.

Gilliland, S.W. (1994) Effects of procedural and distributive justice on reactions to a selection system. *Journal of Applied Psychology*, 79(5): 691–701.

Gilliland, S.W., Groth, M., Baker, R.C., Dew, A.F., Polly, L.M. and Langdon, J.C. (2001) Improving applicants' reactions to rejection letters: An application of fairness theory. *Personnel Psychology*, 54(3): 669–704.

Harari, M.B. and Viswesvaran, C. (2014) Gender differences in work sample assessments: Not all tests are created equal. *Revista de Psicología del Trabajo y de las Organizaciones*, 30(1): 29–34.

Hedge, J.W. and Kavanagh, M.J. (1988) Improving the accuracy of performance evaluations: Comparison of three methods of performance appraiser training. *Journal of Applied Psychology*, 73(1): 68–73.

Hermelin, E., Lievens, F. and Robertson, I.T. (2007) The validity of assessment centres for the prediction of supervisory performance ratings: A meta-analysis. *International Journal of Selection and Assessment*, 15(4): 405–411.

Hogan, J. and Holland, B. (2003) Using theory to evaluate personality and job–performance relations: A socioanalytic perspective. *Journal of Applied Psychology*, 88(1): 100–112.

Hough, L.M. and Oswald, F.L. (2000) Personnel selection: Looking toward the future – Remembering the past. *Annual Review of Psychology*, 51: 631–664.

Hough, L.M., Oswald, F.L. and Ployhart, R.E. (2001) Determinants, detection and amelioration of adverse impact in personnel selection procedures: Issues, evidence and lessons learned. *International Journal of Selection and Assessment*, 9: 152–194.

Huffcutt, A.I., Culbertson, S.S. and Weyhrauch, W.S. (2013) Employment interview reliability: New meta-analytic estimates by structure and format. *International Journal of Selection and Assessment*, 21(3): 264–276.

Hulsheger, U. and Anderson, N. (2009) Applicant perspectives in selection: Going beyond preference reactions. *International Journal of Selection and Assessment*, 17(4): 335–345.

Jackson, D.N. and Rushton, J.P. (2006) Males have greater g: Sex differences in general mental ability from 100,000 17- to 18-year-olds on the Scholastic Assessment Test. *Intelligence*, 34(5): 479–486.

Judge, T.A. and Zapata, C.P. (2015) The person–situation debate revisited: Effect of situation strength and trait activation on the validity of the Big Five personality traits in predicting job performance. *Academy of Management Journal*, 58(4): 1149–1179.

Krause, D.E., Kersting, M., Heggestad, E.D. and Thornton III, G.C. (2006) Incremental validity of assessment center ratings over cognitive ability tests: A study at the executive management level. *International Journal of Selection and Assessment*, 14(4): 360–371.

Kristof-Brown, A.L. (2000) Perceived applicant fit: Distinguishing between recruiter's perceptions of person–job and person–organization fit. *Personnel Psychology*, 53(3): 643–671.

Kuncel, N.R., Ones, D.S. and Sackett, P.R. (2010) Individual differences as predictors of work, educational, and broad life outcomes. *Personality and Individual Differences*, 49(4): 331–336.

Lauver, K.J. and Kristof-Brown, A. (2001) Distinguishing between employees' perceptions of person–job and person–organization fit. *Journal of Vocational Behavior*, 59(3): 454–470.

Lengnick-Hall, M.L., Lengnick-Hall, C.A., Andrade, L.S. and Drake, B. (2009) Strategic human resource management: The evolution of the field. *Human Resource Management Review*, 19(2): 64–85.

Lievens, F. and Burke, E. (2011) Dealing with the threats inherent in unproctored internet testing of cognitive ability: Results from a large-scale operational test program. *Journal of Occupational and Organizational Psychology*, 84: 817–824.

Lievens, F. and Sackett, P.R. (2012) The validity of interpersonal skills assessment via situational judgment tests for predicting academic success and job performance. *Journal of Applied Psychology*, 97(2): 460–468.

Lievens, F., Peeters, H. and Schollaert, E. (2008) Situational judgment tests: A review of recent research. *Personnel Review*, 37(4): 426–441.

Lievens, F., Ones, D.S. and Dilchert, S. (2009) Personality scale validities increase throughout medical school. *Journal of Applied Psychology*, 94: 1514–1535.

McDaniel, M.A. and Nguyen, N.T. (2003) Situational judgment tests: A review of practice and constructs assessed. *International Journal of Selection and Assessment*, 9(1–2): 103–113.

McDaniel, M.A., Whetzel, D.L., Schmidt, F.L. and Maurer, S.D. (1994) The validity of employment interviews: A comprehensive review and meta-analysis. *Journal of Applied Psychology*, 79(4): 599–616.

McDaniel, M., Morgeson, F., Finnegan, E., Campion, M. and Braverman, E. (2001) Use of situational judgment tests to predict job performance: A clarification of the literature. *Journal of Applied Psychology*, 86(4): 730–740.

McDaniel, M.A., Hartman, N.S., Whetzel, D.L. and Grubb, W.L. (2007) Situational judgment tests, response instructions, and validity: A meta-analysis. *Personnel Psychology*, 60(1): 63–91.

Maheshwari, S., Sainani, A. and Reddy, P. (2010) An approach to extract special skills to improve the performance of resumé selection. Paper presented at DNIS'10: Databases in Networked Information Systems, 6th International Workshop, pp. 256–273.

Merkulova, N., Melchers, K.G., Kleinmann, M., Annen, H. and Tresch, T.S. (2014) Effects of individual differences on applicant perceptions of an operational assessment center. *International Journal of Selection and Assessment*, 22(4): 355–370.

Minbashian, A., Earle, J. and Bright, J.E.H. (2013) Openness to experience as a predictor of job performance trajectories. *Applied Psychology: An International Review*, 62: 1–12.

Murphy, K.R. (1986) When your top choice turns you down: Effect of rejected offers on the utility of selection tests. *Psychological Bulletin*, 99(1): 133–138.

Neter, E. and Ben-Shakhar, G. (1989) The predictive validity of graphological inferences: A meta-analytic approach. *Personality and Individual Differences*, 10(7): 737–745.

Nguyen, N.T., Biderman, M.D. and McDaniel, M.A. (2005) Effects of response instructions on faking a situational judgment test. *International Journal of Selection and Assessment*, 13(4): 250–260.

Nicholson, N. and West, M. (1989) Transitions, work histories, and careers, in M.B. Arthur, D.T. Hall and B.S. Lawrence (eds) *Handbook of Career Theory*. New York: Cambridge University Press, pp. 181–201.

Patterson, F. and Ferguson, E. (2007) *Selection into Medical Education and Training*. Edinburgh: Association for the Study of Medical Education.

Patterson, F. and Zibarras, L. (2011) Exploring the construct of perceived job discrimination in selection. *International Journal of Selection and Assessment*, 19(3): 259–265.

Patterson, F., Ferguson, E., Lane, P., Farrell, K., Martlew, J. and Wells, A. (2000) A competency model for general practice: Implications for selection, training, and development. *The British Journal of General Practice*, 50: 188–193.

Patterson, F., Ferguson, E., Norfolk, T. and Lane, P. (2005) A new selection system to recruit general practice registrars: Preliminary findings from a validation study. *British Medical Journal*, 330(7493): 711–714.

Patterson, F., Baron, H., Carr, V., Plint, S. and Lane, P. (2009a) Evaluation of three short-listing methodologies for selection into postgraduate training in general practice. *Medical Education*, 43(1): 50–57.

Patterson, F., Carr, V., Zibarras, L., Burr, B., Berkin, L., Plint, S., Irish, B. et al. (2009b) New machine-marked tests for selection into core medical training: Evidence from two validation studies. *Clinical Medicine*, 9(5): 417–420.

Patterson, F., Zibarras, L., Carr, V., Irish, B. and Gregory, S. (2011) Evaluating candidate reactions to selection practices using organisational justice theory. *Medical Education*, 45(3): 289–297.

Patterson, F., Ashworth, V., Mehra, S. and Falcon, H. (2012a) Could situational judgement tests be used for selection into dental foundation training? *British Dental Journal*, 213(1): 23–26.

Patterson, F., Ashworth, V., Zibarras, L., Coan, P., Kerrin, M. and O'Neill, P. (2012b) Evaluations of situational judgement tests to assess non-academic attributes in selection. *Medical Education*, 46(9): 850–868.

Ployhart, R.E. (2006) Staffing in the 21st century: New challenges and strategic opportunities. *Journal of Management*, 32(6): 868–897.

Ployhart, R.E. and Ryan, A.M. (1998) Applicants' reactions to the fairness of selection procedures: The effects of positive rule violations and time of measurement. *Journal of Applied Psychology*, 83(1): 3–16.

Randall, R., Stewart, P., Farrell, K. and Patterson, F. (2006) Using an assessment centre to select doctors for postgraduate training in obstetrics and gynaecology. *The Obstetrician and Gynaecologist*, 8(4): 257–262.

Rimanoczy, I. and Pearson, T. (2010) Role of HR in the new world of sustainability. *Industrial and Commercial Training*, 42(1): 11–17.

Roberts, B.W. (2006) Personality development and organizational behavior. *Research in Organizational Behavior*, 27: 1–40.

Robertson, I.T. and Smith, M. (2001) Personnel selection. *Journal of Occupational and Organizational Psychology*, 74(4): 441–472.

Robertson, I.T. and Kandola, R.S. (2011) Work sample tests: Validity, adverse impact and applicant reaction. *Journal of Occupational Psychology*, 55(3): 171–183.

Rockstuhl, T., Ang, S., Ng, K.Y., Lievens, F. and Van Dyne, L. (2015) Putting judging situations into situational judgment tests: Evidence from intercultural multimedia SJTs. *Journal of Applied Psychology*, 100(2): 464–480.

Roth, P.L., Bobko, P. and McFarland, L.Y.N.N. (2005) A meta-analysis of work sample test validity: Updating and integrating some classic literature. *Personnel Psychology*, 58(4): 1009–1037.

Schmidt, F. and Hunter, J.E. (1998) The validity and utility of selection methods in personnel psychology: Practical and theoretical implications of 85 years of research findings. *Psychological Bulletin*, 124: 262–274.

Schmitt, N. and Chan, D. (1999) The status of research on applicant reactions to selection tests and its implications for managers. *International Journal of Management Reviews*, 1(1): 45–62.

Schneider, B. (1987) The people make the place. *Personnel Psychology*, 40(3): 437–453.

Scullen, S.E., Mount, M.K. and Goff, M. (2000) Understanding the latent structure of job performance ratings. *Journal of Applied Psychology*, 85(6): 956–970.

Silzer, R. and Church, A.H. (2009) The pearls and perils of identifying potential. *Industrial and Organizational Psychology*, 2(4): 377–412.

Stoughton, J.W., Thompson, L.F. and Meade, A.W. (2015) Examining applicant reactions to the use of social networking websites in pre-employment screening. *Journal of Business and Psychology*, 30(1): 73–88.

Terpstra, D.A., Mohamed, A.A. and Kethley, R.B. (2002) An analysis of federal court cases involving nine selection devices. *International Journal of Selection and Assessment*, 7(1): 26–34.

Thoms, P., McMasters, R., Roberts, M.R. and Dombkowski, D.A. (1999) Resumé characteristics as predictors of an invitation to interview. *Journal of Business and Psychology*, 13(3): 339–356.

Thoresen, C.J., Bradley, J.C., Bliese, P.D. and Thoresen, J.D. (2004) The big five personality traits and individual job performance growth trajectories in maintenance and transitional job stages. *Journal of Applied Psychology*, 89: 835–853.

Truxillo, D.M., Bauer, T.N., Campion, M.A. and Paronto, M.E. (2002) Selection fairness information and applicant reactions: A longitudinal field study. *Journal of Applied Psychology*, 87(6): 1020–1031.

Tsui, A.S., Pearce, J.L., Porter, L.W. and Tripoli, A.M. (1997) Alternative approaches to the employee–organization relationship: Does investment in employees pay off? *Academy of Management Journal*, 40(5): 1089–1121.

Turban, D.B. and Cable, D.M. (2003) Firm reputation and applicant pool characteristics. *Journal of Organizational Behavior*, 24(6): 733–751.

Van der Zee, K.I., Bakker, A.B. and Bakker, P. (2002) Why are structured interviews so rarely used in personnel selection? *Journal of Applied Psychology*, 87(1): 176–184.

Van Vianen, A.E.M., Taris, R., Scholten, E. and Schinkel, S. (2004) Perceived fairness in personnel selection: Determinants and outcomes in different stages of the assessment procedure. *International Journal of Selection and Assessment*, 12(1–2): 149–159.

Wiesner, W.H. and Cronshaw, S.F. (1988) A meta-analytic investigation of the impact of interview format and degree of structure on the validity of the employment interview. *Journal of Occupational Psychology*, 61(4): 275–290.

Woehr, D. (1994) Understanding frame-of-reference training: The impact of training on the recall of performance information. *Journal of Applied Psychology*, 79(4): 525–534.

Woods, S.A. and Anderson, N.A. (2016) Toward a periodic table of personality: Mapping personality scales between the five-factor model and the circumplex model. *Journal of Applied Psychology*, 101(4): 582–604.

Woods, S.A. and Hinton, D.P. (2016) What's in a job? Job design and job analysis, in N. Chmiel (ed.) *Introduction to Work and Organizational Psychology*, 3rd edn. Oxford: Blackwell.

Woods, S.A. and West, M.A. (2014) *The Psychology of Work and Organizations*, 2nd edn. Andover: Cengage Learning EMEA.

Woods, S.A., Lievens, F., De Fruyt, F. and Wille, B. (2013) Personality across working life: The longitudinal and reciprocal influences of personality on work. *Journal of Organizational Behavior*, 34(S1): S7–S25.

Woods, S.A., Patterson, F., Koczwara, A. and Wille, B. (2016) Personality and occupational specialty: An examination of medical specialties using Holland's RIASEC model. *Career Development International*, 21(3): 262–278.

Zibarras, L. and Ballinger, C. (2011) Promoting environmental behaviour in the workplace: A survey of UK organisations, in D. Bartlett (ed.) *The Psychology of Sustainability in the Workplace*. London: BPS Publications, pp. 84–90.

Zibarras, L.D. and Woods, S.A. (2010) A survey of UK selection practices across different organization sizes and industry sectors. *Journal of Occupational and Organizational Psychology*, 83(2): 499–511.

CHAPTER 8

Bassett-Jones, N. (2005) The paradox of diversity management, creativity and innovation. *Creativity and Innovation Management*, 14(2): 169–175.

Bell, M.P. (2012) *Diversity in Organizations,* international edition. Mason, OH: South Western, Cengage Learning.

Benschop, Y. (2001) Pride, prejudice and performance: Relations between HRM, diversity and performance. *International Journal of Human Resource Management*, 12(7): 1166–1181.

Benschop, Y. and Dooreward, H. (1998) Covered by equality: The gender subtext of organizations. *Organization Studies*, 19(3): 787–805.

Bureau of National Affairs (1995) *Affirmative Actions after Adarand*. Special report in the Daily Labor Report series, no. 147. Washington, DC: BNA.

Burstein, P. and Monaghan, K. (1986) Equal employment opportunity and the mobilization of law. *Law and Society Review*, 20: 355–388.

Carlozzi, C.L. (1999) Diversity is good for business. *Journal of Accountancy*, 188(3): 81–86.

Carlsson, M. and Rooth, D.O. (2007) *Is it Your Foreign Name or Foreign Qualifications? An Experimental Study of Ethnic Discrimination in Hiring*. Bonn: Institute for the Study of Labour.

Cassell, C.M. (2001) Managing diversity, in T. Redman and A. Wilkinson (eds) *Contemporary Human Resource Management: Text and Cases*. Harlow: Financial Times/Prentice-Hall.

Chaudhry, S. and Priola, V. (in press) Veiling careers: Comparing gendered work in Islamic and foreign banks in Pakistan, in A. Broadbridge and S. Fielden (eds) *Impact of Diversity on Career Development*. Cheltenham: Edward Elgar.

Cheryan, S., Plaut, V.C., Davies, P.G. and Steele, C.M. (2009) Ambient belonging: How stereotypical cues impact gender participation in computer science. *Journal of Personality and Social Psychology*, 97(6): 1045–1060.

Claire, J.A., Beatty, J.E. and Maclean, T.L (2005) Out of sight but not out of mind: Managing invisible identities in the workplace. *Academy of Management Review*, 30(1): 78–95.

Cooke, F.L. and Saini, D.S. (2012) Managing diversity in Chinese and Indian organizations: A qualitative study. *Journal of Chinese Human Resources Management*, 3(1): 16–32.

Cox, J.T. (1991) The multicultural organisation. *Academy of Management Executive*, 5(2): 34–47.

Cox, T.H. (1993) *Cultural Diversity in Organisations: Theory, Research and Practice*. San Francisco, CA: Berrett-Koehler Publishers.

Cox, T.H. and Blake, S. (1991) Managing cultural diversity: Implications for organisational competitiveness. *The Academy of Management Executive*, 5(3): 45–56.

Crenshaw, K. (1991) Mapping the margins: Intersectionality, identity politics, and violence against women of color. *Stanford Law Review*, 43(6): 1241–1299.

Danowitz, M.A., Hanappi-Egger, E. and Mensi-Klarbach, H. (eds) (2012) *Diversity in Organizations: Concepts and Practices*. New York and Basingstoke: Palgrave Macmillan.

Dick, P. and Cassell, C. (2002) Barriers to managing diversity in a UK constabulary: The role of discourse. *Journal of Management Studies*, 39(7): 953–976.

Dickens, L. (1998) What HRM means for gender equality. *Human Resource Management Journal*, 8(1): 23–40.

Dovidio, J.F. (2013) Included but invisible. *Gender and Work: Challenging Conventional Wisdom*. President of Fellows of Harvard College. Accessed online at: www.hbs.edu/faculty/conferences/2013-w50-research-symposium/Documents/dovidio.pdf

Equality Challenge Unit (2013) *Unconscious Bias and Higher Education*. Accessed online at: www.ecu.ac.uk/wp-content/uploads/2014/07/unconscious-bias-and-higher-education.pdf

Equality and Human Rights Commission (2016) *An Inquiry into Fairness, Transparency and Diversity in FTSE 350 Board Appointments*. Accessed online at: http://ehrcv2oszpjdinzc.devcloud.acquia-sites.com/sites/default/files/ehrc_inquiry_ftd_ftse350_updated_22-4-16.pdf

Fraser, N. (1997) From redistribution to recognition? Dilemmas of justice in a 'postsocialist' age. *Justice Interruptus: Critical Reflections on the 'Postsocialist' Condition*. New York and London: Routledge, pp. 11–40.

Goss, D. (1994) *Principles of Human Resource Management*. London: Routledge.

Greene, A.M. and Kirton, G. (2010) *Diversity Management in the UK: Organizational and Stakeholder Experiences*. Abingdon: Routledge.

Guillaume, Y.R.F., Dawson, J.F., Woods, S.A., Sacramento, C.A. and West, M.A. (2013) Getting diversity at work to work: What we know and what we still don't know. *Journal of Occupational and Organizational Psychology*, 86: 123–141.

Guillaume, Y.R.F., Dawson, J.F., Otaye-Ebede, L., Woods, S.A. and West, M.A. (2015) Harnessing demographic differences in organizations: What moderates the effects of workplace diversity? *Journal of Organizational Behavior*. doi: 10.1002/job.2040

Gutnam, A. (1993) *EEO Law and Personnel Practices*. Newbury Park, CA: Sage.

Harvard Law Review (1989) Rethinking 'Weber': The business response to affirmative action. 102(3): 658–671. Accessed online at: www.jstor.org.libezproxy.open.ac.uk/stable/1341374

Holladay, C.L. and Quiñones, M.A. (2003) Practice variability and transfer of training: The role of self-efficacy generality. *Journal of Applied Psychology*, 88: 1094–1103.

Hoskyns, C. (1996) *Integrating Gender: Women, Law and Politics in the European Union*. London: Verso.

HM Treasury and Virgin Money (2016) *Empowering Productivity: Harnessing the Talents of Women in Financial Services*. Accessed online at: http://uk.virginmoney.com/virgin/assets/pdf/Virgin-Money-Empowering-Productivity-Report.pdf

Jamali, D., Abdullah, H. and Hmaidan, S. (2010) The challenge of moving beyond rhetoric: Paradoxes of diversity management in the Middle East. *Equality, Diversity and Inclusion: An International Journal*, 29(2): 167–185.

Janssens, M. and Zanoni, P. (2005) Many diversities for many services: Theorizing diversity (management) in service companies. *Human Relations*, 58(3): 311–340.

Jewson, N. and Mason, D. (1986) The theory and practice of equal opportunities policies: Liberal and radical approaches. *Sociological Review*, 34(2): 307–334.

Joshi, A. and Roh, H. (2009) The role of context in work team diversity research: A meta-analytic review. *Academy of Management Journal*, 52(3): 599–627.

Joshi, A., Hui, L. and Jackson, S.E. (2006) Cross-level effects of workplace diversity on sales performance and pay. *Academy of Management Journal*, 49: 459–481.

Kang, S.K. and Bodenhausen, G.V. (2015) Multiple identities in social perception and interaction: Challenges and opportunities. *Annual Review of Psychology*, 66: 547–574.

Kellough, J.E. (2006) *Understanding Affirmative Action: Politics, Discrimination, and the Search for Justice*. Washington, DC: Georgetown University Press.

Kelly, E. and Dobbin, F. (1998) How affirmative action became diversity management: Employer response to antidiscrimination law, 1961 to 1996. *American Behavioural Scientist*, 41: 960–984.

Kidder, D.L., Lankau, M.J., Chrobot-Mason, D., Mollica, K.A. and Friedman, R.A. (2004) Backlash toward diversity initiatives: Examining the impact of diversity program justification, personal and group outcomes. *International Journal of Conflict Management*, 15(1): 77–102.

Kossek, E.E. and Lobel, S.A. (1996) Introduction: Transforming human resource systems to manage diversity – An introduction and orienting framework, in E.E. Kossek and S.A. Lobel (eds) *Managing Diversity: Human Resource Strategies for Transforming the Workplace*. Cambridge, MA: Blackwell.

Kumra, S. and Manfredi, S. (2012) *Managing Equality and Diversity: Theory and Practice*. Oxford: Oxford University Press.

Labour Program (2013) *Employment Equity*. Accessed online at: www.labour.gc.ca/eng/standards_equity/eq/emp/

Lebrecht, S., Pierce, L.J., Tarr, M.J. and Tanaka, J.W. (2009) Perceptual other-race training reduces implicit racial bias. *PLoS ONE*, 4(1): e4215.

Legault, L., Gutsell, J.N. and Inzlicht, M. (2011) Ironic effects of antiprejudice messages: How motivational interventions can reduce (but also increase) prejudice. *Psychological Science*, 22(12): 1472–1477.

Liff, S. and Wajcman, J. (1996) 'Sameness' and 'difference' revisited: Which way forward for equal opportunity initiatives? *Journal of Management Studies*, 33(1): 79–94.

Linnehan, F. and Konrad, A.M. (1999) Diluting diversity: Implications for intergroup inequality in organizations. *Journal of Management Inquiry*, 8(4): 399–414.

Mendoza, S.A., Gollwitzer, P.M. and Amodio, D.M. (2010) Reducing the expression of implicit stereotypes: Reflexive control through implementation intentions. *Personality and Social Psychology Bulletin*, 36(4): 512–523.

Miller, J. (1994) *Corporate Responses to Diversity*. New York: Center for the New American Workplace, Queens College.

Monks, K. and McMackin, J. (2001) Designing and aligning an HR system. *Human Resource Management Journal*, 11(2): 57–72.

Nash, J.C. (2008) Re-thinking intersectionality. *Feminist Review*, 89: 1–15.

Nishii, L.H. and Mayer, D.M. (2009) Do inclusive leaders help to reduce turnover in diverse groups? The moderating role of leader-member exchange in the diversity to turnover relationship. *Journal of Applied Psychology*, 94(6): 1412–1426.

Nishii, L.H. and Özbilgin, M. (2007) Global diversity management: Towards a conceptual framework. *The International Journal of Human Resource Management*, 18(11): 1883–1894.

Nkomo, S.M. (1992) The emperor has no clothes: Rewriting 'race in organisation'. *Academy of Management Review*, 17: 487–513.

Ogbonna, E. and Harris, L.C. (2006) The dynamics of employee relationships in an ethnically diverse workforce. *Human Relations*, 59(3): 379–407.

O'Reilly III, C.A., Caldwell, D.F. and Barnett, W.P. (1989) Work group demography, social integration, and turnover. *Administrative Science Quarterly*, 34(1): 21–37.

Ostner, I. and Lewis, J. (1995) Gender and the evolution of European social policies, in S. Leibfried and P. Pierson (eds) *European Social Policy: Between Fragmentation and Integration*. London: The Brookings Institution.

Otaye-Ebede, L. and Tatli, A. (2013) *Shifting Discourses of the Business Case for Diversity: Pre- and Post-Recession Periods in the UK*. Unpublished manuscript.

Özbilgin, M. and Tatli, A. (2008) *Global Diversity Management: An Evidence Based Approach*. London: Palgrave Macmillan.

Özbilgin, M.F. and Tatli, A. (2011) Mapping out the field of equality and diversity: Rise of individualism and voluntarism. *Human Relations*, 64(9): 1229–1253.

Parsons, E. and Priola, V. (2013) Agents for change and changed agents: The micropolitics of change and feminism in the academy. *Gender, Work and Organization*, 20(5): 580–598.

Priola, V., Lasio, D., De Simone, S. and Serri, F. (2014) The sound of silence: Lesbian, gay, bisexual and transgender (LGBT) discrimination in 'inclusive organisations'. *British Journal of Management*, 25(3): 488–502.

Ragins, B.R., Singh, R. and Cornwell, J.M. (2007) Making the invisible visible: Fear and disclosure of sexual orientation at work. *Journal of Applied Psychology*, 92(4): 1103–1118.

Richard, O.C., Barnett, T., Dwyer, S. and Chadwick, K. (2004) Cultural diversity in management, firm performance, and the moderating role of entrepreneurial orientation dimensions. *Academy of Management Journal*, 47(2): 255–266.

Roberson, Q.M. (2006) Disentangling the meanings of diversity and inclusion in organisations. *Group and Organisation Management*, 31(2): 212–236.

Robinson, G. and Dechant, K. (1997) Building a business case for diversity. *Academy of Management Executive*, 11(3): 21–31.

Sabharwal, M. (2014) Is diversity management sufficient? Organizational inclusion to further performance. *Public Administration*, 43(2): 197–217.

Sacco, J.M. and Schmitt, N. (2005) A dynamic multilevel model of demographic diversity and misfit effects. *Journal of Applied Psychology*, 90(2): 203–231.

Shore, L.M., Chung-Herra, B.G., Dean, M.A., Ehrhart, K.H., Jung, D.I., Randel, A.E. and Singh, G. (2009) Diversity in organizations: Where are we now and where are we going? *Human Resource Management Review*, 19: 117–133.

Shore, L., Randel, A., Chung, B., Dean, M., Ehrhart, K. and Singh, G. (2010) Inclusion and diversity in work groups: A review and model for future research. *Journal of Management*, 37(4): 1262–1289.

Sinclair, A. (2006) Critical diversity management practice in Australia: Romanced or co-opted?, in A. Konrad, P. Prasad and J. Pringle (eds) *Handbook of Workplace Diversity*. London: Sage, pp. 511–553.

Subeliani, D. and Tsogas, G. (2005) Managing diversity in the Netherlands: A case study of Rabobank. *International Journal of Human Resource Management*, 16(5): 831–851.

Syed, J. and Özbilgin, M. (2009) A relational framework for international transfer of diversity management practices. *The International Journal of Human Resource Management*, 20(12): 2435–2453.

Taniguchi, M. (2006) Succeeding where others fail to try: A case study of diversity management in the Japanese retail sector. *Career Development International*, 11(3): 216–229.

Tatli, A. (2008) *Understanding the Agency of Diversity Managers: A Relational and Multilevel Investigation*. Unpublished doctoral thesis, Queen Mary, University of London.

Tatli, A. (2011) A multi-layered exploration of the diversity management field: Diversity discourses, practices and practitioners in the UK. *British Journal of Management*, 22: 238–253.

Thomas, D.A. and Ely, R.J. (1996) Making differences matter: A new paradigm for diversity management. *Harvard Business Review*, 74(5): 79–90.

Thomas, R.R., Jr (1990) From affirmative action to affirming diversity. *Harvard Business Review*, 68(March–April): 107–117.

Truss, C. (2001) Complexities and controversies in linking HRM with organizational outcomes. *Journal of Management Studies*, 38(8): 1121–1149.

US Government Accountability Office (2005) *Diversity Management: Expert-Identified Leading Practices and Agency*. Examples: GAO-05-90. GAO Reports, US Government Accountability Office.

Van Knippenberg, D. and Schippers, M.C. (2007) Work group diversity. *Annual Review of Psychology*, 58: 515–541.

Williams, K. and O'Reilly, C. (1998) Forty years of diversity research: A review, in B.M. Staw and L.L. Cummings (eds) *Research in Organisational Behaviour*. Greenwich, CT: JAI Press, pp. 77–140.

Wright, G.L. and Priola, V. (2016) What about a career? The intersection of gender and disability, in A. Broadbridge and S. Fielden (eds) *Impact of Diversity on Career Development*. Cheltenham: Edward Elgar.

Yakura, E.K. (1995) EEO law and managing diversity, in E.E. Kossek and S.A. Lobel (eds) *Managing Diversity: Human Resource Strategies for Transforming the Workplace*. Cambridge, MA: Blackwell.

Ziegert, J. and Hanges, P. (2005) Employment discrimination: The role of implicit attitudes, motivation, and a climate for racial bias. *Journal of Applied Psychology*, 90: 553–562.

CHAPTER 9

Alliger, G. and Janak, E. (1989) Kirkpatrick's levels of training criteria: Thirty years later. *Personnel Psychology*, 42(2): 331–342.

Alpargatas S.A. (2006) Annual Report [electronic version]. Accessed online at: http://ri.alpargatas.com.br/ingles/informacoes...Anual/.../Resp_economica.pdf (accessed 30 June 2013).

Alpargatas S.A. (2013) Profile [electronic version]. Accessed online at: http://ri.alpargatas.com.br/INGLES/alpargatas/perfi l/index.asp (accessed 30 June 2013).

Argyris, C. (1999) *On Organizational Learning*, 2nd edn. Oxford: Blackwell.

Armstrong, M. (2014) *A Handbook of Human Resource Management Practice*, 13th edn. London: Kogan Page.

Bandura, A. (1977) *Social Learning Theory*. Upper Saddle River, NJ: Prentice-Hall.

Barney, J. (1991) Firm resources and sustained competitive advantage. *Journal of Management*, 17: 99–120.

Bass, B.M. and Vaughan, J.A. (1967) *Training in Industry: The Management of Learning*. London: Tavistock Publications.

Bassi, L. and McMurrer, D. (2004) How's your return on people? *Harvard Business Review*, 82(3): 18.

Beattie, R. (2006) Line managers and workplace learning: Learning from the voluntary sector. *Human Resource Development International*, 9(1): 99–119.

Becker, G. (1964) *Human Capital: A Theoretical and Empirical Analysis, with Special Reference to Education*, 2nd edn. New York: Columbia University Press.

Bednall, T.C., Sanders, K. and Runhaar, P. (2014) Stimulating informal learning activities through perceptions of performance appraisal quality and human resource management system strength: A two-wave study. *Academy of Management Learning and Education*, 13(1): 45–61.

Blanchard, N. and Thacker, J. (2013) *Effective Training: Systems, Strategies, and Practices*, 5th edn. Upper Saddle River, NJ: Pearson.

Bowen, D. and Ostroff, C. (2004) Understanding HRM–firm linkages: The role of the 'strength' of the HRM system. *Academy of Management Review*, 29(2): 203–221.

Boxall, P. and Macky, K. (2014) High-involvement work processes, work intensification and employee well-being. *Work, Employment and Society*, 28(6): 963–984.

Bratton, J. and Gold, J. (2007) *Human Resource Management: Theory and Practice*, 4th edn. Mahwah, NJ: Lawrence Erlbaum.

Brown, J. and Duguid, P. (2000) *The Social Life of Information*. Boston, MA: Harvard Business School Press.

Brown, J. and Gray, E. (2008) A short history of learning, in P. Kumar and P. Ramsey (eds) *Learning and Performance Matter*. Hackensack, NJ: World Scientific, pp. 17–32.

Burnes, B. (2009) *Managing Change: A Strategic Approach to Organisational Dynamics*, 5th edn. Harlow: Financial Times/Prentice-Hall.

CIPD (2009) *What is Reflective Learning?* Accessed online at: www.cipd.co.uk/cpd/aboutcpd/refl ectlearn.htm (accessed 19 December 2009).

CIPD (2015) *Learning and Talent Development: Annual Survey Report 2015*. Accessed online at: www.cipd.co.uk/binaries/learning-development_2015.pdf (accessed 11 April 2016).

Conole, G., Dyke, M., Oliver, M. and Seale, J. (2004) Mapping pedagogy and tools for effective learning design. *Computers and Education*, 43(1–2): 17–33.

Dewey, J. (1916) *Democracy and Education*. London: Macmillan.

Division of Skill Development Promotion, Department of Skill Development (2002) *Thailand Skill Development Promotion Act (B.E.2545)*. Asia Pacific Skills and Employability Network. Accessed online at: http://apskills.ilo.org/resources/skill-developmentpromotion-act-b.e.2545 (accessed 5 May 2013).

Easterby-Smith, M. (1994) *Evaluating Management Development, Training and Education*. Aldershot: Gower.

Easterby-Smith, M. and Lyles, M. (2011) Watersheds of organizational learning and knowledge management, in M. Easterby-Smith and M. Lyles (eds) *The Blackwell Handbook of Organizational Learning and Knowledge Management*, 2nd edn. Oxford: Blackwell Publishing, pp. 1–15.

Edvinsson, L. and Malone, M. (1997) *Intellectual Capital*. New York: HarperCollins.

European Commission (2006) *Decision No. 1720/2006/EC of the European Parliament and of the Council of 15 November 2006 Establishing an Action Programme in the Field of Lifelong Learning*. Accessed online at: http://eur-lex.europa.eu/legal-content/EN/TXT/?uri=celex:32006D1720 (accessed 11 April 2016).

Fabac, J. (2006) Project management for systematic training. *Advances in Developing Human Resources*, 8(4): 540–547.

Goldstein, I. and Ford, K. (2001) *Training in Organizations: Needs Assessment, Development and Evaluation*, 4th edn. Boston, MA: Wadsworth Publishing.

Guzzo, R. and Gannet, B. (1989) The nature of facilitators and inhibitors of effective task performance, in F. Schoorman and B. Schneider (eds) *Facilitating Work Effectiveness*. Lexington: Lexington Books, pp. 21–43.

Hager, P. (2004) Lifelong learning in the workplace? Challenges and issues. *Journal of Workplace Learning*, 16(1/2): 22–32.

Harrison, R. (2009) *Learning and Development*, 5th edn. London: CIPD.

HBSExecEd (2010) *Lifelong Learning.* 15 June. Accessed online at: www.youtube.com/watch?v=VjlPOafjLJs&feature=youtu.be (accessed 27 November 2012).

Hofstede, G., Hofstede, G.J. and Minkov, M. (2010) *Cultures and Organizations: Software of the Mind – Intercultural Cooperation and its Importance for Survival.* New York: McGraw-Hill.

Honey, P. and Mumford, A. (2002) *The Learning Styles Helper's Guide.* Maidenhead: Peter Honey Publications.

Huselid, M. (1995) The impact of human resource management practices on turnover, productivity and corporate financial performance. *Academy of Management Journal*, 38: 635–672.

Jarvis, P. (2006) *Towards a Comprehensive Theory of Human Learning: Lifelong Learning and the Learning Society, Volume I.* Abingdon: Routledge.

Kirkpatrick, D.L. (1959) *Evaluating Training Programs*, 2nd edn. San Francisco, CA: Berrett Koehler.

Knowles, M., Holton, E. and Swanson, R. (2015) *The Adult Learner: The Definitive Classic in Adult Education and Human Resource Development*, 8th edn. New York: Routledge.

Kolb, D. (1984) *Experiential Learning: Experience as a Source of Learning and Development.* Englewood Cliffs, NJ: Prentice-Hall.

Kolb, D., Boyatzis, R. and Mainemelis, C. (2001) Experiential learning theory: Previous research and new directions, in R. Sternberg and L. Zhang (eds) *Perspectives on Cognitive, Learning and Thinking Styles.* Mahwah, NJ: Lawrence Erlbaum, pp. 227–247.

Lewin, K. (1951) *Field Theory in Social Science: Selected Theoretical Papers.* New York: Harper & Brothers Publishers.

Lindeman, E.C. (1926) *The Meaning of Adult Education.* New York: New Republic. Republished in a new edition in 1989 by The Oklahoma Research Center for Continuing Professional and Higher Education.

Mankin, D. (2009) *Human Resource Development.* Oxford: Oxford University Press.

Marton, F. and Ramsden, P. (1988) What does it take to improve learning?, in P. Ramsden (ed.) *Improving Learning: New Perspectives.* London: Kogan Page.

Mathews, S. (1997) *Designing and Managing a Training and Development Strategy.* London: Pitman.

Mathieu, J. and Leonard, R. (1987) Applying utility concepts to a training program in supervisory skills: A time-based approach. *Journal of Academic Management*, 30(2): 316–335.

Matthews, J., Megginson, D. and Surtees, M. (2004) *Human Resource Development*, 3rd edn. London: Kogan Page.

Muller-Camen, M., Croucher, R. and Leigh, S. (2009) *Human Resource Management: A Case Study Approach.* London: CIPD.

Mumford, A. (1996) Effective learners in action learning set. *Journal of Workplace Learning: Employee Counselling Today*, 8(6): 3–10.

Nahapiet, J. and Ghoshal, S. (1998) Social capital, intellectual capital, and the organisational advantage. *Academy of Management Review*, 23(2): 242–266.

National Statistical Office (2012) *Informal Employed Persons*. Accessed online at: http://web.nso.go.th/en/survey/data_survey/550712_informal%20labor%202012.pdf (accessed 12 April 2016).

National Statistical Office (2016) *Summary of the Labor Force Survey in Thailand: December 2015*. Accessed online at: http://web.nso.go.th/en/survey/data_survey/LFS_Jan56_eng.pdf (accessed 12 April 2016).

Noe, R. and Tews, M. (2009) Strategic training and development, in J. Storey, P. Wright and D. Ulrich (eds) *The Routledge Companion to Strategic Human Resource Management*. London: Routledge, pp. 262–284.

Nonaka, I. and Takeuchi, H. (1995) *The Knowledge-Creating Company*. New York: Oxford University Press.

Nyfoudi, M. (2016a) Coaching, in A. Wilkinson and S. Johnstone (eds) *Encyclopedia of Human Resource Management*. Cheltenham: Edward Elgar, pp. 46–47.

Nyfoudi, M. (2016b) Learning organization, in A. Wilkinson and S. Johnstone (eds) *Encyclopedia of Human Resource Management*. Cheltenham: Edward Elgar, pp. 258–259.

People Management (19 November 2009) A 'honey bee' with future social media. Accessed online at: www.peoplemanagement. co.uk/pm/articles/2009/11/a-honey-bee-future-with-social-media.htm (accessed 21 December 2009).

Piaget, J. (1954) *The Construction of Reality in the Child*. New York: Basic Books.

Piaget, J. (1970) *Structuralism*. New York: Harper & Row.

Porter, M. (1985) *Competitive Advantage: Creating and Sustaining Superior Performance*. New York: The Free Press.

Roberson, D. (2005) Lifelong learning in the county: A context of nature, community and simplicity. *Rural Educator*, 27(1): 29–40.

Sanders, K., Yang, H., Shipton, H. and Bednall, T. (in press) Effects of human resource management on informal learning, in A. Ellingson and R. Noe (eds) *Autonomous Learning in the Workplace*. SIOP Frontiers Book Series. London: Taylor & Francis.

Schultz, T. (1961) Investment in human capital. *American Economic Review*, 51(1): 1–17.

Shackleton-Jones, N. (2008) Informal learning and the future. *Training Journal*, October: 38–41.

Shipton, H. (2006) Cohesion or confusion? Towards a typology for organizational learning research. *International Journal of Management Reviews*, 8(4): 232–252.

Shipton, H. and Zhou, Q. (2008) Learning and development in organisations, in Aston Centre for Human Resources (ed.) *Strategic HRM: Building Research Based Practice*. London: CIPD, pp. 159–188.

Skinner, B.F. (1953) *Science and Human Behaviour*. New York: Macmillan.

Sloman, M. (1999) *A Handbook for Training Strategy*, 2nd edn. Aldershot: Gower.

Sloman, M. (2007) Making sense of blended learning. *Industrial and Commercial Training*, 39(6): 315–318.

Tai, W. (2006) Effects of training framing, general self-efficacy and training motivation on trainee's training effectiveness. *Personnel Review*, 35(1): 51–65.

Tannenbaum, S. (2002) A strategic view of organizational training and learning, in K. Kraiger (ed.) *Creating, Implementing and Managing Effective Training and Development*. San Francisco, CA: Jossey-Bass, pp. 10–52.

Tuschling, A. and Engemann, C. (2006) From education to lifelong learning: The emerging regime of learning in the European Union. *Educational Philosophy and Theory*, 38(4): 451–469.

Ulrich, D. and Brockbank, W. (2009) The HR business-partner model: Past learnings and future challenges. *People and Strategy*, 32(2): 5–7.

United Nations (2016) *Thailand Info Climate*. Accessed online at: www.un.or.th/service-category/about-thailand/ (accessed 4 April 2016).

Xiao, Y. and Cooke, F.L. (2012) Work–life balance in China? Social policy, employer strategy and individual coping mechanisms, *Asia Pacific Journal of Human Resources*, 50: 6–22.

CHAPTER 10

Abowd, J.M. (1990) Does performance based managerial compensation affect corporate performance? *Industrial and Labour Relations Review*, 45: 52–73.

Adam, S. and Chen, S. (2013) Asia soaring wages mean rising prices worldwide. Bloomberg. Accessed online at: www.bloomberg.com/news/2013-04-02/asia-soaring-wages-stokeinflation-as-factory-costs-rise.html (accessed 2 April 2013).

Armstrong, M. (2006) *A Handbook of Personnel Management Practice*, 10th edn. London: Kogan Page.

Armstrong, M. and Murlis, H. (2004) *Reward Management: A Handbook of Remuneration Strategy and Practice*, 5th edn. London: Kogan Page.

Bevan, S. (2013) Performance related pay and the rhetoric gap. Accessed online at: www.theworkfoundation.com/blog/1479/perform

Bloom, M. (1999) The performance effects of pay dispersion on individuals and organizations. *Academy of Management Journal*, 42(1): 25–40.

Bloom, M. and Milkovich, G.T. (1998) *A SHRM Perspective on International Compensation and Reward Systems*. Center for Advanced Human Resource Studies (CAHRS) Working Paper #98-11. Ithaca, NY: School of Industrial and Labor Relations, Cornell University.

Boselie, P., Paauwe, J. and Jansen, P. (2001) Human resource management and performance: Lessons from the Netherlands. *International Journal of Human Resource Management*, 12: 1107–1125.

Brown, D. (2014) The future of reward management: From total reward strategies to smart rewards. *Compensation and Benefits Review*, 46(3): 147–151.

Brown, L. (2013) Keeping employees engaged: What does it take? Viewpoints. Accessed online at: www.towerswatson.com/en/Insights/IC-Types/Ad-hoc-Point-of-View/2013/11/Keeping-Employees-Engaged-What-Does-It-Take

CIPD (2012) *Reward Risks: Annual Survey Report*. London: Chartered Institute of Personnel and Development.

CIPD (2015) *Reward Management 2014–2015*. London: Chartered Institute of Personnel and Development.

Collins, J.M. and Muchinsky, P.M. (1993) An assessment of the construct validity of three job evaluation methods: A field experiment. *Academy of Management Journal*, 36(4): 895–904.

Delery, J. and Shaw, J. (2001) The strategic management of people in work organisations: Review, synthesis, and an extension. *Research in Personnel and Human Resources Management*, 20: 165–197.

Dishman, L. (2015) Does a huge pay gap between CEO and staff affect employee satisfaction? 25 August. Accessed online at: www.fastcompany.com/3050281/the-future-of-work/does-a-huge-pay-gap-between-ceo-and-staff-affect-employee-satisfaction

Equilar (2015) The New York Times top 200 highest-paid CEOs. Accessed online at: www.equilar.com/reports/18-2-200-highest-paid-CEO-rankings-2015.html

Felipe, J. and Kumar, U. (2011) *Unit Labor Cost in the Eurozone: The Competitiveness Debate Again*. Levy Economics Institute of Bard College and Asia Development Bank, Manila, Philippines, Working Paper No. 651. Accessed online at: http://dx.doi.org/10.2139/ssrn.1773762

Gerhart, B. and Milkovich, G.T. (1990) Organisational differences in managerial compensation and financial performance. *Academy of Management Journal*, 8: 663–691.

Glassdoor (2016) *Global Salary Transparency Survey – Employee Perceptions of Talking Pay*. Accessed online at: https://press-content.glassdoor.com/app/uploads/sites/2/2016/04/GD_Survey_GlobalSalaryTransparency-FINAL.pdf

Gomez-Mejia, L.R., Balkin, D.B. and Cardy, R.L. (2004) *Managing Human Resources*, 4th edn. Upper Saddle River, NJ: Pearson Education.

HayGroup® (2005) *Hay Job Evaluation: Foundations and Applications*. Working Paper. Philadelphia, PA: HayGroup®.

Hays (2016) *Asia at a Crossroads: Can Talent Supply Meet Increasing Demand?* Singapore: Hays Specialist Recruitment Pte Ltd.

Heery, E. (1996) Risk, representation and the new pay. *Personnel Review*, 25(6): 54–65.

Huang, W. and Brown, W. (2007) *Payment Systems in Transition: Case Studies in China's Car Industry*. Cambridge: Judge Business School.

Hutchinson, S. (2013) *Performance Management: Theory and Practice*. London: CIPD.

Lawler, E.E. (1990) *Strategic Pay*. San Francisco, CA: Jossey-Bass.

Lawler, E.E. (1995) The new pay: A strategic approach. *Compensation and Benefits Review*, 27(4): 14–22.

Lawler, E.E. (2011) Creating a new employment deal: Total rewards and the new workforce. *Organizational Dynamics*, 40(4): 302–309.

Lawler, E.E. (2012) Pay secrecy – Why bother. Forbes, 12 September. Accessed online at: www.forbes.com/sites/edwardlawler/2012/09/12/pay-secrecy-why-bother/

Lazear, E.P. and Gibbs, M. (2014) *Personnel Economics in Practice*, 3rd edn. Chichester: John Wiley.

Lin, Z., Kelly, J. and Trenberth, L. (2011) Antecedents and consequences of the introduction of flexible benefit plans in China. *International Journal of Human Resource Management*, 22(5): 1128–1145.

Locke, E.A. (1968) Toward a theory of task motivation and incentives. *Organizational Behavior and Human Performance*, 3: 157–189.

McCormick, E.J., Jeanneret, P.R. and Meacham, R.C. (1972) A study of job characteristics and job dimensions as based on the Position Analysis Questionnaire (PAQ). *Journal of Applied Psychology*, 56(4): 347–368.

McCormick, E.J., Jeanneret, P.R. and Meacham, R.C. (1989) *Position Analysis Questionnaire*. Bellingham, WA: PAQ Services.

McShane, S.L. (1990) Two tests of direct gender bias in job evaluation ratings. *Journal of Occupational Psychology*, 63: 129–140.

Marsden, D. (2009) *The Paradox of Performance Related Pay Systems: 'Why Do We Keep Adopting Them in the Face of Evidence That They Fail to Motivate?'* CEP Discussion Paper #946. London: Centre for Economic Performance.

Marsden, D. and Richardson, R. (1994) Performing for pay? The effects of merit pay on motivation in public services. *British Journal of Industrial Relations*, 32(2): 243–261.

Marsland, P. (2015) *Pay Ratios: Just Do It*. High Pay Centre. Accessed online at: http://highpaycentre.org/pubs/pay-ratios-just-do-it

Martocchio, J.J. (2011) *Strategic Compensation*. New York: Pearson/Prentice-Hall.

Milkovich, G.T., Newman, J.M. and Gerhart, B. (2011) *Compensation*. New York: McGraw-Hill.

Mitchell, T.R. and Mickel, A.E. (1999) The meaning of money: An individual-difference perspective. *The Academy of Management Review*, 24(3): 568–578.

OECD (2015) *Gender Equality*. Accessed online at: www.oecd.org/gender/data/genderwagegap.htm

Pfeffer, J. (1998) Six dangerous myths about pay. *Harvard Business Review*, May–June: 109–119.

Porter, M.E. (1985) *Competitive Advantage: Creating and Sustaining Superior Performance*. New York: The Free Press.

Risher, H. (2014) Pay transparency is coming. *Compensation and Benefits Review*, 46(1): 3–5.

Robinson, S.R. and Morrison, E.W. (1995) Psychological contracts and OCB: The effect of unfulfilled obligations. *Journal of Organizational Behavior*, 16: 289–298.

Rousseau, D.M. (1995) *Psychological Contracts in Organizations: Understanding Written and Unwritten Agreements*. London: Sage.

Rousseau, D.M. and Greller, M.M. (1994) Human resource practices: Administrative contract makers. *Human Resource Management*, 33: 385–401.

Ryan, R.M. and Deci, E.L. (2000) Self-determination theory and the facilitation of intrinsic motivation, social development and well-being. *American Psychologist*, 55: 68–78.

Rynes, S.L., Gerhart, B. and Minette, K.A. (2004) The importance of pay in employee motivation: Discrepancies between what people say and what they do. *Human Resource Management*, 43(4): 381–394.

Rynes, S.L., Gerhart, B. and Parks, L. (2005) Personnel psychology: Performance evaluation and pay for performance. *Annual Review of Psychology*, 56: 571–600.

Schuler, R.S. and Jackson, S.E. (1987) Organisational strategy and organisational level as determinants of human resource management practices. *Human Resource Planning*, 10(3): 125–141.

SEC (Securities and Exchange Commission) (2015) SEC adopts rule for pay ratio disclosure. Press release, 5 August. Accessed online at: www.sec.gov/news/pressrelease/2015-160.html

Shields, J. (2016) *Managing Employee Performance and Reward: Concepts, Practices and Strategies*. Melbourne, Australia: Cambridge University Press.

Simon, H.A. (1991) Organizations and markets. *Journal of Economic Perspectives*, 5(2): 25–44.

Slater, P. (1980) *Wealth Addiction*. New York: Dutton.

Sloane, P., Latreille, P. and O'Leary, N. (2013) *Modern Labour Economics*. London: Routledge.

Strauss, N. and Howe, W. (2000) *Millennials Rising: The Next Great Generation*. New York: Vintage Books.

Towers-Watson (2012) *The Next High Stakes Quest. Balancing Employer and Employee Priorities: 2012–2013 Global Talent Management and Rewards Study*. New York: Towers-Watson.

Trades Union Congress (TUC) (2013) Accessed online at: www.tuc.org.uk

Vroom, V.E. (1964) *Work and Motivation*. Oxford: Wiley.

Welbourne, T. and Trevor, C. (2000) The roles of departmental and position power in job evaluation. *Academy of Management Journal*, 43(4): 761–771.

WorldatWork (2015) *What is Total Rewards?* Accessed online at: www.worldatwork. org/aboutus/html/aboutus-whatis-tr-model.jsp#model

CHAPTER 11

Aguinis, H. (2013) *Performance Management.* Harlow: Pearson Education.

Aycan, Z. (2005) The interplay between cultural and institutional/structural contingencies in human resource management practices. *International Journal of Human Resource Management*, 16(7): 1083–1119.

Bobko, P. and Colella, A. (1994) Employee reactions to performance standards: A review and research propositions. *Personnel Psychology*, 47(1): 1–29.

Cardy, R.L. and Dobbins, G.H. (1986) Affect and appraisal accuracy: Liking as an integral dimension in evaluating performance. *Journal of Applied Psychology*, 71: 672–678.

DeNisi, A.S. (1996) *Cognitive Processes in Performance Appraisal: A Research Agenda with Implications for Practice.* London: Routledge.

DeNisi, A.S. and Pritchard, R.D. (2006) Performance appraisal, performance management and improving individual performance: A motivational framework. *Management and Organization Review*, 2(2): 253–277.

Duguid, M.M. and Thomas-Hunt, M.C. (2015) Condoning stereotyping? How awareness of stereotyping prevalence impacts expression of stereotypes. *Journal of Applied Psychology*, 100(2): 343–359.

Fletcher, C. (2001) Performance appraisal and management: The developing research agenda. *Journal of Occupational and Organizational Psychology*, 74: 473–487.

Graen, G. and Cashman, J. (1975) A role-making model of leadership in formal organizations: A developmental approach, in J.G. Hunt and L.L. Larson (eds) *Leadership Frontiers.* Kent, OH: Kent State University Press, pp. 143–165.

Hofstede, G.H. (1980) *Culture's Consequences: International Differences in Work-Related Values.* Beverly Hills, CA: Sage.

Kahneman, D. (2011) *Thinking, Fast and Slow.* Basingstoke: Macmillan.

Latham, G.P. (2007) *Work Motivation: History, Theory, Research and Practice.* Thousand Oaks, CA: Sage.

Leung, K., Su, S. and Morris, M.W. (2001) When is criticism not constructive? The roles of fairness perceptions and dispositional attributions in employee acceptance of critical supervisory feedback. *Human Relations*, 54(9): 1155–1187.

Locke, E.A. (1968) Toward a theory of task performance and incentives. *Organizational Behavior and Human Performance*, 3: 157–189.

Locke, E.A. (1997) The motivation to work: What we know, in M.L. Maehr and P.R. Pintrich (eds) *Advances in Motivation and Achievement, Vol. 10.* Greenwich, CT: JAI Press, pp. 375–412.

London, M. and Beatty, R.W. (1993) 360-degree feedback as a competitive advantage. *Human Resource Management*, 32: 353–372.

London, M. and Smither, J.W. (1995) Can multisource feedback change perceptions of goal accomplishment, self-evaluations, and performance-related outcomes? Theory-based applications and directions for research. *Personnel Psychology*, 48: 803–839.

Murphy, K.R. and Cleveland, J.N. (1995) *Understanding Performance Appraisal: Social, Organizational, and Goal-Based Perspectives*. Thousand Oaks, CA: Sage.

Pichler, S., Varma, A. and Petty, R. (2008) Rater–ratee relationships, in A. Varma, P.S. Budhwar and A.S. DeNisi (eds) *Performance Management Systems: A Global Perspective*. Global HRM Series. London: Routledge, pp. 55–66.

Pritchard, R.D. and Ashwood, E. (2008) *Managing Motivation*. New York: Taylor & Francis.

Pritchard, R.D. and DiazGranados, D. (2008) Motivation and performance management, in A. Varma, P.S. Budhwar and A.S. DeNisi (eds) *Performance Management Systems: A Global Perspective*. Global HRM Series. London: Routledge, pp. 40–54.

Pucik, V. (1987) Joint ventures with the Japanese: The key role of HRM. *Euro–Asia Business Review*, 6: 36–39.

Schuler, R.S. (1992) Linking the people with the strategic needs of the business. *Organisational Dynamics*, 21(1): 18–32.

Schuler, R.S. and Jackson, S. (1987) Linking competitive strategies with human resource management practices. *Academy of Management Executive*, 1: 207–219.

Shantz, A. and Latham, G. (2011) The effect of primed goals on employee performance: Implications for human resource management. *Human Resource Management*, 50(2): 289–299.

Shih, H.A., Chiang, Y.H. and Kim, I.S. (2005) Expatriate performance management from MNEs of different national origins. *International Journal of Manpower*, 26: 157–176.

Stroh, L.K. and Caligiuri, P.M. (1998) Strategic human resources: A new source for competitive advantage in the global arena. *International Journal of Human Resource Management*, 9: 1–17.

Tung, R.L. and Varma, A. (2008) Expatriate selection and evaluation, in P.B. Smith, M.F. Peterson and D.C. Thomas (eds) *Handbook of Cross-Cultural Management Research*. London: Sage, pp. 367–378.

Varma, A. and Stroh, L.K. (2001) The impact of same-sex LMX dyads on performance evaluations. *Human Resource Management*, 40: 309–320.

Varma, A., DeNisi, A.S. and Peters, L.H. (1996) Interpersonal affect and performance appraisal: A field study. *Personnel Psychology*, 49(2): 341–360.

Varma, A., Budhwar, P.S. and DeNisi, A.S. (eds) (2008) Performance management around the globe: Introduction and agenda, in *Performance Management Systems: A Global Perspective*. Global HRM Series. London: Routledge, pp. 3–14.

Varma, A., Budhwar, P.S. and McCusker, C. (2015) Performance management in the global organization, in D. Collings, G.T. Wood and P.M. Caligiuri (eds) *The Routledge Companion to International Human Resource Management*. Abingdon: Routledge.

Vroom, V. (1964) *Work and Motivation*. New York: Wiley.

CHAPTER 12

Blyton, P. and Turnbull, P. (2004) *The Dynamics of Employee Relations*, 3rd edn. Basingstoke: Palgrave Macmillan.

CIPD/DTI (2004) *High Performance Work Practices: Linking Strategy and Skills to Performance Outcomes*. London: Chartered Institute of Personnel and Development.

Daft, R.L. (2009) *Organisation Theory and Design*, 10th edn. Cincinatti, OH: South-Western College Publishing.

Daniels, K. (2006) *Employee Relations in an Organisational Context*. London: CIPD.

Fox, A. (1966) *Industrial Sociology and Industrial Relations*. Royal Commission Research Paper No. 3. London: HMSO.

Gennard, J. and Judge, G. (2010) *Managing Employment Relations*, 5th edn. London: CIPD.

Marchington, M. and Cox, A. (2007) Employee involvement and participation: Structures, processes and outcomes, in J. Storey (ed.) *Human Resource Management: A Critical Text*, 3rd edn. London: Thomson Learning, pp. 177–194.

Metcalf, D. and Barber, B. (2005) Highway to hell? *People Management*, 11(18): 26–29.

Palmer, G. (1983) *British Industrial Relations*. London: Unwin Hyman.

Salamon, M. (2000) *Industrial Relations: Theory and Practice*, 4th edn. Harlow: Financial Times/Prentice-Hall.

Schein, E. (1988) *Organisation Psychology*, 3rd edn. Englewood Cliffs, NJ: Prentice-Hall.

Webb, S. and Webb, B. (1902) *Industrial Democracy*. London: Longmans Green.

CHAPTER 13

Acs, Z.J. and Armington, C. (2006) *Entrepreneurship, Geography and American Economic Growth*. New York: Cambridge University Press.

Altinay, L., Altinay, E. and Gannon, J. (2008) Exploring the relationship between the human resource management practices and growth in small service firms. *The Service Industries Journal*, 28(7): 919–937.

Anyadike-Danes, M., Bonner, K., Hart, M. and Mason, C. (2009) *Business Growth: High-Growth Firms and their Contribution to Employment in the UK*. London: NESTA.

Atkinson, C. and Curtis, S. (2004) The impact of employment regulation on the employment relationship in SMEs. *Journal of Small Business and Enterprise Development*, 11(4): 486–494.

Audretsch, D. (2002) The dynamic role of small firms: Evidence from the US. *Small Business Economics*, 18(1–3): 13–40.

Bacon, N. and Hoque, K. (2005) HRM in the SME sector: Valuable employees and coercive networks. *International Journal of Human Resource Management*, 16(11): 1976–1999.

Barrett, R. and Mayson, S. (2007) Human resource management in growing small firms. *Journal of Small Business and Enterprise Development*, 14(2): 307–320.

BERR (2008) *The Impact of Regulation on Small Business Performance: Report for the Enterprise Directorate of BERR*. Project Report. London: Department of Business, Enterprise and Regulatory Reform.

Birch, D.L. (1979) *The Job Generation Process: MIT Study on Neighborhood and Regional Change*. Cambridge, MA: MIT.

BIS (2015) *Statistical Release: Business Population Estimates for the UK and Regions*. Sheffield: Department for Business, Innovation and Skills.

Bolton Committee (1971) *Report of the Committee of Enquiry into Small Firms*. Chaired by J.E. Bolton, Cmnd. 4811. London: HMSO.

Boxall, P. (1996) The strategic HRM debate and the resource-based view of the firm. *Human Resource Management Journal*, 6(3): 59–75.

Boxall, P. and Purcell, J. (2000) Strategic human resource management: Where have we come to and where should we be going? *International Journal of Management Reviews*, 2: 183–203.

Brand, M.J. and Bax, E.H. (2002) Strategic HRM for SMEs: Implications for firms and policy. *Education and Training Journal*, 44(8): 451–463.

Brewster, C., Sparrow, P., Vernon, G. and Houldsworth, L. (2011) *International Human Resource Management*. London: CIPD.

Cardon, M.S. and Stevens, C.E. (2004) Managing human resources in small organisations: What do we know? *Human Resource Management Review*, 14: 295–323.

Carmel, E. and Harlock, J. (2008) Instituting the 'third sector' as a governable terrain: Partnership, procurement and performance in the UK. *Policy and Politics*, 36(2): 155–171.

Carroll, M., Marchington, M., Earnshaw, J. and Taylor, S. (1999) Recruitment in small firms: Processes, methods and problems. *Employee Relations*, 21: 236–250.

Chalofsky, N. (1992) A unifying definition for the human resource development profession. *Human Resource Development Quarterly*, 3(2): 175–182.

Crain, N.V. and Crain, W.M. (2010) *The Impact of Regulatory Costs on Small Firms*. Lafayette, PA: US Small Business Administration, Office of Advocacy. Accessed online at: www.sba.gov/advocacy/impact-regulatory-costs-small-firms

Curran, J. and Blackburn, R.A. (2001) *Researching the Small Enterprise*. London: Sage.

Davidsson, P., Delmar, F. and Wiklund, J. (2002) Entrepreneurship as growth: Growth as entrepreneurship, in M.A. Hitt, R.D. Ireland, M.S. Camp and D.L. Sexton (eds) *Strategic Entrepreneurship: Creating a New Mindset*. Oxford: Blackwell, pp. 329–342.

Day, D.L. (1992) Research linkages between entrepreneurship and strategic management or general management, in D.L. Sexton and J.D. Kasandra (eds) *The State of the Art of Entrepreneurship*. Boston, MA: PWS-Kent, pp. 117–163.

Deakins, D. and Freel, M. (2003) *Entrepreneurship and Small Firms*, 3rd edn. London: McGraw-Hill.

De Kok, J. and Uhlaner, L. (2001) Organisation context and human resource management in the small firm. *Small Business Economics*, 17(4): 273–291.

Delaney, J.T. and Huselid, M.A. (1996) The impact of human resource management practices on perceptions of organizational performance. *Academy of Management Journal*, 39: 949–969.

Delery, J.E. and Doty, D.H. (1996) Modes of theorizing in strategic human resource management: Tests of universalistic, contingency and configurational performance predictions. *Academy of Management Journal*, 39(4): 802–835.

Duberley, J. and Walley, P. (1995) Assessing the adoption of HRM by small and medium sized manufacturing organisations. *The International Journal of Human Resource Management*, 6(4): 891–909.

Earnshaw, J., Marchington, M. and Goodman, J. (2000) Unfair to whom? Discipline and dismissal in small establishments. *Industrial Relations Journal*, 31(1): 62–73.

Edwards, P. and Ram, M. (2009) HRM in small firms: Respecting and regulating informality, in A. Wilkinson, N. Bacon, T. Redman and S. Snell (eds) *The Sage Handbook of Human Resource Management*. London: Sage, pp. 524–540.

Edwards, P., Ram, M. and Black, J. (2003) Why does employment legislation not damage small firms? *Journal of Law and Society*, 31(2): 245–265.

European Commission DG Enterprise and Industry (2014) *EU SMEs in 2014: At the Crossroads*. Annual report on small and medium-sized enterprises in the EU. Accessed online at: http://ec.europa.eu/growth/smes/business-friendly-environment/performance-review/files/supporting-documents/2014/annual-report-smes-2014_en.pdf (accessed 18 April 2016).

Ferligoj, A., Prasnikar, J. and Vesa, J. (1997) Competitive advantage and human resource management in SMEs in a transitional economy. *Small Business Economics*, 9(6): 503–514.

Graham, M.E., Murray, B. and Amuso, L. (2002) Stock-related rewards, social identity, and the attraction and retention of employees in entrepreneurial SMEs, in J. Katz and T. Welbourne (eds) *Managing People in Entrepreneurial Organizations*. Amsterdam: Elsevier Science, pp. 107–145.

Guest, D.E. (2011) Human resource management and performance: Still searching for some answers. *Human Resource Management Journal*, 21(1): 3–13.

Guthrie, J. (2001) High-involvement work practices, turnover and productivity: Evidence from New Zealand. *Academy of Management Journal*, 44: 180–192.

Harney, B. and Dundon, T. (2006) Developing an integrated approach to analysing HRM in SMEs. *Human Resource Management Journal*, 16(1): 48–73.

Hayton, J.C. (2003) Strategic human capital management in SMEs: An empirical study of entrepreneurial performance. *Human Resource Management*, 42: 375–391.

Hayton, J.C. (2005) Promoting corporate entrepreneurship through human resource management practices: A review of empirical research. *Human Resource Management Review*, 15(1): 21–41.

Heneman, R.L. and Tansky, J.W. (2002) Human resource management models for entrepreneurial opportunity: Existing knowledge and new directions, in J. Katz and

T.M. Welbourne (eds) *Managing People in Entrepreneurial Organizations*. Amsterdam: JAI Press, pp. 55–82.

Heneman, R.L., Tansky, J.W. and Camp, S.M. (2000) Human resource management practices in small and medium-sized enterprises: Unanswered questions and future research perspective. *Entrepreneurship Theory and Practice*, 25(1): 11–26.

Hitt, M.A., Ireland, R.D., Camp, M.S. and Sexton, D.L. (2001) Guest editors' introduction to the special issue strategic entrepreneurship: Entrepreneurial strategies for wealth creation. *Strategic Management Journal*, 22: 479–505.

Hornsby, J.S. and Kurato, D.K. (1990) Human resource management in small firms: Critical issues for the 1990s. *Journal of Small Business Management*, 28: 9–18.

Hornsby, J.S. and Kurato, D.K. (2003) Human resource management in US small business: A replication and extension. *Journal of Developmental Entrepreneurship*, 8: 73–92.

Huselid, M.A. (1995) The impact of human resource management practices on turnover, productivity and corporate financial performance. *Academy of Management Journal*, 38(3): 635–672.

Huselid, M.A. (2003) Editor's note: Special issue on small and medium sized enterprises – A call for more research. *Human Resource Management*, 42(4): 297.

Huselid, M.A., Jackson, S.E. and Schuler, R.S. (1997) Technical and strategic human resource management effectiveness as determinants of firm performance. *Academy of Management Journal*, 40(4): 704–721.

Jorgensen, D. (1989) *Participant Observation*. Newbury Park, CA: Sage.

Karami, A., Jones, B. and Kakabadse, N. (2008) Does strategic human resource management matter in high-tech sector? Some learning points for SME managers. *Corporate Governance*, 8(1): 7–17.

Katz, J.A., Aldrich, H.E., Welbourne, T.M. and Williams, P.M. (2000) Guest editors' comments: Special issue on human resource management and the SME – Toward a new synthesis. *Entrepreneurship Theory and Practice*, 25(1): 7–10.

Kerr, A. and McDougall, M. (1999) The small business of developing people. *International Small Business Journal*, 17(2): 65–74.

Kerr, G., Way, S. and Thacker, J. (2007) Performance, HR practices and the HR manager in small entrepreneurial firms. *Journal of Small Business and Entrepreneurship*, 20(1): 55–68.

Kidwell, R.E. and Fish, A.J. (2007) High performance human resource practices in Australian family business: Preliminary evidence from the wine industry. *International Entrepreneurship and Management Journal*, 3(1): 1–14.

Klaas, S., McClendon, J. and Gainey, T.W. (2000) Managing HR in the small and medium enterprise: The impact of professional employer organisations. *Entrepreneurship Theory and Practice*, 25: 107–124.

Kotey, B. and Slade, P. (2005) Human resource management practices in small growing firms. *Journal of Small Business Management*, 43(1): 16–40.

McEvoy, G. (1984) Small business personnel practices. *Journal of Small Business Management*, 22(4): 1–8.

Marchington, M., Carrol, M. and Boxall, P. (2003) Labour scarcity and the survival of small firms. *Human Resource Management Journal*, 13: 5–22.

Marlow, S. (2000) Investigating the use of emergent strategic human resource management activity in the small firm. *Journal of Small Business and Enterprise Development*, 7(2): 135–148. Accessed online at: http://go.galegroup.com/ps/i.do?id=GALE%7CA70422176&sid=googleScholar&v=2.1&it=r&linkaccess=fulltext&issn=02662426&p=AONE&sw=w

Marlow, S. (2002) Regulating labour management in small firms. *Human Resource Management Journal*, 12(3): 25–43.

Marlow, S. (2006) Labor management and small business, in S. Carter and D. Jones-Evans (eds) *Enterprise and Small Business.* Harlow: Financial Times/Prentice-Hall, pp. 385–405.

Marlow, S. and Patton, D. (1993) Managing the employment relationship in the smaller firm: Possibilities for human resource management. *International Small Business Journal*, 11(4): 57–64.

Marlow, S., Patton, D. and Ram, M. (2005) *Managing Labour in Small Firms.* London: Routledge.

Marlow, S., Taylor, S. and Thompson, A. (2010) Informality and formality in medium-sized companies: Contestation and synchronization. *British Journal of Management*, 21: 954–966.

Mayson, S. and Barrett, R. (2006) The 'science' and 'practice' of HRM in small firms. *Human Resource Management Review*, 16: 447–455.

Mazzarol, T. (2005) A proposed framework for the strategic management of small entrepreneurial firms. *Small Enterprise Research*, 13(1): 37–53.

NESTA (2009) *The Vital 6 Per Cent: How High-Growth Innovative Businesses Generate Prosperity and Jobs – Research Summary.* October. London: National Endowment for Science, Technology and the Arts.

Nguyen, T.V. and Bryant, S.E. (2004) A study of the formality of human resource management practices in small and medium-size enterprises in Vietnam. *International Small Business Journal*, 22(6): 595–618.

Parry, E., Kelliher, C., Mills, T. and Tyson, S. (2005) Comparing HRM in the voluntary and public sectors. *Personnel Review*, 34(5): 588–602.

Patton, D., Marlow, S. and Hannon, P. (2000) The relationship between training and small firm performance: Research frameworks and lost quests. *International Small Business Journal*, 19(1): 11–27.

Purcell, J., Hutchinson, S., Kinnie, N., Rayton, B. and Swart, J. (2003) *Understanding the Pay and Performance Link: Unlocking the Black Box.* London: CIPD.

Ram, M. and Edwards, P. (2003) Praising Caesar not burying him: What we know about employment relations in small firms. *Work, Employment and Society*, 17(4): 719–730.

Ram, M., Edwards, P., Gilman, M. and Arrowsmith, J. (2001) The dynamics of informality: Employment relations in small firms and the effects of regulatory change. *Work, Employment and Society*, 15(4): 845–861.

Saini, D.S. and Budhwar, P.S. (2008) Managing the human resource in Indian SMEs: The role of indigenous realities. *Journal of World Business*, 43: 417–434.

Sang, C. (2005) *Relationship Between HRM Practices and the Perception of Organisational Performance, Roles of Management Style, Social Capital and Culture: Comparisons between Manufacturing Firms in Cambodia and Taiwan*. Master's Thesis, National Cheng Kung University, Tainan, Taiwan.

Stanworth, J. and Curran, J. (1986) Growth and the small firm, in J. Curran, J. Stanworth and D. Watkins (eds) *The Survival of the Small Firm*. Aldershot: Gower, pp. 81–99.

Storey, D.J. (1994) *Understanding the Small Business Sector*. London: International Thomson Business Press.

Storey, D.J. and Greene, F.J. (2010) *Small Business and Entrepreneurship*. Harlow: Financial Times/Prentice-Hall.

Theodorakopoulos, N. and Figueira, C. (2012) What can situated learning theory tell us about entrepreneurial performance? Lessons from a high technology small firm. *Thunderbird International Business Review*, 54(6): 859–873.

Urwin, P., Karuk V., Buscha, F. and Siara, B. (2008) *Small Businesses in the UK: New Perspectives on Evidence and Policy*. London: Centre for Employment Research, University of Westminster.

USITC (2010) *Small and Medium Sized Enterprises: Overview of Participation in U.S. Exports*. January. Washington, DC: United States International Trade Commission.

Way, S.A. (2002) High performance work systems and intermediate indicators of firm performance within the US small business sector. *Journal of Management*, 28: 765–785.

Wilkinson, A. (1999) Employment relations in SMEs. *Employee Relations*, 21(3): 206–217.

Worthington, I., Britton, C. and Rees, A. (2001) *Economics for Business: Blending Theory and Practice*. Harlow: Financial Times/Prentice-Hall.

Wyer, P., Mason, J. and Theodorakopoulos, N. (2000) An examination of the concept of the 'learning organisation' within the context of small business development. *International Journal of Entrepreneurial Behaviour and Research*, 6(4): 239–259.

CHAPTER 14

Baluch, A.M. (2016) Employee perceptions of HRM and well-being in nonprofit organizations: Unpacking the unintended. *The International Journal of Human Resource Management*. doi: 10.1080/09585192.2015.1136672

Bartram, T., Stanton, P., Leggat, S., Casimir, G. and Fraser, B. (2007) Lost in translation: Exploring the link between human resource management and performance in healthcare. *Human Resource Management Journal*, 17(1): 21–41.

Batt, R. (2002) Managing customer services: Human resource practices, quit rates, and sales growth. *Academy of Management Journal*, 45(3): 587–597.

Bednall, T., Sanders, K. and Runhaar, P. (2014) Stimulating informal learning activities through perceptions of performance appraisal quality and human resource management system strength: A two-wave study. *Academy of Management Learning and Education*, 13(1): 45–61.

Benitez, A., Cruz-Castro, L. and Sanz-Menéndez, L. (2016) Human resources management in higher education: The influence of the policies of regions on hiring and promotion practices at universities. *Human Resources*.

Bennington, L. and Habir, A.D. (2003) Human resource management in Indonesia. *Human Resource Management Review*, 13: 373–392.

Blandford, S. (2012) *Managing Professional Development in Schools*. Education Management Series. London: Routledge.

Boyne, G., Jenkins, G. and Poole, M. (1999) Human resource management in the public and private sectors: An empirical comparison. *Public Administration*, 77(2): 407–420.

Broaden, R., Marchington, M., Hyde, P., Harris, C., Sparrow, P., Pass, S., Carroll, M. and Cortvriend, P. (2008) *Improving Health through Human Resource Management: The Process of Engagement and Alignment*. London: CIPD.

Buchanan, D.A., Addicott, R., Fitzgerald, L., Ferlie, E. and Baeza, J.I. (2007) Nobody in charge: Distributed change agency in healthcare. *Human Relations*, 60(7): 1065–1090.

Budhwar, P.S. and Boyne, G. (2004) Human resource management in the Indian public and private sectors: An empirical comparison. *The International Journal of Human Resource Management*, 15(2): 346–370.

Burns, J.M. (1978) *Leadership*. New York: Harper & Row.

Burton, M.D. and O'Reilly, C. (2004) *Walking the Talk: The Impact of High Commitment Values and Practices on Technology Start-Ups*. Technical Report. Ithaca, NY: Cornell University School of Industrial and Labor Relations Working Papers.

Common, R. (2011) International trends in HRM in the public sector: Reform attempts in the Republic of Georgia. *International Journal of Public Sector Management*, 24(5): 421–434.

Cousins, J.B. (1995) Assessing program needs using participatory evaluation: A comparison of high and marginal success cases, in J.B. Cousins and L.M. Earl (eds) *Participatory Evaluation in Education: Studies in Evaluation Use and Organizational Learning*. London: Routledge, pp. 55–71.

Currie, G. and Procter, S. (2001) Exploring the relationship between human resources and middle managers. *Human Resource Management Journal*, 3(11): 58–69.

Deci, E.L., Koestner, R. and Ryan, R.M. (1999) A meta-analytic review of experiments examining the effects of intrinsic rewards on intrinsic motivation. *Psychological Bulletin*, 125(6): 627–668.

Dick, G. and Metcalfe, B. (2001) Managerial factors and organizational commitment: A comparative study of police officers and civilian staff. *International Journal of Public Sector Management*, 14(2): 111–128.

DiMaggio, P.J. (1998) The new institutionalism: Avenues for collaboration. *Journal of Institutional and Theoretical Economics*, 154(4): 696–705.

DiMaggio, P.J. and Powell, W.W. (1983) The iron cage revisited: Institutional isomorphism and collective rationality in organizational fields. *American Sociological Review*, 48: 147–160.

Faragher, J. (2014) Public and private sector HR in 2014: What are the key differences? *Personnel Today*, 29 April. Accessed online at: www.personneltoday.com/hr/public-and-private-sector-hr-in-2014-what-are-the-key-differences/

Farnham, D. and Horton, S. (1996) *Personnel Management in the Public Sector.* London: Macmillan.

Freeman, M. (1993) *Pemerintah Indonesia: The Indonesian Government System.* Canberra: Country Program Division, Australian International Development Assistance Bureau.

Geldman, A. (2014) Pay trends May 2014: Public-sector wage falls. XpertHR. Accessed online at: www.xperthr.co.uk/survey-analysis/pay-trends-may-2014-public-sector-wage-falls/153143/?cmpid=ILC|PROF|HRPIO-2013-110-XHR_free_content_links|ptod_article&sfid=701w0000000uNMa

Grieves, J. and Hanafin, P. (2005) Human resource management: The Achilles heel of school governance. *Employee Relations*, 27(1): 20–46.

Guest, D., Michie, J., Sheehan, M. and Conway, N. (2000) *Employment Relations, Human Resource Management and Business Performance: An Analysis of the 1998 Workplace Employee Relations Survey.* Development Issue Series. London: CIPD.

Han, Y., Zhang, J. and Huang, S. (2013) China's civil service adopts e-HRM … up to a point: Most offices blend paper-based and electronic systems. *Human Resource Management International Digest*, 21(4): 33–34.

Hartono, A. (2010) *An Investigation into Strategic Human Resource Management in Indonesia: A Grounded Research Approach.* PhD thesis, Murdoch University, Perth, Australia.

Hofstede, G. and Hofstede, G.J. (2005) *Cultures and Organizations: Software of the Mind.* New York: McGraw-Hill.

Hur, Y. (2007) *Organizational Performance, Turnover, and Human Resource Management: Focusing on Municipal Police Services.* University of Kentucky Doctoral Dissertations Paper 524.

Iles, P., Almhedie, A. and Baruch, Y. (2012) Managing human resources in the Middle East: Challenges in the public sector. *Public Personnel Management*, 41(3): 465–492.

Kalidoss, K. and Vijayalakshmi, P. (2016) A comparative study on public and private sector banks in Mayiladuthurai. *International Journal of Advanced Scientific Research and Development*, 3(S1): 66–70.

Kelliher, C. and Parry, E. (2011) Voluntary sector human resource management: Examining the influence of government. *International Journal of Public Sector Management*, 24(7): 650–661.

Kellner, A., Townsend, K. and Wilkinson, A. (2016) 'The mission or the margin?' A high-performance work system in a non-profit organisation. *The International Journal of Human Resource Management*. doi: 10.1080/09585192.2015.1129636

KemenPAN and RB (Kementrian Pendayagunaan Aparatur Negara dan Reformasi Birokrasi) website. Accessed online at: www.menpan.go.id

Khatri, N., Baveja, A., Boren, S. and Mammo, A. (2006) Medical errors and quality of care: From control to commitment. *California Management Review*, 48(3): 115–141.

McConville, T. (2006) Devolved HRM responsibilities, middle-managers and role dissonance. *Personnel Review*, 35(6): 637–653.

Mannion, R., Davies, H.T.O. and Marshall, M.N. (2005) Cultural characteristics of 'high' and 'low' performing hospitals. *Journal of Health Organization and Management*, 19(6): 431–439.

March, J.G. (1994) *Primer on Decision Making: How Decisions Happen*. New York: The Free Press.

Metcalfe, B. and Dick, G. (2000) Is the force still with you? Measuring police commitment. *Journal of Management Psychology*, 15(8): 812–832.

Miao, Q., Newman, A., Sun, Y. and Xu, L. (2013) What factors influence the organizational commitment of public sector employees in China? The role of extrinsic, intrinsic and social rewards. *The International Journal of Human Resource Management*, 24(17): 3262–3280.

Mullins, L.J. (1999) *Management and Organizational Behaviour*, 5th edn. Harlow: Prentice-Hall.

National Civil Service Agency (Badan Kepegawaian Nasional) website (2007) Accessed online at: www.bkn.go.id

OECD (2011) *Teachers Matter: Attracting, Developing and Retaining Effective Teachers – Pointers for Policy Development*. Directorate for Education; Education and Policy Division. Paris: OECD.

Paauwe, J. and Boselie, P. (2003) Challenging 'strategic' human resource management and the relevance of institutional setting. *Human Resource Management Journal*, 13(3): 56–70.

Pei, L., Stanton, P. and Legge, D. (2004) Improving human resource management in Chinese healthcare: Identifying the obstacles to change. *Australian Healthcare Review*, 27(1): 124–130.

Pil, F.K. and Leana, C. (2009) Applying organizational research to public school reform: The effects of teacher human and social capital on student performance. *Academy of Management Journal*, 52(6): 1101–1124.

Purcell, J., Kinnie, N., Hutchinson, S., Swart, J. and Rayton, B. (2003) *Understanding the People and Performance Link: Unlocking the Black Box*. London: CIPD.

Rodriguez, S.B. and Hickson, D.J. (1995) Success in decision making: Different organizations, different reasons for success. *Journal of Management Studies*, 32(5): 655–678.

Rohdewohld, R. (1995) *Public Administration in Indonesia*. Melbourne: Montech Pty Ltd, Monash University School of Government.

Rousseau, D.M. (2004) Research edge: Psychological contracts in the workplace – Understanding the ties that motivate. *The Academy of Management Executive*, 18(1): 120–127.

Runhaar, P.R. and Sanders, K. (2013) Implementing human resources management (HRM) within Dutch VET institutions: Examining the fostering and hindering factors. *Journal of Vocational Education and Training*, 65(2): 236–255.

Sanders, K. and Shipton, H. (2012) The relationship between transformational leadership and innovative behaviour: A team learning versus cohesion perspective. *European Journal of International Management*, 6(1): 83–100.

Schneider, B. (2008) The people still make the place, in D.B. Smith (ed.) *The People Make the Place: Dynamic Linkages between Individuals and Organizations*. Mahwah, NJ: Lawrence Erlbaum, pp. 267–289.

Schwenk, C.R. (1990) Conflict in organizational decision-making: An exploratory study of its effects in for-profit and not-for-profit organizations. *Management Science*, 36(4): 436–448.

Sekretariat Wakil President Republik Indonesia (2012) *Menuju Manajemen Publik Kelas Dunia untuk Reformasi Birokrasi di Indonesia*. Jakarta: Cetakan pertama.

Shipton, H. and Davis, A. (2008) The changing role of human resource management, in Aston Centre for Human Resource Management (ed.) *Strategic Human Resource Management: Building Research Based Practice*. London: CIPD.

Shipton, H., Armstrong, C., West, M. and Dawson, J.F. (2008) The impact of leadership and quality climate on hospital performance. *International Journal for Quality in Healthcare*, 20(6): 439–445.

Shipton, H., Budhwar, P. and Crawshaw, J.R. (2012) Human resource management, organizational capacity for change, and performance: A global perspective. *Thunderbird International Business Review*, 54(6): 777–790.

Sims, R.R. and Slack, J.D. (2007) Public sector human resource management: Minor similarities and major differences, in R.R. Sims (ed.) *Human Resource Management: Contemporary Issues, Challenges and Opportunities*. Charlotte, NC: Information Age Publishing, pp. 37–53.

Sparrow, P. and Cooper, C.L. (2012) *The Employment Relationship: Key Challenges for HR*. Oxford: Butterworth-Heinemann.

Stanton, P. and Manning, K. (2013) High performance work systems, performance and employee participation in the public, in R.J. Burke, A.J. Noblet and C.L. Cooper (eds) *Human Resource Management in the Public Sector*. Cheltenham: Edward Elgar, pp. 255–269.

Storey, J. (1992) *Developments in the Management of Human Resources: An Analytical Review*. Cambridge: Blackwell.

Suharnomo (2009) The impact of culture on human resource management practices: An empirical research finding in Indonesia. Paper presented at Oxford Business and Economics Conference Proceedings, Association for Business and Economic Research (ABER), 24–26 June, Oxford, UK, p. 115. Accessed online at: www.gcbe.us/2009_OBEC/data/Suharnomo.doc

Truss, G., Gratton, L., Hope-Hailey, V., Stiles, P. and Zaleska, J. (2002) Paying the piper: Choice and constraint in changing human resource functional roles. *Human Resource Management Journal*, 12(2): 39–63.

Tsui, A.P.Y. and Lai, K.T. (2009) HRM in the public sector: The hospital authority experience, in A.P.Y. Tsui and K.T. Lai (eds) *Professional Practices of Human Resource Management in Hong Kong: Linking HRM to Organizational Success*. Hong Kong: Hong Kong University Press, pp. 261–278.

Valverde, M., Ryan, G. and Soler, C. (2006) Distributing human resource management responsibilities: A classification of organizations. *Personnel Review*, 35(6): 618–636.

West, M.A., Borill, C., Dawson, J., Scully, J., Carter, M., Anelay, S., Patterson, M. and Waring, J. (2002) The link between management of employees and patient mortality in acute hospitals. *The International Journal of Human Resource Management*, 13(8): 1299–1310.

Woods, D. (2010) Public sector in danger from lack of leadership development. *HR Magazine*, 29 January. Accessed online at: www.hrmagazine.co.uk/article-details/third-sector-in-danger-from-lack-of-leadership-development

Wright, P.C. and Rudolph, J.J. (1994) HRM trends in the 1990s: Should local government buy in? *International Journal of Public Sector Management*, 7(3): 27–43.

GLOSSARY

Armstrong, M. (2012) *A Handbook of Human Resource Management Practice*, 12th edn. London: Kogan Page.

Baron, A., Clarke, R., Pass, S. and Turner, P. (2010) *Workforce Planning: Right People, Right Time, Right Skills*. London: CIPD.

Chalofsky, N. (1992) A unifying definition for the human resource development profession. *Human Resource Development Quarterly*, 3(2): 175–182.

Department of Health (2012) *National Centre for Workforce Intelligence: Leadership Perspectives*. Accessed online at: www.cfwi.org.uk/cfwi-work/social-care/socialcare/leadership/leadership-perspectives

DiMaggio, P.J. and Powell, W.W. (1983) The iron cage revisited: Institutional isomorphism and collective rationality in organizational fields. *American Sociological Review*, 48: 147–160.

Ferrell, O.C., Fraedrich, J. and Ferrell, L. (2008) *Business Ethics: Ethical Decision-Making and Cases*. Boston, MA: Houghton Mifflin.

Matthews, J., Megginson, D. and Surtees, M. (2004) *Human Resource Development*, 3rd edn. London: Kogan Page.

Milkovich, G.T., Newman, J.M. and Gerhart, B. (2011) *Compensation*. New York: McGraw-Hill.

Nyfoudi, M. (2016) Coaching, in A. Wilkinson and S. Johnstone (eds) *Encyclopedia of Human Resource Management*. Cheltenham: Edward Elgar, pp. 46–47.

Porritt, J. (2007) *Capitalism as if the World Matters*. London: Earthscan.

Roberson, D. (2005) Lifelong learning in the county: A context of nature, community and simplicity. *Rural Educator*, 27(1): 29–40.

Rokeach, M. (1973) *The Nature of Human Values*. New York: The Free Press.

Schwartz, S.H. (1999) A theory of cultural values and some implications for work. *Applied Psychology: An International Review*, 48(1): 23–47.

Towers-Watson (2012) The next high stakes quest. *Balancing Employer and Employee Priorities: 2012–2013 Global Talent Management and Rewards Study*. New York: Towers-Watson.

INDEX